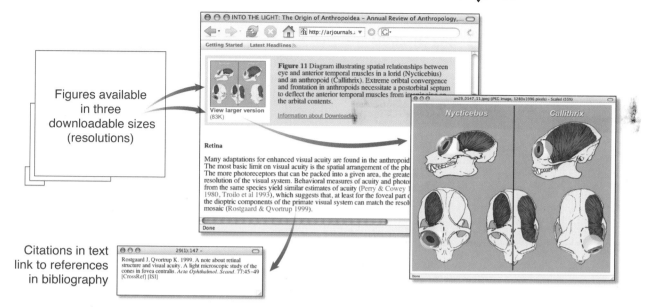

Figures available in three downloadable sizes (resolutions)

Citations in text link to references in bibliography

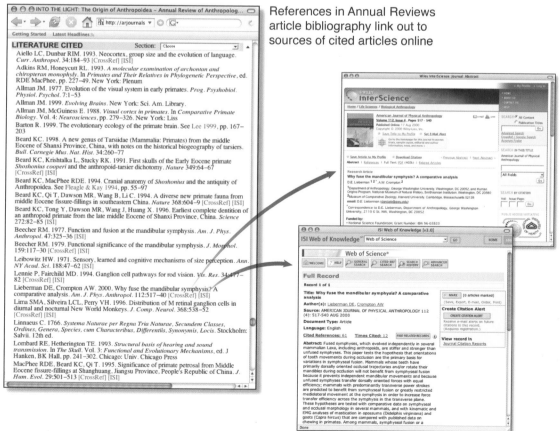

References in Annual Reviews article bibliography link out to sources of cited articles online

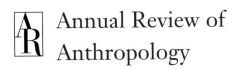

Annual Review of
Anthropology

Annual Review of Anthropology

Volume 37, 2008

William H. Durham, *Editor* (1993–2007)
Stanford University

Donald Brenneis, *Co-Editor*
University of California, Santa Cruz

Peter T. Ellison, *Co-Editor*
Harvard University

www.annualreviews.org • science@annualreviews.org • 650-493-4400

Annual Reviews
4139 El Camino Way • P.O. Box 10139 • Palo Alto, California 94303-0139

Annual Reviews
Palo Alto, California, USA

International Standard Serial Number: 0084-6570
International Standard Book Number: 978-0-8243-1937-3
Library of Congress Catalog Card Number: 72-821360

TYPESET BY APTARA
PRINTED AND BOUND BY MALLOY INCORPORATED, ANN ARBOR, MICHIGAN

Preface: Keep Evolving!

The two themes featured in this volume of the *Annual Review of Anthropology*—"Evolution in Anthropology" "and "Reproduction"—seem especially appropriate this year. First, in recognition of the upcoming Darwin Bicentennial in 2009 (whose many events in diverse locations are listed, for example, at **http://darwin-online.org.uk/2009.html**), the Editorial Committee wanted to bring evolution and the closely related topic of reproduction to the top of our recommended reading list for the year. No matter where your interests lie in anthropology or cognate fields, somehow these two cross-cutting topics impinge on them, even if only remotely or in response. So we have assembled nine chapters for you on evolution and eight more on reproduction, as these topics are currently pursued in vigorous research across the diverse subfields of anthropology. We hope that these timely reviews will help with the, ahem, evolution of your own thinking on these topics as the Bicentennial year progresses.

We also wanted to bring back to the surface the historically productive tension that these two theme areas have generated for anthropology more broadly. No subject in our field has generated more controversy than evolution, on which there is still wide disagreement over the basics (even as to definition and relevance) let alone its extension to or analogs in sociocultural phenomena. The volume before you is no exception in that regard, with controversial content on social evolution, evolutionary linguistics, evolution in religious beliefs, and more. Reproduction and its many consequences are not far behind on the controversy scale, with such topics as sexuality studies in archaeology, alternative kinship, marriage and reproduction, and the cultural impact of assisted reproductive technologies. It is the hope of *ARA*'s Editorial Committee that the intellectual energy released by reviews of these topics will lead to more research, discussion, and debate in the years ahead.

The time has also come to announce our own forms of reproduction and evolutionary change at the *Annual Review of Anthropology*. I am delighted to announce that, starting with the next volume (Volume 38), the series editorship passes to Co-Editors Don Brenneis (UC Santa Cruz) and Peter Ellison (Harvard). Although I have certainly enjoyed the role of editor for the past 15 volumes, and have been nobly assisted by phenomenal teams of associate editors (Val Daniel, Bambi Schieffelin for Volumes 22–31, and Jean Comaroff and Jane Hill for Volumes 31–36), not to mention all the hard work of associated editorial committee members over the years, it is time for both me and the *ARA* to evolve in new directions. For example, anthropology is a far larger and more diverse field than it was when I began working years ago on Volume 22; the evolutionary innovation of co-editors may be seen as an appropriate—some would say "adaptive"—response to all the changes and increasing complexity in our disciplinary environment. I hope that

Peter and Don will enjoy the subfield cross-talk as much as I have and will find new ways to reproduce and sustain the unity and diversity of anthropology.

Looking back in light of the themes of this current volume, I cannot resist offering a self-reflexive thought or two about the *ARA*. Let me suggest that the *ARA* series is itself a provocative example of cultural evolution in action along the lines reviewed and discussed in several chapters here and in other recent reviews (for example, Read 2003, Mesoudi et al. 2006). Using Darwin's simple definition of evolution as "descent with modification," the *ARA* series qualifies as an interesting example in showing iterative replication with change across time. The *ARA* today retains a number of distinctive ancestral features, ranging from the funky, unmistakable orange cover with authors' names in gold leaf (in the printed version) to a table of contents organized largely by conventional subfields. One could clearly infer that today's volumes are unmistakable lineage descendants of earlier volumes. But much has also changed along the way. In format, features, and content, the series certainly has evolved since 1993, including innovations such as theme sections, searchable online access, full-color diagrams and figures, and a narrow-column redesign in the printed version [see Preface to Volume 34 (2005) for more on these and other changes]. Moreover, I like to think that many of these modifications have been selectively retained by the thoughtful choices of the Editorial Committee, rather than by some kind of random drift process. Arguably, we thus have here a fitting example of evolution by value-guided cultural selection (Durham 1991; compare Shennan, this volume). Although I could have fun going on at length with this example, also illustrating David Hull's (1988) arguments about science as an evolutionary process, it would surely tax readers' patience and hold folks back from the intellectual delights of the pages ahead. So I will say only that if *ARA* has shown cultural evolutionary change in the past 15 years, it has been my pleasure to help guide it. And to my successors I leave only this encouragement: Keep evolving!

I dedicate this final Preface to Sam Gubins, Editor-in-Chief at Annual Reviews, for actively encouraging innovation and thoughtful evolutionary change throughout Annual Reviews publications.

William H. Durham
Editor

LITERATURE CITED

Durham WH. 1991. *Coevolution: Genes, Culture, and Human Diversity*. Stanford, CA: Stanford Univ. Press

Hull D. 1988. *Science as a Process: An Evolutionary Account of the Social and Conceptual Development of Science*. Chicago: Univ. Chicago Press

Mesoudi A, Whiten A, Laland K. 2006. Towards a unified science of cultural evolution. *Behav. Brain Sci.* 29:329–83

Read D. 2003. From behavior to culture: an assessment of cultural evolution and a new synthesis. *Complexity* 8(6):17–41

Annual Review of
Anthropology

Volume 37, 2008

Contents

Sociocultural Anthropology

Theme 1: Evolution in Anthropology

Indexes

Errata

An online log of corrections to *Annual Review of Anthropology* articles may be found at
http://anthro.annualreviews.org/errata.shtml

Related Articles

From the ***Annual Review of Law and Social Science***, Volume 3 (2007)

From the ***Annual Review of Nutrition***, Volume 28 (2008)

Ralph L. Holloway

The Human Brain Evolving: A Personal Retrospective

Ralph L. Holloway

Dept. Anthropology, Columbia University, New York, NY 10027; email: rlh2@columbia.edu

Annu. Rev. Anthropol. 2008. 37:1–19

First published online as a Review in Advance on May 29, 2008

The *Annual Review of Anthropology* is online at anthro.annualreviews.org

This article's doi:
10.1146/annurev.anthro.37.081407.085211

Key Words

asymmetries, cerebral cortex, Broca's area, corpus callosum, paleoneurology

Abstract

Minor controversies notwithstanding, the evolution of the human brain has been an intermingled composite of allometric and nonallometric increases of brain volume and reorganizational events such as the reduction of primary visual cortex and a relative increase in both posterior association and (most probably) prefrontal cortex, as well as increased cerebral asymmetries, including Broca's and Wernicke's regions, with some of these changes already occurring in australopithecine times. As outlined in Holloway (1967), positive feedback (amplification-deviation) has been a major mechanism in size increases. Exactly how this mélange of organs evolved will require many more paleontological discoveries with relatively intact crania, an unraveling of the genetic bases for both brain structures and their relationship to behaviors, and a far more complete picture of how the brain varies between male and female and among different populations throughout the world. After all, the human brain is still evolving, but for how long is quite uncertain.

INTRODUCTION

One of my goals is trying to understand how humankind evolved, and in particular, why we have become the most dangerous species on the planet. I attribute this quandary of the species to its brain and the capacity thereby to create by means of arbitrary symbols systems of patterned insanity, that is, delusional systems that nevertheless sustain us. This belief follows and informs my definition of human culture:

> as that biosocial evolutionarily-derived and socially-sustained ability, possessed only by human beings as members of societies, which organizes experiences in a blend of both arbitrary and iconic symbol representations. These representations can be imposed by any level or unit of human social structure, including the individual. (Holloway 1981a; see also Holloway 1967, 1969a, 1996).

The key element here is "imposed" meaning forced upon or done against resistance.

I recognize that this is not a view shared by most people, and I could well be wrong about the patterned insanity I regard as part of human behavior (particularly religion and politics, despite what few eufunctions may attend, at least as far as I understand human history). Because the human brain is the most important constructor of experience and reality, it would be important to know how it came to its present state. Some knowledge of comparative neuroscience, the relationships between individual variation and behavior, molecular neurogenetics, and paleoneurology, or the study of the only truly direct evidence, the endocasts of our fossil ancestors, is necessary. Endocasts, i.e., the casts made of the internal table of bone of the cranium, are rather impoverished objects (the cerebrum is covered by three meningeal tissues) to achieve such an understanding, but these are all we have of the direct evolutionary history of our brains and should not be ignored. Most of my professional career has involved the study of these objects.

To cover all the evidence for human brain evolution would be an impossible task in this retrospective essay. Fortunately, a fine review of human brain evolution has been published by the *Annual Review of Anthropology* (Schoenemann 2006), as well as by Rilling (2006), Buxhoeveden & Casanova 2002, and Preuss et al. 2003, and these articles save me the task of restating all the evidence (see also Grimaud-Hervé 1997, Holloway et al. 2004a, Weaver 2005) and allow me to be more personal in my reflections.

BIOGRAPHICAL

Getting Out of Drexel, New Mexico, Los Angeles

My early college education started at Drexel Institute of Technology in Philadelphia, where I was enrolled in the cooperative program of metallurgical engineering. The cooperative program in the early 1950s meant that half the year was spent in classes, and the other half was spent in industry, meaning some job appropriate to one's major. I was lucky enough to work at Armco Stainless Steel Co. in Baltimore, and although I never did succeed in inventing transparent stainless steel (from my boyhood science fiction fantasies), I was allowed to experiment with extreme temperatures on various alloys of stainless. Three and a half years later, I had my first choice of an elective course, which could be either public speaking for engineers or reading (again) *Huckleberry Finn* and *Tom Sawyer*. I chose the former.

Family matters took me to the University of New Mexico in Albuquerque, and I was admitted on probation because my Drexel grades in calculus left something to be desired. I was thirsting for knowledge and took a course in Anthropology and a course in Geology. These courses affected me profoundly, and I decided to become an anthropologist. My father rebelled, and to shorten this tale, I became a geologist because one was more likely to be employed in the latter pursuit rather than the former. Indeed, upon graduating in 1959 with experience as a roughneck in southwest Texan oil fields, and working in a geophysics lab, I was unable to get a job in geology, there being a major recession at that time. I ended up in Burbank, California, working on heat-resistant metals with Lockheed Aircraft. I remember going to night school and taking a course taught by Dr. Jack Prost at the University of California, Los Angeles, and a course on metal fatigue, just to keep the schizoid quality of my life in motion. A year later, I was admitted to the PhD program in Anthropology at the University of California, Berkeley; I departed Los Angeles and gratefully moved to the Bay Area.

Getting Out of Berkeley

My first mentor at Berkeley was Professor Sherwood Washburn, who was extremely kind to me in offering graduate-student research support. Washburn insisted on my taking various anatomy courses until I suggested to him that I wished to take a course (then taught by Marian Diamond) in neuroanatomy. He was appalled and told me that he would no longer be my mentor if I studied neuroanatomy. I was flabbergasted: How could anyone understand how humankind evolved without understanding how the brain evolved? His response was that I would become too specialized and would not be a physical anthropologist, an argument I found entirely unconvincing. (However, if one looks at the textbooks in physical anthropology of the 1950's through the present, one will find it rare to see more than one page devoted to the brain, and what will be discussed is only the size of the organ.) The recent text by Stanford et al. 2008 is an exception because one author, John Allen, is a neurobiologist who has also studied the lunate sulcus (Allen et al. 2006).

Washburn (and Irvin DeVore) had just come back from field studies in Ambolselie Game Park studying baboon behavior, and I think he wanted me to do the same. At the time, I thought primate studies were interesting, but I could not fathom using baboons as a theoretical model for understanding human evolution because I regarded each species a terminal end product of their own line of evolutionary development. Despite the warning, I took the neu-

roanatomy course and eventually worked with Diamond on the effects of environmental complexity on the rat cortex. In 1966, I wrote the first paper on the effects of environmental complexity training on dendritic branching, using Golgi-Cox methods (Holloway 1966c).

My next mentor was Professor Theodore McCown, who was completely open and supportive regarding my burning interests in the brain. In 1964, I completed my dissertation, after much hassle with Washburn regarding a doctoral dissertation topic, and he was not a member of my committee. My dissertation was of the library variety, a review of quantitative relations in the primate brain [Holloway 1964; the first part of which was published in *Brain Research* (Holloway 1968), but the second half was mysteriously lost between the editors in Holland and Switzerland. . .]. I regarded endocast studies as possibly useless, and this gave me a burning desire to do empirical research and not armchair anthropology. Ironically enough, considering my experiences in geology and engineering, 1964 was a banner year for entering the job market, and I received several offers, most notably from Columbia University and Cornell. Because my first wife's folks were from New York, I took the Columbia position. My father had died prior to this event, so this triumph was unknown to him.

Early Columbia University

My position at Columbia was mostly as a service to sociocultural anthropology, and I taught at both undergraduate and graduate levels. At that time, we were fully committed to the four-field approach, an approach now completely rejected by the cultural anthropologists at Columbia, the majority of which appear strongly postmodern, postcolonialist, feminist, and political. I suppose in the earlier days, had I been more aggressive about constructing a biological anthropology program at Columbia, my stay would have been a more pleasant experience, but I was quickly isolated and marginalized at Columbia, and remain so. Instead, I tried to stay true to scholarship and research, and not to politics.

Fortunately, I was (and am) saved by my mighty tenure.

Harry Shapiro from the American Museum of Natural History was an Adjunct, and he and I shared the responsibilities of educating graduate students in the department. I tried to continue my research on the effects of environmental complexity on dendritic branching; both my children referred to me as the "man who draws spiders," as dendritic branching was done in my darkened office, tracing the dendrites against a sheet of paper attached to the wall, while manipulating the depth of focus on the microscope, there being no joy sticks or computers in those days. My hope was to do research on the quantitative histology of the cerebral cortex of different primates including humans, but no lab facilities were available. I approached my chairman, Morton Fried at the time, and asked for his interceding with the Biology Department, in the hope that they might provide some space and histological help. The answer was brutal. Cyrus Levinthal and Eric Kandel responded to Fried somewhat as follows: "If we do not know what is happening in the brain of *Aplysia*, the sea-slug, how could we possibly learn anything from the primate brain? No." Kandel, of course, went on to win a Nobel Prize for his research. Admittedly, this was a hard lesson for me regarding the hubris of molecular biologists, but I survived it. My early papers in those days were attempts at synthesizing hominid brain evolution (Holloway 1966a,b; 1967; 1968; 1969a,b; 1972a; 1973a) and were of the armchair variety, although I still regard certain papers [1967, 1969a,b; 1975b; 1976; these two latter papers suggested that throwing with force and accuracy selected aspects of brain evolution, well before Calvin's (1983) book, which took this idea much further] as some of my best attempts, despite their speculative hue.

On to Paleoneurology

Indeed, the above experience led me to seek a semester's leave, and my family and I went off to South Africa to look at australopithecines and endocasts under the guidance of Professor Phillip V. Tobias. This was in 1969, and I guess my encounters with the New York police during the 1968 student demonstrations (I experienced testicular trauma at the end of the police blackjacks...) were a sympathetic note to Tobias and the apartheid policies in South Africa that he was fighting. In any event, the experience settled my career, and I became a dedicated paleoneurologist. Ironically, my dissertation had explicitly found endocasts to be useless, particularly when I found that descriptions of *Sinanthropus* were more primitive than *Homo erectus* from Java, despite being later in time.

I met Professor Raymond Dart there, who had so kindly sent me all of his reprints when I was at Berkeley, and I became convinced that the Taung endocast needed independent study, despite the detailed work of George Schepers (Schepers 1946). My main concern at the time was finding accurate volumes for the hominids (Holloway 1970a,b; 1973b) and trying to find an objective method(s) for deciding whether the cortex was reorganized as Dart had previously claimed (Dart 1925, 1926, 1956). This meant trying to determine the exact location of the infamous lunate sulcus, which is almost always the anterior boundary of primary visual cortex, or area 17 of Brodmann. Was it in a typical ape anterior position, as Keith (1931) figured it, or was it indeed in a posterior, more human-like position, as Dart had originally claimed? Little did I realize how contentious this question would turn out to be (30+ years!), as I acquired my long-standing opponent, Dean Falk.

My estimate of the Taung endocast volume came out to 404 ml, double the volume of the 202-ml hemi-endocast I had constructed under the scrutiny of both Tobias and his fabulous assistant, Alun Hughes (Holloway 1970a). This value was quite less than the 525 ml previously reported, and I was pleased that both Alun and Phillip did not find fault with my reconstruction. I particularly enjoyed working on the SK 1587 endocast from Swartkrans (Holloway 1972b) at the Transvaal Museum. Of course, nothing is static in paleoneurology, and the Taung endocast volume has been recently deflated (i.e., 382 ml) by Falk & Clarke (2007) in a paper filled with questionable methods, the most grievous being that they never bothered to define a midsagittal plane, an absolute requisite when trying to mirror-image a half-portion of an endocast (R. Holloway, manuscript in preparation). Falk et al. (2000) proposed some minor deflations of other australopithecine endocast volumes, and replies will ensue in the future.

Apparently, my skills were growing, and I believe Tobias let Louis Leakey know I could be trusted with the fossils. And so in 1971–1972, my family and I spent a sabbatical year in Kenya and South Africa working on australopithecines, habilines, and *H. erectus*. (So many anecdotes, so little space, but I shall always remember Louis's kindness to me and my family when he was in such considerable pain.)

I returned to Kenya a couple more times to work mostly on the habilines, and my visit in the late 1970s, in particular, allowed me to make an undistorted endocast of the famous KNM-ER 1470 cranium. My observations on Broca's area were recorded in Richard Leakey's books (where I had determined that these were of a *Homo*-like form and found a cranial capacity of 752 ml). My method scared the dickens out of Richard because I filled the latex-coated interior of the cranium with plaster of Paris to avoid any distortion while it was still in the cranial portion. When Richard saw this, he asked how in the hell I would get it out, and I told him to come by next day. He did, and lo and behold, there sat the perfect endocast, and there sat the undistorted cranium! (Given the existing breaks in the cranium, simply dissolving the glue joints and extricating the endocast without any damage to the fossil itself was an easy task.)

I believe it was during a 1978 visit, perhaps earlier, that Richard approached me in the Center's lab and asked if Dean Falk could take some impressions ("peels") from the cranium, and I said yes but did not know that she would later publish her observations (Falk 1983a) without either acknowledging my agreement or mentioning my findings, which were discussed in Leakey's books (Leakey 1981, Leakey & Lewin

1978). At the time, I was supposed to be preparing a full description to be included in Bernard Wood's monographic treatment of the Kenyan discoveries (Wood 1991). My results (Holloway 1983d), in very abbreviated form, were published in the journal *Human Neurobiology*, of which Doreen Kimura was a founder but which did not survive very long as a journal. In the latter part of 1972, I went briefly to Indonesia to make endocasts from the newly discovered *Homo erectus* crania (Sangiran 4, 10, 12, and 17) in Dr. Teuku Jacob's lab at Jogjakarta. The hospitality was splendid, but the weather abominable.

The Armchair Stuff, Compulsive Collecting of Data, and More Controversies

Meanwhile, throughout the late 1970s and early 1980s, my interests broadened to more theoretical approaches to human brain evolution (albeit my 1967 paper in *General Systems* was a major beginning) and are reflected in my paper published in 1979, where I tried to synthesize brain size, brain reorganization, structural and regulatory genes, and allometry in the volume edited by Hahn, Jensen, and Dudek (Holloway 1979, in Hahn et al. 1979) (see **Figure 1**). At this time I was in the midst of conceptual battles with my colleague Harry Jerison (1973), who appeared, at least to me, to have little regard for the concept of reorganization (Holloway 1969b, 1974; see also Holloway 1966a for a critique of the extra neuron model Harry had offered in 1963). I was honored to give the James Arthur Lecture on the Evolution of the Human Brain (Holloway 1975b), in which I suggested, as I had in my earlier (Holloway 1967) paper, that selection for social behavioral complexity was what had driven the evolution of the hominid brain. (I would have been wiser to have called it "Machiavellian Intelligence," or the evolution of the "social brain," the current popular jargon, which ignores earlier publications). The paper on relative encephalization quotients (EQ) measures (Holloway & Post 1982) was an important contribution also. My 1969 paper,

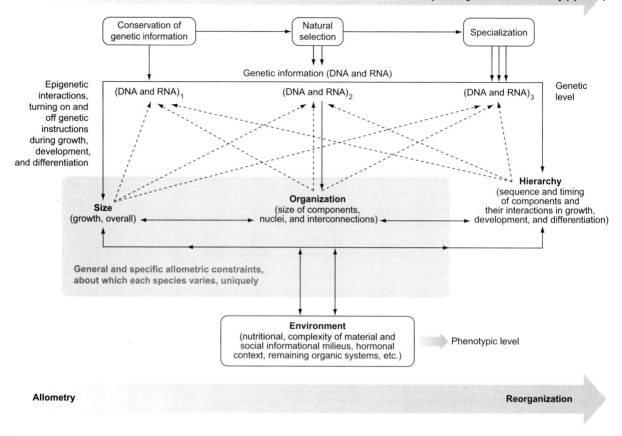

Figure 1

The brain is a composite of size, organization, and hierarchy, which is acted on at the phenotypic level by natural selection throughout the life of the organism. Mathematical formulations and prediction tests are so far applied only to the shaded box containing size and organization. This model conceives of natural selection variously acting on three subsets of genetic information (DNA + RNA_{123}), which also interact with each other and the developing and differentiating organism in epigenetic fashion. Allometrists and brain mass theorists are almost totally working within the framework of the left-hand side of the diagram.

"Culture: A Human Domain," was an attempt to describe what humans did as quite different from what other primates were doing, although if I were to rewrite that paper, I would find many more areas of behavioral continuity between our symbolically mediated behavior, and theirs. At that time, I thought the basis of human language, the use of arbitrary symbols, had aspects of cognitive processes that were shared by stone tool making.

A recent paper by Stout et al. (2008) using fMRI on Nick Toth while he was making stone tools indicates a possible connection between language sites in Broca's and Wernicke's regions of the cerebral cortex and stone tool making, something I had suggested in the above paper on the possible similarities, cognitively, between language and tool-making behavior.

I had, by 1978, made close to 200 latex rubber endocasts of modern humans and apes and monkeys and compulsively collected thousands of data points on a comparative collection of these endocasts, including fossil hominids, apes, and modern humans, using a stereoplotter suggested to me by Alan Walker. This gadget measured the dorsal surface of the endocast every ten degrees in two planes and took the distance from a homologous central point to the endocast surface, thus avoiding problems with allometric corrections. These results (Holloway 1981c) indicated that the region of greatest shape difference was in the posterior parietal region, which I thought was a buttress to my belief that relative expansion of the posterior parietal lobe had occurred early in hominid evolution and was indicated on the Taung endocast, as well as on the AL 162–28 specimen from Hadar, Ethiopia (Holloway 1983a, Holloway & Kimbel 1986). This was also a time in which I published my observations on the Spy Neandertal endocasts, the Indonesian *Homo erectus* endocasts, the Omo endocast, and the Solo endocasts (Holloway 1980a,b; 1981b,d,e; 1983b; 1985b). More recently, I have been making endocasts of modern *Homo sapiens* from sectioned crania in the bone lab at Columbia, and from the Von Lauschan collection at the American Museum of Natural History, adding roughly another 75 specimens to the growing sample size of the 15–20 that I did much earlier. Included among these latter specimens are 5–6 microcephalic endocasts (thanks go to Milford Wolpoff, who lent the crania to me) and a couple of extreme cranial deformation examples. These have all been done using "Dentsply Aquasil LV" dental impression material, which has, hopefully, a much longer shelf life than the earlier latex endocasts, many of which have deteriorated. Thanks to the efforts of Janet Monge and Tom Schoenemann, these endocasts (not the more recent human ones) have been scanned.

THE LUNATE SULCUS

Dart (1925, 1926, 1956) had believed that the Taung child's endocast showed definite signs of reorganization toward a more human-like condition on the basis of his belief that the lunate sulcus, which defines the anterior boundary of primary visual striate cortex, Brodmann's (1909) area 17, was visible on the Taung natural endocast. The cortex anterior to the lunate sulcus would be the parietal and temporal lobe association cortex, where higher cognitive functions occur. I trumpeted the concept of reorganization in my dissertation and early papers (e.g., Holloway 1966b, 1967, 1979) and, indeed, still believe the concept to be of value as an additional set of quantitative changes that are not directly caused by brain size increase alone. How the brain is organized as well as its size is of great importance. (I came to this conclusion before 1964 when I made a seminar presentation in one of Washburn's classes, demonstrating that some human microcephalics with brain sizes that some gorillas might deride as diminutive were nevertheless able to talk. That meant to me that something in their brains was organized differently than in the great apes.)

Most biological anthropologists ignore organization and cathect on brain size, which is a bit unscholarly. Dart, after all, had studied under Grafton Elliot Smith (see Smith 1904), the major claimant and champion of the lunate sulcus, and Dart himself wrote his dissertation on the evolution of the turtle brain, which of course has no lunate sulcus. This history was covered (Holloway 1985a; see also 1988a,b; Holloway et al. 2001a,b; 2003; 2004b) because Falk had previously restudied the Taung endocast and decided that the lunate was represented by a small dimple placed well anterior to the lambdoid suture, and even more anteriorly than would be found in all chimpanzees, gorillas, and orangutans without any measurements based on a comparative sample (Falk 1980; 1983a,b,c; 1985; 1989). It was, however, the question of a possible lunate sulcus in the Hadar AL 162–28 *A. afarensis* that received the most unwelcome confrontation with Falk. She (Falk 1983b) incorrectly oriented the Hadar specimen so that the cerebellar hemispheres protruded beyond the cerebral cortices. Further, the depression along the lambdoid suture region, which she regarded as the lunate sulcus, was placed in an anterior, ape-like position, which simply reflected her own bias. She had apparently accepted my earlier (Holloway 1983c) identification of the posterior end of the interparietal sulcus (IP), which usually abuts the lunate sulcus. I was reluctant to accept the depression as a true lunate sulcus because I had found many of my *Pan* endocasts had a distinct "sulcus" just immediately anterior to the lambdoid suture, which I name the "prelambdoid pseudosulcus," and which is actually caused by the posterior and inferior lip of the parietal bone. Clark et al. (1936) showed this artifact very clearly when they rubbed off the charcoal soot from the endocast surface and compared the endocast to the actual brain. Later, Bill Kimbel and I (Holloway & Kimbel 1986) tried to set the matter straight by pointing out Falk's error of orientation and the fact that the distance between her purported lunate sulcus and the occipital pole was only 15 mm, roughly half the distance that occurs normally in chimpanzee brains of roughly the same volume, i.e., 385–400 ml. Measuring the distance between the occipital pole (the most posterior point on the occipital lobe) and the lunate sulcus on ~80 chimpanzee hemispheres suggested that the Hadar *A. afarensis* AL 162–28 specimen was almost 3 standard deviations outside of the mean chimp value, which varied between 25 and 30+ mm. (Holloway et al. 2001a,b, 2003, 2004b).

This brouhaha was part of a larger theoretical issue, i.e., whether an increase in brain must necessarily precede any organizational shift in brain components, or a reduced primary visual cortex relative to the size of the brain. Jerison (1990), Falk (1983b), and Armstrong et al. (1991) appeared to take the position that the brain did not reorganize until after there was an increase in brain size, and I was taking the position, as had Dart before me, that reorganization took place prior to the increase in brain volume. I believed then and remain convinced today that the earliest hominids, i.e., *Australopithecus africanus, A. afarensis, and A. garhi*, had brains that were definitely different from any ape's, despite their small size, and that natural selection had worked on more complex social behaviors (Holloway 1967, 1975b), as would be expected if the relative reduction in PVC (primary visual cortex) signaled a relative increase in parietal association cortex.

Hopefully, the newer *A. africanus* brain endocast of Stw505 (from Sterkfontein, South Africa), with its clear-cut posterior location of a lunate sulcus (Holloway et al. 2004b), will convince most skeptics that, indeed, the australopithecine hominids had reorganized brains despite their overlapping in size with ape brains. Whether biological anthropology textbooks will recognize this possibility is another matter. As near as I can determine, many of the textbooks in biological anthropology discuss only brain volume in hominids (Stanford et al. 2008 being an exception).

In 1990, I had the honor of being a participant in the Fifth Interdisciplinary Fyssen Symposium, in which I presented a paper "Toward a Synthetic Theory of Human Brain Evolution," eventually published in 1995 (Changeux & Chavaillon 1995, Holloway 1995). This was the first time I tried to present a framework in which brain size increases were interspersed with reorganizational changes. The point here was to suggest that different selection pressures occurred at different times regarding both size and organization. Falk characterized the paper as the same old stuff (Falk 1997), even though this was truly a newer synthesis. If she had disagreed with my premises and outlines and provided her reasons, I would have been pleased and would have regarded such as a positive step in our skirmishes, but instead it was just an opportunity to denigrate and ignore my ideas without ever providing counterevidence or discussing what was wrong with the data presented.

Tables 1, 2, and **3** (updated from Holloway et al. 2004a) present my recent synopsis of the evidence I presented then.

Another major brouhaha with Falk and her colleagues emerged after White & Falk (1999) asserted that the Omo L338y-6 australopithecine from Ethiopia had an occipital-marginal sinus drainage pattern that allied the specimen to robust australopithecines. Having studied and described the original specimen (Holloway 1981b), and not a cast of a cast, I was amazed to see this publication and hear these claims. I examined my original

Table 1 Changes in the reorganization of the hominid brain based on endocasts (After Holloway et al. 2004a)

Brain changes (reorganization)	Taxa	Time (mya)	Endocast evidence
Reduction of primary visual striate cortex, area 17, and relative increase in posterior parietal cortex	*A. afarensis*	3.5 to 3.0	AL 162–28 endocast
	A. africanus	3.0 to 2.0	Taung child, Stw 505 endocast
	A. robustus	~2.0	SK 1585 endocast
Reorganization of frontal lobe (third inferior frontal convolution, Broca's area, widening prefrontal)	*Homo rudolfensis*	2.0 to 1.8	KNM-ER 1470 endocast
	Homo habilis		Indonesian endocasts
	Homo erectus		
Cerebral asymmetries, left occipital, right-frontal petalias	*H. rudolfensis*	2.0 to 1.8	KNM-ER 1470 endocast
	H. habilis, H. erectus		Indonesian endocasts
Refinements in cortical organization to a modern *Homo* pattern	*H. erectus* to present?	1.5 to 0.10	*Homo* endocasts (*erectus, neanderthalensis, sapiens*)

endocast reconstruction and, as I clearly remembered, could find no trace of such a sinus. Tim White and his colleagues were kind enough to secure a new mold of the posterior section of the newly cleaned Omo specimen and serially sectioned it through the purported region claimed by White & Falk. There was absolutely no sign of a marginal sinus on this specimen (Holloway et al. 2002). The presentation of these findings at an American Association of Physical Anthropologists meeting caused an extremely emotionally charged encounter between me and David DeGusta on the one side and Falk and White on the other, each armed with their own endocast copies. (Fortunately, at 430 ml, the endocasts could not do much damage even if thrown, despite being made of plaster.)

One last example might be of interest: In *Braindance*, Falk (2004, pp. 165–66) discusses her "radiator hypothesis" (Falk 1990) as a proven hypothesis and then provides a partial

Table 2 Major cortical regions involved in early hominid evolution (with major emphasis on the evolution of social behavior and adapting to expanding environments) (After Holloway et al. 2004a)

Cortical regions	Brodmann's areas	Functions
Primary visual striate cortex	17	Primary visual
Posterior parietal and anterior occipital (peri- and parastriate cortex)	18, 19	Secondary and tertiary visual integration with area 17
Posterior parietal, superior lobule	5, 7	Secondary somatosensory
Posterior parietal, inferior lobule (mostly right side. Left side processes symbolic-analytical)	39	Angular gyrus perception of spatial relations among objects, face recognition
Posterior parietal, inferior lobule (mostly right side. See above)	40	Supramarginal gyrus spatial ability
Posterior superior temporal cortex	22	Wernicke's area, posterior superior temporal gyrus, comprehension of language
Posterior inferior temporal	37	Polymodal integration, vision, auditory input. Perception and memory of objects' qualities
Lateral prefrontal cortex (including mirror neurons)	44, 45, 47 (also 8, 9, 10, 13, 46)	Broca's area (Broca's Cap), motor control of vocalization, language
		Complex cognitive functioning memory, inhibiton of impulse, foresight, etc.

Table 3 Major size changes in human brain evolution (after Holloway et al. 2004a)

Brain changes	Taxa	Time (mya)	Evidence
Small increase, allometric[a]	*A. afarensis* to *A. africanus*	3.0 to 2.5	Brain size increases from 400 ml to 450 ml, 500+ ml
Major increase, rapid, both allometric and nonallometric	*A. africanus* to *Homo habilis*	2.5 to 1.8	KNM-1470, 752 ml (Ca 300 ml)
Small allometric increase in brain size to 800 ml–1000 ml (Assumes *habilis* was KNM 1470-like)	*Homo habilis* to *Homo erectus*	1.8 to 0.5	*Homo erectus* brain endocasts and postcranial bones, e.g., KNM-ER 17000
Gradual and modest size increase to archaic *Homo sapiens* mostly nonallometric	*Homo erectus* to *Homo sapiens neanderthalensis*	0.5 to 0.10	Archaic *Homo* and neandertal endocasts 1200 to 1700+ ml
Small reduction in brain size among modern *Homo sapiens*, which was allometric	*Homo s. sapiens*	0.015 to present	Modern endocranial capacities

[a]Allometric means related to body size increase or decrease, whereas nonallometric refers to brain size increase without a concomitant body-size increase.

quote from my critique, which appeared in *Brain and Behavioral Sciences* (Holloway 1990a), focusing on my belief that her hypothesis had the structure of a simple just-so story and was unduly speculative. What Falk then left out were my eight points regarding the lack of any empirical demonstration that show an increase in blood cooling associated with cranial capacity increase, upon which the fossil evidence is simply mute. Nor did she respond in any detail to Kimbel's (1984) paper and (1990) critique. My paper (Holloway 1980c) on a reanalysis of the Pakkenberg & Voigt (1964) data on Danish brain weights showed very clearly on p. 113 that body size alone could not explain the difference in male/female brain weights, a result she also finds in her 2004 edition of *Braindance*. Our work (de LaCoste-Utamsing & Holloway 1982, Holloway 1990b, Holloway et al. 1993) on the corpus callosum was not mentioned in her discussions of sexual dimorphism, nor our work on cerebral asymmetries (Holloway & de Lacoste-Lareymondie 1982).

On a more positive note, I was honored in 2007 with a two-day conference ("The Human Brain Evolving: Papers in Honor of Ralph L. Holloway") held on my behalf in Bloomington, Indiana, where 20+ colleagues came together to give papers on various aspects of brain evolution. This conference was sponsored by the Stone Age Institute and the University of Indiana, under the leadership of Drs. Nick Toth

and Kathy Schick and also organized by two former students, Drs. M.S. Yuan and D.C. Broadfield. These papers will appear as a book in the near future. I take these as a validation of my research.

A BRIEF ASIDE ON WHAT CONSTITUTES EVIDENCE FOR HOMINID BRAIN EVOLUTION

This little battle, however, brings forth an interesting question about how valuable paleoneurology and comparative neuroanatomy are in discussing hominid evolution. As I have tried to point out in several places (e.g., Holloway et al. 2004a), the only direct evidence for hominid brain evolution is paleoneurology, the study of endocasts, despite the paucity of that information. Perhaps, in the future, molecular neurogenetics might be able to provide more details regarding what elements of the brain (neurotransmitters to gross neuroanatomy, i.e., gyri, sulci, fiber tracts, overall size; see, for example, Sherwood et al. 2003 regarding Broca's regions in chimpanzees) have changed during hominid evolution. At the moment, however, such data are not available, and comparative neuroanatomy remains the study of extant (not extinct) animal brains, each of which have undergone their own separate evolutionary path development to their present condition, whatever that may be.

Give these questions some serious thought: Is today's chimpanzee brain (against which we do so many comparisons, whether in terms of size or structure) the same as that of the last common ancestor of hominids and chimps? Has the chimpanzee brain evolved during the past 5–7 million years? If so, are our comparisons with the present-day chimpanzee on target? Should the same questions be asked of other areas of comparative primate comparisons, e.g., dentition, locomotion, behavior? The incomplete brain endocast of *Proconsul africanus*, of roughly 12 mya, appears to show an anthropoid pattern of having the lunate sulcus in an anterior position (which all extant anthropoids share) (Radinsky 1974, 1975, 1979). So perhaps with this characteristic, the derived condition (lunate sulcus in a posterior position, indeed an autapomorphy) for *Homo* is a reasonable conclusion that can be translated into functional (i.e., behavioral) terms, such as what we know about the role of the posterior parietal association cortex in perception of objects and their positions, recognition of faces, social behavior, and aspects of language reception. Herein lies the great value of comparative neuroanatomy: It is *the* essential link between neurobiological and behavioral variation writ both large and small.

Still, where are the studies that link what we know of species-specific behavioral patterns and neuroanatomy in the primates? Where is the research that explains, neurologically, the behavioral differences between chimpanzee, gorilla, and orangutan? Even trying to describe the behavioral differences between *Pan troglodytes* and *Homo sapiens* is difficult, despite clear-cut differences in brain anatomy that have been described. I ask these questions not to detract from comparative studies, but simply in the hope of sharpening our analytic abilities and to caution against the wholesale use of extant species' morphology in trying to understand human brain evolution. So much of the primate behavior about which I have read and the speculation that follows regarding hominid evolutions seem to be based on the premise that the chimpanzee has had no further evolution since our split with *Pan*-like hominoids roughly 7 mya.

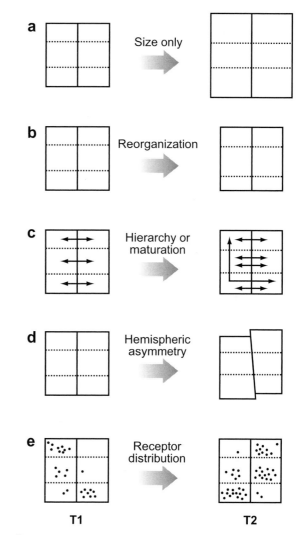

Figure 2

Figure 2 shows several different scenarios where it is possible to reorganize the brain without any apparent increase in size, from T1 (time 1) to T2 (some time after an arbitrary interval of evolution). The horizontal dashed lines represent the central sulcus and lunate sulcus, respectively, with the frontal lobe facing upward. The vertical line divides the two cerebral hemispheres. Thus in part (*a*), Time 1 to Time 2 involves an increase in size without changing any parts of the brain. In part (*b*), the lunate sulcus moves posteriorly, but brain size remains constant from T1 to T2. In part (*c*), different fiber tracts mature at different times and differentially increase or decrease. In part (*d*), the two hemispheres are asymmetric (left-occipital and right-frontal width petalias), but overall brain size remains constant. In part (*e*), brain size is constant, but neuroreceptors are differently distributed between T1 and T2. (Prairie and mountain voles, and oxytocin receptors come to mind.) Needless to say, some of these scenarios cannot be detected on endocasts (parts *c* and *e*, and sometimes *b*). These are a few alternative ways to reorganize a brain without increasing its size.

ENTER THE "HOBBIT," *HOMO FLORESIENSIS*: AN ONGOING TANGO

In the above context, a parallel problem exists with respect to comparing modern-day human pathology with ancient hominid discoveries. The recent controversy over the "hobbit" *Homo floresiensis*, whether it is a true new species of hominid (see Brown et al. 2004 for original claim and description) or a case of pathology, has not been settled (e.g., Henneberg & Thorne 2004, Hershkovitz et al. 2007; see also Richards 2006). I have spent more than two years studying the endocast of this creature and am still sitting on the fence as to whether it is a case of microcephaly or some other pathology, or a new species (Holloway et al. 2006). As cogent as the arguments of Jacob et al. (2006) and Martin et al. (2006a,b) might appear, I agree with the depictions in Falk et al. (2005) of the virtual endocast compared with modern *Homo sapiens*, *Homo erectus*, and chimpanzee [an unfortunate choice of one extremely small microcephalic (278 ml)] and the observation that there are no microcephalic brains yet published showing the suite of features found on the "hobbit" endocast, although the example by Martin et al. (2006b) of the Indian microcephalic comes very close. What I see are (*a*) extreme platycephaly, (*b*) extremely thin and protuberant gyri recti of the prefrontal lobe, (*c*) appearance of a smallish prefrontal lobe and temporal lobes as seen on the undistorted left side, (*d*) unusually spread cerebellar lobes, and (*e*) a peculiar triangular-shaped occipital sinus. These observations leave me sitting on the proverbial fence regarding a new species or pathology argument. The point here is that modern pathology (e.g., primary microcephaly) may not match what appears to be a possible pathology 13–18 thousand years ago. The full spectrum of microcephaly and other pathological conditions affecting the brain has not been available to study or illustrated in recent articles. My consultations with several pediatric neurologists suggest that they see it (the "hobbit") as pathological, but it does not match what they have seen in cases of true primary microcephaly. The original "virtual endocast" published by Falk et al. (2005) shows that they selected the damaged and inferiorly deflected right temporal lobe as a model for their "virtual endocast" when it is the left temporal lobe that was intact, and which, incidentally, appears rather small in comparison to the total size of the endocast. Their 417-ml volume is more likely to be 400 ml. In any event, this tango will not end until more of these creatures are discovered and described.

Having been kindly provided with an endocast made from the stereolith of the LB1 cranium by Peter Brown, I have never once been asked to referee any papers on the LB1 endocast. At the time of these writings, Dean Falk and I are among a small number of practicing paleoneurologists (actually, so are Emiliano Bruner and Dominique Grimaud-Herve, and Anne Weaver) to have worked on these endocasts. Promises made by Mike Morwood to receive the CT scan data so that I could make an independent study of the endocast have never materialized, and I strongly argue that independent study is sorely needed. But this tango is a common occurrence in paleoanthropology, where access to fossil specimens tends to be rigorously guarded (e.g., Atapuerca, Dmanisi, etc.).

BRAIN VARIATION AND TOTTERING ON THE EDGE OF POLITICAL INCORRECTNESS

The 1980s became a period of intensive data collecting. One of the first steps was requesting from Pakkenberg in Denmark the data from their study of Danish autopsies (Pakkenberg & Voigt 1964). These authors kindly sent me the data, which I reanalyzed in 1980 (Holloway 1980c) because I was interested in exploring ranges of variation within a species of derived neuronal statistics such as extra numbers of neurons, EQs (encephalization quotients), and relative brain size. I was intrigued by techniques such as partial correlations, was getting interested in possible sex differences in loss of brain weight with age and EQ's, and indeed was able to show that the difference between male and female brain weights could not be fully explained by differences in body size. I was surprised to find that in males, the brain correlated significantly with stature, but the same effect did not hold for females.

At this time I had a brilliant graduate student, Christine de LaCoste-Lareymondie who was doing her dissertation on the distribution of fibers in the human corpus callosum. I remember approving and encouraging this project but insisted that she had to find out as much as possible about the variation of the corpus callosum, including variation by sex. From a small sample she had collected, Kitty discovered that females appeared to have larger corpus callosa relative to brain size than did males and that the splenium in particular seemed more bulbous in females than in males. We thought this was a very intriguing find and sent a manuscript to *Science*. *Science* then asked for the data because, indeed, our sample was very small. They accepted the paper (de LaCoste-Utamsing & Holloway 1982), and this created a minor cottage industry for the next couple of decades as to whether the corpus callosum was indeed relatively larger in females. Most people argued that it was equal, but seldom used our methods or seemed to understand we were talking about a relative size (Holloway et al. 1993). Blistering commentary depicting us as sexist and worse came [e.g., Fausto-Sterling's (1985) "Myths of Gender," Bishop & Wahlsten (1997). We also were unaware that Bean (1906) had earlier made a similar finding, and his being a well-known racist provided these authors with the necessary guilt by association, which social scientists so savor. Finally, thanks to the sophisticated analytic paper by Richard Smith (2005) in *Current Anthropology*, a case to legitimate ratio data was proven. In those days, sex differences in the brain were really politically incorrect, particularly as a vast sea of feminist literature was being produced. Today, sex differences in the human brain are commonly accepted (e.g., Gur et al. 2002, Kimura 2003, Haier et al. 2005, Narr et al. 2007). These experiences were not pleas-

ant, however, and I found myself sort of a pariah in one realm and a hero in another, and it had a lasting effect on my quest for truth, replication, and letting data trump emotional biases. I am afraid the same principles apply to possible ethnic ("racial") differences in the brain, because without knowing how the brain varies in the human species, it is impossible to understand fully how this organ evolved. Furthermore, given the sensitivity of the brain to environmental insult from conception on, sound knowledge of such variation, whether in overall size, maturation schedules, neuroreceptor sites, etc., is required to determine the most efficient therapeutic measures to take to ensure proper nutrition and other nurturance for the developing brain. A full understanding of the respective roles and interplay of nature and nurture particularly with respect to worldwide distributions on intelligence tests scores is impossible without knowledge of how the human brain varies and why it does so. It would be nice if human variation could be celebrated as our most precious evolutionary heritage and hope instead of prohibiting the study of our variation.

In the late 1970s and early 1980s, I collected autopsy data from the Pathology department at Columbia's College of Physicians and Surgeons (now CUMS). I was interested in age, sex, and ethnic effects on brain size changes through time as might be found in cross-sectional data. Roughly 2000 cases were collected, without personal identifications, and all cases of brain pathology were culled out of the data set. The results, unpublished, were roughly the same as found in the Ho et al. (1980, 1981) work on a sample from Milwaukee, which indicated that African American brains were statistically significantly lower in weight than were European American brains, that is, of course referring to the mean values. Ho et al. (1980) concluded that cultural effects were the reason behind the difference. Interestingly, Lieberman (2005) in his review of Rushton's (2000, 2002) claims regarding ethnic (racial) differences in brain sizes and behaviors ignored this work by Ho et al. Needless to say, Tobias's oft-cited paper on brain weight collecting methods (Tobias 1970) was cited to claim that autopsy data on brain weights are useless. Unfortunately, however problematic such data are, one tends to forget that autopsies are not done discriminately. Once the body is on the morgue slab, the autopsy is conducted in exactly the same fashion irrespective of the cadaver's race, and thus comparisons of such data collected by the same anatomist or medical examiner are surely valid, depending on which variables are being compared. Comparing data collected by different examiners may of course be difficult, and perhaps statistical meta-analyses would be in order. To my knowledge, none exists.

Simply put, this research area remains an intensely political and near-suicidal enterprise. (Indeed, one colleague suggested I should incinerate the data; another suggested this kind of study had led to his relatives perishing in the Nazi concentration camps.) The continuing gap in African American and European-descent test scores on various cognitive tests (particularly IQ) throughout the United States and the world (Lynn & Vanhanen 2006) is a source of tremendous concern and acrimonious debate. Indeed, Jon Marks claimed he "outed" me as a "racist" (Marks 2000; see Holloway 2000 for reply) in his biological section of the *American Anthropologist Newsletter* because I had the temerity to defend Arthur Jensen against Loring Brace's assertion that Jensen was a bigot. I had read much of this literature (e.g., Jensen 1998) including Jensen's infamous 1969 piece in the *Harvard Law Review* and did not find him a racist. I remain appalled at our discipline, which regards him as such and which invented the appellation "Jensenism" to tar and feather him. I remain interested in the possibility that different populations have variation both in their brains and their behavior, but the issue is so politically incorrect that one cannot even approach such a study with anything but trepidation. (For example, the *Annual Review* article by Freedman & DeBoer 1979 was declared by sociocultural students at Columbia as racist and therefore not to be read!) If one disbelieves there are populational differences in the weight and/or structure of the brain, one should examine the papers by Klekamp and his colleagues, particularly regarding the finding that the primary visual striate cortex of Australian aborigines is significantly larger than in brains from people of European descent (Klekamp et al. 1994). This paper is, to my knowledge, the only paper published since the 1930s that demonstrates a real difference in brain morphology between modern populations (the last compilation of some of these earlier studies on brain morphology differences between different populations can be found in C.J. Connolly's 1950 book, *External Morphology of the Primate Brain*, which is a sort of bible for most people working in paleoneurology. See also Kochetkova 1978.) Of course, there is Gould's *Mismeasure of Man*, another bible of sorts, which should be read along with Michael's (1988) *Current Anthropology* paper, which found that Morton's rankings were correct and which Gould ignored in his later editions of the same book. There is certainly no evidence that Paul Broca used his elbow on the scales when measuring brains of peoples of European descent!

Additional autopsy data sets await my attention, including some 5000 cases from Hong Kong, collected by my colleague Philip Beh, and ~7500 cases from Singapore, the latter of multiple ethnicities. I hope to get to these data sets when I retire.

DISCLOSURE STATEMENT

The author is not aware of any biases that might be perceived as affecting the objectivity of this review.

POSTSCRIPT AND ACKNOWLEDGMENTS

On November 27, 2007, the science section of the *New York Times* ran a profile of me and my work (Balter 2007). Although grateful that I could make it within the *New York Times*, I wish more had been said of my other interests in brain research. Thus far, neither my colleagues in the Anthropology department nor the Columbia University Administration have acknowledged the article or the previously mentioned conference.

I am very grateful to the many colleagues who mentioned the honor and to the many students I have encountered over the decades who have truly rewarded me with their intelligence, wit, and support as well as the temerity to disagree. In particular, I mention Michael Yuan, Douglas Broadfield, Chet Sherwood, Francys Subiaul, Sam Marquez, Lynn Copes, and Jill Shapiro, who read earlier versions of this paper and who offered many useful corrections, as well as former students Christine DeLaCoste-Azziz, Peter Heilbroner, Jeffrey Schwartz, Este Armstrong, Joan Witkin, Jason Kaufman, and Peter Post. My special thanks go to Nick Toth and Kathy Schick for their interest in my work and their friendship, and for hosting the conference at the Stone Age Institute. I am grateful to Carole Travis-Henikof for her role in that honor. The encouragement and friendship of the late Clark Howell are sorely missed. My colleagues Janet Monge, Alan Mann, Jason Lewis, Robert D. Martin, Alan Walker, Dominique Grimaud-Hervé, Emiliano Bruner, James Rilling, Tom Schoenemann, Patrick Gannon, Daniel Buxhoeveden, John Allen, Katerina Semendeferi, Milford Wolpoff, John Hawks, Anne H. Weaver, and Carol MacLoed deserve special mention. To Peter Brown goes a special thanks for allowing me to study the LB1 endocast, regardless of whether I agreed with him! I would not have been able to make any contributions to paleoneurology without the cooperation and hospitality I received from the Leakey family in Nairobi, Kenya, and the staff at the Center. I owe a similar debt to the late Raymond Dart, Phillip V. Tobias, Bob Brain, the late Alun Hughes, the late Teuku Jacob and Ralph von Koenigswald, A Leguebe, Roger Saban, Yves Coppens, Ian Tattersall, Eric Delson, Gary Sawyer of the AMNH, and Theya Molleson of the BMNH. I continue to enjoy the collegiality and support of Tim White, Bill Kimbel, Yoel Rak, Gen Suwa, Berhane Asfaw, W. Henry Gilbert, Scott Simpson, and all their colleagues in Ethiopia, and I look forward to continuing studies on more hominid endocasts from there. To Chuck McAlexander and Dr. Graham Kavanagh go special thanks for their support. Lastly, my wife, Dr. Daisy Dwyer, has given me so much and put up with it all.

LITERATURE CITED

Allen JS, Bruss J, Damasio H. 2006. Looking for the lunate sulcus: a magnetic resonance imaging study in modern humans. *Anat. Rec. (A)* 288A:867–76

Armstrong E, Zilles K, Kurtis M, Schleicher A. 1991. Cortical folding, the lunate sulcus and the evolution of the human brain. *J. Hum. Evol.* 20:341–48

Balter M. 2007. In study of human brain evolution, zeal and bitter debate. Profile of scientist at work, Ralph Holloway. *New York Times*, Nov. 27:F2

Bean RB. 1906. Some racial peculiarities of the Negro brain. *Am. J. Anat.* 5:353–432

Bishop KM, Wahlsten D. 1997. Sex differences in the human corpus callosum: myth or reality? *Neurosci. Biobehav. Rev.* 21:581–601

Brodmann K. 1909. *Verleichende Lokalisationslehre der Grosshirnrinde in Ihren Prinzipien Dargestellt auf Grund des Zellenbaues*. Leipzig, Germany: Barth

Brown P, Sutikna T, Morwood MJ, Soejono RP, Jatmiko W, et al. 2004. A new small-bodied hominid from the late Pleistocene of Flores, Indonesia. *Nature* 441:624–28

Buxhoeveden DP, Casanova MF. 2002. The minicolumn and evolution of the brain. *Brain Behav. Evol.* 60:125–51

Calvin W. 1983. *The Throwing Madonna: Essays on the Brain*. New York: McGraw-Hill

Changeux JP, Chavaillon J, eds. 1995. *Origins of the Human Brain*. Oxford, UK: Clarendon

Clark WE, Le Gros, Cooper DM, Zuckerman S. 1936. The endocranial cast of the chimpanzee. *J. R. Anthropol. Inst.* 66:249–68

Connolly CJ. 1950. *External Morphology of the Primate Brain*. Springfield, IL: Thomas

Dart RA. 1925. *Australopithecus africanus*: the man-ape of South Africa. *Nature* 115:195–99

Dart RA. 1926. Taung and its significance. *Nat. Hist.* 26:315–27

Dart RA. 1956. The relationships of brain size and brain pattern to human status. *S. Afr. J. Med. Sci.* 21:23–45

de LaCoste-Utamsing C, Holloway RL. 1982. Sexual dimorphism in the human corpus callosum. *Science* 216:1431–32

Falk D. 1980. A reanalysis of the South African australopithecine natural endocasts. *Am. J. Phys. Anthropol.* 53:525–39

Falk D. 1983a. Cerebral cortices of East African early hominids. *Science* 222:1072–74

Falk D. 1983b. Hadar AL 162–28 endocast as evidence that brain enlargement preceded cortical reorganization in hominid evolution. *Nature* 313:45–47

Falk D. 1983c. The Taung endocast: a reply to Holloway. *Am. J. Phys. Anthropol.* 60:479–90

Falk D. 1985. Apples, oranges, and the lunate sulcus. *Am. J. Phys. Anthropol.* 67:313–15

Falk D. 1989. Ape-like endocast of "ape-man" Taung. *Am. J. Phys. Anthropol.* 80:335–39

Falk D. 1990. Brain evolution in *Homo*: the 'radiator' theory. *Behav. Brain Sci.* 13:333–81

Falk D. 1997. Book review: *Origins of the Human Brain. Am. J. Hum. Biol.* 9:766–67

Falk D. 2004. *Braindance, Revised and Expanded Edition: New Discoveries about Human Origins and Brain Evolution.* Gainesville: Univ. Press Fla.

Falk D, Clarke R. 2007. New reconstruction of the Taung endocast. *Am. J. Phys. Anthropol.* 134(4):529–34

Falk D, Hildebolt C, Smith K, Morwood MJ, Sutikna T, et al. 2005. The brain of LB1 *Homo floresiensis. Science* 308:242–45

Falk D, Redmond JC Jr, Guyer J, Conroy GC, Recheis W, et al. 2000. Early hominid brain evolution: a new look at old endocasts. *J. Hum. Evol.* 38:695–717

Fausto-Sterling A. 1985. *Myths of Gender.* New York: Basic Books

Freedman DG, DeBoer MM. 1979. Biological and cultural differences in early child development. *Annu. Rev. Anthropol.* 8:579–600

Grimaud-Hervé D. 1997. L'évolution de l'encéphale chez *Homo erectus* et *Homo sapiens.* Paris: CNRS Ed.

Gur RC, Gunning-Dixon F, Bilker WB, Gur RE. 2002. Sex differences in temporo-limbic and frontal brain volumes of healthy adults. *Cereb. Cortex* 12:998–1003

Hahn ME, Jensen G, Dudek BC. 1979. *Development and Evolution of Brain Size.* New York: Academic

Haier RJ, Jung RE, Yeo RA, Head K, Alkire MT. 2005. The neuroanatomy of general intelligence: sex matters. *Neuroimage* 25:320–27

Henneberg M, Thorne A. 2004. Flores may be pathological *Homo sapiens. Before Farming* 1:2–4

Hershkovitz I, Kornreich L, Laron Z. 2007. Comparative skeletal features between *Homo floresiensis* and patients with primary growth hormone insensitivity (Laron Syndrome). *Am. J. Phys. Anthropol.* 134:198–208

Ho K-C, Roessmann U, Hause L, Monroe G. 1981. Newborn brain weight in relation to maturity, sex, and race. *Ann. Neurol.* 10:243–46

Ho K-C, Roessmann U, Straumfjord JV, Monroe G. 1980. *Arch. Pathol. Lab. Med.* 104:640–45

Holloway RL. 1964. *Some quantitative relations of the primate brain.* PhD thesis, Univ. Calif., Berkeley. 174 pp.

Holloway RL. 1966a. Cranial capacity and neuron number: a critique and proposal. *Am. J. Phys. Anthropol.* 25:305–14

Holloway RL. 1966b. Cranial capacity, neural reorganization, and hominid evolution: a search for more suitable parameters. *Am. Anthropol.* 68:103–21

Holloway RL. 1966c. Dendritic branching: some preliminary results of training and complexity in rat visual cortex. *Brain Res.* 2:393–96

Holloway RL. 1967. The evolution of the human brain: some notes toward a synthesis between neural structure and the evolution of complex behavior. *Gen. Syst.* 12:3–19

Holloway RL. 1968. The evolution of the primate brain: some aspects of quantitative relations. *Brain Res.* 7:121–72

Holloway RL. 1969a. Culture: a human domain. *Curr. Anthropol.* 10(4):395–412

Holloway RL. 1969b. Some questions on parameters of neural evolution in primates. *Ann. NY Acad. Sci.* 167(1):332–40

Holloway RL. 1970a. Australopithecine endocast (Taung specimen, 1924): a new volume determination. *Science* 168:966–68

Holloway RL. 1970b. New endocranial values for the australopithecines. *Nature* 227:199–200

Holloway RL. 1972a. Australopithecine endocasts, brain evolution in the Hominoidea and a model of hominid evolution. In *The Functional and Evolutionary Biology of Primates*, ed. R Tuttle, pp. 185–204. Chicago: Aldine/Atherton Press

Holloway RL. 1972b. New Australopithecine endocast, SK 1585, from Swartkrans, South Africa. *Am. J. Phys. Anthropol.* 37:173–86

Holloway RL. 1973a. Endocranial volumes of the early African hominids and the role of the brain in human mosaic evolution. *J. Hum. Evol.* 2:449–59

Holloway RL. 1973b. New endocranial values for the East African early hominids. *Nature* 243:97–99

Holloway RL. 1974. On the meaning of brain size. *Science* 184:677–79

Holloway RL. 1975a. Early hominid endocasts: volumes, morphology, and significance. In *Primate Functional Morphology and Evolution*, ed. R Tuttle, pp. 393–416. The Hague: Mouton

Holloway RL. 1975b. *The Role of Human Social Behavior in the Evolution of the Brain*. The 43rd James Arthur Lecture on the Evolution of the Human Brain. New York: Am. Mus. Nat. Hist. 45 pp.

Holloway RL. 1976. Paleoneurological evidence for language origins. In *Origins and Evolution of Language and Speech*, ed. SR Harnad, HD Steklis, J Lancaster, 280:330–48. New York: Ann. NY Acad. Sci.

Holloway RL. 1979. Brain size, allometry, and reorganization: toward a synthesis. In *Development and Evolution of Brain Size: Behavioral Implications*, ed. ME Hahn, C Jensen, BC Dudek, pp. 59–88. New York: Academic

Holloway RL. 1980a. Indonesian "Solo" (Ngandong) endocranial reconstructions: some preliminary observations and comparisons with Neandertal and *Homo erectus* groups. *Am. J. Phys. Anthropol.* 53:285–95

Holloway RL. 1980b. The O.H. 7 (Olduvai Gorge, Tanzania) hominid partial brain endocast revisited. *Am. J. Phys. Anthropol.* 53:267–74

Holloway RL. 1980c. Within-species brain-body weight variability: a reexamination of the Danish data and other primate species. *Am. J. Phys. Anthropol.* 53:109–21

Holloway RL. 1981a. Culture, symbols, and human brain evolution: a synthesis. *Dialect. Anthropol.* 5:287–303

Holloway RL. 1981b. The endocast of the Omo juvenile L338y-6 hominid specimen. *Am. J. Phys. Anthropol.* 54:109–18

Holloway RL. 1981c. Exploring the dorsal surface of hominoid brain endocasts by stereoplotter and discriminant analysis. *Philos. Trans. R. Soc. London B Biol. Sci.* 292:155–66

Holloway RL. 1981d. The Indonesian *Homo erectus* brain endocasts revisited. *Am. J. Phys. Anthropol.* 55:503–21

Holloway RL. 1981e. Volumetric and asymmetry determinations on recent hominid endocasts: Spy I and II, Djebel Ihroud I, and the Sale *Homo erectus* specimens, with some notes on Neandertal brain size. *Am. J. Phys. Anthropol.* 55:385–93

Holloway RL. 1983a. Cerebral brain endocast pattern of *Australopithecus afarensis* hominid. *Nature* 303:420–22

Holloway RL. 1983b. *Homo erectus* brain endocasts: volumetric and morphological observations with some comments on cerebral asymmetries. L'*Homo erectus* et la place de l'homme de Tautavel parmi les hominidés fosiles. *Congr. Int. Paléontol. Hum., 1er, Nice.* 16–21 Oct. 1982, pp. 355–66

Holloway RL. 1983c. Human brain evolution: a search for units, models, and synthesis. *Can. J. Anthropol.* 3:215–32

Holloway RL. 1983d. Human paleontological evidence relevant to language behavior. *Hum. Neurobiol.* 2:105–14

Holloway RL. 1985a. The past, present, and future significance of the lunate sulcus in early hominid evolution. In *Hominid Evolution: Past, Present, and Future*, ed. PV Tobias, pp. 47–62. New York: Liss

Holloway RL. 1985b. The poor brain of *Homo sapiens neanderthalensis*: see what you please. In *Ancestors: The Hard Evidence*, ed. E Delson, pp. 319–24. New York: Liss

Holloway RL. 1988a. "Robust" australopithecine brain endocasts: some preliminary observations. In *The Evolutionary History of the "Robust" Australopithecines*, ed. F Grine. pp. 97–106. New York: Aldine de Gruyter

Holloway RL. 1988b. Some additional morphological and metrical observations on *Pan* brain casts and their relevance to the Taung endocast. *Am. J. Phys. Anthropol.* 77:27–33

Holloway RL. 1990a. Comments on Falk's radiator hypothesis. *Behav. Brain Sci.* 13:360

Holloway RL. 1990b. Sexual dimorphism in the human corpus callosum: its evolutionary and clinical implications. In *From Apes to Angels: Essays in Anthropology in Honor of Phillip V. Tobias*, ed. GH Sperber, pp. 221–28. New York: Wiley-Liss

Holloway RL. 1995. Toward a synthetic theory of human brain evolution. In *Origins of the Human Brain*, ed. J-P Changeux, J Chavaillon, pp. 42–54. Oxford: Clarendon

Holloway RL. 1996. Evolution of the human brain. In *Handbook of Human Symbolic Evolution*, ed. A Lock, C Peters, pp. 74–116. New York: Oxford Univ. Press

Holloway RL. 2000. Holloway denies label. *Anthropol. News* 41(5):4

Holloway RL, Anderson PJ, Defidine R, Harper C. 1993. Sexual dimorphism of the human corpus callosum from three independent samples: relative size of the corpus callosum. *Am. J. Phys. Anthropol.* 92:481–98

Holloway RL, Broadfield DC, Yuan MS. 2001a. The parietal lobe in early hominid evolution: newer evidence from chimpanzee brains. In *Humanity From African Naissance to Coming Millennia*, ed. PV Tobias, MA Raath, J Moggi-Cecchi, GA Doyle, pp. 365–71. Florence, Italy: Florence Univ. Press

Holloway RL, Broadfield DC, Yuan MS. 2001b. Revisiting australopithecine visual striate cortex: newer data from chimpanzee and human brains suggest it could have been reduced during australopithecine times. In *Evolutionary Anatomy of the Primate Cerebral Cortex*, ed. D Falk, K Gibson, pp. 177–86. New York: Cambridge Univ. Press

Holloway RL, Broadfield DC, Yuan MS. 2003. Morphology and histology of the chimpanzee primary visual striate cortex indicate that brain reorganization predated brain expansion in early hominid evolution. *Anat. Rec.* 273A:594–602

Holloway RL, Broadfield DC, Yuan MS. 2004a. *Brain Endocasts: The Paleoneurological Evidence*: Vol. 3, *The Human Fossil Record*. ed. JH Schwartz, I Tattersall. New York: Wiley-Liss

Holloway RL, Brown P, Schoenemann PT, Monge J. 2006. The brain endocast of *Homo floresiensis*: microcephaly and other issues. *Am. J. Phys. Anthropol.* S42:105 (Abstr.)

Holloway RL, Clarke RJ, Tobias PV. 2004b. Posterior lunate sulcus in *Australopithecus africanus:* Was Dart right? *Comptes Rendus Palevol.* 3:1–7

Holloway RL, de Lacoste-Lareymondie MC. 1982. Brain endocast asymmetry in pongids and hominids: some preliminary findings on the paleontology of cerebral dominance. *Am. J. Phys. Anthropol.* 58:101–10

Holloway RL, Kimbel WH. 1986. Endocast morphology of Hadar hominid AL 162–28. *Nature* 321:536

Holloway RL, Post DG. 1982. The relativity of relative brain measures and hominid mosaic evolution. In *Primate Brain Evolution: Methods and Concepts*, ed. E Armstrong, D Falk, pp. 57–76. New York: Plenum

Holloway RL, Yuan MS, Broadfield DC, Degusta D, Richards GD, et al. 2002. Missing Omo L338y-6 occipital-marginal sinus drainage pattern: ground sectioning, computer tomography scanning and the original fossil fail to show it. *Anat. Rec.* 266:249–57

Jacob T, Indriati E, Soejono RP, Hsu K, Frayer DW, et al. 2006. Pygmoid australomelanesian *Homo sapiens* skeletal remains from Liang Bua, Flores: population affinities and pathological abnormalities. *Proc. Natl. Acad. Sci. USA* 103:13421–26

Jensen AR. 1998. *The g Factor: The Science of Mental Ability*. Westport, CT: Praeger

Jerison HJ. 1973. *Evolution of the Brain and Intelligence*. New York: Academic

Jerison HJ. 1990. Fossil evidence on the evolution of the neocortex. In *Cerebral Cortex*, Vol. 8A, ed. EG Jones, A Peters, pp. 285–310. New York: Plenum

Keith A. 1931. *New Discoveries Relating to the Antiquity of Man*. New York: Norton

Kimbel WH. 1984. Variation in the pattern of cranial venous sinuses and hominid phylogeny. *Am. Phys. Anthropol.* 63:243–63

Kimbel WH. 1990. Comments on Falk's radiator hypothesis. *Behav. Brain Sci.* 13:359

Kimura D. 2003. *Sex and Cognition*. Cambridge, MA: Bradford Books

Klekamp J, Riedel A, Harper C, Kretschmann HJ. 1994. Morphometric study on the postnatal growth of the visual cortex of Australian Aborigines and Caucasians. *J. Brain Res.* 35:531–48

Kochetkova VI. 1978. *Paleoneurology*. Washington, DC: Winston

Leakey RE. 1981. *The Making of Mankind*. New York: Dutton

Leakey RE, Lewin R. 1978. *People of the Lake: Mankind and Its Beginnings*. Garden City, NY: Anchor

Lieberman L. 2005. How "Caucasoids" got such big brains and why they shrank. *Curr. Anthropol.* 42(1):69–96

Lynn R, Vanhanen T. 2006. *IQ & Global Inequality*. Augusta, GA: Washington Summit

Marks J. 2000. Scientific racism in your face. *Anthropol. News* 41(2):60

Martin RD, Maclarnon AM, Phillips JL, Dobyns WB. 2006b. Flores hominid: new species or microcephalic dwarf? *Anat. Rec. A Discov. Mol. Cell Evol. Biol.* 288:1123–45

Martin RD, Maclarnon AM, Phillips JL, Dussubieux L, Williams PR, Dobyns WB. 2006a. Comment on *The brain of LB1* Homo floresiensis. *Science* 312:999b

Michael J. 1988. A new look at Morton's craniological research. *Curr. Anthropol.* 29(2):349–54

Narr KL, Woods RP, Thompson PM, Szeszko P, Robinson D, et al. 2007. Relationships between IQ and regional cortical gray matter thickness in healthy adults. *Cereb. Cortex* 17:2163–71

Pakkenberg H, Voigt J. 1964. Brain weight of Danes. *Acta Anat.* 56:297–307

Preuss TM, Cáceres M, Laucher J, Zapala MA, Redmond JC, et al. 2003. Using genomics to identify human brain specializations. *Am. J. Phys. Anthropol.* Suppl. 36:171

Radinsky LB. 1974. The fossil evidence of anthropoid brain evolution. *Am. J. Phys. Anthropol.* 41:15–28

Radinsky LB. 1975. Primate brain evolution. *Am. Sci.* 63:656–63

Radinsky LB. 1979. *The Fossil Record of Primate Brain Evolution*. New York: Am. Mus. Nat. Hist.

Richards GD. 2006. Genetic, physiologic and ecogeographic factors contributing to variation in *Homo sapiens*: *Homo floresiensis* reconsidered. *J. Evol. Biol.* 19:1744–67

Rilling JK. 2006. Human and nonhuman brains: Are they allometrically scaled versions of the same design? *Evol. Anthropol.* 15(2):65–77

Rushton JP. 2000. *Race, Evolution, and Behavior: A Life-History Perspective*. Port Huron, MI: Charles Darwin Res. Inst. 3rd ed.

Rushton JP. 2002. Race, brain size, and IQ. *Gen. Psychol.* 37:28–33

Schepers GWH. 1946. The endocranial casts of the South African ape men. In *The South African Fossil Ape Men: The Australopithecinae*, Transvaal Mus. Mem. 2, ed. R Broom, GHW Schepers. Pretoria: Transvaal Mus.

Schoenemann PT. 2006. Evolution of the size and functional areas of the human brain. *Annu. Rev. Anthropol.* 35(1):379–406

Sherwood CC, Broadfield DC, Hof PR, Holloway RL. 2003. Variability in Broca's area homologue in great apes: implications for language evolution. *Anat. Rec.* 271A:276–85

Smith GE. 1904. The morphology of the occipital region of the cerebral hemispheres in man and apes. *Anat. Anz.* 24:436–51

Smith RJ. 2005. Relative size versus controlling for size. *Curr. Anthropol.* 46(2):249–73

Stanford C, Allen JS, Anton SC. 2008. *Exploring Biological Anthropology: The Essentials*. Upper Saddle River, NJ: Pearson Prentice Hall

Stout D, Toth N, Schick K, Chaminade T. 2008. Neural correlates of Early Stone Age toolmaking: technology, language and cognition in human evolution. *Phil. Trans. R. Soc. London B Biol. Ser.* B:1–11

Tobias PV. 1970. Brain size, grey matter and race-fact or fiction? *Am. J. Phys. Anthropol.* 32:3–26

Weaver AH. 2005. Reciprocal evolution of the cerebellum and neocortex in fossil humans. *Proc. Natl. Acad. Sci. USA* 102:3576–80

White DD, Falk D. 1999. A quantitative and qualitative reanalysis of the endocast from the juvenile *Paranthropus* specimen L338y-6 form Omo, Ethiopia. *Am. J. Phys. Anthropol.* 110:399–406

Wood BA. 1991. *Hominid Cranial Remains*. Oxford: Clarendon

The Effects of Kin on Primate Life Histories

Karen B. Strier

Department of Anthropology, University of Wisconsin, Madison, Wisconsin 53706;
email: kbstrier@wisc.edu

Annu. Rev. Anthropol. 2008. 37:21–36

First published online as a Review in Advance on
April 7, 2008

The *Annual Review of Anthropology* is online at
anthro.annualreviews.org

This article's doi:
10.1146/annurev.anthro.37.081407.085218

0084-6570/08/1021-0021$20.00

Key Words

Reproduction, maternal investment, nepotism, demography, ecology

Abstract

Advances in our understanding of primate life histories and dispersal
patterns provide insights into the ways in which facultative responses to
local ecological and demographic conditions are mediated by phylogenetic constraints. The long life spans characteristic of primates provide
the necessary conditions for overlapping generations of related individuals to maintain extended kin bonds. Dispersal regimes dictate the
opportunities for biological kin to interact with one another and define the range of potential reproductive and social partners within and
beyond their natal groups. Dispersal patterns also affect variation in
components of life histories such as female age at first reproduction,
reproductive rates, and trade-offs between investment in current vs.
future offspring and extended kin. Understanding these dynamics has
important implications for assessing the viability of small populations
and the ability of different primates to adapt.

INTRODUCTION

Mammalian reproductive parameters are defined by life histories, which are the evolutionary products of trade-offs among investment in growth, reproduction, and survival (Stearns 1992). Life-history traits, such as age at first reproduction, interbirth intervals, and life span, set upper limits on female reproductive rates and rates of population growth. Compared with most other mammals of similar body size, primates have relatively large brains and are long lived, with correspondingly slow rates of development that result in long birth intervals, extended juvenile periods, and late maturation (Harvey & Clutton-Brock 1985, Charnov & Berrigan 1993, Ross 1998). These distinctive features of primate life histories also produce overlapping generations that make it possible for extended networks of biological kin to interact. Whether they do so is determined by their dispersal patterns, which affect the composition of primate groups and therefore the potential for long-term associations among diverse configurations of kin (Strier 2004c).

Life histories and dispersal patterns are often regarded as phylogenetically conservative characteristics of species and higher taxonomic units because they tend to cluster together within each of the major adaptive grades (Harvey & Clutton-Brock 1985, Martin & MacLarnon 1985, Lee & Kappeler 2003, Strier 2003). At the same time, however, individual life histories and the kinship structures of primate groups and local communities can vary across populations of the same species in response to local ecological and demographic conditions (Strier 2004c, Jones 2005). Within the phenotypic constraints of a species (sensu Maynard Smith 1978), some components of life histories exhibit considerable phenotypic plasticity (Lee & Kappeler 2003). The duration of lactation and the postpartum delays to both cycling and conception, as well as age at first reproduction, are among the most variable life-history traits because they are sensitive to the effects of ecology and demography, as mediated by energetics and sociality (Fedigan & Rose 1995, Lee 1996).

Interbirth intervals and age at first reproduction are also among the life-history variables that most directly affect intrinsic rates of population growth (Dobson & Lyles 1989, Ross 1998) and are therefore useful indicators for assessing the viabilities of small populations of endangered species and for establishing conservation priorities (Cowlishaw & Dunbar 2000, Strier 2007). Moreover, knowledge of the ways in which these life-history traits respond to local ecological and demographic conditions can provide critical insights into the potential for different primates to adapt to the rapidly changing conditions that now threaten so many of them with extinction (Strier 2001).

Advances in noninvasive methods for obtaining hormonal and genetic data from wild primates have brought new tools for investigating both the mechanisms that regulate reproduction (Whitten et al. 1998, Bercovitch & Ziegler 2002, Ziegler & Wittwer 2005) and the biological relatedness underlying the social relationships that mediate life histories and reproduction (Di Fiore 2003, Di Fiore & Gagneux 2007), respectively. Hormonal data, for example, provide insights into the onset of ovarian cycling and the postweaning resumption of cycling and conception in primates that lack visible cues of ovulation or pregnancy. Similarly, genetic data on paternity and relatedness among other group members provide a basis for evaluating how fathers and both maternal and paternal kin can affect infant survival and thus influence female reproductive rates.

REPRODUCTIVE RATES

Phylogeny, ecology, and the energetics of body size and brain size affect the pace of life histories in general, and gestation and lactation impose additional constraints on the reproductive rates of female mammals (Western 1979, Purvis et al. 2003). Together, these variables account for much of the interspecific variation in primate reproductive rates, which range from the production of twins (or larger litters) at 6 or 7 month intervals in wild female marmosets and tamarins, respectively (Digby et al. 2007) to that of a single infant at 8–9 year intervals in wild female orangutans (Knott 2001, van Noordwijk & van Schaik 2005).

The rapid reproductive rates of marmosets and tamarins have been attributed to the infant care that other group members routinely provide (Garber 1997). Alloparental care releases mothers from the energetic burdens of carrying growing infants during lactation and therefore reduces female interbirth intervals while increasing the infants' probability of survival. In most other primates, the resumption of cycling and conception is postponed until weaning, but marmoset and tamarin mothers resume their cycles and can conceive within a few weeks of giving birth.

The unusually long interbirth intervals of orangutans, by contrast, have been attributed to ecological constraints on their sociality, which preclude the maintenance of extended associations with more than a single offspring at a time. Orangutan mothers cannot meet their own high nutritional requirements while simultaneously nursing a new infant and traveling with an older weaned offspring as female chimpanzees—and most other primates—do because the low primary productivity in the southeast Asian forests they inhabit (Jablonski et al. 2000, Harrison & Chivers 2007) is thought to prevent female orangutans from reproducing before their current offspring are able to travel and forage on their own (van Noordwijk & van Schaik 2005). The long period of time required for orangutans to acquire ecological competence results in interbirth intervals nearly twice as long as those achieved by chimpanzees (Robson et al. 2006).

Despite the phylogenetic distance and morphological and ecological differences between callitrichines and orangutans, the comparison is informative because it illustrates the potential impact that access to nonmaternal infant caretakers can have on female reproductive rates (Mitani & Watts 1997, Ross 1998, Ross & MacLarnon 2000). In wild marmosets and tamarins, biological fathers and older siblings are more likely to carry infants than are unrelated group members (Nievergelt et al. 2000,

Huck et al. 2005), whereas in orangutans, ecological constraints prevent the continuous associations between parents or other kin required for the manifestation of paternal or alloparental care. Most primates, however, fall in between these two extremes in both their reproductive rates and their access to biological kin, which also vary in the levels and types of contributions they make to infant care. The differential ability of male primates to increase female reproductive rates through their behavior may underlie some of the interspecific differences in primate mating and dispersal patterns (Strier 1996a). High levels of paternal care of infants may also be associated with relatively longer male life spans in those species in which it occurs (Allman et al. 1998).

MATERNAL INVESTMENT STRATEGIES

Lactation imposes heavy energetic costs on all mammalian mothers, and even after weaning, many female primates experience temporal delays before cycling resumes and they can conceive again (Altmann 1980, Lee 1996). Intraspecific variation in the nongestational components of interbirth intervals reflect these costs, which vary with maternal nutritional condition and social status, as well as with the strategic allocation of maternal resources in current vs. future offspring. Seasonality in the availability of high-quality foods for mothers or suitable weaning foods for infants can influence both the timing of weaning and the delays from weaning to the resumption of ovarian cycling and from cycling to conception (Lee 1996, Barrett et al. 2006). Among sympatric lemurs at Ranomafana National Park, Madagascar, for example, annual birth seasons are staggered over a six-month period, but weaning in all species is synchronized to coincide with the seasonal availability of weaning foods (Wright 1999).

In northern muriquis, by contrast, maternal condition, instead of weaning foods, appears to regulate the timing of conceptions and births. Northern muriqui females can resume cycling and mate within one week of an infant's death, but they do not usually conceive again until the following conception season (Strier 2004b). Thus, interbirth intervals following the death of an infant during the annual rainy season, when most conceptions occur, may be much shorter than those following the death of an infant during the annual dry season, when conception probabilities are low. The three-year average interbirth intervals following the births of infants that survive through weaning also often include several months before the resumption of ovarian cycling and 2–7 cycles before conception occurs (Strier & Ziegler 1997). These delays in cycling and conception suggest that ecological and energetic constraints on mothers may be responsible for regulating the timing of reproduction in this species (Strier 1996b).

Access to essential resources, such as food and water, varies with female age and rank in hierarchical societies and with territory quality in heterogeneous habitats (Wrangham 1981, Richard et al. 2002, Gould et al. 2003). Differential access to such critical resources at critical times affects the health and survival of mothers and especially of dependent infants. Not surprisingly, age-related maternal condition has a greater effect on infant survival in species with low levels of feeding competition, such as mountain gorillas (Robbins et al. 2006), than does rank-related maternal condition, which may or may not covary with age in hierarchical societies. Among wild Milne Edwards' sifaka, infant mortality varies with maternal age only during years with low rainfall because dental senescence prevents older lactating mothers from obtaining sufficient nutrition from the low-quality foods available in dry years (King et al. 2005). In yellow baboons and chimpanzees, the positive effects of high maternal rank also extend beyond infant survival to the larger sizes of juveniles and their offsprings' earlier ages at sexual maturation (Pusey et al. 1997, Altmann & Alberts 2005).

Variation in maternal investment in current vs. future offspring is affected by the relative importance of intrinsic, or care-dependent, sources of mortality vs. extrinsic, or care-independent, sources of mortality (Barrett et al. 2006). When increased maternal investment can improve infant survival, females tend to invest more heavily in fewer offspring, which are also more likely to survive as a result. By contrast, when maternal investment cannot buffer infants from extrinsic sources of mortality, such as predation, disease, or infanticidal males, mothers tend to invest less in each offspring, which shortens interbirth intervals and results in faster reproductive rates (Jones 1997). Thus, chacma baboons living in harsh climates at high altitudes wean their infants later and have correspondingly longer birth intervals and higher infant and juvenile survival than do conspecifics living at lower altitudes, where predators and disease take a greater toll on offspring survival (Barrett et al. 2006). By contrast, the high frequency of unpredictable catastrophic climatic events such as droughts and storms in Madagascar, which can result in infant mortality rates of up to 52%, may account for why female sifaka pursue a bet-hedging strategy by which they trade off early reproduction in exchange for longer lives over which to reproduce (Richard et al. 2002). Indeed, many of the morphological, physiological, and behavioral adaptations of lemurs in general have been attributed to their unique evolutionary history in an exceptionally unpredictable environment (Wright 1999).

EFFECTS OF KIN

Assistance from allo-caretakers can reduce some of the costs of female reproduction without compromising infant survival, and thereby influences maternal behavior and investment strategies (Ross 1998). Because of their shared genetic interests, biological kin are more likely than nonkin to engage in alloparenting as well as to provide additional support beyond infancy (Hamilton 1964, Hrdy 1981, Silk 2002, Chapais & Berman 2004). Long-term kin bonds, whether between parents and offspring, or among maternal or paternal siblings and extended matrilineal or patrilineal relatives, can also serve other vital social functions that mitigate life-history trade-offs throughout life. (See sidebar on Kinship in Primatology.)

Paternal care involves a wide range of behaviors, including bearing a disproportionate share of infant carrying and food sharing, as occurs in the callitrichines as well as in pairbonded owl monkeys and titi monkeys, where paternity is either presumed (Wright 1990) or known from genetic analyses (Huck et al. 2005). Males can also provide indirect services to females and their infants, such as babysitting while mothers feed unencumbered, providing protection from predators and harassment by conspecifics, including other females and infanticidal males, and defending or providing access to resources that mothers and their infants require (Hrdy 1981, 1995; Whitten 1987; Ross & MacLarnon 2000). Male tolerance toward infants, although not care per se, is also more common in patrilocal societies (Guimaraes and Strier 2001) or when related males disperse together and are therefore related to the offspring sired by other males in their groups (Isbell et al. 2002).

With the exception of twins or larger litters, maternal siblings are always separated in age by at least one birth interval. The long juvenile periods of primates provide maternal siblings with opportunities to become familiar with one another through their ongoing associations with their mothers. Older siblings can carry or monitor infants and therefore simultaneously help as well as gain valuable experience in caring for infants prior to the onset of their own reproductive careers (Paul 1999, Pope 2000, Berman 2004). Paternal siblings, by contrast, are more likely to be members of the same birth cohorts unless their fathers retain their reproductive status long enough to sire another infant with the same mother. Being close in age, paternally related siblings are not usually in a position to care for infants in the ways that older maternal siblings can, and the help paternal siblings may provide each other tends to occur only after they are weaned.

Other older female kin can provide similar kinds of allomaternal care as do adult fathers and may be even more likely to do so when their own reproductive success is not compromised.

KINSHIP IN PRIMATOLOGY

In primatology, kinship usually refers exclusively to the genetic relatedness among individuals and therefore differs from the much more complex concepts and implications associated with descent groups in human kinship systems (Fox 1967, 1975). Primate kinship does not carry any of the inherent assumptions about alliances, exogamy, or inheritance rules associated with human kinship, and there is no equivalent terminology for referring to categories of nonbiological kin, such as those that arise from human marriage practices (Strier 2004a,c). Instead, we use genetic relatedness among individuals to evaluate predictions about the fitness consequences of behaviors and social relationships, which are expected to correspond with the degree of relatedness, and therefore, with the extent to which their genetic interests overlap. Mechanisms of kin recognition, such as various forms of phenotypic matching, are still poorly understood and are difficult to distinguish from familiarity among group members in wild primate societies (Rendall 2004, Widdig 2007). Nonetheless, familiar, closely related biological kin are often powerful allies, particularly in competitive interactions against nonkin or distant relatives. Primate dispersal and residency patterns influence the availability of kin and therefore the extent to which relationships with kin can affect life-history and reproductive patterns.

In provisioned Japanese macaques and captive vervet monkeys, infants were significantly more likely to survive when their maternal grandmothers were still alive in their groups, whether or not they were caring for infants of their own (Fairbanks 1988, 1990; Pavelka et al. 2002). Matrilineally related Hanuman langur females also accounted for some 10% of all cases of infant handling (Hrdy 1977). Indeed, the grandmother hypothesis attributes the evolution of the uniquely human menopause and extended postreproductive life spans of women to the inclusive fitness benefits that older female kin gain by helping to care for the offspring of their daughters or other younger female kin (Hawkes et al. 1998, Alvarez 2000, Hawkes 2003). As with other forms of paternal and allomaternal care, the help provided by extended matrilineal kin may permit the mothers to reproduce at a faster rate while simultaneously increasing their infants' survival.

Kin support that extends after weaning will not directly impact female reproductive rates unless mothers can wean their infants earlier than they otherwise would as a result of the support they can anticipate. In yellow baboons, for example, adult male support of their juvenile offspring may have direct fitness consequences for both parents (Buchan et al. 2003), and the wider social networks that females maintain evidently enhance their infants' survival (Silk et al. 2003). There appears to be a relatedness threshold for altruism, which in the matrilineal societies of Japanese macaques corresponds to the genetic relationship between great-grandmothers and their great-grandoffspring for matrilineal kin, and to that between half siblings for collateral female kin (Chapais et al. 1997, 2001). Below these thresholds, nepotistic support declines to levels that are indistinguishable from support among nonkin, but whether this is because the indirect fitness benefits of supporting more distant kin are too low to outweigh the costs of intervention or because related individuals that fall below the relatedness thresholds are not recognizable as kin is not known (Chapais 2001, Chapais & Bélisle 2004).

Age proximity appears to affect the strength of affiliations among paternally related siblings in populations of rhesus macaques (Widdig et al. 2001, Widdig 2007) and yellow baboons (Alberts 1999, Smith et al. 2003). Primates also require at least some degree of familiarity to recognize even close biological kin as such, and the manifestation of nepotism in any form, such as infant care, cooperation, or agonistic support, requires ongoing spatial proximity (Bernstein 1999, Chapais 2001). This is most easily achieved through coresidence in the same group, but it can also result when kin disperse into the same nonnatal groups or into neighboring groups within their local communities (Kappeler et al. 2002; Lawler et al. 2003; Bradley et al. 2004, 2007; Jack & Fedigan 2004a,b; Strier 2004a; Douadi et al. 2007).

ACCESS TO KIN

Access to kin is dictated by dispersal patterns, which can be male biased, female biased, or bisexual. Examples of bisexual dispersal are found across the primate order, but the distribution of sex-biased dispersal patterns and their corresponding configurations of kin varies with phylogeny. Among anthropoids, male-biased dispersal is more common among Old World cercopithecine monkeys, whereas female-biased dispersal is more common in the African hominoids and New World ateline monkeys (Di Fiore & Rendall 1994, Strier 1994). Bisexual dispersal precludes the maintenance of extended networks of kin, whereas male-biased dispersal promotes these networks among matrilocal females and female-biased dispersal promotes them among patrilocal males.

Dispersal does not necessarily sever the maintenance of all kinds of kin bonds. In many species, for example, familiar males that may also be paternal siblings disperse from their natal groups together, and maternal brothers may join the same groups in succession, where they maintain affiliative associations (e.g., vervet monkeys: Cheney & Seyfarth 1983; long-tailed macaques: van Noordwijk & van Schaik 1985; Peruvian squirrel monkeys: Mitchell 1994; white-faced capuchin monkeys: Jack & Fedigan 2004a; western gorillas: Bradley et al. 2004). Similar patterns have been observed among female northern muriquis that are known to be maternal sisters (Strier et al. 2006), and molecular data have shown that related female lowland gorillas are more likely to disperse into the same groups than would be expected by chance (Bradley et al. 2007). Consequently, the various configurations of primate kin bonds can be envisioned along a continuum reflecting the ranges of possibilities that different dispersal patterns permit.

Dispersal by one or both sexes before the onset of sexual maturity reduces the genetic risks of close inbreeding, but whether inbreeding avoidance is an evolutionary cause of dispersal or a consequence of selection pressures favoring either associations among kin or avoidance of kin is not clear (Moore & Ali 1984, Clutton-Brock 1989). Socioecological models predict the conditions under which the benefits of remaining with kin should outweigh the costs. Briefly, the temporal availability and spatial distribution of primate food resources are thought to determine whether females benefit most by cooperating with or by avoiding competition with their close kin, and the ecological costs and benefits of female dispersal vs. philopatry define the social options available to males (Clutton-Brock & Harvey 1978; Wrangham 1979, 1980; Sterck et al. 1997). Female philopatry may necessitate male dispersal because female primates prefer to mate with unfamiliar partners, whereas female dispersal may permit either male philopatry or male dispersal, depending on whether cooperation among related males improves their ability to collectively defend females from other groups of related males or whether individual males or small teams of dispersing males can successfully defend females or the resources that attract these females into groups.

Demography and Dispersal

Despite the ecological principles underlying variation in primate dispersal and kinship patterns, there are examples in nearly all wild populations studied for any length of time of at least some proportion of individuals that deviate from their species' or local populations' norms (Moore 1984). These deviations can sometimes be explained by local ecological and demographic conditions, which affect different species in different ways (Strier 2000, Isbell et al. 2002). For example, habitat saturation can lead to the dispersal of female Thomas langurs instead of their retention in their natal groups (Sterck 1997, 1998), or it can lead to the retention of sexually mature offspring in the natal groups of marmosets (Ferrari & Digby 1996) and gibbons (Sommer & Reichard 2000), where they remain as subordinates, with limited or no breeding opportunities, until they can inherit a breeding position in their natal group

or favorable dispersal opportunities arise. The same ecological factors that constrain successful dispersal can also increase levels of intergroup competition and therefore increase the value of related allies in cooperative intergroup defense. Concession models of reproductive skew (Hager 2003, Dietz 2004) are predicated on the fitness benefits that dominant individuals gain when they can maintain support from subordinate allies by ceding some share of reproductive opportunities to them.

Unfavorable demographic conditions, such as male-biased sex ratios, are responsible for the secondary dispersal decisions by male yellow baboons (Alberts & Altmann 1995) and male white-fronted capuchin monkeys (Jack & Fedigan 2004b) and can also lead to dispersal attempts by males that are normatively patrilocal. Male dispersal has been reported from an isolated population of chimpanzees at Bossou, Guinea (Sugiyama 1999), and dispersal by a pair of male bonobos (Hohmann 2001) and by two cohorts of male northern muriquis following successive group fissions (Strier et al. 2006) has been attributed to the unfavorable sex ratios in their respective groups relative to the more favorable reproductive opportunities elsewhere.

Indeed, there are a finite number of routes of deviating from particular dispersal or kinship patterns once these become established (Foley & Lee 1989, Lee 1994). Female philopatry appears to be unusually resistant to change, which may reflect the dual reproductive advantages that females gain by remaining in their natal groups, where they simultaneously avoid dispersal costs while benefiting from life-long access to their extended matrilineal kin. When groups of matrilocal female rhesus macaques and savannah baboons fission, females exhibit significant preferences for remaining with their close maternal kin, and secondarily with close paternal kin (Widdig et al. 2006, Van Horn et al. 2007). Genetic studies have also shown that coalitions of related female red howler monkeys that reproduced in their natal groups had higher reproductive success than did coalitions of unrelated females (Pope 2000). Thus, both the costs of dispersal and the advantages of access to extended matrilineal kin appear to contribute to the resilience of matrilocality when ecological conditions permit.

Dispersal Costs

Dispersal is costly to males and females alike because of the ecological and social risks it entails. The ecological and social challenges may begin before an individual of dispersing age has left the natal group, as tolerance by same-sexed adults declines or rates of targeted aggression against them increase. Unless group transfers occur during intergroup encounters, dispersal also requires leaving the safety of a group to travel alone or with one or more partners until an established group or a vacant area of suitable habitat in which to establish a new group can be located. Mortality rates of solitary male yellow baboons during dispersal were estimated to be more than twice as high as those of group-living males because of predation, difficulties in finding adequate food, and susceptibility to disease as a result of stress and poor nutrition (Alberts & Altmann 1995). In red howler monkeys, 27% of dispersing males and 43%–52% of dispersing females are suspected or known to have died; the higher mortality rates among females are attributed to the longer distances over which they dispersed compared with males (Crockett & Pope 1993).

Age at first reproduction generally occurs later among dispersing females than among females that remain and reproduce in their natal groups (**Figure 1**, see color insert). This pattern holds across species among females of similar body sizes, as well as within species in which some, but not all, females disperse. For example, female northern muriquis, yellow baboons, and gibbons are similar to one another in body mass, but age at first reproduction in dispersing muriqui and gibbon females is nearly twice as old as the age at which most matrilocal yellow baboon females reproduce (Strier 2003). Patterns of dental development among female catarrhines also conform to species differences in dispersal patterns, with molar eruptions associated with weaning and maturity occurring

later in species in which females disperse (Dirks & Bowman 2007). Ages at first reproduction in three female muriquis that atypically reproduced in their natal group were more than one year earlier than the median age of 9.75 years at which dispersing females in the same population reproduced (Strier & Ziegler 2000, Strier et al. 2006). Similarly, female red howler monkeys that reproduce in their natal groups do so at 5.1 years, compared with 6.9 years in females that disperse (Crockett & Pope 1993, Pope 2000).

The high costs of dispersal on female reproduction may explain why secondary dispersal by females is so rare (Williams et al. 2002). Dispersing female northern muriquis (Strier et al. 2006) and woolly monkeys (Nishimura 2003) may visit multiple groups before immigrating permanently into one. Unless their groups disintegrate entirely, as can occur in mountain gorilla groups when a silverback dies, most female primates remain in the same groups in which they begin their reproductive careers.

The costs of dispersal on male age at first reproduction are more difficult to assess because the genetic data necessary to confirm paternity, and thus the age at which males sire their first offspring, are still scarce for many species. Although dominance rank affects both male and female reproductive success, it has a stronger influence on male breeding opportunities than it does on most females. Male rank affects the age at which sexually mature males gain access to fertile females, whether or not they remain in their natal groups. Genetic paternity studies indicate a positive relationship between male rank and fertilization success, although the degree of rank-related reproductive skew can vary from less than 40% (e.g., chimpanzees) to 100% (e.g., red howler monkeys) depending on the species, group histories, and abilities of particular males to monopolize reproductive opportunities (Pope 1990, Altmann et al. 1996, Gerloff et al. 1999, Constable et al. 2001, Bradley et al. 2005, Huck et al. 2005, Bales et al. 2006, Nsubuga et al. 2008). Interestingly, the effects of rank on the variance in male reproductive success are more pronounced among related males that either form coalitions to establish their own groups or remain in their natal groups (Strier 2004a).

Advantages of Maintaining Kin Bonds

Philopatry is advantageous to both females and males, which benefit similarly from access to a familiar area and food supply, as well as from access to familiar group members, which can include both maternally and paternally related kin. The effects of these ecological and social advantages on age at first reproduction should vary with population densities, habitat quality, and the degree to which aid or cooperation from allies can affect direct and indirect fitness. Limited dispersal options, either due to habitat fragmentation or habitat saturation, and variance in sex ratios and reproductive opportunities shift the relative costs and benefits of dispersing or remaining in the natal group (Jones 1999, 2005).

Matrilocal females gain life-long access to extended matrilineal kin, some of which may also be paternally related (Altmann et al. 1996, de Ruiter & Geffen 1998). It is rare, however, for matrilocal females to maintain long-term coresidence with their fathers or extended patrilineal kin owing to secondary dispersal by males. Patrilocal males, by contrast, maintain life-long access to their mothers and therefore both their maternal and paternal siblings. Paradoxically, however, there is no evidence for nepotism among paternally related male chimpanzees (Langergraber et al. 2007). Why male chimpanzees appear to recognize and affiliate more strongly with maternally related kin than paternal kin is unclear, but the pattern is consistent with the social support that bonobo mothers provide their adult sons (Furuichi 1997), as well as with the resilience of maternal and matrilineal kin bonds whenever ecological and demographic conditions permit them to persist.

Both males and females can benefit by dispersing with partners instead of alone, but access to same-sexed allies may be more valuable to males, whether they transfer into multimale groups, as Peruvian squirrel monkeys and white-faced capuchin monkeys do (Mitchell 1994, Jack & Fedigan 2004a), or cooperate in taking over or establishing a group. Coalitions of related males are more successful both in take-over attempts and in defending their groups against extragroup challengers, even when the dominant of the codefending males monopolizes all (red howler monkeys: Pope 1990; moustached tamarins: Huck et al. 2005) or a disproportionate share of fertilizations (mountain gorillas: Bradley et al. 2005). Dispersing with maternally related brothers occurs less often because of the age differences among them. Nonetheless, immigration can be easier for young males when they transfer into groups that familiar older siblings have previously joined (Cheney & Seyfarth 1983, van Noordwijk & van Schaik 1985). Secondary dispersal does not always sever these bonds, and the presence of familiar, related males in adjacent groups may result in reduced levels of intergroup aggression (Fuentes 2000, Isbell et al. 2002, Bradley et al. 2004, Jack & Fedigan 2004b).

CONCLUSIONS AND FUTURE DIRECTIONS

Research on primate life histories and kinship has traditionally focused on interspecific comparisons and the refinements that phylogenetic considerations have brought (Purvis et al. 2003). These approaches have been instrumental in identifying critical variables that distinguish primates from other mammals and in illuminating the diversity of trade-offs among growth, reproduction, and survival that account for the normative life-history patterns different species and higher taxonomic units express (Ellison 2001). Equivalent insights into the sources of intraspecific variation in primate life histories have lagged behind our understanding of interspecific variation, however, in part because the comparative individual-based data necessary for distinguishing patterns of plasticity have been so scarce.

Some components of life histories, such as interbirth intervals and age at first reproduction, appear to vary with dispersal and kinship both within and between species. Others, such as maternal investment strategies, which affect interbirth intervals, seem to vary in predictable ways with ecological and demographic conditions that affect intrinsic and extrinsic sources of mortality. Identifying patterns in the ranges of responses to local conditions that different species make in other aspects of their life histories and behavior will require long-term data from a diversity of wild primates.

As pressures on primate populations and their habitats continue to increase, their life-history trade-offs are predicted to change. Contemporary climate change scenarios forecast major shifts in the length and intensity of seasonal rainfall throughout the tropics, which will alter the ecological and demographic conditions to which primate life histories respond. Extreme climatic fluctuations associated with more severe El Niño events are expected to put even greater ecological stress on orangutans than they experience today (Harrison & Chivers 2007). In addition to elevated mortality rates, which have been reported for several primate populations following severe hurricanes (black howler monkeys: Pavelka et al. 2007) and prolonged droughts (e.g., sifaka: Richard et al. 2002; Pochron et al. 2004; ring-tailed lemurs: Gould et al. 2003), corresponding adjustments in the timing of reproduction and weaning and in maternal investment strategies in response to climate change can be widely anticipated.

Stochastic demographic fluctuations, such as skews in group and population-wide sex ratios, have more pronounced effects in small, isolated populations than in large populations, and therefore they represent a major threat to the viabilities of populations of endangered species, which are, by definition, small in size (Cowlishaw & Dunbar 2000). Small, protected populations can show remarkable growth when sex ratios are female biased, as well as rapid declines when male-biased sex ratios persist for any length of time. One population of northern muriquis, for example, quadrupled in 25 years owing to a female-biased infant sex ratio during the first 20 years of the study (Strier et al. 2006). With the maturation of recent cohorts of infants, which have all been strongly male biased, the rate of population growth is expected to decline, and levels of male-male competition are expected to rise. Other shifts in vital rates in this population, including higher infant mortality, shorter interbirth intervals, and later ages at which dispersing females are now reproducing, suggest that a shift in key life-history traits may already be underway.

Documenting individual and population-level responses to ecological and demographic fluctuations is a necessary step for integrating inter- and intraspecific perspectives on primate life histories. Understanding the ways in which primate social relationships, in general, and biological kin, in particular, affect their life histories and reproductive patterns is increasingly critical for assessing the potential of different primates to adapt to the rapidly changing conditions that human primates have caused.

SUMMARY POINTS

1. Biological kin can positively influence primate reproductive success and life histories through their contributions to infant care and social support in obtaining and defending resources.

2. Differential access to kin is determined by dispersal patterns, which vary generally with phylogeny, but are also influenced by local ecological and demographic conditions.

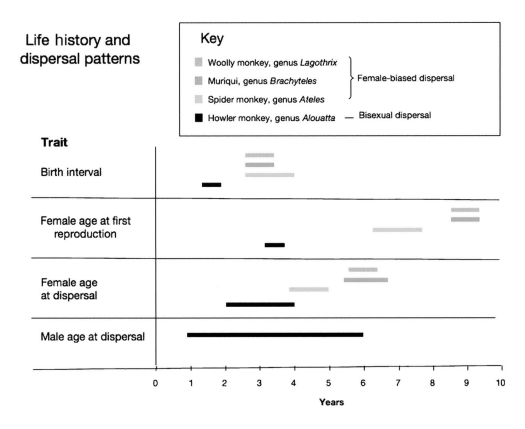

Figure 1

Life-history and dispersal patterns in Atelinae primates. The subfamily, Atelinae, is divided into the howler monkeys (*Alouatta* species) and the atelins, represented by three genera (woolly monkeys, muriquis, and spider monkeys). Bisexual dispersal is characteristic of the howler monkeys, although females in some populations may remain in their natal groups (see text). Female-biased dispersal characterizes the atelins and is associated with later ages at female dispersal and first reproduction, and longer birth intervals compared with those of howler monkeys. Bars represent the ranges of published values for each genus (Strier 1999, Nishimura 2003, Di Fiore & Campbell 2007).

3. Comparisons among closely related species and among populations of the same species provide insights into the mechanisms underlying behavioral plasticity and its affects on reproduction and life histories.

DISCLOSURE STATEMENT

The author is not aware of any biases that might be perceived as affecting the objectivity of this review.

ACKNOWLEDGMENTS

I am grateful to the editorial board for inviting this review and to J. Marks for his comments on an earlier version of this manuscript.

LITERATURE CITED

Alberts SC. 1999. Paternal kin discrimination in wild baboons. *Proc. R. Soc. London B. Biol. Sci.* 266:1501–6

Alberts SC, Altmann J. 1995. Balancing costs and opportunities: dispersal in male baboons. *Am. Nat.* 145:279–306

Allman J, Rosin A, Kumar R, Hasenstaub A. 1998. Parenting and survival in anthropoid primates: Caretakers live longer. *Proc. Natl. Acad. Sci. USA* 95:6866–69

Altmann J. 1980. *Baboon Mothers and Infants*. Cambridge, MA: Harvard Univ. Press. 242 pp.

Altmann J, Alberts SC. 2005. Growth rates in a wild primate population: ecological influences and maternal effects. *Behav. Ecol. Sociobiol.* 57:490–501

Altmann J, Alberts SC, Haines SA, Dubach J, Muruthi P, et al. 1996. Behavior predicts genetic structure in a wild primate group. *Proc. Natl. Acad. Sci. USA* 93:5797–801

Alvarez HP. 2000. Grandmother hypothesis and primate life histories. *Am. J. Phys. Anthropol.* 113:435–50

Bales KL, French JA, McWilliams J, Lake RA, Dietz JM. 2006. Effects of social status, age, and season on androgen and cortisol levels in wild male golden lion tamarins (*Leontopithecus rosalia*). *Horm. Behav.* 49:88–95

Barrett L, Henzi SP, Lycett JE. 2006. Whose life is it anyway? Maternal investment, developmental trajectories, and life history strategies in baboons. In *Reproduction and Fitness in Baboons: Behavioral, Ecological, and Life History Perspectives*, ed. L Swedell, SR Leigh, pp. 199–224. New York: Springer

Bercovitch FB, Ziegler TE. 2002. Current topics in primate socioendocrinology. *Annu. Rev. Anthropol.* 31:45–67

Berman CM. 2004. Developmental aspects of kin bias in behvior. See Chapais & Berman 2004, pp. 317–46

Bernstein IS. 1999. Kinship and the behavior of nonhuman primates. In *The Nonhuman Primates*, ed. P Dohlinhow, A Fuentes, pp. 202–05. Mountain View, CA: Mayfield

Bradley BJ, Doran-Sheehy DM, Lukas D, Boesch C, Vigilant L. 2004. Dispersed male networks in western gorillas. *Curr. Biol.* 14:510–13

Bradley BJ, Doran-Sheehy DM, Vigilant L. 2007. Potential for female kin associations in wild western gorillas despite female dispersal. *Proc. R. Soc. London B. Biol. Sci.* 274:2179–85

Bradley BJ, Robbins MM, Williamson EA, Steklis HD, Steklis NG, et al. 2005. Mountain gorilla tug-of-war: Silverbacks have limited control over reproduction in multimale groups. *Proc. Natl. Acad. Sci. USA* 102:9418–23

Buchan JC, Alberts SC, Silk JB, Altmann J. 2003. True paternal care in a multi-male primate society. *Nature* 425:179–81

Campbell CJ, Fuentes A, MacKinnon KC, Panger M, Bearder SK, eds. 2007. *Primates in Perspective*. New York: Oxford Univ. Press

Chapais B. 2001. Primate nepotism: What is the explanatory value of kin selection? *Int. J. Primatol.* 22:203–29

Chapais B, Bélisle P. 2004. Constraints on kin selection in primate groups. See Chapais & Berman 2004, pp. 365–86

Chapais B, Berman CM, eds. 2004. *Kinship and Behavior in Primates.* New York: Oxford Univ. Press. 507 pp.

Chapais B, Gauthier C, PrudHomme J, Vasey P. 1997. Relatedness threshold for nepotism in Japanese macaques. *Anim. Behav.* 53:1089–101

Chapais B, Savard L, Gauthier C. 2001. Kin selection and the distribution of altruism in relation to degree of kinship in Japanese macaques (*Macaca fuscata*). *Behav. Ecol. Sociobiol.* 49:493–502

Charnov EL, Berrigan D. 1993. Why do female primates have such long lifespans and so few babies? Or life in the slow lane. *Evol. Anthropol.* 1:191–94

Cheney DL, Seyfarth RM. 1983. Non-random dispersal in free-ranging vervet monkeys: social and genetic consequences. *Am. Nat.* 122:392–412

Clutton-Brock TH. 1989. Female transfer and inbreeding avoidance in social mammals. *Nature* 337:70–72

Clutton-Brock TH, Harvey PH. 1978. Mammals, resources and reproductive strategies. *Nature* 273:191–95

Constable JL, Ashley MV, Goodall J, Pusey AE. 2001. Noninvasive paternity assignment in Gombe chimpanzees. *Mol. Ecol.* 10:1279–300

Cowlishaw G, Dunbar R. 2000. *Primate Conservation Biology.* Chicago, IL: Univ. Chicago Press. 518 pp.

Crockett CM, Pope TR. 1993. Consequences of sex differences in dispersal for juvenile red howler monkeys. In *Juvenile Primates: Life History, Development, and Behavior*, ed. ME Pereira, LA Fairbanks, pp. 104–18. New York: Oxford Univ. Press

de Ruiter JR, Geffen E. 1998. Relatedness of matrilines, dispersing males and social groups in long-tailed macaques (*Macaca fascicularis*). *Proc. R. Soc. London B Biol. Sci.* 265:79–87

Dietz JM. 2004. Kins structure and reproductive skew in cooperatively breeding primates. See Chapais & Berman 2004, pp. 223–41

Di Fiore A. 2003. Molecular genetic approaches to the study of primate behavior, social organization, and reproduction. *Yrbk. Phys. Anthropol.* 37:62–99

Di Fiore A, Campbell CJ. 2007. The Atelines. See Campbell et al. 2007, pp. 155–85

Di Fiore A, Gagneux P. 2007. Molecular primatology. See Campbell et al. 2007, pp. 369–93

Di Fiore A, Rendall D. 1994. Evolution of social organization: a reappraisal for primates by using phylogenetic methods. *Proc. Natl. Acad. Sci. USA* 91:9941–45

Digby LJ, Ferrari SF, Saltzman W. 2007. Callitrichines: the role of competition in cooperatively breeding species. See Campbell et al. 2007, pp. 85–106

Dirks W, Bowman JE. 2007. Life history theory and dental development in four species of catarrhine primates. *J. Hum. Evol.* 53:309–20

Dobson AP, Lyles AM. 1989. The population dynamics and conservation of primate populations. *Conserv. Biol.* 3:362–80

Douadi MI, Gatti S, Levrero F, Duhamel G, Bermejo M, et al. 2007. Sex-biased dispersal in western lowland gorillas (*Gorilla gorilla gorilla*). *Mol. Ecol.* 16:2247–59

Ellison PT, ed. 2001. *Reproductive Ecology and Human Evolution.* Chicago: Aldine de Gruyter. 478 pp.

Fairbanks LA. 1988. Vervet monkey grandmothers—interactions with infant grandoffspring. *Int. J. Primatol.* 9:425–41

Fairbanks LA. 1990. Reciprocal benefits of allomothering for female vervet monkeys. *Anim. Behav.* 40:553–62

Fedigan LM, Rose LM. 1995. Interbirth interval variation in three sympatric species of neotropical monkey. *Am. J. Primatol.* 37:9–24

Ferrari SF, Digby LJ. 1996. Wild *Callithrix* groups: stable extended families? *Am. J. Primatol.* 38:19–27

Foley RA, Lee PC. 1989. Finite social space, evolutionary pathways, and reconstructing hominid behavior. *Science* 243:901–6

Fox R. 1967. *Kinship and Marriage.* Baltimore, MD: Penguin. 271 pp.

Fox R. 1975. Primate kin and human kinship. In *Biosocial Anthropology*, ed. R Fox, pp. 9–35. New York: Halstead

Fuentes A. 2000. Hylobatid communities: changing views on pair bonding and social organization in hominoids. *Yrbk. Phys. Anthropol.* 43:33–60

Furuichi T. 1997. Agonistic interactions and matrifocal dominance rank of wild bonobos (*Pan paniscus*) at Wamba. *Int. J. Primatol.* 18:855–75

Garber PA. 1997. One for all and breeding for one: cooperation and competition as a tamarin reproductive strategy. *Evol. Anthropol.* 5:187–99

Gerloff U, Hartung B, Fruth B, Hohmann G, Tautz D. 1999. Intracommunity relationships, dispersal pattern and paternity success in a wild living community of bonobos (*Pan paniscus*) determined from DNA analysis of faecal samples. *Proc. Biol. Sci.* 266:1189–95

Gould L, Sussman RW, Sauther ML. 2003. Demographic and life-history patterns in a population of ring-tailed lemurs (*Lemur catta*) at Beza Mahafaly Reserve, Madagascar: a 15-year perspective. *Am. J. Phys. Anthropol.* 120:182–94

Guimaraes VO, Strier KB. 2001. Adult male-infant interactions in wild muriquis (*Brachyteles arachnoides hypoxanthus*). *Primates* 32:395–99

Hager R. 2003. Models of reproductive skew applied to primates. In *Sexual Selection and Reproductive Competition in Primates: New Perspectives and Directions*, ed. CB Jones, pp. 65–101. Norman, OK: Am. Soc. Primatol.

Hamilton WD. 1964. The genetical evolution of social behaviour. *J. Theor. Biol.* 7:1–51

Harrison ME, Chivers DJ. 2007. The orang-utan mating system and the unflanged male: a product of increased food stress during the late Miocene and Pliocene? *J. Hum. Evol.* 52:275–93

Harvey PH, Clutton-Brock TH. 1985. Life-history variation in primates. *Evolution* 39:559–81

Hawkes K. 2003. Grandmothers and the evolution of human longevity. *Am. J. Hum. Biol.* 15:380–400

Hawkes K, O'Connell JF, Jones NG, Alvarez H, Charnov EL. 1998. Grandmothering, menopause, and the evolution of human life histories. *Proc. Natl. Acad. Sci. USA* 95:1336–39

Hohmann G. 2001. Association and social interactions between strangers and residents in bonobos (*Pan paniscus*). *Primates* 42:91–99

Hrdy SB. 1977. *The Langurs of Abu*. Cambridge, MA: Harvard Univ. Press. 361 pp.

Hrdy SB. 1981. *The Woman That Never Evolved*. Cambridge, MA: Harvard Univ. Press. 256 pp.

Hrdy SB. 1995. The optimal number of fathers. *J. Hum. Evol.* 10:131–44

Huck M, Lottker P, Bohle UR, Heymann EW. 2005. Paternity and kinship patterns in polyandrous moustached tamarins (*Saguinus mystax*). *Am. J. Phys. Anthropol.* 127:449–64

Isbell LA, Cheney DL, Seyfarth RM. 2002. Why vervet monkeys (*Cercopithecus aethiops*) live in multimale groups. In *The Guenons: Diversity and Adaptation in African Monkeys*, ed. ME Glenn, M Cords, pp. 173–87. New York: Klewer Acad./Plenum

Jablonski NG, Whitfort MJ, Roberts-Smith N, Qinqi X. 2000. The influence of life history and diet on the distribution of catarrhine primates during the Pleistocene in eastern Asia. *J. Hum. Evol.* 39:131–57

Jack KM, Fedigan LM. 2004a. Male dispersal patterns in white-faced capuchins, *Cebus capucinus*. Part 1: patterns and causes of natal emigration. *Anim. Behav.* 67:761–69

Jack KM, Fedigan LM. 2004b. Male dispersal patterns in white-faced capuchins, *Cebus capucinus*. Part 2: patterns and causes of secondary dispersal. *Anim. Behav.* 67:771–82

Jones CB. 1997. Life history patterns of howler monkeys in a time-varying environment. *Bol. Primatol. Lat.* 6:1–8

Jones CB. 1999. Why both sexes leave: effects of habitat fragmentation on dispersal behavior. *Endanger. Species UPDATE* 15:70–73

Jones CB. 2005. *Behavioral Flexibility in Primates: Causes and Consequences*. New York: Springer Sci. Bus. Media

Kappeler PM, ed. 2000. *Primate Males: Causes and Consequences of Variation in Group Composition*, ed. PM Kappeler, pp. 159–68. Cambridge, MA: Cambridge Univ. Press

Kappeler PM, Wimmer B, Zinner D, Tautz D. 2002. The hidden matrilineal structure of a solitary lemur: implications for primate social evolution. *Proc. Biol. Sci.* 269:1755–63

King SJ, Arrigo-Nelson SJ, Pochron ST, Semprebon GM, Godfrey LR, et al. 2005. Dental senescence in a long-lived primate links infant survival to rainfall. *Proc. Natl. Acad. Sci. USA* 102:16579–83

Knott C. 2001. Female reproductive ecology of the apes—implications for human evolution. See Ellison, pp. 429–63

Langergraber KE, Mitani JC, Vigilant L. 2007. The limited impact of kinship on cooperation in wild chimpanzees. *Proc. Natl. Acad. Sci. USA* 104:7786–90

Lawler RR, Richard AF, Riley MA. 2003. Genetic population structure of the white sifaka (*Propithecus verreauxi verreauxi*) at Beza Mahafaly Special Reserve, southwest Madagascar (1992–2001). *Mol. Ecol.* 12:2307–17

Lee PC. 1994. Social structure and evolution. In *Behaviour and Evolution*, pp. 266–337. Cambridge, UK: Cambridge Univ. Press

Lee PC. 1996. The meanings of weaning: growth, lactation and life history. *Evol. Anthropol.* 5:87–96

Lee PC, Kappeler PM. 2003. Socioecological correlates of phenotypic plasticity of primate life histories. In *Primate Life Histories and Socioecology*, ed. PM Kappeler, ME Pereira, pp. 41–65. Cambridge, UK: Cambridge Univ. Press

Martin RD, Maclarnon AM. 1985. Gestation period, neonatal size and maternal investment in placental mammals. *Nature* 313:220–23

Maynard Smith J. 1978. Optimization theory in evolution. *Annu. Rev. Ecol. Syst.* 9:31–56

Mitani JC, Watts D. 1997. The evolution of nonmaternal caretaking among anthropoid primates: Do helpers help? *Behav. Ecol. Sociobiol.* 40:213–20

Mitchell CL. 1994. Migration alliances and coalitions among adult male South American squirrel monkeys (*Saimiri sciureus*). *Behaviour* 130:169–90

Moore J. 1984. Female transfer in primates. *Int. J. Primatol.* 5:537–89

Moore J, Ali R. 1984. Are dispersal and inbreeding avoidance related? *Anim. Behav.* 32:94–112

Nievergelt CM, Digby LJ, Ramakrishnan U, Woodruff DS. 2000. Genetic analysis of group composition and breeding system in a wild common marmoset (*Callithrix jacchus*) population. *Int. J. Primatol.* 21:1–20

Nishimura A. 2003. Reproductive parameters of wild female Lagothrix lagotricha. *Int. J. Primatol.* 24:707–22

Nsubuga AM, Robbins MM, Boesch C, Vigilant L. 2008. Patterns of paternity and group fission in wild multimale mountain gorilla groups. *Am. J. Phys. Anthropol.* 135:263–74

Paul A. 1999. The socioecology of infant handling in primates: Is the current model convincing? *Primates* 40:33–46

Pavelka MSM, Fedigan LM, Zohar S. 2002. Availability and adaptive value of reproductive and postreproductive Japanese macaque mothers and grandmothers. *Anim. Behav.* 64:407–14

Pavelka MSM, McGoogan KC, Steffens TS. 2007. Population size and characteristics of Alouatta pigra before and after a major hurricane. *Int. J. Primatol.* 28:919–29

Pochron ST, Tucker WT, Wright PC. 2004. Demography, life history, and social structure in *Propithecus diadema edwardsi* from 1986–2000 in Ranomafana National Park, Madagascar. *Am. J. Phys. Anthropol.* 125:61–72

Pope T. 1990. The reproductive consequences of male cooperation in the red howler monkey: paternity exclusion in multi-male and single-male troops using genetic markers. *Behav. Ecol. Sociobiol.* 27:439–46

Pope TR. 2000. Reproductive success increases with degree of kinship in cooperative coalitions of female red howler monkeys (*Alouatta seniculus*). *Behav. Ecol. Sociobiol.* 48:253–67

Purvis A, Webster AJ, Agapow PM, Jones KE, Isaac NJB. 2003. Primate life histories and phylogeny. In *Primate Life Histories and Socioecology*, ed. PM Kappeler, ME Pereira, pp. 25–40. Cambridge, UK: Cambridge Univ. Press

Pusey A, Williams J, Goodall J. 1997. The influence of dominance rank on the reproductive success of female chimpanzees. *Science* 277:828–31

Rendall D. 2004. "Recognizing" kin: mechanisms, media, minds, modules, and muddles. See Chapais & Berman 2004, pp. 295–316

Richard AF, Dewar RE, Schwartz M, Ratsirarson J. 2002. Life in the slow lane? Demography and life histories of male and female sifaka (*Propithecus verreauxi verreauxi*). *J. Zool.* 256:421–36

Robbins AM, Robbins MM, Gerald-Steklis N, Steklis HD. 2006. Age-related patterns of reproductive success among female mountain gorillas. *Am. J. Phys. Anthropol.* 131:511–21

Robson SL, van Schaik CP, Hawkes K. 2006. The derived features of human life history. In *Evolution of Human Life History*, ed. K Hawkes, RR Paine, pp. 17–44. Sante Fe: Sch. Am. Res. Press

Ross C. 1998. Primate life histories. *Evol. Anthropol.* 6:54–63

Ross C, MacLarnon A. 2000. The evolution of nonmaternal care in anthropoid primates: a test of the hypotheses. *Folia Primatol.* 71:93–113

Silk JB. 2002. Kin selection in primate groups. *Int. J. Primatol.* 23:849–975

Silk JB, Alberts SC, Altmann J. 2003. Social bonds of female baboons enhance infant survival. *Science* 302:1231–34

Smith K, Alberts SC, Altmann J. 2003. Wild female baboons bias their social behaviour towards paternal half-sisters. *Proc. Biol. Sci.* 270:503–10

Sommer V, Reichard U. 2000. Rethinking monogamy: the gibbon case. See Kappeler 2000, pp. 159–68

Stearns SC. 1992. *The Evolution of Life Histories*. Oxford, UK: Oxford Univ. Press. 249 pp.

Sterck EH. 1997. Determinants of female dispersal in Thomas langurs. *Am. J. Primatol.* 42:179–98

Sterck EH. 1998. Female dispersal, social organization, and infanticide in langurs: Are they linked to human disturbance? *Am. J. Primatol.* 44:235–54

Sterck EHM, Watts DP, van Schaik CP. 1997. The evolution of female social relationships in nonhuman primates. *Behav. Ecol. Sociobiol.* 41:291–309

Strier KB. 1994. Myth of the typical primate. *Yrbk. Phys. Anthropol.* 37:233–71

Strier KB. 1996a. Male reproductive strategies in new world primates. *Hum. Nat.* 7:105–23

Strier KB. 1996b. Reproductive ecology of female muriquis. In *Adaptive Radiations of Neotropical Primates*, ed. M Norconk, A Rosenberger, P Garber, pp. 511–32. New York: Plenum

Strier KB. 1999. The atelines. In *Comparative Primate Behavior*, ed. A Fuentes, P Dolhinow, pp. 109–14. New York: McGraw Hill

Strier KB. 2000. From binding brotherhoods to short-term sovereignty: the dilemma of male Cebidae. See Kappeler 2000, pp. 72–83

Strier KB. 2001. Reproductive ecology of New World primates. See Ellison 2001, pp. 351–67

Strier KB. 2003. Primatology comes of age: 2002 AAPA Luncheon Address. *Yrbk. Phys. Anthropol.* 122:2–13

Strier KB. 2004a. Patrilineal kinship and primate behaviour. See Chapais & Berman 2004, pp. 177–99

Strier KB. 2004b. Reproductive strategies of New World Primates: birth intervals and reproductive rates. In *A Primatologia no Brasil-8*, ed. SL Mendes, A Chiarelli, pp. 53–63. Vítoria, Brazil: IPEMA/Soc. Bras. Primatol.

Strier KB. 2004c. Sociality among kin and nonkin in nonhuman primate groups. In *The Origins and Nature of Sociality*, ed. RW Sussman, AR Chapman, pp. 191–214. New York: Aldine de Gruyter

Strier KB. 2007. Conservation. See Campbell et al. 2007, pp. 496–509

Strier KB, Boubli JP, Possamai CB, Mendes SL. 2006. Population demography of northern muriquis (*Brachyteles hypoxanthus*) at the Estação Biológica de Caratinga/Reserva Particular do Patrimônio Natural-Feliciano Miguel Abdala, Minas Gerais, Brazil. *Am. J. Phys. Anthropol.* 130:227–37

Strier KB, Ziegler TE. 1997. Behavioral and endocrine characteristics of the reproductive cycle in wild muriqui monkeys, *Brachyteles arachnoides*. *Am. J. Primatol.* 42:299–310

Strier KB, Ziegler TE. 2000. Lack of pubertal influences on female dispersal in muriqui monkeys, *Brachyteles arachnoides*. *Anim. Behav.* 59:849–60

Sugiyama Y. 1999. Socioecological factors of male chimpanzee migration at Bossou, Guinea. *Primates* 40:61–68

Van Horn RC, Buchan JC, Altmann J, Alberts SC. 2007. Divided destinies: group choice by female savannah baboons during social group fission. *Behav. Ecol. Sociobiol.* 61:1823–37

van Noordwijk MA, van Schaik CP. 1985. Male migration and rank acquisition in wild long-tailed macaques (*Macaca fascicularis*). *Anim. Behav.* 33:849–61

van Noordwijk MA, van Schaik CP. 2005. Development of ecological competence in Sumatran orangutans. *Am. J. Phys. Anthropol.* 127:79–94

Western D. 1979. Size, life-history and ecology in mammals. *Afr. J. Ecol.* 17:185–204

Whitten PL. 1987. Infants and adult males. In *Primate Societies*, ed. BB Smuts, DL Cheney, RM Seyfarth, RW Wrangham, TT Struhsaker, pp. 343–57. Chicago: Univ. Chicago Press

Whitten PL, Brockman DK, Stavisky RC. 1998. Recent advances in noninvasive techniques to monitor hormone-behavior interactions. *Yrbk. Phys. Anthropol.* 41:1–23

Widdig A. 2007. Paternal kin discrimination: the evidence and likely mechanisms. *Biol. Rev. Camb. Philos. Soc.* 82:319–34

Widdig A, Nurnberg P, Bercovitch FB, Trefilov A, Berard JB, et al. 2006. Consequences of group fission for the patterns of relatedness among rhesus macaques. *Mol. Ecol.* 15:3825–32

Widdig A, Nurnberg P, Krawczak M, Streich WJ, Bercovitch FB. 2001. Paternal relatedness and age proximity regulate social relationships among adult female rhesus macaques. *Proc. Natl. Acad. Sci. USA* 98:13769–73

Williams JM, Pusey AE, Carlis JV, Farm BP, Goodall J. 2002. Female competition and male territorial behaviour influence female chimpanzees' ranging patterns. *Anim. Behav.* 63:347–60

Wrangham RW. 1979. On the evolution of ape social systems. *Soc. Sci. Inf.* 18:335–68

Wrangham RW. 1980. An ecological model of female-bonded primate groups. *Behaviour* 75:262–99

Wrangham RW. 1981. Drinking competition in vervet monkeys. *Anim. Behav.* 29:904–10

Wright PC. 1990. Patterns of paternal care in primates. *Int. J. Primatol.* 11:89–102

Wright PC. 1999. Lemur traits and Madagascar ecology: coping with an island environment. *Yrbk. Phys. Anthropol.* 42:31–72

Ziegler TE, Wittwer DJ. 2005. Fecal steroid research in the field and laboratory: improved methods for storage, transport, processing, and analysis. *Am. J. Primatol.* 67:159–74

Linguistic Anthropology of Education

Stanton Wortham

Graduate School of Education, University of Pennsylvania, Philadelphia, Pennsylvania 19104-6216; email: stantonw@gse.upenn.edu

Annu. Rev. Anthropol. 2008. 37:37–51

First published online as a Review in Advance on May 29, 2008

The *Annual Review of Anthropology* is online at anthro.annualreviews.org

This article's doi:
10.1146/annurev.anthro.36.081406.094401

0084-6570/08/1021-0037$20.00

Key Words

schooling, communicative practice, semiotics, pragmatics, language ideology

Abstract

Linguistic anthropological theories and methods have enriched our understanding of education. Almost all education is mediated by language, and linguistic anthropologists use both precise linguistic analyses and powerful anthropological theories to describe how educational language use establishes important social relations. Because educational institutions influence processes of concern to anthropologists—including the production of differentially valued identities, the circulation and transformation of cultural models, and nation states' establishment of official peoples—linguistic anthropological research on education also contributes to cultural and linguistic anthropology more generally. This article defines linguistic anthropology through its focus on language form, use, ideology, and domain, and it reviews linguistic anthropological research that focuses on these four aspects of educational language use.

INTRODUCTION

Linguistic anthropologists study how language use both presupposes and creates social relations in cultural context (Agha 2007, Duranti 1997, Silverstein 1976). Theories and methods from linguistic anthropology have been productively applied to educational processes for the past four decades (Cazden et al. 1972, Collins 1996, Gumperz 1986, Heath 1983, Wortham & Rymes 2003). This article makes two interrelated arguments about the application of linguistic anthropological theories and methods to educational phenomena. First, educational language use and linguistic anthropological concerns illuminate each other. Linguistic anthropological approaches to language use have enriched our accounts of educational processes. The reverse is also true: Educational institutions make important contributions to social, cultural, and linguistic processes that are of central concern to both linguistic and cultural anthropologists (Hall 1999, Levinson 1999), and linguistic anthropological study of educational institutions has illuminated these processes. Second, linguistic anthropological approaches are concerned with four aspects of language use in cultural context, comprising what Silverstein (1985) calls "the total linguistic fact": form, use, ideology, and domain. Successful analyses of socially and culturally situated language use must attend to all four aspects, although individual projects often emphasize one or another.

After presenting introductory sections that define "linguistic anthropology," "linguistic anthropology of education," and "the total linguistic fact," this article reviews work in the linguistic anthropology of education that focuses on form, use, ideology, and then domain. Each section describes how linguistic anthropological approaches to that aspect of language illuminate educational processes and suggests that study of educational institutions can illuminate social and cultural processes of broad interest to anthropologists. Despite having a noun phrase for a title, this article is not intended to describe an entity—a research territory over which battles can be fought and careers built. Instead it describes a process. Linguistic anthropological and educational research are increasingly overlapping, and this overlap enriches both fields.

LINGUISTIC ANTHROPOLOGY

Linguistic anthropologists study language use as social action. Despite prevalent folk ideologies, written and spoken language do more than refer and predicate. They also constitute actions that both presuppose and create social relations in cultural context. Most important social and cultural processes are mediated in significant part by language, and systematic study of language use enriches our understanding of them.

The main historical line of linguistic anthropology runs through Boas (1911), Sapir (1921), and Whorf (1956), to Gumperz (1982), Hymes (1964), and Silverstein (1976). Linguistic anthropology is also an interdisciplinary field. It is one of the four subfields of American anthropology, but it draws on socially oriented linguistics (Jakobson 1960, Labov 1972, Levinson 1983), qualitative sociology (Goffman 1981), philosophy of language (Peirce 1955, Putnam 1975), social theory (Bourdieu 1972), and cultural anthropology (Urban 1996). Exemplary work focuses on the ethnography of communication (Gumperz & Hymes 1964), interactional sociolinguistics (Gumperz 1982), semiotic mediation (Mertz & Parmentier 1985, Hill & Irvine 1993), performance (Bauman & Briggs 1990), metapragmatic discourse (Lucy 1993, Silverstein & Urban 1996), language ideology (Schieffelin et al. 1998), and interevent semiosis (Agha & Wortham 2005). Duranti (1997), Hanks (1996), Mertz (2007), and Parmentier (1997) provide overviews of the field.

Linguistic anthropology distinguishes itself from linguistics in two ways: It focuses on language use, not language form, and it emphasizes the language user's point of view. Duranti (1997), Hymes (1972), and Silverstein (1985) describe how linguistic anthropology takes advantage of linguists' discoveries about phonology and grammar, but only to study how language users deploy linguistic resources to accomplish social action in practice. More contemporary linguistic anthropology takes what Mertz (2007) and Rymes (2007) call a "semiotic" approach to language use, emphasizing the flexible use of language to create sometimes-unexpected relations instead of focusing on stable norms of appropriate use. Linguistic anthropologists also do ethnography, emphasizing language users' points of view and insisting that people themselves explicitly or tacitly recognize the categories that we use to describe their communicative practices (Erickson 2004).

LINGUISTIC ANTHROPOLOGY OF EDUCATION

Linguistic anthropology has made significant contributions to our understanding of educational processes because almost all education is mediated by language use. When educators and students speak and write, they signal things not only about the subject matter they are learning but also about their affiliations with social groups both inside and outside the speech event. These affiliations, some of which are created in educational events and institutions, can both influence how students learn subject matter and shape their life trajectories. Educational researchers need to understand how educational language use presupposes and transforms social relations and how educational actions are influenced by ideologies about language and social personhood. Linguistic anthropologists provide theories and methods for studying these processes, and linguistic anthropological studies have illuminated educational phenomena for decades (Cazden et al. 1972, Cook-Gumperz 1986, Wortham & Rymes 2003).

Educational institutions also play central roles in society and culture. Study of educational institutions, and the language use that mediates them, can illuminate social, cultural, and linguistic processes of interest to many anthropologists (Hall 1999, Levinson 1999). For instance, educational institutions play central roles in authorizing and circulating ideologies of language through which "educated" and "un-educated" language use are associated with differentially valued types of people (González & Arnot-Hopffer 2003, Zentella 1997). Schooling focused on language and literature, in particular, contributes to standardization and the hierarchical ordering of languages and dialects (Lo 2004, Moore 1999, Warriner 2007). Nation states use schools to enforce their views of languages and dialects, often establishing "peoples" associated with official and vernacular languages (Hornberger 2002, Jaffe 1999, Magga & Skutnabb-Kangas 2003). Schools also house complex and sustained interactions among diverse students, and these interactions often establish characteristic, hierarchically organized identities for students (O'Connor 2001, Rex & Green 2008, Rymes 2003, Wortham 1992). Educational language use and school-based ideologies of language thus play essential roles in social processes such as the production of dominant and subordinate identities (Collins & Blot 2003, Varenne & McDermott 1998), the socialization of individuals (Howard 2007, Mertz 1996, Ochs & Schieffelin 2007, Wortham & Jackson 2008), and the formation of nation states, transnational groups, and publics that include colonizer and colonized, "native," and "immigrant" (Lempert 2006, 2007; Rampton 2005, 2006; Reyes 2002, 2005).

This review focuses on events and processes that happen in and around educational institutions, not on informal education. Out-of-school processes make essential contributions to learning, identity, and cultural production, and linguistic anthropological approaches have been productively applied to them (Heath & McLaughlin 1993, Hull & Shultz 2002, Pelissier 1991, Schieffelin & Ochs 1986, Varenne 2007). But informal education is so widespread—taking place in families, workplaces, communities, and other settings—that a short review cannot cover it all. Schools contribute significantly to the creation of important relations, and it is productive to consider how language is used in educational institutions to do this social work.

Three related traditions overlap the linguistic anthropology of education. Language socialization research uses linguistic anthropological theories and methods to explore socialization both in and out of school (Duff & Hornberger 2007, Garrett & Baquedano-López 2002, Riley 2008, Schieffelin & Ochs 1986). Linguistic ethnography draws on American linguistic anthropology as well as applied linguistics and social theory to explore language use and language learning in contemporary Europe (Rampton 2007). Educational linguistics uses linguistic, sociological, and anthropological approaches to study language learning and language policy (Hornberger & Hult 2006, Spolsky & Hult 2008). In this article I define linguistic anthropology of education as research on educational institutions and school-related practices that employs a linguistic anthropological approach focused on form, use, ideology, and domain. Much work in language socialization, linguistic ethnography, and educational linguistics falls within this definition, and some of this research is reviewed below. Other work in these traditions follows what Rymes (2007) calls an "ethnographic" as opposed to a "semiotic" approach—focusing on stable "norms of communication," not on how linguistic "forms are deployed flexibly in interaction to create new forms of culturally relevant action" (p. 31). Because such ethnographic work does not fully explore language use—how linguistic signs come to have meaning in context, across both interactional and historical time—it does not fall within the body of work reviewed here.

THE TOTAL LINGUISTIC FACT

This article reviews linguistic anthropological work that has examined educational institutions and school-related practices organized around the four aspects of what Silverstein (1985) calls the "total linguistic fact": form, use, ideology, and domain. Linguistic anthropologists use linguists' accounts of phonological and grammatical categories, thus studying language form, but they are not primarily interested in how linguistic forms have meaning apart from contexts of use. Instead, they study how linguistic

signs come to have both referential and relational meaning as they are used in social and cultural contexts (Duranti 1997, Hymes 1964, Silverstein 1976). The meaning of any linguistic sign in use cannot be determined by decontextualized rules, whether phonological, grammatical, or cultural. No matter how robust the relevant regularities, language users often deploy signs in unexpected yet meaningful ways (Goffman 1981, Silverstein 1992). Linguistic anthropologists study how language comes to have sometimes-unexpected meanings in interaction. As important as local contexts are, however, the meaning of any linguistic sign cannot be understood without also attending to more widely circulating models of the social world. Linguistic anthropologists often construe these models as language ideologies—models of linguistic signs and the people who characteristically use them, which others employ to understand the social relations signaled through language use (Schieffelin et al. 1998, Silverstein 1979). These ideologies are not evenly distributed across social space. They have a domain—the set of people who recognize the indexical link between a type of sign and the relevant ideology (Agha 2007). Linguistic anthropologists study how linguistic signs and models of language and social relations move from event to event, across time and across social space, and how such movement contributes to historical change.

This article uses the four aspects of form, use, ideology, and domain as an organizing principle to explore linguistic anthropological work that has enriched our understanding of educational phenomena and to show how linguistic anthropological work on education can illuminate processes of broad concern to anthropologists. In practice the four aspects cannot be separated—all language use involves linguistic forms, in use, as construed by ideologies, located within the historical movement of forms and ideologies across events. Any adequate analysis takes into account all four aspects, and ignoring or overemphasizing any one aspect can distort our understanding of how language comes to have meaning in practice.

But many analyses focus on one or two aspects without losing sight of the others.

FORM

A linguistic sign receives part of its meaning from the systematic distribution of the sign with respect to other signs. Linguists describe these distributional patterns in terms of phonological regularities and grammatical categories. "Form" refers to this fraction of meaning, which applies independent of context. Systematic attention to linguistic form has helped linguistic anthropologists illuminate various educational phenomena.

Eckert (2000) presents both an ethnographic and a quantitative sociolinguistic study of students in one suburban high school. Her statistical analyses show how gender and socioeconomic class correlate with the use of phonological variants. By tracing the intersection between gender- and class-based variants and students' peer groups, she explains how systematic differences in phonology help construct the school version of a middle-class/working-class split—the "jock"/"burnout" distinction—as well as gendered models of personhood that involve "sluttiness," aggressive masculinity, and other features. Eckert also shows how individual students use these phonological regularities in practice to navigate relationships and construct identities, and she connects her account to broader analyses of phonological changes taking place across the United States (Labov et al. 2006).

Mendoza-Denton (2007) describes the complex multimodal signs that Latina youth gang members use to distinguish themselves from mainstream peers. She attends to systematic variation in linguistic form, together with other modalities such as paralinguistic features, dress, tattoos, and bodily presentation, as she describes youth positioning themselves both within and against the larger society. Alim (2004) describes style shifting done by black youth as they adjust phonological variants, grammatical categories, and discourse markers according to their interlocutors' social po-

sitions. He explores how black youth use such forms to navigate prevalent models of race and changing socioeconomic conditions in gentrifying areas.

Eckert, Mendoza-Denton, and Alim extend Labov's (1972) variationist sociolinguistics, embedding systematic study of phonological regularities and grammatical categories within ethnographies and exploring the creative positioning that youth do through language and other sign systems. They show how secondary school youth play important roles in linguistic innovation and how language use in and around schools plays an important role in group identification and social stratification. Systematic investigation of linguistic variation and innovation can help anthropologists study the development of youth culture and the production of racialized, gendered, and class-based identities that organize both school-based and broader social relations.

Viechnicki & Kuipers (2006, Viechnicki 2008) describe grammatical and discursive resources through which middle-school students and their teachers objectify experience as scientific fact. The process of transforming experience into evidence is complex, as scientists and science students turn ordinary events into warrants for decontextualizable entities and authoritative laws. Viechnicki & Kuipers describe how science teachers and students use tense and aspect shifts, syntactic parallelism, and nominalization to remove experiences from their immediate circumstances and recontextualize them in an epistemologically authoritative scientific framework, moving from concrete experiences to universal, experience-distant formulations. Their analyses both illuminate science education and describe an important process through which authoritative knowledge is produced in modern societies (Bazerman 1999, Halliday 2004).

USE

Phonological and grammatical regularities are crucial tools for linguistic anthropological analyses, but rules of grammatically correct (or culturally appropriate) usage do not suffice to explain how people use language to create meaningful action in practice. Analyses of language use often err by using as their key tools decontextualized grammatical, pragmatic, or cultural patterns, disregarding how linguistic signs come to have sometimes-unexpected meanings in particular contexts. Silverstein (1992; Silverstein & Urban 1996) provides a systematic account of how signs presuppose and create social relations in context. "Context" is indefinitely large, and language use only makes sense as participants and analysts identify relevant context. They rely on two processes that Silverstein calls "contextualization"—through which signs come to have meaning as they index relevant aspects of the context—and "entextualization"—through which segments of interaction emerge and cohere as recognizable events. Cultural knowledge is crucial to interpreting language use, but we can interpret linguistic signs only by examining how utterances are contextualized in practice.

Erickson & Shultz (1982) study the "organized improvisation" that occurs in conversations between academic counselors and students from nonmainstream backgrounds. Erickson & Shultz do not argue simply that nonmainstream students and mainstream counselors experience a mismatch of styles, resulting in counselors' misjudgments about students. They show how counselors and students use various resources to create, override, resist, and defuse such mismatches. Nonmainstream students are often disadvantaged by their nonstandard habits of speaking and by mainstream counselors' assumptions about what they sometimes construe as deficits, but such disadvantage does not happen simply through a clash of monolithic styles. Erickson and Shultz find that "situationally emergent identity" explains more about the outcome of a gatekeeping encounter than does demographically fixed identity, and they analyze how speakers use social and cultural resources both to reproduce and to overcome disadvantage. Such work goes beyond simple reproductionist accounts to illuminate the more complex improvisations through

which educational institutions both create and restrict social mobility (Erickson 2004).

Rampton (2005) focuses on the hybrid, emergent identities created as students navigate social relations. He describes language "crossing" in urban, multiethnic groups of adolescents in the United Kingdom, as white, South Asian, and Caribbean youth mix features of Panjabi, Caribbean Creole, and Stylized Asian English. Crossing involves sprinkling words or linguistic features from other languages into speech that takes place in a predominant language. Rampton does not argue simply that minority languages are devalued and used to stigmatize nonmainstream youth nor that such youth use their home languages to resist such discrimination. Both of these processes do occur, but Rampton studies how these and other social effects are achieved in practice. Crossing is a discursive strategy in which diverse youth contest and create relations around race, ethnicity, and youth culture. The uses of minority languages involve contestation, teasing, resistance, irony, and other stances with respect to the social issues surrounding minority identities in Britain. Like Erickson (2004, Erickson & Shultz 1982), Rampton (2005, 2006) wants to understand and mitigate the disadvantages faced by minority youth, and he describes the larger social and political forces regimenting language and identity in the United Kingdom. But he does not reduce disadvantage to predictable patterns in which signs of identity routinely signal negative stereotypes. He shows instead how youth use language to navigate among the conflicting forms of solidarity and resistance available to them in multiethnic Britain.

Much other work in the linguistic anthropology of education attends closely to creativity and indeterminacy in language use (Duff 2002, 2003; He 2003; Kamberelis 2001; Kumpulainen & Mutanen 1999; Leander 2002; McDermott & Varenne 1995; Rymes 2001; Sawyer 2004; Wortham 2003, 2006). He (2003), for instance, shows how Chinese heritage language teachers often use three-part "moralized directives" to control disruptive behavior, but she also analyzes how teachers and students sometimes transform these directives as they construct particular stances in context. Rymes (2001) describes typical "dropping out" and "dropping in" autobiographical stories through which academically marginal students construct senses of self and reject or embrace formal education, but she also shows how these "at-risk" students reproduce, contest, ridicule and otherwise rework typical stories. All this work shows that, to study the social relations established through educational language use, we must attend to the sometimes-unexpected ways that educators and students position themselves with respect to both established and emerging models of identity. Because educational institutions are important sites for the reproduction and transformation of social identities, this linguistic anthropological work on creative educational language use addresses broader anthropological concerns about how both established and unexpected social regularities emerge in practice (Bourdieu 1972, Holland & Lave 2001).

IDEOLOGY

Two types of cultural and linguistic knowledge work together to produce meaningful language use in practice. Participants and analysts must know what linguistic and paralinguistic signs index, and they must be familiar with types of events and the types of people who characteristically participate in them (Gumperz 1982; Silverstein 1992, 2003; Silverstein & Urban 1996). All work on language in use attends, explicitly or tacitly, to the second type of knowledge—to more widely distributed social and cultural patterns that form the background against which both routine and innovative usage occurs. Language users rely on models that link types of linguistic forms with the types of people who stereotypically use them, even when the model is deployed in unexpected ways or transformed in practice. Silverstein (1979) describes these models of typical language use as "linguistic ideologies," although they have also been called "language ideologies" (Schieffelin et al. 1998) and "metapragmatic" (Silverstein 1976),

"metadiscursive" (Urban 1996), "metacultural" (Urban 2001), or "metasemiotic" (Agha 2007) models. Any adequate account of language use must include language ideologies and describe how they become salient in practice.

Language ideologies systematically associate types of language use with socially located types of people, and the concept allows linguistic anthropologists to explore relations between the emergent meanings of signs in use and more enduring social structures. Language ideology has been an important topic for the linguistic anthropology of education because schools are important sites for establishing associations between "educated" and "uneducated," "sophisticated" and "unsophisticated," "official" and "vernacular" language use and types of students. Language ideologies thus help explain how schools move students toward diverse social locations, and linguistic anthropological work on these processes helps show how social individuals are produced.

Jaffe (1999) uses the concept of language ideology to trace the policies and practices involved in the recent revitalization of Corsican. She describes one essentialist ideology that values French as the language of logic and civilization and another essentialist ideology that values Corsican as the language of nationalism and ethnic pride, as well as a less essentialist ideology that embraces the use of multiple languages and multiple identities. Her analyses show how schools are a central site of struggle among these ideologies—with some trying to maintain the centrality of French in the curriculum, some favoring Corsican language revitalization, and others wanting some Corsican in the schools but resisting a new standard Corsican as the language of schooling. Jaffe explores both predictable sociohistorical patterns, such as the struggle of a colonized people to value their own language, and less familiar ones such as the celebration of "authentic" Corsican by "natives" who cannot speak the language well.

Bucholtz (2001) and Kiesling (2001) use the concept of language ideology to explore peer relations and ethnic stereotypes among white

Americans. Bucholtz (2001) shows how many white high-school students adopt aspects of Black English Vernacular (BEV) and thereby mark themselves as "cool." She describes how "nerds" reject coolness and mark this rejection by refusing to adopt any features of BEV. Nerds even use what Bucholtz calls "superstandard" English, which includes careful attention to schooled articulation, grammar, and lexis even when most people speak less formally. Bucholtz describes ideologies that associate types of language use—using superstandard, borrowing a few features of BEV, speaking mostly BEV—with types of people—nerds who reject coolness, white students trying to be cool, and white students who go too far toward a racialized other. Kiesling (2001) describes the speech of white middle-class fraternity brothers, exploring how racially linked features of their speech serve interactional functions and reproduce social hierarchies. He shows how fraternity members assert intellectual or economic superiority over each other by marking interlocutors as metaphorically "black." He also shows how they assert physical prowess over each other by speaking like black men themselves and inhabiting a stereotype of physical masculinity. As they jockey for position in everyday life, the fraternity brothers use and reinforce ideologies of BEV speakers as less rational, economically distressed, and physically imposing.

Stocker (2003), Bokhorst-Heng (1999), and Berkley (2001) apply the concept of language ideology to educational situations outside of Europe and North America. Stocker (2003) describes a monolingual Spanish-speaking group in Costa Rica that is believed to speak a stigmatized dialect—despite the fact that their speech is not linguistically distinguishable from their neighbors'—because they live on an artificially bounded "reservation" and are perceived as "indigenous." She shows how high-school language instruction reinforces this ideology. Bokhorst-Heng (1999; see also Wee 2006) describes how Singapore used schools to make Mandarin the mother tongue of ethnically Chinese Singaporeans. In 1957, less than 0.1% of ethnically Chinese Singaporeans spoke Mandarin as their home dialect, but in the 1970s the government selected Malay, Tamil, and Mandarin as the mother tongues of all Singaporeans. The government created an image of Singapore as a multicultural state composed of three homogeneous subgroups and tied this image to the three home languages that students were to use in school. Berkley (2001) describes adult Mayan speakers at school learning to write authentic local stories in their language. He shows how this brought two ideologies into conflict: an ideology of literacy as cognitive skill that emphasized the authority of the young female teacher, and a traditional ideology that presented older men as empowered to tell stories on behalf of others. Berkley shows how the teacher and elders creatively navigated this conflict, with older men telling stories that younger people learned to write down.

Some linguistic anthropologists of education use the concept of language ideology to study broader power relations. Insofar as this work loses touch with the total linguistic fact—most often by failing to attend to the work of producing social relations through flexible language use in and across events—it does not maintain a linguistic anthropological approach. But Blommaert (2005) argues that linguistic anthropological work can both analyze language use in practice and explore enduring power relations that are themselves created partly through language. He focuses on "structural inequalities within the world system" (p. 57) that are both constituted by and yield differential abilities to have voice in educational and other institutional settings. Related linguistic anthropological work describes various ways in which educational institutions establish or reinforce power relations (Harris & Rampton 2003, Macbeth 2003, Varenne & McDermott 1998, Wortham 1992).

Heller (1999) and Blommaert (1999) describe language planning and education within multilingual nation states. They analyze how state and institutional language policies differentially position diverse populations. Heller (1999) studies how French Canadians' arguments for ethnic and linguistic legitimacy have shifted over the past few decades. Before globalization, French Canadians proclaimed the authenticity of their culture and asserted their rights as a minority group in Canada. In recent years, however, they emphasize the benefit of French as an international language. This shift in models of "Frenchness" has changed the value of various French Canadians, with bilinguals now valued more than monolinguals and Standard French valued more than vernaculars. Heller explores how a French-language high-school in Anglophone Ontario handles the resulting tensions between standard and vernacular French and between French and English. Blommaert (1999) describes how the Tanzanian state has used language planning for nation building, trying to make a common nation out of a multilingual society by establishing Swahili as the primary language of government and education. In the process, language planners both deliberately and inadvertently created "symbolic hierarchies," making some types of speakers sound more authoritative.

Other linguistic anthropological work on education and power has addressed literacy (Barton & Hamilton 1998, Blommaert et al. 2006, Bloome et al. 2004, Collins & Blot 2003, Hicks 1996, Kamberelis & Scott 2004, Street 1984). Street (1984) distinguishes between a theory of literacy as "autonomous"—which casts it as a cognitive skill independent of cultural contexts—and theories that emphasize the diverse cultural contexts and activities in which writing is used. He shows how governments and educational institutions favor the autonomous view and how this disadvantages "less literate" peoples and students with nonmainstream literacy practices. Collins & Blot (2003) follow Street in exploring literacy and power, but they also describe how local practices are embedded in global processes such as colonialism and neo-liberalism. They analyze interdependencies between local uses of literacy and larger sociohistorical movements, describing the hegemony of the literate standard and how this has provided cultural capital to some groups while disadvantaging others. They argue against the common assumption that schooled literacy always provides intellectual and economic salvation for the "less developed," and they show how this assumption devalues nonstandard literacies and has been used to justify exploitation.

Many other linguistic anthropologists have explored how educational institutions create social relations as they employ and transform language ideologies (McGroarty 2008, Wortham & Berkley 2001), showing how schools differentially value students from certain groups (Lemke 2002, Warriner 2004), how schools maintain authorized accounts of appropriate and inappropriate speech (Jackson 2008), how governments use school systems to establish visions of national language and identity (Hult 2005), how academic ideologies shape language revitalization efforts (Collins 1998), and how individuals draw on schooled language ideologies to identify others and value them differentially (Baquedano-López 1997). Linguistic anthropological work on educational language ideologies thus helps describe the important role schools play in producing differentially valued social groups.

DOMAIN

Work on language ideology shows how language in use both shapes and is shaped by more enduring social relations. We must not, however, cast this as a simple two-part process—sometimes called the "micro-macro dialectic"—in which events create structures and structures are created in events (Bourdieu 1972, Holland & Lave 2001, Wortham 2006). Agha (2007, Agha & Wortham 2005) provides a useful alternative conceptualization. He argues that all language ideologies, all models that link linguistic features with typifications of people and events, have a domain. They are recognized only by a subset of any linguistic community, and this subset changes as signs and models move across space and time. There is no one "macro" set of models or ideologies universal to a group. Instead, there are models that move across domains ranging from pairs, to local groups, all the way up to global language communities. In analyzing language and social life, we must describe various relevant resources—models drawn from different spatial and temporal scales—that facilitate a phenomenon of interest, and we must describe how models move across events (Agha 2007; Agha & Wortham 2005; Wortham 2005, 2006). Instead of focusing only on speech events, or simply connecting microlevel events to macrolevel structures, we must investigate the many scales of social organization relevant to understanding language in use. We must also, as Agha (2007), Leander & McKim (2003), and Wortham (2005, 2006) argue, follow the chains or trajectories across which individuals, signs, and ideologies move.

In their study of "untracking" as an educational reform, Mehan et al. (1996) go beyond a simple combination of local events and "macro" patterns. They explore various realms that influence at-risk students' school success—ranging from properties of the student him- or herself to parents, family, the classroom, the school, peer groups, the local community, as well as to national educational policy and broader socioeconomic constraints. Instead of describing micro and macro, Mehan and his colleagues describe how resources from many spatial and temporal scales facilitate or impede students' academic success. They give a more complex account of how intelligence, educational success, and other aspects of identity are constructed in practice, describing how resources from various layers of social context together facilitate a student's path. Similarly, Barton & Hamilton (2005) and Barton & Tusting (2005) attend to various "middle" scales that exist between micro and macro, exploring the multiple, changing groups relevant to language and social identities and following the trajectories that individuals and texts take across contexts.

Wortham (2006) describes months-long trajectories across which students' identities emerge in one ninth-grade urban classroom. He traces the development of local models for several types of student one might be in this classroom, showing the distinctive gendered

models that emerge. These local models both draw on and transform more widely circulating models, and they are used in sometimes-unexpected ways in particular classroom events. The analysis follows two students across the academic year, showing how their identities emerge as speakers transform widely circulating models of race and gender into local models of appropriate and inappropriate studenthood and as teachers and students contest these identities in particular interactions. Bartlett (2007) follows one immigrant student's trajectory across several classroom contexts and over many months, exploring how she positions herself with respect to local models of school success. Bartlett describes how the student's local identity stabilized as she kept herself from being acquired by the deficit model often applied to language minority students and instead became "successful" in the school's terms. Rogers (2003) also follows an individual student's trajectory across two years as the student and her family negotiate with authorities about whether she is "disabled." Rogers shows how both institutionalized and local models and practices facilitate the transformation of this student from "low achieving" to "disabled," and she follows the links among official texts, conferences, tests, family conversations, and other events that helped constitute this student's movement toward disability.

Systematic work on what Agha (2007) calls domain, and on the trajectories across which signs and ideologies move, has emerged only recently. In contrast, research on form, use, and ideology—aspects of the total linguistic fact that allow us to treat the speech event as the focal unit of analysis—has been occurring for decades. It has become clear, however, that we cannot fully understand how language constitutes social relations unless we move beyond the lone speech event and attend to domains and trajectories. Even the most sophisticated analyses of linguistic forms, in use, with respect to ideologies, fail to capture how ways of speaking, models of language and social life, and individual identities emerge across events. New linguistic anthropological work on domains and trajectories in educational institutions will show how schools play important roles in the emergence of social relations across various timescales.

CONCLUSIONS

Linguistic anthropologists study linguistic forms, in use, as construed by ideologies, as those forms and language ideologies move across speech events. Linguistic anthropological research on education illuminates educational processes and shows how language and education contribute to processes of broad anthropological concern. Educational language use produces social groups, sanctions official identities, differentially values those groups and identities, and sometimes creates hybrid identities and unexpected social types. Linguistic anthropological accounts of how these processes occur can enrich both educational and anthropological research.

DISCLOSURE STATEMENT

The author is not aware of any biases that might be perceived as affecting the objectivity of this review.

LITERATURE CITED

Agha A. 2007. *Language and Social Relations*. New York: Cambridge Univ. Press

Agha A, Wortham S. 2005. Discourse across speech-events: intertextuality and interdiscursivity in social life. *J. Linguist. Anthropol.* 15(1):Spec. Issue

Alim H. 2004. *You Know My Steez: An Ethnographic and Sociolinguistic Study of Styleshifting in a Black American Speech Community*. Durham, NC: Duke Univ. Press

Baquedano-López P. 1997. Creating social identities through *Doctrina* narratives. *Issues Appl. Linguist.* 8:27–45

Bartlett L. 2007. Bilingual literacies, social identification, and educational trajectories. *Linguist. Educ.* 18:215–31

Barton D, Hamilton M. 1998. *Local Literacies*. New York: Routledge

Barton D, Hamilton M. 2005. Literacy, reification and the dynamics of social interaction. See Barton & Tusting 2005, pp. 14–35

Barton D, Tusting K, ed. 2005. *Beyond Communities of Practice*. New York: Cambridge Univ. Press

Bauman R, Briggs C. 1990. Poetics and performance as critical perspectives on language and social life. *Annu. Rev. Anthropol.* 19:59–88

Bazerman C. 1999. *The Languages of Edison's Light*. Cambridge, MA: MIT Press

Berkley A. 2001. Respecting Maya language revitalization. *Linguist. Educ.* 12:345–66

Blommaert J. 1999. *State Ideology and Language in Tanzania*. Germany: Rüdiger Köppe Verlag

Blommaert J. 2005. *Discourse*. New York: Cambridge Univ. Press

Blommaert J, Creve L, Willaert E. 2006. On being declared illiterate: language-ideological disqualification in Dutch classes for immigrants in Belgium. *Lang. Commun.* 26:34–54

Bloome D, Carter S, Christian B, Otto S, Shuart-Faris N. 2004. *Discourse Analysis and the Study of Classroom Language and Literacy Events*. Mahwah, NJ: Erlbaum

Boas F. 1911. *Handbook of American Indian Languages*. Washington, DC: Smithsonian Inst. Press

Bokhorst-Heng W. 1999. Singapore's "Speak Mandarin Campaign." In *Language Ideological Debates*, ed. J Blommaert, pp. 235–66. Berlin: Mouton de Gruyter

Bourdieu P. 1972/1977. *Outline of a Theory of Practice*, Transl. R. Nice. New York: Cambridge Univ. Press

Bucholtz M. 2001. The whiteness of nerds: superstandard English and racial markedness. *J. Linguist. Anthropol.* 11:84–100

Cazden C, John V, Hymes D, ed. 1972. *Functions of Language in the Classroom*. New York: Teachers Coll. Press

Collins J. 1996. Socialization to text. See Silverstein & Urban 1996, pp. 203–28

Collins J. 1998. *Understanding Tolowa Histories: Western Hegemonies and Native American Responses*. New York: Routledge

Collins J, Blot R. 2003. *Literacy and Literacies*. New York: Cambridge Univ. Press

Cook-Gumperz J, ed. 1986. *The Social Construction of Literacy*. New York: Cambridge Univ. Press

Duff P. 2002. The discursive coconstruction of knowledge, identity and difference: an ethnography of communication in the high school mainstream. *Appl. Linguist.* 23:289–322

Duff P. 2003. Intertextuality and hybrid discourses: the infusion of pop culture in educational discourse. *Linguist. Educ.* 14:231–76

Duff P, Hornberger N, ed. 2007. *Encyclopedia of Language and Education*. Vol. 8: *Language Socialization*. New York: Springer. 2nd rev.

Duranti A. 1997. *Linguistic Anthropology*. New York: Cambridge Univ. Press

Eckert P. 2000. *Linguistic Variation as Social Practice: The Linguistic Construction of Identity in Belten High*. Malden, MA: Blackwell

Erickson F. 2004. *Talk and Social Theory: Ecologies of Speaking and Listening in Everyday Life*. Malden, MA: Polity

Erickson F, Shultz J. 1982. *Counselor as Gatekeeper: Social Interaction in Interviews*. New York: Academic

Garrett P, Baquedano-López P. 2002. Language socialization: reproduction and continuity, transformation and change. *Annu. Rev. Anthropol.* 31:339–61

Goffman E. 1981. *Forms of Talk*. Philadelphia: Univ. Penn. Press

González N, Arnot-Hopffer E. 2003. Voices of the children: language and literacy ideologies in a dual language immersion program. See Wortham & Rymes 2003, pp. 213–43

Gumperz J. 1982. *Discourse Strategies*. New York: Cambridge Univ. Press

Gumperz J. 1986. Interactional sociolinguistics in the study of schooling. In *The Social Construction of Literacy*, ed. J Cook-Gumperz. New York: Cambridge Univ. Press

Gumperz J, Hymes D, ed. 1964. The ethnography of communication. *Am. Anthropol.* 66(No. 6, Pt. 2):Spec. Issue

Hall K. 1999. Understanding educational processes in an era of globalization: the view from anthropology and cultural studies. In *Issues in Educational Research*, ed. E Lagemann, L Shulman, pp. 121–56. San Francisco: Jossey-Bass

Halliday M. 2004. *The Language of Science*. New York: Continuum

Hanks W. 1996. *Language and Communicative Practices*. Boulder, CO: Westview

Harris R, Rampton B. 2003. Introduction. In *The Language, Ethnicity and Race Reader*, eds. R Harris, B Rampton, pp. 1–14. New York: Routledge

He A. 2003. Linguistic anthropology and language education. See Wortham & Rymes 2003, pp. 93–119

Heath S. 1983. *Ways with Words: Language, Life, and Work in Communities and Classrooms*. New York: Cambridge Univ. Press

Heath S, McLaughlin M. 1993. *Identity and Inner-City Youth: Beyond Ethnicity and Gender*. New York: Teachers Coll. Press

Heller M. 1999. *Linguistic Minorities and Modernity*. Paramus, NJ: Prentice Hall

Hicks D. 1996. *Discourse, Learning and Schooling*. New York: Cambridge Univ. Press

Hill J, Irvine J, ed. 1993. *Responsibility and Evidence in Oral Discourse*. New York: Cambridge Univ. Press

Holland D, Lave J, ed. 2001. *History in Person: Enduring Struggles, Contentious Practice, Intimate Identities*. Santa Fe, NM: Sch. Am. Res. Press

Hornberger N. 2002. Multilingual language policies and the continua of biliteracy: an ecological approach. *Lang. Policy* 1:27–51

Hornberger N, Hult F. 2006. Educational linguistics. In *Encyclopedia of Language and Linguistics*, ed. K Brown, pp. 76–81. Oxford, UK: Elsevier

Howard K. 2007. Language socialization and language shift among school-aged children. In *Encyclopedia of Language and Education*. Vol. 8: *Language Socialization*, ed. P Duff, N Hornberger, pp. 187–99. New York: Springer

Hull G, Shultz K. 2002. *School's Out! Bridging Out of School Literacies with Classroom Practice*. New York: Teachers Coll. Press

Hult F. 2005. A case of prestige and status planning: Swedish and English in Sweden. *Curr. Issues Lang. Plan.* 6:73–79

Hymes D. 1964. Introduction: toward ethnographies of communication. *Am. Anthropol.* 66(No. 6, Pt. 2):1–34

Hymes D. 1972. Introduction. See Cazden et al. 1972, pp. xi–lvii

Jackson K. 2008. The social construction of youth and mathematics: the case of a fifth grade classroom. In *Mathematics Teaching, Learning, and Liberation in African American Contexts*, ed. D Martin. Mahwah, NJ: Erlbaum

Jaffe A. 1999. *Ideologies in Action: Language Politics on Corsica*. Berlin: Mouton de Gruyter

Jakobson R. 1960. Closing statement: linguistics and poetics. In *Style in Language*, ed. T Sebeok, pp. 350–77. Cambridge, MA: MIT

Kamberelis G. 2001. Producing heteroglossic classroom (micro)cultures through hybrid discourse practice. *Linguist. Educ.* 12:85–125

Kamberelis G, Scott K. 2004. Other people's voices. In *Uses of Intertextuality in Classroom and Educational Research*, ed. N Shuart-Faris, D Bloome, pp. 201–50. Charlotte: Inf. Age

Kiesling S. 2001. Stances of whiteness and hegemony in fraternity men's discourse. *J. Linguist. Anthropol.* 11:101–15

Kumpulainen K, Mutanen M. 1999. The situated dynamics of peer group interaction: an introduction to an analytic framework. *Learn. Instr.* 9:449–73

Labov W. 1972. *Language in the Inner City*. Philadelphia: Univ. Penn. Press

Labov W, Ash S, Boberg C. 2006. *The Atlas of North American English: Phonetics, Phonology, and Sound*. New York: Mouton de Gruyter

Leander K. 2002. Locating Latanya. *Res. Teach. Engl.* 37:198–250

Leander K, McKim K. 2003. Tracing the everyday "sitings" of adolescents on the internet: a strategic adaptation of ethnography across online and offline spaces. *Educ. Comm. Inf.* 3:211–40

Lemke J. 2002. Ideology, intertextuality, and the communication of science. In *Relations and Functions in Language and Discourse*, ed. P Fries, M Cummings, D Lockwood, W Spruiell, pp. 32–55. London: Cassell

Lempert M. 2006. Disciplinary theatrics: public reprimand and the textual performance of affect at Sera Monastery, India. *Lang. Comm.* 26:15–33

Lempert M. 2007. Conspicuously past: distressed discourse and diagrammatic embedding in a Tibetan represented speech style. *Lang. Comm.* 27:258–71

Levinson B. 1999. Resituating the place of educational discourse in anthropology. *Am. Anthropol.* 101:594–604

Levinson S. 1983. *Pragmatics*. New York: Cambridge Univ. Press

Lo A. 2004. Evidentiality and morality in a Korean heritage language school. *Pragmatics* 14:235–56

Lucy J, ed. 1993. *Reflexive Language*. New York: Cambridge Univ. Press

Macbeth D. 2003. Hugh Mehan's *Learning Lessons* reconsidered: on the differences between the naturalistic and critical analysis of classroom discourse. *Am. Educ. Res. J.* 40:239–80

Magga O, Skutnabb-Kangas T. 2003. Life or death for languages and human beings: experiences from Saamiland. In *Transcending Monolingualism: Linguistic Revitalisation in Education*, ed. L Huss, A Grima, K King, pp. 35–52. Lisse: Swets and Zeitlinger

McDermott R, Varenne H. 1995. Culture *as* disability. *Anthropol. Educ. Q.* 26:324–48

McGroarty M. 2008. The political matrix of linguistic ideologies. In *Handbook of Educational Linguistics*, ed. B Spolsky, F Hult, pp. 98–112. Oxford: Blackwell

Mehan H, Villanueva I, Hubbard L, Lintz A. 1996. *Constructing School Success: The Consequences of Untracking Low Achieving Students*. New York: Cambridge Univ. Press

Mendoza-Denton N. 2007. *Homegirls: Language and Cultural Practice among Latina Youth Gangs*. New York: Wiley

Mertz E. 1996. Recontextualization as socialization: text and pragmatics in the law school classroom. See Silverstein & Urban 1996, pp. 229–49

Mertz E. 2007. Semiotic anthropology. *Annu. Rev. Anthropol.* 36:337–53

Mertz E, Parmentier R, eds. 1985. *Semiotic Mediation*. New York: Academic

Moore L. 1999. Language socialization research and French language education in Africa: a Cameroonian case study. *Can. Mod. Lang. Rev.* 56:329–50

Ochs E, Schieffelin B. 2007. Language socialization: an historical overview. In *Encyclopedia of Language and Education*. Vol. 8: *Language Socialization*, ed. P Duff, N Hornberger, pp. 1–13. Dordrecht: Kluwer Acad.

O'Connor K. 2001. Contextualization and the negotiation of social identities in a geographically distributed situated learning project. *Linguist. Educ.* 12:285–308

Parmentier R. 1997. The pragmatic semiotics of cultures. *Semiotica* 116:1–115

Peirce C. 1955. *Philosophical writings of Peirce*, ed. J Buchler. New York: Dover

Pelissier C. 1991. The anthropology of teaching and learning. *Annu. Rev. Anthropol.* 20:75–95

Putnam H. 1975. The meaning of "meaning." In *Language, Mind and Knowledge*, ed. K Gunderson. Minneapolis: Univ. Minn. Press

Rampton B. 2005. *Crossing*. Manchester, UK: St. Jerome. 2nd ed.

Rampton B. 2006. *Language in Late Modernity: Interaction in an Urban School*. New York: Cambridge Univ. Press

Rampton B. 2007. Neo-Hymesian linguistic ethnography in the United Kingdom. *J. Sociolinguist.* 11:584–607

Rex L, Green J. 2008. Classroom discourse and interaction: reading across the traditions. In *Handbook of Educational Linguistics*, ed. B Spolsky, F Hult, pp. 571–84. Oxford: Blackwell

Reyes A. 2002. "Are you losing your culture?": poetics, indexicality and Asian American identity. *Discourse Stud.* 4:183–99

Reyes A. 2005. Appropriation of African American slang by Asian American youth. *J. Sociolinguist.* 9:509–32

Riley K. 2008. Language socialization. In *Handbook of Educational Linguistics*, ed. B Spolsky, F Hult, pp. 398–410. Oxford: Blackwell

Rogers R. 2003. *A Critical Discourse Analysis of Family Literacy Practices: Power In and Out of Print*. Mahwah, NJ: Erlbaum

Rymes B. 2001. *Conversational Borderlands: Language and Identity in an Alternative Urban High School*. New York: Teachers Coll. Press

Rymes B. 2003. Relating word to world: indexicality during literacy events. See Wortham & Rymes 2003, pp. 121–50

Rymes B. 2007. Language socialization and the linguistic anthropology of education. In *Encyclopedia of Language and Education*. Vol. 8: *Language Socialization*, ed. P Duff, N Hornberger, pp. 29–42. New York: Springer. 2nd ed.

Sapir E. 1921. *Language: An Introduction to the Study of Speech*. New York: Harcourt Brace

Sawyer K. 2004. Improvised lessons: collaborative discussion in the constructivist classroom. *Teach. Educ.* 15:189–201

Schieffelin B, Ochs E, ed. 1986. *Language Socialization across Cultures*. New York: Cambridge Univ. Press

Schieffelin B, Woolard K, Kroskrity P, ed. 1998. *Language Ideologies: Practice and Theory*. New York: Oxford Univ. Press

Silverstein M. 1976. Shifters, linguistic categories, and cultural description. In *Meaning in Anthropology*, ed. K Basso, H Selby, pp. 11–55. Albuquerque: Univ. N. M. Press

Silverstein M. 1979. Language structure and linguistic ideology. In *The Elements: A Parasession on Linguistic Units and Levels*, ed. P Clyne, W Hanks, C Hofbauer, pp. 193–247. Chicago: Chicago Ling. Soc.

Silverstein M. 1985. Language and the culture of gender: at the intersection of structure, usage and ideology. See Mertz & Parmentier 1985, pp. 219–59

Silverstein M. 1992. The indeterminacy of contextualization: When is enough enough? In *The Contextualization of Language*, ed. A DiLuzio, P Auer, pp. 55–75. Amsterdam: John Benjamins

Silverstein M. 2003. Indexical order and the dialectics of sociolinguistic life. *Lang. Comm.* 23:193–229

Silverstein M, Urban G, eds. 1996. *Natural Histories of Discourse*. Chicago: Univ. Chicago Press

Spolsky B, Hult F, ed. 2008. *Handbook of Educational Linguistics*. Oxford: Blackwell

Stocker K. 2003. "Ellos se comen las eses/heces." See Wortham & Rymes 2003, pp. 185–211

Street B. 1984. *Literacy in Theory and Practice*. Cambridge, UK: Cambridge Univ. Press

Urban G. 1996. *Metaphysical Community*. Austin: Univ. Tex. Press

Urban G. 2001. *Metaculture: How Culture Moves through the World*. Minneapolis, MN: Univ. Minn. Press

Varenne H. 2007. Difficult collective deliberations: anthropological notes toward a theory of education. *Teach. Coll. Rec.* 109:1559–88

Varenne H, McDermott R. 1998. *Successful Failure: The School America Builds*. Boulder, CO: Westview

Viechnicki G. 2008. "The evidence from your experiment is a weight loss": grammatical processes of objectification in a middle school science classroom. *Linguist. Educ.* 19:In press

Viechnicki G, Kuipers J. 2006. "It's all human error!": when a school science experiment fails. *Linguist. Educ.* 17:107–30

Warriner D. 2004. "The days now is very hard for my family": the negotiation and construction of gendered work identities among newly arrived women refugees. *J. Lang. Identity Educ.* 3:279–94

Warriner D. 2007. Transnational literacies: immigration, language learning, and identity. *Linguist. Educ.* 18:201–14

Wee L. 2006. The semiotics of language ideologies in Singapore. *J. Sociolinguist.* 10:344–61

Whorf B. 1956. *Language, Thought and Reality*. Cambridge, MA: MIT Press

Wortham S. 1992. Participant examples and classroom interaction. *Linguist. Educ.* 4:195–217

Wortham S. 2003. Accomplishing identity in participant-denoting discourse. *J. Linguist. Anthropol.* 13:1–22

Wortham S. 2005. Socialization beyond the speech event. *J. Linguist. Anthropol.* 15:95–112

Wortham S. 2006. *Learning Identity: The Mediation of Social Identity through Academic Learning*. New York: Cambridge Univ. Press

Wortham S, Berkley A, eds. 2001. *Language ideology and education. Linguist. Educ.* 12(3):Spec. issue

Wortham S, Jackson K. 2008. Educational constructionisms. In *Handbook of Constructionist Research*, ed. J Holstein, J Gubrium, pp. 107–27. New York: Guilford

Wortham S, Rymes B, eds. 2003. *Linguistic Anthropology of Education*. Westport, CT: Praeger

Zentella A. 1997. *Growing Up Bilingual: Puerto Rican Children in New York*. Cambridge, MA: Blackwell

Evolutionary Models of Women's Reproductive Functioning

Virginia J. Vitzthum

Anthropology Department and Kinsey Institute, Indiana University, Bloomington, Indiana 47405-7100; email: vitzthum@indiana.edu

Annu. Rev. Anthropol. 2008. 37:53–73

First published online as a Review in Advance on May 29, 2008

The *Annual Review of Anthropology* is online at anthro.annualreviews.org

This article's doi: 10.1146/annurev.anthro.37.081407.085112

Key Words

life history theory, reproductive ecology, evolutionary endocrinology, ovarian steroids, adaptation

Abstract

Life history theory posits that natural selection leads to the evolution of mechanisms that tend to allocate resources to the competing demands of growth, reproduction, and survival such that fitness is locally maximized. (That is, among alternative allocation patterns exhibited in a population, those having the highest inclusive fitness will become more common over generational time.) Strategic modulation of reproductive effort is potentially adaptive because investment in a new conception may risk one's own survival, future reproductive opportunities, and/or current offspring survival. Several physiological and behavioral mechanisms modulate reproductive effort in human females. This review focuses on the hormonal changes that vary the probability of ovulation, conception, and/or continuing pregnancy and discusses evolutionary models that predict how and why these hormonal changes occur. Anthropological field studies have yielded important insights into the environmental correlates of variation in ovarian steroids, but much remains to be learned about the evolutionary determinants, proximate mechanisms, and demographic significance of variation in women's reproductive functioning.

INTRODUCTION

" . . . [T]he maximization of individual reproductive success will seldom be achieved by unbridled fecundity." George C. Williams (1966a, p. 161)

Williams's deceptively simple observation is a perceptive appraisal of the nature of evolutionary adaptation. Because concepts of adaptation are so closely linked to successful reproduction, it might appear contradictory to propose that reducing reproductive effort (RE), or even suppressing it entirely, could ever be adaptive. But an organism inevitably faces trade-offs in the allocation of available resources (Gadgil & Bossert 1970). Energy devoted to somatic maintenance may prolong life but is then unavailable for reproduction. On the other hand, a new investment in reproduction can place one's own survival and future reproductive opportunities at risk. Hence, in a given opportunity, modulating RE may be a woman's best strategy for maximizing lifetime reproductive success (Wasser & Barash 1983, Ellison 1990, Haig 1990, Peacock 1990, Vitzthum 1990).

The application of evolutionary theory to explain women's reproductive functioning is a relatively recent development in the study of human biological variation. The approach caught on quickly and is now a central focus of human reproductive ecology. Although there is not a single perspective or evolutionary model shared by all reproductive ecologists (see the contributions in Campbell & Wood 1994 and Ellison 2001), it is widely agreed that there are physiological mechanisms that modulate RE (Voland 1998, Worthman 2003). The most thoroughly studied mechanism thus far is the suppressive effect of infant suckling on the maternal hypothalamic-pituitary-ovarian (HPO) axis (Konner & Worthman 1980, Vitzthum 1994, Wood 1994). Many questions regarding the optimal adjustment of RE throughout a woman's lifetime are yet to be as well understood as that of lactational suppression of ovulation, but current research efforts are promising.

The full breadth of thinking and relevant evidence regarding a woman's investment in reproduction is beyond the scope of a single paper. This review focuses on evolutionary models of women's reproductive functioning and the physiological mechanisms by which women modulate RE in a potential or recent conception, either by varying the probability of conceiving or by terminating an extant conception at its earliest stages. It is useful to consider these two mechanisms in tandem because both involve the loss of perhaps only one or two opportunities for reproduction and because there is some evidence that both involve varying ovarian steroid levels.

Modulating hormone levels is only one of several potential avenues for adjusting RE. A vast array of behavioral, cultural, and sociopolitical factors can influence human fertility. Demographers have organized these into a small tractable set of "proximate determinants" (e.g., proportion married, use of contraception, pregnancy loss) through which all other variables must operate (Davis & Blake 1956, Bongaarts & Potter 1983). Wood (1994) and his colleagues have developed a detailed specification of the biological proximate determinants of natural fertility (e.g., ovarian cycle length, duration of fertile period). Although this demographic approach is not informed by evolutionary theory, it is a valuable tool in modeling the relative importance of proximate and more distal sources of variation in human fertility. Among the advantages of Wood's (1994) model, it can be used to evaluate the impact of interpopulational differences in reproductive physiology on fertility.

This review begins with a brief description of the two principal frameworks that have informed an evolutionary study of women's reproductive functioning: human adaptability research and life history theory (LHT). Next, I outline the evolutionary models that have been developed to explain adaptive variability in women's reproductive functioning. These models attempt to link theoretical descriptions of modulating RE to the physiological mechanisms by which RE is allocated in a living organism. The subsequent section reviews the

---

Adaptation: depending on context, may refer to a trait (an adaptation) or to the process of becoming adapted

Reproductive effort (RE): the allocation of resources to producing a live offspring that survives to maturity; comprises mating effort and parental investment

Modulating RE: any physiological or behavioral change that varies the opportunities for reproduction and/or the probability of a live offspring reaching maturity

HPO axis: hypothalamic-pituitary-ovarian axis

Life history theory (LHT): an analytical framework within evolutionary theory for studying behavioral and physiological resource-allocation mechanisms and related maturational and reproductive traits

evidence on variation in ovarian steroids relevant to testing the hypotheses generated by these models. I close with a brief mention of several research questions deserving greater attention in the continuing effort to understand the evolution of women's reproductive functioning.

CONCEPTS OF EVOLUTION AND ADAPTATION IN BIOLOGICAL ANTHROPOLOGY

Biological anthropology's chief concern is with understanding the processes that generate variation in biological form and functioning in humans and other primates. Since the mid-twentieth century (Washburn 1951), the principal framework for much of the research in this field has been the synthetic theory of evolution, which emerged from the integration, initiated in the mid-1930s, of Darwin's theory of natural selection and Mendel's theory of genetic inheritance.

According to this "modern synthesis" (Huxley 1942), evolution is an intergenerational change in the genetic structure (allele frequencies) of a population of breeding individuals as a result of natural selection, genetic drift, gene flow, and mutation. Heritable phenotypes are the outcome of interactions between genotypes and environments. Hence, phenotypic change in a species over time is often presumed to reflect genetic variation and to be the outcome of one or more evolutionary processes. Natural selection of heritable traits is considered to be the principal, and perhaps only, process that can lead to adaptations (Williams 1966a).

This succinct description belies the tumultuous debates among evolutionary biologists regarding, among other issues, the concept of adaptation. One approach (Williams 1966a, Gould & Lewontin 1979) restricts adaptations to those features that have evolved through selection on heritable phenotypes for a specific function as the result of an associated increase in fitness (Gould & Vrba 1982). These are recognizable as well-engineered solutions for specific challenges to survival and reproduction (i.e.,

the "argument from design") (Williams 1966a, Lauder 1996). However, there appear to be very few cases for which the necessary data to assess a trait by these criteria are of sufficient quality, or even available (Leroi et al. 1994). More importantly, an organism's morphology and physiology operate as an integrated unit in which any one component may serve multiple purposes. Because natural selection is more like a tinkerer than an engineer (Jacob 1977), many morphological, physiological, and behavioral features of an organism are not readily perceivable as having been shaped by selection to meet a specific challenge.

Another approach considers a phenotypic variant to be adaptive if its current possessor has a higher inclusive fitness compared with some other variant in the same population (Clutton-Brock & Harvey 1979, Fisher 1985, Caro & Borgerhoff Mulder 1987). Defining adaptation by its effects (on fitness) rather than its causes (selection among heritable variants) avoids faulty perceptions of design and the misleading notion of "goal" implicit in an argument from design, dispels speculations about unknown genetic influences and past selection pressures, and specifies a clear criterion for testing hypotheses. However, this approach to identifying an adaptation usually begs the question of whether the phenotype under study is heritable, and hence subject to natural selection, and ignores rather than solves the difficulties encountered in evaluating the evolutionary origins and maintenance of a character.

Befitting their focus on understanding variation in a widespread, phenotypically diverse, long-lived, flexible, culture-bearing species, many human biologists have adopted an ecologically oriented concept of adaptation that emphasizes an individual's ability to "surmount the challenges to life" (Lasker 1969, Mazess 1975, Thomas et al. 1989). This biocultural approach explicitly acknowledges that human behavior and its cultural, social, institutional, technological, and symbolic manifestations can have consequences for human biological variation potentially as significant as the effects of the physical environment (Lasker 1969,

Inclusive fitness: an individual's number of offspring surviving to reproductive maturity plus those of its kin discounted by the degree of relationship

Mazess 1975, Wiley 1992). Any biological or behavioral response that affords a beneficial adjustment to physical or social conditions is considered adaptive, even if it is not the direct consequence of natural selection on a heritable phenotype. Thus, physiological acclimatization, learning, and other mechanisms of adjustment join genetic change as one of several processes that can result in adaptations. Adaptations can be identified by measuring fitness or its presumed proxies (health, energy efficiency, longevity) (Thomas et al. 1989, Wiley 1992).

This conceptualization of adaptive responses informed the Human Adaptability Project, a series of investigations on human adaptation to different environments (Lasker 1969). Among their many contributions, these studies produced a large body of empirical evidence refuting the assumption that all humans respond in a similar manner to comparable stimuli ("biological uniformitarianism," Leslie & Little 2003) and documented the influence of developmental conditions on adult form and functioning. Human stature, for example, has been especially well studied (Lasker 1969, Bogin 1999) and is widely used as a barometer of environmental quality and population health (Komlos 1994, WHO 1995).

An ecological perspective on adaptation is an elaboration of the synthetic theory of evolution, predicated on the assumption that selection has favored the phenotypes associated with beneficial responses to environmental challenges. However, natural selection need not enhance individual well-being or congruity with the environment. Consider the relationships among agriculture, malaria, and an increase in the allele for sickle cell hemoglobin (lethal when homozygous, barring biomedical intervention) because of heterozygote advantage (Livingstone 1958). The outcome of heterozygote advantage is maximization of mean (not individual) fitness because the pool of heterozygous parents unavoidably produces homozygous offspring of lower fitness [referred to as genetic load (Rose & Lauder 1996)]. Although the sickle-cell adaptation is wasteful (lost offspring), the inefficiency is an inevitable outcome of the interaction between this particular genetic variant and a specific environment. Such a genetic adaptation to malaria is not the manifestation of any engineered design.

The assumption that selection yields an optimal solution to some challenge can promote the mistaken expectation that a genuinely adaptive response is efficient and not detrimental to the individual. But selection favors those phenotypes with the highest reproductive success in a specific population, even if this greater fitness comes at substantial cost to individuals. For this and other reasons, there is merit in distinguishing adaptations (based on inclusive fitness) from individual adaptability (responsiveness to challenge). Yet while there is no necessary relationship between reproductive fitness and measures of individual well-being or efficiency (Voland 1998), neither is there any reason to assume that such a relationship is rare (Wiley 1992). Rather, life history theory (discussed below) provides a framework for elucidiating the fitness benefits and costs of allocating resources to self-maintenance over the course of a lifetime. With regard to individual well-being, studies of adaptation and adaptability can yield valuable insights into the patterns of morbidity, growth, fertility, and mortality in human populations across different environments (see Wiley 1992; Chisholm 1993; Geronimus et al. 1999; and Walker et al. 2006, 2008 for examples).

Bioanthropologists generally agree that evolution involves an intergenerational change in allele frequency (and/or gene expression), but there is a growing effort to enrich (or replace) this gene-centric model with a framework that includes developmental (ontogenetic) processes and dynamic interactions between organisms and environments (Pigliucci & Kaplan 2000, Jablonka & Lamb 2006). Over time, evolution by natural selection will maximize multigenerational inclusive fitness in a specific population and environment. The interplay of this mechanism with other processes that may lead to adaptations is not yet clear. Bioanthropologists hold several positions on how to define adaptation, how to demonstrate that adaptation is occurring (or has occurred), and which processes other than natural selection could lead to adaptation (Lasker 1969, Wiley 1992, Worthman 2003, Bogin et al. 2007). As each of these viewpoints has its merits, the preferred approach in a given study can be dictated as much by the specific question and available data as by the superiority of any particular criterion for recognizing adaptation.

LIFE HISTORY THEORY

LHT is an analytical framework comprising models and observations concerned with the allocation of finite resources within a finite lifetime to the competing demands of growth, maintenance, and reproduction (Gadgil & Bossert 1970, Borgerhoff Mulder 1992, Charnov 1993, Stearns 1992, Hill & Kaplan 1999). LHT may be thought of as evolutionary economics. Life history strategies (LHSs), suites of reproductive and developmental traits (e.g., age and size at initiating reproduction; the number, quality, and timing of offspring; age at death), are investment schedules subject to natural selection. These traits are often flexible in their expression, depending on the specific environmental conditions encountered by the individual. The theoretically optimal LHS for an organism in a given environment is that which maximizes its multigenerational inclusive fitness.

LHT began to inform anthropological research in the 1970s. Human behavioral ecology, developed as an alternative to the then-dominant ecosystem and energy-flow schools in ecological anthropology (Winterhalder 2002), adapted both LHT and optimal foraging models to explain human behavioral variation. The use of LHT to explain human biological variation is more recent.

There are at least 45 recognized trade-offs among life history traits (e.g., quantity vs. quality of offspring, current vs. future reproduction) (Stearns 1992). The formalization of allocation trade-offs began with Fisher (1930), who defined reproductive value (RV) as the mean future reproductive success (i.e., how many more offspring the organism can expect will survive to reproductive maturity) for those of a given age and sex in that population. Williams (1966b) partitioned RV into that which is immediately at stake (current reproduction, CR) and residual reproductive value ($RV = CR + RRV$). He defined a as the proportional gain to CR and c as the proportional cost to RRV when a positive allocation decision is made by the organism (e.g., ovulate, defend). Given a negative allocation decision (e.g., do not forage, do not mate), he defined b as the proportional decrement to CR. Hence,

RV given positive decision:

$$RV_p = (1 + a)CR + (1 - c)RRV,$$

and

RV given negative decision:

$$RV_n = (1 - b)CR + RRV.$$

If RV_p (the increased CR from investing plus the reduced future RRV due to the current investment) exceeds RV_n (the reduced CR by not investing plus the future RRV), then selection will favor the positive allocation decision and it will become the normative decision. Alternatively, the negative allocation decision would become normative if $RV_n > RV_p$. Over time, selection has favored those physiological and behavioral mechanisms by which the most successful LHSs are implemented, and these mechanisms respond accordingly given the available resources throughout an organism's lifetime.

Depending on the species, resources comprise the energy and other nutrients available to support a growing conceptus and live offspring; the availability of a suitable habitat, mate, and social group; and the physical and psychological status of the mother. Information is another "good in limited supply" because knowledge facilitates access to material and social resources (Worthman 2003). All these resources contribute to the relative values of RV_p and RV_n at any given reproductive opportunity. Hence, selection will favor RE whenever $RV_p > RV_n$, even if some single resource (e.g., food availability) does not appear to be

Life history strategy (LHS): a suite of reproductive and developmental traits subject to natural selection

Reproductive value (RV): for an individual of a given age and sex, how many more offspring are expected to survive to reproductive maturity

Fertility: the production of a live offspring

particularly propitious. Likewise, selection will favor delaying or avoiding RE whenever $RV_n > RV_p$, even if some relevant resources are favorable (Williams 1966b).

Time until the termination of reproductive capacity (either death or menopause) is a particularly critical resource contributing to the relative values of RV_p and RV_n. Rapid maturation is advantageous because it yields more generations per unit time, but it is also costly because it precludes growth to a larger size with its own advantages (e.g., predator reduction). However, in environments with high mortality risk, an organism cannot afford to take the time to grow (see Walker et al. 2006 and Migliano et al. 2007 for evidence of this relationship between mortality risk and human growth). Analytically, the impact of time on the trade-offs among life history traits is represented by the Euler-Lotka equation, which is parameterized by age-specific fertility and mortality schedules, and allows RV to be expressed as a function of these demographic variables (Stearns 1992). Conceptually, one should appreciate that the optimal LHS for an organism is a consequence of numerous competing costs and benefits, which vary with locally specific risks of mortality.

EVOLUTIONARY MODELS OF WOMEN'S REPRODUCTIVE FUNCTIONING

LHT predicts that, given parental resources, selection favors that combination of offspring number and size that maximizes the number of offspring reaching reproductive maturity (Lack 1954). This quantity-quality trade-off has been observed in numerous species (Stearns 1992) and across mammals (Charnov & Ernest 2006) but has only rarely been documented in humans (e.g., Strassmann & Gillespie 2002). A recent analysis of 17 natural-fertility populations supports a quantity-quality trade-off in nonindustrial societies (Walker et al. 2008). Across populations, offspring size at age five years (a measure of parental investment) varied inversely with the energy-corrected fertility

rate (i.e., those with smaller offspring had more offspring).

In mammals, lactation is a principal pathway by which ovarian functioning, and hence RE in another conception, is suppressed (Vitzthum 1994). Shorter breastfeeding duration may yield a smaller-sized infant at weaning but permits a new conception sooner. The upper limit on this fertility-size trade-off depends on the increasing risk of infant mortality with progressively younger weaning age.

In addition to lactational suppression, physiological mechanisms that modulate RE in human females include (but are not limited to) varying the age at reproductive maturation; hormonal changes in the HPO axis that vary the probability of ovulation, conception, and/or implantation; and early pregnancy termination (Frisch & Revelle 1970, Wasser & Barash 1983, Ellison 1990, Haig 1990, Peacock 1990, Vitzthum 1990, Chisholm 1993). Anthropologists have repeatedly emphasized the role of developmental conditions in shaping adult morphology and physiology, including reproductive functioning (Purifoy 1981, Ellison 1990, Vitzthum 1990, Chisholm 1993).

Wasser & Barash (1983) explored the potential advantages of adjusting RE in female mammals under a broad array of circumstances including variation in resource availability. Their formulation (the reproductive suppression model) is a special case of Williams's (1966b) model. They proposed that age (an indicator of time remaining until the end of reproduction) and its associated physical changes are perhaps the most reliable predictors of RV, whereas nutritional status, disease, and psychosocial stress are less reliable cues. They examined the evidence for social suppression resulting from "one's interactions with, and the reproductions of, other individuals." During periods of strong social competition, they argued, it could be beneficial to delay conception (or terminate a recent conception) until conditions have become less competitive. In addition, a female might also increase her own reproductive success by manipulating reproduction in the other members of her social group.

Drawing on LHT and studies of human adaptability, Vitzthum (1990, 1997, 2001) developed the flexible response model (FRM) to explain an apparent paradox: Why are the ovarian cycles of healthy U.S. women easily disrupted by dieting and exercise, whereas women in nonindustrialized countries have high fertility despite arduous physical labor and poor nutrition? The resolution of this paradox lies in an organism's ability to integrate the information garnered from the prevailing conditions during maturation, which are likely to approximate future conditions, into resource evaluation during adulthood. RE is delayed in U.S. women experiencing temporarily poor conditions because the environment is expected to improve shortly. Where suboptimal conditions are normative, an improvement is unlikely; hence, delaying RE is not advantageous. Reducing RE is potentially advantageous when conditions are worse than those prevailing during development; increasing RE is potentially advantageous when conditions are better than those prevailing during development.

The FRM predicts that selection favors a flexible reproductive system reflective of and responsive to local conditions. Fecundity is hypothesized to be a function of both current conditions (including one's own status) and long-term average conditions (viewed as an estimate of likely future conditions). Hence, the decision to reproduce depends on (a) the probability of successful reproduction in the present conditions, (b) the probability of conditions changing (for better or worse) within a finite period, (c) the risk to future reproductive opportunities, and (d) the expected duration until the end of the reproductive life span.

The FRM also predicts that a woman able to acclimate to persistently suboptimal conditions (i.e., able to resume reproductive functioning) will have a selective advantage over one who does not, as long as the probability of a successful birth in these poorer conditions is >0. This prediction is consistent with numerous studies of the adaptability of human physiology in the face of conditions that initially perturb normal functioning (e.g., physiological acclimatization

to high altitude in sea-level sojourners (Beall et al. 2002) and is supported by experimental studies in other mammals (Barker-Gibb & Clarke 1996). The argument can also be understood in terms of RV. As time progresses, the inequality between RV_p and RV_n changes, even if environmental conditions do not improve, because there is less time during which to reproduce before one dies. Selection favors physiological mechanisms that adjust RE in accordance with time-related changes in RV. In an independent examination of widespread pregnancy wastage in humans and other animals, Peacock (1990, 1991) likewise proposed that selection favors mechanisms that permit reproduction under persistently suboptimal conditions.

Another explicitly adaptationist approach to women's reproductive functioning argues that energetics (energy intake, expenditure, flux, and balance) are of paramount importance in generating adaptive variation in ovarian functioning (Ellison 1990, 1994, 2003; Ellison et al. 1993, 2007; Jasienska 2001; Lipson 2001). The hypothesis that selection favors efficient energy utilization has a long history (Lotka 1922a,b). But the role of energy in human reproduction did not receive much attention until Frisch proposed that a critical body-fat threshold must be exceeded to initiate and maintain ovarian cycling (Frisch & Revelle 1970, Frisch & McArthur 1974). Although her specific threshold hypothesis has been refuted (Bongaarts 1980, Scott & Johnston 1982), there is substantial evidence for Frisch's fundamental premise that energy intake and expenditure influence the functioning of the human HPO axis.

In particular, extensive research on the precise causes of exercise-associated amenorrhea (the loss of menstrual cycling in some exercising women) has yielded valuable insights into the effects of energetic stressors. The dose-dependent relationship between increasing exercise and decreasing integrity of the menstrual cycle led Prior (1985, 1987) to propose that such changes in ovarian functioning should not be seen as disease processes but rather as a progressive series of adaptive responses to

FRM: flexible response model

Fecundity: the biological capacity to conceive

escalating energetic stress, a view also advanced by Ellison (1990). Studies in monkeys (reviewed in Cameron 1996) and women in nonindustrialized populations (e.g., Ellison et al. 1989) have also reported a dose-dependency, similar to that of exercising women, between increasing energetic imbalance and reductions in ovarian steroid levels.

Ellison (1990, 1994) proposed a developmental energetics model, elaborated by his colleagues (Jasienska 2001, Lipson 2001), to explain interpopulational variation in ovarian steroid levels and other aspects of ovarian functioning. This model predicts that women born in energetically demanding conditions will grow more slowly, mature later, have a greater sensitivity to energetic stress, have lower fecundity (evidenced by lower ovarian steroid levels), and have fewer offspring during their lives than would be the case if they had developed in resource-rich conditions. This pattern of growth and reproduction is seen as adaptive because it avoids investment in a pregnancy with a poor probability of success, thereby conserving energy and increasing the probability of maternal survival. Energetics models posit that selection favors reproducing only if a woman's nutritional status is substantially adequate and/or there is some indication of "the potential for sustaining an ongoing investment" (Ellison 2003, p. 345); fecundity is hypothesized to be a function of trends in energetic status and/or current energetic status.

The curtailment of RE is not only a matter of the adequacy of maternal resources and environmental conditions. Offspring must be of sufficient quality to merit maternal investment (Temme 1986, Kozlowski & Stearns 1989, Haig 1990). The quick termination of RE in a defective conceptus increases the RE available for other offspring (existing or future) of higher quality. Genetic defects that preclude normal development can be expected to terminate on their own accord, but selection will also favor any maternal mechanism, presumably hormonal, that detects and eliminates poor-quality offspring as early as possible. Haig (1993) proposed that a principal cue by which human mothers evaluate an offspring's quality is its ability to produce hCG. Production of hCG indicates the embryo's capacity to carry out protein synthesis [a minimal requirement of viability (Haig 1993)] and promotes maternal production of progesterone, without which the pregnancy would terminate.

An evolutionary perspective on RE challenges the view that, having been designed by natural selection for reproduction, any deviations of the HPO axis from this function must be pathologies or failures of adaptation. Rather, just as lactational suppression of ovulation is potentially adaptive, so might other instances of reducing RE be adaptive. The argument that modulating RE can be considered adaptive only if an initially negative effect on fertility is "countered by an even larger positive effect at some later time" (Wood 1994, p. 528) misconstrues evolutionary processes. Natural selection maximizes lifetime (and over time, multigenerational) reproductive success (having offspring that live to reproduce), not fecundity or fertility. A given instance of suppressing RE is rightly considered adaptive if the inclusive fitness of the individual is greater than it would be if RE had occurred in that instance. Furthermore, the optimal LHS is specific to a local environment. Nothing can be inferred about the relative adaptiveness of two populations if the optimal number of offspring in one locality happens to be less than the number in a population in a different locality.

A women's reproductive system is not an autonomous machine, unflagging in its production if given sufficient fuel. Nor is it limping along if resources are less than optimal. Rather, an evolutionary perspective of women's reproductive functioning sees the HPO axis as an integral component of a whole organism in which adjustments in RE and other functions are responsive to local resources and mortality schedules. For example, if energy availability is low, the number of offspring can be maintained by reducing the size of each or by decreasing maternal body size (which increases the proportion of acquired energy available for RE), or by making other investment trade-offs (Stearns

1992). Because selection inexorably favors the LHS that has the highest inclusive fitness in the local context, the locally optimal LHS likely comprises a combination of several such trade-offs. LHT does not yet have the tools to predict which combination has been favored by selection in a specific population (Stearns 1992).

EVOLUTIONARY ENDOCRINOLOGY

"It would be instructive to know . . . by what physiological mechanisms a just apportionment is made between the nutriment devoted to the gonads and that devoted to the rest of the parental organism . . . ." Fisher (1930, pp. 43–44)

Efforts to understand the mechanisms by which LHSs are implemented have coalesced into the emerging field of evolutionary endocrinology. The endocrine system plays a central role in orchestrating an organism's response to external signals and stimuli (Finch & Rose 1995; Worthman 1995, 2003; Wade et al. 1996; Dufty et al. 2002; Nepomnaschy et al. 2006a). Hormonal changes can, for example, trigger or suppress gene transcription and modify metabolic rates.

Modulating RE logically involves neurohormonal changes in the HPO axis including (but not limited to) varying the fraction of ovulatory cycles and the levels of estradiol and progesterone. Because many experimental protocols are precluded in humans, testing this and related hypotheses usually requires hormonal data from a reasonably large sample of free-living women. The development of field-friendly collection protocols and assays that measure hormones and their metabolites in saliva, urine, and blood spots have removed many, but not all, of the technological barriers to such studies (Ellison 1988, Worthman & Stallings 1997, O'Connor et al. 2006). Saliva is a particularly useful medium when frequent measurements are needed, as during a menstrual cycle. Comparisons of salivary steroid levels presume that the ratio of salivary to serum levels is roughly comparable across individuals and populations. [This assumption was questioned by Chatterton and colleagues (2006), but their statistical approach was seriously flawed (Thornburg et al. 2008).]

Methodological Challenges in the Study of Ovarian Steroid Variation

Efforts to determine the extent, causes, and demographic significance of interpopulational variation in levels of reproductive hormones have been hampered by several significant methodological issues including selection bias and inadequate control of confounders. These sources of error should be considered when evaluating the literature and must be addressed when designing new studies and conducting analyses.

The ecological (or epidemiological) fallacy refers to the (often unsupportable) assumption that factors that covary among populations are causally linked in individuals and arises from the extraordinary difficulty of controlling for all potential confounders that differ among populations (Robinson 1950). For example, among U.S. states, Florida has one of the highest cancer rates, not because being a Floridian causes cancer but rather because so many retirees move to Florida (McCoy et al. 1992).

Selection bias is the unintended preferential sampling of only a segment of the variation in a population. For example, if many sexually active women in a population are not using contraception, those with the highest fecundity are more likely to be either pregnant or lactating and not included in a study of ovarian cycle steroids. Unavoidably, a cross-sectional sample would disproportionately represent women with the lowest fecundity. There is clear evidence of such within-population variation in fecundity. The probability of conceiving was higher in lactating than nonlactating menstruating married Bolivian women (Vitzthum et al. 2000b), and recent data from Europe indicate a fourfold difference in fecundability among non-contracepting women of the same age (Dunson et al. 2002). If comparable variation is typical across populations, then this selection bias will

Fecundability: the monthly probability of conception

be more severe in cross-sectional samples from nonindustrialized natural fertility populations, where anthropologists have focused their research efforts, than in industrialized societies.

Comparisons of normal ovarian steroid levels must control for confounders (e.g., age, season of collection) (Vitzthum et al. 2000a, Vitzthum 2007). Progesterone levels, for example, are lower at younger and older ages (Ellison 1994). Therefore, samples having different age distributions (even if their mean ages are identical) could erroneously appear to differ in progesterone levels. Because progesterone levels first rise with age and then later fall, modeling the age variation in progesterone as linear over the full reproductive life span does not correct for this bias (Thornburg 2007). Instead, a quadratic or other non-linear functional form must be used.

Comparisons should also be restricted to samples of ovulatory cycles (Vitzthum et al. 2002, 2004; Vitzthum & Thornburg 2008). The inclusion of anovulatory cycles inappropriately lowers the estimates of mean hormone levels and obscures the sources of steroid variation. Because populational samples often differ in the rate of anovulation, this bias can easily corrupt cross-populational comparisons of mean hormone levels. Several methods have been developed by which to infer ovulation; each has its advantages and drawbacks (Kassam et al. 1996, Vitzthum et al. 2004, O'Connor et al. 2006). Caution is required when comparing ovulation rates across samples that used different methods or sampling regimes. For example, one commonly used algorithm assumes ovulation has occurred when at least one observed luteal progesterone value is >2 standard deviations above the daily mean of follicular progesterone. However, even without a systematic rise in progesterone due to ovulation, this chance probability is $0.08 (= 1–0.975^{3.5})$ in sampling every 4 days, $0.16 (= 1–0.975^{7})$ in every-other-day sampling, and 0.30 in daily sampling. Hence, in the hypothetical case where all cycles are anovulatory, women sampled every day would appear to have a rate of ovulation two to four times higher than do other women sampled less frequently simply because of differences in the sampling regimes (Vitzthum et al. 2002, 2004).

Interpopulational Variation in Ovarian Steroid Levels

Statistically significant differences exist in ovarian steroid levels between populations and among ethnic subpopulations, but much of this variation remains unexplained.

Early studies reported estrogen levels in Asians to be ~55%–90% of those observed in "white" women in the United States and the United Kingdom (MacMahon et al. 1974, Purifoy 1981, Trichopoulos et al. 1984, Key et al. 1990, Wang et al. 1991). The range among studies in relative estrogen concentrations of Asians to whites is attributable to different methodologies and several confounders. In a study with greater control of covariates (age, weight, height, pregnancy history, and day of the menstrual cycle), luteal-phase estradiol levels were ~20% higher in Los Angeles whites compared with women in Shanghai, but progesterone levels were not significantly different (Bernstein et al. 1990).

van der Walt and colleagues (1978) reported low ovarian steroids in !Kung San and suggested that these may be a mechanism to restrict conception to seasons of better nutrition. Compared with Bostonians, salivary progesterone levels were lower (and also varied seasonally) in agricultural populations in Zaire (Ellison et al. 1989), Nepal (Panter-Brick et al. 1993), and Poland (Jasienska & Ellison 1998). The age composition, season of collection, and inclusion of anovulatory cycles differed in these samples, hence comparisons that did not adjust for these confounders may not be valid. Restricting the samples to data collected during the least energetically stressful season from women aged 25–35 years, researchers found that rural Bolivians at high altitude had progesterone levels statistically comparable to or higher than these three agricultural populations from lower altitudes (Vitzthum et al. 2000a). In another study controlling for known confounders (e.g., age, lactation, season), salivary

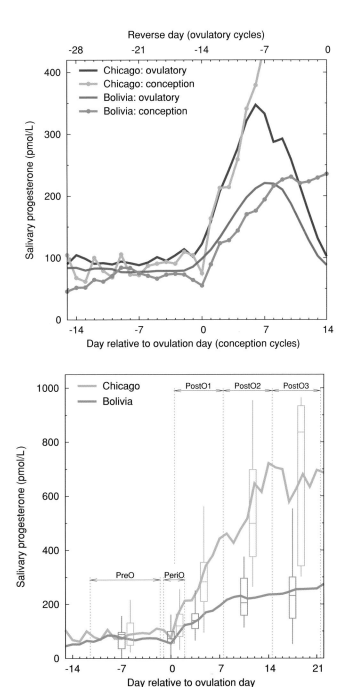

Figure 1

Top: Salivary progesterone (P) profiles in conception and ovulatory nonconception cycles in women from Chicago and rural Bolivia (cycle days 1–28). Ovulatory cycles are aligned on the first day of the subsequent cycle (days numbered backward); conception cycles are aligned on the putative day of ovulation (day 0). P levels in ovulatory cycles are significantly lower in Bolivian women than in women from Chicago throughout the ovarian cycle; in each sample, conception and ovulatory cycles have comparable P levels. *Bottom*: P profiles in conception cycles through implantation. Boxplots display median, quartiles, and range of P indices corresponding to the range of days delimited by vertical dashed lines to the respective left and right of box plot. PreO, preovulatory; PeriO, periovulatory; PostO, postovulatory. P levels do not significantly differ in women from Bolivia and Chicago during the follicular phase but are significantly different during and subsequent to ovulation and through implantation (redrawn after Vitzthum et al. 2004).

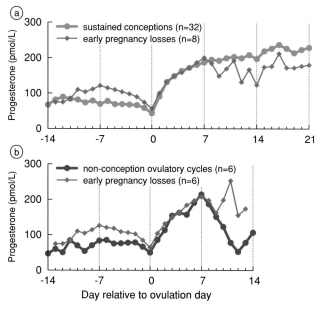

Figure 2

Salivary progesterone (P) levels (daily geometric mean) before and after ovulation (day 0) in naturally occurring conception and nonconception cycles. Luteal-phase (days 0 to 7) P levels did not differ among the samples. Follicular-phase (days –14 to 0) P was significantly higher in conceptions lost early compared with those pregnancies sustained ≥5 weeks after conception (panel *a*) and compared with nonconception ovulatory cycles from the same women (panel *b*) (redrawn after Vitzthum et al. 2006).

progesterone levels in the ovulatory cycles of Bolivian women were ~70% of those in Chicago women of comparable age (Vitzthum et al. 2002), and serum estradiol levels were significantly lower than published values for U.S. women (Vitzthum et al. 2007).

Three studies reported ethnic differences in steroid levels, but the findings are inconsistent despite each study's effort to control for several known confounders. Among northern Californians (Windham et al. 2002), Asians had lower and Hispanics had higher estrogen levels compared with whites, but progesterone metabolites did not vary with ethnicity. In Los Angeles (Haiman et al. 2002), both African Americans and Latinas had higher luteal estradiol and progesterone levels compared with non-Latina whites. Matched samples from the Nurses' Health Study II (Pinheiro et al. 2005) reported elevated estradiol levels in African Americans and Asian Americans compared with Caucasians but showed no ethnic differences in progesterone. Whether the reported hormonal variation among these ethnicities is rightly attributable to genetic variation, environmental factors, or some interaction of these remains unknown. Other than education level and current employment status in the study of northern Californians (Windham et al. 2002), none of the studies included socioeconomic indicators.

Developmental Conditions and Adult Ovarian Steroid Variation

A better understanding of interpopulational variation requires considerably more study of the determinants of hormonal variation between individuals. For a given woman, ovarian steroid levels vary with age, health, lactation, psychosocial stress, energy intake, and activity level (Prior 1985, 1987; Ellison & Lager 1986; Ellison 1994, 2003; Vitzthum 1994; Bentley 1999; Nepomnaschy et al. 2004). Once these factors are excluded, substantial unexplained differences between women still remained (Landgren et al. 1980, Bernstein et al. 1990, Haiman et al. 2002, Windham et al. 2002).

Reflecting the field's century-long interest in the consequences of early environments for adult biology (Boas 1911, Lasker 1969), bioanthropologists have proposed that more arduous conditions during development may underlie lower ovarian steroid levels in adulthood (Ellison 1990, Vitzthum 1990). Under the assumption that U.S. white women grew up in generally favorable environments, this hypothesis is consistent with lower progesterone levels in nonindustrialized populations compared with U.S. women (Ellison et al. 1989, Panter-Brick et al. 1993, Jasienska & Ellison 1998, Vitzthum et al. 2000a), lower estradiol levels and older age at menarche in Shanghai women than those in a Los Angeles white sample (Bernstein et al. 1990), and lower progesterone and estradiol levels in poorer compared with better-off Bolivians (Vitzthum et al. 2002, 2007). On the other hand, the relatively lower steroid levels observed in whites compared with other ethnic groups in California (Haiman et al. 2002, Windham et al. 2002) and the Nurses Health Study (Pinheiro et al. 2005) do not support this hypothesis. Such inconsistencies aside, because of the ecological fallacy, population-level associations should be viewed cautiously.

Two studies of individual-level variation provide strong evidence of a link between developmental conditions and adult ovarian steroid levels (Vitzthum et al. 2002, Windham et al. 2002). Each study avoided the selection bias described above, restricted samples to ovulatory cycles, and used an established biological indicator of childhood conditions [either adult height, which is substantially determined by environmental factors (e.g., food, disease) during the first two years of postnatal life (WHO 1995, Bogin 1999), or age at menarche, which is typically later in resource-poor environments (Wood 1994)]. As predicted, in urban Bolivian women, mean luteal progesterone level was positively correlated with height ($r = 0.35$, $P = 0.015$). A somewhat stronger correlation ($r = 0.40$, $P = 0.005$) was also observed between an index of overall progesterone level and an index of overall body size (a principal component factor that loaded mainly

NCEPS: North Carolina Early Pregnancy Study

Project REPA: Project on Reproduction and Ecology in Província Aroma

on height). Likewise, in a sample of U.S. women, estrogen metabolites were significantly lower in those whose menarche was ≥14 years (Windham et al. 2002). Yet even in these two studies, only a modest proportion of the variance is explained by developmental conditions as captured by the proxy variables. A third individual-level study suggests that prenatal energetic conditions do not influence the unstressed levels of adult ovarian steroids. Among Polish women engaged in only low physical activity, mean estradiol levels did not vary with ponderal index [(body weight in kg)/(body length in m)^3] at birth (Jasienska et al. 2006).

Fecundity, Pregnancy Loss, and Ovarian Steroid Variation

Considerable evidence supports the hypothesis that fecundity covaries with temporal (within-woman) variation in ovarian steroids (Ellison 1990, 1994, 2003; Wood 1994). In contrast, findings regarding the demographic significance of between-woman (within population) hormonal variation are inconsistent. Some studies have reported higher estrogen levels in conception vs. nonconception cycles (Stewart et al. 1993, Lipson & Ellison 1996, Venners et al. 2006), but in the North Carolina Early Pregnancy Study (NCEPS) urinary estrogen levels did not differ once other hormonal confounders were controlled (Baird et al. 1999). Li and colleagues (2001) reported higher serum estradiol on the day that follicular stimulating hormone peaked but demonstrated comparable total urinary estradiol metabolite levels in conception vs. nonconception cycles. Two studies observed higher luteal-phase progesterone levels in conception cycles (Stewart et al. 1993, Baird et al. 1999), but four studies did not (Lipson & Ellison 1996, Li et al. 2001, Vitzthum et al. 2004, Venners et al. 2006).

Extrapolating from the within-woman association between lower ovarian steroid levels and subfecundity, and the between-woman association between hormone levels and conception reported by some studies, proponents of energetic models have hypothesized that variation in steroid levels across populations is necessarily associated with variation in fecundity (Ellison et al. 1993, Ellison 1994, Lipson 2001). LHT does not make an explicit prediction about ovarian steroids and fecundity but does hypothesize that age-specific fertility schedules will vary with mortality schedules (Williams 1966a, Stearns 1992). For example, if mortality risk is high, it can be selectively advantageous to begin reproduction early (Chisholm 1993, Geronimus et al. 1999, Migliano et al. 2007) and have many smaller offspring (Charnov & Ernest 2006). Hence, the FRM (Vitzthum 1990, 1997, 2001) predicts that fecundity is not necessarily reduced in women living in suboptimal conditions but would depend on the four probabilities noted above (see section on Evolutionary Models of Women's Reproductive Functioning). The association between higher fertility and smaller offspring body size reported by Walker et al. (2008) implies that fecundity is not necessarily depressed (and may even be enhanced) in human populations where body size is small (as is often the case in suboptimal conditions).

A single study has tested the hypothesis that fecundity is necessarily lower in populations characterized by lower ovarian steroid levels (Vitzthum et al. 1998, 2004). Project REPA (Reproduction and Ecology in Província Aroma) recruited 316 rural Bolivian women without regard to lactational or menstrual status (to avoid selection bias) and followed each longitudinally. All women who menstruated during the study ($n = 191$; the remaining 125 women were pregnant and/or lactating and non-cycling throughout their participation in the study) contributed every-other-day saliva samples for up to 8 sequential cycles; late-luteal-phase urine samples were tested for hCG (human chorionic gonadotrophin), indicating implantation. Conceptions were followed until loss or birth. Salivary progesterone levels in the ovulatory cycles of these women averaged ∼70% of those in women from Chicago, and similarly lower progesterone levels also accompanied conception and implantation (**Figure 1**, see color insert).

These relatively low progesterone levels continued through pregnancy and were not associated with a higher probability of pregnancy loss (Vitzthum et al. 2006). The fertility levels of the Bolivian participants also suggested that their relatively lower progesterone levels had little or no effect on fecundity. Between the ages of 20 and 30 years, these women averaged four live births. A woman breastfed each of her infants on demand for 1–2 years; postpartum amenorrhea lasted ~1 year on average. Adding time for gestation, the live birth rate was neither so low as to be clear evidence of a reduction in fecundability nor so high as to rule out a small reduction (Vitzthum et al. 2004). Analyses are currently underway to quantify fecundability more precisely in this Bolivian population.

Indirect evidence also suggests that interpopulational variation in ovarian steroids may not be associated with comparable variation in fertility. Bongaarts (1980) observed that only a very small percentage of the fertility differences among human populations could be attributed to nutritional status, except in the case of famine. If the relatively lower levels of ovarian steroids reported for a handful of samples from nonindustrialized populations are generally representative of developing countries, then Bongaarts's observation contradicts the hypothesis that ovarian steroid levels covary with fecundity across populations. A recent cross-populational comparison of progesterone levels also appears to contradict this hypothesis; although progesterone levels in residents of Sylhet, Bangladesh, were reported to be less than half those of U.K. women of European descent (Núñez-de la Mora et al. 2007), the region has high fertility (Islam et al. 2004). However, because of selection bias and inadequate control for confounders (see section on Methodological Challenges in the Study of Ovarian Steroid Variation), progesterone levels in Sylhet may not be as low as reported (Thornburg 2007, Vitzthum 2007).

Although famine can reduce fecundity in adult women, decades-long follow-up on the effects of the Dutch famine during 1944–1945 found no impact of in utero famine exposure on subsequent fertility in adulthood and no effect of childhood famine exposure on menarcheal age; childhood famine exposure had only a modest effect on the probability of conceiving a first or second child in adulthood (Elias et al. 2005). These observations differ from the documented effects of chronic undernutrition on menarcheal age (Bogin 1999) and are consistent with the argument (Vitzthum 1990, 2001) that acute and chronic energetic stressors differ in their effects on reproductive functioning.

Three prospective studies tested the hypothesis that early pregnancy loss (EPL) is associated with relatively lower levels of ovarian steroids (Baird et al. 1991, Venners et al. 2006, Vitzthum et al. 2006). None of the studies found any significant differences in progesterone with respect to pregnancy loss. EPL detected in Project REPA had luteal-phase progesterone levels comparable to those in

AXIS CROSS-TALK MAY MODULATE REPRODUCTIVE EFFORT

Hormonal communication between the HPO and hypothalamic-pituitary-adrenal (HPA) axes may mediate the probability of conception and/or pregnancy termination. The adrenal cortex is the main source of progesterone during most of the follicular phase (Judd et al. 1992, De Geyter et al. 2002). In controlled experiments, adrenal progesterone rose in response to stress, triggering surges in lutenizing hormone that could impair follicular development (Puder et al. 2000). In Mayan women, 90% of those conceptions characterized by elevated cortisol were lost, a termination risk that was 2.7 times greater than in those with normal cortisol levels (Nepomnaschy et al. 2006b). In Bolivians, follicular-phase progesterone was significantly higher in early pregnancy losses than in either sustained conceptions or prior ovulatory cycles from the same women (**Figure 2**). Hence, elevated follicular-phase progesterone was specific to the pregnancy-loss conception cycle, as would be expected if the elevated progesterone was a signal of current maternal habitats (Vitzthum et al. 2006). Emotional stress, physical activity, and food restriction can all stimulate the HPA; elevations in cortisol and/or adrenal progesterone may be acting as signals of suboptimal maternal habitats as part of a mechanism to modulate maternal RE.

ovulatory cycles from the same women and comparable to those in sustained pregnancies (**Figure 2**, see color insert) (Vitzthum et al. 2006). The NCEPS reported no difference in estrogen metabolites with conception outcome (Baird et al. 1991), but a more recent study with a much larger sample reported that EPL was more likely to be associated with very low levels of estrone conjugates than were continuing conceptions (Venners et al. 2006). Intriguingly, cross-talk between the neuroendocrine axes that regulate reproduction and responses to stressors appears to be an important mechanism for the strategic modulation of RE (see sidebar on "Axis Cross-Talk May Modulate Reproductive Effort").

CONCLUDING REMARKS

The foundation has been laid for developing a comprehensive evolutionary explanation of temporal, individual, and populational variation in women's reproductive functioning. LHT provides a powerful framework for the construction of testable hypotheses, and theorists are actively engaged in advancing these models to better fit the complexities of human life histories (e.g., Winterhalder & Leslie 2002, Gage 2003). Models of the proximate determinants of natural fertility (e.g., Wood 1994) help to delineate the specific biological and behavioral pathways by which varying environmental conditions influence human fertility. Not surprisingly, the full breadth of thinking and evidence relevant to human reproduction is far more than can be addressed here.

This review has focused on the physiological mechanisms by which women modulate RE in a potential or recent conception. Both theory and present evidence argue that the reproductive functioning of women born and living in arduous conditions is not analogous to that of athletes or dieters in wealthier populations. Nor is it much the same as the lower end of the range of HPO functioning in women accustomed to more propitious environments. Rather, for each individual, there is an ontogenetic interplay of genotype and environment such that the behavioral and physiological mechanisms that modulate RE are responding to locally specific physical, biotic, and social conditions. A better grasp of this nexus promises to advance understanding of the evolutionary determinants of women's reproductive functioning and, more broadly, to inform theoretical and analytical frameworks in anthropology, demography, physiology, and medicine.

SUMMARY POINTS

1. The modern synthesis, begun in the 1930s, defines evolution as an intergenerational change in allele frequencies and identifies natural selection as the principal, and perhaps only, process that can lead to adaptations. Biological anthropologists hold several positions on how to define adaptation, how to demonstrate that adaptation is occurring (or has occurred), and which processes other than natural selection could lead to adaptation.

2. Darwinian natural selection favors those phenotypes with the highest multigenerational inclusive fitness in a population, even at substantial cost to individuals. There is no necessary relationship between inclusive fitness and measures of individual well-being or efficiency.

3. Life history theory posits that natural selection leads to the evolution of mechanisms that tend to allocate resources to the competing demands of growth, reproduction, and survival such that fitness is locally maximized. (That is, among alternative allocation patterns exhibited in a population, those having the highest inclusive fitness will become more common over generational time.) Strategic modulation of reproductive effort (RE) is potentially adaptive because investment in a new conception may risk one's own survival, future reproductive opportunities, and/or current offspring survival.

4. Evolutionary models of women's reproductive functioning link theoretical descriptions of modulating RE to variability in the physiological mechanisms by which RE is allocated in a living organism. These mechanisms include (but are not limited to) adjusting the age at reproductive maturation; lactational suppression of the HPO axis; hormonal changes that reduce the probability of ovulation, conception, and/or implantation; and early pregnancy termination.

5. Substantial evidence supports the hypothesis that temporal (within-woman) modulation of RE is a response to energetic and other stressors, but much of the hormonal variation between women remains unexplained. The response to a given stressor also varies markedly among women, for unknown reasons. Developmental conditions may be a significant factor in determining adult ovarian steroid levels and responsiveness to stressors.

6. The extent, causes, and demographic significance of interpopulational variation in reproductive hormone levels are uncertain. Populational comparisons have often been hampered by the ecological fallacy, selection bias, failure to identify anovulatory cycles, and inadequate control for confounding variables (e.g., participant age and season of collection).

7. Evidence from Project REPA, a longitudinal study of salivary progesterone levels at conception and during pregnancy in rural Bolivian women, supports the hypothesis that there is no necessary relationship between fecundity and mean ovarian steroid levels across populations.

8. Three studies reported that the risk of early pregnancy loss (EPL) in naturally occurring conceptions did not covary with progesterone levels. One study found that EPLs were more likely to be associated with very low levels of estrone conjugates than were continuing conceptions.

FUTURE ISSUES

1. The determinants of interwoman variation in reproductive hormones are far from certain. The observed correlations between steroid levels and height or menarcheal age suggest developmental conditions probably play a role, but this hypothesis requires further study. Dietary composition has been implicated in steroidal variation but has proven difficult to study because childhood diet may be much more important than adult eating patterns. Potential genetic contributions to variation in ovarian steroid levels deserve greater attention.

2. Little is known about populational variation in the gonadotrophins (lutenizing hormone and follicular stimulating hormone), the pituitary hormones that participate in the regulation of ovarian functioning. In both the !Kung San (van der Walt et al. 1978) and Bolivians (Vitzthum et al. 2007), gonadotrophin levels are similar to those in comparative samples even though ovarian steroids are relatively lower. The levels of lutenizing hormone and follicular stimulating hormone suggest that the HPO axis is functioning normally in both these populations, but it is unknown if gonadotrophin levels are comparable across most populations despite substantial variability in ovarian steroid levels.

3. It has yet to be demonstrated that temporal (within-woman) variability in the functioning of the HPO axis in women is, in fact, adaptive (i.e., increases inclusive fitness). Because of the difficulties of collecting the necessary data from humans, demonstrating the putative adaptiveness of such variability will require considerable ingenuity.

4. The HPO axis is an integrated component of a living organism. Much greater effort should be made to evaluate the dynamic cross-talk between the HPO and other regulatory axes and the intersection of these hormonal communications with environmental variation.

DISCLOSURE STATEMENT

The author is not aware of any biases that might be perceived as affecting the objectivity of this review.

ACKNOWLEDGMENTS

The maximization of scientific insight will seldom be achieved in isolation. My apologies to the authors of the numerous publications that informed my thinking but were not cited because of space limitations. I thank the many colleagues who have graciously shared their insights over the years, and especially Jonathan Thornburg, Andrea Wiley, and an anonymous reviewer for their thoughtful comments on this paper. I also thank the Fulbright Scholar Program and the Max Planck Institute for Evolutionary Anthropology for their support while completing the writing of this review. My abiding gratitude goes to Dr. Hilde Spielvogel and Esperanza Caceres (Bolivian Institute for High Altitude Biology, La Paz) for two decades of collaboration and friendship, and to the women of the Bolivian *altiplano* for their generosity, despite grinding poverty, and their patience, despite having much better things to do than giving me some spit.

LITERATURE CITED

Baird DD, Weinberg CR, Wilcox AJ, McConnaughey DR, Musey PI, Collins DC. 1991. Hormonal profiles of natural conception cycles ending in early, unrecognized pregnancy loss. *J. Clin. Endocrinol. Metab.* 72:793–800

Baird DD, Weinberg CR, Zhou H, Kamel F, McConnaughey DR, et al. 1999. Preimplantation urinary hormone profiles and the probability of conception in healthy women. *Fertil. Steril.* 71:40–49

Barker-Gibb ML, Clarke IJ. 1996. Increased galanin and neuropeptide-Y immunoreactivity within the hypothalamus of ovariectomised ewes following a prolonged period of reduced body weight is associated with changes in plasma growth hormone but not gonadotropin levels. *Neuroendocrinology* 64:194–207

Beall CM, Decker MJ, Brittenham GM, Kushner I, Gebremedhin A, Strohl KP. 2002. An Ethiopian pattern of human adaptation to high-altitude hypoxia. *Proc. Natl. Acad. Sci. USA* 99:17215–18

Bentley GR. 1999. Aping our ancestors: comparative aspects of reproductive ecology. *Evol. Anthropol.* 7:175–85

Bernstein L, Yuan JM, Ross RK, Pike MC, Hanisch R, et al. 1990. Serum hormone levels in premenopausal Chinese women in Shanghai and white women in Los Angeles: results from two breast cancer case-control studies. *Cancer Causes Control* 1:51–58

Boas F. 1911. *Changes in Bodily Form of Descendants of Immigrants.* Washington, DC/New York: US GPO/Columbia Univ. Press

Bogin B. 1999. *Patterns of Human Growth.* Cambridge, UK: Cambridge Univ. Press. 2 ed. 455 pp.

Bogin B, Silva MI, Rios L. 2007. Life history trade-offs in human growth: adaptation or pathology? *Am. J. Hum. Biol.* 19:631–42

Bongaarts J. 1980. Does malnutrition affect fecundity? A summary of evidence. *Science* 208(4444):564–69

Bongaarts J, Potter RG. 1983. *Fertility, Biology, and Behavior: An Analysis of the Proximate Determinants.* New York: Academic. 230 pp.

Borgerhoff Mulder M. 1992. Reproductive decisions. In *Evolutionary Ecology and Human Behavior*, ed. EA Smith, B Winterhalder, pp. 339–74. New York: Aldine de Gruyter

Cameron JL. 1996. Regulation of reproductive hormone secretion in primates by short-term changes in nutrition. *Rev. Reprod.* 1:117–26

Campbell KL, Wood JW, eds. 1994. *Human Reproductive Ecology: Interactions of Environment, Fertility and Behavior*, Vol. 709. New York: Ann. N. Y. Acad. Sci. 429 pp.

Caro TM, Borgerhoff Mulder M. 1987. The problem of adaptation in the study of human behavior. *Ethol. Sociobiol.* 8:61–72

Charnov EL. 1993. *Life History Invariants: Some Explorations of Symmetry in Evolutionary Ecology.* Oxford, UK: Oxford Univ. Press. 186 pp.

Charnov EL, Ernest SK. 2006. The offspring-size/clutch-size trade-off in mammals. *Am. Nat.* 167:578–82

Chatterton RT Jr, Mateo ET, Lu D, Ling FJ. 2006. Interpopulational differences in the concentrations and ratios of salivary and serum progesterone. *Fertil. Steril.* 86:723–25

Chisholm JS. 1993. Death, hope, and sex: life history theory and the development of reproductive strategies. *Curr. Anthropol.* 34:1–24

Clutton-Brock TH, Harvey PH. 1979. Comparison and adaptation. *Proc. R. Soc. London B* 205:547–65

Davis K, Blake J. 1956. Social structure and fertility: an analytic framework. *Econ. Dev. Cult. Change* 4:211–35

De Geyter C, De Geyter M, Huber PR, Nieschlag E, Holzgreve W. 2002. Progesterone serum levels during the follicular phase of the menstrual cycle originate from crosstalk between the ovaries and the adrenal cortex. *Hum. Reprod.* 17:933–39

Dufty AM, Clobert J, Moller AP. 2002. Hormones, developmental plasticity and adaptation. *Trends Ecol. Evol.* 17:190–96

Dunson DB, Colombo B, Baird DD. 2002. Changes with age in the level and duration of fertility in the menstrual cycle. *Hum. Reprod.* 17:1399–403

Elias SG, van Noord PA, Peeters PH, den Tonkelaar I, Grobbee DE. 2005. Childhood exposure to the 1944–1945 Dutch famine and subsequent female reproductive function. *Hum. Reprod.* 20:2483–88

Ellison PT. 1988. Human salivary steroids: methodological considerations and applications in physical anthropology. *Yearb. Phys. Anthropol.* 31(S9):115–42

Ellison PT. 1990. Human ovarian function and reproductive ecology: new hypotheses. *Am. Anthropol.* 92:933–52

Proposed an evolutionary model for explaining energetic effects on ovarian functioning (see also Ellison et al. 1993, Ellison 1994)

Ellison PT. 1994. Advances in human reproductive ecology. *Annu. Rev. Anthropol.* 23:255–75

Ellison PT, ed. 2001. *Reproductive Ecology and Human Evolution.* New York: Aldine. 478 pp.

Ellison PT. 2003. Energetics and reproductive effort. *Am. J. Hum. Biol.* 15:342–51

Ellison PT, Lager C. 1986. Moderate recreational running is associated with lowered salivary progesterone profiles in women. *Am. J. Obstet. Gynecol.* 154:1000–103

Ellison PT, Lipson SF, Jasienska G, Ellison PL. 2007. Moderate anxiety, whether acute or chronic, is not associated with ovarian suppression in healthy, well-nourished, Western women. *Am. J. Phys. Anthropol.* 134:513–19

Ellison PT, Panter-Brick C, Lipson LF, O'Rourke M. 1993. The ecological context of human ovarian function. *Hum. Reprod.* 8:2248–58

Ellison PT, Peacock NR, Lager C. 1989. Ecology and ovarian function among Lese women of the Ituri Forest, Zaire. *Am. J. Phys. Anthropol.* 78:519–26

Finch CE, Rose MR. 1995. Hormones and the physiological architecture of life history evolution. *Q. Rev. Biol.* 70:1–52

Fisher DC. 1985. Evolutionary morphology; beyond the analogous, the anecdotal, and the ad hoc. *Paleobiology* 11:120–38

Fisher RA. 1930. *The Genetical Theory of Natural Selection.* Oxford, UK: Clarendon. 272 pp.

Frisch RE, McArthur JW. 1974. Menstrual cycles: fatness as a determinant of minimum weight for height necessary for their maintenance or onset. *Science* 185:949–51

Frisch RE, Revelle R. 1970. Height and weight at menarche and a hypothesis of critical body weights and adolescent events. *Science* 169:397–99

Gadgil M, Bossert WH. 1970. Life historical consequences of natural selection. *Am. Nat.* 104:1–24

Gage TB. 2003. The evolution of human phenotypic plasticity: age and nutritional status at maturity. *Hum. Biol.* 75:521–37

Geronimus AT, Bound J, Waidmann TA. 1999. Health inequality and population variation in fertility-timing. *Soc. Sci. Med.* 49:1623–36

Gould SJ, Lewontin RC. 1979. The spandrels of San Marco and the Panglossian paradigm: a critique of the adaptationist programme. *Proc. R. Soc. London B* 205:581–98

Gould SJ, Vrba ES. 1982. Exaptation—a missing term in the science of form. *Paleobiology* 8:4–15

Haig D. 1990. Brood reduction and optimal parental investment when offspring differ in quality. *Am. Nat.* 136:550–66

Haig D. 1993. Genetic conflicts in human pregnancy. *Q. Rev. Biol.* 68:495–532

Haiman CA, Pike MC, Bernstein L, Jaque SV, Stanczyk FZ, et al. 2002. Ethnic differences in ovulatory function in nulliparous women. *Br. J. Cancer* 86:367–71

Hill K, Kaplan H. 1999. Life history traits in humans: theory and empirical studies. *Annu. Rev. Anthropol.* 28:397–430

Huxley J. 1942. *Evolution, The Modern Synthesis*. New York: Harper. 645 pp.

Islam MM, Islam MA, Chakroborty N. 2004. Fertility transition in Bangladesh: understanding the role of the proximate determinants. *J. Biosoc. Sci.* 36:351–69

Jablonka E, Lamb MJ. 2006. *Evolution in Four Dimensions: Genetic, Epigenetic, Behavioral, and Symbolic Variation in the History of Life*. Boston: MIT Press. New ed. 474 pp.

Jacob F. 1977. Evolution and tinkering. *Science* 196:1161–66

Jasienska G. 2001. Why energy expenditure causes reproductive suppression in woman. See Ellison 2001, pp. 59–84

Jasienska G, Ellison PT. 1998. Physical work causes suppression of ovarian function in women. *Proc. Biol. Sci.* 265(1408):1747–51

Jasienska G, Thune I, Ellison PT. 2006. Fatness at birth predicts adult susceptibility to ovarian suppression: an empirical test of the Predictive Adaptive Response hypothesis. *Proc. Natl. Acad. Sci. USA* 103:12759–62

Judd S, Terry A, Petrucco M, White G. 1992. The source of pulsatile secretion of progesterone during the human follicular phase. *J. Clin. Endocrinol. Metab.* 74:299–305

Kassam A, Overstreet JW, Snow-Harter C, De Souza MJ, Gold EB, Lasley BL. 1996. Identification of anovulation and transient luteal function using a urinary pregnanediol-3-glucuronide ratio algorithm. *Environ. Health Perspect.* 104:408–13

Key TJ, Chen J, Wang DY, Pike MC, Boreham J. 1990. Sex hormones in women in rural China and in Britain. *Br. J. Cancer* 62:631–36

Komlos J, ed. 1994. *Stature, Living Standards, and Economic Development: Essays in Anthropometric History*. Chicago: Univ. Chicago Press. 264 pp.

Konner M, Worthman C. 1980. Nursing frequency, gonadal function, and birth spacing among !Kung hunter-gatherers. *Science* 207:788–791.

Kozlowski J, Stearns SC. 1989. Hypotheses for the production of excess zygotes: models of bet-hedging and selective abortion. *Evolution* 43:1369–77

Lack D. 1954. *The Natural Regulation of Animal Numbers*. London: Oxford Univ. Press. 344 pp.

Landgren BM, Unden AL, Diczfalusy E. 1980. Hormonal profile of the cycle in 68 normally menstruating women. *Acta Endocrinol. (Cph.)* 94:89–98

Lasker GW. 1969. Human biological adaptability. *Science* 166:1480–86

Lauder GV. 1996. The argument from design. In *Adaptation*, ed. MR Rose, GV Lauder, pp. 55–92. San Diego: Academic

Leroi AM, Rose MR, Lauder GV. 1994. What does the comparative method reveal about adaptation? *Am. Nat.* 143:381–402

Leslie PW, Little MA. 2003. Human biology and ecology: variation in nature and the nature of variation. *Am. Anthropol.* 105:28–37

Li H, Nakajima ST, Chen J, Todd HE, Overstreet JW, Lasley BL. 2001. Differences in hormonal characteristics of conceptive versus nonconceptive menstrual cycles. *Fertil. Steril.* 75:549–53

Empirical support for the life history hypothesis that early fertility timing mitigates costs associated with excess mortality and morbidity in impoverished African American populations

An influential polemic on the excesses of "adaptationism"

Examines consequences of conflicts between maternal and fetal genes during pregnancy; challenges the assumption of maternal-fetal cooperation

Lipson SF. 2001. Metabolism, maturation, and ovarian function. See Ellison 2001, pp. 235–48

Lipson SF, Ellison PT. 1996. Comparison of salivary steroid profiles in naturally occurring conception and nonconception cycles. *Hum. Reprod.* 11:2090–96

Livingstone FB. 1958. Anthropological implications of sickle cell gene distribution in West Africa. *Am. Anthropol.* 60:533–62

Lotka AJ. 1922a. Contribution to the energetics of evolution. *Proc. Natl. Acad. Sci. USA* 8:147–51

Lotka AJ. 1922b. Natural selection as a physical principle. *Proc. Natl. Acad. Sci. USA* 8:151–54

MacMahon B, Cole P, Brown JB, Aoki K, Lin TM, et al. 1974. Urine oestrogen profiles of Asian and North American women. *Int. J. Cancer* 14:161–67

Mazess RB. 1975. Biological adaptation: aptitudes and acclimatization. In *Biosocial Interrelationships in Population Adaptation*, ed. ES Watts, FE Johnston, GW Lasker, pp. 9–18. The Hague: Mouton

McCoy HV, Ritchey PN, McCoy CB. 1992. Effects of migration on cancer incidence and resources for prevention and treatment in Florida. *Public Health Rep.* 107:389–96

Migliano AB, Vinicius L, Lahr MM. 2007. Life history trade-offs explain the evolution of human pygmies. *Proc. Natl. Acad. Sci. USA* 104:20216–19

Nepomnaschy PA, Vitzthum VJ, Flinn M. 2006a. Evolutionary endocrinology: integrating proximate mechanisms, ontogeny, and evolved function. *Am. J. Hum. Biol.* 20:236 (Abstr.)

Nepomnaschy PA, Welch KB, McConnell DS, Low BS, Strassmann BI, England BG. 2006b. Cortisol levels and very early pregnancy loss in humans. *Proc. Natl. Acad. Sci. USA* 103:3938–42

Nepomnaschy PA, Welch K, McConnell D, Strassmann BI, England BG. 2004. Stress and female reproductive functioning: a study of daily variations in cortisol, gonadotrophins, and gonadal steroids in a rural Mayan population. *Am. J. Hum. Biol.* 16:523–32

Núñez-de la Mora A, Chatterton RT, Choudhury OA, Napolitano DA, Bentley GR. 2007. Childhood conditions influence adult progesterone levels. *PLoS Med.* 4(5):e167

O'Connor KA, Brindle E, Miller RC, Shofer JB, Ferrell RJ, et al. 2006. Ovulation detection methods for urinary hormones: precision, daily and intermittent sampling and a combined hierarchical method. *Hum. Reprod.* 21:1442–52

Panter-Brick C, Lotstein DS, Ellison PT. 1993. Seasonality of reproductive function and weight loss in rural Nepali women. *Hum. Reprod.* 8:684–90

Peacock N. 1990. Comparative and cross-cultural approaches to the study of human female reproductive failure. In *Primate Life History and Evolution*, ed. J DeRousseau, pp. 195–220. New York: Wiley-Liss

Peacock N. 1991. An evolutionary perspective on the patterning of maternal investment in pregnancy. *Hum. Nat.* 2:351–85

Pigliucci M, Kaplan J. 2000. The fall and rise of Dr Pangloss: adaptationism and the Spandrels paper 20 years later. *Trends Ecol. Evol.* 15:66–70

Pinheiro SP, Holmes MD, Pollak MN, Barbieri RL, Hankinson SE. 2005. Racial differences in premenopausal endogenous hormones. *Cancer Epidemiol. Biomarkers Prev.* 14:2147–53

Prior JC. 1985. Luteal phase defects and anovulation: adaptive alterations occurring with conditioning exercise. *Sem. Reprod. Endocrinol.* 3:27–33

Prior JC. 1987. Physical exercise and the neuroendocrine control of reproduction. *Baillieres Clin. Endocrinol. Metab.* 1:299-317

Puder JJ, Freda PU, Goland RS, Ferin M, Wardlaw SL. 2000. Stimulatory effects of stress on gonadotropin secretion in estrogen-treated women. *J. Clin. Endocrinol. Metabol.* 85:2184–88

Purifoy FE. 1981. Endocrine-environment interaction in human variability. *Annu. Rev. Anthropol.* 10:141–62

Robinson WS. 1950. Ecological correlations and the behavior of individuals. *Am. Sociol. Rev.* 15:351–57

Rose MR, Lauder GV. 1996. *Adaptation*. San Diego: Academic

Scott EC, Johnston FE. 1982. Critical fat, menarche, and the maintenance of menstrual cycles: a critical review. *J. Adolesc. Health Care* 2:249–60

Stearns SC. 1992. *The Evolution of Life Histories*. Oxford: Oxford Univ. Press

Stewart DR, Overstreet JW, Nakajima ST, Lasley BL. 1993. Enhanced ovarian steroid secretion before implantation in early human pregnancy. *J. Clin. Endocrinol. Metab.* 76:1470–76

Strassmann BI, Gillepsie B. 2002. Life-history theory, fertility and reproductive success in humans. *Proc. Biol. Sci.* 269:553–62

Temme DH. 1986. Seed size variability: a consequence of variable genetic quality among offspring? *Evolution* 40:414–17

Thomas RB, Gage TB, Little MA. 1989. Reflections on adaptive and ecological models. In *Human Population Biology*, ed. MA Little, JD Haas, pp. 296–319. New York: Oxford Univ. Press

Thornburg J. 2007. Failure to control for age variation in progesterone levels (response on 14 December 2007 to Núñez-de la Mora et al. 2007). *PLoS Med.* 4(5):e167, doi: 10.1371/journal.pmed.0040167#r1795

Thornburg J, Spielvogel H, Vitzthum VJ. 2008. Are there significant interpopulational differences in the ratio of salivary to serum progesterone? *Am. J. Phys. Anthropol. Suppl.* 43:206 (Abstr.)

Trichopoulos D, Yen S, Brown J, Cole P, MacMahon B. 1984. The effect of westernization on urine estrogens, frequency of ovulation, and breast cancer risk. A study of ethnic Chinese women in the Orient and the USA. *Cancer* 53:187–92

van der Walt LA, Wilmsen EN, Jenkins T. 1978. Unusual sex hormone patterns among desert-dwelling hunter-gatherers. *J. Clin. Endocrinol. Metab.* 46:658–63

Venners SA, Liu X, Perry MJ, Korrick SA, Li Z, et al. 2006. Urinary estrogen and progesterone metabolite concentrations in menstrual cycles of fertile women with nonconception, early pregnancy loss or clinical pregnancy. *Hum. Reprod.* 21:2272–80

Vitzthum VJ. 1990. An adaptational model of ovarian function. *Res. Rep. No. 90–200*, Popul. Stud. Cent., Univ. Mich., Ann Arbor

Proposed a life history model (FRM) to explain variation in responsiveness of ovarian functioning to stressors (see also Vitzthum 1997, 2001)

Vitzthum VJ. 1994. The comparative study of breastfeeding structure and its relation to human reproductive ecology. *Yearb. Phys. Anthropol.* 37:307–49

Vitzthum VJ. 1997. Flexibility and paradox: the nature of adaptation in human reproduction. In *The Evolving Female: A Life History Perspective*, ed. ME Morbeck, A Galloway, A Zihlman, pp. 242–58. Princeton, NJ: Princeton Univ. Press

Vitzthum VJ. 2001. Why not so great is still good enough: flexible responsiveness in human reproductive functioning. See Ellison 2001, pp. 179–202

Vitzthum VJ. 2007. Significant problems in study design and analyses (response on 10 September 2007 to Núñez-de la Mora et al. 2007). *PLoS Med.* 4(5):e167, doi: 10.1371/journal.pmed.0040167#r1795

Vitzthum VJ, Bentley GR, Spielvogel H, Caceres E, Heidelberg K, et al. 1998. Salivary progesterone levels at conception and during gestation in rural Bolivian women. *FASEB J.* 12(20 March):A726

Vitzthum VJ, Bentley GR, Spielvogel H, Caceres E, Thornburg J, et al. 2002. Salivary progesterone levels and rate of ovulation are significantly lower in poorer than in better-off urban-dwelling Bolivian women. *Hum. Reprod.* 17:1906–13

Vitzthum VJ, Ellison PT, Sukalich S, Caceres E, Spielvogel H. 2000a. Does hypoxia impair ovarian function in Bolivian women indigenous to high altitude? *High Alt. Med. Biol.* 1:39–49

Vitzthum VJ, Spielvogel H, Caceres E, Gaines J. 2000b. Menstrual patterns and fecundity among nonlactating and lactating cycling women in rural highland Bolivia: implications for contraceptive choice. *Contraception* 62:181–87

Vitzthum VJ, Spielvogel H, Thornburg J. 2004. Interpopulational differences in progesterone levels during conception and implantation in humans. *Proc. Natl. Acad. Sci. USA* 101:1443–48

Vitzthum VJ, Spielvogel H, Thornburg J, West B. 2006. A prospective study of early pregnancy loss in humans. *Fertil. Steril.* 86:373–79

Vitzthum VJ, Thornburg J. 2008. Analyses do not support *CYP17* genotype-estradiol association. *Cancer Epidemiol. Biomark. Prevent.* 17(6):1550

Vitzthum VJ, Worthman CM, Spielvogel H, Thornburg J. 2007. Adequacy of steroid levels for the regulation of gonadotrophin secretion during the ovarian cycles of Bolivian women. *Am. J. Hum. Biol.* 19:286 (Abstr.)

A comprehensive review of reproductive ecology calling for the importation of life history theory, evolutionary psychology, and physiology into demographic research

Voland E. 1998. Evolutionary ecology of human reproduction. *Annu. Rev. Anthropol.* 27:347–74

Wade GN, Schneider JE, Li H-Y. 1996. Control of fertility by metabolic cues. *Am. J. Physiol.* 270:E1–19

Walker RS, Gurven M, Migliano AB, Chagnon N, De Souza R, et al. 2006. Growth rates and life histories in twenty-two small-scale societies. *Am. J. Hum. Biol.* 18:295–311

Walker RS, Gurven M, Burger O, Hamil MJ. 2008. The trade-off between number and size of offspring in humans and other primates. *Proc. R. Soc. London B Biol. Ser.* 275:827–33

Wang DY, Key TJ, Pike MC, Boreham J, Chen J. 1991. Serum hormone levels in British and rural Chinese females. *Breast Cancer Res. Treat.* 18(Suppl. 1):S41–S45

Washburn S. 1951. The new physical anthropology. *Trans. NY Acad. Sci.* 13:298–304

Wasser SK, Barash DP. 1983. Reproductive suppression among female mammals: implications for biomedicine and sexual selection theory. *Q. Rev. Biol.* 58:513–38

WHO (World Health Organ.) 1995. *Physical Status: The Use and Interpretation of Anthropometry.* Geneva: WHO

Wiley AS. 1992. Adaptation and the biocultural paradigm in medical anthropology: a critical review. *Med. Anthropol. Q.* 6:213–36

Williams GC. 1966a. *Adaptation and Natural Selection: A Critique of Some Current Evolutionary Thought.* Princeton, NJ: Princeton Univ. Press. 307 pp.

Williams GC. 1966b. Natural selection, the cost of reproduction, and a refinement of Lack's principle. *Am. Nat.* 100:687–90

Windham GC, Elkin E, Fenster L, Waller K, Anderson M, et al. 2002. Ovarian hormones in premenopausal women: variation by demographic, reproductive and menstrual cycle characteristics. *Epidemiology* 13:675–84

Winterhalder B. 2002. Behavioral and other human ecologies: critique, response and progress through criticism. *J. Ecol. Anthropol.* 6:4–23

Winterhalder B, Leslie P. 2002. Risk-sensitive fertility: the variance compensation hypothesis. *Evol. Hum. Behav.* 23:59–82

Wood JW. 1994. *Dynamics of Human Reproduction: Biology, Biometry, Demography.* New York: Aldine de Gruyter. 653 pp.

Worthman CM. 1995. Hormones, sex, and gender. *Annu. Rev. Anthropol.* 24:593–617

Worthman CM. 2003. Energetics, sociality, and human reproduction: life history theory in real life. In *Offspring: Human Fertility Behavior in Biodemographic Perspective*, ed. KW Wachter, RA Bulatao, pp. 289–321. Washington, DC: Natl. Acad. Press, Natl. Res. Counc.

Worthman CM, Stallings JF. 1997. Hormone measures in finger-prick blood spot samples: new field methods for reproductive endocrinology. *Am. J. Phys. Anthropol.* 104:1–21

Proposed the reproductive suppression model and examined the evidence for social influences on reproductive functioning

A classic essay expounding on the sufficiency of natural selection among individuals (and not groups) for explaining biological variation and adaptation

An impressive effort to integrate biological and demographic approaches to human reproduction

Provocative essay calling for greater attention to sociality, multitasking, and epigenetic processes in the study of human reproduction

RELATED RESOURCES

Elton S, O'Higgins P. 2008. *Medicine and Evolution: Current Applications, Future Prospects.* Boca Raton, FL: CRC Press. 360 pp.

Hill K, Hurtado AM. 1996. *Ache Life History: The Ecology and Demography of a Foraging People.* New York: Aldine de Gruyter. 561 pp.

Lewontin R. 2000. *The Triple Helix: Gene, Organism, and Environment.* Cambridge, MA: Harvard Univ. Press. 129 pp.

Morbeck ME, Galloway A, Zihlman A, ed. 1997. *The Evolving Female: A Life History Perspective.* Princeton, NJ: Princeton Univ. Press

Towner MC, Luttbeg B. 2007. Alternative statistical approaches to the use of data as evidence for hypotheses in human behavioral ecology. *Evol. Anthropol.* 16:107–18

Winterhalder B, Smith EA. 2000. Analyzing adaptive strategies: human behavioral ecology at twenty-five. *Evol. Anthropol.* 9:51–72

Evolution in Archaeology

Stephen Shennan

Institute of Archaeology and AHRC Center for the Evolution of Cultural Diversity, University College London, London, WC1H 0PY, United Kingdom; email: s.shennan@ucl.ac.uk

Annu. Rev. Anthropol. 2008. 37:75–91

First published online as a Review in Advance on June 5, 2008

The *Annual Review of Anthropology* is online at anthro.annualreviews.org

This article's doi:
10.1146/annurev.anthro.37.081407.085153

0084-6570/08/1021-0075$20.00

Key Words

Darwinian archaeology, cultural transmission, cultural lineages, dual inheritance theory, human behavioral ecology, optimality modeling

Abstract

This review begins with a brief outline of the key concepts of Darwinian archaeology. Its history is then summarized, beginning with its emergence as a significant theoretical focus within the discipline in the early 1980s; its main present-day currents are then presented, citing examples of recent work. The developments in archaeology are part of broader trends in anthropology and psychology and are characterized by the same theoretical disagreements. There are two distinct research traditions: one centered on cultural transmission and dual inheritance theory and the other on human behavioral ecology. The development of specifically archaeological methodologies within these two traditions for testing evolutionary hypotheses relating to diachronic questions using archaeological data is discussed. Finally, this review suggests that the greatest challenge for the future lies in finding ways of using archaeological data to address current major debates in evolutionary social science as a whole concerning, for example, the emergence of large-scale cooperation.

INTRODUCTION

The term evolution in archaeology has accumulated an enormous range of meanings, with different implications, over many years. Traditionally, however, when not referring to the biological evolution of putatively ancestral species, it has occurred most commonly in the phrase cultural evolution (sometimes used interchangeably with social or sociocultural evolution), referring to the history of what are conceived as the key long-term trends in human history: from foraging to farming, or from farming to the origins of civilization and the state, accompanied by such developments as increased population, greater social complexity and inequality, and more complex technologies. More recently, the term has increasingly come to refer to the idea that the processes producing cultural stability and change are analogous in important respects to those of biological evolution: On this view, just as biological evolution is characterized by changing frequencies of genes in populations through time as a result of such processes as natural selection, so cultural evolution refers to the changing distributions of cultural attributes in populations, likewise affected by processes such as natural selection but also by others that have no analog in genetic evolution. In fact, to understand changing patterns of human behavior and organization we need to take account of both the biological and the cultural dimensions. It is this latter, Darwinian rather than Spencerian, sense of evolution that will be the focus of this review, but the reader will see that the Darwinian perspective also has things to say about social evolution in the traditional sense.

In this review I briefly outline the key concepts that form the basis of what it is useful to call Darwinian archaeology, then provide a summary review of its history beginning with its emergence as a significant theoretical focus within the discipline in the early 1980s, and finally outline its main present-day currents, citing examples of recent work. The developments in archaeology are part of broader trends in anthropology and psychology more generally (see e.g., Aunger 2000, Cronk et al. 2000,

Dunbar & Barrett 2007, Durham 1991, Smith & Winterhalder 1992b, Sperber 1996), but the types of data dealt with by archaeologists and the diachronic questions they generally address have led to an emphasis on some theoretical perspectives rather than others and to the development of specifically archaeological methodologies for obtaining information relevant to testing evolutionary hypotheses.

THE PROCESSES OF CULTURAL EVOLUTION

The extent to which cultural processes may be modeled in evolutionary terms remains disputed (e.g., Bamforth 2002; Fracchia & Lewontin 1999, 2005), although the way in which cultural entities and processes closely match Darwin's original formulation of the theory of evolution has recently been shown in detail by Mesoudi et al. (2006). In the most general terms, they involve parallel mechanisms for inheritance, mutation, selection, and drift.

In the case of culture, the inheritance mechanism is social learning: People learn ways to think and act from others. Of course, the routes through which culture is inherited are much more diverse than those for genes (Cavalli-Sforza & Feldman 1981), and different routes have different consequences for the patterning of cultural change through time. Variation in what is inherited is generated by innovations. These may be unintended copying errors, but they can also be intentional changes, perhaps arising from trial-and-error experimentation, that lead an individual to stop doing what they had previously learned and to start doing it differently, or even to do something different altogether. Whether this will be widely adopted depends on a range of selection and bias mechanisms, many of which have no equivalent in genetic evolution but whose existence and importance have formed the subject of major developments in the theory of cultural evolution over the past 30 years (especially Boyd & Richerson 1985, Cavalli-Sforza & Feldman 1981). These mechanisms form the theoretical foundation for what follows and, given the complexities involved, it is important to spell them out (see also Eerkens & Lipo 2007).

Natural selection in the narrowest sense affects humans as it does members of all other species; for example, other things being equal, individuals whose genes give them dispositions toward behavior that is more advantageous in enabling survival and reproductive success are more likely to survive and reproduce than are those who do not have such dispositions and those genes will be more widely represented in future generations. However, natural selection can also act on cultural attributes in the sense that those individuals who inherit or acquire certain cultural attributes may have a greater probability of surviving and/or reproducing than would those who do not, a process that will continue so long as those possessing the cultural attributes pass them on to their children; thus, those cultural attributes will become increasingly prevalent. For example, in many parts of the world, adopting an agricultural rather than a hunting-and-gathering way of life clearly led to greater reproductive success because population densities increased considerably; as a result, the cultural traits that characterize agriculture spread and, in some cases, subsequently influenced genetic evolution (e.g., the ability to digest lactose: Burger et al. 2007). An analogous process of cultural selection can also operate if individuals with certain cultural traits are more likely to be taken as models for imitation than others are, by virtue of those traits, and these in turn become successful models. The traits concerned will become more prevalent even if they have no bearing on reproductive success whatsoever, and indeed, even if they are deleterious to it. This is because if an attribute is passed on other than by parents to children, there is no reason for its success to depend on the reproductive success of the individuals concerned. For example, if celibate priests are more likely than other adults to be teachers and if, as a result of what they teach, their pupils are more likely to become celibate priests and teachers, then the values they teach will increase in frequency relative to others.

However, in addition to these selection mechanisms, a number of bias processes can affect what is transmitted; these refer to factors that affect what and who people try to copy when they are learning from others. Thus, results bias refers to the situation where people look at what other people do, for example, the crops they plant, compare the results with what they are doing themselves, and then change what they do because the other way of doing things seems to be more effective. Content biases are affected by features of transmissible phenomena that make them intrinsically more or less memorable for reasons relating to the structure of the mind or the strong reactions they provoke; examples might be fairy tales or so-called urban myths (see also Washburn 2001). Context biases are aspects of the context of learning that affect what is transmitted; thus, something may be copied simply because the person initially doing it is prestigious (prestige bias) or because it is what most people locally do (conformist bias). In these latter two cases, whether a particular cultural attribute or practice becomes more prevalent in a population has nothing to do with its intrinsic properties but only with the context of learning.

Finally, there is the cultural equivalent of genetic drift. The frequencies of particular cultural attributes can change for essentially chance reasons not involving any preference for a particular attribute. Who or what one copies may simply be a random choice dependent on who or what one meets.

None of these different mechanisms in themselves specify the tempo or mode of cultural evolution, whether it occurs gradually or in a punctuated fashion, or by means of episodes of branching cladogenesis or continuity within a single lineage. Many views assume, implicitly or explicitly, that the emergence of new culturally inherited phenomena with natural selection consequences for human populations, such as agricultural practices, is the key motor for episodes of branching cladogenesis, especially through population dispersal (e.g., Bellwood 2001; Prentiss & Chatters 2003), but here too drift processes may play a key role in the initial stages of the process (Rosenberg 1994).

HBE: human behavioral ecology

A BRIEF CONCEPTUAL HISTORY OF DARWINIAN ARCHAEOLOGY

Darwinian archaeology attempts to account for the patterns observed in the archaeological record in terms of the processes outlined above. The work carried out under this heading is extremely varied but can be roughly divided up into two categories: studies that emphasize the role of natural selection in affecting human behavior and do not attach that much importance to culture, and those that emphasize the importance of understanding changing cultural traditions. These two approaches are generally seen as opposed to one another, although in many respects they are complementary. The opposition goes back to the beginnings of Darwinian archaeology, which had its origins in two very different traditions.

One was Dunnell's (1980) evolutionary archaeology, which took the view that the material remains making up the archaeological record could be seen, like human skeletal remains, as an element of the hard part of the human phenotype, which had the property of surviving after death; they were therefore analogous to the paleontological fossil record. Artifacts, or attributes of artifacts, either had a function, in which case they would be subject to natural selection, or they did not, in which case the only process affecting their frequency over time would be drift (Dunnell 1978). The job of evolutionary archaeology was to distinguish the operation of these factors in different cases. One could criticize many things in Dunnell's approach (see e.g., Shennan & Wilkinson 2001), and his terminology was a source of confusion rather than clarification. For example, under natural selection he included all forces affecting the replicative success of particular artifact forms, not just those relating to the reproductive success of their makers and users (see Bentley et al. 2008 for further discussion), but the key importance of his approach for archaeology was that it focused on the archaeological record. Whereas other varieties of evolutionary anthropology focused on human decision makers and the factors affecting their decisions, Dunnell asked what the operation of evolutionary forces would look like from the point of view of the cultural attributes or artifacts themselves—their prevalence over time and the modifications that occur in them—when we do not have direct observational access to people's decision making. This perspective has its origins in the culture historical archaeology of the first half of the twentieth century. It remains an issue of central importance for archaeology.

The other evolutionary perspective was human behavioral ecology (HBE), one of the two evolutionary approaches that emerged out of the human socio-biology of the 1970s (the other being evolutionary psychology, which has had much less influence on archaeology and is therefore not considered in this review). HBE postulates that people are behaviorally plastic in the context of general dispositions toward courses of action that tend to lead to improved survival and reproductive success and of an ability to perceive and react appropriately to relevant environmental cues; these perceptions and reactions may be conscious or unconscious. Accordingly, people should tend to respond optimally from the point of view of survival and reproductive success to the various challenges posed by their local adaptive environment, even if that is a novel one. It is the environment that is the motor for change or stability; people are sufficiently plastic behaviorally to respond to new conditions and cultural traditions have no role, a position very close to the cultural ecology of processual archaeology. HBE research is carried out using naturalistic studies that identify the adaptive constraints and opportunities that characterize particular situations and then collect data to test whether people are indeed acting optimally.

The differences between evolutionary archaeology (sensu Dunnell) and HBE emerged most clearly in a debate between Lyman &

O'Brien (1998) and Boone & Smith (1998). It revolved around the role of transmission and selection and focused specifically on an ethnographic example, the process by which Cree Indians gave up using snow shoes for snowmobiles (Ramenofsky 1995). For Boone & Smith it was a matter of cost-benefit decision-making based on behavioral plasticity underpinned by selection-influenced capacities. For Lyman & O'Brien, the demise of the snow shoe, an artifact type with a long history conditioned by its functional requirements, i.e., subject to selection, and its replacement by the snowmobile, a different artifact with essentially a shorter but more complex history of transmission, could indeed be seen as a Darwinian process in the strictest terms—involving the increasing replicative success of snowmobiles compared with snowshoes, although that process need not be related to the survival or otherwise of the population of users. Clearly both are right in this case—the difference is one of perspective—and the complementarity of the two approaches has been increasingly recognized. Nevertheless, the distinction between those evolutionary approaches that attach importance to the role of culture and cultural transmission and those that see relatively little role for them remains an important one and will provide the basis for structuring the remainder of this review.

CULTURAL TRANSMISSION AND THE ARCHAEOLOGY OF CULTURAL TRADITIONS

In the past 15 years there have been major theoretical and methodological developments in this domain as well as a rapid growth in the number of concrete case studies putting the ideas and methods to work. The main theoretical development has been the absorption of Dunnellian evolutionary archaeology within the framework of Boyd & Richerson's dual inheritance theory (DIT). This combination has broadened the range of concepts and mechanisms now considered relevant to understanding the evolution of culture (Eerkens & Lipo 2007). Dunnell's natural selection can now be seen as a catch-all category covering a range of very diverse forces acting on what is transmitted through time, and the distinctions are important ones. Thus, in the famous example discussed above, snowmobiles became more prevalent among the Cree as a result of results bias, not natural selection on the survival and reproductive success of the users. Indeed, making this distinction is at the root of some of the most long-standing debates in archaeology, for example, whether the spread of farming into Europe was a process of indigenous adoption (involving results bias) or demographic expansion and extinction (natural selection acting on the bearers of cultural traditions). In effect, evolutionary archaeology sensu Dunnell has to be seen as an artifact-focussed subset of the dual inheritance approach. However, the match is not perfect. As formulated by Boyd & Richerson and their students, DIT focuses on the individual decision-making and does not take what might be called the meme's eye view that the evolutionary study of archaeological traditions requires. Thus, whether it is possible to distinguish the different mechanisms on the basis of archaeological data and to identify the operation of one rather than another is an area of active research (see below). However, the basic procedures of an evolutionary archaeology of cultural traditions are now clear. It is necessary to identify histories of transmission to show that an ancestor-descendant relationship exists, if indeed it does (O'Brien & Lyman 2000), and then attempt to understand the forces shaping it, all on the basis of patterned variation in the archaeological record. In practice, however, these operations are not necessarily sequential, and the information to make the distinctions required may simply not exist. Thus, if a particular cultural attribute, for example, the sharpness of a lithic cutting edge, is very strongly determined by its function, then it will contain no signal of its transmission history, even though it is likely that it had one (as opposed to being discovered anew by every novice flint knapper through trial-and-error learning).

Characterizing Cultural Lineages

The first issue to address is whether a given diachronic sequence of archaeological observations is the result of a transmission process. Clearly, transmission implies continuity but continuity does not necessarily imply transmission. It might arise, for example, from the continuity of environmental conditions or of a particular function. In practice, probably the most important technique for characterizing transmission has been seriation. This is a very well-known technique with a long history and involves putting phenomena in a linear order on the basis of some measure of their similarity to one another (Lyman & O'Brien 2006, O'Brien & Lyman 2000). The assumption that things that are more similar to one another are close together in time provided an important basis for culture-historical chronology building. However, with independent evidence of the chronological order, we can test whether the phenomena that are most similar to one another are indeed closest to one another in time. To the extent that they are, continuity is implied. Thus, if successive assemblages linked by transmission, for example, of counts of different ceramic types, are put in order, then the changing frequencies of the types will show the characteristic battleship curve pattern of first appearance, increasing popularity, and decline. Ultimately, however, our conviction that cultural transmission is the predominant force accounting for the pattern is also based on other knowledge, for example, that the making of pottery is an activity acquired by social learning. Other situations are a priori less clear cut. Thus Schibler (2004) showed that through-time fluctuations in the proportional and absolute frequencies of wild and domestic animal bones did not relate to changing cultural preferences but to climatic fluctuations because hunting became predominant at times of a cool, wet climate, which could be demonstrated by independent evidence.

As Lyman and O'Brien (2006) have pointed out, seriation is based on the idea of tracing a single cultural lineage through time, but if we take the example of frequency seriation of ceramic assemblages, based on the successive appearance, rise, and decline of new variants within the assemblages, then the new variants can also be looked at from a different perspective: They represent new branches on the evolutionary tree of that ceramic tradition, characterized by innovations that differentiate them from the ancestral state. Of course, the idea that cultural relationships can be represented as an evolutionary tree analogous to those that are used to represent the relationships among biological species is the basis of traditional historical linguistics. It also has a very long history in cultural anthropology, as does the idea that the branches of cultural trees can grow back together again, split, and join together once more, producing complex patterns of hybridization or reticulation. In recent years, the nature of cultural evolutionary trees has once again become the center of major debate because of the use of modern methods of cladistics derived from evolutionary biology as a basis for inferring the existence of cultural lineages and the relationships among them.

These methods are based on the assumption of branching evolution from a single origin; the entities under study, specific artifact types, for example, are placed on a tree such that those branches that have the most similar common histories in terms of shared mutations with respect to particular characters are most closely linked (O'Brien & Lyman 2003). This notion presupposes that the characters are homologous, that is, the artifact types or other entities share specific values for those characters because they are linked by descent from a common ancestor, rather than because they have undergone similar selection pressures (analogous characters or homoplasies; see e.g., O'Brien & Lyman 2003 for the complex terminology of cladistic analysis). A given set of descriptive traits of, for example, an artifact type may be made up of a mixture of homologous and analogous attributes, and these need to be distinguished or reconciled by methods that produce an overall cladogram consistent with the largest number of characters (see, e.g., Collard et al. 2008). Moreover, not all the traits that characterize a complex object or entity will have had a common history (Boyd et al. 1997). Some of the attributes of a given ceramic tradition, decorative motifs, for example, may have been borrowed from a different ceramic tradition by a process of horizontal transmission, and tree-building methods based on the assumption of branching differentiation from a single ancestor will not do this justice. These issues have resulted in a great deal of debate (for doubts and concerns see Borgerhoff Mulder 2001, Lipo 2006, Temkin & Eldredge 2007, Terrell et al. 1997; contra, e.g., Gray & Jordan 2000, Kirch & Green 2001, Mace & Pagel 1994) and critical analysis (e.g., Eerkens et al. 2006, Nunn et al. 2006) but also produced important methodological developments (e.g., Bryant et al. 2005, Page 2003; for an archaeological example, see Riede 2008). Gray et al. (2008) argue on a variety of methodological and theoretical grounds that pessimistic conclusions about the role of cultural phylogenetics are unjustified.

Many examples of the use of such phylogenetic techniques to construct cultural lineages and identify the forces affecting them have appeared in the archaeological literature in recent years (e.g., Coward et al. 2008, Darwent & O'Brien 2006, Foley & Lahr 1997, Harmon et al. 2006). Many examples from anthropology have major archaeological implications. Gray & Atkinson (2003), for example, used phylogenetic methods to estimate the most probable date of the root of the Indo-European language family tree, obtaining a result that fits much better with Renfrew's (1987) agricultural dispersal model of Indo-European spread than with the so-called Kurgan hypothesis, which fits the dates estimated by traditional historical linguists.

In fact, as Neff (2006) has emphasized, formal seriation and phylogenetic analyses are not the only means of characterizing cultural lineages and the forces acting on them. He himself uses scientific methods of ceramic composition analysis which he links to raw material zones to develop and test hypotheses concerning cultural lineages in Mesoamerican pottery and the factors that affected them.

Modelling Lineage Change

As noted above, to identify and characterize cultural lineages, indeed to claim their existence, is already to make inferences about the processes that produced them and to exclude some of the possible reasons for similarity among different phenomena, for example, that they arise from environmental continuities or convergent adaptations. Distinguishing the action of different forces such as those postulated by DIT requires researchers to make many more distinctions than Dunnell did (see above), which has caused problems for archaeologists. Although the basic mathematical framework of DIT was defined more than 20 years ago, progress has been slow in finding ways to operationalize it through the analysis of patterned variation in archaeological data (Eerkens & Lipo 2007).

One example is Bettinger & Eerkens's (1999) analysis of variation in arrow points in the western United States. They examined the patterns of correlation among different attributes of early arrowheads in central Nevada and eastern California and found that there was a generally high level of attribute intercorrelation among the arrowheads in the former area and many more variable correlations between different attributes in the latter. On this basis, they proposed that in central Nevada, arrowheads were adopted by a process of prestige bias without examining the functional efficacy of their different attributes, but in eastern California, local populations experimented with the different attributes, which led to greater variation and more independence between them. In effect, the size and nature of the covarying package of attributes (Boyd et al. 1997) can be extremely informative about specific processes of cultural transmission and the factors affecting them.

There is clearly much more scope for taking forward the identification and analysis of cultural packages, but the main single topic on which the characterization of processes has focused is the identification of drift. The key achievement here was Neiman's (1995) demonstration of the way the mathematics of the neutral theory of evolution could be used to generate quantitative expectations of what a distribution of artifact frequencies should look like if drift is the only factor affecting it, rather than simply making a priori judgments. In effect, the methods provide the basis for a null hypothesis. If a particular distribution fails to depart from neutrality, there is no reason to postulate anything other than drift as the process producing it (Bentley et al. 2004). If there is a departure, then something further needs to be invoked to account for it (Shennan & Wilkinson 2001). It is important to note that drift as a process can exist only in the context of an evolutionary model, which includes transmission. It has no role in HBE, nor in any other approach that lacks an inheritance concept.

Following the logic of genetic drift, in cultural drift, variation is the result of random copying of cultural attributes, with some possibility of innovation, and the results of the process depend solely on the innovation rate and the effective population size, itself dependent on the scale of interaction. It is very unlikely that any individual act of copying, for example, of a ceramic decorative motif, will be random, but if everyone has their own reasons for copying one person rather than another, the result will be that there are no directional forces affecting what or who is copied. Neiman's original case study indicated that patterning in the rim attributes of eastern North American Woodland period pottery was a result of drift, but Shennan & Wilkinson (2001) showed that patterning in the frequency of decorative attributes of early Neolithic pottery from a small region of Germany indicated a pronovelty bias in the later periods and Kohler et al. (2004) in a case study from the U.S. Southwest were able to show a departure in the direction of conformity. Thus, these methods do provide a potential basis for distinguishing some of the transmission forces postulated by DIT. All these studies followed Neiman in using an assemblage diversity measure to identify drift, but subsequently Bentley & colleagues (2004) also showed that the frequencies of different variants resulting from a random copying process followed a power law,

with a small number of the variants attaining very high frequencies but most occurring only very few times. In such cases, although one can predict that a small number of variants will attain very high frequencies, it is impossible to predict which ones. It is increasingly clear that such processes occur in an enormous range of phenomena and follow universal laws (Bentley & Maschner 2008).

Eerkens & Lipo (2005) have developed a similar approach to the characterization of neutral variation in continuous measurements and the measurement of departures from it. They applied it to explaining variation in projectile point dimensions in Owens Valley and in Illinois Woodland ceramic vessel diameters. They showed that drift was sufficient to explain the variation in projectile point thickness, but base width showed less variation than expected, so some biasing process leading to a reduction in variation must have been operating while, in the case of the pottery vessel diameters, variation-increasing mechanisms were at work.

One of the points that emerges very clearly from all the work with drift models is that there cannot be a radical separation between function and style, or between the operation of selection and biasing forces and drift. There is a continuous spectrum from pure drift to very strong selection/bias, just as certain activities depend very strongly on transmission and others are most strongly conditioned by variation in the environment facilitated by behavioral plasticity.

HUMAN BEHAVIORAL ECOLOGY IN ARCHAEOLOGY

As noted above, the starting point for HBE is the assumption that humans, like other animals, have evolved under the pressure of natural selection to maximize their reproductive success, and that behavioral plasticity enables them to respond speedily and adaptively to changes in the environment. In effect, of all the different evolutionary forces listed above, this approach assumes that natural selection acting on humans as it does on other animals is the only one that matters, by giving them adaptive capacities to make good decisions. Some of HBE's advocates believe strongly that this is substantively the case and that culture and cultural transmission are therefore unimportant; however, it is not necessary to accept this idea to believe that HBE provides a powerful starting point for many kinds of archaeological investigation because of the specific hypotheses that follow from its assumptions, which are underwritten by their success in accounting for behavioral strategies in nonhuman animals.

Thus, HBE theory provides the basis for setting up cost-benefit models of what is optimal to do in specific circumstances, which may depend on what other people are doing (the province of evolutionary game theory, e.g., Skyrms 1996). For archaeologists, it provides a strong basis for generating specific hypotheses to account for patterning in the archaeological record so long as certain conditions can be satisfied, but those conditions are arguably quite stringent. It is necessary to know, or have a sound basis for making assumptions about, the range of options available, the currency in terms of which they will be evaluated, and therefore by implication the relevant goals of the people concerned, as well as constraints that affect the payoffs (Bird & O'Connell 2006, p. 5; Lupo 2007, p. 146; Winterhalder & Kennett 2006, pp. 13–14). The area of research where these criteria have been most fully developed and discussed has been in the use of optimal foraging theory to account for patterning in the remains of plants and animals found at archaeological sites, especially those of nonagriculturalists. However, archaeologists are increasingly using HBE ideas to explain patterning in archaeological data relating to a wide range of other areas of human activity in response to theoretical developments within HBE and their application in other areas of anthropology. Although it is impossible to cover even a small fraction of the work that is now being carried out, the main areas of research will be indicated below (see also reviews by Bird & O'Connell 2006, Lupo 2007).

Optimal Foraging

Over the past 20 years, optimal foraging theory (OFT) has been the basis of numerous studies. Researchers usually assume that people are seeking to maximize their rate of calorific intake when they are engaged in food-getting activities, on the further assumption that, other things being equal, natural selection will favor those individuals that are most efficient. The diet breadth model postulates that an individual will make the choice whether to exploit a particular encountered resource by determining whether the postencounter returns obtained after pursuing (if necessary) and processing it into a form in which it can be eaten will be greater than those to be obtained by ignoring that resource and looking for something better. Thus, resources can be ranked in terms of their postencounter returns. Highly ranked resources will always be taken on encounter, but lower ranked ones will be ignored. This principle is important and, in some respects, counterintuitive. Whether a resource is exploited does not depend on its own abundance but on that of the resources ranked higher than it. Resource ranks may be assessed on the basis of experimental or ethnographic work in the present (e.g., Barlow 2002, Kaplan & Hill 1992). In terms of archaeological evidence, significant taphonomic and sampling issues potentially arise, but assuming that these can be overcome, faunal assemblages, for example, can be evaluated in terms of some measure of their likely productivity or resource rank. Because animal body size is correlated with handling costs and is readily assessable using archaeological faunal data, the proportion of large-bodied vs. small-bodied animal bones has very frequently been used as a diet-breadth measure (e.g., Broughton 1994; see also Ugan 2005; for within-species size variation see, e.g., Mannino & Thomas 2002). Stiner and colleagues (2000) have used the proportions of slow-moving vs. fast-moving (and therefore hard to catch) small game as a diet breadth measure in their studies of faunal exploitation in the east Mediterranean later Palaeolithic. Despite its simplicity, the diet breadth model has been remarkably successful in accounting for variation in faunal assemblages, especially in the context of diachronic sequences showing resource depression (e.g., Broughton 1997, Butler 2000).

This simple model can be modified in various ways. For example, central place-foraging models (Lupo 2007, pp. 151–53) have been developed to make predictions about the effects of transport costs on what resources will be exploited where and the extent to which they will be processed before being brought back to a base for consumption (Metcalfe & Barlow 1992). Nagaoka (2002) relates changing prey representation at the Shag River Mouth site in New Zealand to changing hunting and transport distances as a result of resource depression.

Many of the most interesting issues arise when initial predictions of such optimal foraging models are apparently not met. Thus, Stiner & Munro's (2002) analysis of the faunal remains from the Natufian period (~13–10 ka) at Hayonim cave in the Levant found that for the first three phases, the proportion of fast-moving small game was high and of slow-moving game was low, but, contrary to the resource depression that might be expected as a result of long-term occupation, in the final two phases the situation was reversed, with slow-moving game now in a majority. It appears that these slow-moving game populations were able to recover and exploitation was now not sufficiently intense to reduce them again. In fact, we know independently, from regional data on site sizes and occupation intensities, that in the Early Natufian phase sites were large and occupation intensity was high, whereas in the Later Natufian, population declined as a result of the onset of the Younger Dryas cold and dry climatic phase ~11 ka.

Clearly the matter of distinguishing causes for patterns observed in faunal and plant remains assemblages is fundamental. Inferences of resource depression as a result of human overexploitation, for example, need to exclude factors such as climate change. However, some of the most interesting recent debates have concerned the nature of the fitness-related cur-

rency which is being maximized in a particular context. As noted above, standard models assume that the rate of energy extraction is being maximixed. However, some researchers have proposed that, as far as big-game hunting is concerned, it is more probably prestige, in the context of costly signaling. The basis of this argument is that ethnographically big-game hunting does not seem to lead to calorie maximization for the hunter and his immediate family when compared with possible alternatives, but the sharing of meat that results from hunting success gives prestige and other political benefits in alliances, which lead to greater reproductive success (Hawkes 1991). Costly signaling theory, another set of ideas from BE, proposes that apparently costly or wasteful behavior can be favored by natural selection if it provides an honest signal of underlying, otherwise invisible, fitness-related qualities that are of interest to observers such as potential mates or rivals. Only individuals of high quality can afford to pay the costs of the most expensive signals. Bliege Bird & Smith's review (2005) of costly signaling in the context of human behavior showed that in many ethnographic contexts, costly signaling provides a coherent explanation of instances of apparently extravagant generosity or consumption. Hildebrandt & McGuire (2002, McGuire & Hildebrandt 2005) have proposed that the increase in big-game hunting in the Middle Archaic of the Great Basin should be seen as representing an increase in costly signaling, which occurred because populations were increasing, leading to increased social competition and larger numbers of receivers of the costly signals being produced (cf. Neiman 1997). They contrast the pattern in presumptively male-dominated hunting with that indicated by the plant remains, which suggests increasing diet breadth and intensification. They reject the counter arguments proposed by Byers & Broughton (2004) that the increase in big-game hunting resulted from an increase in animal populations as a result of climate change and is explicable in OF terms. However, their proposal has been further criticized by Codding & Jones (2007) on the grounds, among others, that provisioning activities would always have been dominant and would therefore make up the vast proportion of faunal remains in the archaeological record, even if prestige hunting was occurring. McGuire et al. (2007) respond with an analysis of faunal remains, which suggests that the logistically organized hunting of bighorn sheep, which was driving the increase in big-game hunting, could not have been efficient in terms of gaining calories under even the most advantageous assumptions. It is clearly important to be able to distinguish the factors affecting hunting priorities in particular cases rather than assuming a priori that one or the other must be the case. As Bird & O'Connell (2006) point out, the interesting question then becomes understanding the factors that lead the priorities to vary. Thus, for example, differences in social status may affect the currencies that individuals maximize in particular contexts (Lupo 2007).

OFT is increasingly being applied to understanding past plant exploitation and food production (e.g., Barlow 2002, 2006; Kennett et al. 2006b), and issues of risk and time-discounting are also being introduced (e.g., Tucker 2006).

Technology

Technology potentially raises problems for HBE approaches in the sense that the assumption of immediate adaptive responses to environmental change effectively implies that technological solutions will automatically arise when specific problems appear that the technology could solve. Although this notion may be more or less true in the case of some simple technologies, it is very unlikely for more complex ones, which will have a specific culturally transmitted history of accumulated successful innovation. Nevertheless, this does not make it any the less worthwhile to analyze technology from an HBE perspective in terms of how the costs and benefits of available alternatives affect the likelihood of their adoption.

The issues are clearly laid out by Ugan et al. (2003, pp. 1315–16). Determining how much time and effort it is worth to put into producing an artifact depends on a number of factors—what it is used for and how frequently, the extent to which increased effort in manufacture produces improved performance—as well as on the opportunity cost of the time spent in making the artifact—time that could have been used for some other activity. Many artifacts figure directly in the optimal foraging calculus because they are concerned in some way with improving the postencounter handling costs of particular resources. The optimality assumption predicts maximizing efficiency in this context, while acknowledging that there may be conflicting priorities leading to the need for trade-offs. Conversely, of course, demonstration of a lack of efficiency in production may indicate that costly signaling considerations are relevant (Bliege Bird & Smith 2005, pp. 230–31).

Bettinger et al. (2006) propose a model different from that of Ugan et al. but within the same optimality framework. It leads to different results for the comparison between different technologies in terms of the number of hours of use required for a more expensive technology to substitute for a less expensive one. Bettinger et al. use the method to explore the history of projectile weapons in prehistoric California.

Social Evolution

As noted above, one of the triggers for the emergence of a specifically Darwinian evolutionary archaeology was the rejection of the study of social evolution in the sense of trends toward increasing complexity. In fact, many HBE concepts are relevant to understanding social processes and changing patterns of social organization and have been used in illuminating ways to understand ethnographic and historical phenomena. They include the contrast between scramble and contest competition (Boone 1992), parental investment theory (Mace 1998), reproductive skew theory (Bird & O'Connell 2006, pp. 26–27; Summers 2006; Vehrencamp 1983), and theory concerning the relation between the density and predictability of resources and territoriality (Dyson-Hudson & Smith 1978; see also Shennan 2002 for a general discussion of these and other issues). These theories and their existing applications demonstrate that HBE is not a set of ideas restricted to the analysis of optimal foraging in hunter-gatherer societies but is relevant to a vast range of social processes in societies of all sorts [and is closely akin in many respects to the so-called New Institutional Economics (North 1981)]. These ideas have been much slower to enter the specifically archaeological literature, partly because they raise significant issues about how they can be operationalized in terms of archaeological data, but also because, whereas students of hunter-gatherer foraging behavior very often have a strong background in biological evolution, this is much less the case with students of, for example, state-level complex societies.

One example that has entered the literature is costly signaling theory, as described above; other studies, more wide-ranging in their use of HBE theory, have begun to appear (e.g., Fitzhugh 2003, Kennett 2005). Like Kennett (2005, also Kennett et al. 2006a), Shennan (2007) used the concepts of the "ideal free distribution" and the "ideal despotic distribution" (Fretwell & Lucas 1970, Sutherland 1996) to provide a basis for understanding the consequences of the patch colonization process represented by the spread of farming into Central Europe. The ideal free distribution proposes that, as new areas are colonized, individuals occupy the resource patch that gives them the best returns. As more individuals occupy the patch, the returns to each individual decline to the point that the returns to an individual from the best patch are no better than those from the next best patch, which has no occupants. Once the returns from both patches are equal, they will be occupied indiscriminately until population growth reaches the point at which an equal benefit can be gained by occupying a still worse patch, and the process is repeated. When there is territoriality, however, the situation is different. Here the ideal despotic distribution applies. The first individual occupying the area can select the best territory in the best patch. Subsequent individuals settling there do not affect the first arrival but have to take the next best territory, and so on, until there comes a point at which the next settler will do just as well by taking the best territory in the next best patch. Subsequent individuals will then take territories in either patch where the territories are equally suitable. In contrast to the ideal free distribution, where new settlers decrease the mean return for everybody, including those who arrived first, in the case of the ideal despotic distribution, the returns depend on the order of settlement so that the initial settlers of the best territory in the patch will do best.

In the case of the expansion of farmers into Central Europe, the first to arrive at favorable settlement patches settled in the best locations; indeed, the founding settlements almost invariably remained the most important ones. Individual microregions filled up relatively rapidly, as the detailed local data make clear. Cemeteries came into existence to represent an ancestral claim to territory in the face of increasing competition as local carrying capacities were reached. Isotope analyses point to the emergence of patrilineal corporate groups (e.g., Bentley et al. 2002). One can postulate that over time the senior line of the lineage in a given patch would have maintained control of the prime location and its territory and is represented archaeologically by the larger houses in the founding settlements. The junior branches, however, would be in increasingly inferior positions and would have relatively little option to go elsewhere (Vehrencamp 1983), hence the increasing number of smaller houses in the settlements.

In the later occupation phases of many settlement microregions, ditched and/or palisaded enclosures appeared. These may have been ritual and/or defensive, but they represent the emergence of a new type of social institution integrating large numbers of people. Once institutions emerged that integrated larger numbers of people into a cooperating unit that could be more successful in competition than groups not integrated in this way, other groups had little option but to copy them if they wished to avoid potentially disastrous consequences.

The nature of those disastrous consequences is indicated by the evidence for massacres occurring at this time; the evidence for large numbers of dead—more than 60 in one case—points to a large number of attackers. This situation may be seen as a prisoner's dilemma. The fates of individual households would have become increasingly dependent on those of the larger entities of which they became a part (Read & LeBlanc 2003). Not adopting this new form of organization was not an option at the local level, but at the global level it might have been better for all concerned if it had not occurred, in the sense that the conditions of life deteriorated with the appearance of warfare; the extent of exchange, visible in the materials making up lithic assemblages, declined drastically and so too did population, leading to regional abandonment in some places.

One could argue that what has been presented is no more than a plausible scenario described in evolutionary terms. Nevertheless, the model provides a strong set of natural-selection-based predictions about the kinds of things that happen during colonization and population-expansion processes, and the available archaeological evidence corresponds closely to the predictions. Others who have not adopted an HBE framework have interpreted the settlement and social patterns of these colonizing farmers in ways that are similar to those outlined above (e.g., van der Velde 1990), so the description is not simply a circular consequence of the framework and models adopted.

FUTURE DEVELOPMENTS

Developments in all areas of evolutionary archaeology will continue, but two key areas may be identified: comparing and testing in specific cases the predictions of HBE approaches with those of DIT perspectives in which culture plays a significant explanatory role, and especially developing and testing social evolutionary hypotheses involving the sorts of mechanisms outlined above. Indeed, the number of different theoretical models and hypotheses framed within a Darwinian perspective available in the literature, usually on the basis of evolutionary game theory and often making evolutionary psychology assumptions, is now almost overwhelming. Many such studies refer more or less in passing to archaeological evidence, make assumptions about prehistoric states of affairs on the basis of ethnographic generalizations, or have archaeological consequences that have not been explored. It is only possible to give one example here.

Many of the most important current debates in evolutionary social science concern the emergence of human altruism and large-scale cooperation. Some (e.g., Henrich 2004) depend on cultural group selection. Others propose very different mechanisms. Choi & Bowles (2007), for example, have developed a model of what they call parochial altruism and warfare, which shows that altruism to the members of one's own group and hostility to nongroup members could evolve if such attitudes contributed to the group's success in warfare and the parochial attitudes actually encouraged intergroup conflict. Their simulations show that in conditions such as those that were likely relevant to late Pleistocene societies, neither altruism nor parochialism could have been successful on their own, but they could have prevailed jointly by encouraging intergroup warfare.

It remains to be seen how much archaeology will contribute to such debates. As always, the extent to which it can do so depends on archaeologists' ability to identify and characterize variation in the archaeological record in relevant ways that lead to the development and testing of causal hypotheses.

DISCLOSURE STATEMENT

The author is not aware of any biases that might be perceived as affecting the objectivity of this review.

ACKNOWLEDGMENTS

I thank Lucia Nagib for comments on an earlier draft and acknowledge the inspiration provided by my colleagues in the AHRC Center for the Evolution of Cultural Diversity.

LITERATURE CITED

Aunger R, ed. 2000. *Darwinizing Culture: The Status of Memetics as a Science*. Oxford: Oxford Univ. Press

Bamforth DB. 2002. Evidence and metaphor in evolutionary archaeology. *Am. Antiq.* 67:435–52

Barlow KR. 2002. Predicting maize agriculture among the Fremont: an economic comparison of farming and foraging in the American Southwest. *Am. Antiq.* 67:65–88

Barlow KR. 2006. A formal model for predicting agriculture among the Fremont. See Kennett & Winterhalder 2006, pp. 87–102

Bellwood P. 2001. Early agriculturalist population diasporas? Farming, languages and genes. *Annu. Rev. Anthropol.* 30:181–207

Bentley RA, Hahn MW, Shennan SJ. 2004. Random drift and culture change. *Proc. R. Soc. London B* 271:1443–50

Bentley RA, Lipo C, Maschner HDG, Marler B. 2008. Darwinian archaeologies. See Bentley et al. 2008, pp. 109–30

Bentley RA, Maschner HDG. 2008. Complexity theory. See Bentley et al. 2008, pp. 245–70

Bentley RA, Maschner HDG, Chippindale C, eds. 2008. *Handbook of Archaeological Theories*. Lanham, MD: Altamira

Bentley RA, Price TD, Lüning J, Gronenborn D, Wahl J, et al. 2002. Human migration in early neolithic Europe. *Curr. Anthropol.* 43:799–804

Bettinger RL, Eerkens J. 1999. Point typologies, cultural transmission, and the spread of bow-and-arrow technology in the prehistoric Great Basin. *Am. Antiq.* 64:231–42

Bettinger RL, Winterhalder B, McElreath R. 2006. A simple model of technological intensification. *J. Archaeol. Sci.* 33:538–45

Bird DW, O'Connell JF. 2006. Behavioral ecology and archaeology. *J. Archaeol. Res.* 14:143–88

Bliege Bird R, Smith EA. 2005. Signaling theory, strategic interaction, and symbolic capital. *Curr. Anthropol.* 46:221–48

Boone JL. 1992. Competition, conflict and development of social hierarchies. See Smith & Winterhalder 1992a, pp. 301–38

Boone JL, Smith EA. 1998. Is it evolution yet? A critique of evolutionary archaeology. *Curr. Anthropol.* 39:S141–74

Borgerhoff Mulder M. 2001. Using phylogenetically based comparative methods in anthropology: more questions than answers. *Evol. Anthropol.* 10:99–111

Boyd R, Borgerhoff-Mulder M, Durham WH, Richerson PJ. 1997. Are cultural phylogenies possible? In *Human By Nature*, ed. P Weingart, SD Mitchell, PJ Richerson, S Maasen, pp. 355–86. Mahwah, NJ: Erlbaum

Boyd R, Richerson PJ. 1985. *Culture and the Evolutionary Process*. Chicago: Univ. Chicago Press

Broughton JM. 1994. Declines in mammalian foraging efficiency during the late Holocene, San Francisco Bay, California. *J. Anthropol. Archaeol.* 13:371–401

Broughton JM. 1997. Widening diet breadth, declining foraging efficiency, and prehistoric harvest pressure: ichthyofaunal evidence from the Emeryville Shellmound, California. *Antiquity* 71:845–62

Bryant D, Filimon F, Gray RD. 2005. Untangling our past: languages, trees, splits and networks. In *The Evolution of Cultural Diversity: A Phylogenetic Approach*, ed. R Mace, CJ Holden, SJ Shennan, pp. 67–83. London: UCL Press

Burger J, Kirchner M, Bramanti B, Haak W, Thomas MG. 2007. Absence of the lactase-persistence-associated allele in early Neolithic Europeans. *Proc. Natl. Acad. Sci. USA* 104:3736–41

Butler VL. 2000. Resource depression on the Northwest Coast of North America. *Antiquity* 74:649–61

Byers DA, Broughton JM. 2004. Holocene environmental change, artiodactyl abundances, and human hunting strategies in the Great Basin. *Am. Antiq.* 69:235–56

Cavalli-Sforza LL, Feldman MW. 1981. *Cultural Transmission and Evolution: A Quantitative Approach*. Princeton, NJ: Princeton Univ. Press

Choi JK, Bowles S. 2007. The evolution of parochial altruism and war. *Science* 318:636–40

Codding BF, Jones TL. 2007. Man the showoff? Or the ascendance of a just-so story: a comment on recent applications of costly signalling theory in American archaeology. *Am. Antiq.* 72:349–57

Collard M, Shennan SJ, Buchanan B, Bentley RA. 2008. Evolutionary biological methods and cultural data. See Bentley et al. 2008, pp. 203–23

Coward F, Shennan SJ, Colledge S, Conolly J, Collard M. 2008. The spread of Neolithic plant economies from the Near East to Northwest Europe: a phylogenetic analysis. *J. Archaeol. Sci.* 35:42–56

Cronk L, Chagnon N, Irons W, eds. 2000. *Adaptation and Human Behavior*. New York: Aldine de Gruyter

Darwent J, O'Brien M. 2006. Using cladistics to construct lineages of projectile points from northeastern Missouri. See Lipo et al. 2006, pp. 185–208

Dunbar R, Barrett L, eds. 2007. *Handbook of Evolutionary Psychology*. Oxford: Oxford Univ. Press

Dunnell RC. 1978. Style and function: a fundamental dichotomy. *Am. Antiq.* 43:192–202

Dunnell RC. 1980. Evolutionary theory and archaeology. *Adv. Archaeol. Method Theory* 3:35–99

Durham WH. 1991. *Coevolution: Genes, Culture and Human Diversity*. Stanford, CA: Stanford Univ. Press

Dyson-Hudson R, Smith EA. 1978. Human territoriality: an ecological reassessment. *Am. Anthropol.* 80:21–41

Eerkens J, Bettinger RL, McElreath R. 2006. Cultural transmission, phylogenetics and the archaeological record. See Lipo et al. 2006, pp. 169–84

Eerkens JW, Lipo CP. 2005. Cultural transmission, copying errors, and the generation of variation in material culture in the archaeological record. *J. Anthropol. Archaeol.* 24:316–34

Eerkens JW, Lipo CP. 2007. Cultural transmission theory and the archaeological record: providing context to understanding variation and temporal changes in material culture. *J. Archaeol. Res.* 15:239–74

Fitzhugh B. 2003. *The Evolution of Complex Hunter-Gatherers: Archaeological Evidence from the North Pacific*. New York: Plenum

Foley R, Lahr M. 1997. Mode 3 technologies and the evolution of modern humans. *Camb. Archaeol. J.* 7:3–36

Fracchia J, Lewontin RC. 1999. Does culture evolve? *Hist. Theory Theme Issue* 38:52–78

Fracchia J, Lewontin RC. 2005. The price of metaphor. *Hist. Theory* 44:14–29

Fretwell SD, Lucas HL Jr. 1970. On territorial behavior and other factors influencing habitat distribution in birds: I. theoretical development. *Acta Biotheoretica* 19:16–36

Gray RD, Atkinson QD. 2003. Language-tree divergence times support the Anatolian theory of Indo-European origin. *Nature* 426:435–39

Gray RD, Greenhill SJ, Ross RM. 2008. The pleasures and perils of Darwinizing culture (with phylogenies). *Biol. Theory* 2(4):In press

Gray RD, Jordan FM. 2000. Language trees support the express-train sequence of Austronesian expansion. *Nature* 405:1052–55

Harmon MJ, VanPool TL, Leonard RD, VanPool CS, Salter LA. 2006. Reconstructing the flow of information across time and space: a phylogenetic analysis of ceramic traditions from Prehispanic western and northern Mexico and the American southwest. See Lipo et al. 2006, pp. 209–30

Hawkes K. 1991. Showing off: tests of an hypothesis about men's foraging goals. *Ethology Sociobiol.* 12:29–54

Henrich J. 2004. Cultural group selection, coevolutionary processes and large-scale cooperation. *J. Econ. Behav. Organ.* 53:3–35

Hildebrandt WR, McGuire KR. 2002. The ascendance of hunting during the California Middle Archaic: an evolutionary perspective. *Am. Antiq.* 67:231–56

Kaplan HS, Hill K. 1992. The evolutionary ecology of food acquisition. See Smith & Winterhalder 1992a, pp. 167–202

Kennett DJ. 2005. *The Island Chumash: Behavioral Ecology of a Maritime Society*. Berkeley: Univ. Calif. Press

Kennett DJ, Anderson A, Winterhalder B. 2006a. The ideal free distribution, food production and the colonization of Oceania. See Kennett & Winterhalder 2006, pp. 265–88

Kennett DJ, Voorhies B, Martorana D. 2006b. An ecological model for the origin of maize-based food production on the Pacific coast of southern Mexico. See Kennett & Winterhalder 2006, pp. 103–36

Kennett DJ, Winterhalder B, eds. 2006. *Behavioral Ecology and the Transition to Agriculture*. Berkeley: Univ. Calif. Press

Kirch P, Green RC. 2001. *Hawaiki, Ancestral Polynesia: An Essay in Historical Anthropology*. Cambridge, UK: Cambridge Univ. Press

Kohler TA, VanBuskirk S, Ruscavage-Barz S. 2004. Vessels and villages: evidence for conformist transmission in early village aggregations on the Pajarito Plateau, New Mexico. *J. Anthropol. Archaeol.* 23:100–18

Lipo CP. 2006. The resolution of cultural phylogenies using graphs. See Lipo et al. 2006, pp. 89–108

Lipo CP, O'Brien MJ, Collard M, Shennan SJ, eds. 2006. *Mapping Our Ancestors: Phylogenetic Approaches in Anthropology and Prehistory*. New Brunswick, NJ: Aldine Transaction

Lupo KD. 2007. Evolutionary foraging models in zooarchaeological analysis: recent applications and future challenges. *J. Archaeol. Res.* 15:143–89

Lyman RL, O'Brien MJ. 1998. The goals of evolutionary archaeology: history and explanation. *Curr. Anthropol.* 39:615–52

Lyman RL, O'Brien MJ. 2006. Seriation and cladistics: the difference between anagenetic and cladogenetic evolution. See Lipo et al. 2006, pp. 65–88

Mace R. 1998. The coevolution of human fertility and wealth inheritance strategies. *Philos. Trans. R. Soc. London B* 353:389–97

Mace R, Pagel MD. 1994. The comparative method in anthropology. *Curr. Anthropol.* 35:549–64

Mannino MA, Thomas KD. 2002. Depletion of a resource? The impact of prehistoric human foraging on intertidal mollusk communities and its significance for human settlement, mobility and dispersal. *World Archaeol.* 33:452–74

McGuire K, Hildebrandt WR. 2005. Re-thinking Great Basin foragers: prestige hunting and costly signaling during the Middle Archaic period. *Am. Antiq.* 70:695–712

McGuire KR, Hildebrandt WR, Carpenter KL. 2007. Costly signaling and the ascendance of no-can-do archaeology: a reply to Codding and Jones. *Am. Antiq.* 72:358–65

Mesoudi A, Whiten A, Laland KN. 2006. Towards a unified science of cultural evolution. *Behav. Brain Sci.* 29:329–83

Metcalfe D, Barlow KR. 1992. A model for exploring the optimal tradeoff between field processing and transport. *Am. Anthropol.* 94:340–56

Nagaoka L. 2002. Explaining subsistence change in Southern New Zealand using foraging theory models. *World Archaeol.* 34:84–102

Neff H. 2006. Archaeological-materials characterization as phylogenetic method: the case of Copador pottery from southeastern Mesoamerica. See Lipo et al. 2006, pp. 231–48

Neiman FD. 1995. Stylistic variation in evolutionary perspective: inferences from decorative diversity and interassemblage disstance in Illinois Woodland ceramic assemblages. *Am. Antiq.* 60:7–36

Neiman FD. 1997. Conspicuous consumption as wasteful advertising: a Darwinian perspective on spatial patterns in Classic Maya terminal monument dates. In *Rediscovering Darwin: Evolutionary Theory in Archaeological Explanation*, ed. CM Barton, GA Clark, pp. 267–90. Arlington, VA: Am. Anthropol. Assoc.

North DC. 1981. *Structure and Change in Economic History*. New York: Norton

Nunn CL, Borgerhoff Mulder M, Langley S. 2006. Comparative methods for studying cultural trait evolution: a simulation study. *Cross-Cultur. Res.* 40:1–33

O'Brien MJ, Lyman RL. 2000. *Applying Evolutionary Archaeology*. New York: Plenum

O'Brien MJ, Lyman RL. 2003. *Cladistics and Archaeology*. Salt Lake City: Univ. Utah Press

Page RD. 2003. *Tangled Trees: Phylogeny, Cospeciation, and Coevolution*. Chicago: Univ. Chicago Press

Prentiss WC, Chatters JC. 2003. Cultural diversification and decimation in the prehistoric record. *Curr. Anthropol.* 44:33–58

Ramenofsky AF. 1995. Evolutionary theory and native artifact change in the post contact period. In *Evolutionary Archaeology: Methodological Issues*, ed. PA Telster, pp. 129–47. Tucson: Univ. Ariz. Press

Read DW, LeBlanc SA. 2003. Population growth, carrying capacity, and conflict. *Curr. Anthropol.* 44:59–85

Renfrew C. 1987. *Archaeology and Language: The Puzzle of Indo-European Origins*. London: Cape

Riede F. 2008. Tangled trees: modeling material culture evolution as host-associate co-speciation. In *Pattern and Process in Cultural Evolution*, ed. SJ Shennan. Berkeley: Univ. Calif. Press

Rosenberg M. 1994. Pattern, process and hierarchy in the evolution of culture. *J. Anthropol. Archaeol.* 13:307–40

Schibler J. 2004. Kurzfristige Klimaschwankungen aufgrund archäologischer Daten und ihre Auswirkungen auf die prähistorischen Gesellschaften. In *Alpenwelt—Gebirgswelten. Inseln, Brücken, Grenzen. Tagungsbericht und Wissenschaftliche Abhandlungen. 54. Deutscher Geographentag Bern 2003*, ed. W Gamerith, P Messerli, P Meusburger, H Wanner, pp. 87–93. Heidelberg

Shennan SJ. 2002. *Genes, Memes and Human History: Darwinian Archaeology and Cultural Evolution*. London: Thames and Hudson

Shennan SJ. 2007. The spread of farming into Central Europe and its consequences: evolutionary models. In *The Model-Based Archaeology of Socionatural Systems*, ed. TA Kohler, SE van der Leeuw, pp. 141–56. Santa Fe, NM: SAR Press

Shennan SJ, Wilkinson JR. 2001. Ceramic style change and neutral evolution: a case study from Neolithic Europe. *Am. Antiq.* 66:577–93

Skyrms B. 1996. *Evolution of the Social Contract*. Cambridge, UK: Cambridge Univ. Press

Smith EA, Winterhalder B, eds. 1992a. *Evolutionary Ecology and Human Behavior*. New York: Aldine de Gruyter

Smith EA, Winterhalder B. 1992b. Natural selection and decision making: some fundamental principles. See Smith & Winterhalder 1992a, pp. 25–60

Sperber D. 1996. *Explaining Culture: A Naturalistic Approach*. Oxford: Blackwell

Stiner MC, Munro ND. 2002. Approaches to prehistoric diet breadth, demography, and prey ranking systems in time and space. *J. Archaeol. Method Theory* 9:181–214

Stiner MC, Munro ND, Surovell TA. 2000. The tortoise and the hare—small-game use, the broad-spectrum revolution, and paleolithic demography. *Curr. Anthropol.* 41:39–73

Summers K. 2006. The evolutionary ecology of despotism. *Evol. Hum. Behav.* 26:106–35

Sutherland WJ. 1996. *From Individual Behaviour to Population Ecology*. Oxford: Oxford Univ. Press

Tëmkin I, Eldredge N. 2007. Phylogenetics and material cultural evolution. *Curr. Anthropol.* 48:146–53

Terrell JE, Hunt TL, Gosden C. 1997. The dimensions of social life in the Pacific: human diversity and the myth of the primitive isolate. *Curr. Anthropol.* 38:155–96

Tucker B. 2006. A future discounting explanation for the persistence of a mixed foraging-horticulture strategy among the Mikea of Madagascar. See Kennett & Winterhalder 2006, pp. 22–40

Ugan A. 2005. Does size matter? Body size, mass collecting, and their implications for understanding prehistoric foraging behaviour. *Am. Antiq.* 70:75–90

Ugan A, Bright J, Rogers A. 2003. When is technology worth the trouble? *J. Archaeol. Sci.* 30:1315–29

van der Velde P. 1990. Banderamik social inequality—a case study. *Germania* 68:19–38

Vehrencamp S. 1983. A model for the evolution of despotic versus egalitarian societies. *Anim. Behav.* 31:667–82

Washburn DK. 2001. Remembering things seen: experimental approaches to the process of information transmittal. *J. Archaeol. Method Theory* 8:67–99

Winterhalder B, Kennett DJ. 2006. Behavioral ecology and the transition from hunting and gathering to agriculture. See Kennett & Winterhalder 2006, pp. 1–21

A Historical Appraisal of Clicks: A Linguistic and Genetic Population Perspective

Tom Güldemann[1,3] and Mark Stoneking[2]

Departments of [1]Linguistics and [2]Evolutionary Genetics, Max Planck Institute for Evolutionary Anthropology, D-04103 Leipzig, Germany; email: gueldema@rz.uni-leipzig.de, stoneking@eva.mpg.de

[3]Seminar für Allgemeine Sprachwissenschaft, Universität Zürich, CH-8032 Zurich, Switzerland

Annu. Rev. Anthropol. 2008. 37:93–109

First published online as a Review in Advance on May 29, 2008

The *Annual Review of Anthropology* is online at anthro.annualreviews.org

This article's doi:
10.1146/annurev.anthro.37.081407.085109

Key Words

Khoisan, Africa, mtDNA, Y chromosome, genealogical inheritance, language contact

Abstract

Clicks are often considered an exotic feature of languages, and the fact that certain African "Khoisan" groups share the use of clicks as consonants and exhibit deep genetic divergences has been argued to indicate that clicks trace back to an early common ancestral language (Knight et al. 2003). Here, we review the linguistic evidence concerning the use of click sounds in languages and the genetic evidence concerning the relationships of African click-speaking groups. The linguistic evidence suggests that genealogical inheritance and contact-induced transmission are equally relevant for the distribution of clicks in African languages. The genetic evidence indicates that there has been substantial genetic drift in some groups, obscuring their genetic relationships. Overall, the presence of clicks in human languages may in fact not trace back to the dawn of human language, but instead reflect a much later episode in the diversification of human speech.

INTRODUCTION

Clicks are among the few features of modern languages that attract the attention of nonlinguists when trying to ascertain the early history of humans. In particular, popular thinking holds that because clicks are highly unusual, and because the African groups that use clicks extensively are mostly hunter-gatherers that have maintained this "primitive" lifestyle since the origin of modern humans, clicks must also be an old feature whose distribution today reflects genealogical inheritance from a common ancestral language. More recently, genetic studies have been used to reinforce this notion (Knight et al. 2003). It is thus of widespread interest to determine how the present distribution of clicks across human populations arose.

A linguistic feature, such as clicks, comes to be shared between two languages in three ways: inheritance from a common proto-language,, transfer via language contact, or independent innovation (**Figure 1**). As we discuss later, these three scenarios may lead to different outcomes concerning the phonotactic employment and functional load of clicks in particular languages and would also make different predictions for the genetic relationships between groups. We thus focus on individual click-speaking groups and examine their genetic relationships, which in turn allows us to infer how clicks came to be associated with certain populations. However, discrepancies between genetic and linguistic relationships may arise in the case of significant language contact (scenario 2, **Figure 1**) without genetic contact or vice versa. Additionally, genetic relationships can be obscured by genetic drift (random changes in allele frequencies), which has a particularly strong effect in small populations and may be a relevant factor for some click-speaking groups.

Discussion of these issues has been hampered by inconsistent terminology (see Box 1 online. Follow the **Supplemental Material link** from the Annual Reviews home page at **http://www.annualreviews.org**). In particular, the term Khoisan has, without much evidence, come to be used in a linguistic sense (Greenberg 1963), when in fact it was originally coined for a purely biologically intended affinity between two populations in the Cape (Schultze 1928): the pastoral Khoekhoe, speaking Khoe languages, and the foraging "San," there speaking Tuu languages. The terminology used here is as follows:

- Khoisan: biological profile in southern Africa as opposed to non-Khoisan African
- San (formerly Bushmen): ethnic groups with foraging subsistence in southern Africa
- Khoe: subfamily of Khoe-Kwadi, one of the three click language families in southern Africa

Genealogical inheritance: the transfer of a linguistic feature by way of normal language transmission from one to another generation of speakers

Phonotactic: concerns the possible combinations of phonemic segments in words, syllables, etc.

Functional load: the importance of a certain feature for making distinctions in a language

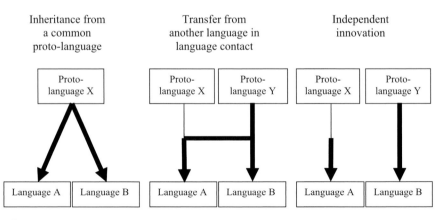

Figure 1

Three scenarios as to how two languages come to share a linguistic feature.

- Pastoral Khoekhoe (formerly Hottentot): ethnic groups with pastoral subsistence confined to South Africa and Namibia

Individual groups will be identified by linguistic affiliation and location, unless there are unambiguous terms such as Hadza, Sandawe, and Dama.

It must be emphasized from the outset that the physical classification of Khoisan vs. non-Khoisan does not overlap with either linguistic or subsistence-based classifications of African populations (**Figure 2**). Although all groups subsumed biologically under Khoisan do speak click languages, other groups who do not resemble Khoisan groups also speak click languages (Nurse et al. 1985). These include (*a*) the Dama in Namibia; (*b*) the Kwadi in Southwest Angola; (*c*) the so-called Black Bushmen or Negroid hunter-gatherers, known locally inter alia as Kwengo (=Khwe) or Masarwa and spreading from Southeast Angola over the Namibian Caprivi Strip to the entire northern and eastern flank of the Kalahari in Botswana; and (*d*) the eastern African groups Hadza and Sandawe.

THE DISTRIBUTION OF CLICKS IN THE LANGUAGES OF THE WORLD

Clicks as Nonphonemic Speech Sounds

When ascertaining the occurrence of clicks across the world's languages, it is necessary to distinguish between two employments of clicks: phonemic speech sounds, which distinguish lexical meaning, or paralinguistic speech sounds, which do not play a role in the lexicon. The latter use of clicks is quite frequent according to the first worldwide survey of this phenomenon (Gil 2005). Non-phonemic clicks involve such different functions as the expression of "yes" and/or "no," of "positive" and/or "negative" attitude (compare the English dental click [|]), turn-taking in conversation, and communication with babies or with animals (compare the English lateral click [||] for driving

horses). The geographical distribution shown in **Figure 3** does not provide complete coverage of the globe; in particular, an area without dots does not imply the absence of paralinguistic clicks, but two general conclusions can be drawn: Clicks per se are geographically and genealogically widespread across human languages and, as a consequence, should not be viewed as unusual speech sounds in terms of production and in-principle usability in language.

Clicks as Phonemic Speech Sounds

Clicks as phonemes are found in just three geographical locations (**Figure 3**): two in Africa and one in Australia (Maddieson 2005). **Table 1** provides a complete list of attested language groups or single languages with click phonemes. There are eight independent linguistic lineages; that is, each of these units has not (yet) been shown to have a relative among the attested languages of the world. This classification is based on commonly accepted linguistic methodology, namely historical-comparative work and diachronic typology.

Greenberg (1963) claimed that units 1–5 form a genealogical language group Khoisan, and units 1–3 form a lower-order group Southern African Khoisan (see **Figure 2**). This hypothesis is not accepted by most specialists (Güldemann & Vossen 2000). Although future research might well strengthen or newly bring up viable hypotheses regarding higher-order relationships between some lineages, a very "optimistic" guess brings down the number of independent lineages to no less than three or four.

The languages concerned are not homogeneous in terms of the functional load as well as the phonotactic properties of clicks. The functional load of clicks in a language can be ascertained by two parameters: (*a*) the complexity of the click phoneme system and (*b*) the importance of clicks for the distinction of lexical meaning. The complexity of systems is measured conveniently by the size of the segment inventory, which ranges between 3 clicks in

Paralinguistic: refers to consciously or unconsciously used nonverbal elements of communication, which can express emotion and/or modify meaning

Phoneme: sound distinguishing meaning in words in opposition to other sounds with the same function (e.g., /b/ and /t/ in "bank" versus "tank")

Figure 2

Southern African non-Bantu groups and their basic linguistic (Tuu vs. Ju-ǂHoan vs. Khoe-Kwadi), biological (Khoisan vs. non-Khoisan), and cultural (forager vs. pastoralist) classifications. Larger geographical overlaps between distinct population categories generally involve the pastoral Khoekhoe, i.e., (*a*) Tuu and Khoekhoe languages in western South Africa and southeastern Namibia, (*b*) non-Khoisan and Khoisan in the Dama-Nama contact zone in central Namibia, and (*c*) foragers and pastoralists again in South Africa and Namibia. The map is idealized in two major respects: First, all South African populations no longer exist today as distinct ethnolinguistic groups, except for tiny remnants of Nama and N‖ng; and second, Bantu populations are omitted, although they are distributed all over the area and thus overlap widely with the groups considered here.

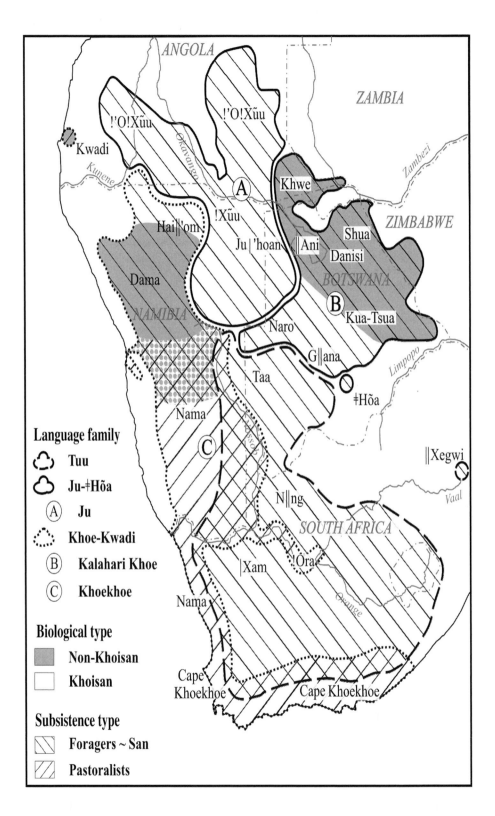

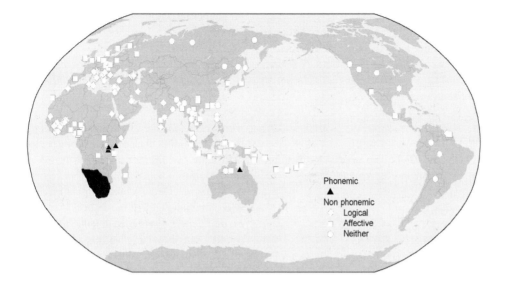

Figure 3

The global distribution of clicks (Gil 2005, Güldemann 2007).

Table 1 Attested language groups with click phonemes

Language or LANGUAGE FAMILY	Area	Highest linguistic affiliation
All TUU (=Southern Khoisan)	Southern Africa	Isolate family
All JU (=Northern Khoisan) + ǂHoan	Southern Africa	Isolate family (Honken 2008)
All KHOE (=Central Khoisan) + Kwadi	Southern Africa	Isolate family (Güldemann 2004, Güldemann & Elderkin 2008)
Sandawe	Eastern Africa	Isolate language (? or related to Khoe-Kwadi; Elderkin 1989, Güldemann & Elderkin 2008)
Hadza	Eastern Africa	Isolate language (Sands 1998)
Dahalo (CUSHITIC)	Eastern Africa	Afroasiatic
Some BANTU	Southern Africa	Niger-Congo
Damin (speech register of Lardil, TANGKIC)	Northern Australia	Australian

Dahalo and 83 in East !Xõo. The importance of clicks in the lexicon can be measured in a language by the relative frequency of items with and without clicks, ranging between less than 5% in Dahalo and well over 60% in many languages in southern Africa. Although the lexical frequency of clicks in a language does not necessarily correlate with the click inventory size, both measurements can be conflated so that a language can be assigned to an approximate position on a scalar continuum of the functional load of clicks, namely high in Tuu, Ju-ǂHoan,

and Khoe; intermediate in Sandawe, Hadza, Kwadi, and some Bantu languages (Nguni, Yei); and low in Dahalo, Damin, and some other Bantu languages (Southern Sotho, Kavango).

Languages also differ with respect to the phonotactic characteristics of clicks, that is their syntagmatic distribution vis-à-vis other speech sounds within words. In Tuu, Ju-ǂHoan, and Khoe-Kwadi, clicks are associated with the following structure of lexical items C(C)VCV [C, consonant; V, vowel; CC, a consonant cluster], where clicks are restricted to the first consonant position. Traces of this phonotactic pattern are found in Sandawe. Although Damin does not have the same stem structure, its clicks are also initial. The only exceptions to this property are Bantu languages as well as Hadza and Dahalo.

Summary

The following can be summarized for the modern distribution and function of clicks:

1. Clicks as such are common as human speech sounds,
2. clicks as phonemes are cross-linguistically exceptionally rare, and
3. click phonemes have a high functional load only in Tuu, Ju-‡Hoan, and Khoe-Kwadi.

Although overall there are few languages from which generalizations about the history of clicks can be drawn, the data are sufficiently diverse to assess claims concerning the origin of clicks in particular languages as well as the properties of clicks as a phoneme class in general.

THE HISTORY OF CLICK PHONEMES IN MODERN LANGUAGES

Nongenealogical Click Origin

All three scenarios of click origin as given in the introduction will be evaluated for the languages concerned. Because the inheritance of clicks is well attested, to the extent that this is in fact assumed to be the default scenario (Knight et al. 2003), we first address in more detail the two neglected nongenealogical explanations.

There is one case for independent innovation of click phonemes, namely Damin. This is a so-called register—a fully functional speech form used formerly by second-degree male initiates in an Australian Aboriginal community. The normal language Lardil and the Damin register are mutually unintelligible, so the latter can be considered to a certain extent a language of its own (Hale 1973). The set of five click

phonemes in Damin are clearly a conscious innovation associated with the creation of the register. An important fact is that Damin clicks "are in all essential respects like those of the Khoisan languages of southern Africa" (Hale 1973, Hale & Nash 1997)—among other things, they comprise the same basic types and occur only in word-initial position. One must thus conclude that independent click origin is not necessarily detectable by different properties of the relevant sounds.

Although other theoretical possibilities exist for the independent innovation of clicks, for example, their emergence in language-internal sound change starting with nonclick consonants, this need not be discussed here because there are no known examples.

The second type of nongenealogical origin of clicks involves contact between populations with languages that are distinguished by the presence/absence of clicks. Contact provides four basic scenarios for the proliferation of these sounds across linguistic or genetic population types (each scenario on its own represents an idealization because more than one scenario can be involved in a particular case). First, a population with a click language can experience extensive gene flow from a population with a click-less language, leading to apparent genetic similarity between populations with click and click-less languages. A second possibility is that clicks are borrowed by a population with a click-less language from a click language. Two additional scenarios involve language shift. First, a population can undergo shift from a click language to a click-less language whereby clicks enter the target language from the language that is given up—so-called substrate interference (Thomason & Kaufman 1988). Second, a population can shift from a click-less language to a click language whereby clicks in the target language—the linguistic superstrate—are retained. With respect to the presence/absence of clicks, a given language does not change in the two scenarios of gene flow and click language superstrate; it does change in the case of click borrowing and click language substrate because clicks newly enter it. With respect to

Table 2 Contact scenarios for the proliferation of clicks across populations

Contact scenario	Language change regarding clicks	Expected genetic change
Gene flow into a click language population	No	High
Borrowing from a click language	Yes	⇑
Language shift from a click language	Yes	⇓
Language shift to a click language	No	Low

genetic properties of the population, a rough probabilistic generalization would be a cline of salience of genetic change across different contact scenarios: Heavy gene flow would involve the highest degree; borrowing from a click language is also likely to leave some trace in the genetic record of the relevant population; and the language shift scenarios from and to a click language are indeterminate—they can, but need not, be associated with easily detectable genetic change. The scenarios are summarized in **Table 2**.

That certain languages have acquired clicks through contact can be discerned from several facts. Most importantly, click sounds cannot be reconstructed to the respective proto-language. Also, language contact is historically attested or can be assumed because unrelated click languages are found in the geographical vicinity. Finally, there is direct linguistic evidence that click words are borrowings from one or the other click language. These considerations help to identify several cases of contact-induced click origin in Africa.

The historically least clear case is that of Dahalo, a Cushitic language in eastern Africa. Clicks cannot be reconstructed to Proto-Cushitic. Because there is no apparent source for Dahalo click words in other languages, an independent click origin cannot be excluded. However, owing to the existence of other click languages in the geographical vicinity, a contact scenario in the more remote past is quite probable.

Click origin due to contact is certain for the relevant southern African Bantu languages. The sounds cannot be reconstructed for Proto-Bantu, and contact between Bantu and local click languages occurred from prehistoric times up to the present (Herbert 1990b, Voßen

1997). The evidence from these secondarily acquired systems provides three important conclusions to the effect that clicks, once borrowed, have a life of their own in the borrowing language (Güldemann 2007). First, click inventories of some Bantu languages are as complex as, or even more complex than, systems of such click languages as Standard Khoekhoe, Kwadi, Sandawe, and Hadza. Second, there exist click types in Bantu that are not attested in any of the possible source languages. Finally, Nguni gives clear indications that a considerable number of click words are not directly due to borrowing or substrate interference but have been innovated on the basis of the inherited Bantu lexicon (Herbert 1990b).

Furthermore, the salience and degree of click integration in the southernmost Bantu languages correlate with a sociolinguistic feature observed already in Damin, i.e., the existence and importance of a specialized speech register (Finlayson 1982, Herbert 1990a). As part of a complex of avoidance customs, known as "hlonipha," married women are obliged in Nguni (and to a lesser extent Southern Sotho) to linguistically disguise words that sound similar to the names of male in-laws. A major strategy to achieve this is the substitution of an original consonant by another consonant, whereby clicks were recruited particularly frequently. This helps to explain why Southern Nguni, where hlonipha is most salient, displays the highest degree of click integration.

Shift-induced click origin can involve the proliferation of any linguistic feature into another population. Important here is that genetic changes can be virtually absent if the shifting population maintains its distinct identity. Classic cases where hunter-gatherer populations almost certainly underwent language

Speech register: subsystem of a language used for special purposes and/or in a special social environment, reflecting socially determined linguistic variation

shift, but kept (initially) fairly separate from their contact groups are the Negrito in the Philippines and the Pygmies in central Africa. The possible shift of a population to a click language is particularly challenging because it need not considerably affect the genetic profile of the shifting population and does not involve a change within a language regarding clicks. Although click languages are unlikely targets of language shift today because of the low social position of their speakers, who were mostly hunter-gatherers, this cannot be assumed for the past. First, some evidence demonstrates that languages of foraging cultures did expand and thereby were targets of language shift just like other languages, such as the cases of Athapascan in North America (Ives 1990, Golla 2000) and Pama-Nyungan in Australia (Evans & McConvell 1998, McConvell 2001); this must have been particularly relevant before the global expansion of food production. Second, click languages are not necessarily associated with low prestige; some have been and still are targets of language shift such as Sandawe in eastern Africa (Newman 1994) as well as languages of pastoral Khoekhoe in southern Africa (Traill 1995).

Clicks and the Khoisan Languages

Although the genealogical unity of Khoisan languages is no longer entertained by most specialists, it is still widely maintained that the existence of clicks in these languages is due to inheritance from some (but not necessarily the same) ancestor language. **Table 1** shows that Khoisan comprises five independent lineages, i.e., Tuu, Ju-ǂHoan, Khoe-Kwadi, Sandawe, and Hadza. Khoe-Kwadi-Sandawe is a higher-order unit that is promising but insufficiently proven; its acceptance would reduce to four the number of independent lineages. For the respective protolanguages of all family-like units, one can safely assume that they possessed clicks because all their daughter languages possess this feature. In Tuu and Ju-ǂHoan, the number and use of clicks are overall so extensive that even their protolanguages must be reconstructed with a very

elaborate system, which allows one to project the age of clicks even further back in time. This hypothesis is not warranted to the same degree for Proto-Khoe-Kwadi, and Sandawe because their click systems are considerably smaller.

Hadza is the most problematic case in this respect because the profile of its restricted click system is compatible with all possible historical explanations (Güldemann 2007). Although there is no clear positive evidence suggesting inheritance from an ancient ancestor language (it is an isolate), the contact scenario is quite probable: Hadza is spoken in eastern Africa, where phonemic clicks are attested in two other unrelated languages, Dahalo and Sandawe, suggesting that in the past the area hosted more, diverse click languages, which were mostly obliterated by later colonization.

It is still an open question whether click phonemes have emerged in Africa more than once, i.e., in eastern and southern Africa independently. Although this is possible, it is also conceivable that all clicks attested in African languages today ultimately trace back to a single historical event: Click phonemes would have developed just once in a single lineage and expanded later in areal and genealogical distribution by means of language and population contacts. Synchronic linguistic evidence indicates that there existed a linguistic-areal connection between eastern and southern Africa, which was submerged by the recent Bantu expansion (Heine & Voßen 1981; Güldemann 1999, 2008), leading to the extinction of numerous languages, which may have been of different type and genealogical affiliation but shared at least some linguistic features—inter alia clicks as a common phoneme type. Under such a scenario, it is unwarranted to expect a clear linguistic or other affinity among all the different African populations speaking click languages. In general, the historical processes that have brought about the modern click distribution in Africa likely involve a complex scenario of divergence, convergence, and obliteration of distinct languages and populations across space and time, including language shifts that leave few linguistic and genetic traces.

Summary

All three scenarios in **Figure 1** are attested in the case of clicks. The cases of nongenealogical origin involve at least three of the eight linguistic lineages in **Table 1**, i.e., Bantu of Niger-Congo, Dahalo of Afroasiatic, and Damin of Australian; moreover, the Bantu languages reflect more than one case of click borrowing (at least one in the northwest and one in the southeast of the Kalahari). The controversial case of Hadza aside, these cases represent more than one third of all attested lineages. In view of this observation and the fact that both independent innovation and contact-induced origin of clicks may not be detectable in the click inventory and the lexicon, there are no empirical grounds for underestimating, let alone excluding, nongenealogical explanations for the presence of clicks in a language.

THE GENETIC RELATIONSHIPS OF AFRICAN CLICK-SPEAKING POPULATIONS

Classical Genetic Markers

Classical markers include blood groups, serum proteins, red cell enzymes, and some immunological loci such as Gm and HLA and represent the first genetic markers to be studied in human populations. Nurse et al. (1985) analyzed 32 alleles belonging to 11 systems in 23 sub-Saharan African populations, including Nama-speaking Khoekhoe from Namibia (there Khoi), Ju-speaking San from Botswana (there Dobe !Kung), Naro (Khoe)-speaking San from Botswana (there Nharo), Dama from Namibia, and Hadza and Sandawe from eastern Africa. A principal components analysis of these data indicates that the Ju and Naro are similar to one another and distinct from the other tested southern African groups, and the Nama are in between (and somewhat closer to) non-Khoisan groups and these two Khoisan groups, in agreement with other studies based on fewer loci (Excoffier et al. 1987). The Dama and the Sandawe cluster with non-Khoisan groups. The Hadza do not group with Khoisan either, but

instead with a Pygmy group. Finally, Nurse et al. (1985) also indicate a genetic similarity between click-speaking non-Khoisan groups such as the Khwe and neighboring non-Khoisan groups, with little or no detectable admixture with Khoisan.

MtDNA Data

MtDNA is maternally inherited and thus gives insight into the maternal history of populations. The relationships of some southern African click-speaking groups have been examined in some detail with a low-resolution approach for determining mtDNA types that is based on polymorphisms detected with six restriction enzymes (Johnson et al. 1983, Merriwether et al. 1991, Soodyall & Jenkins 1992, Soodyall & Jenkins 1993). Overall, Ju-speaking San from Botswana and Angola (there !Kung and Sekele !Kung, respectively) and Nama (there Khoi) cluster together, while the Dama cluster with non-Khoisan groups (Merriwether et al. 1991). However, one mtDNA type is present at high frequency in the two Ju groups (26%–43%) but is completely absent in the Nama (and all other groups). Thus, either the Nama and Ju have an ancient shared origin and have since diverged considerably via genetic drift, or they have experienced admixture with different groups; more detailed studies of these groups and their neighbors are required to distinguish between these possible explanations.

Low-resolution mtDNA studies have been largely supplanted in recent years by studies that rely on sequencing the first hypervariable segment (HV1) of the noncoding mtDNA control region. HV1 sequences are available from samples of Hadza (Knight et al. 2003), Ju (there !Kung) from Botswana (Vigilant et al. 1991), Ju (there Vasikela !Kung) from Angola, and Khwe (there Kwengo) from Namibia (Chen et al. 2000); both Ju and Khwe are listed by Chen et al. (2000) as South African but only settled there from Angola/Namibia around 1990. In **Figure 4**, we present the results of a multidimensional scaling (MDS) analysis of 26 sub-Saharan African populations, including the

Multidimensional scaling (MDS) analysis: a means of visualizing the relationships among a set of populations based on a matrix of their pairwise genetic distances

Genetic drift: random changes in allele frequencies over generations that lead to loss of genetic variation and increased genetic differentiation

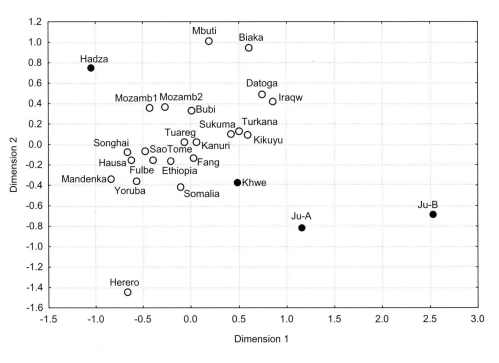

Figure 4

MDS plot of the first two dimensions for 26 sub-Saharan African populations, based on F_{st} distances for mtDNA HV1 sequences. Solid symbols denote groups with click languages. Ju-A, Ju from Angola; Ju-B, Ju from Botswana. The stress value is 0.079.

above four click-speaking groups, using published data (Vigilant et al. 1991, Chen et al. 2000, Salas et al. 2002, Knight et al. 2003). The results indicate that the two Ju groups are distinct from all other African groups (and from each other). The Khwe group clusters with Bantu-speaking and other non-Khoisan groups, in good agreement with previous results based on classical markers (Nurse et al. 1985) and low-resolution mtDNA types (Soodyall & Jenkins 1992), although their position in between this cluster and the two Ju groups indicates some admixture between Khwe and Ju. The Hadza are also outliers in the MDS plot, as are the Herero—possibly due to a recent bottleneck (Vigilant et al. 1991, Soodyall & Jenkins 1993)—and the two Pygmy groups.

Previously, Knight et al. (2003) analyzed mtDNA sequences in a smaller number of sub-Saharan African groups and concluded that the Hadza and the Ju from Botswana are separated by the largest genetic distance of any pair of African populations, thereby indicating that the earliest genetic split among human populations was between the ancestors of east African and south African click-speaking groups. The MDS

analysis also shows that the Hadza and Ju are separated by large genetic distances, indicating that they are indeed quite distinct genetically, according to mtDNA HV1 sequences. However, this does not necessarily indicate that the earliest split was between the ancestors of east African and south African click-speaking groups. Another possible explanation is genetic drift. Genetic drift due to small population size or a reduction in population size, even for a brief period of time, can drastically alter patterns of genetic variation, thereby making it difficult, if not impossible, to accurately reconstruct population relationships.

Has genetic drift influenced variation in Hadza and some southern African Khoisan groups? One indication of genetic drift is low levels of genetic diversity, and it is telling that all the groups that appear as outliers in the MDS plot (**Figure 4**) also have low levels of genetic diversity (**Supplemental Figure 1**). Therefore, the extreme positions of the Hadza and Ju (as well as the Herero and the Biaka and Mbuti Pygmies) in the MDS plot most likely reflect greatly altered frequencies of mtDNA HV1 sequences in these groups, as a consequence of genetic drift. This means that one cannot, with any degree of certainty, draw any conclusions about the genetic relationships of these groups using these data.

Y-Chromosome Data

The Y-chromosome is transmitted from father to son and thus provides insight into the paternal history of populations. Eastern and southern African click-speaking groups were previously analyzed at 8 Y-chromosome markers (Knight et al. 2003), but recently, data for 50 Y-chromosome markers in 40 African populations were published (Wood et al. 2005). Data are available from the latter study for two Ju groups sampled in Namibia (there Sekele !Kung and Tsumkwe), Nama from Namibia (there Khoi), and Dama. Knight et al. (2003) provided data on Hadza, as well as additional published data (Underhill et al. 2000, Cruciani et al. 2002) for the same markers for two additional Ju groups (there Sekele !Kung and Ju|'hoansi) and the Khwe. To combine the data from Wood et al. (2005) with the data from Knight et al. (2003), we collapsed the Y-chromosome types (haplogroups) identified by the former into the 8 haplogroups that would have been identified if they had analyzed only those Y-chromosome markers that were studied by the latter. After excluding northern African groups, and all those groups with sample sizes less than 10, we calculated genetic distances, using the Y-chromosome marker frequencies, for the remaining 40 groups. An MDS plot based on the genetic distances is shown in **Figure 5**.

In contrast with the mtDNA results, the Ju groups do not stand out as outliers for the Y-chromosome; instead, they are arranged along a line extending outward from a central cluster of southeastern Bantu-speaking groups and other groups. The Nama are close to the Ju, whereas the Dama and Khwe are grouped with Bantu-speaking groups, in agreement with the results for other genetic markers discussed above. In contrast with the mtDNA results, for the Y-chromosome, the Hadza are near the southern African click-speaking groups, along with Pygmy groups. Here, the available genetic diversity values do not indicate a particularly low level of Y-chromosome diversity in the Hadza (**Supplemental Figure 2**).

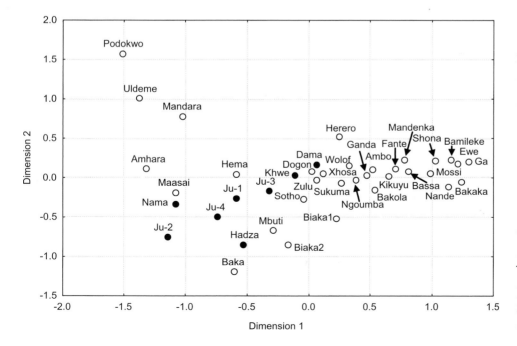

Figure 5

MDS plot of the first two dimensions for 40 African populations, based on Fst distances for eight Y-SNP haplogroups (Knight et al. 2003, Wood et al. 2005). Solid symbols denote groups with click languages. Ju-1 denotes the Sekele !Kung and Ju-2, the Tsumkwe of Wood et al. (2005), whereas Ju-3 denotes the Sekele !Kung and Ju-4, the Ju|'hoansi of Knight et al. (2003). The stress value is 0.074.

Our conclusion that the Hadza and southern African click-speaking groups are not genetically distant, based on Y-chromosome haplogroups, differs from the conclusions of Knight et al. (2003). These authors did not actually analyze population relationships on the basis of Y-chromosome haplogroups, but rather estimated a large relative population divergence time between the Hadza and the Ju from eight short tandem repeat (STR) loci on the background of one Y-chromosome marker, M112. However, this analysis is based on just 12 Hadza and 6 Ju Y-chromosomes and hence cannot be viewed as very reliable.

The clustering of Pygmy, southern African click-speaking groups, and Hadza in the MDS plot for the Y-chromosome is intriguing because these are all associated with a hunter-gatherer subsistence. This grouping most likely reflects haplogroup B2b (defined by the M112 marker), which is at high frequency in these groups (10%–67%) but essentially absent from agricultural African groups (Knight et al. 2003, Wood et al. 2005). This haplogroup may thus represent a marker for hunting-gathering groups, which is both widespread (occurring in southern, eastern, and central Africa) and relatively ancient, a conclusion based on associated Y-STR diversity in a small number of individuals (Knight et al. 2003)]. Further characterization of this haplogroup would be desirable.

Summary

In sum, the genetic results indicate the following. First, pastoral Khoekhoe and at least the Ju-speaking San are genetically closely related to one another and relatively distinct from other African groups, supporting a biological basis for a Khoisan group as proposed by Schultze (1928). Second, click-speaking non-Khoisan groups, such as the Dama and Khwe, are genetically distinct from this Khoisan group and instead are related to non-Khoisan Africans. Third, although the mtDNA differs significantly between the Hadza and the sampled click-speaking South African groups, the reason for this is not clear yet. Although it may be due to a very ancient population split, it is also likely that internal genetic drift has obscured their original relationship(s). Finally, the Y-chromosome data indicate a shared ancient ancestry of southern, eastern, and central African hunter-gatherers that is not confined to click-speaking groups.

Recently, a more extensive analysis of mtDNA and Y-chromosome variation in Hadza and Sandawe click-speaking groups from Tanzania, and Ju (Ju|'hoansi) and mixed Ju (!Xun)/Khwe groups from South Africa, indicates that the initial divergence between southern and eastern African groups occurred ~35,000–50,000 years ago, and the Sandawe and Hadza groups either diverged ~15,000–20,000 years ago or diverged earlier and then came into extensive contact ~15,000–20,000 years ago (Tishkoff et al. 2007). In either event, there has been little genetic contact between the Sandawe and Hadza since 15,000–20,000 years ago, although the genetic results indicate contact between all these groups and neighboring (nonclick-speaking) groups in the past 5000 years. The authors of this study favor a single ancient origin (35,000–50,000 years ago) of clicks in an ancestral population of Hadza, Sandawe, and the South African click-speaking groups but do not consider the alternative possibilities discussed above of the acquisition of clicks in one (or more) of these groups via contact.

Moreover, these conclusions are based on just two genetic loci (mtDNA and the Y-chromosome) and a small sample of the existing click-speaking groups. The entire southern and eastern sphere of click-speaking southern Africa is not yet represented at all in genetic studies, e.g., most Kalahari Khoe-speaking San in Botswana and further northeast, all Tuu-speaking San in Namibia, Botswana, and South Africa, and the Khoekhoe-speaking pastoralists of South Africa (**Figure 2**). Given the considerable genetic diversity among the few click-speaking groups that have been studied (**Figures 4** and **5**), and the rapid rate of disappearance of click-speaking groups via assimilation into neighboring groups, it is vital to sample the genes of these groups as soon as possible to preserve their genetic heritage.

GENERAL HISTORICAL ASPECTS OF CLICK PHONEMES

The preceding discussion of linguistic and genetic aspects of click-speaking groups does not suggest, but also does not exclude, a single ancient origin of clicks. This hypothesis, however, implies that click phonemes have (*a*) been lost in the great majority of linguistic lineages on the globe and were (*b*) only locally retained in a few African languages. That is, while clicks are very old, they are at the same time somehow unstable.

The intuition that clicks are difficult and hence unstable as a sound class, favoring their loss over time, seems to be corroborated by attested cases of click loss in southern Africa (Traill & Voßen 1997). However, this phenomenon shows an interesting geographical pattern in that the languages thus affected are all situated at the periphery of the core click language area and share an intimate contact history with click-less Bantu languages, which are sociolinguistically more prestigious and often the ultimate targets of language shift (Traill & Voßen 1997). Thus, the frequent click loss in these languages might well be a later phenomenon associated with an extralinguistic factor rather than motivated by properties inherent to the speech sounds themselves. This is corroborated by the observation that clicks are stable in relatively undisturbed sociolinguistic environments (Traill 1974).

There are yet other indications that clicks are not inherently prone to loss. Clicks in a typical southern African language normally outnumber other consonants, both in the phoneme inventory and in the lexicon. Cross-linguistically no other sound class is subject to such an extensive series formation—inter alia by combining with a second, i.e., the pulmonic, air-stream mechanism. And finally, the evidence presented above that clicks can emerge independently, be transferred to click-less languages, and expand over time does not support

the idea that this sound class is an inherently recessive linguistic feature. Hence, any theory that assumes proto-world to have been a click language has to invoke more than just the alleged instability of clicks to account for their absence in most of the world's languages. At the same time, fanciful ideas such as clicks enhancing hunter-gatherer survival (Knight et al. 2003) are, apart from being unfounded (Box 2 online), not needed to motivate click retention in a small subset of human populations.

The view that there is something inherently "archaic" to clicks has a long tradition in the relevant research history (Bleek 1862, Ginneken 1938, Stopa 1960, Grolier 1990), and until fairly recently could hardly be separated from the stereotypical idea that the peoples speaking these languages are themselves "archaic" and "primitive." In modern treatments, the old age of click phonemes is often simply asserted without giving supporting evidence (Kohler 1998). Although it is indeed probable that clicks are "archetypal" elements of human communication as a nonphonemic, paralinguistic phenomenon (see above), this is not the case for clicks as phonemes.

An alternative hypothesis is that clicks have been widely available as a paralinguistic aspect of communication throughout human history but made it only occasionally into the phoneme inventory of a language. There are two uncontroversial cases in which clicks in modern languages were innovated, completely so in Damin and partly in Nguni Bantu. Significantly, in both cases the innovative "promotion" of clicks from nonphonemic to phonemic speech sounds involves more than just their availability: They are associated with a marked sociolinguistic phenomenon in the form of an avoidance language. This suggests a more general scenario according to which clicks are initially recruited for phonemic purposes in a marked speech register but then spill over into the "normal language," eventually consolidating and gradually expanding both in the phoneme system and across the lexicon. That is, the special register serves as a permeable mediator between the partly distinct sound inventories of paralinguistic and linguistic communication. Under this scenario, the cross-linguistic rarity of phonemic clicks is expected because the full cycle where clicks enter a phoneme system through a kind of bottle-neck passage—the special register—should and need only be assumed in an exceptionally small number of cases (apart from the incipient one in Damin, possibly only one other, but much older case in Africa). That is, instead of trying to explain the widespread absence of clicks, we consider it to be simpler to account for their very rare presence.

Because the evidence on phonemic clicks does not itself support the old-age hypothesis, the feature is often tied to the old age of either a linguistic lineage or a population type. However, the rigor of even the most ambitious linguistic method presently available fades out from 10,000 years backwards so that chance, inheritance, and contact can no longer be securely distinguished in the case of a similarity. Regarding clicks, there is no good reason for associating even the oldest relevant lineage with some linguistic entity spoken, say, 20,000, 30,000, or 40,000 years ago. From a genetic perspective, the distinct Khoisan profile associated with click sounds is indeed old. But in view of nongenealogical click origins and the relevant time depth, the emergence of click phonemes within the modern populations cannot be tied securely to their origin in genetic terms. In conclusion, there is no good reason as yet to assume with any confidence that phonemic clicks were among the earliest speech sounds. That their emergence in Africa represents a far later episode in the diversification of human speech is a very real possibility.

CONCLUSIONS

The first conclusion of the above discussion is something that has been known for a long time but is insufficiently appreciated in certain scientific contexts: There is not only enormous diversity among all African peoples characterized by phonemic clicks in terms of all major criteria for classifying human populations, but also there is a significant absence of overlap in the linguistic, cultural, and biological characteristics of these populations (see **Figure 2**). This observation also requires a more careful approach to terminology: Because the term Khoisan is vacuous in terms of language classification and social organization, its generalized use in and outside science can only lead to misunderstanding.

Second, the idea that modern click phonemes have their ultimate origin in the linguistic feature of a very ancient human language, as has been proposed for a long time (Bleek 1862, Grolier 1990, Kohler 1998) and is entertained yet again on the basis of genetic data (Knight et al. 2003), is a possible hypothesis not falsified by the present discussion. However, the available linguistic and genetic data do not single it out in favor of other hypotheses. It remains just one among several (speculative) ideas, still inspired by the outdated default assumption that genetic, cultural, and linguistic features correlate: Because Khoisan groups are among the oldest genetically, because most groups are hunter-gatherers and thus associated with the oldest subsistence pattern of our species, and because all their languages are characterized by clicks, clicks must also be an old feature of language. Unspectacular as our present conclusion may appear, there is no new information supporting this line of thinking.

There is, however, another lesson to be learned from the present problem: The tempting combination of genetic and linguistic data is potentially confronted with a serious problem, namely the possible incompatibility of time depths. The enormous time depths that can be reached by modern genetic research have so far no counterpart in linguistic methodology. That is, a time depth of several tens of thousands of years invokes highly different connotations of "old"/"early" versus "young"/"late." If clicks in Africa had an age of, say, 20,000 years, they would be a relatively "young" phenomenon vis-à-vis the identifiable time depths of human genetic profiles; in linguistic terms, they would be exceptionally "old" in the sense that available methods of this discipline are incapable of identifying such an early date.

It is also necessary to appreciate the different historical dynamics of the primary research objects of the two disciplines: linguistic features, languages, and language groups on the one hand and genetic features and populations on the other hand. More reliable hypotheses about the early development of language can be reached only by truly interdisciplinary research in the disciplines concerned, here genetics and linguistics. Moreover, information on other aspects that can influence the outcome of contact between populations, such as environmental conditions and social and economic differences, just to mention a few, needs to be included when seeking explanations for the rich genetic and linguistic diversity of human populations.

DISCLOSURE STATEMENT

The authors are not aware of any biases that might be perceived as affecting the objectivity of this review.

ACKNOWLEDGMENTS

Parts of this paper were presented at a number of previous occasions—we are grateful to the different audiences for interesting discussions on the topic. We also thank Antonio Salas for kindly providing African mtDNA sequences, and Brigitte Pakendorf for pointing out the association between Y-chromosome haplogroup B2b and foraging groups and for valuable comments. Our research is supported by the Max Planck Society and the Deutsche Forschungsgemeinschaft.

LITERATURE CITED

Bleek W. 1862. *A Comparative Grammar of South African Languages, Part 1: Phonology*. Cape Town/London: Juta & Trübner

Chen YS, Olckers A, Schurr TG, Kogelnik AM, Huoponen K, Wallace DC. 2000. mtDNA variation in the South African Kung and Khwe and their genetic relationships to other African populations. *Am. J. Hum. Genet.* 66:1362–83

Cruciani F, Santolamazza P, Shen P, Macaulay V, Moral P, et al. 2002. A back migration from Asia to sub-Saharan Africa is supported by high-resolution analysis of human Y-chromosome haplotypes. *Am. J. Hum. Genet.* 70:1197–214

Elderkin E. 1989. *The significance and origin of the use of pitch in Sandawe*. PhD thesis. Univ. York

Evans N, McConvell P. 1998. The enigma of Pama-Nyungan expansion in Australia. In *Archaeology and Language II: Correlating Archaeology and Linguistic Hypotheses*, ed. R Blench, M Spriggs, pp. 174–92. London: Routledge

Excoffier L, Pellegrini B, Sanchez-Mazas A, Simon C, Langaney A. 1987. Genetics and history of sub-Saharan Africa. *Yearb. Phys. Anthropol.* 30:151–94

Finlayson R. 1982. Hlonipha—the women's language of avoidance among the Xhosa. *S. Afr. J. Afr. Lang.* Suppl. 1:35–60

Gil D. 2005. Paralinguistic usages of clicks. See Haspelmath et al. 2005, pp. 572–75

Ginneken J. 1938. Les clics, les consonnes et les voyelles dans l'histoire de l'humanité. *Proceedings of the Third International Congress of Phonetic Sciences*, pp. 321–26. Ghent: Univ. Ghent

Golla V. 2000. Language history and communication strategies in aboriginal California. In *Languages of the Pacific Rim*, pp. 43–64. Suita, Japan: Fac. Inform., Osaka Gakuin Univ.

Greenberg J. 1963. *The Languages of Africa*. Bloomington: Indiana Univ. Press

Grolier E. 1990. Toward a tentative "reconstruction" of homo sapiens sapiens language(s): an essay in glosso-genetics theory. In *Geneses of Language*, ed. W Koch, pp. 135–63. Bochum: Universitätsverlag Dr. Norbert Brockmeyer

Güldemann T. 1999. Head-initial meets head-final: nominal suffixes in eastern and southern Bantu from a historical perspective. *Stud. Afr. Linguist.* 28:49–91

Güldemann T. 2004. Reconstruction through 'deconstruction': the marking of person, gender, and number in the Khoe family and Kwadi. *Diachronica* 21:251–306

Güldemann T. 2007. *Clicks, Genetics, and "Proto-World" from a Linguistic Perspective.* Leipzig: Inst. für Afr., Univ. Leipzig

Güldemann T. 2008. Typology. In *The Khoisan Languages*, ed. R Voßen. London: Routledge

Güldemann T, Elderkin E. 2008. On external genealogical relationships of the Khoe family. In *Khoisan Languages and Linguistics: The Riezlern Symposium 2003*, ed. M Brenzinger, C König. Köln: Rüdiger Köppe

Güldemann T, Vossen R. 2000. Khoisan. In *African Languages: An Introduction*, ed. B Heine, D Nurse, pp. 99–122. Cambridge, UK: Cambridge Univ. Press

Hale K. 1973. Deep-surface canonical disparities in relation to analysis and change: an Australian example. In *Current Trends in Linguistics*, ed. T Sebeok, pp. 401–58. The Hague: Mouton

Hale K, Nash D. 1997. Damin and Lardil phonotactics. In *Boundary Rider: Essays in Honour of Geoffrey O'Grady*, ed. D Tryon, M Walsh, pp. 247–59. Canberra: Aust. Natl. Univ.

Haspelmath M, Dryer M, Gil D, Comrie B, eds. 2005. *The World Atlas of Language Structures*. Oxford: Oxford Univ. Press

Heine B, Voßen R. 1981. Sprachtypologie. In *Die Sprachen Afrikas*, ed. B Heine, T Schadeberg, E Wolff, pp. 407–44. Hamburg: Buske

Herbert R. 1990a. Hlonipha and the ambiguous woman. *Anthropos* 85:455–73

Herbert R. 1990b. The sociohistory of clicks in Southern Bantu. *Anthropol. Linguist.* 32:295–315

Honken H. 2008. Eastern ǂHoã as an NK language. In *Essays in Honour of Anthony Traill*, ed. K Keuthmann, G Sommer, R Voßen. Köln: Rüdiger Köppe. In press

Ives J. 1990. *A Theory of Northern Athabascan Prehistory*. Boulder, CO: Westview

Johnson MJ, Wallace DC, Ferris SD, Rattazzi MC, Cavalli-Sforza LL. 1983. Radiation of human mitochondria DNA types analyzed by restriction endonuclease cleavage patterns. *J. Mol. Evol.* 19:255–71

Kohler K. 1998. The development of sound systems in human language. In *Approaches to the Evolution of Language: Social and Cognitive Bases*, ed. J Hurford, M Studdert-Kennedy, C Knight, pp. 265–78. Cambridge, UK: Cambridge Univ. Press

Knight A, Underhill PA, Mortensen HM, Zhivotovsky LA, Lin AA, et al. 2003. African Y chromosome and mtDNA divergence provides insight into the history of click languages. *Curr. Biol.* 13:464–73

Maddieson I. 2005. Presence of uncommon consonants. See Haspelmath et al. 2005, pp. 82–85

McConvell P. 2001. Language shift and language spread among hunter-gatherers. In *Hunter-Gatherers: An Interdisciplinary Perspective*, ed. RH Layton, P Rowley-Conwy, pp. 143–69. Cambridge, UK: Cambridge Univ. Press

Merriwether DA, Clark AG, Ballinger SW, Schurr TG, Soodyall H, et al. 1991. The structure of human mitochondrial DNA variation. *J. Mol. Evol.* 33:543–55

Newman J. 1994. Reconfiguring the Sandawe puzzle. *Sprache Gesch. Afrika* 12:159–70

Nurse G, Weiner J, Jenkins T. 1985. *The Peoples of Southern Africa and their Affinities*. Oxford: Oxford Univ. Press

Salas A, Richards M, De la Fe T, Lareu MV, Sobrino B, et al. 2002. The making of the African mtDNA landscape. *Am. J. Hum. Genet.* 71:1082–111

Sands B. 1998. *Eastern and Southern African Khoisan: Evaluating Claims of Distant Linguistic Relationships*. Köln: Rüdiger Köppe

Schultze L. 1928. *Zur Kenntnis des Körpers der Hottentoten und Buschmänner*. Jena: Gustav Fischer 17:147–228

Soodyall H, Jenkins T. 1992. Mitochondrial DNA polymorphisms in Khoisan populations from Southern Africa. *Ann. Hum. Genet.* 56:315–24

Soodyall H, Jenkins T. 1993. Mitochondrial DNA polymorphisms in Negroid populations from Namibia: new light on the origins of the Dama, Herero and Ambo. *Ann. Hum. Biol.* 20:477–85

Stopa R. 1960. *The Evolution of Click Sounds in Some African Languages*. Kraków: Uniwersytet Jagiellonski

Thomason S, Kaufman T. 1988. *Language Contact, Creolization and Genetic Linguistics*. Berkeley: Univ. Calif. Press

Tishkoff SA, Gonder MK, Henn BM, Mortensen H, Knight A, et al. 2007. History of click-speaking populations of Africa inferred from mtDNA and Y chromosome genetic variation. *Mol. Biol. Evol.* 24:2180–95

Traill A. 1974. *The Compleat Guide to the Koon*. Johannesburg: Afr. Stud. Inst., Univ. Witwatersrand

Traill A. 1995. The Khoesan languages of South Africa. In *Language and Social History: Studies in South African Sociolinguistics*, ed. R Mesthrie, pp. 1–18. Cape Town: David Philip

Traill A, Voßen R. 1997. Sound change in the Khoisan languages: new data on click loss and click replacement. *J. Afr. Lang. Ling.* 18:21–56

Underhill PA, Shen P, Lin AA, Jin L, Passarino G, et al. 2000. Y chromosome sequence variation and the history of human populations. *Nat. Genet.* 26:358–61

Vigilant L, Stoneking M, Harpending H, Hawkes K, Wilson AC. 1991. African populations and the evolution of human mitochondrial DNA. *Science* 253:1503–7

Voßen R. 1997. What click sounds got to do in Bantu: reconstructing the history of language contacts in southern Africa. In *Human Contact Through Language and Linguistics*, ed. B Smieja, M Tasch, pp. 353–66. Frankfurt am Main: Peter Lang

Wood ET, Stover DA, Ehret C, Destro-Bisol G, Spedini G, et al. 2005. Contrasting patterns of Y chromosome and mtDNA variation in Africa: evidence for sex-biased demographic processes. *Eur. J. Hum. Genet.* 13:867–76

Evolutionary Perspectives on Religion

Pascal Boyer[1,2] and Brian Bergstrom[1]

Departments of Psychology[1] and Anthropology[2], Washington University, St. Louis, Missouri 63130; email: pboyer@wustl.edu, bdbergst@artsci.wustl.edu

Annu. Rev. Anthropol. 2008. 37:111–130

First published online as a Review in Advance on May 29, 2008

The *Annual Review of Anthropology* is online at anthro.annualreviews.org

This article's doi: 10.1146/annurev.anthro.37.081407.085201

Key Words

cognition, cooperation, beliefs, morality, institutions

Abstract

Recent work in biology, cognitive psychology, and archaeology has renewed evolutionary perspectives on the role of natural selection in the emergence and recurrent forms of religious thought and behavior, i.e., mental representations of supernatural agents, as well as artifacts, ritual practices, moral systems, ethnic markers, and specific experiences associated with these representations. One perspective, inspired from behavioral ecology, attempts to measure the fitness effects of religious practices. Another set of models, representative of evolutionary psychology, explain religious thought and behavior as the output of cognitive systems (e.g., animacy detection, social cognition, precautionary reasoning) that are not exclusive to the religious domain. In both perspectives, the question remains open, whether religious thought and behavior constitute an adaptation or a by-product of adaptive cognitive function.

INTRODUCTION

Understanding religious thought and behavior as consequences of human nature is an old project, perhaps as old as the systematic, reflective examination of belief in gods and spirits. A notion of "natural religion" as the result of fundamental human propensities is familiar, for instance, in both Western and Muslim traditions (Pailin 1984, Reinhart 1986). Understanding religion as a result of evolution by natural selection is obviously a more recent research program, even though the first rudiments of such a project can be found in Darwin himself (Darwin 1871). In the past 20 years, a number of psychologists, anthropologists, religious scholars, and evolutionary biologists have put forward a new evolutionary perspective, understanding religion as one among the many domains of cultural activity that were shaped by human evolutionary history (Hinde 1999).

THE RELIGIOUS DOMAIN

What the term religion denotes is widely disputed in contemporary anthropology and religious studies (Saler 1993), so it may be of help to start with a rough demarcation of the field of inquiry. Evolutionary models are supposed to explain a whole collection of behaviors and mental representations that are found in many different human groups, including the following:

- mental representations of nonphysical agents, including ghosts, ancestors, spirits, gods, ghouls, witches, etc., and beliefs about the existence and features of these agents;
- artifacts associated with those mental representations, such as statues, amulets, or other visual representations or symbols;
- ritual practices associated with stipulated nonphysical agents;
- moral intuitions as well as explicit moral understandings that people in a particular group connect to nonphysical agency;
- specific forms of experience intended to either bring about some proximity to nonphysical agents or communicate with them;
- ethnic affiliation and coalitional processes linked to nonphysical agents; and
- evolutionary models, such as other explanatory models in anthropology, assume cross-cultural commonalities in each of these domains of thought and behavior.

Does this collection of features constitute a domain of "religion"? As we demonstrate below, the models described here do not assume that the features listed above are always found together. The only assumption is that evolution provides the context for understanding some or many of the phenomena listed. In this sense the term religion is to an evolutionary anthropologist what "tree" is to an evolutionary botanist, a common prescientific category that may need to be replaced with other, causally grounded, scientific categories.

Are religious phenomena sui generis? A related but distinct question is whether "religious" is a specific property of the phenomena listed above, such that they would all differ from their "nonreligious" counterparts. For instance, is a religious ritual different from a nonreligious one, and religious morality intrinsically different from the nonreligious kind? The models reviewed here make no strong assumption about that. Indeed, most of them lead to deflationary accounts of religion, in which the phenomena in question are explained in terms of processes that would operate in the same way in other contexts (Lawson & McCauley 1990). In this sense, what explains religious thought or behavior may also explain many other domains of cultural thought and behavior (Saler 1993). This pits evolutionary models, like most other anthropological accounts, against classical assumptions in the study of religion, following which there is a specific quality of religious phenomena (thought, experience, emotion, etc.) that requires explanation [see Eliade (1959), Otto (1959) and a discussion in Wiebe (1998)].

Are there religious universals? Some features of religion may well constitute substantive cultural universals (Brown 1991). This however is not crucial to using evolutionary models, whose aim is to explain the variance observed in terms of some common factors. Thus explanations should be sought for all cultural phenomena whose recurrence is clearly above chance. In many domains, evolution resulted in dispositions that render humans sensitive to particular contextual input, but evolved human dispositions do not always result in uniform behaviors or cultural outputs.

Was religion present in ancestral times? If religion, or at least the phenomena described above, were influenced by natural selection, we should expect at least some of these behaviors to be ancient as well as widespread. In the archaeological record, we find evidence for a variety of nonpragmatic behaviors, such as elaborate burial procedures, from the earliest stages of the Paleolithic and perhaps also in Neanderthals (Trinkaus & Shipman 1993). Also, we find evidence for supernatural concepts, chimeras for instance, from early stages of modern human cultures (Mithen 1999). Did these behaviors and concepts already constitute "religion"? The question only makes sense if we assume that "religion" stands for a natural kind, an integrated package, which is probably not the case. More important, the archaeological evidence shows that many of the phenomena discussed here appear at the same point (about 50 kya) along with other phenomena typical of modern humans, such as regional "cultural" differences (Richerson & Boyd 2006), sophisticated tool-equipment (Mithen 1996), body ornamentation and make-up (Hovers et al. 2003), and probably the first musical instruments (Falk 2000).

What was early "religion" like? There is no straightforward way of connecting inferred past practices to their modern equivalents, especially to the beliefs and experiences associated with religious thoughts. Some of the evidence, such as rock art similar to the visual phenomena induced by trance and altered states of consciousness (Pearson 2001), would point to a Paleolithic form of shamanism (Hayden 2003) and ecstatic experience (Dornan 2004). This would be consistent with a traditional assumption made by religious scholars that shaman-

ism is the most archaic form of religious behavior (Eliade & Trask 1964, Shirokogoroff 1935). However, such inferences are fraught with problems, as we discuss below (see Experience and Commitment). Cues to special experience do not necessarily indicate that such experience was interpreted in terms of nonphysical agency or that religious specialists like modern shamans existed.

Most evolutionary approaches to religion actually eschew speculation on archaic forms of religious behavior and experience. Rather, a common strategy is to identify the capacities and behaviors universally involved in religious thought or behavior and to relate them to plausible selective pressure. In this sense, evolutionary anthropologists of religion adopt the same strategy as other evolutionary behavioral scientists do—that of measuring the contributions of various behaviors and behavioral strategies to fitness.

EVOLUTIONARY BACKGROUND

Genetic and Cultural Evolution

The theoretical background to models of religion is a specific approach to cultural phenomena and was developed in the past 20 years by evolutionarily inspired cultural anthropologists (Boyd & Richerson 1985, Durham 1991, Lumsden & Wilson 1981, Sperber 1985). A common assumption among these different, partly overlapping frameworks is that what we observe as cultural representations and practices are variants (of cultural traits), found in roughly similar forms in a particular place or group because they have resisted change and distortion through innumerable processes of acquisition, storage, inference, and communication.

In these models, the spread of specific variants of cultural representations (such as a particular religious belief or concept represented by a human mind) is seen as partly analogous to the spread of alleles in a gene pool. In particular, the tools of population genetics can be applied to the spread of cultural traits and allow us to predict their spread, given such parameters as the initial prevalence of a trait, the likelihood of transmission, and various biases (Boyd & Richerson 1985). Such models allow scholars to describe formally the different possible connections between genetic evolution and cultural transmission (Durham 1991). Particularly relevant to modeling the cultural transmission of religion are specific cognitive and behavioral biases that result from evolution, such as for instance a frequency bias (a general trend toward cultural conformism) and a prestige bias (toward imitation of successful models) (Boyd & Richerson 1985, 1996).

Epidemiological models of cultural transmission (Sperber 1985, 1996) also aim to describe a number of evolved biases that constrain cultural transmission. They focus specifically on a cognitive description of the communicative processes involved in cultural learning, as well as the evidence for a host of specialized cognitive dispositions that canalize emergent representations and inferences. Human communication never consists in the downloading of information among brains or in straightforward imitation of others' behavior. Rather, it consists in complex processes whereby people build new mental representations as a result, among other causes, of information inferred from other people's behavior and speech (Sperber 1996, 2000). This process is highly entropic—communication creates many different representations in different minds—so that the existence of commonalities, of "cultural" information found in roughly similar versions in different minds, requires a special explanation (Sperber 1985). This is where cognitive dispositions are relevant. In many domains, people's representations are similar—despite exposure to nonidentical input—because their inferences are guided by tacit principles that happen to be identical in all normal minds (see Sperber & Hirschfeld 2004 for more detail, and see Cognitive Turn, below, for an application to religion).

In sum, genetic evolution produced a suite of psychological dispositions, typical of modern *sapiens*, that provides a vast amount of information (mostly from conspecifics), but also creates dispositions for acquiring certain kinds of information. Evolutionary models do not assume that acquiring more information from the environment implies less information specified in the genome. On the contrary, as comparison among species invariably confirm, acquiring more information from the environment requires richer cognitive dispositions to render such information sensible, and therefore requires more genetic specification.

How does this perspective relate to ethnographic evidence? In contrast with most mainstream cultural anthropology, but in parallel to linguistic anthropology or archaeology, evolutionary models of culture are crucially dependent on cross-cultural comparisons. A common strategy in the field consists in (*a*) identifying specific adaptive challenges encountered by *Homo* in its ancestral conditions of evolutionary adaptation; (*b*) specifying information-processing mechanisms that could meet these challenges and accrue fitness benefits—on the basis of what is independently established in experimental psychology, neuroscience, etc.; (*c*) designing new experimental protocols to establish or disconfirm the existence of these specific information-processing mechanisms; (*d*) specifying the kind of concepts and norms that would be widespread among humans, if these mechanisms operated as theoretically expected; and (*e*) testing the latter prediction against the ethnographic record from scientific publications or databases. Obviously, this is a normative ideal and the distinct steps are often shuffled out of order in actual scientific work. The main point, however, lies in the appeal to external, independently established models of mental functioning (step *b*, above). In this view, the concepts and norms specific to a given population of study are the outcome of the encounter between a unique history and the common dispositions of the species.

Two Reductive Strategies

All evolutionary models are reductive in the sense that they attempt to show that a number of variables account for a significant part of the variance in the cultural phenomena at hand. It is important at the outset to be specific about this reductive enterprise. In the social sciences, the strategy of evolutionary modeling is often misconstrued as one of "just-so" storytelling, that is, observing a particular human behavior and then producing a posthoc evolutionary story whereby that particular behavior could have been adaptive (Kurzban 2001). True, this *ex post facto* approach was typical of early applications of Darwinism to social phenomena, including models of religious behavior (Wilson 1975). For instance, Reynolds and colleagues collected comparative data on potential fitness consequences of membership in different modern religious traditions (Reynolds & Tanner 1983). Given that most religious systems include moral prescriptions about sexuality, contraception, polygamy, and infanticide, one should expect some impact on reproductive potential. Despite this empirical grounding, such studies were ultimately unsatisfactory for several reasons. First, fitness differences between historically evolving, recent traditions occur on such a short timescale that genetic evolution is an unlikely factor in accounting for these differences. Second, these studies could not address the more general question of the evolutionary background of religion, beyond cultural differences.

The strategy of current evolutionary modeling is to analyze natural function in terms that lead to nontrivial predictions that can then be tested against the evidence (Ketelaar & Ellis 2000). Two main explanatory strategies have been developed in this direction. One considers cross-culturally recurrent features of religious behaviors and their potential or actually measured effects on fitness. The other focuses on the evolved psychology that led to religious thought and behavior. Although both types of models hinge on the notion of evolved adaptations, they differ in the emphasis placed on proximate causation (if any) that is involved in such adaptations and the empirical consequences (if any) that follow. The first strategy tries to proceed directly from religious behav-

ior to hypotheses about evolutionary processes that would have led to such phenomena. This is close to the general approach of early sociobiology (Wilson 1975) and behavioral ecology (Krebs & Davies 1984). Alternatively, religious behavior may be explained in terms of underlying capacities or dispositions, which themselves are seen as outcomes of evolution. This is closer to the general approach in recent nonhuman sociobiology (Kacelnik 2003) and in evolutionary psychology (Kirkpatrick 2006). Here, we discuss these two strategies.

COST AND COMMITMENT

Commitment and Signals

A striking characteristic of most religious thought and behavior is that they do not seem to confer any direct fitness advantage on the practitioners. So, from an evolutionary viewpoint, most religious phenomena might seem to be either maladaptive or adaptively neutral (Durham 1991). However, evolutionary biology also documents specific ways in which fitness costs can become adaptive. This is particularly so in the case of signaling, an area of intense work in recent evolutionary biology (Grafen 1990). Signaling requires the coevolution of sender and receiver capacities (Rowe 1999). A central problem is the evolution of honest signals, which reliably inform an organism about qualities of others. In recent years, biologists have focused especially on costly signals, which are reliable because they are difficult to fake and thereby provide direct indices of the fitness qualities they are supposed to advertise (Zahavi & Zahavi 1997). For example, gazelles advertise their strength and dexterity by stotting (high-jumping) in front of a predator. The direct fitness cost of this relative vulnerability is offset if the predator chooses to redirect its attention to less nimble prey. Under such specific conditions, costly signaling can become an evolutionarily stable strategy (Grafen 1990). Some human cultural behaviors may also be described in these terms, as costly signals that provide ultimate fitness advantages.

Signals are especially important in intensely social species like humans, who can be said to live in the "cognitive niche" (Tooby & DeVore 1987), that is, to survive on information extracted from the natural and social environment. Information about conspecifics is crucial to social exchange, especially information about their intentions and dispositions, because there are clear and immediate rewards for opportunistic defection, that is, for reaping the benefits of social exchange without paying its costs. So how could exchange and cooperation ever evolve? A number of capacities may be involved. Reciprocal altruism, for instance, simply requires one to recall which individuals cooperated and which defected, together with a disposition to return the favor (Trivers 1971). However, human cooperation goes much further than that, and people often display costly, nonopportunistic behaviors. Humans are more altruistic than expected utility would predict. This disposition to cooperate is manifest in economic games (Smith 2003) and everyday behaviors (Frank 1988). Why is that the case?

Cooperation often requires that people sacrifice an immediate benefit for a delayed reward, an arrangement that goes against the grain of evolved discounting strategies (Ainslie 2005, Rachlin 2006). A possible solution is to evolve a system of emotions that provide immediate negative rewards (e.g., guilt) for opportunistic behaviors and positive ones (e.g., pride) for cooperation. However, these dispositions are worthwhile only if they override rational self-interest and are honestly signaled. This may be why some emotions and moral feelings associated with cooperation are neither rational nor easy to conceal (Frank 1988). According to Frank, they constitute commitment devices whereby one ties one's own hands to signal a disposition to cooperate, thereby garnering the benefit of being seen as a reliable partner (Frank 1988).

Another possible factor is the evolution of "tribal instincts" (Richerson & Boyd 2001). Humans are notable for their demonstration of strong reciprocity, typically within small ethno-linguistic groups or within modern nations that mimic the language of tribal affiliation (common ancestry territory, mores, etc.) (Gintis 2000, 2003). The specific norms of the community become the object of great emotional commitment (Nichols 2002), and norm violations trigger punitive attitudes (Price et al. 2002). Modern humans may have evolved a propensity to cooperate within groups that share common norms, a propensity that may have spread by group selection at the cultural, not genetic, level (Boyd & Richerson 1990). This would provide the background against which sharing or other nonopportunistic dispositions naturally develop in human beings.

Religion as Signals

Is religion a form of costly signaling? As one author has noted, "most religions are expressed in elaborate rituals that are costly in time and sometimes in other ways" (Irons 2001). Initiation rites are generally painful, and many rites require expensive preparations. In a more general way, religious thought and behavior would seem to mobilize cognitive resources away from survival and reproduction, being focused on nonphysical imagined agency. Assuming that religious activity is costly, does it provide signals? To a large extent it does, given that most activity of this kind is both public and formalized, so that people's commitments to the local ritual system are observable by all (Sosis 2003). On the basis of a comparative study of small communities, Sosis showed that cost is indeed an important factor. Religious groups that require a greater investment in costly rituals tend to remain more cohesive (Sosis & Bressler 2003).

This framework requires a significant change of perspective in our understanding of religious activity. First, it describes religion mostly in terms of communication rather than internal beliefs. What matters here is what people demonstrate to others. Second, it suggests that internal states, beliefs, and emotions may be tools recruited in the development of such demonstrations, which is why this approach is best seen as a complement to commitment and strong reciprocity models.

In its current formulation, the costly signal hypothesis suggests that religion is a straightforward adaptation. Dispositions to entertain religious thought and communicate them to others emerged because of their impact on fitness (Bulbulia 2004), distinct from the notion that religious solidarity provides benefit to the group (Wilson 2002). Obviously, such a strong claim requires equally strong empirical evidence, which in turn depends on more precise hypotheses. First, one must specify to what extent "religion" is actually costly and signaling, in the precise sense required by biological models (Cronk 2005). Second, the framework implies that costly behaviors are the original ones, and noncostly ones are a by-product. This way of thinking might imply psychological predictions, e.g., as to the relative impact of costly vs. noncostly practices on receiver psychology, on the mental states of potential believers. These models perhaps need to be supplemented with the psychological proximate causation that is currently missing.

EXPERIENCE AND BELIEF

What is the role of exceptional experience in the acquisition and transmission of religious concepts and behaviors? This is an old theme in the study of religion, which William James saw as foundational: people having such experiences becoming inspired leaders or prophets (James 1902). Experience might be a powerful factor in the diffusion of religious belief because it provides undeniable subjective grounding to concepts and norms acquired from other people. Diverse attempts have been made to relate evolutionary history and prehistory to a disposition for religious thought and behavior. However, one must first be specific about the range of "experience" considered relevant. Religious scholars sometimes extend the notion of "experience" to long-term processes of conversion (Edwards & Lewis 2001), whereas the anthropological or psychological understanding of the term is narrower, denoting such phenomena as trance, possession, and the feeling of a supernatural presence (Argyle 1990, Boyatzis 2001). Although such experiences are very diverse, potential similarities include a loss of control, positive valence, benevolence and compassion, a bird's eye perspective on one's surroundings, and an impression of personal, actual, though nonphysical presence of supportive agents (Moehle 1983).

The occurrence of such experiences is beyond doubt, but many anthropologists and religious scholars have debated their relevance to religion, asking first whether such experience is *sui generis*, and second whether it has anything to do with the persuasive power of religious cognition. On the first front, it is very difficult to argue that what is described as religious experience forms a natural kind, distinct from other kinds, of altered states of consciousness (e.g., those experienced by nonreligious individuals) (Pyysiäinen 2004, Ratcliffe 2006). Although a number of recent studies have documented the specific neural correlates of meditation and trance (Azari et al. 2001, Persinger 1999), these states do not require that individuals perceive any link to nonphysical agency. Indeed, disciplines of meditation and trance can support diametrical interpretations, either in terms of powerful agency (Sufism) or agency as an illusion (Lamaism).

Exceptional experience could be related to the evolution of religion if it had an impact on belief and commitment. Some archaeologists and anthropologists assume that experience-based commitment was a general feature of archaic religion (Dornan 2004, Winkelman 2000). This however remains hypothetical. Although altered states of consciousness were not absent among early modern humans (Hayden 2003), we do not know how widespread these practices were. In all modern groups, such states are exceptional in one's lifetime and are typically the preserve of specialists (James 1902) or particular subgroups (Bourguigon 1973). More important, most religious rituals in most places do not require exceptional experience. "Sensory pageantry" in religious ritual often includes aesthetic displays, music, euphoria, and fear or torture, but little if any disruptions of consciousness (McCauley & Lawson 2002). So the persuasive power of extraordinary experience may constitute only one of the many factors in the general diffusion of religious concepts and norms.

One may also wonder about the possible evolutionary background to a general capacity for religious belief. This question is difficult for several reasons. First, most people (including anthropologists and religious scholars) think of belief in terms of conscious, deliberate, evidence-based decisions and thereby ignore a vast complexity of underlying cognitive processes (Stich 1983). Second, our best models of mental functioning are still altogether rudimentary, as far as belief fixation is concerned (Gazzaniga 1998, Stich 1990). It is tempting to assume that acceptance of one's local religion stems from a general tendency to accept all culturally transmitted material (Dawkins 1998), but this is probably not sufficient to explain the recurrent features of religious thought, or indeed of cultural transmission in general (Sperber 1996).

In religious scholarship, commitment to religious ideas is often construed in terms of the relative weighing of belief vs. unbelief, given a set of accessible arguments (Vergote 1985). However, this way of thinking about commitment may be a residue of defensive, post-Enlightenment religious institutions, in which "religion" is construed as an intellectual territory to be defended against other forms of knowledge more than a property of belief in general. Indeed, it would seem that for most people in most human groups, norms and concepts are made compelling by processes that largely escape conscious scrutiny, which may explain why the notion of "belief" is alien to most religious traditions (Needham 1972).

Cognitive scientists have emphasized two features of everyday beliefs that may be relevant here. First, to entertain a representation, e.g., of a particular situation, inferences are generated (possible causes, consequences, associations with similar situations) that would determine if the representation was true, even in cases where that representation is clearly perceived as false (Gilbert 1991). Second, most religious statements are represented not as simple propositions but as complex formulae of the form "Proposition p is x," in which the "x" may stand for "true," "guaranteed by the ancestors," "said by the prophets," etc. Such statements are meta-represented (Cosmides & Tooby 2000, Sperber 1997). They constitute "reflective beliefs," distinct from intuitive beliefs (e.g., that a table is a solid object) by the fact that reflective beliefs are explicitly represented along with comments on their validity (Sperber 1997).

This view would suggest that two processes are involved in generating commitment to religious statements. First, particular statements are meta-represented so that the propositional content is specifically linked to particular authorities, which may strengthen their plausibility even when the content is not entirely elucidated (Koenig et al. 2004). Second, people establish particular associations among these socially transmitted statements, particular events, and background cognitive principles (Boyer 1994)—a process we describe in the following section.

THE COGNITIVE TURN

Domain-Specific Dispositions

A proper understanding of cultural phenomena should start with an understanding of the cognitive processes whereby cultural representations are acquired, stored, and transmitted (Sperber 1996). In the past 15 years, this "cognitive turn" has resulted in what could be called a standard cognitive model of religious thought (Atran 2002; Barrett 2000, 2004; Boyer 1992, 2001; Lawson & McCauley 1990; Pyysiäinen 2001). This is the consequence of remarkable progress in experimental psychology, developmental psychology, and cognitive neuroscience, which are converging toward a description of mental functioning as the operation of many different functional systems, each of which is geared to representing a particular domain of reality (Hirschfeld &

Gelman 1994). For instance, children develop from infancy an understanding of physical and mechanical processes (Baillargeon 2004) and number (Feigenson et al. 2004, Xu et al. 2005), as well as early understandings of biological animacy (Rochat et al. 1997) and the mental states of other agents (Song et al. 2005). All these processes are based on specific epigenetic principles that initialize domain-specific learning processes (Gelman 1994, Gelman & Brenneman 1994). Young humans are disposed to extract enormous amounts of information from their social and natural environment precisely because they are equipped with sophisticated prior principles that guide learning and development (Boyer & Barrett 2005). Despite important developmental changes in knowledge, these early principles also inform adult intuitive expectations about physical objects, intentional agents, and biological processes.

As a result of these largely tacit learning principles, some types of representations and associations are intrinsically easier to acquire, remember, and communicate than others. This would suggest a fractionated model of religion, in which different aspects of religious thought and behavior activate different mental capacities.

Religious Ontologies: Agents and Objects

The central feature of religious thought and behavior is a set of beliefs about nonphysical agents. In cognitive terms, such beliefs are a subset of a larger repertoire of supernatural concepts, found in religion but also in fantasy, dreams, superstitions, etc. Supernatural concepts are highly constrained by domain-specific assumptions about persons, solid objects, and biological beings. For instance, a spirit is a special kind of person, a magic wand a special kind of artifact, a talking tree a special kind of plant. Such notions are salient and inferentially productive because they combine specific features that violate some default expectations for the domain with nonviolated expectations held by default as true of the entire domain (Boyer

1994). These combinations of explicit violation and tacit inference are culturally widespread and constitute a memory optimum (Barrett & Nyhof 2001, Boyer & Ramble 2001). This may be because explicit violations of expectations are attention-grabbing, whereas preserved nonviolated expectations allow one to reason about the postulated agents or objects (Boyer 1994).

A notion of god or spirit combines salient, explicitly transmitted violations of expectations (a god can move through physical objects, be at several places at once, etc.) and tacit, standard expectations of intuitive psychology (a god perceives what happens, remembers what he perceived, believes what he remembers, acts to bring about desired states of affairs, etc.). The human imagination tends to project humanlike and person-like features onto nonhuman or nonperson-like aspects of the environment; such representations are attention-grabbing or enjoyable; they are found in all religious traditions (Guthrie 1993). But anthropomorphism in religious concepts is also rather selective. That is, the domain of intuitions and inferences that is projected is intentional agency, more frequently and consistently projected than any other domain of human characteristics (Barrett & Keil 1996).

In this sense, concepts of religious agency can be described as derived from (and a possible by-product of) evolved dispositions to represent physical objects and intentional agents. But what is remarkable in religion is not just the production of supernatural concepts but also their social and emotional importance, which in a cognitive account also derives from evolved dispositions to morality and social interaction (Boyer 2000).

Morality and Religion

In many human groups, supernatural agency is associated with moral understandings. This may take the form of explicit moral codes supposedly laid down by gods or ancestors or stories of exemplary semimythical ethical paragons. More generally, people assume that supernatural agents keep a watch on them and are concerned about moral behavior (Boyer 2001). A cognitive-evolutionary account may explain why this latter assumption is "natural" enough to be found in nonliterate groups but also in the spontaneous religious thinking of most religious believers.

Developmental evidence suggests that young children have an early understanding of moral imperatives. In particular, even preschoolers judge that moral norms, especially concerning justice or harm to others, are compelling whether or not they are expressed by an authority, apply to all places and contexts, and justify punishment when violated (Turiel 1983). These intuitions are remarkably stable across cultures (Song et al. 1987, Yau & Smetana 2003). Moral understandings, far from being dependent on socially transmitted (e.g., religious) conceptual frames, develop before such concepts are intelligible to children, and regardless of which religious concepts are entertained by adults around the child (indeed, regardless of whether there are any religious concepts in the child's cultural environment).

Interestingly, many early-developing and strongly emotional norms focus on social coordination (e.g., norms about sharing, cooperating, not harming others) and coalitional signals (e.g., norms about etiquette, disgust at strangers' typical behaviors) (Nichols 2002, Stich 2006). This is why it makes sense to describe the development of moral feelings and intuitions in the context of evolved dispositions for social interaction (Katz 2000, Krebs 1998). Moral understandings are an outcome of the commitment and solidarity mechanisms described above (see Commitment and Signals section). In this view, it is not surprising that moral intuitions exist prior to and outside of religious commitment, in much the same form across individuals, and with the same compelling force (Krebs & Van Hesteren 1994). Nor should it be surprising, then, that when people associate their moral understandings with nonphysical agency, the association tends to be a posthoc rationalization. Although religious believers generally hold that nonphysical agency is the origin of morality, a cogni-

tive model would suggest the reverse: that our moral feelings emerge independently but are consequently recruited to lend plausibility to the moral notions of religious agents.

Religious morality is special only in that it adds an imagined agent (a god or ancestor) as a morally competent witness of one's own actions. In a series of experiments with children and adults, Bering has demonstrated that subjects readily consider nonphysical or dead agents as participants in their current situation. Children and adults are prepared to entertain the notion that nonphysical agents are trying to communicate with them, and—importantly—these agents are generally (though implicitly) construed as having full access to morally relevant aspects of a situation, such as people's motivations and the moral value of their actions. Supernatural agents thereby come to be involved in representing how our actions would appear to others, particularly in terms of moral judgment (Bering 2002, 2006; Boyer 2001).

Ritualized Behavior

Central to our intuitive definition of religion is the performance of rituals, more or less directly connected to beliefs about nonphysical agents. The notion of "ritual" is notoriously ambiguous, a fact that some authors see as a manifestation of a highly flexible form of symbolism (Bell 1992). Others have argued that the vagueness lies in our categories and that all sorts of behaviors could be considered rituals by virtue of a very loose family resemblance so that the term is effectively useless (Lienard & Boyer 2006). By contrast, there are some precise empirical criteria for what could more selectively be called "ritualized behavior" (Rappaport 1979). We can detect that specific sequences of action, in a particular human group, are compelling (one must perform them, given particular circumstances), rigidly scripted (one must perform them in the precise manner described), divorced from goals (specific actions are performed without connection to usual empirical goals) and often internally redundant (the actions are reiterated, often a prescribed number of times) (Rappaport 1979). Also, recurrent features of ritualized behavior include the use of special colors, a focus on numbers, the urge to delimit a specially protected space, an interest in cleansing and purity, and an insistence on order and symmetry (Dulaney & Fiske 1994, Fiske & Haslam 1997). These themes are found in socially acquired ceremonial behaviors, including religion, but also in obsessive-compulsive pathologies (Freud 1906[1948]) and in normal child development (Evans et al. 1997).

Classical anthropology and psychology of religion assumed that rituals made it possible to convey deep symbolic meanings (Bell 1992, Gluckman 1975, Turbott 1997). This view seems less than compelling to cognitive anthropologists, given that many rituals include vague, incoherent, paradoxical, or just plain meaningless elements (Humphrey & Laidlaw 1993, Staal 1990). Indeed, ritualization reduces rather than increases the amount of information potentially conveyed (Bloch 1974). So why should there be a disposition for such behaviors?

Several authors have proposed that ritualized behavior is, in fact, derivative. First, ritual scripts activate an intuitive understanding of action that is also present in the representation of ordinary, nonritual behavior (Lawson & McCauley 1990). Second, the particular themes of ritualized behavior may emerge from evolved cognitive and motivational systems geared to the representation of indirect threats to fitness (Lienard & Boyer 2006). Humans can detect indirect cues of unobservable danger, such as the potential presence of predators and enemies (Barrett 2005), the risk of contagion (Siegal 1988), and threats to status and coalitional protection (Harcourt & de Waal 1992). The ritualized behaviors of patients and young children seem to include many behavioral routines that are appropriate, species-specific preparations against such dangers. Culturally transmitted ritual sequences may be attention-grabbing and compelling to the extent that they implicitly trigger associations with these protective routines (Lienard & Boyer 2006).

This notion would explain the cultural spread of these ritualized sequences in epidemiological terms, as a consequence of their cognitive effects on evolved dispositions. In this view, there is no special urge or capacity to perform rituals, religious or not. Rather, human minds are such that any sequence of action that is thematically related to precautionary concerns and explicitly associated with invisible danger will appear attention-grabbing and potentially more compelling than action sequences that lack these characteristics (Lienard & Boyer 2006). Over long-term cultural transmission, this would result in apparently compelling, highly prescribed sequences of nonpragmatic actions that people can readily associate with their concepts of nonphysical agency.

Magic and Misfortune

The themes of magical routines and recipes very often overlap with the precaution themes listed above. Many forms of magic constitute precautionary behaviors against real but unobservable dangers (Sørensen 2002), yet a recurrent finding is that the actions prescribed seem to have little direct causal connection to the desired result; no intermediate mechanism is represented (Needham 1976). This may not be so surprising, given that magical prescriptions typically effect changes on invisible objects, such as sources of contamination or other people's mental states. Indeed, this may be a general feature of precautionary thinking. In the domains of contagion, predation, or social relations, people are prepared to accept as plausibly efficacious recipes whose causal mechanisms are opaque (Fiddick 2004).

Magical associations also frequently activate social cognitive capacities, particularly in the representation of misfortune. People assume that the ancestors or gods are involved in various occurrences (bad crops, illness, death, etc.) but generally do not bother to represent in what way they bring about those states of affairs. That is, people's reasoning, when thinking about such situations, is entirely centered on the reasons why an ancestor would want them to fall ill or have many children and not on the causal process by which they make it happen (Boyer 2000).

This is also true of the explanation for mishaps and disorders in terms of witchcraft. Witchcraft and evil eye notions may not really seem to belong in the domain of religion, but they show that there is a tendency to focus on the possible reasons for why some agents would cause misfortune, rather than the processes whereby they could do it. In a great majority of cases, the expression of these reasons is supported by our social exchange intuitions. People refused to follow God's orders, they polluted a house against the ancestors' prescriptions, they had more wealth or good fortune than their God-decreed fate allocated them, and so on (Boyer 2000). All this supports what anthropologists have been saying for a long time on the basis of evidence gathered in the most various cultural environments: Misfortune is generally interpreted in social terms. But by itself, this familiar conclusion conceals the deeper indications that the evolved cognitive resources people bring to their understanding of interaction are crucial to their construal of misfortune.

Social Cognition

The foregoing cognitive examples indicate that, in principle, people's concepts of gods or ancestors may recruit or exploit any of the diverse psychological systems that govern social relations, simply by virtue of the gods' representations as social agents. Various other programs of research have begun teasing out additional aspects of social cognition that appear to interact meaningfully with people's notions of supernatural agents.

For example, one line of inquiry has suggested that people can form "attachment relationships" with God or other noncorporeal agents (Granqvist 2006, Kirkpatrick 2005). These proposals draw from a rich literature on attachment dynamics in cognitive development and show that under some circumstances gods or spirits can simulate a real-world attachment figure: that is, offer a safe emotional haven in times of distress, enable a sense of security, and provide a secure base from which to explore life. Such a perspective illuminates certain aspects of religion that are not easily explained by the dynamics of coalition or social exchange. For example, the need for physical proximity to icons, churches, or written texts; the importance of prayer in moments of extreme psychological distress; the importance of spiritual relationships to those in a state of bereavement all receive some explanatory purchase from attachment dynamics.

Other aspects of religious cognition, such as teleological reasoning and afterlife beliefs, may also be rooted in basic operational characteristics of social cognition (Bering 2006, Kelemen et al. 2005). Consistent with an interpretation of misfortune in social terms, an overarching bias to perceive events generally as manifestations of intentionality may contribute to a chronic sense of supernatural presence and intentional activity—a bias demonstrated even by children, e.g., with regard to the origin of natural objects (a view dubbed "intuitive theism") (Kelemen et al. 2005). Taking intentionality and social considerations a step further, another proposal considers that afterlife beliefs may originate from the interplay of theory of mind capacities, overperception of intentionality, and prosocial concerns regarding "moral" behavior vs. opportunistic behaviors (Bering 2006).

Some of these new avenues of inquiry take the big religions as their empirical purview (e.g., Christianity), so it remains to be seen to what extent their explanatory reach will extend to other forms of religion.

RELIGIOUS INSTITUTIONS

Most of humankind now lives in large-scale societies where religion is widely institutionalized. People acquire their religious concepts and practices from large-scale institutions with specially trained, officially sanctioned religious officers, rather than from face-to-face interactions with personally known ritual specialists. Also, many religious concepts and norms are acquired through literacy and electronic media rather than via oral transmission. To what extent do these changes affect the relevance of evolutionary approaches?

Two Aspects of Religious Thought and Behavior

Anthropologists have long emphasized the contrast between doctrinal systems, such as those of the "world religions," which are supported by large scale institutions, and "traditional" systems, such as village or tribe-based ancestor cults (Weber 1922), a distinction sometimes expressed as "great" vs. "small" traditions. These labels denote important differences in terms of types of institutions, kinds of practices, and the kinds of concepts and norms. First, the competence of tribal religious specialists is typically sanctioned by their audience or clients rather than by an impersonal institution. Second, the services that tribal specialists provide are highly variable and often attached to particular locations or groups. All this changes with the appearance of large-scale agrarian states, which produce religious institutions as we know them (Gellner 1989). These changes may seem beyond the scope of evolutionary approaches because they have occurred only in recent historical times. However, evolutionary considerations are still relevant for two reasons.

First, experimental studies show that institutional or organized religion has only a limited effect on people's religious cognitions, even in modern societies. Believers cultivate an explicit representation of their own beliefs that is largely in agreement with official doctrine, what Barrett has called "theological correctness" (Barrett & Keil 1996). But implicit tests show that their spontaneous, everyday judgments are based not on doctrine but on intuitive expectations similar to the various domain-specific principles described above (Barrett 2001, 2002), regardless of differences in religious traditions (Barrett 1998, Malley 2004, Slone 2004). Thus, religion as a cognitive phenomenon is generally much closer to the tribal version than to the official one. These findings are crucial for a cognitively valid anthropology of religion. They show that the raw material of much anthropological description, people's explicit statements about their own beliefs, is a fragmentary and highly misleading source of information about people's religious thoughts.

Second, the way religious institutions are built, work, and perpetuate themselves illustrates particular cognitive adaptations that predate these historical developments. Institutions themselves are constrained by evolved cognitive capacities and therefore fall within the remit of an evolutionary perspective.

Priestly Guilds and Doctrines

Kingdoms and city-states gradually evolved out of the tribes and chiefdoms that were more typical of incipient agricultural societies (Maryanski & Turner 1992). They provided economic niches for individuals and groups specialized in the provision of specific services, such as lineages or castes of specialized craftsmen, servants, functionaries, and scribes. Groups of craftsmen or other specialists are generally organized in ways that optimize each member's potential share of a limited market. This is why we find that the development of large polities with tradesmen and craftsmen also heralds the development of guilds and other such professional groups (Greif 2006). Among these are groups of "priests" as distinct from local specialists. Priests are exclusive providers of particular religious services, whose competence is guaranteed by an impersonal institution.

Institutionalization has a deep influence on religious concepts and on the use of particular cognitive capacities. Reformulating Weber's contrast between traditional and routinized forms of religion (Weber 1922), Whitehouse points out that most organized religion is centered on "doctrinal religiosity," with frequently repeated rituals and explicit religious statements taught in the form of tightly argued propositional sermons (Whitehouse 2000). These rituals are usually not ethnically or locally based, they potentially recruit members far from their point of origin, they maintain a high degree of uniformity, and they generally involve specialized personnel with a centralized organization. They recruit semantic memory in the construction of elaborate doctrines, as opposed to the unexplained, salient, "imagistic" episodes of many tribal rituals (Whitehouse 2004).

The differences in doctrine may be seen as a consequence of the specific markets and commodities involved. Religious specialists supply something (rituals, a guarantee that rituals are efficacious, a specific link to supernatural agents) that could be easily provided by competitors. Indeed, in most places with castes of religious priests, other providers exist: local witch doctors, healers, shamans, holy men, and knowledgeable elders whose claims may be just as persuasive (Gellner 1994). An optimal path for priestly guilds is to gain political influence and use it against local, informal competition, a universal phenomenon in religious history. Also, most priestly groups try to turn their services into a brand, that is, a type of service that is (*a*) delivered by all providers from a same organization in the same form, (*b*) exclusive to that organization, and (*c*) recognized as such (Giannias & Giannias 2003). The effort toward greater coherence and stability in the religious concepts and practices, as well as the systematic use of literacy, which strengthens coherence and logical structure (Goody 1986), may be a response to this new market for religious services.

The special conditions of modern industrial societies reinforce the dynamics of competition and branding (Ekelund et al. 2006), as sociologists of religion have noted, mostly on the basis of modern U.S. religion (Greeley 1982). Such economic behavior is deeply influenced by evolved cognitive capacities, a point many economists have recently emphasized (McCabe & Smith 2001, Smith 2008).

EPILOGUE

Evolutionary accounts of religious concepts and behaviors stand in contrast to other traditions in the study of religion. First, the varieties of evolutionary-cognitive framework outlined here are clearly reductionistic. Their aim is not to describe what it feels like to entertain religious thoughts, or in what way these thoughts could make sense, but to explain their occurrence and their contents (Spilka et al. 1985). Second, this account suggests that religious processes are not *sui generis*. They do not require that we assume a specific religious organ or religious mode of function in the mind (Boyer 1992). Third, even though there is a strong social demand for explaining religion in terms of a unique "origin," evolutionary and cognitive models suggest that this project makes little sense. Religion denotes a variety of behaviors and cognitive processes likely with different evolutionary backgrounds.

Evolutionary considerations are relevant beyond early, archaic religion because they illuminate cognitive processes generally present in the transmission of culture, either in ancestral times or in modern societies. They may also help address some of the current issues that confront modern attitudes toward religion. The apparent resurgence of religious extremism and its tragic consequences has prompted a flurry of commentary on how religion leads to self-sacrifice and murder. Reflection on these issues may benefit from a better description of what is involved in religious affiliation and its fundamentalist varieties (Marty & Appleby 1991, 1994). Biologically inspired models of commitment and affiliation explain how people can be persuaded of the value of extremist action (Sageman 2004) and why the connection between religion and self-sacrifice is less direct than we generally presume (Pape 2005).

Is religion an adaptation? An evolutionary perspective implies that manifest behaviors are enabled and supported by functional systems, which are the outcome of natural selection. Some of these functional systems can be construed as adaptations, that is, reliably developing capacities or traits that provide evidence of complex functional design and confer potential reproductive advantages (or did so under ancestral conditions) (Symons 1992, Williams 1966). Also, the trait would have evolved gradually from previous versions; adaptive advantages would have been conferred by each incremental change because evolution does not look ahead. These stringent criteria indicate that few of the features involved in serving some function can be described as evolutionary adaptations. Many features of organisms can be parsimoniously explained in terms of preadaptations and by-products of adaptations, as well as the outcome of genetic drift and other nonevolutionary processes (Buss et al. 1998). As far as religion is concerned, one can distinguish between models that tend to present religion (or some part thereof) as an adaptation (like the capacity to learn a natural language) (Irons 2001, Wilson 2002) and models couched in terms of by-products (like the capacity to read and write) (Barrett 2004; Boyer 1992, 2001). However, note that general statements about adaptations and by-products are conclusions, not starting points. Before we can say anything about the adaptive function of religious thoughts or behaviors, we must analyze what makes them possible, which is the substantial contribution of the models reviewed here.

So far, traditional cultural anthropology, contrary to archaeology and other subfields, has made little use of the tools and findings of evolutionary biology (Durham 1991). Indeed, the field has evinced a considerable hostility to the introduction of evolution and genetics in the study of culture (Brown 1991, Cronk 1999, Fox 1975, Tooby & Cosmides 1992). More generally, a widespread reluctance to entertain explanatory scientific reduction (D'Andrade 1995) has hindered an integration of cultural phenomena in the study of human nature (Wilson 1998). Resolution of such

paradigmatic disputes lies less in philosophical debates than in comparing the relative explanatory power of different approaches. That is why proponents of an integrated, evolutionary-cognitive approach to cultural phenomena will need to provide more empirical evidence, particularly more cross-cultural studies, to overcome the discipline's preference for "segregation" models, which depict human cultures as lying outside the influence of evolution and genetics.

Religion may be a particularly apposite test case for the evolutionary cognitive approach. The domain is a priori unconstrained—people might let their imaginations run freely when it comes to representing nonphysical agency. But we do find an impressive set of recurrent features, for which classical anthropological theory has no coherent, predictive, independently based explanatory hypotheses. By contrast, the models reviewed above show that evolutionary perspectives can help us make sense of specifically human, and otherwise puzzling, cultural phenomena. Religion is only one among various domains in which very different socially transmitted input results in highly similar, recurrent cultural traits. Notions of nonphysical agency, their powers, and their connections to human beings are so widespread that explanations couched purely in terms of local knowledge are clearly missing the point. What is needed is a more detailed investigation into an evolved psychology shaped by natural selection.

DISCLOSURE STATEMENT

The authors are not aware of any biases that might be perceived as affecting the objectivity of this review.

LITERATURE CITED

Ainslie G. 2005. Précis of breakdown of will. *Behav. Brain Sci.* 28:635–73

Argyle M. 1990. The psychological explanation of religious experience. *Psyke Logos* 11:267–74

Atran SA. 2002. *In Gods We Trust. The Evolutionary Landscape of Religion*. Oxford: Oxford Univ. Press. 374 pp.

Azari NP, Nickel J, Wunderlich G, Niedeggen M, Hefter H, et al. 2001. Neural correlates of religious experience. *Eur. J. Neurosci.* 13:4

Baillargeon R. 2004. Infants' physical world. *Curr. Dir. Psychol. Sci.* 13:89–94

Barkow JH, Cosmides L, Tooby J, eds. 1992. *The Adapted Mind: Evolutionary Psychology and the Generation of Culture*. New York: Oxford Univ. Press

Barrett HC. 2005. Adaptations to predators and prey. See Buss 2005, pp. 200–23

Barrett JL. 1998. Cognitive constraints on Hindu concepts of the divine. *J. Sci. Study Relig.* 37:608–19

Barrett JL. 2000. Exploring the natural foundations of religion. *Trends Cogn. Sci.* 4:29–34

Barrett JL. 2001. How ordinary cognition informs petitionary prayer. *J. Cogn. Cult.* 1(3):259–69

Barrett JL. 2002. Smart gods, dumb gods, and the role of social cognition in structuring ritual intuitions. *J. Cogn. Cult.* 2(3):183–93

Barrett JL. 2004. *Why Would Anyone Believe in God?* Walnut Creek, CA: Altamira. 200 pp.

Barrett JL, Keil FC. 1996. Conceptualizing a nonnatural entity: anthropomorphism in God concepts. *Cogn. Psychol.* 31:219–47

Barrett JL, Nyhof M. 2001. Spreading non-natural concepts: the role of intuitive conceptual structures in memory and transmission of cultural materials. *J. Cogn. Cult.* 1(1):69–100

Bell CM. 1992. *Ritual Theory, Ritual Practice*. New York: Oxford Univ. Press. x, 270 pp.

Bering JM. 2002. Intuitive conceptions of dead agents' minds: the natural foundations of afterlife beliefs as phenomenological boundary. *J. Cogn. Cult.* 2:263–308

Bering JM. 2006. The folk psychology of souls. *Behav. Brain Sci.* 29:453–62

Bloch M. 1974. Symbols, song, dance, and features of articulation: Is religion an extreme form of traditional authority? *Eur. J. Sociol.* 15:55–81

Bourguignon E, ed. 1973. *Religion, Altered States of Consciousness and Social Change*. Columbus: Ohio State Univ. Press

Boyatzis CJ. 2001. A critique of models of religious experience. *Int. J. Psychol. Relig.* 11:247–58

Boyd R, Richerson PJ. 1985. *Culture and the Evolutionary Process*. Chicago: Univ. Chicago Press

Boyd R, Richerson PJ. 1990. Culture and cooperation. In *Beyond Self-Interest*, ed. JJ Mansbridge, pp. 111–32. Chicago: Univ. Chicago Press

Boyd R, Richerson PJ. 1996. Why culture is common, but cultural evolution is rare. In *Evolution of Social Behaviour Patterns in Primates and Man*, ed. WG Runciman, JM Smith, pp. 77–93. Oxford: Oxford Univ. Press

Boyer P. 1992. Explaining religious ideas: outline of a cognitive approach. *Numen* 39:27–57

Boyer P. 1994. Cognitive constraints on cultural representations: natural ontologies and religious ideas. See Hirschfeld & Gelman 1994, pp. 391–411

Boyer P. 2000. Functional origins of religious concepts: conceptual and strategic selection in evolved minds [Malinowski Lecture 1999]. *J. R. Anthropol. Inst.* 6:195–214

Boyer P. 2001. *Religion Explained. Evolutionary Origins of Religious Thought*. New York: Basic Books. 403 pp.

Boyer P, Barrett HC. 2005. Evolved intuitive ontology. See Buss 2005, pp. 96–118

Boyer P, Ramble C. 2001. Cognitive templates for religious concepts: cross-cultural evidence for recall of counter-intuitive representations. *Cogn. Sci.* 25:535–64

Brown DE. 1991. *Human Universals*. New York: McGraw Hill

Bulbulia J. 2004. Religious costs as adaptations that signal altruistic intention. *Evol. Cogn.* 10:19–42

Buss DM, ed. 2005. *Handbook of Evolutionary Psychology*. Hoboken, NJ: Wiley

Buss DM, Haselton MG, Shackelford TK, Bleske AL, Wakefield JC. 1998. Adaptations, exaptations, and spandrels. *Am. Psychol.* 53:533–48

Cosmides L, Tooby J. 2000. Consider the source: the evolution of adaptations for decoupling and metarepresentation. In *Metarepresentations: A Multidisciplinary Perspective*, ed. D Sperber, pp. 53–115. New York: Oxford Univ. Press

Cronk L. 1999. *That Complex Whole. Culture and the Evolution of Behavior*. Boulder, CO: Westview

Cronk L. 2005. The application of animal signaling theory to human phenomena: some thoughts and clarifications. *Soc. Sci. Inf.* 44:603–20

D'Andrade RG. 1995. *The Development of Cognitive Anthropology*. Cambridge/New York: Cambridge Univ. Press. xiv, 272 pp.

Darwin C. 1871. *The Descent of Man, and Selection in Relation to Sex*. London: Murray

Dawkins R. 1998. *Unweaving the Rainbow: Science, Delusion, and the Appetite for Wonder*. Boston: Houghton Mifflin. xiv, 336 pp.

Dornan JL. 2004. Beyond belief: religious experience, ritual, and cultural neuro-phenomenology in the interpretation of past religious systems. *Camb. Archaeol. J.* 14:12–21

Dulaney S, Fiske AP. 1994. Cultural rituals and obsessive-compulsive disorder: Is there a common psychological mechanism? *Ethos* 22:243–83

Durham WH. 1991. *Coevolution. Genes, Cultures and Human Diversity*. Stanford, CA: Stanford Univ. Press

Edwards AC, Lewis MJ. 2001. The Batson-Schoenrade-Ventis model of religious experience: critique and reformulation. *Int. J. Psychol. Relig.* 11:215–34

Ekelund RBJ, Hébert RF, Tollison RD. 2006. *The Marketplace of Christianity*. Cambridge, MA: MIT Press. 328 pp., 8 illus. pp.

Eliade M. 1959. *The Sacred and the Profane. The Nature of Religion.* New York: Harcourt Brace Jovanovich

Eliade M, Trask WR. 1964. *Shamanism: Archaic Techniques of Ecstasy*. New York: Pantheon. xxiii, 610 pp.

Evans DW, Leckman JF, Carter A, Reznick JS, et al. 1997. Ritual, habit, and perfectionism: the prevalence and development of compulsive-like behavior in normal young children. *Child Dev.* 68:58–68

Falk D. 2000. Hominid brain evolution and the origins of music. In *The Origins of Music*, ed. NL Wallin, B Merker, pp. 197–216. Cambridge, MA: MIT Press

Feigenson L, Dehaene S, Spelke E. 2004. Core systems of number. *Trends Cogn. Sci.* 8:307–14

Fiddick L. 2004. Domains of deontic reasoning: resolving the discrepancy between the cognitive and moral reasoning literatures. *Q. J. Exp. Psychol. Hum. Exp. Psychol.* 57A:447–74

Fiske AP, Haslam N. 1997. Is obsessive-compulsive disorder a pathology of the human disposition to perform socially meaningful rituals? Evidence of similar content. *J. Nerv. Ment. Dis.* 185:211–22

Fox R. 1975. *Biosocial Anthropology*. New York: Wiley. xii, 169 pp.

Frank RH. 1988. *Passions within Reason. The Strategic Role of the Emotions.* New York: Norton

Freud S. 1906[1948]. Zwangsbehandlungen und religionsübungen. In *Gesammelte Werke von Sigmund Freud, Chronologisch Geordnet*, ed. Aea Freud, pp. 107–16. London: Imago

Gazzaniga MS. 1998. *The Mind's Past*. Berkeley: Univ. Calif. Press. xv, 201 pp.

Gellner DN. 1994. Priests, healers, mediums and witches: the context of possession in the Kathmandu Valley, Nepal. *Man* 29:27–48

Gellner E. 1989. *Plough, Sword, and Book: The Structure of Human History*. Chicago: Univ. Chicago Press. 288 pp.

Gelman R. 1994. Constructivism and supporting environments. In *Implicit and Explicit Knowledge: An Educational Approach*, ed. D Tirosh, pp. 55–82. Norwood, NJ: Ablex

Gelman R, Brenneman K. 1994. First principles can support both universal and culture specific learning about number and music. See Hirschfeld & Gelman, pp. 369–90

Giannias DA, Giannias GA. 2003. Branding in microeconomics: a modelling approach and an application. *RISEC Int. Rev. Econ. Bus.* 50:109–20

Gilbert DT. 1991. How mental systems believe. *Am. Psychol.* 46:107–19

Gintis H. 2000. Strong reciprocity and human sociality. *J. Theor. Biol.* 206:169–79

Gintis H. 2003. The hitchhiker's guide to altruism: gene-culture coevolution, and the internalization of norms. *J. Theor. Biol.* 220:407–18

Gluckman M. 1975. Specificity of social-anthropological studies of ritual. *Ment. Health Soc.* 2:1–17

Goody J. 1986. *The Logic of Writing and the Organization of Society*. Cambridge, UK: Cambridge Univ. Press

Grafen A. 1990. Biological signals as handicaps. *J. Theor. Biol.* 144:517–46

Granqvist P. 2006. Religion as a by-product of evolved psychology: the case of attachment and implications for brain and religion research. See McNamara 2006, pp. 105–50

Greeley AM. 1982. *Religion, A Secular Theory*. New York/London: Free Press/Collier Macmillan. viii, 192 pp.

Greif A. 2006. *Institutions and the Path to the Modern Economy: Lessons from Medieval Trade*. Cambridge, UK/New York: Cambridge Univ. Press. xix, 503 pp.

Guthrie SE. 1993. *Faces in the Clouds. A New Theory of Religion.* New York: Oxford Univ. Press

Harcourt AH, de Waal FB, eds. 1992. *Coalitions and Alliances in Humans and other Animals*. Oxford: Oxford Univ. Press

Hayden B. 2003. *Shamans, Sorcerers, and Saints: A Prehistory of Religion*. Washington, DC: Smithsonian. xi, 468 pp.

Hinde RA. 1999. *Why Gods Persist: A Scientific Approach to Religion*. London/New York: Routledge. vi, 288 pp.

Hirschfeld LA, Gelman SA, eds. 1994. *Mapping The Mind: Domain-Specificity in Culture and Cognition*. New York: Cambridge Univ. Press

Hovers E, Ilani S, Bar-Yosef O, Vandermeersch B. 2003. An early case of color symbolism: ochre use by modern humans in Qafzeh cave with CA* comment. *Curr. Anthropol.* 44:491–522

Humphrey C, Laidlaw J. 1993. *Archetypal Actions. A Theory of Ritual as a Mode of Action and the Case of the Jain Puja*. Oxford: Clarendon

Irons W. 2001. Religion as a hard-to-fake sign of commitment. See Nesse 2001, pp. 292–309

James W. 1902. *The Varieties of Religious Experience: A Study in Human Nature. Being the Gifford Lectures on Natural Religion Delivered at Edinburgh in 1901–1902*. New York: Mod. Libr. xviii, 526 pp.

Kacelnik A. 2003. The evolution of patience. In *Time and Decision: Economic and Psychological Perspectives on Intertemporal Choice*, ed. G Loewenstein, D Read, R Baumeister, pp. 115–38. New York: Russell Sage

Katz LD, ed. 2000. *Evolutionary Origins of Morality: Cross-Disciplinary Perspectives*. Thorverton, UK: Imprint Acad. xvi, 352 pp.

Kelemen D, Callanan MA, Casler K, Pâerez-Granados DR. 2005. Why things happen: teleological explanation in parent-child conversations. *Dev. Psychol.* 41:251–64

Ketelaar T, Ellis BJ. 2000. Are evolutionary explanations unfalsifiable? Evolutionary psychology and the Lakatosian philosophy of science. *Psychol. Inq.* 11:1–21

Kirkpatrick LA. 2005. *Attachment, Evolution, and the Psychology of Religion*. New York: Guilford. xvi, 400 pp.

Kirkpatrick LA. 2006. Religion is not an adaptation. In *Where God and Science Meet: How Brain and Evolutionary Studies Alter Our Understanding of Religion*. Vol. 1: *Evolution, Genes, and the Religious Brain*, ed. P McNamara, pp. 173–93. Westport, CT: Praeger/Greenwood

Koenig MA, Clément F, Harris PL. 2004. Trust in testimony: children's use of true and false statements. *Psychol. Sci.* 15:694–98

Krebs D. 1998. The evolution of moral behaviors. In *Handbook of Evolutionary Psychology: Ideas, Issues, and Applications*, ed. CB Crawford, DL Krebs, pp. 337–68. Mahwah, NJ: Lawrence Erlbaum

Krebs D, Van Hesteren F. 1994. The development of altruism: toward an integrative model. *Dev. Rev.* 14:103–58

Krebs JR, Davies NB. 1984. *Behavioural Ecology: An Evolutionary Approach*. Sunderland, MA: Sinauer. xi, 493 pp.

Kurzban R. 2001. The social psychophysics of cooperation: nonverbal communication in a public goods game. *J. Nonverbal Behav.* 25:241–59

Lawson ET, McCauley RN. 1990. *Rethinking Religion: Connecting Cognition and Culture*. Cambridge, UK: Cambridge Univ. Press

Lienard P, Boyer P. 2006. Why cultural rituals? A cultural selection model of ritualized behaviour. *Am. Anthropol.* 108:814–27

Lumsden CJ, Wilson EO. 1981. *Genes, Minds and Culture*. Cambridge, MA: Harvard Univ. Press

Malley B. 2004. *How the Bible Works: An Anthropological Study of Evangelical Biblicism*. Walnut Creek, CA: Altamira. ix, 173 pp.

Marty ME, Appleby RS, eds. 1991. *Fundamentalisms Observed*. Chicago: Univ. Chicago Press

Marty ME, Appleby RS, eds. 1994. *Accounting for Fundamentalisms. The Dynamic Character of Movements*. Chicago: Univ. Chicago Press

Maryanski A, Turner JH. 1992. *The Social Cage. Human Nature and the Evolution of Society*. Stanford, CA: Stanford Univ. Press

McCabe KA, Smith VL. 2001. Goodwill accounting and the process of exchange. In *Bounded Rationality: The Adaptive Toolbox*, ed. G Gigerenzer, R Selten, pp. 319–40. Cambridge, MA: MIT Press

McCauley RN, Lawson ET. 2002. *Bringing Ritual to Mind: Psychological Foundations of Cultural Forms*. Cambridge, UK: Cambridge Univ. Press. 225 pp.

McNamara P, ed. *Where God and Science Meet: How Brain and Evolutionary Studies Alter Our Understanding of Religion*. Vol. 2: *The Neurology of Religious Experience*. Westport, CT: Praeger/Greenwood

Mithen SJ. 1996. *The Prehistory of the Mind*. London: Thames & Hudson

Mithen SJ. 1999. Symbolism and the supernatural. In *The Evolution of Culture*, ed. R Dunbar, C Knight, C Power, pp. 147–71. New Brunswick, NJ: Rutgers Univ. Press

Moehle D. 1983. Cognitive dimensions of religious experiences. *J. Exp. Soc. Psychol.* 19:122–45

Needham R. 1972. *Belief, Language and Experience.* Chicago: Chicago Univ. Press

Needham R. 1976. Skulls and causality. *Man* 11:71–88

Nesse R, ed. 2001. *Evolution and the Capacity for Commitment.* New York: Russell Sage

Nichols S. 2002. Norms with feeling: towards a psychological account of moral judgment. *Cognition* 84:221–36

Otto R. 1959. *The Idea of the Holy.* London: Oxford Univ. Press

Pailin DA. 1984. *Attitudes to Other Religions: Comparative Religion in Seventeenth- and Eighteenth-Century Britain.* Manchester, UK/Dover, NH: Manchester Univ. Press. ix, 339 pp.

Pape RA. 2005. *Dying to Win: The Strategic Logic of Suicide Terrorism.* New York: Random House. viii, 335 pp.

Pearson JL. 2001. *Shamanism and the Ancient Mind: A Cognitive Approach to Archaeology.* Walnut Creek, CA: AltaMira. ix, 195 pp.

Persinger MA. 1999. Near-death experiences and ecstasy: a product of the organization of the human brain. In *Mind Myths: Exploring Popular Assumptions about the Mind and Brain*, ed. SD Sala, pp. 85–99. Chichester, UK: Wiley

Price ME, Cosmides L, Tooby J. 2002. Punitive sentiment as an antifree rider psychological device. *Evol. Hum. Behav.* 23:203–31

Pyysiäinen I. 2001. *How Religion Works. Towards a New Cognitive Science of Religion.* Leiden: Brill. 272 pp.

Pyysiäinen I. 2004. *Magic, Miracles, and Religion: A Scientist's Perspective.* Walnut Creek, CA: AltaMira. xx, 277 pp.

Rachlin H. 2006. Notes on discounting. *J. Exp. Anal. Behav.* 85:425–35

Rappaport RA. 1979. *Ecology, Meaning and Religion.* Berkeley, CA: N. Atl. Books

Ratcliffe M. 2006. Neurotheology: a science of what? See McNamara 2006, pp. 81–104

Reinhart AK. 1986. *Before Revelation: The Boundaries of Muslim Moral Knowledge.* Albany, NY: State Univ. N. Y. Press

Reynolds V, Tanner RES. 1983. *The Biology of Religion.* New York: Longman

Richerson P, Boyd R. 2001. The evolution of subjective commitment to groups: a tribal instincts hypothesis. See Nesse 2001, pp. 186–220

Richerson PJ, Boyd R. 2006. *Not by Genes Alone: How Culture Transformed Human Evolution.* Chicago/Bristol: Univ. Chicago Press/Univ. Presses

Rochat P, Morgan R, Carpenter M. 1997. Young infants' sensitivity to movement information specifying social causality. *Cogn. Dev.* 12:441–65

Rowe C. 1999. Receiver psychology and the evolution of multicomponent signals. *Anim. Behav.* 58:921–31

Sageman M. 2004. *Understanding Terror Networks.* Philadelphia: Univ. Penn. Press. ix, 220 pp.

Saler B. 1993. *Conceptualizing Religion. Immanent Anthropologists, Transcendent Natives and Unbounded Categories.* Leiden: Brill

Shirokogoroff SM. 1935. *Psychomental Complex of the Tungus.* London: K. Paul Trench Truebner

Siegal M. 1988. Children's knowledge of contagion and contamination as causes of illness. *Child Dev.* 59:1353–59

Slone DJ. 2004. *Theological Incorrectness: Why Religious People Believe What They Shouldn't.* Oxford/New York: Oxford Univ. Press. ix, 156 pp.

Smith VL. 2003. Constructivist and ecological rationality in economics. *Am. Econ. Rev.* 93:465–508

Smith VL. 2008. *Rationality in Economics: Constructivist and Ecological Forms.* Cambridge/New York: Cambridge Univ. Press

Song H-J, Baillargeon R, Fisher C. 2005. Can infants attribute to an agent a disposition to perform a particular action? *Cognition* 98:B45–55

Song M-J, Smetana JG, Kim SY. 1987. Korean children's conceptions of moral and conventional transgressions. *Dev. Psychol.* 23:577–82

Sørensen J. 2002. *The Morphology and Function of Magic* revisited. In *Current Approaches in the Cognitive Study of Religion*, ed. V Anttonen, I Pyysiäinen, pp. 35–43. London: Continuum

Sosis R. 2003. Why aren't we all hutterites? Costly signaling theory and religious behavior. *Human Nat.* 14:91–127

Sosis R, Bressler ER. 2003. Cooperation and commune longevity: a test of the costly signaling theory of religion. *Cross-Cult. Res. J. Comp. Soc. Sci.* 37:211–39

Sperber D. 1985. Anthropology and psychology. Towards an epidemiology of representations. *Man* 20:73–89

Sperber D. 1996. *Explaining Culture: A Naturalistic Approach*. Oxford: Blackwell

Sperber D. 1997. Intuitive and reflective beliefs. *Mind Lang.* 12:67–83

Sperber D. 2000. An objection against memetics. In *Darwinizing Culture. The Status of Memetics as a Science*, ed. R Aunger, pp. 163–73. London: Oxford Univ. Press

Sperber D, Hirschfeld LA. 2004. The cognitive foundations of cultural stability and diversity. *Trends Cogn. Sci.* 8:40–46

Spilka B, Hood RW, Gorsuch RL. 1985. *The Psychology of Religion: An Empirical Approach*. Englewood Cliffs, NJ: Prentice-Hall

Staal F. 1990. *Rules Without Meaning: Ritual, Mantras, and the Human Sciences*. New York: P. Lang. xix, 490 pp.

Stich S. 1983. *From Folk-Psychology to Cognitive Science: The Case Against Belief*. Cambridge, MA: MIT. Press

Stich S. 2006. Is morality an elegant machine or a kludge? *J. Cogn. Cult.* 6:181–89

Stich SP. 1990. *The Fragmentation of Reason: Preface to a Pragmatic Theory of Cognitive Evaluation*. Cambridge, MA: MIT Press. x, 181 pp.

Symons D. 1992. On the use and misuse of Darwinism in the study of human behavior. See Barkow et al. 1992, pp. 137–59

Tooby J, Cosmides L. 1992. The psychological foundations of culture. See Barkow et al. 1992, pp. 19–136

Tooby J, DeVore I. 1987. The reconstruction of hominid behavioral evolution through strategic modeling. In *Primate Models of Hominid Behavior*, ed. W Kinzey, pp. 183–237. New York: SUNY Press

Trinkaus E, Shipman P. 1993. *The Neandertals: Changing the Image of Mankind*. New York: Knopf

Trivers RL. 1971. The evolution of reciprocal altruism. *Q. Rev. Biol.* 46:35–57

Turbott J. 1997. The meaning and function of ritual in psychiatric disorder, religion and everyday behaviour. *Aust. N. Z. J. Psychiatry* 31:835–43

Turiel E. 1983. *The Development of Social Knowledge. Morality and Convention*. Cambridge, UK: Cambridge Univ. Press

Vergote A. 1985. Psychology of religion as the study of the conflict between belief and unbelief. In *Advances in the Psychology of Religion. International Series in Experimental Social Psychology*, Vol. 11, ed. BB Laurence, pp. 52–61. Oxford: Pergamon

Weber M. 1922. *Wirtschaft und Gesellschaft*. Tübingen: J.C.B. Mohr (P. Siebeck). 840 pp.

Whitehouse H. 2000. *Arguments and Icons. Divergent Modes of Religiosity*. Oxford: Oxford Univ. Press

Whitehouse H. 2004. *Modes of Religiosity*. Walnut Creek, CA: Altamira. 200 pp.

Wiebe D. 1998. *The Politics of Religious Studies: The Continuing Conflict with Theology in the Academy*. New York: St. Martin's. xx, 332 pp.

Williams GC. 1966. *Adaptation and Natural Selection. A Critique of Some Current Evolutionary Thought*. Princeton, NJ: Princeton Univ. Press

Wilson DS. 2002. *Darwin's Cathedral: Evolution, Religion and the Nature of Society*. Chicago: Univ. Chicago Press. 268 pp.

Wilson EO. 1975. *Sociobiology: The New Synthesis*. Cambridge, MA: Belknap Press of Harvard Univ. Press. ix, 697 pp.

Wilson EO. 1998. *Consilience: The Unity of Knowledge*. London: Little Brown. 374 pp.

Winkelman M. 2000. *Shamanism: The Neural Ecology of Consciousness and Healing*. Westport, CT: Bergin & Garvey. xvi, 309 pp.

Xu F, Spelke ES, Goddard S. 2005. Number sense in human infants. *Dev. Sci.* 8:88–101

Yau J, Smetana JG. 2003. Conceptions of moral, social-conventional, and personal events among Chinese preschoolers in Hong Kong. *Child Dev.* 74:647–58

Zahavi A, Zahavi A. 1997. *The Handicap Principle: A Missing Piece of Darwin's Puzzle*. New York: Oxford Univ. Press. xvi, 286 pp.

Linguistic Diversity
in the Caucasus

Bernard Comrie

Department of Linguistics, Max Planck Institute for Evolutionary Anthropology,
D-04103 Leipzig, Germany; Department of Linguistics, University of California,
Santa Barbara, California, 93106-3100; email: comrie@eva.mpg.de

Annu. Rev. Anthropol. 2008. 37:131–43

First published online as a Review in Advance on
June 27, 2008

The *Annual Review of Anthropology* is online at
anthro.annualreviews.org

This article's doi:
10.1146/annurev.anthro.35.081705.123248

Key Words

accretion zone, exogamy, genealogical diversity, linguistic area,
structural diversity

Abstract

The Caucasus is characterized by a relatively high level of linguistic
diversity, whether measured in terms of number of languages, number
of language families, or structural properties. This is in stark contrast
to low levels of linguistic diversity in neighboring areas (Europe, the
Middle East), although the Caucasus does not reach such high levels of
linguistic diversity as are found in New Guinea. There is even a variation
between greater diversity in the North Caucasus and less diversity in
the South Caucasus. Illustrative structural properties show not only
idiosyncratic properties of individual languages and families but also
features that have spread across the boundaries separating languages
and families, sometimes with variation across languages with regard to
finer points of detail, although few features characterize the Caucasus
as a single linguistic area. Social factors have probably played at least
as important a role as has geography in the development of linguistic
diversity in the Caucasus.

INTRODUCTION

As noted by Catford (1977) in an earlier *Annual Review* contribution on languages of the Caucasus, to the medieval Arab geographers the Caucacus was the "mountain of tongues," characterized by a high degree of internal linguistic diversity, certainly relative to the large surrounding areas of Europe and the Middle East, which are characterized rather by large speech communities, their languages spoken by millions of speakers. If one includes as languages of the Caucasus languages that are spoken predominantly in the Caucasus, or at least have geographically consolidated large numbers of speakers in the Caucasus, then one is looking at ~45 languages. A map showing the geographical distribution of languages of the Caucasus is available online at **http://titus.uni-frankfurt.de/didact/karten/kauk/kaukasm.htm;** for more detail, though restricted to the three families of Kartvelian, West Caucasian, and East Caucasian, see Korjakov (2006).

A distinction must be made, however, between the North Caucasus (roughly, the part of the Caucasus region within the Russian Federation) and the South Caucasus (also known as Transcaucasia, corresponding roughly to the combined territory of Georgia, Armenia, and Azerbaijan). In the South Caucasus, we do find in general languages with larger numbers of speakers, with Georgian having ~4 million speakers (nearly all in the Caucasus), Armenian having ~3.4 million in the Caucasus (and about as many again in the diaspora), and Azerbaijani (Azeri) having ~7 million in the Caucasus (mainly Azerbaijan, with a significant spillover into the south of Daghestan, the southernmost constituent republic of the Russian Federation; there are perhaps three times as many speakers of Azerbaijani in Iran). [Except where otherwise indicated, statistics on numbers of speakers refer to native speakers and are taken either from Gordon (2005) or from the 2002 census of the Russian Federation (*Itogi 2004*). For further discussion, see Comrie (2007).] By contrast, the North Caucasus is

an area of real linguistic diversity: The languages with the largest number of speakers are Chechen (~1.3 million speakers) and Avar and Talyshi (each ~800,000 speakers), with other languages ranging down from approximately half a million to a few hundred, as detailed below.

One might characterize linguistic diversity in several ways. Above, I have implicitly concentrated on the number of languages spoken and the relatively small number of speakers of each. However, perhaps even more important is the fact that these languages belong to several different language families—an area containing many genealogically closely related languages would be less striking by far—and this aspect is addressed in the next section. Another way of assessing linguistic diversity is in terms of the structural differences across languages (see Divergence and Convergence Among Languages of the Caucasus). In terms of the concepts introduced by Nichols (1992) and using the terminology of Nichols (1997), the Caucasus is a good general example of an accretion zone, i.e., an area with high genealogical diversity (a large number of language families relative to population and area), high structural diversity, deep language families (i.e., with a common ancestor spoken far back in time), no large-scale spreading of individual languages (see, however, the discussion of Azerbaijani in The Extra-Linguistic Basis of Linguistic Diversity in the Caucasus, below), no clear center of innovation (although there may be areal features common to all or a substantial subpart of the area), increasing diversity with the passage of time, and no lingua franca.

THE LANGUAGES AND THEIR GENEALOGICAL AFFILIATION

As is indicated by the term languages of the Caucasus, the topic of this article is determined geographically, namely those languages that are spoken in the geographical area defined by the Caucasian isthmus, although for practical purposes we exclude languages that are represented in the Caucasus but the overwhelming majority of whose speakers live elsewhere, such as Greek and Russian. There is no implication that these languages form a genealogical unit, either a language family or a branch of a language family, and this is agreed by all researchers, whatever stand they take on the validity of more wide-ranging genealogical units in linguistics. Although some of the families to which languages of the Caucasus belong are virtually restricted to the Caucasus, several families are also well represented outside the Caucasus, indeed have the majority of their representatives there.

Of the branches of the Indo-European family (Ramat & Ramat 1998), which geographically covers most of Europe and northern South Asia, as well as parts of the Middle East, two have representatives among the languages of the Caucasus: Armenian and Iranian (the latter is actually a subbranch of Indo-Iranian). Armenian has two modern written varieties, Eastern and Western Armenian, of which Eastern Armenian is the standard language of Armenia itself, Western Armenian being used by most speakers in the diaspora; as noted above, Armenian has ~3.4 million speakers in the Caucasus. Three Iranian languages clearly count as languages of the Caucasus (although there are also smaller numbers of speakers of other Iranian languages in the area, such as speakers of varieties of Kurdish); they belong to three of the four subdivisions of Iranian. Ossetian, spoken by about half a million speakers divided between the Republic of North Ossetia-Alania in the Russian Federation and the break-away South Ossetia region of Georgia, is (despite its geographical location) a northeastern Iranian language. Talyshi, a northwestern Iranian language, has ~800,000 speakers in Azerbaijan (though this figure may include the diaspora in the rest of the former USSR) and more than 100,000 in Iran, whereas Tat, a southwestern Iranian language, has of the order of 20,000 speakers in Azerbaijan.

The Turkic family (Johanson & Csató 1998) is also represented in the Caucasus by three languages: Azerbaijani, as mentioned above, plus Kumyk, with ~460,000 speakers in northeastern Daghestan, and Karachay-Balkar, with ~300,000 speakers in the northwestern Caucasus.

Three language families are virtually restricted to the Caucasus and are often collectively referred to as "the Caucasian languages" (as opposed to "the languages of the Caucasus"), though without any presupposition that they form a genealogical unit, on which see below. The Kartvelian (South Caucasian) family is spoken predominantly in Georgia: Georgian itself, as noted above, has ~4 million speakers, whereas Megrelian (Mingrelian) has ~500,000 in northwestern Georgia, Svan has ~15,000 speakers in northern Georgia, and Laz (Chan) is spoken predominantly on the Black Sea coast in Turkey, with perhaps 30,000 speakers there and only a couple of thousand speakers across the border in Georgia. As in many instances across the world, there is no unanimity, because of conflicting linguistic, political, and sociopsychological factors, as to where exactly to draw the line between language and dialect; in some sources, Megrelian and Laz are considered dialects of a single language (Zan).

The West Caucasian (Northwest Caucasian, Abkhaz-Adyghe) family officially comprises four living languages: Abkhaz, with ~100,000 speakers in the breakaway Republic of Abkhazia (de jure part of Georgia), and Abaza, with ~35,000 speakers in the northwest Caucasus; and Kabardian, with ~600,000 speakers, and Adyghe, with ~125,000 in the northwest Caucasus. Alternatively, one might recognize only two languages, grouping Abkhaz and Abaza together, and likewise Kabardian and Adyghe (as Circassian). All four languages have significant diasporas, especially in Turkey, reflecting emigration when the North Caucasus was absorbed by Russia in the nineteenth century, and a fifth language of the family, representing a third subgroup distinct from Abkhaz-Abaza and Circassian, namely Ubykh, was spoken only in Turkey from the nineteenth-century emigration until it became extinct at the end of the twentieth century.

The real linguistic diversity of the Caucasus, however, is provided by the East Caucasian

(Northeast Caucasian, Nakh-Daghestanian) family. This is an old family, with a time depth comparable to that of Indo-European (Nichols 1992, p. 14), and contains a number of branches. Although there is some disagreement on the details, one analysis would provide a primary bifurcation into the Nakh and Daghestanian branches, with the latter further dividing into Avar-Andic-Tsezic [in turn dividing into Avar-Andic and Tsezic (Didoic)], Lak, Dargi (Dargwa), Lezgic, and Khinalugh. The Nakh languages are Chechen (~1.3 million speakers, mainly in the Republic of Chechnya in the Russian Federation), Ingush (~400,000 speakers, mainly in the Republic of Ingushetia, Russian Federation), and Tsova-Tush (Batsbi), the last a heavily endangered language with a little more than 3000 speakers in northeastern Georgia. Avar, with ~800,000 speakers, is spoken in western Daghestan. The Andic languages Andi, Botlikh, Godoberi, Karata, Akhvakh, Bagvalal, Tindi, and Chamalal are spoken in the far west of Daghestan, with numbers of speakers in the general range from 2500 to 9000 or higher (although the 2002 census figure of nearly 24,000 for Andi seems inflated and may include speakers of other Andic languages). The Tsezic (Didoic) languages Khwarshi, Tsez (Dido), Hinuq (Ginukh), Bezhta (Kapuchi), and Hunzib are spoken to the south of the Andic languages, with numbers of speakers ranging from ~500 for Hinuq (spoken in a single village wedged between the Tsez- and Bezhta-speaking areas) to perhaps 15,000 or more for Tsez. Accurate numbers of speakers for Andic and Tsezic languages are particularly hard to come by because they were not listed separately in Soviet censuses, and in the 2002 census, some speakers seem to have instead identified with Avar, which they speak as a second language.

Lak is a single, rather homogeneous language with ~150,000 speakers in central Daghestan, with Dargi to its east. Dargi is officially considered a single language, with about half a million speakers, but in fact the diversity across varieties of Dargi is considerable, with several so-called dialects being mutually unintelligible.

Korjakov (2006), for instance, recognizes two large dialect groups plus three isolated varieties. The Lezgic branch contains two outliers, Archi (in western Daghestan, ~1000 speakers) and Udi (~6000 speakers divided between northern Azerbaijan and an émigré settlement in eastern Georgia), and seven languages within Nuclear Lezgic, spoken in southeastern Daghestan with some spillover into northern Azerbaijan: Tsakhur, Rutul, Agul (all three with ~30,000 speakers each), Tabasaran (130,000), Lezgian (over half a million), Kryz (Dzhek, ~6000), and Budukh (~1000). Khinalugh (~1500 speakers in northern Azerbaijan) is either the most aberrant Lezgic language or a Daghestanian language standing outside this group.

Thus, the areas of greatest linguistic diversity are western Daghestan and northern Azerbaijan. This discussion shows clearly on the map of density of languages spoken in different parts of the world in Gordon (2005), viewable online (**http://www.ethnologue.com/show_map.asp?name_=_World&seq_=_10**). The Caucasus, and especially its eastern part, show as an area of high density relative to surrounding areas. Equally clearly, however, the Caucasus does not match the levels of language density found in some other parts of the world, such as New Guinea, where Gordon (2005) lists only three languages (plus the lingua franca Tok Pisin) out of more than 1000 with 100,000+ speakers and none with more than 200,000. Nonetheless, the Caucasus is one of the areas that frequently needs to be shown as an enlarged inset map in Haspelmath et al. (2005), reflecting the large number of languages in a relatively small area.

The classification into language families followed so far has been conservative, essentially along the lines of that presented by Dryer (2005). Does the situation change if one adopts a more sympathetic attitude toward macrofamilies, i.e., larger genealogical groupings that have not yet gained the support of most linguists and are of the type advocated, for instance, in Ruhlen (1991)? Under this kind of approach, Indo-European and Turkic (the latter via the intermediate genealogical unit Altaic) would both form part of a large family called Nostratic or Eurasiatic, to which some linguists would also add Kartvelian; other components of this macrofamily would include Uralic, Chukotko-Kamchatkan, and Eskimo-Aleut. West Caucasian and East Caucasian would group together as a single North Caucasian family (Nikolayev & Starostin 1994), which would in turn be part of Dene-Caucasian, which would include, among others, the Sino-Tibetan family and the Na-Dene languages of northwestern North America, perhaps also Basque in the Pyrenees. The number of macrofamilies in the Caucasus would thus reduce to two, but the Caucasus would still be the meeting place of two of the three major macrofamilies of Eurasia (the third being Austro-Tai, in Southeast Asia). (It should be noted that Ruhlen (1991) does not group Kartvelian with North Caucasian, in contrast to the classification adopted in his first edition from 1987.) Resources relating to the historical-comparative study of each of the three Caucasian families have increased in recent years, e.g., Klimov (1998) and Fähnrich (2007) on Kartvelian, Chirikba (1996) on West Caucasian, and Alekseev (2003) on East Caucasian.

DIVERGENCE AND CONVERGENCE AMONG LANGUAGES OF THE CAUCASUS

This section addresses the question of structural diversity among the languages of the Caucasus. In large measure, this discussion is facilitated by the much better availability of good overviews of and comprehensive descriptions of Caucasian languages in comparison to the state of affairs when Catford (1977) was published. [Of other languages of the Caucasus, Armenian is by far the best documented language; a recent descriptive grammar of Eastern Armenian is Minassian (1980).] Recent English-language overviews of the Caucasian languages are van den Berg (2005), which consists of extended articles on each of the three Caucasian families, and

the four-volume series comprising Harris (1991), Hewitt (1989), Job (2004), and Smeets (1995), consisting of articles on the individual languages (a selection of languages in the case of some groupings). For Georgian, Hewitt (1995) is a comprehensive reference source in English. For many of the other Caucasian languages, at least traditional monograph descriptions written in Russian were available by the 1970s, or chapter-length descriptions in monographs devoted to a group of languages, sometimes written by native speakers or speakers of other Caucasian languages. In the past three decades, the number of extensive grammatical descriptions has increased considerably, including the following in particular: Hewitt & Khiba (1989) for Abkhaz, Colarusso (1992) and Kumaxov (2005) for Kabardian, Kibrik (2001) for Bagvalal, van den Berg (1997) for Hunzib, Haspelmath (1993) for Lezgian, Kibrik & Testelec (1999) for Tsakhur, and Kibrik (1977) for Archi, with grammars of other languages in preparation. Dictionary resources have also grown substantially for the traditionally less well known languages: for example, Gudjedjiani & Palmaitis (1985) for Svan & Nichols (2004) for Ingush [for Ingush more generally, see the home page of the Ingush Language Project at the University of California, Berkeley (**http://ingush.berkeley.edu:7012/**)]. Also available is the series *Dictionaries of Unwritten Languages of Daghestan*, including so far Saidova (2006) for Godoberi, Magomedova & Xalidova (2001) for Karata, Magomedova (2004) for Bagvalal, Magomedova (2003) for Tindi, Magomedova (1999) for Chamalal, Xalilov (1999) for Tsez, Xalilov & Isakov (2005) for Hinuq, Xalilov (1995) for Bezhta, Isakov & Xalilov (2001) for Hunzib, and Ganieva (2002) for Khinalugh.

This section is headed "divergence and convergence" because it should not be assumed that the Caucasus is an area of purely fissional tendencies, with linguistic boundaries becoming ever more potent barriers to transmission of linguistic features. This can be seen perhaps most clearly in vocabulary because languages of the Caucasus have all borrowed vocabulary from their neighbors, and because the latter have also borrowed vocabulary from their neighbors, long chains of lexical borrowings can often be established, especially from traditionally culturally prestigious languages and language families such as Arabic, Persian, and Turkic. Two recent illustrative studies in this area are Xalilov (2004), showing how Daghestanian languages, in particular the Tsezic languages, have borrowed vocabulary from Georgian, including vocabulary transmitted through Georgian from other languages (including Russian during the period before there was direct contact with Russia), and Zabitov & Efendiev (2001) tracing Arabic and Persian loans into Lezgian. This section's emphasis, however, is on structural, grammatical features.

Several groups of languages spoken in the Caucasus illustrate cross-linguistically rare phenomena. Languages of the Caucasus overall tend to have large consonant inventories, especially in the case of the three Caucasian families, and especially in the case of West Caucasian. Some Indo-European languages also end up with at least moderately large consonant inventories, with Eastern Armenian, for instance, having a set of consonants almost exactly congruent with that of Georgian; Turkic languages of the Caucasus, by contrast, do not share in this phenomenon and, like Turkic languages in general, have an average number of consonants. Maddieson (2005a) considers languages with more than 34 consonants to have large inventories and those in the range 26–33 to have moderately large inventories. It is clear from his map that languages of the Caucasus, more specifically the Caucasian families plus Armenian represented in his sample, are a local cluster of such languages. (Unfortunately, two errors have crept into the physical maps: Abkhaz should be shown as having a large consonant inventory, Armenian as having a moderately large consonant inventory; both are shown as having small inventories.) By contrast, the West Caucasian languages have small vowel inventories, which Maddieson (2005c) defines as being in the range 2–4. Although suggestions have been made that Kabardian—a typical West Caucasian language

with respect to its vowel inventory—can be analyzed as having one vowel phoneme or maybe even none, all phonetic vowel qualities being predictable from other information, in particular consonants and stress, an analysis with three vowels is now usually advocated, as argued for instance by Hewitt (2005).

Although the Kartvelian languages are in many respects more like mainstream European languages than are their East and especially West Caucasian neighbors, they nonetheless provide instances of rarities and complexities. Although Georgian verbs can in principle show agreement with three of their arguments— subject, direct object, and indirect object— in practice, there are cooccurrence constraints that prevent all three from being realized simultaneously. Usually these are cooccurrence constraints on the overt realization of arguments, but as shown by Boeder (2005), there are instances where even a covert agreement marker can block the occurrence of another agreement marker. Suppose one wants to say "she paints you for herself." In the verb form *ixat'avs*, the only overt agreement marker is the suffix -*s* indexing the third-person singular subject. Because there is no overt agreement marker with the indirect object "for herself," one might expect that the second-person direct object would be able to be indexed. But in fact, it cannot. The verb form *ixat'avs* includes a covert agreement marker indexing the indirect object so that a more accurate representation might be Ø-*ixat'av-s*, marking not only the overt third-person singular subject agreement but also the third-person singular indirect object agreement. The only way to express the second-person direct object is by using a separate noun phrase, *ixat'avs šens tavs*. The direct object noun phrase *šens tavs* means literally "your head," although this expression has been grammaticalized as a pronominal expression to be used when indexing in the verb is excluded. But the noun phrase is grammatically third person, and third-person direct objects are not indexed in Georgian verbs, so there is nothing to compete with the covert indirect object marker. Not all linguists are happy with the concept of a zero morpheme, Ø, but Georgian does seem to provide one of the few clear pieces of evidence that a zero morpheme is not the same as nothing.

A number of languages of the Caucasus, including the East Caucasian languages Lak, Tsakhur (Kazenin 1999, 2002), and Udi (Harris 2002), and also the Indo-European language Armenian (Comrie 1984), show variations on a theme with respect to the marking of focus, i.e., the essential new information conveyed by a sentence, such as the noun phrase "the house" in "John built the house" in answer to the question, "What did John build?" (Focus will be indicated by underlining.) In Lak, an ordinary sentence without focus marking will have a structure as in Sentence 1. If one wants to mark the object as focus, then the agreement marker that appears as a suffix on the verb in Sentence 1 shifts to the object, as in Sentence 2.

1. na   qqatri   d-ullalissa-ra.
   I   house   IV-build-1SG
   "I am building a house."

2. na   qqatri-ra   d-ullalissa.
   I   house-1SG   IV-build
   "I am building a house."

Here, 1 denotes first person, and SG, singular. In Sentence 1, the verb agrees with both its subject (through the first-person singular suffix, which derives etymologically from a form of the copular verb) and its object (through the noun class IV prefix, the noun *qqatri* "house" being of noun class IV). In Sentence 2, one might be inclined to say that the suffix -*ra* on *qqatri* should rather be analyzed as a focus suffix, and in a sense this is correct; however, it is then odd that this suffix agrees not with the focus noun phrase to which it is attached (it is neither third-person singular nor noun class IV), but rather with the subject of the sentence (first-person singular). To mark a noun phrase as focus, whether or not it is subject, one attaches to it the suffix indicating agreement not with the focused noun phrase but with the subject. This puzzling phenomenon can be related to more mainstream phenomena in other languages of the Caucasus. In Armenian, the focus of a sentence must

be placed immediately in front of the finite verb, i.e., the one that shows agreement with the subject, as in Sentence 3.

3. mard-ik-ə   mi   xənjor   kera-n.
   man-PL-DEF   a   apple   ate-3PL
   "The men ate an apple."

Here, 3 denotes third person; DEF, definite; and PL, plural. What if the verb is complex, like English "are eating," where the finite auxiliary verb form "are" combines with the nonfinite verb form "eating"? Although the Armenian for "are eating" normally has the order with the nonfinite form preceding the finite form, i.e., *utum en*, if one wishes to focus a noun phrase, then this noun phrase must immediately precede the finite form, i.e., the auxiliary "are," and the nonfinite verb form will then follow, as in Sentence 4.

4. mard-ik-ə   mi   xənjor   e-n   utum.
   man-PL-DEF   a   apple   be-3PL eating
   "The men are eating an apple."

In an Armenian example such as Sentence 4, it might look as if *e-n* is a focus marker immediately following the focused element but agreeing with the subject, irrespective of whether the focus is subject. However, examples such as Sentence 3 show that the more general principle is that the focus must immediately precede the finite verb. The difference between Lak and Armenian is that Lak lacks the kind of construction illustrated in Sentence 3 so that what must formally have been a finite auxiliary verb (namely, -*ra*) can now be interpreted as a focus marker that follows the focused element but, paradoxically, agrees with the subject of its clause. Incidentally, placement of the focused constituent immediately before the finite verb is found in a wide range of languages (Kim 1988). In a number of other languages of the Caucasus, focus is expressed by a cleft sentence, as in English, "it is an apple that the men ate," and reinterpretation of such a construction is another possible path leading to constructions such as Sentence 2 in Lak (Harris 2002, pp. 226–43).

Another unusual syntactic phenomenon whose distribution crosses the boundary separating the various language families of the Caucasus is so-called backward control, found in both the East Caucasian language Tsez and the West Caucasian language Kabardian (Kumaxov & Vamling 1998, Polinsky & Potsdam 2002). In Tsez example Sentence 5a, one finds the subject of the intransitive verb *oq* "begin" as expected, in the absolutive case. In the alternative Sentence 5b, however, the subject appears in the ergative case, appropriate for the subject of a transitive verb, a possibility that is allowed only if the verb of the subordinate clause is transitive (in this case, "feed"), i.e., in this variant, the case of "girl" is determined not by the main clause verb "begin" but by the subordinate clause verb "feed."

5. *a.* kid   ziya b-išr-a   y-oq-si.
     girl.ABS cow III-feed-INF F-begin-PAST
  b. kid-bā ziya b-išr-a   y-oq-si.
     girl.ERG cow III-feed-INF F-begin-PAST
     "The girl began to feed the cow."

Here, III indicates class III, including all nouns denoting animals; ABS indicates absolutive, a case used for the subject of an intransitive verb and for the object/patient of a transitive verb; ERG indicates ergative, a case used for the subject/agent of a transitive verb; F indicates feminine; and INF indicates the infinitive.

A good example of increasing linguistic differentiation is provided by Bezhta, one of the Tsezic languages, and in particular the Bezhta Proper dialect of this language, which has developed a number of areally unusual features even relative to the two other main dialects of Bezhta (Khashar-Khota and Tladal). (Information on Bezhta derives primarily from ongoing collaborative research with M. Xalilov.) The Bezhta Proper dialect has lost the opposition between the sounds [r] and [y], which are distinguished in almost every language of the Caucasus, neutralizing both to [y]; interestingly, this neutralization affects early loan words, for instance, from Avar (*beyten* "wedding" < Avar *berten*), but not more recent ones, such as *bercinab* "beautiful," also from Avar; these more recent loans have thus reintroduced the phoneme into the language. The Bezhta

Proper dialect has lost the pharyngeal [ʕ], replacing it with a glottal stop, but with concomitant umlauting (fronting) of adjacent vowels, giving rise to new vowel phonemes [ä], [ö], [ü], pronounced much as in German, and giving the Bezhta Proper dialect a very distinctive sound in comparison even with other Bezhta dialects. But the innovations in Bezhta extend even to syntax—I do not have data from dialects other than Bezhta Proper, so it is unclear whether there is also internal variation across Bezhta dialects—as in the following example discussed by Comrie (2001), which contrasts Bezhta on the one hand with two other Tsezic languages, Tsez and Hunzib, on the other. In Tsez and Hunzib, it is not directly possible to form imperatives from verbs of emotion and perception such as "to love" or "to see"; rather the verb must first be causativized so that examples such as Sentence 6 (Tsez) and Sentence 7 (Hunzib) might be translated more literally as something like "cause your enemies to be lovable [sc. to you]" or "cause him to be visible [sc. to you]."

6.
mež-ā   mežu-s   tušman-bi   b-eti-r.
you.PL-ERG you.PL-GEN1 enemy-PL.ABS M.PL-love-CAUS.IPR
"Love your enemies!"

7.   ãc'-k'(-o).
     M. see-CAUS-IPR
     "See [him]!"

In Bezhta, by contrast, it is directly possible to express an imperative such as "love your enemies" in much the same way as it is in English, as in Sentence 8.

8. mizo-s   tušmal-la   b-āt'.
   you.PL-GEN1 enemy-PL.ABS M.PL-love.PL.IPR
   "Love your enemies!"

Here, CAUS denotes causative; GEN, genitive; IPR, imperative; and M, masculine. The partial syntactic treatment of verbs of emotion and perception as ordinary transitive verbs in Bezhta is unusual for a Daghestanian language and seems to be a spontaneous innovation. In some other respects, however, such verbs still follow the pattern of other Daghestanian languages, e.g., "I love you" is expressed literally as "to-me is-lovable you."

In looking at convergence, the question arises as to whether the languages of the Caucasus might constitute a Sprachbund or linguistic area, i.e., a region where languages from different genealogical families nonetheless share structural features that are absent from neighboring areas (including, where relevant, genealogically related languages spoken outside the Sprachbund area). One classic example of such a Sprachbund is South Asia, where features are shared by Indo-Aryan (a branch of Indo-European), Dravidian, Munda (a branch of Austroasiatic), and Himalayan (subgroups of Sino-Tibetan) languages (Masica 1976). Tuite (1999) examines the Caucasus as a linguistic area with special reference to ergativity, a phenomenon whereby the subject/agent of a transitive verb stands in one morphological case (ergative), whereas the subject of an intransitive verb and also the object/patient of a transitive verb stand in another case (absolutive). He concludes that the differences among languages of the Caucasus showing ergativity are sufficient to question any significance regarding the similarities. Without entering into the general question of whether the Caucasus constitutes a Sprachbund, it is clear that even where there are general similarities across languages of the Caucasus, there are often differences in detail.

For instance, one of the phonetic characteristics of languages of the Caucasus are so-called ejective consonants, whereby the glottis (vocal folds) is completely closed and the larynx is raised to produce the air pressure necessary for the articulation of the consonant, rather than using air directly from the lungs. Cross-linguistically, ejective consonants are rather rare; in the worldwide survey reported in Maddieson (2005b), only 95 out of 566 languages, or 16.8%, have ejective consonants. In the Caucasus, however, they are widespread, occurring in all three Caucasian families as well as in some other languages of the area, such as Ossetian, Eastern Armenian (some dialects), and

some varieties of Kurdish. All these languages have a basic three-way opposition among stop consonants, with a voiced consonant (e.g., [d]), a voiceless ejective (e.g., [t']), and a voiceless aspirate (e.g., [tʰ], pronounced with a slight puff of breath after the consonant). However, the markedness/frequency relations between ejective and aspirated stops vary. In Georgian and Armenian, for instance, the aspirates seem to be marked/less frequent, whereas in the West and East Caucasian languages, the situation seems to be rather the inverse. A phonological analysis might therefore maintain that languages such as Georgian and Armenian really distinguish aspirated and ordinary stops, the latter happening to have an ejective articulation (which, in the case of Armenian, varies according to dialect), whereas languages such as Tsez and Bezhta really distinguish ejective and ordinary stops, the latter having concomitant aspiration. This is apparent, for instance, in the ways in which the voiceless stops of Russian (which are phonetically neither ejective nor aspirated) are interpreted by speakers of the different languages. In loans from Russian into Georgian, they show up as ejectives; in loans from Russian into Tsez and Bezhta, they show up as aspirates. Indeed, in Bezhta, it is even possible to recognize words that have been borrowed from Russian through Georgian because these do show ejectives, e.g., Bezhta *p'alt'o* < Georgian *p'alt'o* < Russian *pal'to* "raincoat," contrasting with a direct loan from Russian into Bezhta such as Bezhta *peč* < Russian *peč'* "stove." (The free-standing acute in the Russian forms is an orthographic indication of palatalization and has nothing to do with ejectives or aspirates.)

In connection with the discussion of Sentences 1–3 above, some languages of the Caucasus, and Daghestanian languages in particular, express psychological predicates such as "to love" and "to believe" not in the form "A loves B" but rather in the form "to-A is-lovable B." One might therefore wonder how such languages would express notions such as "A loves him/herself": Would this come out as "to-A is lovable him/herself," or rather as A is lovable "to-him/herself"? The answer is that we find variation—i.e., again we have a phenomenon, the so-called affective, or dative-subject, or oblique-subject construction, that is shared by languages of the Caucasus but where there can be striking differences among languages that share the same overall phenomenon. In Tsez example Sentence 9, the literal translation is "Fatima is lovable to herself" (barring differences in word order between Tsez and English, and likewise for the other languages); in Tsakhur example Sentence 10, the literal translation is "to Rasul is lovable himself"; Bagvalal allows both variants (Sentences 11a,b). [See further Comrie & van den Berg (2006).]

9. pat'i   neɫāneɫo-r   y-eti-x.
    Fatima.ABS   REFL-DAT   F-love-PRS
    'Fatima loves herself.'

10. rasulu-s   ǯuswuǯ   ikkan.
    Rasul-DAT   REFL.ABS   M.love.IPF
    'Rasul loves himself.'

11.
    a. ʕali   in-ššʷa-da   w-ož-urōw.
       Ali.ABS   REFL-SUP-REFL   M-believe-IPF

    b. ʕali-la   e-w-da   w-ož-urōw.
       Ali-SUP   REFL-ABS-REFL   M-believe-IPF
       'Ali believes himself.'

In these examples, DAT is dative; IPF, imperfect; REFL, reflexive; and SUP, superessive, a case corresponding to the English preposition "on," though also with a number of idiomatic uses.

THE EXTRALINGUISTIC BASIS OF LINGUISTIC DIVERSITY IN THE CAUCASUS

An obvious solution to explaining linguistic diversity in the Caucasus might seem to be to relate the degree of linguistic diversity to the terrain, with the highest levels of linguistic diversity being found in the most mountainous areas, where communication is most difficult, and lower levels being found in the plains of the South Caucasus, for instance. And in the Caucasus, a correlation does indeed exist between terrain and linguistic diversity, with ar-

eas of great diversity such as western Daghestan (where Tsezic and Andic languages are spoken) or northern Azerbaijan (where some smaller Lezgic languages and Khinalugh are spoken) being in particularly mountainous areas. This can seen particularly clearly in the maps in Korjakov (2006), which include rivers, and thus show that even some more localized local instances of small languages (such as Archi) or of fragmentation (such as the internal dialect diversity of Dargi) correlate with locations close to the sources of streams. However, this cannot be the whole story because there are other parts of the world where one does not find this correlation. Indeed in the New Guinea area, the correlation is, if anything, the inverse: The languages with more speakers tend to be found in the Highlands, the smaller ones on the coast; see Ross (1998) for the fissiparous social factors that lead to language fission in New Guinea. This finding suggests that it might also be worth considering social factors in the case of the Caucasus. A major concern in the Caucasus is shortage of agricultural, especially arable, land, and this shortage is particularly acute in the most mountainous areas. Practicing endogamy provides a high level of guarantee that outsiders will not be able to lay claim to land, and because it also constrains membership of the speech community, it minimizes outside influence and maximizes the effects of internal change, thus increasing the level of differentiation among neighboring communities. Incipient effects of this kind can be seen in Tsez: Although probably all dialects of Tsez are still mutually intelligible [with perhaps some hesitation with regard to the most aberrant Sahada (Sagada) dialect], it is nonetheless the case that clear differences exist between the speech varieties of any pair of villages and that even a short text will reveal the speaker's village of origin.

If endogamy is a major factor in the preservation of linguistic diversity, then one would predict that a move away from endogamy would endanger linguistic diversity. D. Forker's recent observations on the language situation in Ginukh, home to the 500 speakers of Hinuq, suggest that this is indeed the case: In Ginukh, increasing marriage to speakers of the neighboring languages Tsez and Bezhta is leading to increased use of these languages and decreased use of Hinuq. Although the languages of the Caucasus are not, in general, endangered, developments such as that in Bezhta show that their ecology, especially in the case of smaller languages, is nonetheless fragile.

How, then, do large languages such as Azerbaijani achieve their spread? Recent work in genetics suggests at least part of the answer. History shows that Turkic languages such as Azerbaijani are relatively recent arrivals in the Caucasus, having made their way to the Caucasus only ~1000 years ago. As would be expected given such a recent dispersal, Turkic languages of the area are still relatively close to one another so that Azerbaijani, for instance, is still to a large extent mutually intelligible with Turkish. Nasidze et al. (2004) show that from a genetic perspective, speakers of Azerbaijani fall within the general range of variation found among populations of the Caucasus and are quite distinct from speakers of Turkic languages in Turkey or Central Asia; this finding applies, incidentally, to both mitochondrial and Y-chromosomal DNA, i.e., to both female and male lines, which strongly suggests the following scenario. A relatively small group of Turkic speakers, not large enough to have any significant effect on the genetics of the population, arrived in Azerbaijan. Culturally, however, they were able to establish themselves as an elite and gradually, by the process of language shift (Thomason & Kaufman 1988), assimilate the rest of the population linguistically, thus giving rise to the now observed discrepancy between the linguistic and genetic affiliations of Azerbaijani speakers. The final stages of this process can still be observed in the far north of Azerbaijan, where small languages such as Budukh, Kryz, and Khinalugh still survive but are increasingly endangered by the spread of Azerbaijani.

DISCLOSURE STATEMENT

The author is not aware of any biases that might be perceived as affecting the objectivity of this review.

LITERATURE CITED

Alekseev ME. 2003. *Sravnitel'no-Istoričeskaja Morfologija Naxsko-Dagestanskix Jazykov*. Moscow: Academia
Boeder W. 2005. The South Caucasian languages. In van den Berg 2005, pp. 5–89
Catford JC. 1977. Mountain of tongues: the languages of the Caucasus. *Annu. Rev. Anthropol.* 6:283–314
Chirikba VA. 1996. *Common West Caucasian*. Leiden: CNWS
Colarusso J. 1992. *A Grammar of the Kabardian Language*. Calgary: Univ. Calgary Press
Comrie B. 1984. Some formal properties of focus in Modern Eastern Armenian. *Ann. Arm. Ling.* 5:1–21
Comrie B. 2001. "Love your enemies": affective constructions in two Daghestanian languages. In *Perspectives on Semantics, Pragmatics, and Discourse: A Festschrift for Ferenc Kiefer*, ed. I Kenesei, RM Harnish, pp. 59–72. Amsterdam: Benjamins
Comrie B. 2007. The languages of northern Asia and eastern Europe. In *Atlas of the World's Languages*, ed. C Moseley, RE Asher, pp. 229–56. London: Routledge. 2nd ed.
Comrie B, van den Berg H. 2006. Experiencer constructions in Daghestanian languages. In *Semantic Role Universals and Argument Linking: Theoretical, Typological, and Psycholinguistic Perspectives*, ed. I Bornkessel, M Schleswesky, B Comrie, AD Friederici, pp. 127–54. Berlin: Mouton de Gruyter
Dryer MS. 2005. Genealogical languages list. In Haspelmath et al. 2005, pp. 584–644
Fähnrich H. 2007. *Kartwelisches Etymologisches Wörterbuch*. Leiden: Brill
Ganieva FA. 2002. *Xinalugsko-Russkij Slovar'*. Makhachkala: IJaLI DNC RAN
Gordon RG Jr, ed. 2005. *Ethnologue: Languages of the World*. Dallas: SIL Int. 15th ed. **http://www.ethnologue.com**

Gudjedjiani C, Palmaitis L. 1985. *Svan-English Dictionary*. Delmar: Caravan

Harris AC, ed. 1991. *The Indigenous Languages of the Caucasus*, Vol. I: *The Kartvelian Languages*. Delmar: Caravan

Harris AC. 2002. *Endoclitics and the Origins of Udi Morphosyntax*. Oxford, UK: Oxford Univ. Press

Haspelmath M. 1993. *A Grammar of Lezgian*. Berlin: Mouton de Gruyter

Haspelmath M, Dryer MS, Gil D, Comrie B, eds. 2005. *The World Atlas of Language Structures*. Oxford, UK: Oxford Univ. Press

Hewitt BG, ed. 1989. *The Indigenous Languages of the Caucasus*, Vol. II: *The North West Caucasian Languages*. Delmar: Caravan

Hewitt BG. 1995. *Georgian: A Structural Reference Grammar*. Amsterdam: Benjamins

Hewitt BG. 2005. North West Caucasian. In van den Berg 1997, pp. 91–145

Hewitt BG in collaboration with Khiba ZK. 1989. *Abkhaz*. London: Routledge

Isakov IA, Xalilov MSh. 2001. *Gunzibsko-Russkij Slovar'*. Moscow: Nauka

Itogi Vserossijskoj Perepisi Naselenija 2002 Goda. Tom 4: Nacional'nyj Sostav i Vladenie Jazykami, Graždanstvo. 2004. Moscow: Federal'naja Služba Gosudarstvennoj Statistiki. Distributed by East View Publ., Minneapolis. **http://www.perepis2002.ru/index.html?id=17**

Job M, ed. 2004. *The Indigenous Languages of the Caucasus*, Vol. III: *The North East Caucasian Languages, Part 1*. Delmar: Caravan

Johanson L, Csató ÉÁ, eds. 1998. *The Turkic Languages*. London: Routledge

Kazenin KI. 1999. Fokusnaja konstrukcija. In Kibrik & Testelec 1999, pp. 582–608

Kazenin KI. 2002. Focus in Daghestanian and word order typology. *Ling. Typol.* 6:289–316

Kibrik AE, ed. 1977. *Opyt Strukturnogo Opisanija Arčinskogo Jazyka*, Vols. 1–3. Moscow: Izd-vo Moskovskogo Universiteta

Kibrik AE, ed. 2001. *Bagvalinskij Jazyk: Grammatika, Teksty, Slovari*. Moscow: Nasledie

Kibrik AE, Testelec JaG, eds. 1999. *Èlementy Caxurskogo Jazyka v Tipologičeskom Osveščenii*. Moscow: Nasledie

Kim AH-O. 1988. Preverbal focussing and type XXIII languages. In *Studies in Syntactic Typology*, ed. M Hammond, E Moravcsik, J Wirth, pp. 147–69. Amsterdam: Benjamins

Klimov GA. 1998. *Etymological Dictionary of the Kartvelian Languages*. Berlin: Mouton de Gruyter

Korjakov JuB. 2006. *Atlas Kavkazskix Jazykov*. Moscow: Institut Jazykoznanija, RAN

Kumaxov MA, ed. 2005. *Kabardino-Čerkesskij Jazyk*, vols. 1–2. Moscow: Inst. Jazykoznanija, RAN

Kumaxov MA, Vamling K. 1998. *Dopolnitel'nye Konstrukcii v Kabardinskom Jazyke*. Lund: Lund Univ., Dep. Ling.

Maddieson I. 2005a. Consonant inventories. In Haspelmath et al. 2005, pp. 12–15

Maddieson I. 2005b. Glottalized consonants. In Haspelmath et al. 2005, pp. 34–37

Maddieson I. 2005c. Vowel inventories. In Haspelmath et al. 2005, pp. 16–19

Magomedova PT. 1999. *Čamalinsko-Russkij Slovar'*. Makhachkala: IJaLI DNC RAN

Magomedova PT. 2003. *Tindinsko-Russkij Slovar'*. Makhachkala: IJaLI DNC RAN

Magomedova PT. 2004. *Bagvalinsko-Russkij Slovar'*. Makhachkala: IJaLI DNC RAN

Magomedova PT, Xalidova RS. 2001. *Karatinsko-Russkij Slovar'*. Makhachkala: IJaLI DNC RAN

Masica CP. 1976. *Defining a Linguistic Area: South Asia*. Chicago, IL: Univ. Chicago Press

Minassian M. 1980. *Grammaire d'Arménien Oriental*. Delmar: Caravan

Nasidze I, Ling EYS, Quinque D, Dupanloup I, Cordaux R, et al. 2004. Mitochondrial DNA and Y-chromosome variation in the Caucasus. *Ann. Hum. Gen.* 68:205–21

Nichols J. 1992. *Linguistic Diversity in Space and Time*. Chicago: Univ. Chicago Press

Nichols J. 1997. Modeling ancient population structures and movement in linguistics. *Annu. Rev. Anthropol.* 26:359–84

Nichols J. 2004. *Ingush-English and English-Ingush Dictionary*. London: Routledge Curzon

Nikolayev SL, Starostin SA. 1994. *A North Caucasian Etymological Dictionary*. Moscow: Asterisk

Polinsky M, Potsdam E. 2002. Backward control. *Ling. Inq.* 33:245–82

Ramat P, Ramat AG, eds. 1998. *The Indo-European Languages*. London: Routledge

Ross M. 1998. Sequencing and dating linguistic events in Oceania: the linguistics/archaeology interface. In *Archaeology and Language II: Archaeological Data and Linguistic Hypotheses*, ed. R Blench, M Spriggs, pp. 141–73. London: Routledge

Ruhlen M. 1991. *A Guide to the World's Languages*, Vol. 1: *Classification, With a Postscript on Recent Developments*. Stanford, CA: Stanford Univ. Press

Saidova PA. 2006. *Godoberinsko-Russkij Slovar'*. Makhachkala: IJaLI DNC RAN

Smeets R, ed. 1995. *The Indigenous Languages of the Caucasus*, Vol. IV: *The North East Caucasian Languages, Part 2*. Delmar: Caravan

Thomason S, Kaufman T. 1988. *Language Contact, Creolization and Genetic Linguistics*. Berkeley: Univ. Calif. Press

Tuite K. 1999. The myth of the Caucasian Sprachbund: the case of ergativity. *Lingua* 108:1–29

van den Berg H. 1997. *A Grammar of Hunzib (With Texts and Lexicon)*. Munich: Lincom Europa

van den Berg H, ed. 2005. *Special issue: Caucasian. Lingua* 115:1–2

Xalilov MSh. 1995. *Beztinsko-Russkij Slovar'*. Makhachkala: IJaLI DNC RAN

Xalilov MSh. 1999. *Cezsko-Russkij Slovar'*. Moscow: Academia

Xalilov MSh. 2004. *Gruzinsko-Dagestanskie Jazykovye Kontakty*. Moscow: Nauka

Xalilov MSh, Isakov IA. 2005. *Ginuxsko-Russkij Slovar'*. Makhachkala: IJaLI DNC RAN

Zabitov SM, Efendiev II. 2001. *Slovar' Arabskix i Persidskix Leksičeskix Zaimstvovanij v Lezginskom Jazyke*. Makhachkala: Dagestanskij Gosudarstvennyj Universitet

Reproduction and Inheritance: Goody Revisited

Chris Hann

Max Planck Institute for Social Anthropology, 06017 Halle, Germany;
email: hann@eth.mpg.de

Annu. Rev. Anthropol. 2008. 37:145–58

First published online as a Review in Advance on
June 6, 2008

The *Annual Review of Anthropology* is online at
anthro.annualreviews.org

This article's doi:
10.1146/annurev.anthro.37.081407.085222

Key Words

property, devolution, kinship, law, Eurasia

Abstract

According to Jack Goody, in a body of work that dates back to the
1950s, differences in the mode of inheritance between Eurasia and sub-
Saharan Africa have multiple connections to domestic groups, kin terminology, politics and stratification, and above all, productive systems.
Goody's theory is built on evolutionist assumptions and draws in part on
statistical analysis of the *Ethnographic Atlas*. Theoretically and methodologically unfashionable among sociocultural anthropologists, his work
has been largely ignored in recent decades. This article considers the
standard criticisms and reviews pertinent recent work on kinship and
property in rural Europe and in legal anthropology. Inheritance was
supposed to lose its fundamental social significance in socialist societies, and it also came to play a smaller role in the social reproduction
of advanced capitalist societies. However, this eclipse may prove to be
temporary, and a reengagement with the topic on the part of anthropologists is overdue.

INTRODUCTION

The notion of reproducing economic relations, or relations of political domination, or the reproduction of society itself, has been frequently deployed in the social sciences from Marx and Engels to Bourdieu and Meillassoux. The topic is potentially broad enough to include virtually everything that sociocultural anthropologists study, but this article focuses on property transmission. Inheritance is best conceptualized broadly as the intergenerational devolution of valuables, including many forms of *inter vivos* transfer. It links the sphere of production to that of kinship and marriage and has far-reaching implications for the development of social institutions in general. The key figure in the elaboration of these links is Jack Goody, who in an oeuvre stretching over more than five decades has placed "diverging devolution" (a term he prefers to bilateral inheritance) at the center of a *longue durée* account of Eurasian history since the urban revolution of the late Bronze Age. In the first part of this review, I outline Goody's vision, which was set out most concisely and comprehensively in *Production and Reproduction* (1976). Both in terms of theory, where he addressed an agenda shaped by Maine, McLennan, and Morgan in the nineteenth century, and in terms of methods, where he relied heavily on the data coded in Murdock's *Ethnographic Atlas*, Goody's work went against the dominant grain of the twentieth-century discipline. The fields he sought to draw together are nowadays fragmented; I discuss some recent work in just two of these fields. Large-scale comparisons over millennia remain unfashionable in sociocultural anthropology. Yet between the detail of localized ethnographies and the universalist aims of new cognitive approaches, Goody's diverging devolution hypothesis remains an outstanding example of middle range theory, notable for both its non-Marxist materialism and its engagement with the work of archaeologists and historians.

THE GOODY ARGUMENT

Goody's abiding interest in mechanisms of property transmission originated in his fieldwork in Northern Ghana in the early 1950s and drew on traditions of comparative legal scholarship, which had strong influence on the descent theorists of the British school (Goody 1962). Although he is often associated with these earlier theorists, Goody frequently criticizes the circularity, holism, and synchronicism of structural-functionalism, which led some scholars to project African descent models onto Eurasia without paying attention to fundamental differences in productive systems, the devolution of property, and ensuing differences in domestic roles and succession strategies. Instead of male property passing to men (sons inherit from their fathers or from their mother's brother in matrilineal societies) and female property to women, the dominant pattern in Eurasia is for both male and female offspring to inherit from a conjugal estate. Drawing on Human Relations Area Files (HRAF) data, Goody links this observation to the predominance of monogamy over polygyny and of "vertical" dowry transfers (an important form of premortem inheritance) over "horizontal" payments of bridewealth. The contrast is further developed in terms of roles and quasi-kinship relationships: Monogamy is associated with concubinage, and emotional tensions, which in Africa are focused on cowives, are directed in Eurasia toward the stepmother. Adoption is also shown to be primarily a Eurasian institution to provide an heir; it is largely superfluous in Africa, where polygyny and fostering provide flexible alternatives (Goody 1982). Late marriage and high rates of celibacy are further consequences in some parts of Eurasia. Outside the domestic domain, diverging devolution is linked to increased social stratification and complex polities. Finally, it is linked to individualizing (i.e., descriptive rather than classificatory) kin terminologies.

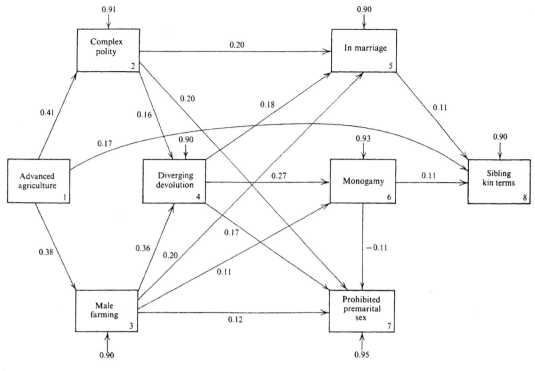

Figure 1

Causal model tested by path analysis (Goody 1976, p. 39).

But diverging devolution is not the ultimate cause of the fundamental contrast between Eurasia and sub-Saharan Africa. Generalizations about causality are hazardous, but the strong links between the domestic, sociological, and productive domains are incontrovertible (**Figure 1**). Diverging devolution is associated with advanced agriculture (defined by use of the plough and/or irrigation), which requires new gendered divisions of labor, enables higher yields, and converts land into a new kind of property object. In its general thrust, Goody's argument is consistent with the evolutionism of Morgan (1877) and also with Marxist historical materialism (Engels 1972), though he largely avoids the language of class struggle and exploitation.

Much of Goody's later work is devoted to detailed historical elaboration of the hypotheses outlined in *Production and Reproduction*. Two volumes address developments in Europe (Goody 1983, 2000), but his principal purpose,

exemplified in Goody (1990), a *magnum opus* devoted mainly to Asian materials, has been to criticize a basic Western bias in the most influential accounts of the emergence of the modern world. The impressive economic performances of East Asian countries have not been inhibited by "primitive" domestic institutions or by Confucian or other maladaptive mentalities. Anticipating arguments that have recently been advanced in other quarters (Frank 1998), Goody shows that Western teleological accounts have "stolen" Eurasian history by misrepresenting East Asian contributions (Goody 1996, 2006b). He recently (2006a) reiterated his debt in this line of thinking to archaeologist Gordon Childe, who traced the ultimate unity of the landmass back to the urban revolution of the late Bronze Age.

Although most of his work is devoted to the preindustrial era, Goody has also provided suggestive insights into the property and inheritance dilemmas of both modern capitalist societies (1998b) and of socialist societies (2003). I briefly consider both variants below. What I do not attempt here is to provide an assessment either of the vast literature on property or of Goody's entire oeuvre; property transmission is a central theme in his work, but it by no means exhausts it.

GENERAL ASSESSMENTS

Goody's work has occasionally been dismissed as reductionist and crudely materialist.[1] Some enduring criticisms were formulated by Yanagisako (1979). She was respectful of some parts of his thesis, particularly concerning the contrast between bridewealth and dowry, but questioned both "the empirical generality and analytic utility of his typology" (p. 172). As we have seen, Goody aims at more than just a typology, but Yanagisako was scornful in her predictions:

> His causal model in which technological factors of production are the primary movers in the evolution of domestic organization probably will not stand so well against the test of time.... The problem, of course, is inherent in any evolutionary scheme that rests on a crude succession of types. For however sophisticated the quantitative hardware, one cannot derive historical process from ahistorical, cross-sectional data. (p. 172)

Despite Goody's pursuit of the contrasts in domestic role sets between Eurasia and Africa, for Yanagisako he is as guilty as Malinowski in generalizing from a genealogical grid and taking the nuclear family as society's basic and natural unit.

These criticisms would probably still be endorsed by most sociocultural anthropologists. Goody's hopes that new computing technologies would enable the thorny issues of causality to be addressed in more sophisticated ways have not yet been realized. Instead those questions have largely been avoided. Some scholars continue to use the HRAF to pursue cross-cultural comparison, but the agendas seem to have narrowed. Thus the authors of a recent study of polygyny conclude that its best predictors are high rates of male mortality in warfare (as suggested in the nineteenth century by Herbert Spencer) and high exposure to pathogens (Ember et al. 2007). They acknowledge the arguments of Goody (following Ester Boserup) concerning the negative association with plough agriculture and land scarcity but point out that all these models remain frustratingly crude because we still lack any means of measuring land scarcity.[2]

In the tradition of Yanagisako (and behind her David Schneider), ethnographers have continued creatively to extend the study of kinship (Carsten 2000, Schweitzer 2000, Strathern 1992). Goody did much work at that level himself, and his own interest in institutions such as concubinage and adoption presaged some of the recent work on cultures of relatedness. But he also believes that ethnographic studies should be complemented by more general, bird's eye perspectives, including long-term historical trends as best we can infer or conjecture them. Perhaps the most significant effort of this kind in recent decades has been a theory of house-based societies as a transitional form between simple and complex structures of kinship. But Lévi-Strauss's (1983) definition of the house is vague: "a corporate body holding an estate made up of both material and immaterial wealth, which perpetuates itself through the transmission of its name, its goods and its titles down a real or imaginary line" (p. 174). Goody's

---

[1]Goody (1976) noted Althusser's formulation that the mode of production dominates "in the last instance," but he took no part in the neo-Marxist debates of the 1970s concerning the forces and relations of the productive "base." This did not prevent his being classified by Hindess & Hirst (1975) as a vulgar materialist, to which he replied that theirs was a highly vulgar form of idealism (see Goody 1980, p. 17). His aversion to truly reductionist approaches is made clear in his criticisms of Diamond (Goody 1998b).

[2]For Goody, exercises of this sort have little value because they distort the broader picture of social reproduction: "[T]o start by trying to explain polygyny is to start from the wrong end" (1976, p. 51).

work is not addressed in the ensuing literature (Carsten & Hugh-Jones 1995).

Indeed the Goody approach is nowadays largely ignored in anthropological research and curricula, and the terms devolution and social reproduction may be slipping into oblivion. New forms of property—biogenetic, cultural, intellectual etc.—attract plenty of attention, reflecting intensified commoditization and globalization (Hart 2008, Verdery & Humphrey 2004). Some anthropologists have emphasized radical cross-cultural differences in subject-object relations (Strathern 1999), but others insist that it is still useful to apply analytic definitions of property and inheritance for comparative analysis (von Benda-Beckmann et al. 2006). Whereas the latter volume emphasizes legal anthropology, the collection edited by Gilman & Hunt (1998) addresses a broad range of economic anthropology. But the role of property in long-term change and the precise mechanisms of its devolution receive little attention in either of these volumes.

Why the neglect? Goody's approach has an undeniable affinity to the unpopular paradigm of modernization theory, which posited monogamy and the nuclear family as the domestic institutions to which other forms would eventually have to give way. Goody is emphatic in rejecting the transfer of Western models to postcolonial Ghana, but in taking this position he explicitly relates the African models to a less developed economy and implies that, at some later stage, the Western (or rather Eurasian) patterns are likely to emerge. In short, he represents an evolutionist perspective, which has long been as unfashionable in the mainstream of the discipline as has the use of the HRAF data sets.

Even among those anthropologists who continue to view their discipline as historical comparative sociology, few feel comfortable at the level of continents. Most sociocultural anthropologists have preferred to focus more narrowly on single societies or ethnographic cases. It is simply not possible to appreciate or to refute Goody's theories at this level. Goody was well aware from his own work in Ghana that not all African polities were so undifferentiated and that land was not equally abundant everywhere.[3] Within Eurasia, the regional and local variety are bewildering, but it is pointless to seize on details to question the Goody model, e.g., by pointing to the widespread occurrence of horizontal transfers at marriage, because nowhere does Goody claim that bridewealth and dowry are fully exclusive. One of the few to tackle the big picture (though both his time span and his spatial frame of reference remain restricted compared with those of Goody) is Macfarlane, who in his early work celebrated the uniqueness of English ego-centered kinship and traced individualist attitudes toward property, exemplified in testamentary freedom, back to the origins of the Common Law. Later, an engagement with the Japanese case obliged Macfarlane (1997) to recognize that quite different domestic institutions were equally compatible with rapid accumulation. Macfarlane places more emphasis than Goody on demographic trends. The ultimate causes of the success of England and Japan in escaping from the Malthusian traps are traced to similarly favorable geographical and political circumstances ("islandhood"). Impartible inheritance was also crucial, but the associated mechanisms differed radically. Whereas the Japanese solved the problem of farm succession primarily through the adoption of nonkin, in England (as Goody acknowledges but does not explain) adoption was not legally codified until the twentieth century and farm labor needs were met through the extensive use of servants and hired hands. Through these mechanisms, according to Macfarlane, England and Japan became the first agrarian societies to drive a wedge between production and reproduction, thereby paving the way for industrial modernity.

---

[3] In a striking contrast on the island of Madagascar, Bloch (1975) showed how the endogamous practices of the Merina distinguished them from the neighboring Zafamaniry, always potentially keen to expand their local groups. Bloch's neo-Marxist explanation emphasized Merina investment in rice terraces as the key to the "end of affinity." This conforms to the predictions of Goody's model under conditions of intensified agriculture; the point is that such investments in land were rare in Africa.

INHERITANCE AND SUCCESSION IN RURAL EUROPE

Macfarlane's is a work of grand synthesis rare in contemporary anthropology, but it is also worth looking more closely at more narrowly focused studies in Europe, where the abundance of records has allowed anthropologists to continue close cooperation with historians and other scholars (Kertzer & Barbagli 2001–2003). Scholars have oscillated between macro- and microregional classifications (Viazzo 2007). Although some spatial patterns are robust over centuries, Viazzo warns against excessively broad models such as the "Mediterranean family". Noting that behavior toward close kin can change with astonishing speed, he questions "cultural fault lines" and also the use of quantitative evidence in interpreting kinship: Frequency of contact and levels of financial support may not be adequate indicators of the quality of relationships.

These warnings are pertinent to the theme of inheritance. Older notions of a common north-west European pattern of impartible inheritance (little stressed by Goody) have had to be modified as more and more microregions are detected. In Spain, for example, most regions are characterized by partible inheritance, the principle commonly favored in the legislation of modern nation states. In Catalonia, however, "unipersonal succession" is assured through the prevalence of "stem family" formations (Barrera-Gonzaléz 1998). Following Skinner on Japan (1993), Barrera-Gonzaléz questions whether the egalitarian fragmentation of property can be considered a form of succession at all. Catalan primogeniture is associated with strong traditions of literacy and the written law, along with larger households, late marriage, active matchmaking, high rates of celibacy, and a strong ideological emphasis on the ancestral house. However, this particular succession system is Oriental rather than European inasmuch as the patriarch does not retire but retains effective authority even after the marriage of the eldest son and heir, who is obliged to await his father's death before he fully succeeds to the role. Barrera-Gonzaléz concludes (following Habakkuk 1955) by speculatively associating Catalonia with England and virtuous causal chains: In both cases, impartible inheritance tended to promote social mobility, more efficient agriculture, and the first shoots of industrial development.

A significant earlier contribution was Bourdieu's investigation of high rates of celibacy in Béarn (1962). Bourdieu and Goody share an underlying concern with "property transfers as tactics for maintaining status and power and reproducing symbolic capital" (de Haan 1994, p. 161). Bourdieu's later elaboration (1976) of how ideals of honor provided scope for individual agency in the manipulation of marriage and inheritance rules is viewed by de Haan as undermining Goody's arguments, but it can equally be seen as filling in an ideological dimension neglected by the latter. In any case, changing marriage patterns too can be related to material factors, as in early modern Württemberg, where the shift toward more endogamous marriages resulted from rising populations and the increased value of land in a region of partible inheritance (Sabean 1990). de Haan (1994) makes the important point that the functional vagueness of Bourdieu's notion of "habitus" may be hard to sustain in the conditions of an increasingly commoditized agriculture, when the "rules of the game" become more explicit and rigid (p. 166).

One way to formalize succession rules is that of state law. Yet regional diversity has persisted, even within a small country such as the Netherlands. The farmers of the eastern district of Twente maintained viable farms through a system of impartible inheritance long after state law had decreed equal rights for all siblings. de Haan draws on Lévi-Strauss's (1983) notion of the *société à maison* to explain how ideas about the land as an estate and obligations to kin continue to play a role in the present day, defying the application of any narrow economic calculus to farmers' decisions concerning the transmission of their property. Kinship loyalties based on the continuity of the house are similarly central in Catalonia and in Bourdieu's Béarn case. By contrast, the farmers of Brittany have continuously divided and recombined their farms (Segalen 1991). Echoing a very old distinction in the anthropological literature, Augustins (1990) argues that in the Breton case kinship rather than residence is the basic principle of social organization.

The ideological dimension is well treated in Cole & Wolf's comparative study in South Tyrol (1974). Whereas the German-speaking residents of St. Felix have an ideology of impartible inheritance, the Romance speakers of Tret insist on partibility. The difference has considerable implications for interpersonal relations, but it transpires that average farm size is the same in the two communities. Although the authors were initially inclined to emphasize cultural factors as prior to and independent of ecology and economics, in the final analysis they had to recognize complex interaction. (Similar conclusions emerge from many other studies.) Two decades after the original research Cole was astonished by the changes he found in St. Felix (2003). A plethora of wage employment opportunities had helped transform peasants into farmers and converted the inheritance norm from male primogeniture to female ultimogeniture. Farming was no longer the basis of the economy, land ownership had lost its crucial function, and typically it was now the youngest daughter who stayed on to provide care for the aging parents; also striking was the fact that villagers told the ethnographer that this had always been their custom.

Summarizing the contributions to their rich volume, which include several explorations of the *longue durée* by historians as well as case studies of contemporary change from both Eastern and Western Europe, Heady & Grandits (2003) suggest cautiously that

> [o]ver the very long-term there is evidence of a movement away from systems that stressed communal inheritance and defined kinship identity in patrilineal terms, towards systems of partible or impartible inheritance and a conception of identity that emphasizes property

over kinship, conceptualizing kinship in bilateral terms. However, the shifts involved are neither uniform nor complete. (p. 6)

LAW, LAWYERS, LEGAL PLURALISM

The European studies discussed above reveal ubiquitous tensions between state law and local norms. The distinction between partible and impartible inheritance may be clear in theory, but it is often muddy in practice. Customary law diverges from state codes, the norms articulated by villagers may be different again, and what people actually do with their resources must be analyzed at a different level altogether. Notarial documents may create the impression that status is giving way to contract, that state law is penetrating the intimacy of the family; yet villagers may manipulate the law to serve their traditional, nonindividualist purposes, e.g., when making wills or registering "fictional" transfers *inter vivos* to gain tax benefits or cement informal pension arrangements within the kin group (Abrahams 1991).

These discrepancies point to broader analytic issues in legal anthropology. Goody has been criticized for failing to maintain a consistent distinction between inheritance transfers and other forms of alienation (von Benda-Beckmann 1979, 1994). If a property owner has testamentary freedom to bequeath wealth at his death to whomever he wishes, then it is clearly insufficient to consider only dowry and transfers to legal heirs as forms of *inter vivos* inheritance: Account should also be taken of other transfers made before death, including the gifts that Goody treats as "counter-inheritance" strategies. von Benda-Beckmann calls for a more rigorous approach to inheritance in terms of "nonreciprocal diachronic transfers." He distinguishes four types of transfer pertaining to "actions of last will," including "property transfers—donations—which are retroactively drawn into the diachronic dimension and subjected to different criteria of validity than obtained during the property holder's lifetime" (1994, p. 118). This analytic clarity is a prerequisite for grasping how inheritance is shaped in practice, often by different systems of law simultaneously. In his Ambon case study, von Benda-Beckmann documents the complex mixing of local (*adat*) law, religious (*sharia*) law, and state (Dutch) law in colonial Indonesia. As in Sabean's European study (1990), the diachronic flows are continuous, not concentrated at the moment of death. The long-term story in both these cases is that devolution is increasingly concentrated on direct descendants, and individuals come to enjoy greater freedom both to give away their property during their lifetimes and to bequeath it.

Islamic inheritance law in Indonesia differed considerably from the *adat* systems, notably in establishing heirs bilaterally, but Islamic jurisprudence is itself far from static and homogenous. Contrary to some Orientalist "superimposition" theories, women in at least some regions of the Middle East received their share long before the writings of the Prophet, which in key respects resembled the provisions of Christianity and Judaism (Mundy 1988). Local diversity persisted long after the introduction of written codes of inheritance law, and Mundy has illustrated this in two major empirical studies, first in Yemen (1995) and later in a historical study of what is now a region of northern Jordan (Mundy & Saumarez Smith 2007). The latter develops a powerful tripartite model to analyze the "three moments of property": The first is the law, the second its administration in the wider context of governance, and the third consists in concrete realities of ecology and production; it is usually the last that holds the key to understanding why women should be endowed with land in some places but not in others. Mundy's intensive focus on property devolution challenges prevalent idealist models of "tribal" societies in the Middle East, with their one-sided focus on agnatic descent. Goody would surely approve of the way in which her work modifies his model (see Goody 1990) because the incidence of diverging devolution is shown to depend more on agrarian sociology than on legal texts or that least satisfactory of variables, "culture."

For Goody, one of the distinctive features of the Middle East is its high divorce rate. In a more recent contribution (1998b), he draws attention to a recent sharp rise in the divorce rate in Western societies, which, together with the increased incidence of single mothers, is generating new social tensions and excessive demands on taxpayers. His solution is to revive practices of endowment and to make inventories of all the property that the partners bring to a marriage to facilitate that property's redistribution in the event of divorce. Although dowry has long had a bad press, notably in India (see Basu 2005), Goody argues that it should not automatically be opposed by feminists. Far from reducing women to the status of property, it is more likely to strengthen their position. More generally, the earmarking of valuables should facilitate the earlier devolution of property by the elder generation and minimize recourse to artful lawyers, whose involvement generally benefits men rather than women but above all, the lawyers themselves.

Whereas Goody argues that "keeping matters out of the hands of courts and lawyers must remain a major personal and social objective, if only because of the expense involved to individuals or to the community" (1998b, p. 211), for dynastic families in the United States, state law has long insinuated itself into the heart of the kin group (Marcus 1992). Descendants of these elites perceive their wealth and their relations to each other not in terms of an idealized kin group but through the legal instruments provided by trusts and foundations. Fiduciary professionals, many of them lawyers, assume the managerial responsibilities for the fortune and, in a sense, become the true heirs. The symbolic or mystical significance of the dynasty comes to exceed the economic: Family idioms serve to give inherited wealth a cloak of moral legitimacy and provide an object onto which wider sections of the population can project their desires. However, Marcus is also sensitive to changing political economy and sociological relations. In an afterword to his chapter on the fiduciary, he points out that the British structural functionalist anthropologists drew heavily on a nineteenth-century legal scholarship in their constructions of African descent groups (pp. 81–82). Whereas Goody was critical of Maine's assumptions for Eurasia (1976, pp. 77–81), Marcus (echoing Bourdieu 1976) was skeptical of the value of such legalistic models anywhere in the preindustrial world. However, he argued persuasively that legal categories must be given due recognition in any cultural analysis of contemporary Western societies, where they feature so prominently.

CAPITALISM AND SOCIALISM

For most of the population in Western societies, in recent generations the inheritance of family property has been less significant in determining the life course than has the individual acquisition of skills and qualifications. Change has been a gradual, uneven process. Long after land had ceased to be the dominant factor of production, the "new men" of Britain's industrial revolution still strove to convert their wealth into status and political power through the acquisition of a landed estate, which they could pass on in the family line.[4] The estate, ranch, and even the modest summer house have retained much of their cultural significance as transgenerational familial property (Balfe 1999).

The continuing economic and stratificational significance of property has been neglected in recent years and Marcus's work is exceptional among contemporary anthropologists. It has been left to sociologists to document the continued importance of intergenerational transfers in family life (Kohli 2004) and in the macrostructuration of capitalist societies (Miller & McNamee 1998). The topic of inheritance also lends itself well to the development of sociological theory. Beckert has shown that normative "discourses of evaluation" have

developed in significantly different ways in the United States, France, and Germany since the eighteenth century (2007, 2008).[5] These cultural discourses can be related to political and economic developments in these three countries (the absence of a revolutionary moment in the eighteenth century is one key to the German case) and also to their institutions and legal codes. Beckert argues that the key ideas have created a "cognitive lock-in" over the past two centuries, shaping the perceptions and thereby the rational actions of individual actors. His theories have a multidimensional ambition comparable to those of Goody. The major contrast is that the *longue durée* of this sociologist covers two centuries, whereas that of the anthropologist extends over some five millennia. Perhaps it is his longer time frame that leads Goody to privilege material causation, whereas the economic sociologist Beckert gives priority to ideas.

If the revolutions at the end of the eighteenth century placed a new ideological emphasis on equality and the *Code Napoléen* proclaimed the egalitarian treatment of siblings, in practice, even after the introduction of inheritance taxation to offset the expanding services provided by the state, equality (of opportunity as well as of outcome) has remained a chimera. The transmission of cultural capital has helped to ensure that the deep inequalities characteristic of preindustrial Eurasia have persisted in new forms. At this point it is instructive to consider the more radical attempt to resolve the Eurasian property problem: Whereas in Africa, mild forms of social differentiation could evoke accusations of sorcery, the structural inequalities of Eurasia produced socialism (Goody 2003).

Engels's (1972) historical materialism outlined an evolution from "primitive communism," defined in terms of the absence of

---

[4]As Habakkuk (1994) explains for the nineteenth century, "land was the most visible and therefore the most effective way of exhibiting wealth. No one could tell the worth of a money fortune or assess the value of the units in which it was held. But anyone could make a shrewd guess at the value of 1000 acres" (p. 403).

[5]Whereas American discourses emphasize individual testamentary freedom, in France this individualism is modified by a concern with the family, which in Germany takes even stronger form and affects the very definition of property (e.g., in the work of Hegel).

property, to the predominance of private property under capitalism. Accordingly, twentieth-century socialist regimes set out to eliminate the inheritance of private productive property. Whereas (at least in principle) liberal property codes do not rank property forms, the Soviet Union discriminated against private ownership, which was inferior to cooperative (collective) ownership, which was in turn inferior to state ownership. Under Marxist-Leninist-Maoist socialism, land and other means of production were nationalized (collectivized) in broadly similar ways. The irony was that this socialist revolution began not in the advanced industrial regions of Western Europe, as Marx had anticipated, but in economically backward Russia.

The most ambitious attempt by an anthropologist to theorise socialism is that of Verdery (1996), who emphasizes the inefficiency of bureaucratic domination compared with the market. The notorious "economies of shortage" were dealt with in very different ways, but some degree of "informality" and "manipulable resources" was to be found even in the more rigid of the planned economies and was arguably crucial to their reproduction (Humphrey 1983). By the 1980s, Hungarian socialists had greatly diluted collectivist principles governing access to and control over resources (Hann 1990). Goody (2003) echoed many previous critics in suggesting that poor economic performance must be connected to the lack of incentive that resulted from the impossibility of passing on productive wealth to one's offspring; however, when this restriction was removed under the "shock therapy" of the 1990s, the results were an economic disaster.

In fact, most types of nonproductive property could be inherited under socialism as under capitalism.[6] The consequences for social re-

production can be compared in Berlin, where Borneman (1992) documented the considerable differences in kinship, marriage patterns, and the life course that developed in just a few decades between East and West. The socialists in the east were ideologically committed to improving the position of women and went even further than did most other socialist states to draw women into the labor force and provide child care from a very early age. However, inheritance per se plays only a minor role in the contrasts drawn by Borneman for the era of the Cold War: Even in the capitalist West, for the great majority of citizens, material transfers were no longer decisive in determining life chances and sustaining parental power. But there are some signs in the era of "neoliberalism" that the pendulum might be swinging back again in all parts of Eurasia. Thus the role of inheritance in the constitution of English kinship seems to be increasing as many more people now have an estate to pass on, thanks mainly to a sharp rise in home ownership in recent decades (Finch & Mason 2000).[7]

In those Eastern European countries where private property was well established before the imposition of collectivization, there was strong interest in reestablishing those rights in the 1990s (Hann 1993, Verdery 2004). In some countries, the retention of legal title to land, generally viewed as a legal irrelevance following the imposition of collectivization, suddenly turned out to be crucially significant. Citizens were angry when legislation made it difficult or impossible to regain one's previous property or when local factors obstructed implementation (Hann et al. 2003). In Russia, by contrast, entrepreneurial farming was much slower to

---

[6]The devolution of nonproductive property grew in social significance in most countries of the Soviet bloc before its collapse. The high rates of social mobility achieved in the wake of the revolution were seldom sustained. Inequalities were particularly acute in the housing market (see Szelenyi 1983).

[7]A recent survey in Germany indicated that almost 90% of respondents were in basic agreement with the statement that "[i]t is just that parents should transmit their property to their children, even when this means that the children of richer parents have better life chances." In legislative changes currently under discussion in parliament it is proposed to reduce the taxation of wealth that is passed to one's own children and grandchildren, thereby strengthening the privileged position of the nuclear family vis-à-vis wider kin groups (Bernau 2007).

develop, inhibited by communal sentiments and envy (Heady & Miller 2003). Here one finds little evidence of a dominating urge to accumulate and pass on private productive property, although this did not prevent governments and their Western advisers from pressing ahead with privatization schemes.

That states which call themselves socialist are capable of flexible property arrangements and high rates of economic growth is well demonstrated by China and Vietnam over the past three decades. Much productive property, along with other valuables, can now be owned and inherited. At present, land is leased for periods of up to 30 years, within which period use rights are inherited within the family. According to critics, these arrangements fail to satisfy either the criteria of equity or the criteria of efficiency (because they preclude farm expansion and provide no secure incentive for long-term improvements). Western proponents of a property rights approach question whether China can possibly sustain high rates of growth, given citizens' lack of confidence in impartial legal codes. So far, however, the reform model has maintained its momentum. Diverging devolution combines with the norm of unipersonal succession consequent on the one-child policy, and individual claims to property have undermined notions of familial as well as collective property (see Oi 1999, Yan 2003). Overall, the recent Chinese experience confirms Goody's account of East Asia as resembling Europe in the long-term "fit" between domestic institutions and rapid modernization, and as profoundly hierarchical.[8] Meanwhile it would seem that the challenges of how to develop new systems of welfare and social security to support a rapidly aging population are fundamentally the same for East and for West.

Like the former East Germany, now incorporated into the Federal Republic, the "reform socialist" countries continue to exhibit distinctive features. However, the challenge of developing new social security systems to support rapidly aging populations, and the proper role of inheritance in such systems, is now fundamentally the same throughout Eurasia.

CONCLUSION

No anthropologist has argued more convincingly than Goody against Eurocentric accounts of the emergence of the modern world, and few have undertaken comparative work across the levels and time frames that he has addressed. For most anthropologists of his generation and since, the ambition of Wolf (1982) (corresponding to Wallerstein's notion of the "modern world system") is already very *longue durée*. Historical sociologists have begun to develop new forms of "civilizational analysis," and the notion of the "axial age" has been rediscovered (Arnason et al. 2005). Yet even these cover only a fraction of the period tackled by Goody.

In recent sociocultural anthropology, Goody's panorama has been truncated temporally and fragmented thematically. His work is little used even in the subfields to which he has contributed prominently. I have discussed some of these above; space has precluded a review of many others. Europeanist work continues to improve our understanding of the links between property and kinship, legal anthropology has the potential to invigorate theoretical frames, and the study of socialist societies reveals some of the grim consequences of dispensing with the private ownership and transmission of productive property. Another subfield in which more research is needed is the interface between anthropology and demography because fertility obviously has profound consequences for inheritance (Kertzer & Fricke 1997). As noted above, Macfarlane (1997) saw England and Japan as the pioneers of what elsewhere took the form of "demographic transition." Instead of the "natural" tendency to maximize births, these privileged islanders began to calculate the costs and benefits of additional offspring.

---

[8]Much has been made of China's success in raising hundreds of millions of citizens out of absolute poverty, but statistics suggest that income distribution has become even more unequal than that of the United States (*Economist* 2007, p. 50).

Similar economistic assumptions have continued to dominate the literature, including studies of why fertility levels have plunged to below replacement levels in many parts of Europe (see Kertzer & Fricke 1997). Whereas Goody (1976) cautioned against the export of European models of the family to Africa on the grounds that the African economies of that era could not possibly sustain welfare states of the sort that had evolved in modern Europe, it has recently become clear that this model of welfare cannot be sustained in Europe either. It seems likely that lower fertility is one of a number of factors working to increase the significance of familial material inheritance for life chances, but more careful analysis of changing "generational contracts" is needed (Wrigley 2003).

Most of the demographic arguments are grounded primarily in individualist economic calculations. However, Heady (2007) has suggested that fertility rates may be better explained if we think of reproduction in terms of intergenerational Maussian gift exchange. He argues that only in exceptional situations of turbulence will the fundamental moral norm of meeting replacement needs not be fulfilled. Heady has recently led a large-scale comparative investigation of European kinship. Data on inheritance have not yet been analyzed, but early results confirm the persistence of macroregional variations in kin recognition and demographic strategies. With its combination of large-scale statistical analysis and ethnography, the *Kinship and Social Security in Europe* project is in some respects a belated realization of Goody's methodological blueprint, even though the investigations have so far been restricted to eight European countries (Heady & Grandits 2008).

DISCLOSURE STATEMENT

The author is not aware of any biases that might be perceived as affecting the objectivity of this review.

LITERATURE CITED

Abrahams R. 1991. *A Place of Their Own: Family Farming in Eastern Finland*. Cambridge, UK: Cambridge Univ. Press

Arnason JP, Eisenstadt SN, Wittrock B, eds. 2005. *Axial Civilizations and World History*. Leiden: Brill

Augustins G. 1990. *Comment se Perpétuer? Devenirs des Lignées et Destins des Patrimoines dans les Paysanneries Européennes*. Nanterre: Société d'ethnologie

Balfe JH. 1999. *Passing It On: The Inheritance and Use of Summer Houses*. Montclair, NJ: Pocomo

Barrera-Gonzalez A. 1998. Domestic succession, property transmission, and family systems in the agrarian societies of contemporary Spain. *Hist. Fam.* 3(2):221–46

Basu S, ed. 2005. *Dowry and Inheritance*. London: Zed

Beckert J. 2007. The *longue durée* of inheritance law; discourses and institutional development in France, Germany, and the United States since 1800. *Arch. Eur. Sociol.* 48(1):79–120

Beckert J. 2008. *Inherited Wealth*. Princeton, NJ: Princeton Univ. Press

Bernau P. 2007. Die neue Erbschaftsteuer wird gerechter. *Frankf. Allg. Sonntagszeitung* Nov. 11:58

Bloch M. 1975. Property and the end of affinity. In *Marxist Analyses and Social Anthropology*, ed. M Bloch, pp. 203–28. London: Malaby

Borneman J. 1992. *Belonging in the Two Berlins: Kin, State, Nation*. Cambridge, UK/New York: Cambridge Univ. Press

Bourdieu P. 1962. Célibat et condition paysanne. *Etudes Rural.* 5–6:32–135

Bourdieu P. 1976. Marriage strategies as strategies of social reproduction. In *Family and Society. Selections from the Annales*, ed. R Forster, O Ranum, pp. 117–44. Baltimore: Johns Hopkins Univ. Press

Carsten J, ed. 2000. *Cultures of Relatedness: New Approaches to the Study of Kinship*. Cambridge, UK: Cambridge Univ. Press

Carsten J, Hugh-Jones S, eds. 1995. *About the House: Lévi-Strauss and Beyond*. Cambridge, UK/New York: Cambridge Univ. Press

Cole J. 2003. The last becomes first: the rise of ultimogeniture in contemporary South Tyrol. See Grandits & Heady 2003, pp. 263–74

Cole J, Wolf E. 1974. *The Hidden Frontier: Ecology and Ethnicity in an Alpine Valley*. New York: Academic

de Haan H. 1994. *In the Shadow of the Tree: Kinship, Property and Inheritance Among Farm Families*. Amsterdam: Het Spinhuis

Economist. 2007. For whosoever hath, to him shall be given, and he shall have more. *Economist* Aug. 11:50

Ember M, Ember CR, Low BS. 2007. Comparing explanations of polygyny. *Cross-Cult. Res.* 41(4):428–40

Engels F. 1972. *The Origin of the Family, Private Property and the State*. London: Lawrence & Wishart

Finch J, Mason J. 2000. *Passing On: Kinship and Inheritance in England*. London: Routledge

Frank AG. 1998. *ReOrient: Global Economy in the Asian Age*. Berkeley: Univ. Calif. Press

Gilman A, Hunt RC, eds. 1998. *Property in Economic Context*. Lanham, MD: Univ. Press Am.

Goody E. 1982. *Parenthood and Social Reproduction: Fostering and Occupational Roles in West Africa*. Cambridge, UK: Cambridge Univ. Press

Goody JR. 1962. *Death, Property and the Ancestors: A Study of the Mortuary Customs of the Lodagaa of West Africa*. London: Tavistock

Goody JR. 1976. *Production and Reproduction: A Comparative Study of the Domestic Domain*. Cambridge, UK: Cambridge Univ. Press

Goody JR. 1980. Slavery in time and space. In *African and Asian Systems of Slavery*, ed. JL Watson, pp. 16–42. Oxford: Basil Blackwell

Goody JR. 1983. *The Development of Family and Marriage in Europe*. Cambridge, UK: Cambridge Univ. Press

Goody JR. 1990. *The Oriental, the Ancient and the Primitive: Systems of Marriage and the Family in the Pre-Industrial Societies of Eurasia*. Cambridge, UK: Cambridge Univ. Press

Goody JR. 1996. *The East in the West*. Cambridge, UK: Cambridge Univ. Press

Goody JR. 1998a. Dowry and the rights of women to property. In *Property Relations: Renewing the Anthropological Tradition*, ed. CM Hann, pp. 201–13. Cambridge, UK: Cambridge Univ. Press

Goody JR. 1998b. *Food and Love: A Cultural History of East and West*. London: Verso

Goody JR. 2000. *The European Family: An Historico-Anthropological Essay*. Oxford: Blackwell

Goody JR. 2003. Sorcery and socialism. See Grandits & Heady 2003, pp. 391–408

Goody JR. 2006a. Gordon Childe, the urban revolution, and the haute cuisine: an anthropo-archaeological view of modern history. *Comp. Stud. Soc. Hist.* 48(3):503–19

Goody JR. 2006b. *The Theft of History*. Cambridge, UK: Cambridge Univ. Press

Grandits H, Heady P, eds. 2003. *Distinct Inheritances: Property, Family and Community in a Changing Europe*. Münster: LIT

Habakkuk HJ. 1955. Family structure and economic change in nineteenth century Europe. *J. Econ. Hist.* 15:1–12

Habakkuk J. 1994. *Marriage, Debt and the Estates System: English Landownership, 1650–1950*. Oxford: Clarendon

Hann C, ed. 1990. *Market Economy and Civil Society in Hungary*. London: Frank Cass

Hann C. 1993. From production to property: decollectivization and the family-land relationship in contemporary Hungary. *Man* 28(3):299–320

Hann C, and the Prop. Relat. group. 2003. *The Postsocialist Agrarian Question: Property Relations and the Rural Condition*. Münster: LIT

Hart K. 2008. Intellectual property. In *The New Keywords: Neoliberalism in Contemporary Social Theory. Curr. Anthropol.* Spec. Issue: In press

Heady P. 2007. Fertility as a process of social exchange. *Demogr. Res.* 17(16):465–93

Heady P, Grandits H. 2003. Introduction. Property, family and community in a changing Europe: a system and historical approach. See Grandits & Heady 2003, pp. 1–30

Heady P, Grandits H, eds. 2008. *Kinship and Social Security in Europe*. Frankfurt am Main: Peter Lang. 3 Vols.

Heady P, Miller LG. 2003. Cooperation, power, and community: economy and ideology in the Russian countryside. See Hann and the Prop. Relat. group, pp. 257–92

Hindess B, Hirst P. 1975. *Pre-Capitalist Modes of Production*. London: Routledge

Humphrey C. 1983. *Karl Marx Collective: Economy, Society and Religion in a Siberian Collective Farm*. Cambridge, UK: Cambridge Univ. Press

Kertzer D, Barbaglis M, eds. 2001–2003. *The History of the European Family*, Vols. 1–3. New Haven: Yale Univ. Press

Kertzer D, Fricke T. 1997. *Anthropological Demography: Toward a New Synthesis*. Chicago: Univ. Chicago Press

Kohli M. 2004. Intergenerational transfers and inheritance: a comparative view. In *Annual Review of Gerontology and Geriatrics*. Vol. 24: *Intergenerational Relations Across Time and Place*, ed. M Silverstein, pp. 266–89. New York: Springer

Lévi-Strauss C. 1983. *The Way of the Masks*. London: Cape

Macfarlane A. 1997. *The Savage Wars of Peace: England, Japan and the Malthusian Trap*. Oxford: Blackwell

Marcus G. 1992. *Lives in Trust: The Fortunes of Dynastic Families in Late Twentieth-Century America*. Boulder: Westview

Miller RK, McNamee SJ, eds. 1998. *Inheritance and Wealth in America*. New York: Plenum

Morgan LH. 1877. *Ancient Society, or Researches in the Lines of Human Progress from Savagery, Through Barbarism to Civilization*. London: Macmillan

Mundy M. 1988. The family, inheritance and Islam: a reexamination of the sociology of farâ'id law. In *Islamic Law: Social and Historical Contexts*, ed. A al-Azmeh, pp. 1–123. London: Routledge

Mundy M. 1995. *Domestic Government: Kinship, Community and Polity in Northern Yemen*. London: I. B. Tauris

Mundy M, Saumarez Smith R. 2007. *Governing Property, Making the Modern State: Law, Administration and Production in Ottoman Syria*. London: I. B. Tauris

Oi JC, ed. 1999. *Property Rights and Economic Reform in China*. Berkeley: Univ. Calif. Press

Sabean DW. 1990. *Property, Production and Family in Neckarhausen 1700–1870*. Cambridge, UK: Cambridge Univ. Press

Schweitzer PP, ed. 2000. *Dividends of Kinship: Meanings and Uses of Social Relatedness*. London: Routledge

Segalen M. 1991. *Fifteen Generations of Bretons: Kinship and Society in Lower Brittany, 1720–1980*. Cambridge, UK: Cambridge Univ. Press

Skinner GW. 1993. Conjugal power in Tokugawa Japanese families: a matter of life and death. In *Sex and Gender Hierarchies*, ed. BD Miller, pp. 236–70. London: Cambridge Univ. Press

Strathern M. 1992. *After Nature: English Kinship in the Late Twentieth century*. Cambridge, UK: Cambridge Univ. Press

Strathern M. 1999. *Property, Substance and Effect: Anthropological Essays on Persons and Things*. London: Athlone

Szelenyi I. 1983. *Urban Inequalities Under State Socialism*. Oxford, UK: Oxford Univ. Press

Verdery K. 1996. *What Was Socialism and What Comes Next?* Princeton, NJ: Princeton Univ. Press

Verdery K. 2004. *The Vanishing Hectare: Property and Value in Postsocialist Transylvania*. Ithaca, NY: Cornell Univ. Press

Verdery K, Humphrey C, eds. 2004. *Property in Question: Value Transformation in the Global Economy*. Oxford: Berg

Viazzo PP. 2007. *Macro-regional differences in European kinship culture*. Presented at Conf. Kinship Soc. Secur. Eur., Nov., Halle/Saale

von Benda-Beckmann F. 1979. *Property in Social Continuity: Continuity and Change in the Maintenance of Property Relationships through Time in Minangkabau, West Sumatra*. The Hague: Nijhoff

von Benda-Beckmann F. 1994. Acts of last will in Indonesian local laws. In *Actes à Cause de Mort—Acts of Last Will. Transactions of the Jean Bodin Society*, No. LXII, 4th part, pp. 115–43. Bruxelles: De Boeck Univ.

von Benda-Beckmann F, von Benda-Beckmann K, Wiber M, eds. 2006. *Changing Properties of Property*. Oxford: Berghahn

Wolf ER. 1982. *Europe and the People Without History*. Berkeley: Univ. Calif. Press

Wrigley EA. 2003. Intrinsic growth rates and inheritance strategies: a perspective from historical demography. See Grandits & Heady 2003, pp. 69–95

Yan Y. 2003. *Private Life Under Socialism: Love, Intimacy, and Family Change in a Chinese Village 1949–1999*. Stanford, CA: Stanford Univ. Press

Yanagisako S. 1979. Family and household: the analysis of domestic groups. *Annu. Rev. Anthropol.* 8:161–205

The Archaeology
of Childhood

Jane Eva Baxter

Department of Anthropology, DePaul University, Chicago, Illinois 60614;
email: jbaxter@depaul.edu

Annu. Rev. Anthropol. 2008. 37:159–75

First published online as a Review in Advance on
June 17, 2008

The *Annual Review of Anthropology* is online at
anthro.annualreviews.org

This article's doi:
10.1146/annurev.anthro.37.081407.085129

Key Words

children, gender, identity, material culture

Abstract

The archaeology of childhood has grown over the past decade and a
half as a vibrant field of specialized interest within archaeology as a
whole. A thematic treatment of the literature highlights a variety of
approaches to how and why archaeologists should study children using
the archaeological record. These themes are organized chronologically
and begin with critiques of archaeological approaches that do not include children and an exploration of the relationship between childhood
studies and studies of gender, identity, and agency in the archaeological
record. Theoretical and methodological developments that draw attention to new ways of looking at the archaeological record to identify
cultural constructions of childhood and lived experiences of children
are presented. Finally, current tensions and pluralities in the literature
are explored as the archaeology of childhood reaches a new stage in its
own maturity as a field of inquiry.

INTRODUCTION: A THEMATIC APPROACH TO THE ARCHAEOLOGY OF CHILDHOOD

The archaeology of childhood is an emerging field of interest within archaeology. Theoretical developments and methodological innovations are integral features of this continually evolving body of literature, and conversations about childhood are taking place among an ever diversifying pool of scholars in the discipline.

The piece most often regarded as the seminal work on the topic of children in archaeology is Lillehammer's article, "A Child is Born: The Child's World in an Archaeological Perspective." Her work underscored the lack of consideration that children had received previously in archaeological interpretations despite ample evidence of children in the material record of the past (Lillehammer 1989, p. 90). This work was seen as a call to action by many archaeologists, and since the late 1990s, a proliferation of literature on children and childhood has been published. Most of this work is found in edited, topical volumes (Ardren & Hutson 2006; Baxter 2006a; Kamp 2002a; Moore & Scott 1997; Sofaer Derevenski 1994a, 2000a), although a few monograph-length works (Baxter 2000, 2005; Wileman 2005) and several significant articles (Crown 1999, 2001; Kamp 2001a,b; Park 1998; Roveland 2001) have been devoted to children, childhood, and archaeology.

Even a casual perusal of publication dates suggests that children and childhood studies are emergent topics in archaeology. The pronounced florescence of work after the year 2000 also indicates that this area of scholarship is still developing its own sense of intellectual history. Early ideas that set the agenda for childhood studies in archaeology are still tightly intertwined with thoughts about future directions for scholarship.

Thematic considerations of the archaeology of childhood have been undertaken previously. One approach to addressing this literature presented themes that are common categories for thinking about children in contemporary, western cultural traditions (Kamp 2001b, Wileman 2005). Another approach focused on the categories of evidence typically encountered by archaeologists, such as burials, iconography, artifacts, and space (Baxter 2005). The approach taken toward the literature in this review is somewhat different from previous works. Although certainly chronological, this review is primarily a thematic consideration of theoretical and methodological approaches to studying children and childhood through the archaeological record. This review, therefore, privileges works that contribute to the conversations taking place about how and why archaeologists should engage questions about children and childhood when studying the past.

SOLVING A PROBLEM: THE ABSENCE OF CHILDREN IN ARCHAEOLOGICAL INTERPRETATIONS

Two significant, early articles on the archaeology of childhood were entitled "Where Are the Children? (Sofaer Derevenski 1994b) and "Where Have All the Children Gone?" (Kamp 2001b). Rhetorical questions about the absence of children in archaeological studies were matched by a question posed of anthropology in general in a leading article in *American Anthropologist* whose title begged the question, "Why Don't Anthropologists Like Children?" (Hirschfeld 2002).

Archaeologists and anthropologists interested in the study of children were readily convinced of the importance of children in understanding human societies and of their significance as a topic of study in their own right (Schwartzman 2006). Hirschfeld (2002) stated that anthropology is based on the premise that culture is learned and not inherited, making studies of children and childhood among the most natural areas of interest for all anthropologists. Many authors have noted that children comprised significant demographic portions of all documented social groups, making incomplete any interpretation of the past that does not consider them (Ardren 2006, Baxter 2005, Chamberlain 2000). Similarly, several authors have presented evidence that children are significant social and economic actors in their own right and that the organization of families, communities, and societies often prioritizes the care and training of children (Ardren 2006; Baxter 2005, 2006a; Kamp 2001b; Sofaer Derevenski 1997, 2000a).

Asking why children have been omitted with such regularity from archaeological interpretations seems to be very reasonable, given the compelling reasons to study children. An examination of archaeological literature prior to the emergent disciplinary interest in children led scholars to identify two main barriers that kept, and continue to keep, children marginalized in archaeological thinking and research.

Questioning the Universal, Biological, and Natural in Western Constructions of Childhood

Archaeologists have always sought analogs from the historical and ethnographic records because they presupposed that cultures in the past were, in many ways, fundamentally different from the cultural traditions lived and experienced by archaeologists themselves. Archaeological thought regarding children and childhood has not followed this trend traditionally, and some researchers have tended to make assumptions about children and childhood on the basis of the idea that childhood is a natural and universal experience. This tendency has stemmed from ideas held about childhood in the contemporary, western cultures from which most archaeologists derive and from the fact that everyone has experienced childhood at some point (Baxter 2005; Kamp 2001b; Sofaer Derevenski 1994b, 1997, 2000b).

In direct contradiction, scholars across disciplines have acknowledged that childhood is a sociocultural construct that is shaped and formed around the ontological development of human beings (Baxter 2000, 2005; Joyce 2000; Kamp 2001b; Rothschild 2002; Sofaer Derevenski 1994b, 1997, 2000b; Stephens 1995). Specific biological changes occur as individual humans mature, but the meaning, definitions, and ideals imposed on these changes are arbitrary and vary cross-culturally (Kamp 2001b). It is the specific, cultural constructions of childhood in contemporary, western cultures that have been identified as being particularly detrimental to the archaeology of childhood, and the implications of these constructions on archaeologists' attitudes toward children and childhood have been recognized as twofold.

First, contemporary constructions of children and childhood are cast in relation to the concepts of adult and maturity (Sofaer Derevenski 1997), and they stem from a relatively recent and historically traceable phenomenon that grew around bourgeois notions of family, home, individuality, and privacy (Stephens 1995, pp. 4–5). Children are associated with dependence and innocence, and childhood is most often identified as a time for learning and training in preparation for adulthood. Children should be cared for, controlled, and kept secure and happy during this liminal stage between birth and adulthood (Kamp 2001b). These ideas about the nature and care of children are paired with the assumption that political, economic, and social control are held exclusively by adults (Sofaer Derevenski 1997).

Second, contemporary, western definitions of childhood emphasize individuals' biological and physical development through the human life cycle (Kamp 2001b). Ontological categories defined by western medicine and psychology represent a biological reality that includes readily identifiable stages of personhood, such as infant, toddler, child, adolescent, young adult, adult, and elderly. This rhetoric of science and biology has led to the naturalization of western understandings of childhood and the extension of other aspects of childhood into the universal realm.

The idea of a universal childhood can be seen in archaeological reconstructions of the past in textbooks and museum exhibits (Kamp & Whittaker 2002). This idea of a biologically based, universal childhood also has made it very easy for archaeologists to discount children as viable subjects of study, particularly because this construction suggests they were not the individuals making significant contributions to past social groups.

Finding the Invisible, Unknowable Child

A second barrier to including children in archaeological interpretations has stemmed from children's perceived invisibility in the archaeological record. Children are frequently underrepresented in mortuary contexts (Chamberlain 2000), are often considered to have relationships with material culture that are unconventional and unpredictable, and are often thought to be the sole users of very few artifacts and spaces (Baxter 2000, Kamp 2001b). Thus children have not been investigated with the same rigor as adults in mortuary contexts and have been absent in settlement studies and studies of space, work, and household (Sofaer Derevenski 1994b).

Baxter (2005) has identified ways that early archaeological literature treated children as subjects of inquiry. The first early role of children in archaeological literature was to explain the presence of otherwise "uninterpretable" artifact categories at archaeological sites such as miniature objects or other objects thought to be toys. The second role was to use ethnographic information about children to create cautionary tales where children's behaviors acted as spoilers to more traditional and conventional archaeological interpretations. Children's behaviors were characterized as randomizing or distorting because they often altered the deposits of materials created by adults. Children were also reported as using objects in atypical, unconventional, or unexpected ways that deviated from the normative uses of those objects by adults. The fact that children used different material culture than adults did, or used the same objects in different ways than adults did, deemed them an unknowable category of people in the past (Baxter 2000, pp. 4–6; 2005; 2006b).

LEARNING FROM OUR PAST: CHILDHOOD AND GENDER STUDIES IN ARCHAEOLOGY

Cultural constructions that result in marginalization and presumed archaeological invisibility are themes that have led scholars to draw direct parallels between the archaeology of childhood and the archaeology of gender (Ardren 2006; Baker 1997; Baxter 2005; Joyce 2000; Kamp 2001b, 2006; Rothschild 2002; Sofaer Derevenski 1994b, 1997, 2000b). Scholars have asserted that the absence of children in archaeological interpretations has stemmed, at least in part, from the association between children and women. Like women, children are categorized at the weaker end of the male/female and adult/child dimensions and are therefore feminized (other than male) and exist in a category of the disempowered (Baker 1997, Rothschild 2002).

This shared history of disempowerment, marginalization, and invisibility has directed scholars to study the history of gender research in archaeology as way of approaching the archaeological study of childhood (Kamp 2001b, p. 3). The historical movement from marginalization to widespread acceptance of gender as a topic of archaeological inquiry is often described as the desired trajectory for children and childhood as well. Parallel arguments about the cultural construction of gender and childhood, and the necessity to alter underlying assumptions about who was present in the past and therefore responsible for the archaeological record, are often invoked to underscore this move toward becoming part of the archaeological mainstream (Ardren 2006; Baker 1997; Baxter 2005, 2006b; Kamp 2001b, 2002b; Sofaer Derevenksi 1994b, 1997, 2000b; Wilkie 2000).

The relationship between gender and archaeology has developed on more sophisticated theoretical levels through associations with more general trends and emphases on identity and agency as important ways of understanding the archaeological record (King 2006). Archaeological investigations of identity often consider how individuals come to embody a series of overlapping and intersecting identities that can include age, sex, gender, class, race, and other categories (Meskell 2001). Shifting emphases in research prioritize how cultural identities such as childhood are actively embodied and practiced rather than passively constructed (Lillehammer 2000; Lopiparo 2006, p. 134). This consideration of identity in general and the overlapping constructions of age and gender specifically have been central in attempts to expand understandings of what childhood meant in different times and places.

EXPANDING DEFINITIONS OF CHILDHOOD

As all these critiques suggest, age categories are culturally defined and cannot be assumed or transplanted from one time period to another. Rothschild (2002) explicitly warned archaeologists not to export ideas about modern lives into the past and not to impose ethnographical and historical expectations on past lives. Indeed, Rothschild noted that if childhood is a cultural construct, then perhaps at certain times and places in the past no such marked stage of personhood existed (2002, pp. 3–4). Similarly, the term child or category of childhood subsumes a large amount of diversity in terms of developmental stages, roles, dependence, and independence that may be elaborated selectively in different cultural contexts (Sofaer Derevenski 1997). Given the possibility for infinite variation in how childhood was constructed, Kamp (2001b) argued that we should assume that definitions of childhood were different in the past, making imperative the need to define children in specific contexts.

Seeking the Dominant Discourse: Representation, Ritual, and Childhood

Recently, Kamp (2006) noted that cultural constructions of childhood are part of a dominant discourse recognized by all members of a social group. How an individual is supposed to progress through his or her life cycle and how changes in status are marked by biological or cultural milestones are important parts of this dominant discourse. Although these ideals may be contested and not always actualized in practice, it is this ideal cultural construction that becomes depicted in symbolic and ritual contexts.

Archaeologists seeking to explore alternative constructions of childhood are often seeking the dominant discourse. Idealized categories often involve how stages in the life cycle were marked through language, ceremony, ritual, objects, and performance and how specified sets of roles, behaviors, expectations, and limitations became associated with particular individuals. James & Prout (1990, p. 220) suggested that transitions are particularly important for the study of childhood because changes are often symbolically marked. Rituals marking transitions in status and identity often include particular bodily modifications and changes in clothing and hairstyles and can be associated with particular places and objects that leave archaeological traces.

One category of evidence that has been used successfully to identify emic constructions of childhood identity are images of individuals found in literary, artistic, and iconographic sources (e.g., Beaumont 2000, Joyce 2000, King 2006). King (2006) noted that archaeologists tend to prioritize visually expressive cultural traditions in their investigations of individual identities. These artistic and iconographic representations of children are not the products of children's activities but rather represent adult idealizations of individuals at different phases and stages of life (Baxter 2005). As such, these images are thought to be imbued with particular meanings for the adults who created and viewed such images, including invoking a sense of memory (Lillehammer 2000) and nostalgia (Joyce 2006) for their own childhoods.

A particularly useful example of how images of individuals have been used to investigate categories of identity in the past comes from the Aztec *Florentine Codex* and *Codex Mendoza* (Joyce 2000). Joyce used the textual and visual narratives found in these texts to investigate the social construction of gender identities. Described in the texts were a variety of individuals including infants, children, and young adults of both sexes and of different classes (Joyce 2000, p. 474). Through changes in objects and rhetoric surrounding individuals at different stages in the life cycle, she identified three distinct categories of identity marked by rites and symbols, which reflected differences in gender, achievement, and status. The first of these identities was infants, who were considered to be unformed individuals at birth and, through habitual action, costumes, and ornaments, were shaped into one of three genders in their early teens (Joyce 2000).

Prehistoric rock art and ethnographic sources have also been used in the American Southwest to identify particular life stages that were ritually and materially marked (Hays-Gilpin 2002). The particular whorled style of hair associated with Pueblo puberty rituals for girls was known as "wearing a butterfly" and was part of an extended ritual marking a biological milestone. Examining rock art from the Pueblo regions resulted in the identification of girls "wearing a butterfly" along with others who were not, suggesting a particular status of the wearer. Hays-Gilpin (2002) argued that this combination of ethnographic and iconographic evidence points to a unique category of personhood that extended more than 1500 years into prehistory.

More often, archaeologies of identity that have focused on culturally constructed ideas of childhood have used mortuary data where intersections of the biological and cultural can be explored through skeletal remains (Sofaer Derevenski 2000b). Mortuary studies that employed the concept of children have a long history in archaeology and relied on an unproblematized equation between a subadult skeleton and a child (Rothschild 2002). These types of studies used the placement and treatment of subadult skeletons to answer broad questions of social organization, such as status, or to shed light on adult identities (Sofaer Derevenski 2000b, Perry 2006).

Mortuary studies undertaken to investigate the lives of children and the individual identities embodied by young people are relatively recent phenomena and take very different approaches to the skeletal remains and mortuary treatment of children (Bradley 2002, Crawford 2000, Lucy 1994, Janik 2000, McCafferty & McCafferty 2006, Meskell 1994, Mizoguchi 2000, Perry 2006, Sofaer Derevenski 2000b, Storey & McAnany 2006).

Defining categories of identity using mortuary populations requires a decoupling of biological distinctions of immaturity from cultural meanings that are placed on individuals' bodies (Sofaer Derevenski 2000b; Perry 2006). It also requires seeking overlapping categories of identity, including age and gender, to understand social constructions of individuals in the past (Janik 2000, Meskell 1994, Mizoguchi 2000). Perry (2006) provided a comprehensive overview of bioarchaeological analyses of subadult skeletons, or individuals identified as being under the age of 18. Rather than equating subadult skeletons with children, she noted that biological transformations, such as weaning and puberty, are often marked by ritual and emphasized in ideological and social constructions of identity categories. These events also leave discernable traces on subadult skeletons. Using a case study from the Byzantine Near East, Perry (2006) demonstrated how bioarchaeology may be used to define childhood in a particular time and place by seeking ways that biological transformations were elaborated or downplayed in mortuary treatment.

Two recent studies in Mesoamerica used skeletal and mortuary analyses to identify categories of identity in subadult populations. At the Mexican site of Cholula, categories of identity found in Aztec Codices (Joyce 2000) were investigated using skeletal and mortuary evidence (McCafferty & McCafferty 2006). Although researchers identified a cohesive burial tradition through analyzing the evidence, they found a series of significant differences among burials of infants, young children, older children, and adults. Infants had few or no burial goods, suggesting they were perceived as incomplete persons much as they were in the codices. Young children had unique markers of identity, such as musical instruments and toys, included in their burials. Older children and young teens were interred with the same materials as adults, suggesting that certain statuses of age and gender were recognized in those individuals.

Seeking differences among burials of children as well as comparing child and adult burials, archaeologists undertook a similar analysis at the Maya site of K'axob. Differences in how children were buried at different stages of life were interpreted as both communal ideals of appropriate commemoration and representations of how adults valued individual children (Storey & McAnany 2006). Four patterns of age differentiation were revealed: neonates, toddlers, older children, and near adults. Mortuary treatment for each category of individual showed increasing elaboration with age, although at no time were the treatments as elaborate as those for adults. This pattern has been interpreted to indicate how children were valued as they matured and as adult perceptions of, and investments in, children changed.

Seeking New Analogs: Social and Economic Roles for Children Across Cultures

Approaching the archaeological record to explore constructed identities of children is related to research designed to expand the variety of ways children may be involved in economic and ritual activities. These types of studies are designed to redress the tendency to universalize western childhood experiences and to offer new analogs to expand ways of thinking about childhood in the past.

Understanding that archaeologists tend to divide tasks along gender lines, Kamp (2002b, p. 71) noted that children are generally not seen as providing significant labor in archaeological interpretations. Ethnographic sources, in contrast, point to the strategic, important uses of children's work in a variety of contexts, including child care, tending animals, gathering, food preparation, housework, agricultural activities, and wage labor.

The largest body of literature investigating children's social and economic roles comes from the study of hunter-gatherer populations (Lamb & Hewlett 2005). Ethnoarchaeological sources have indicated that child labor does not vary in relationship to subsistence strategy; rather children's labor is valued using social as well as economic variables (Bugarin 2006, Kamp 2002b, Lamb & Hewlett 2005). This assertion was explored using a systematic evaluation of the ethnographic and ethnoarchaeological record of African foragers, pastoralists, and agriculturalists (Bugarin 2006). This study documented a wide variety of economic roles for children and identified implements, ceremonial goods, spatial behaviors, and special purpose areas that were related to children. Some of these goods related to child rearing and training, whereas others were objects and areas that were child-specific; all pointed to the potential visibility of children's economic roles in the African past (Bugarin 2006).

Similarly, ethnoarchaeological investigations of children of the Meriam, Eastern Torres, have shown that children's foraging behaviors included a series of age-based practices that were archaeologically visible in the composition of shell middens (Bird & Bliege Bird 2000). Comparisons of shellfish foraging strategies between children and adults found that children engaged in unique foraging strategies that maximized their efficiency in the present, rather than attempting practices that were preparatory for adult foraging. Children's choices in prey reflected their physiological development around areas of manual dexterity, limb size, and strength. The result was a unique profile of prey types that made their contributions to midden deposits unique. Interpreting the archaeological record without considering the possibility of children foraging would not only mask their contributions in the past, but also would result in erroneous interpretations of the archaeological record.

Children as Participants in Transformation: Ritual and Childhood in the Past

Children's contributions in the past are not always economic in nature, and expanding the definitions of childhood requires an exploration of the different arenas in which children may be engaging in activities that become archaeologically visible. Different cultural groups imbue the time of childhood with particular meanings that can make them significant actors in ritual contexts (Berrelleza & Chavez Balderas 2006, Bradley 2002, Hays-Gilpin 2002, Sillar 1994). Several archaeologists have explored cultural constructions of children that cast them as unique repositories of sacred knowledge and power.

Perhaps the first archaeologist to take such an approach was Sillar (1994), who used ethnographic, historical, and archaeological data for the Inca custom of *capacocha*, the ritual sacrifice of children, to seek unique identities of children in Incan culture. His work found that Incan children often played with miniature vessels created specifically for their use. The act of play had strong symbolic significance because their culture believed that skills were given to people by gods and were learned through play. Those who engaged in play were seen as being active communicants with deities, making children the most effective people to communicate with the gods and the most suitable offerings through sacrifice.

Child sacrifice in Aztec cultures has also been used to interpret the particular ritual significance of children (Berrelleza & Chavez Balderas 2006). The Aztec codices, child burial treatment, and osteological analyses were used to investigate which children were selected for sacrifice and why. Profiles of skeletal remains showed that male children in poor health were chosen as sacrifices to particular deities. The specific characteristics of these children suggested that the gender and illness they represented made them significant communicants with deities who were also gendered male and who were believed to be the givers of particular illnesses. Individuals who possessed the same traits early in life were seen as particularly powerful offerings for the placation of gods, which gave particular children cultural power and significance in their lifetimes.

Rituals and childhood have not been investigated just as they pertain to the context of sacrifice. Bradley (2002) studied skeletal remains from Sand Canyon Pueblo and discovered that children at that ritual center showed evidence for better health and nourishment than did contemporary populations from other sites. She argued that it was the specific ideological construction of childhood that allowed children to be included in ritual feasting, which resulted in a skeletal profile that reflected health and good nutrition prior to death.

MATERIALIZING CHILDREN

Childhood as a defined stage of life and a category of identity is not the same as the lived experiences of children (Kamp 2006). Identifying children as individual cultural actors in the past requires alternative approaches to knowing the past and engaging the archaeological record (Sofaer Derevenksi 1994b, p. 10). An essential step in identifying traces of children's lived experiences is shifting assumptions about who is present and visible in the past (Wilkie 2000). Baker (1997) noted that archaeologists have always assumed that men were present at archaeological sites, but that women and children had to be found.

One of the earliest examples of archaeology being written with a different set of assumptions is Spector's *What This Awl Means* (1991), which is often acknowledged as revolutionary because it recreated a past that was not focused on male actors and instead interpreted the archaeological record with women and children as the central figures. The person who made and used the awl in Spector's recreation of the past was a young girl who "had a reputation... for hard work, creativity, and excellence through her skills in quill and bead work" (Spector 1991, p. 398).

Shifting assumptions must also be paired with new theoretical and methodological approaches in the archaeological record. Children have been identified archaeologically using a variety of categories of archaeological data including burials and burial objects; toys and play things; the spatial organization of objects and activity areas; representations of children in art, artifacts, and monuments; artifacts produced by children; and skeletal remains (Baxter 2005, Kamp 2001b, Lillehammer 1989). Children, therefore, are not archaeologically invisible, but it is necessary to identify their activities as opposed to other agents in the archaeological record (Sofaer Derevenski 1997).

Children as Producers of Material Goods: Learning Culture, Shaping Traditions, Pushing Boundaries

One of the most prolific areas of archaeological research on children has been the investigation of child participation in craft production activities, including stone tool production, ceramic manufacture, and weaving (Bagwell 2002; Crown 1999, 2001, 2002; Finlay 1997; Greenfield 2000; Grimm 2000; Kamp 2001b, 2002b; Kamp et al. 1999). Craft production is a natural place to look for children archaeologically because crafting requires the acquisition of technical skills and cultural knowledge and must be learned. Because proficiency in learning a craft can take several years, it is often assumed that individuals started learning crafts at a young age; ethnographic evidence has documented children as young as 2–5 years old learning crafts (Kamp 2001b, p. 13). This does not mean that all apprentice craftspeople were children, but it does suggest that many novice crafters were likely starting their learning at younger ages.

Archaeological evidence for novice crafters has been defined in a variety of ways. Objects displaying evidence of inexpert workmanship are often thought to be the work of novice crafters, and further refinements to this approach have discerned deficiencies in manufacture that are attributable to conceptual under-

standings of crafting and motor skill development (Crown 1999, Finlay 1997, Kamp 2001b). Other scholars have argued that the standardization in finished products is indicative of proficiency and have associated a high degree of variability with novice and child crafters (Bagwell 2002). Other variables that have been identified as potential indicators include the types of raw materials available to crafters of different skill levels and the apparent divergences from local norms resulting from the inadvertent skipping of certain technological steps in production (Kamp 2001b, Finlay 1997, Grimm 2000).

Crown (1999, 2001, 2002) has advocated using psychological studies of child development to identify children as apprentice crafters in prehistory, and she has tested this approach by studying painted designs on ceramics from a variety of cultural traditions in the American Southwest, including Hohokam, Mimbres, and Salado. She noted that the ability to conceive, plan, and execute painted designs on ceramics is an indicator for levels of psychological development (Crown 1999) and that certain types of errors can be directly related to stages of cognitive development rather than to a lack of experience or expertise. This distinction allowed for the identification of novice crafters who were old enough to have fully developed cognitive skills versus those at earlier stages in the life cycle when cognitive skills were still developing. Focusing on ceramics that she identified as inexpertly made, Crown was able to analyze painted designs for material signatures of particular features of development, such as symmetry, and suggested that two age groups of children, those between the ages of 9 and 12 and another between the ages of 4 and 6, were responsible for creating some of the painted designs.

Bagwell (2002) built on Crown's work and studied variations in two-dimensional and three-dimensional abilities in children by age; she used variables of development to create a "skill score" that may be used to provide the minimum age of a potter who produced a particular vessel. She tested her skill score system using 78 miniature and poorly made vessels from Pecos Pueblo in New Mexico and several larger vessels from the same collection. She analyzed variables of construction techniques, standardization, and symmetry, which were designed to measure the ability to make recognizable types of ceramics. She identified three different skill levels among the community of crafters at Pecos Pueblo and determined a subset of miniature vessels that were most likely manufactured by children.

Another technique for identifying children among novice crafters has been to study fingerprint measurements left in clay figurines, miniature vessels, and full-sized vessels in Sinagua ceramic assemblages (Kamp 2001b; Kamp et al. 1999). Fingerprints were examined in the context of other variables of manufacture, such as the complexity of the manufacturing technique employed, the presence of symmetry, vessel thickness, vessel finish, vessel size, and the presence or absence of cracks upon firing. The association of children's fingerprints with relatively simply and poorly made vessels and figurines suggested that children may have been learning to become crafters in the context of play and that making and using toys would have been culturally associated (Kamp 2001b).

Evidence for children as producers of lithic technology has also been explored, particularly in Europe. Finlay (1997) observed variation in the lithic assemblage from the Mesolithic site of Coulererarch in Scotland and found poorly worked low-quality flint pebbles alongside evidence for fine blade production, reflecting the presence of knappers of various abilities. Other scholars have demonstrated that novice flint knappers may be identified through differences in how cores are prepared and manipulated; their studies suggest that children would have different sized hands and levels of manual dexterity, which may or may not have enabled the direct imitation of adult knappers (Finlay 1997, Grimm 2000, Pigeot 1990). Other variables associated with novice lithic production include the peripheral location of debitage from novice knappers in relationship to master crafters, the use of poor-quality materials

in novice knapping, and the observation that products of novice knappers were often not ultimately worked into tools (Grimm 2000, Pigeot 1990). Pigeot (1990) suggested that one could use these variables to identify master knappers, occasional knappers, and novices who seemed to be reducing materials for their own sakes. Grimm (2000) used these variables to study an apprentice flint knapper at the Upper Paleolithic site of Solvieux. In addition to analyzing the archaeological evidence for this apprentice operating in a community of master crafters, she employed the idea of "legitimate peripheral participation" (Lave & Wenger 1991) to assert that prehistoric apprenticeship was a social practice by which individuals were being socialized into a community. She used this concept to hypothesize the types of nonproduction-related activities that would have enabled an apprentice to observe the workings of the crafters at Solvieux while making valuable contributions to the community.

Analyzing the social context of production has been a growing theme that extends this literature about children and craft production beyond methods for identifying children archaeologically. Crown (2002) used ethnographic literature and archaeological samples to consider how children would have learned to become artisans and potters. She identified ethnographic and archaeological cases relating to a variety of learning frameworks in the American Southwest, including observation and imitation, verbal instruction, hands-on demonstration, and self-teaching as ways of communicating skill sets and cultural knowledge.

Greenfield (2000) explored how children learned to weave textiles in the Maya community of Zincantan in Highland Chiapas and demonstrated how learning frameworks among weavers shifted with other cultural changes in the community. She followed two families of weavers from the 1970s to the 1990s and identified how patterns of teaching and learning were altered when the community transitioned from living as a self-sustaining agricultural community to being a part of a larger cash economy. When the community was focused on agricultural production in the 1970s, weavers taught children in highly supervised and scaffolded ways that emphasized observation and the replication of traditional design patterns. When agriculture was replaced by cash economies, weaving was no longer taught directly by adults, but rather was learned independently by children through a great deal of trial and error. The result was a shift away from cultural conservativism in designs and technique toward variation and innovation on the part of child weavers.

Smith (2006) studied the role children played as innovators in ceramic production in prehistoric Huron communities in the Great Lakes region. She studied a category of vessels traditionally identified as juvenile ceramics on the basis of small size and poor quality of manufacture. A comparison of juvenile and adult vessels from the same assemblages revealed children to be active agents in their own socialization because they chose to copy only certain motif elements found in the decorative repertoire of larger vessels. These types of selections on the part of children have been interpreted to reflect the symbolic association through stylistic appropriation between a child potter and particular adults within a group of crafters.

Children learning crafts as part of a community has also been studied at the household level in the Ulua Valley, Honduras (Lopiparo 2006). Mold-constructed ceramic figurines were identified across this region and are a type of technology that would have allowed for all levels of crafters, including children, to participate in the manufacturing process. Children learning to produce crafts in the context of their households would have been an activity that imparted ideas about aesthetics, personhood, social roles, and identity and, through that process, reproduced and transformed important cultural elements. When these figurines were then used in important rituals of renewal, these objects would have linked spheres of household creation and ritual performance as children learned to become and perform in a variety of cultural contexts.

Children Moving and Doing: Children's Spaces, Places, and Things

Another way that children have been materialized in the archaeological record is through investigations of how children used social space, as seen through the patterned distributions of artifacts at archaeological sites. Some of the earliest literature to discuss children in the archaeological record explored the effects of children's behavior on archaeological deposits (Bonnichsen 1973, Hammond & Hammond 1981). These early studies demonstrated that children had an affect on the patterning of archaeological materials, but they also labeled those effects as distorting and randomizing as they masked the distributions of artifacts created by adults (Baxter 2000).

More recently, studies of children and social space have made theoretical arguments that children do not use space in random fashions because they interact with a material world that is filled with messages and meanings that shape their behavior (Baxter 2000, 2006c). Children's behaviors are shaped by contemporary expectations of children of different genders and at different ages, by functional and symbolic associations in the built environment, and by competing spheres of social influence. The assertion that children's behaviors would produce non-random patterns in the archaeological record was tested by investigating the spatial distribution of material culture that could be historically identified as child-specific, such as toys and child-rearing devices, at five nineteenth-century domestic sites across the United States (Baxter 2000, 2006c). At four of the five sites, these artifacts demonstrated clear patterning that did not mirror the distributional patterns of the overall artifact assemblage, demonstrating the archaeological visibility of children through the spatial distribution of artifacts. Moreover, these artifact distributions were interpreted in light of nineteenth-century cultural constructions of childhood as evidenced in published sources, and ideals of gender, parenting, and learning were identified as well as distributions that suggested children were creating autonomous spaces in domestic landscapes (Baxter 2000).

Similarly, Buchli & Lucas (2000) studied deposits in an abandoned home in 1990s Britain to study the nature and arrangement of children's material culture. The home had been occupied by a single mother and her two children, a four-year-old boy and a six-year-old girl. The investigators found that artifacts relating to the children far outnumbered those that were specifically attributable to the mother, a finding that is consistent with contemporary ideals of child rearing that emphasize the appropriate accessorizing of children with child-rearing devices and play things. They also identified segregated spaces of childhood activity, including gender-specific areas in bedrooms and mixed-gender child activity areas elsewhere in the home. These distributional patterns in materials witnessed upon the abandonment of the household were consistent with expectations of children's play and the appropriate domains for gender segregation and integration among children.

More recently, Hutson (2006) undertook a relational study between children and the built environment at the site of Chunchucmil as a way to make children visible where no traditional forms of evidence were present. He challenged archaeologists to move away from understanding children on the basis of an assumed essence or set of characteristics and to take a phenomenological approach that considers children in the context of the world in which they lived and the relationships they had with others. Looking to the built environment that could be observed archaeologically, he sought evidence for how children would have encountered these spaces in the past and how these relational encounters would have mutually affected the children and the spaces themselves. His research led to an interpretation of concentrations of shells fragments, which could not be explained by other types of site formation processes as the actions of children interacting with abandoned spaces within buildings. This phenomenological approach to children and space facilitated an interpretation of the archaeological record that was inclusive of children without the presence of identifiable child-specific artifacts.

BECOMING OR BEING? NEW DIRECTIONS IN INTERPRETATION AND INTEGRATION

Childhood is a viable and significant topic for archaeological research, and scholars have undertaken a variety of projects to identify children and conceptualize childhood using an array of archaeological and ethnographic evidence. Within this cohesive movement focused on redressing the absence of children in archaeological research is an emerging division around how children should be interpreted in the past (Ardren 2006, Baxter 2007). Some of the works presented in this review emphasize childhood as a stage of life that is preparatory for adulthood and prioritize the transmission of cultural knowledge across generations. Other works emphasize the distinct identities and specific characteristics of children, and they stress qualities and experiences unique to childhood. This tension points to future directions in the archaeology of childhood and is worth exploring here in a preliminary fashion.

Children Becoming: Socialization, Cultural Transmission, and Preparation for Adulthood

Hirschfeld's (2002) assertion that anthropology is based on the premise that culture is learned and not inherited is fundamental to how many archaeologists approach the study of childhood. Childhood is often described in the archaeological literature as a time when skills and belief systems are learned, when personality is formed, and when attitudes and values are inculcated (Kamp 2001b). Although strict ideas of socialization that emphasize a unilateral transmission of information from adults to children have been rejected (Baxter 2005, Sofaer Derevenski 1997), ideas about how cultural information is imparted across generations have been central to many theoretical conversations about childhood in archaeology (Ardren 2006; Baxter 2005; Kamp 2001b; Sofaer Derevenski 1997, 2000b).

Research on "children becoming" includes studies that explicitly wish to understand the implications of child-rearing practices on social organization as a whole (Keith 2006), whereas others are interested in how adult identities emerge through transitional identities in childhood (Joyce 2000, McCafferty & McCafferty 2006). Many studies that emphasize socialization are interested in how cultural knowledge is transmitted and negotiated through the creation and use of artifacts and social space (Bagwell 2002; Baxter 2000, 2005, 2006c; Crown 1999, 2001, 2000; Finlay 1997; Greenfield 2000; Grimm 2000; Kamp 2001b; Park 2006; Wilkie 2000).

Interests in socialization, the transmission of cultural knowledge, and how identities are related over the course of the human life cycle particularly make sense in archaeology. Studies of cultural change and continuity over time are integral components of all archaeological research, and the study of children offers ways to learn about the negotiated transmission of cultural information across generations.

Studying Children for Children's Sake

The trend that emphasizes childhood as preparatory for adulthood has recently been critiqued by cultural anthropologist Helen Schwartzman (2006), who suggested that archaeology currently has a "focus challenge" where claims about the importance of children need to become aligned with research that is actually studying children. She suggested it is important that archaeologists address children as "topics not tools" and understand childhood as a particular time during which unique powers, associations, and knowledge may be found exclusively in the realm of children. Her critique comes from an appreciation of the disciplinary history of studying childhood in cultural anthropology, and her admonishments encourage archaeologists to learn from previous work.

The study of childhood has been marginalized in cultural anthropology as well as archaeology (Hirschfeld 2002, Schwartzman 2006), and one of the ways to make research more acceptable to a broad audience has been to assert that children were useful ways to study topics considered truly important within the discipline. The results were studies that presented "oversocialized" children who were busy preparing for their roles as adults, at which time they would be engaged in all the social, economic, political, and ritual practices considered to be valid topics for research.

Archaeologists who are focusing on children as children have not stated their focus to be in direct opposition to studies that emphasize socialization and cultural transmission. Rather, their work is informed by general theoretical interests in identity that tacitly embrace the basic anthropological assumption that cultural knowledge is differentially distributed among all members of a particular group (Baxter 2007). These studies emphasize the ways that childhood and its subcategories are unique identities that are embodied and performed by individuals and imbued with meanings, privileges, and obligations through the dominant discourse (Ardren 2006, Hutson 2006, King 2006, Sillar 1994). This approach to children is part of a more general idea that the archaeology of childhood will ultimately become the archaeology of age, where age-based categories throughout the human life cycle become important ways of understanding identity in the past (Kamp 2001b).

These dual approaches to interpreting childhood in the past are not in opposition, but are in fact complementary and represent an area in which childhood studies in archaeology are shaping theoretical understandings of identity in general (Ardren 2006, Baxter 2007). Developing these emerging themes in scholarship on children and childhood is essential. One common assertion is that the archaeology of childhood should not be a specialized interest within the discipline, but rather all archaeologists should be studying children in the past because they were present at all archaeological sites (Baxter 2006b). For this integration to take place, there needs to be a sense of what the study of children and childhood can uniquely contribute to our understanding of past societies (Baxter 2007, Lopiparo 2006). Literature to date has created a theoretical space for the archaeology of childhood to exist, provided alternative definitions and constructions of childhood that are culturally situated, and demonstrated that the archaeological record cannot be interpreted accurately without children as cultural actors. As the archaeology of childhood itself matures, these new explorations of how cultural knowledge is embodied by individuals and transmitted across generations and life stages present new directions for interpretation and integration so that all archaeology becomes the archaeology of childhood.

SUMMARY POINTS

1. Archaeologists have traditionally disregarded children as subjects of archaeological inquiry because they have perceived children as unimportant and invisible.

2. The archaeology of childhood is linked to broader theoretical trends in archaeology, including growing emphases on gender, agency, and identity.

3. Alternative cultural constructions of childhood are necessary to address questions of childhood in the past and are addressed through theoretical, ethnographic, historical, and archaeological sources.

4. The lived experiences of children may be investigated through a variety of evidence types, but these investigations require that archaeologists rethink assumptions about the archaeological record and develop new methodological approaches.

5. Current literature on the archaeology of childhood suggests that there are two emerging directions for childhood studies in archaeology. One approach emphasizes the study of childhood as a topic in its own right, whereas the other emphasizes childhood as a time that is preparatory for adulthood.

DISCLOSURE STATEMENT

The author is not aware of any biases that might be perceived as affecting the objectivity of this review.

LITERATURE CITED

Ardren T. 2006. Setting the table: why children and childhood are important in an understanding of ancient Mesoamerica. See Ardren & Hutson 2006, pp. 3–24

Ardren T, Hutson S, eds. 2006. *The Social Experience of Childhood in Ancient Mesoamerica*. Boulder: Univ. Press Colo. 309 pp.

Bagwell E. 2002. Ceramic form and skill: attempting to identify child producers at Pecos Pueblo, New Mexico. See Kamp 2002a, pp. 90–107

Baker M. 1997. Invisibility as a symptom of gender categories in archaeology. See Moore & Scott 1997, pp. 183–91

Baxter JE. 2000. *An archaeology of childhood: children, gender, and material culture in 19th century America*. PhD thesis. Univ. Mich., Ann Arbor. 298 pp.

Baxter JE. 2005. *The Archaeology of Childhood: Children, Gender, and Material Culture*. Walnut Creek, CA: Alta Mira

Baxter JE, ed. 2006a. *Children in Action: Perspectives on the Archaeology of Childhood*. Vol. 15: *Archaeological Papers of the American Anthropological Association*. Berkeley: Univ. Calif. Press

Baxter JE. 2006b. Introduction: the archaeology of childhood in context. See Baxter 2006a, pp. 1–9

Baxter JE. 2006c. Making space for children in archaeological interpretations. See Baxter 2006a, pp. 77–88

Baxter JE. 2007. *A different way of seeing: casting children as social actors in archaeological interpretations*. Presented at Annu. Meet. Am. Anthropol. Assoc., 106th, Washington, DC

Beaumont L. 2000. The social status and artistic presentation of "adolescence" in fifth century Athens. See Sofaer Derevenski 2000a, pp. 39–50

Berrelleza AJR, Chavez Balderas X. 2006. The role of children in the ritual practices of the great temple of Tenochtitland and the great temple of Tlateloco. See Ardren & Hutson 2006, pp. 233–48

Bird D, Bliege Bird R. 2000. The ethnoarchaeology of juvenile foragers: shellfishing strategies among Meriam children. *J. Anthropol. Archaeol.* 19:461–76

Bonnichsen R. 1973. Millie's camp: an experiment in archaeology. *World Archaeol.* 4(3):277–91

Bradley C. 2002. Thoughts count: ideology and the children of Sand Canyon Pueblo. See Kamp 2002a, pp. 169–95

Buchli V, Lucas G. 2000. Children, gender and the material culture of domestic abandonment in the late twentieth century. See Sofaer Derevenski 2000a, pp. 131–38

Bugarin F. 2006. Constructing an archaeology of children: studying children and child material culture from the African past. See Baxter 2006a, pp. 13–26

Chamberlain AT. 2000. Minor concerns: a demographic perspective on children in past societies. See Sofaer Derevenski 2000a, pp. 206–12

Crawford S. 2000. Children, grave goods and social status in Anglo-Saxon England. See Sofaer Derevenski 2000a, pp. 169–79

Crown P. 1999. Socialization in American southwest pottery decoration. In *Pottery and People: A Dynamic Interaction*, ed. J Skibo, G Feinman, pp. 25–43. Salt Lake City: Univ. Utah Press

Crown P. 2001. Learning to make pottery in the prehispanic American Southwest. *J. Anthropol. Res.* 57:451–69

Crown P. 2002. Learning and teaching in the prehispanic American Southwest. See Kamp 2002a, pp. 108–24

Finlay N. 1997. Kid knapping: the missing children in lithic analysis. See Moore & Scott 1997, pp. 203–12

Greenfield P. 2000. Children, material culture and weaving: historical change and developmental change. See Sofaer Derevenski 2000a, pp. 72–86

Grimm L. 2000. Apprentice flintknapping: relating material culture and social practice in the Upper Paleolithic. See Sofaer Derevenski 2000a, pp. 53–71

Hammond G, Hammond N. 1981. Child's play: a distorting factor in archaeological distribution. *Am. Antiq.* 46(3):634–36

Hays-Gilpin K. 2002. Wearing a butterfly, coming of age: a 1,500 year old Pueblo tradition. See Kamp 2002a, pp. 196–210

Hirschfeld L. 2002. Why don't anthropologists like children? *Am. Anthropol.* 104:611–27

Hutson S. 2006. Children not at Chunchcmil: a relational approach to young subjects. See Ardren & Hutson 2006, pp. 103–32

Janik L. 2000. The construction of the individual among North European fisher-gatherer-hunters in the Early and Mid-Holocene. See Sofaer Derevenski 2000a, pp. 117–30

Joyce RA. 2000. Girling the girl and boying the boy: the production of adulthood in ancient Mesoamerica. *World Archaeol.* 31(30):473–83

Joyce RA. 2006. Where we all began: archaeologies of childhood in the Mesoamerican past. See Ardren & Hutson 2006, pp. 283–302

Kamp K. 2001a. Prehistoric children working and playing: a Southwestern case study in learning ceramics. *J. Anthropol. Res.* 57:427–50

Kamp K. 2001b. Where have all the children gone? The archaeology of childhood. *J. Archaeol. Method Theory* 8(1):1–34

Kamp K, ed. 2002a. *Children in the Prehistoric Puebloan Southwest*. Salt Lake City: Univ. Utah Press

Kamp K. 2002b. Working for a living: children in the prehistoric Southwestern Pueblos. See Kamp 2002a, pp. 71–89

Kamp K. 2006. Dominant discourses; lived experiences: studying the archaeology of children. See Baxter 2006, pp. 115–22

Kamp K, Whittaker JC. 2002. Prehistoric Puebloan children in archaeology and art. See Kamp 2002a, pp. 14–40

Kamp K, Timmerman N, Lind G, Graybill J, Natowski I, et al. 1999. Discovering childhood: using fingerprints to find children in the archaeological record. *Am. Antiq.* 64(2):309–15

Keith K. 2006. Childcare, learning, and the distribution of knowledge in foraging societies. See Baxter 2006, pp. 27–40

King S. 2006. The marking of age in ancient coastal Oaxaca. See Ardren & Hutson 2006, pp. 169–202

Lamb M, Hewlett B, ed. 2005. *Hunter-Gatherer Childhoods: Evolutionary, Developmental, and Cultural Perspectives.* Somerset, NJ: Aldine

Lave J, Wenger E. 1991. *Situated Learning: Legitimate Peripheral Participation.* Cambridge, UK: Cambridge Univ. Press

Lillehammer G. 1989. A child is born: the child's world in an archaeological perspective. *Nor. Archaeol. Rev.* 22(2):89–105

Lillehammer G. 2000. The world of children. See Sofaer Derevenski 2000a, pp. 17–26

Lopiparo J. 2006. Crafting children: materiality, social memory, and the reproduction of terminal classic house societies in the Ulua Valley, Honduras. See Ardren & Hutson 2006, pp. 133–68

Lucy S. 1994. Children in early medieval cemeteries. *Arch. Rev. Camb.* 13(2):21–34

McCafferty G, McCafferty S. 2006. Boys and girls interrupted: mortuary evidence of children from Postclassic Cholula, Puebla. See Ardren & Hutson 2006, pp. 25–52

Meskell L. 1994. Dying young: the experience of death at Deir El Medina. *Archaeol. Rev. Camb.* 13(2):35–46

Meskell L. 2001. Archaeologies of identities. In *Archaeological Theory Today*, ed. I Hodder, pp. 187–213. Cambridge, UK: Polity

Mizoguchi K. 2000. The child as a node of past, present, and future. See Sofaer Derevenski 2000a, pp. 141–50

Moore J, Scott E, eds. 1997. *Invisible People and Processes: Writing Gender and Childhood into European Archaeology.* London/New York: Leicester Univ. Press

Park R. 1998. Size counts: the miniature archaeology of childhood in Inuit societies. *Antiquity* 72:269–81

Park R. 2006. Growing up north: childhood in the Thule and Dorset cultures of arctic Canada. See Baxter 2006, pp. 53–64

Perry M. 2006. Redefining childhood through bioarchaeology: towards an archaeological and biological understanding of children in antiquity. See Baxter 2006, pp. 89–114

Pigeot N. 1990. Technical and social actors: flintknapping specialists at Magdalenian Etoilles. *Archaeol. Rev. Camb.* 9(1):126–41

Prout A, James A. 1990. A new paradigm for the sociology of childhood: provenance, promise, and problems. In *Constructing and Reconstructing Childhood: Contemporary Issues in the Sociological Study of Childhood*, ed. A James, A Prout, pp. 7–34. London: Falmer

Rothschild N. 2002. Introduction. See Kamp 2002a, pp. 1–13

Roveland B. 2001. Archaeological approaches to the study of prehistoric children: past trends and future directions. In *Children and Anthropology: Perspectives for the 21st Century*, ed. H Schwartzman, pp. 39–56. Westport, CT: Bergin and Garvey

Schwartzman H. 2006. Materializing children: challenges for the archaeology of childhood. See Baxter 2006, pp. 123–32

Sillar B. 1994. Playing with God: cultural perceptions of children, play, and miniatures in the Andes. *Archaeol. Rev. Camb.* 13(2):47–63

Smith PE. 2006. Children and ceramic innovation: a study in the archaeology of children. See Baxter 2006, pp. 65–76

Sofaer Derevenski J, ed. 1994a. *Archaeological Review from Cambridge: Perspectives on Children and Childhood.* Vol. 13, Issue 2

Sofaer Derevenski J. 1994b. Where are the children? Accessing children in the past. *Archaeol. Rev. Camb.* 13(2):7–20

Sofaer Derevenski J. 1997. Engendering children: engendering archaeology. See Moore & Scott 1997, pp. 192–202

Sofaer Derevenski J. 2000a. *Children and Material Culture*. New York: Routledge

Sofaer Derevenski J. 2000b. Material culture shock: confronting expectations in the material culture of children. See Sofaer Derevenski 2000a, pp. 3–16

Spector J. 1991. *What This Awl Means: Feminist Archaeology at a Wahpeton Dakota Village*. Minneapolis: Minn. Hist. Soc. Press

Stephens S. 1995. Children and the politics of culture in "late capitalism." In *Children and the Politics of Culture*, ed. S Stephens, pp. 1–50. Princeton, NJ: Princeton Univ. Press

Storey R, McAnany P. 2006. Children of K'axob: premature death in a formative Maya village. See Ardren & Hutson 2006, pp. 53–72

Wileman J. 2005. *Hide and Seek: The Archaeology of Childhood*. Stroud, UK: Tempus

Wilkie L. 2000. Not merely child's play: creating a historical archaeology of children and childhood. See Sofaer Derevenski 2000a, pp. 100–14

Assisted Reproductive Technologies and Culture Change

Marcia C. Inhorn[1]
and Daphna Birenbaum-Carmeli[2]

[1]Department of Anthropology, Yale University, New Haven, Connecticut 06520-8277;
email: marcia.inhorn@yale.edu

[2]University of Haifa, Haifa 31905, Israel; email: daphna@research.haifa.ac.il

Annu. Rev. Anthropol. 2008. 37:177–96

First published online as a Review in Advance on
June 17, 2008

The *Annual Review of Anthropology* is online at
anthro.annualreviews.org

This article's doi:
10.1146/annurev.anthro.37.081407.085230

Key Words

infertility, globalization, gender, kinship, religion, ethics

Abstract

In 1978, the world's first "test-tube" baby was born via in vitro fertilization (IVF). The past 30 years have seen the rapid evolution of many other assisted reproductive technologies (ARTs)—some are simple variants of IVF, whereas others bridge the fields of assisted reproduction and human genomics. As ARTs have evolved over time, so have social, cultural, legal, and ethical responses to them. Indeed, ARTs are a key symbol of our times, representing the growing prominence of biotechnologies in the configuration of individual, familial, and collective identities around the globe. This review highlights the scholarship of more than 50 anthropologists who are studying the effects of ARTs in many areas of social life, including the traditional anthropological domains of kinship, marriage, and the family, gender, religion, and biomedicine. Their research bespeaks both the destabilizing and the generative impacts of ARTs at the interface between science and society.

INTRODUCTION

In 1978, the world's first "test-tube" baby—England's Louise Brown—was born via in vitro fertilization (IVF), a technique whereby sperm and eggs are retrieved from bodies, allowed to fertilize in a petri dish, and then transferred as fertilized embryos back to the woman's uterus. The past 30 years have seen the rapid evolution of many other assisted reproductive technologies (ARTs), which have evoked a variety of social, cultural, legal, and ethical responses. As we show below, assisted reproduction has diversified, globalized, and denaturalized the taken-for-granted binaries of, inter alia, sex/procreation, nature/culture, gift/commodity, informal/formal labor, biology/sociality, heterosexuality/homosexuality, local/global, secular/sacred, and human/nonhuman. Such challenges suggest that there is much to consider in thinking through what is "new" about these so-called new reproductive technologies.

At the present time, more than 50 anthropologists around the globe are producing a rich body of ART scholarship, which is cited in this review and comprehensive bibliography. Their work is concerned primarily with key anthropological debates surrounding kinship and gender in Euro-America. However, in recent years, ART ethnography has also flourished outside Euro-America, particularly in Israel and the Muslim countries, where anthropologists have made significant contributions to the understanding of local moral economies. With the exception of HIV/AIDS scholarship, no single topic seems to have attracted so much attention in medical anthropology, particularly over the past decade. Why are anthropologists so fascinated by the ARTs?

First, ARTs ramify in many areas of social life, including the traditional anthropological domains of kinship, marriage, and the family, religion, and biomedicine (Becker 1990, Franklin 2006a, Franklin & Ragoné 1998). As Rapp (2001) has also noted, the feminist anthropological concern with gender and the body has "dragged" reproduction, including assisted reproduction, into the center of social theory in anthropology. Second, the ARTs might be described as "mutating technologies": Namely, emerging variants of older technological forms have led to significant new practices, new dilemmas, and new realms of anthropological research. In short, technological innovation has led to anthropological proliferation. Finally, the concern with ARTs at this particular historical juncture signifies medical anthropology's millennial intersection with science and technology studies (STS) (Inhorn 2006a, 2007a) and the development of a newer generation of anthropological scholars who are well versed in STS perspectives. Indeed, ARTs provide a key lens through which to view the relationship between science and society.

Given this medical anthropology–STS nexus, our broad theoretical assumption in this article is that technologies are socio-technical products, which are shaped by human and nonhuman factors, including the technical features of the ARTs themselves, as well as by the economic, political, cultural, and moral environs in which they unfold. This assumption implies that technologies are deeply culturally embedded, intimately linked with power relations, and eventually accepted by professionals and potential recipients only when perceived as reasonable in the context of existing social relations, cultural norms, and knowledge systems (Webster 2002). Within this general perspective, society/technology relations become both pivotal and mutually constitutive, with each being at once a source and a consequence of the other (Ong & Collier 2005). By situating technologies within networks of power/knowledge, as well as the surrounding cultural and social order, we can begin to unpack the multifaceted repercussions and cultural transformations currently being induced by ARTs around the world.

GLOBALIZATION AND INEQUALITIES

ARTs were initially developed to overcome intractable infertility—i.e., intrauterine insemination (IUI) and donor insemination (DI) for cases of male infertility and in vitro fertiliza-tion (IVF) for infertile women with blocked fallopian tubes. It is always important to keep the problem of infertility in clear view when discussing ARTs. Infertility affects more than 15% of all reproductive-aged couples world-wide at some point in their lives (Vayena et al. 2002). The scope and gravity of the infertil-ity problem is much more severe in the non-Western world, owing largely to the problem of untreated reproductive tract infections (RTIs) (Bentley & Mascie-Taylor 2000; Brady 2003; Inhorn 2003a,b; Nachtigall 2006; Van Balen & Inhorn 2002). Infertility affects ~80 million women and men worldwide (Vayena et al. 2002), with the highest prevalence being in central and southern Africa, where the pres-ence of an "Infertility Belt" has been repeatedly reaffirmed in cross-national studies (Feldman-Savelsberg 2002, Leonard 2002a, Van Balen & Inhorn 2002). Unfortunately, effective infertil-ity treatments and ARTs are generally inacces-sible in these poor and mostly rural nations, leading to a grim scenario of untreated and intractable infertility across large portions of the non-Western world (Bhatti et al. 1999, Leonard 2002b, Nahar et al. 2000, Richards 2002, Sundby 2002, Unisa 1999, Van Balen & Gerrits 2001). The nonexistence of IVF and other ARTs in these countries is often ratio-nalized in terms of population control, scarcity of health care resources, and the heavy bur-den of other life-threatening diseases such as HIV/AIDS and maternal mortality (Macklin 1995, Okonofua 1996). Although these con-cerns raise major questions about prioritizing infertility as a global reproductive health prob-lem (Inhorn 2003b), the silence surrounding infertility in resource-poor countries may also reflect a tacit eugenic view that the infertile poor are unworthy of treatment; thus, overcoming their infertility problems, including through provision of ARTs, contradicts Western inter-ests in global population control (Greenhalgh 1995).

Nonetheless, studies consistently show that the social consequences of infertility in non-Western countries lead to profound human suffering, particularly on the part of women (Boerma & Mgalla 2001, Feldman-Savelsberg 1999, Hollos 2003, Pearce 1999). Strong prona-talist norms frequently translate into blaming women for reproductive failure, to the point of divorce and social ostracism in some cases (Inhorn 1994, 1996; Inhorn & Bharadwaj 2007). Life-long childlessness also implies se-vere difficulties in achieving old-age security in a majority of countries that lack strong social safety nets (Inhorn 2000, Inhorn & Van Balen 2002). Thus, the provision of ARTs to infertile women in pronatalist settings may lead to social empowerment and the alleviation of gender-based suffering and violence.

Even in the Western world, access to ARTs reflects pronounced class- and race-based in-equalities (Inhorn et al. 2008, Spar 2006). In the United States, relatively few states man-date full or even partial insurance coverage for ARTs, meaning that infertile American couples must pay for ARTs out of pocket, at the aver-age cost of $12,400 per IVF cycle as of 2003 (Spar 2006). As a result, only 36% of infer-tile women in the United States seek any form of medical assistance, and only 1% resort to any form of ART (Spar 2006). Low-income ethnic minority populations, be they African American (Ceballo 1999), Latino (Becker et al. 2006, Nachtigall et al. 2009), Native American (Quiroga 2007), Arab American (Inhorn & Fakih 2006), or South Asian (Culley et al. 2006, Culley & Hudson 2005/2006), may be unable to access these technologies. All Western health care systems—both public and private—set re-strictive eligibility criteria that limit consumers' access, despite some state subsidization in most of the countries of Western Europe (Melhuus 2005, Vanderlinden 2009, Yebei 2000).

The financial burden of ARTs is even heavier in non-Western countries, where state subsi-dization rarely exists (Inhorn 2001, Nachtigall 2006). ARTs provide a prime example of stratified reproduction (Colen 1995, Ginsburg & Rapp 1995): Namely, technologically as-sisted reproduction is largely restricted to global elites, whereas the infertile poor, who are at highest risk of infertility, are devalued and even despised as reproducers (Inhorn 2003a, Spar 2006). Numerous "arenas of constraint," or structural, ideological, and practical obstacles and apprehensions, serve to limit access to these technologies (Inhorn 2003a–c). Nonetheless, ART services are gradually reaching larger populations in some non-Western countries. Anthropologists have documented the globalization of ARTs to China (Handwerker 2002), Ecuador (Roberts 2006), Egypt (Inhorn 1994; 2002a,b; 2003a,b), India (Bharadwaj 2000, Gupta 2006), Iran (Tremayne 2006), Lebanon (Clarke 2007, Inhorn 2007a), Mali (Horbst 2006), and Vietnam (Pashigian 2009).

By ethnographic interrogation of the varied reception and practice of ARTs in these diverse non-Western settings, anthropologists have elucidated some of the cross-cultural similarities as well as differences that arise when a technology travels along multiple pathways and trajectories. The transformations and innovations that ARTs undergo in their global travel enable us to test our assumptions about biotechnological Eurocentrism, namely, that technologies always develop in the West then travel elsewhere (Birenbaum-Carmeli & Inhorn 2009). Although controversial, the first IVF pregnancies were actually reported in India (Bharadwaj 2000, 2002), with China, Russia, Israel, and Australia also playing leading roles in ART development. In non-Western settings such as Egypt, located on the "receiving" end of ART globalization (Inhorn 2003a,b), ARTs may translate into a collective symbol of the technological know-how shared by the advanced, wealthy nations of the world. By providing and deploying ARTs, both practitioners and consumers in non-Western countries may come to pride themselves on keeping pace with the "modern," industrialized world (Blyth & Landau 2004). In this sense, then, ARTs not only reflect, but contribute to, the construction of global power relations and new notions of local modernity (Bharadwaj 2006a, Kanaaneh 2002, Paxson 2006, Raspberry 2009, Roberts 2008, Tremayne 2006).

GENDER, EMBODIMENT, AND SUBJECTIVITIES

Among those who are able to access ARTs, gender identities are often deeply implicated in the process of ART utilization (Becker & Nachtigall 1994, Haelyon 2006, Inhorn 2002a, Nachtigall et al. 1992, Throsby 2004). ARTs themselves are gendered technologies, with highly specific and differentiated applications on men's and women's bodies (Konrad 1998). Generally speaking, ARTs are applied more invasively to women's bodies, for example, by inducing superovulation with powerful oral and injectable hormones and in invasive procedures to harvest oocytes and transfer embryos back to the uterus. The enactment of ARTs on the female body may facilitate the mistaken view that women bear the responsibility for reproductive problems (Inhorn 2003a, Van Balen & Inhorn 2002). As an unintended consequence, the very existence of ARTs may serve to reinforce cultural "motherhood mandates" for women in many societies, mandates that have been challenged by generations of Western feminist scholars (Thompson 2002).

Women's heightened embodiment of ARTs also manifests in men being treated as "the second sex" in ART practices and discourses (Inhorn et al. 2009) despite the fact that more than half of all infertility cases around the world involve a so-called male factor (Inhorn 2003d, 2004; Vayena et al. 2002). Although their experience is marginalized, infertile men also experience embodied suffering via powerful hormonal medications and genital surgeries (Inhorn 2007b,c). Furthermore, the precisely timed collection of semen—"man's most precious fluid" (Moore 2007)—can produce deep anxiety and even impotence but is imperative for all ART procedures (Inhorn 2002b, 2007b). Occasionally, sperm are extracted surgically from the testicles (Inhorn 2007b,c) or posthumously from dead men's bodies (Simpson 2001), creating physical discomforts and ethical concerns. In some cultural contexts and circumstances, the uses of ARTs may entirely marginalize men in the reproductive process, configuring an exclusively female fertility domain, wherein problems are not only detected but also resolved within a female network, supported by female relationships and resources (Birenbaum-Carmeli et al. 1995, Goldberg 2009, Roberts 2009).

In most societies, male infertility remains deeply hidden because of its conflation with impotency and emasculation (Birenbaum-Carmeli et al. 2000, Carmeli & Birenbaum-Carmeli 2000, Tjørnhøj-Thomsen 2009, Upton 2002). Until the early 1990s, the only solution to severe male-factor infertility was DI—the oldest of the "new" reproductive technologies, but one still shrouded in secrecy and stigma (Becker 2002; Becker et al. 2005; Bharadwaj 2003; Birenbaum-Carmeli & Carmeli 2002a,b; Grace et al. 2007; Hanson 2001; MacDougall et al. 2007; Nachtigall et al. 1997, 1998). The introduction of intracytoplasmic sperm injection (ICSI) in Belgium in 1992 has created new possibilities for infertile men and supplanted DI to some degree. Designed to overcome male infertility through micromanipulation and injection of "weak" spermatozoa directly into oocytes under a high-powered microscope, ICSI has led to the birth of biological offspring to thousands of infertile men who would never before have fathered their genetic children (La Rochebrochard 2003). The coming of this new "hope technology" (Franklin 1997) has repaired masculinity in men who were once silently suffering from their infertility (Inhorn 2003a, 2004). However, ICSI also has other important gender effects, not always beneficial, suggesting that ARTs have the potential to destabilize a given society's gender order. Whereas the fecundity of older men can often be enhanced through ICSI, women's fertility is highly age sensitive, often requiring donor eggs at later stages of the reproductive life cycle (Friese et al. 2006, 2008). ART-induced time may thus become a thoroughly gendered problematic in some societies, giving new powers to men (including divorce of once-fertile wives) and creating new feelings of stigma among aging women (Inhorn 2003a, 2005). Thus,

another effect of the ARTs is the enhancement of gendered notions of time and life-course disruption (Becker 1994, 1997; Friese et al. 2006, 2008; Kirkman 2003).

At the same time, gender scripts surrounding conjugality are also being reworked in complex ways as ARTs reach wider audiences. The very growth of a global ART industry, including in "seats of patriarchy" (Ghoussoub & Sinclair-Webb 2000), bespeaks the love, companionate marriage, and financial commitments of spouses around the globe (Inhorn 2007d, Inhorn & Bharadwaj 2007). Increasingly, couples are staying in long-term childless marriages while trying repeated cycles of ARTs (Inhorn 2003a, Birenbaum-Carmeli & Dirnfeld 2007). Although ART success rates have improved over time—leading to the birth of five million test-tube babies—only ~27% of all IVF cycles result in a live birth, even in the technologically advanced United States (Spar 2006). Most couples, therefore, experience the "emotional rollercoaster" and "never enough" quality of repeated but unsuccessful ART cycles (Franklin 1997; Sandelowski 1991, 1993). Becker (2000) has captured most vividly the discourses of hope and despair among infertile American couples in their pursuit of what she calls "the elusive embryo." Thompson (1996, 2005), meanwhile, has unpacked the complex "ontological choreography" required to make a viable embryo. To do so, numerous actors (e.g., physicians, nurses, patients) must enact a complex choreography of precisely timed biological actions (e.g., injections of hormones, ejaculation of sperm, cryopreservation of gametes) in the IVF clinic. According to Thompson, this choreography increasingly includes the "strategic naturalization" of so-called third parties—gestational surrogates and gamete donors—whose contributions to the world of ARTs and new forms of kinship have piqued the anthropological imagination.

NEW KINSHIP STUDIES

Of all the anthropological work that has been written about ARTs, the most substantial and

Intracytoplasmic sperm injection (ICSI): variant of IVF that overcomes male infertility by micromanipulation and injection of "weak" sperm directly into oocytes under a high-powered microscope

Cryopreservation: long-term freezing of sperm, embryos, and ova, as well as human ovaries for later use in postmenopausal women and cancer survivors

Surrogacy: the use of third parties to gestate the fetuses of both heterosexual and single-sex couples

most foundational, in some sense, is that which explores the effects of these technologies on kinship and notions of family. Strathern's book, *Reproducing the Future: Anthropology, Kinship, and the New Reproductive Technologies* (1992a), paved the way for the new anthropology of kinship (Carsten 2004, 2007; Edwards et al. 1999; Franklin & McKinnon 2001; Strathern 1992b) and stimulated burgeoning interest among anthropologists of reproduction in how ARTs might redefine and expand notions of relatedness (Bonaccorso 2008, Clarke 2007a, Edwards 2000, Franklin 1997, Konrad 2005, Thompson 2005).

Strathern's major contribution was to question how ARTs might denaturalize and therefore blur the so-called nature/culture intersection: Namely, if kinship, as a set of social relations, is seen to be rooted in the natural facts of biological reproduction, then the nature of kinship itself might be called into question by ARTs, which, in effect, destabilize the biological within parenthood through the assistance of technologies and third parties. As noted by Strathern (1992a, pp. 27–28), ARTs have created "a new convention, the distinction between social and biological parenting, out of an old one, kinship as the social construction of natural facts." This early insight by Strathern served to spur a wide range of empirical research on ARTs and kinship in Euro-America (Bonaccorso 2008, Edwards 2000, Edwards et al. 1999, Franklin 1997, Franklin & Ragoné 1998, Harrington et al. 2008, Konrad 2005, Melhuus 2007, Ragoné 1994, Thompson 2005), as well as in various non-Western societies where kinship is probably even more central to social organization (Clarke 2006a,b, 2007a,b, 2008; Inhorn 2006a,b; Kahn 2000; Roberts 2009; Tremayne 2009).

What are some of the major findings of this large body of work? First, given that Euro-American notions of kinship are biogenetically based (Schneider 1980), many infertile couples now "chase the blood tie" (Ragoné 1996) in a relentless quest to produce biogenetically related offspring through the ART-assisted manipulation of their own gametes (Becker

2000, Franklin 1997, Inhorn 2003a, Ragoné 1994). Indeed, the very presence of ARTs has served to marginalize, to some degree, alternate means of family formation through adoption (Bharadwaj 2003, Birenbaum-Carmeli & Carmeli 2009, Storrow 2006), once regarded in Euro-America as the "natural solution" to infertility (Becker 2000, Carsten 2000).

Second, ARTs have pluralized notions of relatedness and led to a more dynamic notion of "kinning" (Howell 2006), namely, kinship as a process, as something under construction, rather than a natural given (Carsten 2004, 2007; Strathern 2005). In fact, ARTs can be thought of as deconstructive in introducing ambiguity and uncertainty into kinship relations, including the fundamental categories of motherhood and fatherhood (Collard & de Parseval 2007). As ARTs are applied to an ever-expanding range of people and problems, they are unseating core notions of kinship and undermining the traditional family by introducing a whole range of quasi-, semi-, or pseudobiological forms of parenting (Franklin & Ragoné 1998; Thompson 2001, 2005).

Surrogacy, for example, threatens dominant Western ideologies that presume an indissoluble mother-child bond (Baslington 1996, Birenbaum-Carmeli 2007, Markens 2007, Ragoné 1994), gradually deconstructing motherhood into genetic, birth, adoptive, and surrogate maternities, with the potential for three "biological" mothers to a single child (Sandelowski 1993, Thompson 1998). The "hybridized fusion" of the surrogate with the intended mother that is introduced by surrogacy can create alliances between women (Teman 2003a,b), as well as hierarchies, especially when gestational surrogates come from different ethnic and class backgrounds than do the intended parents (Ragoné 2000). Furthermore, the raft of antisurrogacy legislation around the world, as well as the many court cases, bespeak the societal discomfort with the very notion of maternal multiplicity (Baslington 1996, Birenbaum-Carmeli 2007, Collard & de Parseval 2007, Pashigian 2009, Weisberg 2005).

ARTs are also unseating traditional notions of heterosexual parenthood by creating previously inconceivable offspring for single-sex couples (Agigian 2004, Cadoret 2008, Kahn 2000, Mamo 2007). The introduction of ARTs—particularly donor insemination for lesbians and gestational surrogacy for gay men—has led to the "queering of reproduction" in the United States (Mamo 2007), with specialty clinics and Web sites designed to assist would-be gay parents, as well as nonmarried couples and single women and men (Spar 2006). Nonetheless, antigay ART legislation, even in the most "progressive" countries (e.g., Denmark; Bryld 2001), serves as a potent reminder of these technologies' subversive effects on social norms, as well as states' ability to channel governmentality in conservative directions through legislation (Franklin 1997, Melhuus 2005, Ong & Collier 2005).

Furthermore, gamete and embryo donations—in which one or more third parties transmit genetic material to a resulting child—have led to a variety of interesting consequences (Collard & de Parseval 2007, Konrad 2005, Spilker & Lie 2007). Sperm donation, which is undertaken anonymously in most cases, has led to an increase in secretive family space (Becker 2002, Birenbaum-Carmeli et al. 2000) in a variety of ways: (*a*) Most donors prefer to remain anonymous (although laws now mandate the disclosure of donor identity in some countries such as Sweden, the United Kingdom, and Australia); (*b*) most infertile men base their donor selection on purported physiognomy to create family resemblances; (*c*) most infertile men, feeling emasculated by their condition, prefer to hide from family and friends their use of donor sperm; (*d*) many parents who have used donor sperm decide not to disclose this information to the resulting child; and (*e*) finally, many parents engage in "resemblance talk" to mask the child's origins (Becker 2002; Becker et al. 2005; Birenbaum-Carmeli & Carmeli 2002a,b; Birenbaum-Carmeli et al. 2000; Nachtigall et al. 1997, 1998).

Egg donation, on the other hand, has created kin-like female alliances, including those among actual kin (e.g., sisters) who donate their ova to relatives (Roberts 2009, Tremayne 2009) as well as those among unrelated women who "share" their ova with other women in infertility clinics or "donate" them for a fee (Bonaccorso 2008, Edwards 2000, Konrad 2005). Ova donation in particular invokes the notion of altruistic "gift exchange" (Konrad 2005), even though ova are increasingly sold on the market for up to $50,000 (Almeling 2007, Spar 2006). As with surrogacy, ova donation has produced new forms of labor among reproductive "assistors," who, in this case, undergo risky forms of hormonal stimulation and egg harvesting (Pollock 2003). Concerns over the potential harm of such bodily commodification are mounting, given the newly recognized category of the "traveling foreign egg donor," who seeks economic mobility through the sale of her body parts (Heng 2007; Storrow 2005a,b). Indeed, legal scholars are beginning to worry that significant "reproductive tourism" between countries involves the search for human gametes in countries with relaxed legal and regulatory environments (Blyth & Farrand 2005; Deech 2003; Jones 2008; Jones & Keith 2006; Pennings 2002; Spar 2005; Storrow 2005a,b). Anthropologists are beginning to confirm that these concerns are warranted because infertile couples travel from countries where gamete donation is outlawed (including in "progressive" countries such as Norway) to those where it is available (including in "traditional" countries such as Lebanon and Iran), usually for hefty fees (Clarke 2007a,b, 2008; Inhorn 2009; Melhuus 2003, 2006, 2008; Nahman 2006).

MORAL ECONOMIES AND EMBRYO ETHICS

The processes of assisted reproduction described above introduce ever more problematic global and local divisions (Spilker & Lie 2007, Thompson 2008a), threatening to augment domestic and transnational disparities and

Third-party donation: the use of embryos and gametes (sperm and ova) from third parties, including for assisted conception among single-sex couples

perpetuate social injustice (Deech 2003). Multiple sets of inequalities surface in the practice of assisted reproduction, reflecting intersecting oppressions based on gender, race, class, and nationality (Quiroga 2007, Thompson 2008a). For example, poor minority women in some countries are being "recruited" (some would say "coerced") as gestational surrogates, similar in some ways to their domestic servitude as low-paid maids and nannies (Ragoné 2000). Similarly, racially preferential "white" women from the economically dislocated post-Soviet societies are being recruited as egg donors for affluent Western European and Israeli couples (Nahman 2006), a form of reproductive "trafficking" that is being compared with sex tourism (Storrow 2006).

ARTs and the bodily commodification that has accompanied them bring into sharp relief the moral economies surrounding reproductive technoscience that may serve to exacerbate transnational inequalities and challenge, even rupture, local legal, religious, and ethical orders (Bharadwaj 2006a,b; Gupta 2006; Inhorn 2003a). As ARTs have made their way around the globe, they have often invoked fervent ethical and legal debates (Hudson et al. 2008, Kitzinger & Williams 2005, Macklin 1995, Melhuus 2005, Tsuge 2005), debates that are deeply embedded within particular "local moral worlds" of religion and culture (Kleinman 1995, Thompson 2006). In the Western countries, religion-science rifts are normally addressed in plurivocal public debates, while leaving a moral vacuum to be filled by ethicists and lawyers. For example, the ART industry in the United States is often described as "The Wild West," with little if any regulation and a profession that is largely free market regulated and profit driven (Spar 2006). In the United States, any federal foray into ARTs would probably fall prey to the intense politics of abortion (Morgan & Michaels 1999, Nachtigall et al. 2005, Spar 2006). As a result, cases of ART negligence and abuse are handled in the legal system, with the courts forced to chart new legal terrain (Blyth & Landau 2004). A different model is the United Kingdom's government-commissioned Warnock Committee, which has tackled the thorny ethical issues surrounding ARTs and has been very influential throughout Europe (Franklin 1997, Hudson et al. 2008).

Outside of Euro-America, religion may impact the practices of assisted reproduction more directly. For example, across the Sunni Muslim world, gamete donation and surrogacy have been religiously prohibited (Culley 2006; Culley & Hudson 2008; Inhorn 2003a, 2006b,d,e; Zuhur 1992), although minority Shia *fatwas* (religious decrees) issued by leading clerics in Iran and Lebanon have opened the door to third-party donation in these two Middle Eastern countries (Abbasi-Shavazi et al. 2008; Clarke 2006a,b, 2007a,b, 2008; Inhorn 2006b,c; Tremayne 2006, 2009). By contrast, in neighboring Israel, all attempts to restrict ART provision have failed in both court and Parliament, where, in the name of the Biblical commandment to "be fruitful and multiply," permissive treatment options have consistently outweighed opposing voices (Shalev & Gooldin 2006). Only in Israel is IVF almost completely state subsidized (Birenbaum-Carmeli 2004, Kahn 2000, Rabinerson et al. 2002), even for Palestinian citizens of Israel (Inhorn & Birenbaum-Carmeli 2009, Kanaaneh 2002). Israeli society is ardently pronatalist, with ARTs viewed as a way to reproduce the nation through the birth of Jewish babies. The religious emphasis on procreation, plus the fear of being outnumbered by non-Jews on Israeli soil (Kanaaneh 2002), has served to promote one of the most aggressive and proactive ART regimes in the world, in which single and lesbian women, surrogates, gamete donors, and recipients all participate in the ontological choreography of making Jewish babies in Israeli IVF clinics (Birenbaum-Carmeli & Carmeli 2009; Goldberg 2009; Haelyon 2006; Kahn 2000, 2009; Nahman 2008, Prainsack 2006, 2007; Seeman 2009). Halakhic (rabbinical) law has shown remarkable flexibility in accommodating technologies such as sperm donation, interpreting them in ways that are consistent with religious views of kinship and family formation, even in ultraorthodox communities (Kahn 2000, 2002, 2006).

Similarly pronounced, albeit in the opposite direction, is the Roman Catholic Church, which denounces all forms of assisted reproduction, as evident in anti-ART legislation in Catholic countries such as Costa Rica, Ireland, and Italy (Bonaccorso 2004a,b; 2008). However, despite the Vatican's ban on ARTs, IVF and related technologies are widely practiced in most Catholic countries around the world, including the nations of Latin America (Raspberry 2009; Roberts 2008, 2009). However, IVF practitioners there are particularly cautious about embryo disposition because the Vatican's discomfort with ARTs centers on the perceived status of the embryo as a human life (Raspberry 2009; Roberts 2006, 2007). With most ARTs, embryos are created outside the human body, without the requirement of sexual intercourse; they are returned to a woman's uterus two to five days following fertilization. During this process, embryos may be manipulated, tested, frozen, discarded, used for research, or utilized in the manufacture of human embryonic stem cells (hESCs) (Bharadwaj 2005, 2007, 2009a; Franklin 2006b; Ganchoff 2004; Krones et al. 2006; Roberts & Throsby 2007). In terms of embryo ethics, pressing questions include, When does life begin—namely, does an embryo constitute a human life (James 2000, Morgan & Michaels 1999)? Should embryos be transferred to or "adopted" by other nonrelated infertile couples (Nachtigall et al. 2005, Tremayne 2009)? Are all embryos created equal, or can/should some be culled before embryo transfer for the purposes of research, disposal, or stem cell manufacture (Nachtigall et al. 2005)? These questions are beginning to be studied in earnest by anthropologists, particularly in the new era of so-called reproductive genetics (Franklin 2007, Franklin & Roberts 2006, Hashiloni-Dolev 2007, Hashiloni-Dolev & Shkedi 2007, Roberts & Throsby 2007, Williams et al. 2007).

At the same time that IVF and gamete donation practices were evolving in laboratories in the West, genetic tests were being developed to detect heritable diseases in ART-created human embryos. Preimplantation genetic diagnosis (PGD) is a screening test that can detect genetic abnormalities in IVF- or ICSI-created embryos outside the woman's body, thus enabling implantation of only mutation-free embryos (Franklin & Roberts 2006, Krones et al. 2006). Initially developed to screen for rare but life-threatening genetic illnesses, such as cystic fibrosis or Tay-Sachs disease in high-risk families, the application of PGD is currently expanding (Remennick 2006, Williams et al. 2007). PGD is now used for sex selection—either to ensure so-called family balancing among couples with existing children or to guarantee male offspring in areas of the world characterized by son preference (Lock 2009, Van Balen & Inhorn 2003). In some IVF clinics in the West, PGD is also used as a routine screening measure for couples with severe male-factor infertility (of a potentially heritable origin) and among women with so-called advanced maternal age (AMA) whose IVF outcomes may be improved through embryo screening (for aneuploidy reduction) (Franklin & Roberts 2006, Williams et al. 2007). In addition, PGD is being used to select for genetically matching embryos who will grow up to donate cord blood or bone marrow to save an older ailing sibling (Franklin & Roberts 2006, Hashiloni-Dolev & Shkedi 2007).

Unsurprisingly, PGD has spawned a bevy of ethical concerns surrounding the sanctity of life in its very early stages, the culling and disposal of female embryos, the right to life of the genetically impaired, and the creation of so-called "designer" babies (Franklin & Roberts 2006, Lock 2008, Van Balen & Inhorn 2002). Moreover, PGD has played a pivotal role in relation to other controversial technologies—cloning and human embryonic stem cells—by providing the first bridge between assisted conception and clinical genetics (Bowring 2004, Franklin 2007, Franklin & Roberts 2006). Indeed, the ability to reprogram cell development is at the heart of both cloning and stem cell technology (Franklin 2006b, Kitzinger & Williams 2005, Prainsack & Spector 2006). By now, IVF,

Human embryonic stem cells (hESCs): cells derived from excess embryos and used for research into future therapeutic interventions

Preimplantation genetic diagnosis (PGD): a technique used to screen IVF embryos for genetic defects, sex selection, and, potentially, certain "designer" traits

AMA: advanced maternal age

Cloning: asexual, autonomous reproduction of animals (e.g., Dolly, the sheep) and potentially humans

PGD, and embryonic stem cell research have become so inextricable that it is virtually impossible to debate any one technology separately (Franklin & Roberts 2006, Thompson 2008b).

In the IVF-hESC encounter, infertile couples must decide whether to "donate" their spare embryos for stem cell research (Bharadwaj 2005, 2008, 2009a,b; Roberts & Throsby 2007), thereby "trans-substantiating" their embryo from being their own to becoming an anonymous, publicly owned, human embryonic cell line and part of a shared, collective commitment to scientific progress (Franklin 2006b). In the United States, embryo disposition decisions (i.e., to discard or to donate to other infertile couples or to stem cell research) appear to be emotionally significant for couples and are frequently unresolved (Nachtigall et al. 2005; see also Britt & Evans 2007 on multifetal pregnancy reduction decisions). In India, however, such donations are seen as an act of altruism (Bharadwaj 2009a), a willingness that has helped place India at the forefront of the global stem cell industry (Bharadwaj & Glasner 2008). Currently, India provides the West with generous supplies of hESC materials—a global outsourcing that has resulted from American abortion politics and restrictions on, and short-

age of, hESC materials in Europe. Whereas the Indian state is a major promoter of this biotechnology, it does not fully regulate stem cell research, thus exposing Indians, mostly women, to the potential for gender-based exploitation (Bharadwaj 2005, 2008, 2009a,b; Bharadwaj & Glasner 2008).

CONCLUSION

As seen in the many examples in this article, ARTs are a key symbol of our times, representing the growing prominence of biotechnologies in the configuration of individual, familial, and collective identities. ARTs are clearly prompting transformations in many domains of culture. As such, ARTs provide an illuminating lens through which to examine contemporary social relations during a very fluid, complex epoch. Indeed, the burgeoning corpus of theoretical and empirical research being produced by anthropologists bespeaks the centrality of ARTs at the science-society interface. As ARTs continue to evolve in the new millennium, a central goal of our discipline should be to follow these technologies into the future, elucidating their destabilizing and generative impacts as they make their way around the globe.

FUTURE ISSUES

1. Embryo disposition, or the decisions couples make regarding their excess embryos, is a critical issue for future study. This is particularly true in countries with abortion restrictions and in those where large numbers of excess embryos are frozen in IVF laboratories.

2. Multifetal pregnancy reduction, a form of selective abortion undertaken in high-order (i.e., triplets and beyond) ART-assisted pregnancies, is an especially critical issue in the non-Western world, where up to six embryos may be returned to a woman's uterus to increase IVF success rates. High-order, high-risk ART pregnancies themselves require further investigation.

3. Male infertility and the use of ICSI are poorly studied, but are especially significant in pronatalist societies where male infertility may impinge significantly on manhood. Male infertility may be especially prominent as a genetic disorder in societies where consanguineous (i.e., cousin) marriage is practiced.

4. Postmenopausal pregnancies are increasing among women older than 50, who achieve IVF pregnancies through hormonal assistance and the use of donor eggs. The ramifications of ART-assisted parenthood among older women (and men) require further study.

5. Pregnancy loss, which is a frequent occurrence in ART-assisted pregnancies, especially among older women, can be particularly devastating, given the financial and emotional investments in the ART pregnancy. However, little is known about the impact of pregnancy loss following ARTs.

6. Preimplantation genetic diagnosis is increasingly employed in non-Western countries, where it may be used for the purpose of sex selection in societies characterized by son preference. Sex-selective PGD is an important topic of future scholarship.

7. Reproductive tourism (a.k.a. fertility tourism) is the movement of infertile individuals, couples, reproductive "assistors," and their gametes across national borders in search of conception (or, in the case of assistors, in search of financial compensation). Reproductive tourism is a burgeoning form of medical tourism, which requires additional study.

8. Stem cell research occurs through the donation of excess IVF embryos in some countries. The relationship between the IVF and stem cell industries requires investigation around the world.

9. Issues of ART access are still of paramount concern for infertile couples in most resource-poor societies around the world. This is especially true in sub-Saharan Africa, where rates of infertility are highest but ARTs are not widely available. ARTs in Africa should be studied as they emerge in the context of the HIV/AIDS epidemic.

10. ART access may be restricted among minority populations (be they racial, ethnic, or religious minorities) within dominant societies. Minority experiences of infertility and ART access are topics for future research on health disparities within Euro-American settings.

11. Further study on religion and ARTs is recommended. Attitudes toward ARTs in Catholic, Jewish, Muslim, and Hindu countries have been relatively well studied by anthropologists. But more research is needed for other religious traditions, including Protestant, Evangelical, and Orthodox Christianity and various forms of Buddhism.

12. The ART "industry" is a complex world involving, among others, scientists, medical professionals, pharmaceutical industries, sperm banks, surrogacy agencies, egg brokers, and others. The components of this complex social world should be studied ethnographically. The industry as a whole is a rich site for future investigation by science and technology scholars.

DISCLOSURE STATEMENT

The authors are not aware of any biases that might be perceived as affecting the objectivity of this review.

ACKNOWLEDGMENTS

The authors thank Aditya Bharadwaj, Kirk Hooks, Stanley Inhorn, Robert Nachtigall, Charis Thompson, Soraya Tremayne, and Emily Wentzell for their various contributions to the development of this review, including comments on the first draft. Special thanks go to Susan Martha Kahn for generously sharing her bibliographic materials. We dedicate our essay to the memory of Gay Becker, whose anthropological scholarship and many important insights on assisted reproductive technologies have been an inspiration.

LITERATURE CITED

Abbasi-Shavazi M, Inhorn MC, Razeghi-Nasrabad HB, Toloo G. 2008. The "Iranian ART revolution": infertility, assisted reproductive technology, and third-party donation in the Islamic Republic of Iran. *J. Middle East Women's Stud.* 4:1–28

Agigian A. 2004. *Baby Steps: How Lesbian Insemination is Changing the World*. Middletown, CT: Wesleyan Univ. Press

Almeling R. 2007. Selling genes, selling gender: egg agencies, sperm banks, and the medical market in genetic material. *Am. Sociol. Rev.* 72:319–40

Baslington H. 1996. Anxiety overflow: implications of the IVF surrogacy case and the ethical and moral limits of reproductive technologies in Britain. *Women's Stud. Int. Forum* 19:675–84

Becker G. 1990. *Healing the Infertile Family: Strengthening Your Relationship in the Search for Parenthood*. Berkeley: Univ. Calif. Press

Becker G. 1994. Metaphors in disrupted lives: infertility and cultural constructions of continuity. *Med. Anthropol. Q.* 8:383–410

Becker G. 1997. *Disrupted Lives: How People Create Meaning in a Chaotic World*. Berkeley: Univ. Calif. Press

Becker G. 2000. *The Elusive Embryo: How Women and Men Approach New Reproductive Technologies*. Berkeley: Univ. Calif. Press

Becker G. 2002. Deciding whether to tell children about donor insemination: an unresolved question in the United States. See Inhorn & Van Balen 2002, pp. 119–33

Becker G, Butler A, Nachtigall RD. 2005. Resemblance talk: a challenge for parents whose children were conceived with donor gametes in the U.S. *Soc. Sci. Med.* 61:1300–9

Becker G, Castrillo M, Jackson R, Nachtigall RD. 2006. Infertility among low-income Latinos. *Fertil. Steril.* 85:882–87

Becker G, Nachtigall RD. 1994. "Born to be a mother": the cultural construction of risk in infertility treatment in the U.S. *Soc. Sci. Med.* 39:507–18

Bentley GR, Mascie-Taylor N, eds. 2000. *Infertility in the Modern World: Present and Future Prospects*. Cambridge, UK: Cambridge Univ. Press

Bharadwaj A. 2000. How some Indian baby makers are made: media narratives and assisted conception in India. *Anthropol. Med.* 7:63–78

Bharadwaj A. 2002. Conception politics: medical egos, media spotlights, and the contest over test-tube firsts in India. In *Infertility Around the Globe: New Thinking on Childlessness, Gender, and Reproductive Technologies*, ed. MC Inhorn, F Van Balen, pp. 315–33. Berkeley: Univ. Calif. Press

Bharadwaj A. 2003. Why adoption is not an option in India: the visibility of infertility, the secrecy of donor insemination, and other cultural complexities. *Soc. Sci. Med.* 56:1867–80

Bharadwaj A. 2005. Cultures of embryonic stem cell research in India. In *Crossing Borders: Cultural, Religious and Political Differences Concerning Stem Cell Research*, ed. W Bender, C Hauskeller, A Manzei, pp. 325–41. Munster: Agenda Verlag

Bharadwaj A. 2006a. Sacred modernity: religion, infertility, and technoscientific conception around the globe. *Cult. Med. Psychiatry* 30:423–25

Bharadwaj A. 2006b. Sacred conceptions: clinical theodicies, uncertain science, and technologies of procreation in India. *Cult. Med. Psychiatry* 30:451–65

Bharadwaj A. 2008. Biosociality and biocrossings: encounters with assisted conception and embryonic stem cells in India. In *Biosocialities, Genetics and the Social Sciences: Making Biologies and Identities*, ed. S Gibbon, C Novas, pp. 98–116. New York: Routledge

Bharadwaj A. 2009a. Assisted life: the neoliberal moral economy of embryonic stem cells in India. See Birenbaum-Carmeli & Inhorn 2009. In press

Bharadwaj A. 2009b. Reproductive viability and the state: the embryonic stem cell research in India. In *Reproduction, Globalization, and the State*, ed. CH Browner, CF Sargent. Durham, NC: Duke Univ. Press. In press

Bharadwaj A, Glasner P. 2008. *Local Cells, Global Science: The Rise of Embryonic Stem Cell Research in India*. London: Routledge

Bhatti LI, Fikree F, Khan A. 1999. The quest of infertile women in squatter settlements of Karachi, Pakistan: a qualitative study. *Soc. Sci. Med.* 49:637–49

Birenbaum-Carmeli D. 2004. "Cheaper than a newcomer": on the social production of IVF policy in Israel. *Sociol. Health Illn.* 26:897–924

Birenbaum-Carmeli D. 2007. Contested surrogacy and the gender order: an Israeli case study. *J. Middle East Women's Stud.* 3:21–44

Birenbaum-Carmeli D, Carmeli YS. 2002a. Physiognomy, familialism and consumerism: references among Jewish Israeli recipients of donor insemination. *Soc. Sci. Med.* 54:363–76

Birenbaum-Carmeli D, Carmeli YS. 2002b. Hegemony and homogeneity: donor preferences of recipients of donor insemination. *J. Mater. Cult.* 7:73–94

Birenbaum-Carmeli D, Carmeli YS, eds. 2009a. *Kin, Gene, Community: Reproductive Technology among Jewish Israelis*. New York: Berghahn. In press

Birenbaum-Carmeli D, Carmeli YS. 2009b. Adoption and assisted reproduction technologies: a comparative reading of Israeli policies. See Birenbaum-Carmeli & Carmeli 2009a. In press

Birenbaum-Carmeli D, Carmeli YS, Capser R. 1995. Discrimination against men in fertility treatments: the underprivileged male. *J. Reprod. Med.* 40:590–93

Birenbaum-Carmeli D, Carmeli YS, Yavetz H. 2000. Secrecy among Israeli recipients of donor insemination. *Polit. Life Sci.* 19:69–76

Birenbaum-Carmeli D, Dirnfeld M. 2007. *Women's experiences following repeated IVF treatments in Israel*. Eur. Soc. Hum. Reprod. Embryol. (ESHRE), Lyon, Fr., July

Birenbaum-Carmeli D, Inhorn MC, eds. 2009. *Assisting Reproduction, Testing Genes: Global Encounters with New Biotechnologies*. New York: Berghahn. In press

Blyth E, Farrand A. 2005. Reproductive tourism—a price worth paying for reproductive autonomy? *Crit. Soc. Policy* 25:91–114

Blyth E, Landau R, eds. 2004. *Third Party Assisted Conception across Cultures*. London: Jessica Kingley

Boerma JT, Mgalla Z, eds. 2001. *Women and Infertility in Sub-Saharan Africa: A Multi-Disciplinary Perspective*. Amsterdam: R. Trop. Inst., KIT

Bonaccorso M. 2004a. Making connections: family and relatedness in clinics of assisted conception in Italy. *Mod. Italy J.* 9:59–68

Bonaccorso M. 2004b. Gamete donation: strategies in (private) clinics of assisted conception. In *Reproductive Change, Medicine and the State: Ethnographic Explorations of Agency in Childbearing*, ed. M Unnithan, pp. 82–102. New York: Berghahn

Bonaccorso ME. 2008. *Conceiving Kinship: Family and Assisted Conception in South Europe*. New York: Berghahn

Bowring F. 2004. Therapeutic and reproductive cloning: a critique. *Soc. Sci. Med.* 58:401–9

Brady M. 2003. Preventing sexually transmitted infections and unintended pregnancy, and safeguarding fertility: triple protection needs of young women. *Reprod. Health Matters* 11:134–41

Britt DW, Evans MI. 2007. Sometimes doing the right thing sucks: frame combinations and multi-fetal pregnancy reduction decision difficulty. *Soc. Sci. Med.* 65:2342–56

Bryld M. 2001. The infertility clinic and the birth of the lesbian: the political debate on assisted reproduction in Denmark. *Eur. J. Women's Stud.* 8:299–312

Cadoret A. 2008. The contribution of homoparental families to the current debate on kinship. In *Kinship Matters: European Cultures of Kinship in the Age of Biotechnology*, ed. J Edwards, C Salazar. New York: Berghahn. In press

Carmeli YS, Birenbaum-Carmeli D. 2000. Ritualizing the "natural family": secrecy in Israeli donor insemination. *Sci. Cult.* 9:301–24

Carsten J, ed. 2000. *Cultures of Relatedness: New Approaches to the Study of Kinship*. Cambridge, UK: Cambridge Univ. Press

Carsten J. 2004. *After Kinship*. Cambridge, UK: Cambridge Univ. Press

Carsten J. 2007. Constitutive knowledge: tracing trajectories of information in new contexts of relatedness. *Anthropol. Q.* 80:403–26

Ceballo R. 1999. "The only black woman walking the face of the earth who cannot have a baby": Two women's stories. In *Women's Untold Stories: Breaking Silence, Talking Back, Voicing Complexity*, ed. M Romero, AJ Stewart, pp. 3–19. New York: Routledge

Clarke M. 2006a. Shiite perspectives on kinship and new reproductive technologies. *ISIM Rev.* 17:26–27

Clarke M. 2006b. Islam, kinship and new reproductive technology. *Anthropol. Today* 22:17–20

Clarke M. 2007a. Closeness in the age of mechanical reproduction: debating kinship and biomedicine in Lebanon and the Middle East. *Anthropol. Q.* 80:379–402

Clarke M. 2007b. Children of the revolution: Ali Khamane'i's "liberal" views on in vitro fertilization. *Br. J. Middle East. Stud.* 34:287–303

Clarke M. 2008. *Islam and New Kinship: Reproductive Technology, Anthropology and the Shari'ah in Lebanon*. New York: Berghahn. In press

Colen S. 1995. "Like a Mother to Them": Stratified Reproduction and West Indian Childcare Workers and Employers in New York. In *Conceiving the New World Order: The Global Politics of Reproduction*, ed. FD Ginsburg, R Rapp, pp. 78–102. Berkeley: Univ. Calif. Press

Collard C, de Parseval GD. 2007. La gestation pour autrui: un bricolage des representations de la paternite et de la maternite euro-americaine. *L'Homme* 183:1–26

Culley L. 2006. Public perceptions of gamete donation in British South Asian communities. *Econ. Soc. Res. Counc. Res. Rep.*, Fac. Health Life Sci., De Montfort Univ., Leicester, UK

Culley L, Hudson N. 2005/2006. Diverse bodies and disrupted reproduction. *Int. J. Divers. Org. Commun. Nations* 5:117–25

Culley L, Hudson N. 2008. Public understandings of science: British South Asian men's perceptions of third party assisted conception 2:79–86

Culley LA, Hudson N, Rapport FL, Katbamna S, Johnson MRD. 2006. British South Asian communities and infertility services. *Hum. Fertil.* 9:37–45

Deech R. 2003. Reproductive tourism in Europe: infertility and human rights. *Glob. Gov.* 9:425–32

Edwards J. 2000. *Born and Bred: Idioms of Kinship and New Reproductive Technologies in England*. Oxford: Oxford Univ. Press

Edwards J, Franklin S, Hirsch E, Price F, Strathern M. 1999. *Technologies of Procreation: Kinship in the Age of Assisted Conception*. London: Routledge. 2nd ed.

Feldman-Savelsberg P. 1999. *Plundered Kitchens, Empty Wombs: Threatened Reproduction and Identity in the Cameroon Grassfields*. Ann Arbor: Univ. Mich. Press

Feldman-Savelsberg P. 2002. Is infertility an unrecognized public health and population problem? A view from the Cameroon Grassfields. See Inhorn & Van Balen 2002, pp. 215–32

Franklin S. 1997. *Embodied Progress: A Cultural Account of Assisted Conception*. London: Routledge

Franklin S. 2006a. Origin stories revisited: IVF as an anthropological project. *Cult. Med. Psychiatry* 30:547–55

Franklin S. 2006b. The cyborg embryo: our path to transbiology. *Theory Cult. Soc.* 23:167–89

Franklin S. 2007. *Dolly Mixtures: The Remaking of Genealogy*. Durham, NC: Duke Univ. Press

Franklin S, McKinnon S, eds. 2001. *Relative Values: Reconfiguring Kinship Studies*. Durham, NC: Duke Univ. Press

Franklin S, Ragoné H, eds. 1998. *Reproducing Reproduction: Kinship, Power, and Technological Innovation*. Philadelphia: Univ. Penn. Press

Franklin S, Roberts C. 2006. *Born and Made: An Ethnography of Preimplantation Genetic Diagnosis*. Princeton: Princeton Univ. Press

Friese C, Becker G, Nachtigall RD. 2006. Rethinking the biological clock: eleventh hour moms, miracle moms and meanings of age-related infertility. *Soc. Sci. Med.* 63:1550–60

Friese C, Becker G, Nachtigall RD. 2008. Older motherhood and the changing life course in the era of assisted reproductive technologies. *J. Aging Stud.* 22:65–73

Ganchoff C. 2004. Regenerating movements: embryonic stem cells and the politics of potentiality. *Sociol. Health Illn.* 26:757–74

Ghoussoub M, Sinclair-Webb E, eds. 2000. *Imagined Masculinities: Male Identity and Culture in the Modern Middle East*. London: Saqi

Ginsburg FD, Rapp R, eds. 1995. *Conceiving the New World Order: The Global Politics of Reproduction*. Berkeley: Univ. Calif. Press

Goldberg H. 2009. The sex in the sperm: male infertility and its challenges to masculinity in an Israeli Jewish context. See Inhorn et al. 2009. In press

Grace VM, Daniels KR, Gillett W. 2007. The donor, the father, and the imaginary constitution of the family: parents' constructions in the case of donor insemination. *Soc. Sci. Med.* 66:301–14

Greenhalgh S, ed. 1995. *Situating Fertility: Anthropology and Demographic Inquiry*. Cambridge, UK: Cambridge Univ. Press

Gupta JA. 2006. Towards transnational feminisms: some reflections and concerns in relation to the globalization of reproductive technologies. *Eur. J. Women's Stud.* 13:23–38

Haelyon H. 2006. "Longing for a child": perceptions of motherhood among Israeli-Jewish women undergoing in vitro fertilization (IVF) treatments. *Nashim: J. Women's Stud. Gender Iss.* 12:177–203

Handwerker L. 2002. The politics of making modern babies in China: reproductive technologies and the "new" eugenics. See Inhorn & Van Balen 2002, pp. 298–314

Hanson FA. 2001. Donor insemination: eugenic and feminist implications. *Med. Anthropol. Q.* 15:287–311

Harrington J, Becker G, Nachtigall RD. 2008. Non-reproductive technologies: remediating kin structure with donor gametes. *Sci. Tech. Hum. Values* 33:393–418

Hashiloni-Dolev Y. 2007. *A Life (Un)Worthy of Living: Reproductive Genetics in Israel and Germany*. Secaucus, NJ: Springer

Hashiloni-Dolev Y, Shkedi S. 2007. On new reproductive technologies and family ethics: preimplantation genetic diagnosis for sibling donor in Israel and Germany. *Soc. Sci. Med.* 65:2081–92

Heng BC. 2007. Regulatory safeguards needed for the traveling foreign egg donor. *Hum. Reprod.* 22:2350–52

Hollos M. 2003. Problems of infertility in Southern Nigeria: Women's Voices from Amakiri. *Afr. J. Reprod. Health* 7:46–56

Horbst V. 2006. Infertility and in-vitro fertilization in Bamako, Mali: women's experience, avenues for solution and social contexts impacting on gynaecological consultations. *Curare* 29:35–46

Howell S. 2006. *The Kinning of Foreigners: Transnational Adoption in a Global Perspective*. New York: Berghahn

Hudson N, Culley L, Rapport F, Johnson M, Bharadwaj A. 2008. "Public" perceptions of gamete donation: a research review. *Public Underst. Sci.* In press

Inhorn MC. 1994. *Quest for Conception: Gender, Infertility, and Egyptian Medical Traditions*. Philadelphia: Univ. Penn. Press

Inhorn MC. 1996. *Infertility and Patriarchy: The Cultural Politics of Gender and Family Life in Egypt*. Philadelphia: Univ. Penn. Press

Inhorn MC. 2000. Missing motherhood: infertility, technology, and poverty in Egyptian women's lives. In *Ideologies and Technologies of Motherhood*, ed. H Ragoné, FW Twine, pp. 139–68. New York: Routledge

Inhorn MC. 2001. Money, marriage, and morality: constraints on IVF treatment seeking among infertile Egyptian couples. In *Cultural Perspectives on Reproductive Health*, ed. CM Obermeyer, pp. 83–100. Oxford: Oxford Univ. Press

Inhorn MC. 2002a. The "local" confronts the "global": infertile bodies and new reproductive technologies in Egypt. See Inhorn & Van Balen 2002, pp. 263–82

Inhorn MC. 2002b. Sexuality, masculinity, and infertility in Egypt: potent troubles in the marital and medical encounters. *J. Men's Stud.* 10:343–59

Inhorn MC. 2003a. *Local Babies, Global Science: Gender, Religion, and In Vitro Fertilization in Egypt*. New York: Routledge

Inhorn MC. 2003b. Global infertility and the globalization of new reproductive technologies: illustrations from Egypt. *Soc. Sci. Med.* 56:1837–51

Inhorn MC. 2003c. The risks of test-tube baby making in Egypt. In *Risk, Culture, and Health Inequality: Shifting Perceptions of Danger and Blame*, ed. BH Harthorn, L Oaks, pp. 57–78. Westport, CT: Praeger

Inhorn MC. 2003d. "The worms are weak": male infertility and patriarchal paradoxes in Egypt. *Men Masc.* 5:238–58

Inhorn MC. 2004. Middle Eastern masculinities in the age of new reproductive technologies: male infertility and stigma in Egypt and Lebanon. *Med. Anthropol. Q.* 18:34–54

Inhorn MC. 2005. Gender, health, and globalization in the Middle East: male infertility, ICSI, and men's resistance. In *Women, Globalization, and Health*, ed. I Kickbusch, KA Hartwig, JM List, pp. 113–25. New York: Palgrave Macmillan

Inhorn MC. 2006a. Medical anthropology at the intersections. *Med. Anthropol. Q.* 21:249–55

Inhorn MC. 2006b. Making Muslim babies: IVF and gamete donation in Sunni versus Shi'a Islam. *Cult. Med. Psychiatry* 30:427–50

Inhorn MC. 2006c. "He won't be my son": Middle Eastern Muslim men's discourses of adoption and gamete donation. *Med. Anthropol. Q.* 20:94–120

Inhorn MC. 2006d. *Fatwa*s and ARTS: IVF and gamete donation in Sunni v. Shi'a Islam. *J. Gender, Race Justice* 9:291–317

Inhorn MC. 2006e. Islam, IVF, and everyday life in the Middle East: the making of Sunni versus Shi'ite test-tube babies. *Anthropol. Middle East* 1:37–45

Inhorn MC, ed. 2007a. *Reproductive Disruptions: Gender, Technology, and Biopolitics in the New Millennium*. New York: Berghahn

Inhorn MC. 2007b. Masculinity, reproduction, and male infertility surgeries in Egypt and Lebanon. *J. Middle East Women's Stud.* 3:1–20

Inhorn MC. 2007c. Masturbation, semen collection, and men's IVF experiences: anxieties in the Muslim world. *Body Soc.* 13:37–53

Inhorn MC. 2007d. Loving your infertile Muslim spouse: notes on the globalization of IVF and its romantic commitments in Sunni Egypt and Shi'ite Lebanon. In *Love and Globalization: Transformations of Intimacy in the Contemporary World*, ed. MB Padilla, JS Hirsch, M Munoz-Laboy, R Sember, RG Parker, pp. 139–60. Nashville, TN: Vanderbilt Univ. Press

Inhorn MC. 2009. Globalization and reproductive tourism in the Muslim Middle East: IVF, Islam, and the Middle Eastern state. In *Reproduction, Globalization, and the State*, ed. CH Browner, CF Sargent. Durham NC: Duke Univ. Press. In press

Inhorn MC, Bharadwaj A. 2007. Reproductively disabled lives: infertility, stigma, and suffering in Egypt and India. In *Disability in Local and Global Worlds*, ed. B Ingstad, SR Whyte, pp. 78–106. Berkeley: Univ. Calif. Press

Inhorn MC, Birenbaum-Carmeli D. 2009. Male infertility, chronicity, and the plight of Palestinian men in Israel and Lebanon. In *Chronic Conditions, Fluid States: Globalization and the Anthropology of Illness*, ed. L Manderson, C Smith-Morris. New Brunswick, NJ: Rutgers Univ. Press. In press

Inhorn MC, Ceballo R, Nachtigall R. 2008. Marginalized, invisible, and unwanted: American minority struggles with infertility and assisted conception. In *Marginalised Reproduction: Ethnicity, Infertility and Assisted Conception*, ed. L Culley, N Hudson, F Van Rooij. London: Earthscan. In press

Inhorn MC, Fakih MH. 2006. Arab Americans, African Americans, and infertility: barriers to reproduction and medical care. *Fertil. Steril.* 85:844–52

Inhorn MC, Tjørnhøj-Thomsen T, Goldberg H, Mosegaard MlC, eds. 2009. *Reconceiving the Second Sex: Men, Masculinity, and Reproduction*. New York: Berghahn. In press

Inhorn MC, Van Balen F, eds. 2002. *Infertility around the Globe: New Thinking on Childlessness, Gender, and Reproductive Technologies*. Berkeley: Univ. Calif. Press

James WR. 2000. Placing the unborn: on the social recognition of new life. *Anthropol. Med.* 7:169–89

Jones CA. 2008. Ethical and legal conundrums of postmodern procreation. *Int. J. Obstet. Gynecol.* 100:208–10

Jones CA, Keith LG. 2006. Medical tourism and reproductive outsourcing: the dawning of a new paradigm for healthcare. *Int. J. Fertil.* 51:1–5

Kahn SM. 2000. *Reproducing Jews: A Cultural Account of Assisted Conception in Israel*. Durham, NC: Duke Univ. Press

Kahn SM. 2002. Rabbis and reproduction: the uses of new reproductive technologies among ultraorthodox Jews in Israel. See Inhorn & Van Balen 2002, pp. 283–97

Kahn SM. 2006. Making technology familiar: Orthodox Jews and infertility support, advice, and inspiration. *Cult. Med. Psychiatry* 30:467–80

Kahn SM. 2009. The mirth of the clinic: the banality of conception in an Israeli fertility clinic. See Birenbaum-Carmeli & Carmeli 2009a. In press

Kanaaneh RA. 2002. *Birthing the Nation: Strategies of Palestinian Women in Israel*. Berkeley: Univ. Calif. Press

Kirkman M. 2003. Egg and embryo donation and the meaning of motherhood. *Women Health* 38:1–18

Kitzinger J, Williams C. 2005. Forecasting science futures: legitimizing hope and calming fears in the embryo stem cell debate. *Soc. Sci. Med.* 61:731–40

Kleinman A. 1995. *Writing at the Margin: Discourse between Anthropology and Medicine*. Berkeley: Univ. Calif. Press

Konrad M. 1998. Ova donation and symbols of substance: some variations on the theme of sex, gender and the partible body. *J. R. Anthropol. Inst.* 4:643–67

Konrad M. 2005. *Nameless Relations: Anonymity, Melanesia and Reproductive Gift Exchange between British Ova Donors and Recipients*. New York: Berghahn

Krones T, Schlüter E, Neuwohner E, El Ansari S, Wissner T, Richter G. 2006. What is the preimplantation embryo? *Soc. Sci. Med.* 63:1–20

La Rochebrochard de E. 2003. Men medically assisted to reproduce: AID, IVF, and ICSI, an assessment of the revolution in the medical treatment of male factor infertility. *Population* 58:487–522

Leonard L. 2002a. Problematizing fertility: "scientific" accounts and Chadian women's narratives. See Inhorn & Van Balen 2002, pp. 193–214

Leonard L. 2002b. "Looking for children": the search for fertility among the Sara of Southern Chad. *Med. Anthropol.* 21:79–112

Lock M. 2009. Globalization and the state: is an era of neo-eugenics in the offing? In *Embodiment and the State: Health, Politics and the Intimate Life of State Powers*, ed. G Pizza, H Johannessen. New York: Berghahn. In press

MacDougall K, Becker G, Scheib J, Nachtigall RD. 2007. Strategies for disclosure: how parents approach telling their children that they were conceived with donor gametes. *Fertil. Steril.* 87:524–33

Macklin RB. 1995. Reproductive technologies in developing countries. *Bioethics* 9:276–82

Mamo L. 2007. *Queering Reproduction: Achieving Pregnancy in the Age of Technoscience*. Durham, NC: Duke Univ. Press

Markens S. 2007. *Surrogate Motherhood and the Politics of Reproduction*. Berkeley: Univ. Calif. Press

Melhuus M. 2003. Exchange matters: issues of law and the flow of human substances. In *Globalisation: Anthropological Perspectives*, ed. TH Eriksen, pp. 170–97. London: Pluto

Melhuus M. 2005. "Better safe than sorry": legislating assisted conception in Norway. In *State Formation: Anthropological Perspectives*, ed. C Krohn-Hansen, KG Nustad, pp. 212–33. London: Pluto

Melhuus M. 2006. The possibility of going abroad or lessons in how to resolve problems of conception: issues of law and practice in assisted conception in Norway. In *Circulation of Human Body Parts: Local, National and Beyond*, ed. A Deguchi, pp. 11–29. Tokyo: Res. Inst. Lang. Cult. Asia, Africa, Tokyo Univ. For. Stud.

Melhuus M. 2007. Procreative imaginations: when experts disagree on the meanings of kinship. In *Holding Worlds Together: Ethnographies of Knowing and Belonging*, ed. ME Lien, M Melhuus, pp. 37–56. New York: Berghahn

Melhuus M. 2008. The inviolability of motherhood or why egg donation is not allowed in Norway. In *Les Défis Contemporains de la Parente*, ed. E Porqueres. Paris: Ed. de L'HESS. In press

Moore LJ. 2007. *Sperm Counts: Overcome by Man's Most Precious Fluid*. New York: NYU Press

Morgan LM, Michaels MW, eds. 1999. *Fetal Subjects, Feminist Positions*. Philadelphia: Univ. Penn. Press

Nachtigall RD. 2006. International disparities in access to infertility services. *Fertil. Steril.* 85:871–75

Nachtigall RD, Becker G, Friese C, Butler A, MacDougall K. 2005. Parents' conceptualization of their frozen embryos complicates the disposition decision. *Fertil. Steril.* 84:431–34

Nachtigall RD, Becker G, Szkupinski-Quiroga SS, Tschann JM. 1998. The disclosure decision: concerns and issues of parents of children conceived through donor insemination. *Am. J. Obstet. Gynecol.* 178:1165–70

Nachtigall RD, Becker G, Wozny M. 1992. The effects of gender-specific diagnosis on men's and women's response to infertility. *Fertil. Steril.* 57:113–21

Nachtigall RD, Castrillo M, Shah N, Turner D, Harrington J, Jackson R. 2009. The challenge of providing infertility services to a low-income immigrant Latino population. *Fertil. Steril.* In press

Nachtigall RD, Tschann JM, Pitcher L, Szkupinski-Quiroga SS, Becker G. 1997. Stigma, disclosure, and family functioning among parents of children conceived through donor insemination. *Fertil. Steril.* 68:83–89

Nahar P, Sharma A, Sabin K, Begum L, Ahsan SK, Baqui A. 2000. Living with infertility: experiences among urban slum populations in Bangladesh. *Reprod. Health Matters* 8:33–44

Nahman M. 2006. Materializing Israeliness: difference and mixture in transnational ova donation. *Sci. Cult.* 15:199–213

Nahman M. 2008. Synecdochic ricochets: biosocialities in a Jerusalem IVF clinic. In *Biosocialities, Genetics, and the Social Sciences: Making Biologies and Identities*, ed. S Gibbon, C Novas, pp. 117–35. London: Routledge

Okonofua FE. 1996. The case against new reproductive technologies in developing countries. *Br. J. Obstet. Gynecol.* 103:957–62

Ong A, Collier SJ, eds. 2005. *Global Assemblages: Technology, Politics, and Ethics as Anthropological Problems.* Oxford: Blackwell

Pashigian M. 2009. Inappropriate relations: the ban on surrogacy with in vitro fertilization and the limits of state renovation in contemporary Vietnam. See Birenbaum-Carmeli & Inhorn. In press

Paxson H. 2006. Reproduction as spiritual kin work: orthodoxy, IVF, and the moral economy of motherhood in Greece. *Cult. Med. Psychiatry* 30:481–505

Pearce TO. 1999. She will not be listened to in public: perceptions among the Yoruba of infertility and childlessness in women. *Reprod. Health Matters* 7:69–79

Pennings G. 2002. Reproductive tourism as moral pluralism in motion. *J. Med. Ethics* 28:337–41

Pollock A. 2003. Complicating power in high-tech reproduction: narratives of anonymous paid egg donors. *J. Med. Humanit.* 24:241–63

Prainsack B. 2006. Negotiating life: the regulation of embryonic stem cell research and human cloning in Israel. *Soc. Stud. Sci.* 36:173–205

Prainsack B. 2007. Research populations: biobanks in Israel. *New Genet. Soc.* 26:85–103

Prainsack B, Spector TD. 2006. Twins: a cloning experience. *Soc. Sci. Med.* 63:2739–52

Quiroga SS. 2007. Blood is thicker than water: policing donor insemination and the reproduction of whiteness. *Hypatia* 22:143–61

Rabinerson D, Dekel A, Orvieto R, Feldberg D, Simon D, Kaplan B. 2002. Subsidised oocyte donation in Israel (1998–2000): results, costs and lessons. *Hum. Reprod.* 17:1404–6

Ragoné H. 1994. *Surrogate Motherhood: Conception in the Heart.* Boulder, CO: Westview Press

Ragoné H. 1996. Chasing the blood tie: surrogate mothers, adoptive mothers and fathers. *Am. Ethnol.* 23:352–65

Ragoné H. 2000. Of likeness and difference: how race is being transfigured by gestational surrogacy. In *Ideologies and Technologies of Motherhood*, ed. H Ragoné, FW Twine, pp. 56–75. New York: Routledge

Rapp R. 2001. Gender, body, biomedicine: how some feminist concerns dragged reproduction to the center of social theory. *Med. Anthropol. Q.* 15:466–77

Raspberry K. 2009. The genesis of embryos and ethics in vitro: practicing preimplantation genetic diagnosis in Argentina. See Birenbaum-Carmeli & Inhorn 2008. In press

Remennick L. 2006. The quest for the perfect baby: why do Israeli women seek prenatal genetic testing? *Sociol. Health Illn.* 28:21–53

Richards SC. 2002. "Spoiling the womb": definitions, aetiologies and responses to infertility in North West Province, Cameroon. *Afr. J. Reprod. Health* 6:84–94

Roberts C, Throsby K. 2007. Paid to share: IVF patients, eggs and stem cell research. *Soc. Sci. Med.* 66:159–69

Roberts EFS. 2006. God's laboratory: religious rationalities and modernity in Ecuadorian in vitro fertilization. *Cult. Med. Psychiat.* 30:507–36

Roberts EFS. 2007. Extra embryos: the ethics of cyropreservation in Ecuador and elsewhere. *Am. Ethnol.* 34:181–99

Roberts EFS. 2008. Biology, sociality and reproductive modernity in Ecuadorian in-vitro fertilization: the particulars of place. In *Biosocialities, Genetics and the Social Sciences: Making Biologies and Identities*, ed. S Gibbon, C Novas, pp. 79–97. New York: Routledge

Roberts EFS. 2009. The traffic between women: female alliance and familial egg donation in Ecuador. See Birenbaum-Carmeli & Inhorn 2009. In press

Sandelowski M. 1991. Compelled to try: the never-enough quality of conceptive technology. *Med. Anthropol. Q.* 5:29–47

Sandelowski M. 1993. *With Child in Mind: Studies of the Personal Encounter with Infertility*. Philadelphia: Univ. Penn. Press

Schneider DM. 1980. *American Kinship: A Cultural Account*. Chicago: Univ. Chicago Press. 2nd ed.

Seeman D. 2009. On ethnography, Jewish ethics, and assisted reproductive technologies in Israel. See Birenbaum-Carmeli & Carmeli 2009a. In press

Shalev C, Gooldin S. 2006. The uses and misuses of in vitro fertilization in Israel: some sociological and ethical considerations. *Nashim: J. Jew. Women's Stud. Gend. Iss.* 12:151–76

Simpson B. 2001. Making "bad" deaths "good": the kinship consequences of posthumous conception. *J. R. Anthropol. Inst.* 7:1–18

Spar DL. 2005. Reproductive tourism and the regulatory map. *N. Engl. J. Med.* 352:531–33

Spar DL. 2006. *The Baby Business: How Money, Science, and Politics Drive the Commerce of Conception*. Boston: Harvard Bus. School Press

Spilker K, Lie M. 2007. Gender and bioethics intertwined: egg donation within the context of equal opportunities. *Eur. J. Women's Stud.* 4:327–40

Storrow RF. 2005a. *The Handmaid's Tale* of fertility tourism: passports and third parties in the religious regulation of assisted conception. *Tex. Wesleyan Law Rev.* 12:189–211

Storrow RF. 2005b. Quest for conception: fertility tourists, globalization and feminist legal theory. *Hastings Law J.* 57:295–330

Storrow RF. 2006. Marginalizing adoption through the regulation of assisted reproduction. *Cap. Univ. Law Rev.* 35:479–516

Strathern M. 1992a. *Reproducing the Future: Essays on Anthropology, Kinship and the New Reproductive Technologies*. New York: Routledge

Strathern M. 1992b. *After Nature: English Kinship in the Late Twentieth Century*. Cambridge, UK: Cambridge Univ. Press

Strathern M. 2005. *Partial Connections*. Landham, MD: AltaMira

Sundby J. 2002. Infertility and health care in countries with less resources: case studies from Sub-Saharan Africa. See Inhorn & Van Balen 2002, pp. 247–59

Teman E. 2003a. The medicalization of "nature" in the "artificial body": surrogate motherhood in Israel. *Med. Anthropol. Q.* 17:78–98

Teman E. 2003b. "Knowing" the surrogate body in Israel. In *Surrogate Motherhood: International Perspectives*, ed. R Cook, SD Sclater, F Kaganas, pp. 261–79. Oxford: Hart

Thompson C. 1996. Ontological choreography: agency through objectification in infertility clinics. *Soc. Stud. Sci.* 26:575–610

Thompson C. 1998. "Quit sniveling cyro-baby, we'll work out which one's your mama": kinship in an infertility clinic. In *Cyborg Babies: From Techno-Sex to Techno-Tots*, ed. R Davis-Floyd, J Dumit, pp. 40–66. London: Routledge

Thompson C. 2001. Strategic naturalizing: kinship in an infertility clinic. See Franklin & McKinnon 2001, pp. 175–202

Thompson C. 2002. Fertile ground: feminists theorize infertility. See Inhorn & Van Balen 2002, pp. 52–78

Thompson C. 2005. *Making Parents: The Ontological Choreography of Reproductive Technologies*. Cambridge, MA: MIT Press

Thompson C. 2006. God is in the details: comparative perspectives on the intertwining of religion and assisted reproductive technologies. *Cult. Med. Psychiatry* 30:557–61

Thompson C. 2008a. Skin tone and the persistence of biological race in egg donation for assisted reproduction. In *Shades of Difference*, ed. EN Glenn. Palo Alto, CA: Stanford Univ. Press. In press

Thompson C. 2008b. Stem cells, women, and the new gender and science. In *Gender Innovations in Science and Engineering*, ed. L Schiebinger, pp. 109–30. Palo Alto, CA: Stanford Univ. Press

Throsby K. 2004. *When IVF Fails: Feminism, Infertility and the Negotiation of Normality*. New York: Palgrave Macmillan

Tjørnhøj-Thomsen T. 2009. "It feels unmanly, in a way": men and infertility in Denmark. See Inhorn et al. 2009. In press

Tremayne S. 2006. Not all Muslims are luddites. *Anthropol. Today* 22:1–2

Tremayne S. 2009. Law, ethics and donor technologies in Shia Iran. See Birenbaum-Carmeli & Inhorn 2009. In press

Tsuge A. 2005. How society responds to desires of childless couples: Japan's position on donor conception. *Meijigakuin Univ. J.* 35:21–34

Unisa S. 1999. Childlessness in Andhra Pradesh, India: treatment-seeking and consequences. *Reprod. Health Matters* 7:54–64

Upton R. 2002. Perceptions of and attitudes towards male infertility in Northern Botswana: some implications for family planning and AIDS prevention policies. *Afr. J. Reprod. Health* 3:103–11

Van Balen F, Gerrits T. 2001. Quality of infertility care in poor-resource areas and the introduction of new reproductive technologies. *Hum. Reprod.* 16:215–19

Van Balen F, Inhorn MC. 2002. Introduction—interpreting infertility: a view from the social sciences. See Inhorn & Van Balen 2002, pp. 3–23

Van Balen F, Inhorn MC. 2003. Son preference, sex selection, and the "new" new reproductive technologies. *Int. J. Health Serv.* 33:235–52

Vanderlinden L. 2009. East in west? Turkish migrants and the conception of the ethnic other in Germany. See Birenbaum-Carmeli & Inhorn 2009. In press

Vayena E, Rowe PJ, Griffin PD, eds. 2002. *Current Practices and Controversies in Assisted Reproduction.* Geneva: WHO

Webster A. 2002. Innovative health technologies and the social: redefining health, medicine and the body. *Curr. Sociol.* 50:443–57

Weisberg DK. 2005. *The Birth of Surrogacy in Israel.* Gainesville: Univ. Fla. Press

Williams C, Ehrich K, Farsides B, Scott R. 2007. Facilitating choice, framing choice: staff views on widening the scope of preimplantation diagnosis in the UK. *Soc. Sci. Med.* 65:1094–105

Yebei VN. 2000. Unmet needs, beliefs and treatment-seeking for infertility among migrant Ghanaian women in the Netherlands. *Reprod. Health Matters* 8:134–41

Zuhur S. 1992. Of milk-mothers and sacred bonds: Islam, patriarchy, and new reproductive technologies. *Creighton Law Rev.* 25:1725–38

Detecting the Genetic Signature of Natural Selection in Human Populations: Models, Methods, and Data

Angela M. Hancock and Anna Di Rienzo

Department of Human Genetics, University of Chicago, Chicago, Illinois 60637;
email: ahancock@uchicago.edu, dirienzo@uchicago.edu

Annu. Rev. Anthropol. 2008. 37:197–217

First published online as a Review in Advance on
June 17, 2008

The *Annual Review of Anthropology* is online at
anthro.annualreviews.org

This article's doi:
10.1146/annurev.anthro.37.081407.085141

0084-6570/08/1021-0197$20.00

Key Words

genetic adaptations, selective sweeps, neutrality tests

Abstract

Patterns of DNA sequence variation in the genome contain a record of past selective events. The ability to collect increasingly large data sets of polymorphisms has allowed investigators to perform hypothesis-driven studies of candidate genes as well as genome-wide scans for signatures of adaptations. This genetic approach to the study of natural selection has identified many signals consistent with predictions from anthropological studies. Selective pressures related to variation in climate, diet, and pathogen exposure have left strong marks on patterns of human variation. Additional signals of adaptations are observed in genes involved in chemosensory perception and reproduction. Several ongoing projects aim to sequence the complete genome of 1000 individuals from different human populations. These large-scale projects will provide data for more complete genome scans of selection, but more focused studies aimed at testing specific hypotheses will continue to hold an important place in elucidating the history of adaptations in humans.

INTRODUCTION

Genetic drift: the change in frequency of a mutation due to the random sampling of alleles from one generation to the next

Fitness: a measure of the contribution of an organism to the next generation, related to the capacity to survive and reproduce

From a genetic perspective, evolution can be defined as changes in allele frequencies over time due to mutation, genetic drift, migration, and natural selection. The investigation of natural selection and genetic adaptations in humans has held a central place in biological anthropology as well as in disciplines such as human genetics and evolutionary biology. Although these disciplines differ slightly in the questions they address and the approaches they use, they intersect in the field of human population genetics, which uses genetic variation data to learn about the past demographic events and the history of natural selection in human populations.

Traditional approaches to identifying adaptations to local environments have often relied on comparing the distribution of a phenotype to an environmental variable hypothesized to mirror a selective pressure. This was, for example, pertinent to the malaria hypothesis, which explains the geographic distribution of the β-thalassemia (Haldane 1949) and HbS (Allison 1954) alleles in terms of the resistance they confer to malaria. Additional notable examples of this approach focused on quantitative phenotypes, such as the relationship between body mass and temperature (Katzmarzyk & Leonard 1998, Roberts 1978), skin pigmentation and solar radiation (Jablonski & Chaplin 2000), and oxygen saturation of arterial hemoglobin and altitude (Beall et al. 1997). If the phenotypes are heritable, the correlation between the distribution of phenotype and environmental variable constitutes evidence for an adaptation at the genetic level (as opposed, for example, to acclimatization). The argument for positive selection is especially strong if a correlation can also be shown between the phenotype of interest (e.g., high oxygen saturation at high altitude) and a measure of fitness (e.g., number of surviving offspring) (e.g., Beall et al. 2004).

Although these traditional approaches directly test the hypothesis that natural selection acted on a given genetic variant, their application on a large scale is hampered by several limitations. They require investigators to collect phenotype data, which is expensive and time consuming, and analyze large samples to achieve adequate statistical power. More recently, an approach based on the genetic signature of natural selection on patterns of variation has found wide applicability in studies of adaptations in humans and other species. This approach is based on the idea that natural selection introduces a local perturbation in the patterns of neutral genetic variation surrounding an advantageous allele relative to regions of the genome where variation is shaped only by genetic drift. This approach has two major advantages: First, it does not require investigators to collect phenotype information, and second, it can detect adaptive changes resulting from selection coefficients, e.g., 1%, that would be very hard to detect by traditional phenotype-based approaches (Gillespie 1991). The recent development of technologies and resources for studying human genetic variation on an unprecedented scale has allowed investigators to scan the entire human genome for signals of positive natural selection. Moreover, as the same technologies are being applied to the study of the genetic bases of common diseases, signals of natural selection can be connected to genotype-phenotype association signals, where both signals arise from unbiased genome-scale analyses.

Despite the somewhat separate trajectories of anthropological, human genetic, and evolutionary genetic studies of human adaptations, by weaving together strands from these disciplines, it may soon be possible to reconstruct the history of selective events that occurred during human evolution and to infer the role of human adaptations in health and disease. Here, we briefly review models of selection and methods for detecting its signature. In describing the main signals of selection reported so far, we focus on those that pertain to variation that is still segregating in humans, rather than to mutations that became fixed between humans and closely related primates. Our goal is to provide a starting point for the synthesis of findings from the different disciplines that are contributing to our understanding of human adaptations.

MODELS OF POSITIVE NATURAL SELECTION

Natural selection can be defined as the process by which beneficial heritable traits increase in frequency over time and unfavorable heritable traits become less common. This process can occur according to a variety of models; the resulting signatures vary considerably across selection models and for different values of the relevant parameters (e.g., strength of selection, mode of inheritance, age of the selective pressure). Therefore, consideration of these models is crucial for interpreting empirical patterns of variation in regions of the genome that experienced positive selection.

Standard selection models involve loci that have two alleles, and selection occurs if the fitness differs across the three genotypes. Directional selection occurs when one of the two alleles is favored over the other so that its frequency may increase until it reaches fixation. The time needed for a new beneficial allele to become fixed is a function of the selection coefficient and mode of inheritance, with favored dominant and additive alleles increasing in frequency much faster than recessive ones (see **Figure 1a**, see color insert). Under balancing selection, the heterozygote has fitness greater than that of both homozygotes; in this case, a new allele quickly reaches a stable equilibrium frequency and fluctuates around that frequency for as long as the selective pressure is present (see **Figure 1b**). Therefore, although both directional and balancing selection will result in the rapid increase in frequency of a new beneficial allele, the former ultimately eliminates variation from a population while the latter tends to maintain it. If balancing selection is due to a long-standing selective pressure, a polymorphism may be maintained in the population well beyond the expected lifetime of a neutral polymorphism (i.e., $4N_e$ generations for an autosomal locus, where N_e is

the effective population size). Another classical model is diversifying selection in which two or more phenotypes are simultaneously favored. This model generally predicts an increase in levels of genetic variation.

In addition to the models above, scenarios with temporally and spatially varying selection may be particularly relevant to humans (Gillespie 1991). Temporal variation in selective pressures probably resulted from the climatic changes of the Ice Ages, the diversity of habitats to which humans became exposed during their dispersal, and the environmental changes arising from the impact of human activities, e.g., the spread of agriculture. The new selective pressures may favor new alleles—as described in the models above—or standing (previously neutral) alleles, which may afford a faster adaptive response to environmental shifts. These two models make different predictions about the population dynamics of the favored allele and the expected signature of selection. The difference in predictions is mainly because a beneficial allele that was previously neutral underwent an initial phase of random drift before being driven to high frequency by selection; this initial neutral phase has important consequences for the expected patterns of linked variation. In addition to environmental and selective changes over the time span of human evolution, there is also ample evidence for spatial variation in selective pressures; this may be the consequence of variation in features of the physical environment, such as climate, or of the different subsistence strategies adopted by humans, which in turn influence other aspects of the environment, e.g., diet or pathogen exposure. In some cases, selective pressures may vary spatially in a graded fashion, e.g., climate or ultraviolet (UV) exposure, with important implications for the expected geographic distribution of favored alleles. Finally, differences across environments may lead to spatial variation in the intensity of purifying selection (i.e., selection removing deleterious mutations); for example, a gene that was under strong purifying selection in a given environment may

Fixation: the process by which a mutation reaches 100% frequency in the population

undergo relaxation of selective constraints when the population migrates to a different location or adopts a different lifestyle.

METHODS FOR DETECTING THE SIGNATURE OF NATURAL SELECTION

As shown in **Figure 1**, natural selection acting on a beneficial variant has a dramatic impact on its rate of frequency change over time, resulting in a trajectory that is distinct from that expected for neutral variants. Under directional selection or during the initial phase of a balanced polymorphism, beneficial alleles are characterized by a rapid rise in frequency. Because of the low recombination distance, the histories of the beneficial allele and the nearby neutral alleles are strongly correlated. Because of this correlation, natural selection generates a local perturbation in the pattern of variation tightly linked to the selected site. In contrast, patterns of variation in neutrally evolving genomic regions are influenced only by genetic drift and, therefore, by properties of the population, including the history of population size and population structure. Therefore, detecting the signature of natural selection essentially consists in distinguishing the patterns of variation that are shaped solely by demographic history from those that are influenced by natural selection, in addition to demography.

Briefly, as shown in **Figure 2** (see color insert), when a new advantageous allele is introduced into the population by the mutation process, it will be associated with a particular haplotype background. As this allele is driven quickly to an intermediate or high frequency, the neutral alleles that define the haplotype and that are tightly linked to the selected site will also tend to increase in frequency. Owing to the rapid increase in frequency of the advantageous allele, recombination does not erode the association between the selected site and the surrounding neutral sites, thereby generating a local pattern of extended identical haplotypes [referred to as extended haplotype homozygosity (EHH)] that

occur at intermediate to high frequencies. This process is often referred to as a partial or incomplete selective sweep. A number of statistical tests have been developed to detect this haplotype pattern (Hanchard et al. 2006, Hudson et al. 1994, Innan et al. 2005, Sabeti et al. 2002, Voight et al. 2006). If selection is directional, the advantageous allele may go to fixation. In this case, which is referred to as a complete selective sweep, all variation near the selected site will also be fixed and only new mutations arising during the sweep will segregate in the population at low frequencies. Therefore, the expected pattern near a fixed advantageous allele consists of a reduction in polymorphism levels and a relative abundance of rare alleles. At a greater distance from the selected site, recombination events will tend to uncouple the advantageous allele from the neutral alleles. This may result in a pattern characterized by high frequency derived alleles (i.e., new mutations); because such alleles tend to be rare under neutrality, the occurrence of multiple high frequency derived alleles within a small region constitutes a strong signal of selection. Therefore, different aspects of the data (i.e., polymorphism levels, allele frequency spectrum, haplotype structure) will be informative to detect complete versus incomplete selective sweeps. A number of statistical tests have been developed to capture the impact of positive natural selection under different models (see Appendix); we refer the reader to several recent reviews for details (Biswas & Akey 2006, Nielsen 2005, Nielsen et al. 2007, Sabeti et al. 2006).

When selection acts on a variant that is advantageous only in a subset of populations, the frequency of that variant may differ across populations to a greater extent than predicted for variants evolving neutrally in all populations. Several approaches have been devised to detect such adaptations to local environments. Historically, the most widely used is based on the statistic F_{ST} and its modifications (Beaumont & Balding 2004, Consortium 2005), which simply summarize allele frequency differences between pairs of populations or among multiple populations (Weir 1996). Variants with unusually large F_{ST} values are typically interpreted as being the targets of local selective pressures (Lewontin & Krakauer 1973).

If the intensity of selection varies spatially in a graded fashion, advantageous allele frequencies may vary across populations following the geographic distribution of the selective pressure. Therefore, if the selective pressure—or a good proxy for it—is known, a test of the correlation between the advantageous allele frequency and the value of the environmental variable may provide evidence for spatially varying selection. This approach is particularly appropriate when the advantageous phenotype is known to have a clinal distribution; for example, this is true for human skin pigmentation as well as body mass and proportionality, which are correlated with UV radiation and temperature, respectively (Jablonski & Chaplin 2000, Katzmarzyk & Leonard 1998).

Additional information regarding the action of natural selection on genetic variation may be extracted by comparing the pattern of variation within species and among species (i.e., humans and a close outgroup) for synonymous and nonsynonymous variants within a coding region. If a gene is evolving neutrally, the ratios of nonsynonymous to synonymous mutations within species and among species are expected to be the same. However, if natural selection drives multiple advantageous mutations to fixation within the same gene, this action may generate an excess of nonsynonymous relative to synonymous changes among species compared with the ratio observed within species. Alternatively, an excess of nonsynonymous mutations may be observed in the variation within species relative to among species. One possible interpretation for this pattern is that diversifying selection maintains a higher number of nonsynonymous variants; this explanation likely applies to the HLA genes (see below). However, a more common interpretation of this pattern, which is often observed in human genes, is that weak purifying (rather than positive) selection acts on nonsynonymous polymorphisms. Under this scenario, the nonsynonymous variants in excess are slightly deleterious mutations that reach nontrivial frequency in populations but are unlikely to become fixed.

Assessing Statistical Significance of Selection Signals

From the statistical standpoint, two main approaches have been used to detect the signature of natural selection: model-based and empirical approaches. In the model-based approach, a theoretical model of population history in which all variation is neutral is used to develop quantitative expectations about patterns of variation (quantitative expectations for different models of demography under neutrality can be readily obtained using simulations). If a test locus exhibits variation patterns that are significantly different from those expected under the model, the null hypothesis of neutrality is rejected. A variant of this approach is to compare the likelihood of the data under neutrality with that under a specified model of selection, using the statistical framework of the likelihood ratio test (Kim & Stephan 2002, Nielsen et al. 2005, Przeworski 2003). The drawback of model-based methods is that, if the assumptions about population history are violated, one may falsely reject neutrality. Although much progress has been made in reconstructing the broad picture of human population history (Schaffner et al. 2005, Stajich & Hahn 2005 Voight et al. 2005), it is widely recognized that the details of the true history are too complex to be captured by simple models. Unlike the model-based method, the empirical method is agnostic about population history, and, under the assumption that most loci in the human genome evolve neutrally, it aims at identifying the loci with the most unusual patterns compared with large-scale data sets of genetic variation. For example, empirical patterns of variation may be summarized by means of one or more test statistics, which are used to rank loci in the genome; those loci falling above an arbitrary cut-off (typically the top 5%) are identified as unusual and are often referred to as outliers. A recently developed composite likelihood method attempts to integrate the advantages of both approaches

Nonsynonymous mutations: mutations that change the amino acid sequence of a protein

Synonymous mutations: mutations that do not change the amino acid sequence of a protein

HLA: human leukocyte antigen

International HapMap Project: a project to characterize the haplotype structure of the human genome by genotyping more than 3.1 million SNPs in diverse populations

Perlegen Project: a project to characterize patterns of genetic variation 1.6 million SNPs in three diverse populations

by comparing a model without selection that is fitted to genome-wide variation data with a model in which selection acted in a particular region of the genome (Nielsen et al. 2005). This method, which is tailored to the detection of complete selective sweeps, is remarkably robust to deviations from the demographic assumptions (Williamson et al. 2007).

Because it relies on large-scale variation data, the outlier approach has gained wider applicability since the completion of genome-wide projects, such as the International HapMap Project (Consortium 2005, Frazer et al. 2007) and the Perlegen Project (Hinds et al. 2005). This approach already generated many interesting candidate targets of selection. However, to reconstruct accurately the history of selective events, all or the vast majority of adaptations must be detected, and this is unlikely to occur with outlier approaches alone. This is because there is a trade-off between false positives and false negatives, the extent of which is sensitive to a number of factors that affect the statistical power of neutrality tests (see below) (Teshima et al. 2006). To complement outlier approaches, investigators can compare the strength of the evidence for positive selection across groups of genes in different biological processes; a significant excess in one group of genes suggests that the biological process as a whole evolved genetic adaptations, even though the signals at individual genes may not reach genome-wide significance (Akey et al. 2002, Tang et al. 2007, Voight et al. 2006, Wang et al. 2006).

Considerations about Statistical Power

The power of neutrality tests based on polymorphism levels, the spectrum of allele frequency, and haplotype structure is affected by a number of factors, most notably the age of the selective event and the strength of selection, whereby younger and more strongly advantageous alleles are more easily detected. In addition, it is important to note that the process illustrated in **Figure 2** applies most directly to mutations that are immediately ad-

vantageous and that are dominant or codominant. If selection acts on standing—previously neutral—mutations or on recessive new mutations, the expected pattern of variation may not be distinguishable from that typical of neutrally evolving regions of the genome, leading to a marked reduction in power (Hermisson & Pennings 2005; Pennings & Hermisson 2006a,b; Przeworski et al. 2005). The similarity in expected variation patterns under neutrality and under the above selection models is due to the fact that the frequency trajectory of previously neutral or recessive new mutations is characterized by a longer initial phase, prior to the rapid rise in frequency, during which mutation and recombination events can generate substantial diversity in the chromosomal background of the mutation. For the case of selection on standing variation, the signature of selection is unlikely to be detectable if the frequency of the variant at the onset of selection is higher than 5% (Przeworski et al. 2005).

The above factors affect the power of different tests to a varying degree. Therefore, the results of genome-wide selection scans are inherently biased toward the type of signals most powerfully detected by the test used in the scan. This bias complicates the analysis of the overlap of signals across studies and potentially distorts the reconstruction of the overall history of selective pressures. Approaches that combine different summaries of the data have also been implemented in hopes of achieving greater power and accuracy (Tang et al. 2007, Zeng et al. 2006).

SIGNALS OF GENETIC ADAPTATIONS IN HUMAN POPULATIONS

Here, we review briefly the main signals of selection observed in studies of genetic variation within and among human populations. Some of these studies tested specific hypotheses arising from the anthropological literature on phenotypic variation and on its adaptive significance (see, for example, Biasutti 1959; Roberts 1953, 1978; Roberts & Kahlon 1976). With the advent of genome-wide scans for selection signals, investigators can evaluate the evidence for positive selection in an unbiased manner. Genome-wide scans have identified many selection targets that are consistent with previous anthropological studies. In addition, these scans implicated other, perhaps less expected signals of selection.

Climate and the Physical Environment

That climate and the physical environment played an important role in shaping human phenotypic variation is evident from the strong correlations between traits such as body mass, basal metabolic rate, or skin reflectance and variables such as temperature, latitude, and UV radiation (Henry & Rees 1991, Jablonski & Chaplin 2000, Leonard et al. 2005, Roberts & Kahlon 1976). Other phenotypes likely to have similar geographic distributions include those related to sodium homeostasis, salt and water retention, and thermogenesis. Overall, studies of phenotypic variation have provided strong support for the notion that heat and cold stress as well as UV radiation have exerted strong selective pressures on humans; genetic studies of selection have largely supported these predictions.

UV radiation. Among the phenotypes with complex patterns of inheritance, skin pigmentation is one of the more completely characterized phenotypes at the genetic level (Rees 2003 and references therein), with contributions from studies of animal models [e.g., Kelsh et al. 1996, Mammalian phenotype ontology database (see Related Resources)], Mendelian pigmentation disorders, and genotype-phenotype association (Bonilla et al. 2005; Duffy et al. 2004, 2007; Flanagan et al. 2000; Graf et al. 2005, 2007; Kanetsky et al. 2002; Lamason et al. 2005; Palmer et al. 2000; Rebbeck et al. 2002; Smith et al. 1998; Stokowski et al. 2007; Sulem et al. 2007).

An early study of the genetic signature of selection on skin pigmentation examined variation at the melanocortin 1 receptor (*MC1R*) locus, which influences variation in skin and hair color. The authors found a larger proportion of nonsynonymous variants in non-African compared with African samples, which was interpreted as evidence for strong purifying selection against nonsynonymous mutations in Africa and relaxation of constraints outside Africa (Harding et al. 2000). A recent study focused on a strong candidate gene for skin pigmentation, *SLC24A5*, which, when mutated, causes a pigmentation defect in zebrafish that can be rescued by the human gene (Lamason et al. 2005). In humans, a nonsynonymous alanine to threonine polymorphism at position 111 is associated with variation in skin pigmentation among African American and African Caribbean individuals. The light pigmentation allele is fixed or nearly fixed in Europeans, and, consistent with the expectations for a complete selective sweep, the genomic region spanning *SLC24A5* exhibits low levels of polymorphism.

The availability of extensive variation data allowed investigators to search for selection signatures in candidate genes for skin pigmentation on the basis of strong population differentiation (i.e., high F_{ST}) and EHH (Izagirre et al. 2006, Lao et al. 2007, Myles et al. 2007, Norton et al. 2007). The geographic distribution of some of these candidate single nucleotide polymorphisms (SNPs) was characterized in further detail; these analyses found evidence for variation leading to lighter pigmentation at *OCA2* in both Europe and Asia and at *ASIP* worldwide, whereas the *SLC24A5*, *MATP* and *TYR* genes showed evidence for selection only in Europeans. Because signatures of selection for lighter pigmentation are not found at the same genes in Europe and Asia, convergent evolution for reduced pigmentation appears to be relatively common for this trait (Norton et al. 2007).

Unbiased scans for signals of adaptations using genome-wide data have also provided strong evidence for selection on skin pigmentation. Strong signals were detected using haplotype structure [*OCA2*, *TYRP1*, *DNTPB1*, *SLC24A5* and *MYO5A* by Voight et al. (2006) and Tang et al. (2007)], EHH and

SNP: single nucleotide polymorphism

strong population differentiation [*SLC24A5*, *SLC45A2* by Sabeti et al. (2007)], strong population differentiation alone [*ABCC11*, *SLC45A2, SLC24A5* by Barreiro et al. (2008)], and frequency spectrum [*KITLG, MATP, SILV, OCA2, TRPM1, SLC24A5, RAB27A, MC2R, ATRN* by Williamson et al. (2007)].

Heat and cold stress. The role of heat stress as a selective pressure in humans has been summarized in the sodium-retention hypothesis, which posits that, in hot, humid environments, selection for high sodium retention was strong because salts are lost quickly through sweat but are important for maintaining temperature homeostasis (Denton 1982, Gleibermann 1973). One prediction of this hypothesis is that genetic variation underlying adaptations to heat stress is correlated with climatic variables (e.g., temperature and potential evaporation) or latitude as a proxy for climate. In addition, signals consistent with complete or partial selective sweeps may be observed within individual populations. Consistent with these predictions, the frequency of genetic variants implicated in interindividual variation in sodium retention and risk to hypertension was significantly correlated with latitude. Researchers observed this pattern in a number of genes including those coding for angiotensinogen (*AGT*), which plays a vital role in the renin-angiotensin pathway, cytochrome P450 3A5 (*CYP3A5*), which activates cortisol in the kidney, and the G-protein beta-3 subunit, which is involved in signal transduction in a number of tissues (Thompson et al. 2004, Young et al. 2005). In the case of the *AGT* and the *CYP3A5* genes, investigators also observed signals of natural selection using tests of the frequency spectrum or haplotype structure (Nakajima et al. 2004, Thompson et al. 2004).

In addition to heat tolerance, selective pressures related to climate probably acted to increase cold tolerance by shaping genetic variation in energy metabolism. Consistent with a role for positive selection on cold tolerance–enhancing variation, Mishmar et al. (2003) and Ruiz-Pesini et al. (2004) showed that the number and frequencies of nonsynonymous mu-

tations in mitochondrial genes increase with distance from Africa. Furthermore, we recently investigated a large number of candidate susceptibility genes for common metabolic disorders (e.g., type 2 diabetes, obesity) to determine whether there was widespread evidence for spatially varying selection in energy metabolic genes (Hancock et al. 2008). As with the sodium-retention genes, we found that variation in these genes was significantly correlated with climate variables in worldwide population samples. Several of the strongest signals included variants previously associated with disease, and several of these fell in thermogenesis pathway genes.

The results of genome-wide selection scans have generally been consistent with those from hypothesis-driven studies. Carlson et al. (2005) scanned the human genome for signals of selection using the frequency spectrum and found evidence for selection at *CYP3A5*. Voight et al. (2006) used the genotype data from the HapMap project to test for evidence of an incomplete selective sweep by detecting regions of EHH across the genome (Voight et al. 2006); this study found significant signals at the *CYP3A5* and the leptin receptor (*LEPR*) genes, both showing strong correlations between allele frequency and climate variables. In addition to individual signals, they found a significant excess of signals in genes involved in biological processes related to energy metabolism, such as carbohydrate metabolism and electron transport (in Asians and Europeans, respectively). Tang et al. (2007) used a different measure of EHH that preferentially targeted signals in high frequency alleles; this study found signals for the *CYP3A5* region and for a group of genes with similar function (i.e., oxidoreductase activity). Williamson et al. (2007) used a composite likelihood test to scan the genome for signals of complete selective sweeps (Williamson et al. 2007); this study identified several strong signals in genes that may be important for heat or cold stress adaptations, including those coding for sterol carrier protein 2 (*SCP2*), farnesoid X receptor (*NR1H4*), and activator of heat shock 90kDa protein ATPase homolog 1 (*AHSA1*).

Diet and Food Availability

Specific dietary components. Lactase persistence is the production, after infancy, of the enzyme lactase, which breaks down the milk sugar lactose into glucose and galactose so that it can be further processed in the intestines. Although uncommon in nonhuman species, in some human populations lactase persistence is relatively common. Prevalence of lactase persistence varies greatly among human populations and has been shown to cooccur with cultural traits that involve the inclusion of dairy products in the diet. A cline in the lactase persistence phenotype exists within Europe such that persistence is highest among populations in the Northwest and lowest among those in the Southeast (Swallow 2003 and references therein). But the observed pattern is not restricted to Europe: Pastoral populations in the Middle East (e.g., Bedouin) and sub-Saharan Africa (e.g., Fulani and Tutsi) also have high prevalence of lactase persistence. These findings led to the hypothesis that alleles causing lactase persistence were advantageous when populations adopted dairy farming and shifted to a diet in which milk is a major adult staple (Kretchmer 1972, McCracken 1971, Simoons 1970).

In Europeans, lactase persistence was shown to be due to a polymorphism about 14 kb upstream of the gene coding for the lactase enzyme (*LCT*). This polymorphism, denoted C/T_{-13910}, is likely to affect lactase production via changes in transcription levels. The genomic region containing this polymorphism was investigated for signatures of positive natural selection in ethnically diverse population samples, with a special focus on the haplotype associated with persistence in Europeans (Bersaglieri et al. 2004). Consistent with the idea that lactase persistence was advantageous in European populations, multiple polymorphisms displayed unusually large differences in allele frequencies between European and non-European populations, and the haplotype structure exhibited extremely high EHH in European populations. The time since expansion of

the C/T_{-13910} variant in Europeans was estimated to be 2188–20650 years, roughly consistent with the likely time of onset of dairy farming. The above findings were bolstered by genome-wide scans for selection, which showed that the *LCT* gene in Europeans contains the strongest signal of a partial selective sweep in the human genome (Consortium 2005, Sabeti et al. 2007, Voight et al. 2006, Williamson et al. 2007).

Although it is common in Europeans, the C/T_{-13910} variant is absent or very rare in some African and Middle Eastern populations where lactase persistence is high, which led to the hypothesis that different variants underlie the lactase persistence phenotype across populations. Indeed, genotype-phenotype association studies in African pastoral populations found that several polymorphisms near the C/T_{-13910} (G/T_{-14010}, T/G_{-13915}, and C/G_{-13907}) may cause lactase persistence. Furthermore, in vitro studies showed that these alleles affected *LCT* transcription levels. These findings suggested that convergent evolution occurred for lactase persistence in Europeans and in African pastoralist populations that regularly drink milk (Tishkoff et al. 2007). The high frequency of the lactase persistence allele(s) in African pastoralists compared with nonpastoralists and the high EHH among pastoralists are consistent with the notion that these alleles were driven quickly to high frequency by positive natural selection. As with European populations, the time estimated since the expansion of the lactase persistence allele in Africa, i.e., 3000–7000 years ago, is consistent with selection beginning around the time when a pastoral subsistence strategy was adopted in Africa. Enattah et al. (2008) described a high frequency haplotype in Saudi Arabians that is defined by two polymorphisms (G_{-13915} and C_{-3712}) upstream to the *LCT* gene and is correlated with lactase persistence; *in vitro* assays showed that the variants defining this haplotype influenced *LCT* transcription (Enattah et al. 2008). As with the European and African lactase persistence haplotypes, they found evidence that this haplotype had been driven quickly to high frequency by positive selection. They estimated the age for the haplotype to be ~4000 years, broadly consistent with the timing of camel domestication in the region.

Starch consumption, like adult milk consumption, varies greatly across populations with different subsistence, most notably across agricultural versus nonagricultural populations. Therefore, the ability to digest and absorb starch is likely to have become advantageous since the spread of agriculture. Perry et al. (2007) recently presented evidence supporting this hypothesis. They examined variation in the number of copies of the amylase gene (*AMY1*), which encodes an enzyme important in starch hydrolysis, between agricultural and nonagricultural populations. They found that the agricultural populations had, on average, more copies of *AMY1* than did the combined hunter-gatherer and pastoralist populations, whose copy numbers were intermediate between those of the agricultural populations and chimpanzees and bonobos.

Alcohol dehydrogenase genes in the *ADH1* cluster, which play an important role in ethanol metabolism, harbor variation associated with susceptibility to alcoholism. This includes a nonsynonymous polymorphism (R47H) in the *ADH1B* gene, which has near-fixation frequency in Asian populations and is rare elsewhere (Osier et al. 2002a,b). Indeed, a genome-wide selection scan based on population differentiation found that the value for *ADH1B* R47H was exceptionally high (Consortium 2005). Osier et al. (2002b) reported that several variants on the same haplotype showed high population differentiation, such that the haplotype was common in East Asian populations and was rare or absent elsewhere. Additionally, in their genome-wide scan, Voight et al. (2006) found evidence for selection at the *ADH1* gene cluster on the basis of strong EHH in East Asian populations (Voight et al. 2006). These results strongly argue for a selective advantage conferred by the *ADH1* polymorphism(s). However, whereas *ADH1* polymorphisms clearly affect variation in the processing of a common dietary component, i.e., ethanol, it is unclear whether ethanol consumption itself was the selective pressure underlying the observed population genetic pattern. Because the high-activity *ADH1* alleles result in an accumulation of acetaldehyde in response to alcohol load and because acetaldehyde has antiprotozoal activity, Goldman & Enoch (1990) proposed that these alleles are selectively advantageous because they protect against severe infectious diseases by protozoans.

Other specific dietary components may also be important. For example, two genome scans found evidence for selection from EHH for genes important in vitamin transporter activity and cofactor transporter activity (Tang et al. 2007, Voight et al. 2006). In addition, Wang et al. (2006) found signatures of positive selection for several genes involved in protein metabolism (*ADAMTS19-20*, *APEH*, *PLAU*, *HDAC8*, *UBR1*, and *USP26*) and a significant excess of signals in the group of genes in this biological category compared with other groups.

Food availability. In addition to variation in dietary components, fluctuation in food availability likely exerted strong selective pressures on the human genome. More than 40 years ago, Neel proposed the thrifty genotype hypothesis to explain why variants that increase risk to type 2 diabetes and obesity may be at high frequency in human populations (Neel 1962). He reasoned that because ancestral populations underwent seasonal cycles of feast and famine, they would have benefited from having extremely efficient fat and carbohydrate storage. When food production and storage resulted in more reliable food availability, this ancestral thriftiness became detrimental, and in contemporary populations, it contributes to the increased prevalence of diabetes and obesity. Consistent with the notion that thriftiness is an ancestral state, many alleles that increase risk to type 2 diabetes and other metabolic disorders are ancestral (i.e., shared with chimpanzee), whereas the alternative alleles at those polymorphic sites protect against the disease (*Chimpanzee Seq. Anal. Consort.* 2005, Di Rienzo & Hudson 2005).

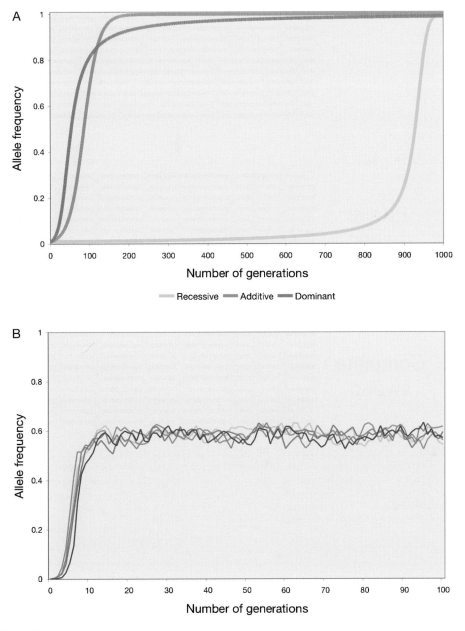

Figure 1

Allele frequency change over time under a directional selection model (*a*) and a balancing selection model (*b*). In the case of directional selection, different modes of inheritance of the advantageous allele are considered.

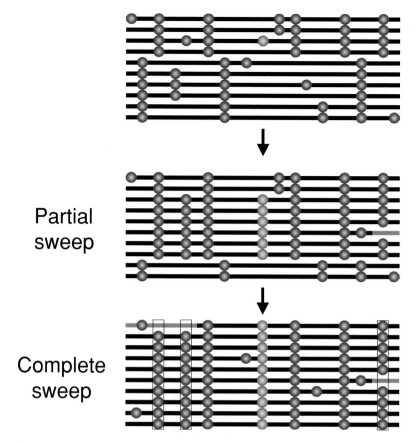

Figure 2

The impact of selective sweeps on patterns of neutral variation tightly linked to an advantageous mutation. Neutral mutations are shown as blue circles, whereas advantageous mutations are shown as red
circles. Gray bars indicate the results of recombination events involving a chromosome not carrying the
advantageous mutation. Black line boxes mark mutations segregating at a high frequency; a large number of such mutations is a strong signal of selection.

Although researchers have well documented that the transition to a Western lifestyle and diet results in major prevalence increases of type 2 diabetes (O'dea 1991; Szathmary 1986, 1990; Weiss et al. 1984), it is unclear whether this is also true for the transition from hunting-gathering to agriculture. In a revision of the original thrifty genotype hypothesis, Neel proposed that the changes that likely accompanied the spread of agriculture, including the reduction in dietary diversity to a diet composed mainly of carbohydrates, represented an important step in the shift to overall environmental conditions that favor the development of type 2 diabetes in individuals carrying the thrifty genotype (Neel 1999). However, whether food availability and reliability were indeed higher in agriculturalists compared with foragers is arguable (Cohen & Armelagos 1984, Larsen 2003). For example, Benyshek & Watson (2006) compared the quantity of available food as well as the frequency and intensity of food shortages between contemporary agricultural and hunter-gatherer populations and found no significant differences. However, some interesting trends were observed: Occasional and mild-to-moderate food shortages were more common among agricultural populations, whereas frequent and severe shortages were more common among hunter-gatherers.

A corollary of the thrifty genotype hypothesis is that populations with reliable, steady access to food resources may have evolved adaptations that slowed the insulin response and decreased the storage of energy as fat, thus resulting in a decrease in type 2 diabetes prevalence over time. In this context, Diamond (2003) proposed that the low prevalence of type 2 diabetes in Europeans reflects a longer history of stable food supply in these populations. Under this scenario, alleles that protect against type 2 diabetes are expected to have increased in frequency and to carry a signature of positive selection (e.g., be associated with high EHH). It is important to note that changes of allele frequencies, even if driven by strong positive selection, take at least hundreds of generations. Therefore, the above scenario applies only if the change in diet and life style and the resulting shift in selective pressures occurred long before Westernization, possibly with the transition to agriculture as suggested by Neel (1999).

Until now a comprehensive test of the thrifty genotype hypothesis has not been possible because only few susceptibility variants are known; however, studies of individual genes have suggested some signals of selection. Fullerton et al. (2002) found that susceptibility variants in the calpain 10 (*CAPN10*) gene had large differences in allele frequencies between African and non-African populations and suggested that natural selection had favored different alleles across populations (Fullerton et al. 2002). Another study of the same gene found both a significant reduction in variability for the alleles carrying the putative protective allele, consistent with positive selection acting on this subset of alleles, and a region of unusually high polymorphism and decay of linkage disequilibrium (LD), consistent with balancing selection in the region (Vander Molen et al. 2005). More recently, Grant et al. (2006) showed that variation in the *TCF7L2* gene affects risk to type 2 diabetes. The haplotype carrying the protective allele at *TCF7L2* is associated with a signature of positive selection on the basis of tests of population differentiation and haplotype homozygosity (Helgason et al. 2007).

Response to Pathogens

Response to pathogens was likely an important selective pressure during human evolutionary history. Although selection in response to pathogen attack has probably been important throughout human evolutionary history, selection likely intensified over the past 10–20 kya as a result of a warming climate, more recent localized changes in environments, and the shifts to agriculture and animal husbandry.

Malaria. Whereas selection for resistance to several pathogens has been studied, response to malaria pathogens has received an exceptional amount of attention owing to the large number of people affected and the high resultant

kya: thousand years ago

G6PD: glucose-
6-phosphate
dehydrogenase

mortality. The most deadly strain by far, *Plasmodium falciparum*, is likely to have gained prominence rather recently; its prevalence is thought to have increased as a consequence of the transition to agriculture. A less deadly but widespread strain, *Plasmodium vivax*, is associated with high levels of morbidity; it is unclear if the spread of *P. vivax* occurred after the spread of agriculture, as for *P. falciparum*. A number of common polymorphisms confer resistance to malaria infection, including a number of hemoglobin variants such as Hb S, Hb C, Hb E, β-thalassemia, α-thalassemia, G6PD deficiency, and the null allele of the Duffy blood group (Kwiatkowski 2005). Most of these variants carry a genetic signature of selection.

Deficiency of the enzyme G6PD is correlated with reduced risk of malaria infection, and signatures of positive selection have been observed for alleles that confer this deficiency (Sabeti et al. 2002, Saunders et al. 2005, Tishkoff et al. 2001, Verrelli et al. 2002). Tishkoff et al. (2001) and Saunders et al. (2005) found reduced variability in the subset of haplotypes carrying the deficiency alleles, evidence for EHH associated with the haplotypes carrying these alleles, and long branches separating the deficiency alleles from other alleles. The ages of the G6PD deficiency alleles were estimated using different methods and yielded values ranging from 2.5 to 45 kya (Coop & Griffiths 2004, Saunders et al. 2005, Tishkoff et al. 2001, Verrelli et al. 2002); the younger estimates are consistent with an increase in malaria infection with the transition to agriculture, but the older ones are not.

Carriers of the Duffy null (*FY*0*) mutation do not express a protein on the red blood cells to which *P. vivax* binds to invade the cells. As a result, *FY*0* homozygotes are resistant to this variety of malaria (Livingstone 1984); Kasehagen et al. (2007) recently showed that *FY*0* heterozygosity may also afford some degree of protection against vivax malaria. This allele has a striking geographic distribution in that it is fixed or nearly fixed in most Sub-Saharan African populations and is virtually absent elsewhere. This degree of differenti-

ation in the frequency of the *FY*0* allele is highly unusual relative to genome-wide patterns (Consortium 2005) and is consistent with the notion that this allele underwent a complete selective sweep in Sub-Saharan African populations. Consistent with this hypothesis, Hamblin and colleagues showed that polymorphism levels in sub-Saharan Africans are low compared with divergence and that there is an excess of high frequency derived alleles near the *FY* gene (Hamblin & Di Rienzo 2000, Hamblin et al. 2002). Interestingly, the *FY*0* allele is found on two major haplotypes, which suggests that this is a case of selection on standing neutral variation.

Several hemoglobin variants, the most common of which include Hb S, Hb C, and Hb E, represent well-documented cases of balanced polymorphism whereby heterozygotes are resistant to *P. falciparum*, whereas homozygotes have reduced fitness. Accordingly, signatures of positive selection have been observed at the *HBB* locus on the basis of extensive haplotype homozygosity and strong population differentiation for HbS (Hanchard et al. 2006, Sabeti et al. 2007) and strong haplotype structure for HbC (Wood et al. 2005) and HbE (Ohashi et al. 2004). Consistent with the idea that the onset of malaria selection coincided with the spread of agriculture, the ages of the HbS, HbE, and HbC variants have been estimated to be 1350–2100 years (Currat et al. 2002), 1240–4440 years (Ohashi et al. 2004), and 1875–3750 years (Wood et al. 2005), respectively.

HLA region. Genes in the HLA region have received a great deal of attention in studies of mechanisms and selection for pathogen defense as a result of their roles in response to a broad range of pathogens. Balancing selection appears to have been pervasive in this region owing to the need for different HLA peptides to confer resistance to disease, but there is also evidence for strong directional selection on specific alleles. Although the HLA region contains at least 120 genes, many of which are involved in immune function, most studies have focused on nine, which are considered to be the classical

HLA genes. Several lines of evidence suggest a history of natural selection at the classical HLA genes. As a group, these genes show exceptionally high levels of polymorphism especially in functional (peptide binding) regions (Meyer & Thomson 2001, Satta et al. 1994), and many genes have an excess of nonsynonymous compared with synonymous mutations (Hughes & Nei 1988). In addition to the high levels of polymorphism and nonsynonymous variation, the frequency spectrum tends to be skewed toward intermediate frequency variants relative to neutral expectation. Large sequence differences are observed among the HLA haplotypes, suggesting that the alleles are old, consistent with a model of long-term balancing selection (Meyer & Thomson 2001).

In addition to studies directed at single genes and small groups of related genes, multigene and genome-wide studies of selection have detected significant signals in immune response genes, either individually [*CD226*, *IG7* (Akey et al. 2002, Carlson et al. 2005, Williamson et al. 2007); *ABO*, *IL1A*, *IL1RN*, *KEL* (Akey et al. 2002), *ABO*, *KEL* (Carlson et al. 2005)] or as a group. Tang et al. (2007) found signals of positive selection for interleukin-1 receptor antagonist activity and cytokine activity. Using a test based on haplotype structure, Voight et al. (2006) found an enrichment for MHC-I-mediated immunity genes, and Wang et al. (2006) found signals in several genes (*CSF2*, *CCNT2*, *DEFB118*, *STAB1*, *SP*, *Zap70*) and an enrichment for pathogen response genes. Sabeti et al. (2007) found signals of positive selection based on haplotype structure and population differentiation at *LARGE* and *DMD*.

Other Signals of Selection

Chemosensory perception. The ability to sense aspects of the environment is necessary for survival and reproduction, and the array of cues encountered in different environments may be especially diverse for some senses, such as olfaction and taste. Olfaction may be important to detect and identify food and mates,

whereas taste is likely crucial to identify suitable foods. Evidence that genes responsible for olfaction and taste evolved under positive selection is beginning to emerge.

Gilad et al. (2003) found evidence of positive selection on the human lineage compared with chimpanzees on the basis of the ratio of nonsynonymous to synonymous substitutions, low levels of polymorphism, and an excess of rare variants. Additional evidence for adaptation in olfactory receptor genes was detected in genome-wide scans. One study identified a signal for a complete selective sweep in a region within a cluster of olfactory receptor genes (Williamson et al. 2007); other studies found evidence for selection based on the frequency spectrum in several olfactory receptor genes (Carlson et al. 2005) and an enrichment of signals based on haplotype structure in genes involved in olfaction (Voight et al. 2006).

Inter-individual variation in the ability to taste PTC has been known for more than 70 years, but the genetic basis for this trait was only recently elucidated (Drayna et al. 2003 and references therein). Identification of the region that influences the PTC phenotype allowed testing for evidence of positive selection at the genetic level (Wooding et al. 2004). Two high-frequency haplotypes, defined by three nonsynonymous variants, were observed, consistent with the action of balancing selection at this locus. An additional 21 bitter taste receptor genes have been analyzed for evidence of selection: the average ratio of nonsynonymous to synonymous substitutions was high compared with that observed in 151 other genes; in addition, polymorphism levels tended to be high in the bitter taste receptor genes (Kim et al. 2005).

Fertility and reproduction. Genes that affect fertility and reproduction are expected to be subject to especially strong selection owing to their direct effects on fitness-related traits. This class of proteins evolves rapidly both within and among species (Swanson & Vacquier 2002). Significant variation in fertility exists among human populations with different subsistence patterns (Bentley et al. 1993). To the extent

PTC:
phenylthiocarbamide

that variation in fertility within populations is heritable (Pettay et al. 2005), it is possible that natural selection has acted on this trait to influence variation among populations.

Stefansson et al. (Stefansson et al. 2005) showed that female carriers of a large inversion polymorphism, which shows evidence of selection based on population differentiation and long-range haplotype structure, have higher fertility than do noncarriers. Follicle stimulating hormone is important for fertility in both males (for Sertoli cell proliferation and in maintaining sperm quality in the testes) and females (for stimulation of ovarian follicles). Grigorova et al. (2007) examined sequence patterns for the follicle stimulating hormone receptor-binding beta-subunit (*FSHB*) in several human populations and found low overall diversity combined with an excess of intermediate frequency variants, consistent with balancing selection at this locus. The authors also found that one of the two high-frequency haplotypes was associated with increased fertility and hypothesized that balancing selection at this locus may act on birth intervals.

Although relatively few single gene studies have been conducted for genes involved in fertility and reproduction, several signatures of selection have been found for genes in this class from genome-wide scans for selection. Williamson et al. (2007) found evidence for a complete sweep in European Americans and Han Chinese for *SPAG6*, a gene involved in sperm motility, and others found evidence for an excess of signals of partial selective sweeps in genes related to fertility, gametogenesis, spermatogenesis, sperm motility, and fertilization (Voight et al. 2006, Wang et al. 2006).

CONCLUSIONS

Early studies examined evidence for positive selection from the distribution of phenotypic traits and their cooccurrence with variables that were expected to represent underlying selective pressures. With the advent of DNA sequencing and genotyping technologies and the development of methods to detect evidence of selec-

tion from sequence variation data, testing for evidence of genetic adaptations in single genes became feasible. More recently, the availability of dense, genome-wide genotype data for multiple populations and the development of methods for detecting selection using SNP data have elicited many genome-wide scans for evidence of positive selection in human populations. Now, the HapMap project is expanding to include genotype data for additional populations as well as genome-wide resequencing data for some HapMap individuals. In addition, the 1000 Genomes Project was recently launched, which aims to resequence completely the genomes of 1000 individuals from diverse worldwide populations. The continued collection of data from large-scale projects will be useful for conducting more complete genome scans to detect evidence for positive selection. At the same time, more focused studies to test specific hypotheses or to follow up on results from genome-wide scans will continue to have an important place in reconstructing the overall history of selective pressures among human populations.

APPENDIX: STATISTICAL TESTS OF NEUTRALITY

Several methods have been developed to evaluate statistically whether empirical patterns of variation are consistent with the expectations of the null hypothesis of evolutionary neutrality. These tests, which are briefly described here, can be grouped on the basis of the aspect of variation that they use.

Amount of Variation Within and Between Species

The most widely used test to detect departures from neutrality based on polymorphism levels is the so-called HKA (Hudson-Kreitman-Aguade) test (Hudson et al. 1987), which is based on the notion that polymorphism levels within species and sequence divergence between species are proportional to the same underlying mutation rate. Therefore, by comparing polymorphism and divergence at two or more loci, one can test for departures from neutrality due to a deficit or an excess of polymorphism.

Spectrum of Allele Frequencies

The standard neutral model provides quantitative expectations for the spectrum of allele frequencies, whereby the expected fraction of alleles that occur i times in a sample is proportional to $1/i$. The most widely used test statistic summarizing information about the frequency spectrum is Tajima's D (TD) (Tajima 1989), which is based on the standardized difference between two estimators of the same parameter, $4N_e\mu$ (where N_e is the effective population size and μ is the mutation rate per site per generation). Under the standard neutral model, TD is expected to be near zero; an excess of intermediate frequency variants will generate a positive TD value, whereas an excess of rare variants will give rise to a negative TD value (because TD does not use information about the ancestral state of the polymorphisms, it does not distinguish between rare and high-frequency new mutations). A different test, referred to as H (Fay & Wu 2000), uses information from an outgroup sequence to infer the ancestral allele at each polymorphic site and tests specifically for an excess of high-frequency nonancestral alleles.

Haplotype Structure

This family of tests relies on the property of partial sweeps to generate an extended region of haplotype homozygosity surrounding the selected site (**Figure 2**) (Hudson et al. 1994). In general, the extent of haplotype homozygosity is a function of the age of the mutation, with younger mutations exhibiting homozygosity over larger regions than would older ones. Under neutrality, young mutations are expected

to be rare, whereas equally young advantageous mutations tend to occur at higher frequency. Therefore, tests based on the haplotype structure aim to capture the discrepancy between the extent of haplotype homozygosity in a region and the frequency of that haplotype in the population. The EHH in a region can be calculated for a core haplotype or a core SNP allele and then compared with that for other core haplotypes or the alternative allele at the core SNP. To perform a statistical test of neutrality, the relative EHH at a candidate region is compared with that for other core haplotypes or core SNPs within the same frequency range, obtained either by simulations or from empirical patterns (Sabeti et al. 2002, Voight et al. 2006).

Spatial Distribution of Allele Frequencies

Tests to detect the impact of selection on the extent of allele frequency differentiation have historically relied on the summary statistic F_{ST}, which is the proportion of the total genetic variance that occurs among populations. The spatial distribution of allele frequencies can also be tested for a correlation with an environmental variable, e.g., latitude or temperature, which is likely to reflect a selective pressure. For both F_{ST} and the correlation between allele frequency and an environmental variable, a statistical test of neutrality can be constructed by comparing the value of the test statistic at a candidate locus with the distribution of values expected for a null neutral model of subdivided populations. Because the models of human population structure investigated so far are too simplistic to provide an appropriate null model, an empirical approach is usually taken in which the value of the test statistic at the candidate locus is compared with the distribution of the statistic observed for a large set of independent loci.

Effective population size (N_e): the size of an ideal population with the same rate of genetic drift of gene frequencies as the actual population

DISCLOSURE STATEMENT

The authors are not aware of any biases that might be perceived as affecting the objectivity of this review.

ACKNOWLEDGMENTS

We thank Cynthia Beall and William Leonard for helpful comments on the manuscript. We gratefully acknowledge funding from National Institutes of Health grants DK56670 and GM79558. A.M.H. was partially supported by a predoctoral fellowship from the American Heart Association.

LITERATURE CITED

Akey JM, Zhang G, Zhang K, Jin L, Shriver MD. 2002. Interrogating a high-density SNP map for signatures of natural selection. *Genome Res.* 12:1805–14

Allison AC. 1954. Protection afforded by sickle-cell trait against subtertian malareal infection. *Br. Med. J.* 1:290–94

Barreiro LB, Laval G, Quach H, Patin E, Quintana-Murci L. 2008. Natural selection has driven population differentiation in modern humans. *Nat. Genet.* 40:340–45

Beall CM, Song K, Elston RC, Goldstein MC. 2004. Higher offspring survival among Tibetan women with high oxygen saturation genotypes residing at 4,000 m. *Proc. Natl. Acad. Sci. USA* 101:14300–4

Beall CM, Strohl KP, Blangero J, Williams-Blangero S, Decker MJ, et al. 1997. Quantitative genetic analysis of arterial oxygen saturation in Tibetan highlanders. *Hum. Biol.* 69:597–604

Beaumont MA, Balding DJ. 2004. Identifying adaptive genetic divergence among populations from genome scans. *Mol. Ecol.* 13:969–80

Bentley GR, Goldberg T, Jasienska G. 1993. The fertility of agricultural and nonagricultural traditional societies. *Popul. Stud. A J. Demogr.* 47:269–81

Benyshek DC, Watson JT. 2006. Exploring the thrifty genotype's food-shortage assumptions: a cross-cultural comparison of ethnographic accounts of food security among foraging and agricultural societies. *Am. J. Phys. Anthropol.* 131:120–26

Bersaglieri T, Sabeti PC, Patterson N, Vanderploeg T, Schaffner SF, et al. 2004. Genetic signatures of strong recent positive selection at the lactase gene. *Am. J. Hum. Genet.* 74:1111–20

Biasutti R. 1959. *Le Razze e i Popoli Della Terra*. Torino: Unione Tipografico/Editrice Torinese

Biswas S, Akey JM. 2006. Genomic insights into positive selection. *Trends Genet.* 22:437–46

Bonilla C, Boxill LA, Donald SA, Williams T, Sylvester N, et al. 2005. The 8818G allele of the agouti signaling protein (*ASIP*) gene is ancestral and is associated with darker skin color in African Americans. *Hum. Genet.* 116:402–6

Carlson CS, Thomas DJ, Eberle MA, Swanson JE, Livingston RJ, et al. 2005. Genomic regions exhibiting positive selection identified from dense genotype data. *Genome Res.* 15:1553–65

Chimpanzee Seq. Anal. Consort. 2005. Initial sequence of the chimpanzee genome and comparison with the human genome. *Nature* 437:69–87

Cohen MN, Armelagos GJ. 1984. *Paleopathology at the Origins of Agriculture*. Orlando, FL: Academic. 635 pp.

Consortium IH. 2005. A haplotype map of the human genome. *Nature* 437:1299–320

Coop G, Griffiths RC. 2004. Ancestral inference on gene trees under selection. *Theor. Popul. Biol.* 66:219–32

Currat M, Trabuchet G, Rees D, Perrin P, Harding RM, et al. 2002. Molecular analysis of the beta-globin gene cluster in the Niokholo Mandenka population reveals a recent origin of the beta(S) Senegal mutation. *Am. J. Hum. Genet.* 70:207–23

Denton D. 1982. *The Hunger for Salt: An Anthropological, Physiological and Medical Analysis*. New York: Springer-Verlag

Diamond J. 2003. The double puzzle of diabetes. *Nature* 423:599–602

Di Rienzo A, Hudson RR. 2005. An evolutionary framework for common diseases: the ancestral-susceptibility model. *Trends Genet.* 21:596–601

Drayna D, Coon H, Kim UK, Elsner T, Cromer K, et al. 2003. Genetic analysis of a complex trait in the Utah Genetic Reference Project: a major locus for *PTC* taste ability on chromosome 7q and a secondary locus on chromosome 16p. *Hum. Genet.* 112:567–72

Duffy DL, Box NF, Chen W, Palmer JS, Montgomery GW, et al. 2004. Interactive effects of *MC1R* and *OCA2* on melanoma risk phenotypes. *Hum. Mol. Genet.* 13:447–61

Duffy DL, Montgomery GW, Chen W, Zhao ZZ, Le L, et al. 2007. A three-single-nucleotide polymorphism haplotype in intron 1 of *OCA2* explains most human eye-color variation. *Am. J. Hum. Genet.* 80:241–52

Enattah NS, Jensen TG, Nielsen M, Lewinski R, Kuokkanen M, et al. 2008. Independent introduction of two lactase-persistence alleles into human populations reflects different history of adaptation to milk culture. *Am. J. Hum. Genet.* 82:57–72

Fay JC, Wu CI. 2000. Hitchhiking under positive Darwinian selection. *Genetics* 155:1405–13

Flanagan N, Healy E, Ray A, Philips S, Todd C, et al. 2000. Pleiotropic effects of the melanocortin 1 receptor (*MC1R*) gene on human pigmentation. *Hum. Mol. Genet.* 9:2531–37

Frazer KA, Ballinger DG, Cox DR, Hinds DA, Stuve LL, et al. 2007. A second generation human haplotype map of over 3.1 million SNPs. *Nature* 449:851–61

Fullerton SM, Bartoszewicz A, Ybazeta G, Horikawa Y, Bell GI, et al. 2002. Geographic and haplotype structure of candidate type 2 diabetes susceptibility variants at the calpain-10 locus. *Am. J. Hum. Genet.* 70:1096–106

Gilad Y, Bustamante CD, Lancet D, Paabo S. 2003. Natural selection on the olfactory receptor gene family in humans and chimpanzees. *Am. J. Hum. Genet.* 73:489–501

Gillespie JH. 1991. *The Causes of Molecular Evolution.* New York: Oxford Univ. Press. 336 pp.

Gleibermann L. 1973. Blood pressure and dietary salt in human populations. *Ecol. Food Nutr.* 2:143–56

Goldman D, Enoch MA. 1990. Genetic epidemiology of ethanol metabolic enzymes: a role for selection. *World Rev. Nutr. Diet.* 63:143–60

Graf J, Hodgson R, van Daal A. 2005. Single nucleotide polymorphisms in the *MATP* gene are associated with normal human pigmentation variation. *Hum. Mutat.* 25:278–84

Graf J, Voisey J, Hughes I, van Daal A. 2007. Promoter polymorphisms in the *MATP* (*SLC45A2*) gene are associated with normal human skin color variation. *Hum. Mutat.* 28:710–17

Grant SF, Thorleifsson G, Reynisdottir I, Benediktsson R, Manolescu A, et al. 2006. Variant of transcription factor 7-like 2 (*TCF7L2*) gene confers risk of type 2 diabetes. *Nat. Genet.* 38:320–23

Grigorova M, Rull K, Laan M. 2007. Haplotype structure of *FSHB*, the beta-subunit gene for fertility-associated follicle-stimulating hormone: possible influence of balancing selection. *Ann. Hum. Genet.* 71:18–28

Haldane JBS. 1949. *The rate of mutation of human genes.* Presented at Int. Congr. Genet., 8th, Stockholm, Sweden

Hamblin MT, Di Rienzo A. 2000. Detecting the signature of natural selection in humans: evidence from the Duffy blood group locus. *Am. J. Hum. Genet.* 66:1669–79

Hamblin MT, Thompson EE, Di Rienzo A. 2002. Complex signatures of natural selection at the Duffy blood group locus. *Am. J. Hum. Genet.* 70:369–83

Hanchard NA, Rockett KA, Spencer C, Coop G, Pinder M, et al. 2006. Screening for recently selected alleles by analysis of human haplotype similarity. *Am. J. Hum. Genet.* 78:153–59

Hancock AM, Witonsky DB, Gordon AS, Eshel G, Pritchard JK, et al. 2008. Adaptations to climate in candidate genes for common metabolic disorders. *PLoS Genet.* 4(2):e32

Harding RM, Healy E, Ray AJ, Ellis NS, Flanagan N, et al. 2000. Evidence for variable selective pressures at MC1R. *Am. J. Hum. Genet.* 66:1351–61

Helgason A, Palsson S, Thorleifsson G, Grant SF, Emilsson V, et al. 2007. Refining the impact of *TCF7L2* gene variants on type 2 diabetes and adaptive evolution. *Nat. Genet.* 39:218–25

Henry CJ, Rees DG. 1991. New predictive equations for the estimation of basal metabolic rate in tropical peoples. *Eur. J. Clin. Nutr.* 45:177–85

Hermisson J, Pennings PS. 2005. Soft sweeps: molecular population genetics of adaptation from standing genetic variation. *Genetics* 169:2335–52

Hinds DA, Stuve LL, Nilsen GB, Halperin E, Eskin E, et al. 2005. Whole-genome patterns of common DNA variation in three human populations. *Science* 307:1072–79

Hudson RR, Bailey K, Skarecky D, Kwiatowski J, Ayala FJ. 1994. Evidence for positive selection in the superoxide dismutase (Sod) region of *Drosophila melanogaster*. *Genetics* 136:1329–40

Hudson RR, Kreitman M, Aguade M. 1987. A test of neutral molecular evolution based on nucleotide data. *Genetics* 116:153–59

Hughes AL, Nei M. 1988. Pattern of nucleotide substitution at major histocompatibility complex class I loci reveals overdominant selection. *Nature* 335:167–70

Innan H, Zhang K, Marjoram P, Tavare S, Rosenberg NA. 2005. Statistical tests of the coalescent model based on the haplotype frequency distribution and the number of segregating sites. *Genetics* 169:1763–77

Izagirre N, Garcia I, Junquera C, de la Rua C, Alonso S. 2006. A scan for signatures of positive selection in candidate loci for skin pigmentation in humans. *Mol. Biol. Evol.* 23:1697–706

Jablonski NG, Chaplin G. 2000. The evolution of human skin coloration. *J. Hum. Evol.* 39:57–106

Kanetsky PA, Swoyer J, Panossian S, Holmes R, Guerry D, Rebbeck TR. 2002. A polymorphism in the agouti signaling protein gene is associated with human pigmentation. *Am. J. Hum. Genet.* 70:770–75

Kasehagen LJ, Mueller I, Kiniboro B, Bockarie MJ, Reeder JC, et al. 2007. Reduced Plasmodium vivax erythrocyte infection in PNG Duffy-negative heterozygotes. *PLoS ONE* 2:e336

Katzmarzyk PT, Leonard WR. 1998. Climatic influences on human body size and proportions: ecological adaptations and secular trends. *Am. J. Phys. Anthropol.* 106:483–503

Kelsh RN, Brand M, Jiang YJ, Heisenberg CP, Lin S, et al. 1996. Zebrafish pigmentation mutations and the processes of neural crest development. *Development* 123:369–89

Kim U, Wooding S, Ricci D, Jorde LB, Drayna D. 2005. Worldwide haplotype diversity and coding sequence variation at human bitter taste receptor loci. *Hum. Mutat.* 26:199–204

Kim Y, Stephan W. 2002. Detecting a local signature of genetic hitchhiking along a recombining chromosome. *Genetics* 160:765–77

Kretchmer N. 1972. Lactose and lactase. *Sci. Am.* 227:71–78

Kwiatkowski DP. 2005. How malaria has affected the human genome and what human genetics can teach us about malaria. *Am. J. Hum. Genet.* 77:171–92

Lamason RL, Mohideen MA, Mest JR, Wong AC, Norton HL, et al. 2005. *SLC24A5*, a putative cation exchanger, affects pigmentation in zebrafish and humans. *Science* 310:1782–86

Lao O, de Gruijter JM, van Duijn K, Navarro A, Kayser M. 2007. Signatures of positive selection in genes associated with human skin pigmentation as revealed from analyses of single nucleotide polymorphisms. *Ann. Hum. Genet.* 71:354–69

Larsen CS. 2003. Animal source foods and human health during evolution. *J. Nutr.* 133:3893S–97S

Leonard WR, Snodgrass JJ, Sorensen MV. 2005. Metabolic adaptation in indigenous Siberian populations. *Annu. Rev. Anthropol.* 34:451–71

Lewontin RC, Krakauer J. 1973. Distribution of gene frequency as a test of the theory of the selective neutrality of polymorphisms. *Genetics* 74:175–95

Livingstone FB. 1984. The Duffy blood groups, Vivax malaria, and malaria selection in human populations: a review. *Hum. Biol.* 56:413–25

McCracken RD. 1971. Origins and implications of the distribution of adult lactase deficiency in human populations. *J. Trop. Pediatr. Environ. Child Health* 17:7–10

Meyer D, Thomson G. 2001. How selection shapes variation of the human major histocompatibility complex: a review. *Ann. Hum. Genet.* 65:1–26

Mishmar D, Ruiz-Pesini E, Golik P, Macaulay V, Clark AG, et al. 2003. Natural selection shaped regional mtDNA variation in humans. *Proc. Natl. Acad. Sci. USA* 100:171–76

Myles S, Somel M, Tang K, Kelso J, Stoneking M. 2007. Identifying genes underlying skin pigmentation differences among human populations. *Hum. Genet.* 120:613–21

Nakajima T, Wooding S, Sakagami T, Emi M, Tokunaga K, et al. 2004. Natural selection and population history in the human angiotensinogen gene (*AGT*): 736 complete *AGT* sequences in chromosomes from around the world. *Am. J. Hum. Genet.* 74:898–916

Neel JV. 1962. Diabetes mellitus: a "thrifty" genotype rendered detrimental by "progress"? *Am. J. Hum. Genet.* 14:353–62

Neel JV. 1999. Diabetes mellitus: a "thrifty" genotype rendered detrimental by "progress"? 1962. *Bull. World Health Organ.* 77:694–703; discussion 692–93

Nielsen R. 2005. Molecular signatures of natural selection. *Annu. Rev. Genet.* 39:197–218

Nielsen R, Hellmann I, Hubisz M, Bustamante C, Clark AG. 2007. Recent and ongoing selection in the human genome. *Nat. Rev. Genet.* 8:857–68

Nielsen R, Williamson S, Kim Y, Hubisz MJ, Clark AG, Bustamante C. 2005. Genomic scans for selective sweeps using SNP data. *Genome Res.* 15:1566–75

Norton HL, Kittles RA, Parra E, McKeigue P, Mao X, et al. 2007. Genetic evidence for the convergent evolution of light skin in Europeans and East Asians. *Mol. Biol. Evol.* 24:710–22

O'dea D. 1991. Traditional diet of Australian Aboriginal hunter-gatherers. In *Foraging Strategies and Natural Diet of Monkeys, Apes, and Humans*, ed. A Whiten, EM Widdowson, pp. 73–81. Oxford, UK: Oxford Univ. Press

Ohashi J, Naka I, Patarapotikul J, Hananantachai H, Brittenham G, et al. 2004. Extended linkage disequilibrium surrounding the hemoglobin E variant due to malarial selection. *Am. J. Hum. Genet.* 74:1198–208

Osier MV, Pakstis AJ, Goldman D, Edenberg HJ, Kidd JR, Kidd KK. 2002a. A proline-threonine substitution in codon 351 of *ADH1C* is common in Native Americans. *Alcohol Clin. Exp. Res.* 26:1759–63

Osier MV, Pakstis AJ, Soodyall H, Comas D, Goldman D, et al. 2002b. A global perspective on genetic variation at the *ADH* genes reveals unusual patterns of linkage disequilibrium and diversity. *Am. J. Hum. Genet.* 71:84–99

Palmer JS, Duffy DL, Box NF, Aitken JF, O'Gorman LE, et al. 2000. Melanocortin-1 receptor polymorphisms and risk of melanoma: Is the association explained solely by pigmentation phenotype? *Am. J. Hum. Genet.* 66:176–86

Pennings PS, Hermisson J. 2006a. Soft sweeps II—molecular population genetics of adaptation from recurrent mutation or migration. *Mol. Biol. Evol.* 23:1076–84

Pennings PS, Hermisson J. 2006b. Soft sweeps III: the signature of positive selection from recurrent mutation. *PLoS Genet.* 2:e186

Perry GH, Dominy NJ, Claw KG, Lee AS, Fiegler H, et al. 2007. Diet and the evolution of human amylase gene copy number variation. *Nat. Genet.* 39:1256–60

Pettay JE, Kruuk LE, Jokela J, Lummaa V. 2005. Heritability and genetic constraints of life-history trait evolution in preindustrial humans. *Proc. Natl. Acad. Sci. USA* 102:2838–43

Przeworski M. 2003. Estimating the time since the fixation of a beneficial allele. *Genetics* 164:1667–76

Przeworski M, Coop G, Wall JD. 2005. The signature of positive selection on standing genetic variation. *Evol. Int. J. Org. Evol.* 59:2312–23

Rebbeck TR, Kanetsky PA, Walker AH, Holmes R, Halpern AC, et al. 2002. P gene as an inherited biomarker of human eye color. *Cancer Epidemiol. Biomarkers Prev.* 11:782–84

Rees JL. 2003. Genetics of hair and skin color. *Annu. Rev. Genet.* 37:67–90

Roberts DF. 1953. Body weight, race and climate. *Am. J. Phys. Anthropol.* 11:533–58

Roberts DF. 1978. *Climate and Human Variability*. Menlo Park, CA: Cummings

Roberts DF, Kahlon DP. 1976. Environmental correlations of skin colour. *Ann. Hum. Biol.* 3:11–22

Ruiz-Pesini E, Mishmar D, Brandon M, Procaccio V, Wallace DC. 2004. Effects of purifying and adaptive selection on regional variation in human mtDNA. *Science* 303:223–26

Sabeti PC, Reich DE, Higgins JM, Levine HZ, Richter DJ, et al. 2002. Detecting recent positive selection in the human genome from haplotype structure. *Nature* 419:832–37

Sabeti PC, Schaffner SF, Fry B, Lohmueller J, Varilly P, et al. 2006. Positive natural selection in the human lineage. *Science* 312:1614–20

Sabeti PC, Varilly P, Fry B, Lohmueller J, Hostetter E, et al. 2007. Genome-wide detection and characterization of positive selection in human populations. *Nature* 449:913–18

Satta Y, O'HUigin C, Takahata N, Klein J. 1994. Intensity of natural selection at the major histocompatibility complex loci. *Proc. Natl. Acad. Sci. USA* 91:7184–88

Saunders MA, Slatkin M, Garner C, Hammer MF, Nachman MW. 2005. The extent of linkage disequilibrium caused by selection on *G6PD* in humans. *Genetics* 171:1219–29

Schaffner SF, Foo C, Gabriel S, Reich D, Daly MJ, Altshuler D. 2005. Calibrating a coalescent simulation of human genome sequence variation. *Genome Res.* 15:1576–83

Simoons FJ. 1970. Primary adult lactose intolerance and the milking habit: a problem in biologic and cultural interrelations. II. A culture historical hypothesis. *Am. J. Dig. Dis.* 15:695–710

Smith R, Healy E, Siddiqui S, Flanagan N, Steijlen PM, et al. 1998. Melanocortin 1 receptor variants in an Irish population. *J. Invest. Dermatol.* 111:119–22

Stajich JE, Hahn MW. 2005. Disentangling the effects of demography and selection in human history. *Mol. Biol. Evol.* 22:63–73

Stefansson H, Helgason A, Thorleifsson G, Steinthorsdottir V, Masson G, et al. 2005. A common inversion under selection in Europeans. *Nat. Genet.* 37:129–37

Stokowski RP, Pant PV, Dadd T, Fereday A, Hinds DA, et al. 2007. A genomewide association study of skin pigmentation in a South Asian population. *Am. J. Hum. Genet.* 81:1119–32

Sulem P, Gudbjartsson DF, Stacey SN, Helgason A, Rafnar T, et al. 2007. Genetic determinants of hair, eye and skin pigmentation in Europeans. *Nat. Genet.* 39:1443–52

Swallow DM. 2003. Genetics of lactase persistence and lactose intolerance. *Annu. Rev. Genet.* 37:197–219

Swanson WJ, Vacquier VD. 2002. Reproductive protein evolution. *Annu. Rev. Ecol. Syst.* 33:161–79

Szathmary EJE. 1986. Diabetes in arctic and sub-arctic populations undergoing acculturation. *Coll. Antropol.* 10:145–58

Szathmary EJE. 1990. Diabetes in Amerindian populations: the Dogrib studies. In *Diseases in Populations in Transition: Anthropological and Epidemiological Perspectives*, ed. AC Swedlund, GJ Armelagos, pp. 75–103. New York: Bergin and Garvey

Tajima F. 1989. Statistical method for testing the neutral mutation hypothesis by DNA polymorphism. *Genetics* 123:585–95

Tang K, Thornton KR, Stoneking M. 2007. A new approach for using genome scans to detect recent positive selection in the human genome. *PLoS Biol.* 5:e171

Teshima KM, Coop G, Przeworski M. 2006. How reliable are empirical genomic scans for selective sweeps? *Genome Res.* 16:702–12

Thompson EE, Kuttab-Boulos H, Witonsky D, Yang L, Roe BA, Di Rienzo A. 2004. *CYP3A* variation and the evolution of salt-sensitivity variants. *Am. J. Hum. Genet.* 75:1059–69

Tishkoff SA, Reed FA, Ranciaro A, Voight BF, Babbitt CC, et al. 2007. Convergent adaptation of human lactase persistence in Africa and Europe. *Nat. Genet.* 39:31–40

Tishkoff SA, Varkonyi R, Cahinhinan N, Abbes S, Argyropoulos G, et al. 2001. Haplotype diversity and linkage disequilibrium at human *G6PD*: recent origin of alleles that confer malarial resistance. *Science* 293:455–62

Vander Molen J, Frisse LM, Fullerton SM, Qian Y, del Bosque-Plata L, et al. 2005. Population genetics of *CAPN10* and *GPR35*: implications for the evolution of type 2 diabetes variants. *Am. J. Hum. Genet.* 76:548–60

Verrelli BC, McDonald JH, Argyropoulos G, Destro-Bisol G, Froment A, et al. 2002. Evidence for balancing selection from nucleotide sequence analyses of human *G6PD*. *Am. J. Hum. Genet.* 71:1112–28

Voight BF, Adams AM, Frisse LA, Qian Y, Hudson RR, Di Rienzo A. 2005. Interrogating multiple aspects of variation in a full resequencing data set to infer human population size changes. *Proc. Natl. Acad. Sci. USA* 102:18508–13

Voight BF, Kudaravalli S, Wen X, Pritchard JK. 2006. A map of recent positive selection in the human genome. *PLoS Biol.* 4:e72

Wang ET, Kodama G, Baldi P, Moyzis RK. 2006. Global landscape of recent inferred Darwinian selection for *Homo sapiens*. *Proc. Natl. Acad. Sci. USA* 103:135–40

Weir BS. 1996. *Genetic Data Analysis II: Methods for Discrete Population Genetic Data*. Sunderland, MA: Sinauer

Weiss KM, Ferrell RF, Hanis CL. 1984. A new world syndrome of metabolic diseases with a genetic and evolutionary basis. *Yearb. Phys. Anthropol.* 27:153–78

Williamson SH, Hubisz MJ, Clark AG, Payseur BA, Bustamante CD, Nielsen R. 2007. Localizing recent adaptive evolution in the human genome. *PLoS Genet.* 3:e90

Wood ET, Stover DA, Slatkin M, Nachman MW, Hammer MF. 2005. The beta-globin recombinational hotspot reduces the effects of strong selection around HbC, a recently arisen mutation providing resistance to malaria. *Am. J. Hum. Genet.* 77:637–42

Wooding S, Kim UK, Bamshad MJ, Larsen J, Jorde LB, Drayna D. 2004. Natural selection and molecular evolution in *PTC*, a bitter-taste receptor gene. *Am. J. Hum. Genet.* 74:637–46

Young JH, Chang YP, Kim JD, Chretien JP, Klag MJ, et al. 2005. Differential susceptibility to hypertension is due to selection during the out-of-Africa expansion. *PLoS Genet.* 1:e82

Zeng K, Fu YX, Shi S, Wu CI. 2006. Statistical tests for detecting positive selection by utilizing high-frequency variants. *Genetics* 174:1431–39

RELATED RESOURCES

1000 Genomes Project. **http://www.1000genomes.org/#**
HapMap Project. **http://www.hapmap.org/**
Mammalian Phenotype Ontology database. **http://www.informatics.jax.org/**
NCBI Entrez Gene. **http://www.ncbi.nlm.nih.gov/sites/entrez?db=gene**
Perlegen Genotype Browser. **http://genome.perlegen.com/browser/index_v2.html**

Evolutionary Linguistics

William Croft

Department of Linguistics, University of New Mexico, Albuquerque, New Mexico 87131;
email: wcroft@unm.edu

Annu. Rev. Anthropol. 2008. 37:219–34

First published online as a Review in Advance on
June 17, 2008

The *Annual Review of Anthropology* is online at
anthro.annualreviews.org

This article's doi:
10.1146/annurev.anthro.37.081407.085156

Key Words

replicator, selection, phylogeny, comparative method

Abstract

Both qualitative concepts and quantitative methods from evolutionary
biology have been applied to linguistics. Many linguists have noted the
similarity between biological evolution and language change, but usually
have employed only selective analogies or metaphors. The development
of generalized theories of evolutionary change (Dawkins and Hull) has
spawned models of language change on the basis of such generalized
theories. These models have led to the positing of new mechanisms of
language change and new types of selection that may not have biological parallels. Quantitative methods have been applied to questions of
language phylogeny in the past decade. Research has focused on widely
accepted families with cognates already established by the comparative
method (Indo-European, Bantu, Austronesian). Increasingly sophisticated phylogeny reconstruction models have been applied to these families to resolve questions of subgrouping, contact, and migration. Little
progress has been made so far in analyzing sound correspondences in
the cognates themselves.

INTRODUCTION

Phylogeny: a graph structure, usually a tree, representing the evolutionary history of a set of individuals (organisms, species, languages)

Selection: the process by which the interaction of the interactor with its environment causes differential replication of the relevant replicators

Evolutionary models have come to be employed in several areas of the study of language in the past two decades. The use of evolutionary models is naturally found in historical linguistics and also in the study of the origins of language. In the latter case, however, the employment of evolutionary models is handicapped by the absence of data regarding the transition from our primate ancestors to the emergence of modern human language, which is found in all societies. All that we can go by is the archaeological record and the comparison of the social-cognitive abilities and communication systems of humans and other animals, particularly nonhuman primates. Because the study of the origin of human language does not depend on linguistic data, it is not discussed in this article. Even so, the area under review is vast and growing, and therefore this review is restricted to research in which qualitative concepts and quantitative methods from evolutionary biology have been applied to the analysis of language, in particular language change and language phylogeny.

EVOLUTIONARY THEORY AND THEORIES OF LANGUAGE CHANGE

In historical linguistics, the parallels between biological and linguistic evolution have been observed since Darwin himself first took notice (for a historical survey, see Atkinson & Gray 2005). However, the differences in the domains of biology and language appear to have outweighed the similarities, and Darwinian evolutionary theory has developed over time. In the meantime, the advent of structuralism and generative grammar has led to the dominance of an ahistorical approach to the study of language (Croft 2002). As a consequence, linguistics has rarely used models from evolutionary biology. Nevertheless, the similarities between the two have led historical linguists to employ evolutionary analogies or metaphors. Analogies/metaphors indicate similarities between the two domains (biological evolution and language change) but do not imply an overarching generalized theory.

An isolated analogy from evolutionary biology that has proven to be useful in explaining language change is Lass's application of exaptation to historical linguistic phenomena (Lass 1990). Exaptation in biology is the employment of a phylogenetic trait for a function different from the one for which it was originally adapted; Lass slightly changes the definition to apply to linguistic structures that have lost their function but have come to be employed for another function.

A recent example of the employment of a biological metaphor is Blevins's theory of evolutionary phonology (Blevins 2004). Evolutionary phonology proposes to account for synchronic phonological patterns as the result of phonetically motivated changes in the transmission of sound systems from adult to child over time. It uses the notions of inheritance (via the child learning the adults' language), variation generated by "errors" in replication (mechanisms by which the listener alters what he hears from the speaker), and natural selection (certain sound changes are more/less likely in particular phonetic contexts). However, because of disanalogies between biological evolution and language change, Blevins explicitly rejects an evolutionary approach to sound change that is more than metaphorical.

Although analogies or metaphors between biological evolution and language change can be fruitful, one does not know which parallels between the two domains are legitimate to draw and which are not, or even more important, which parallel structures must be present for the analogy/metaphor to make sense. In particular, it is common to assume that the mechanisms that cause variation and selection in biological evolution must be the same in other domains such as language change, yet the mechanisms are domain specific. What is required is a generalized theory of evolutionary change that subsumes biological evolution, language change, and other phenomena of evolutionary change such as cultural evolution. Researchers have derived models of cultural evolution from biological evolution (Boyd & Richerson 1985, Cavalli-Sforza & Feldman 1981, Durham 1991, Richerson & Boyd 2005). But the generalized theories of evolutionary change that have attracted the most attention in historical linguistics are those developed by Dawkins (1989, 1982) and Hull (1988, 2001).

The most crucial feature of a generalized theory of evolutionary change is that evolutionary change is change by replication, a process by which some entity is copied in such a way that most or all of the structure of the replicate is the same as that of the original. The replication process is cumulative and iterative, leading to lineages. Second, evolutionary change is a two-step process: the generation of variation in the replication process, and the selection of variants via some mechanism. Dawkins' and Hull's models have these properties, as do the models of cultural evolution mentioned above. In the context of language change, Lass notes that these properties are necessary to understand languages as historical entities (Lass 1997, pp. 109–11), although he does not develop a detailed theory of language change on this basis (see also Nettle 1999, Wedel 2006). Evolutionary theory also rejects any notion of progress.

Dawkins' and Hull's models are related but differ in important respects. Dawkins generalizes the concept of a gene as a replicator. The replicator possesses a structure that can be copied. Variation occurs through the copying process. Dawkins also generalizes the concept of an organism as a vehicle. For Dawkins, a vehicle has been constructed by the replicator to aid in its replication. Selection is differential replication, but for Dawkins it is focused on the replicator (the selfish gene concept), whereas in more standard neo-Darwinian models, selection is a function of the organism/vehicle.

Dawkins proposed that there are units of culture with heritable structure that replicate; he called them memes and proposed a science of memetics to study them. Memes have been interpreted as cognitive entities in the minds of humans, instances of human behavior, or artifacts. Most memeticists, including Dawkins himself, assume memes to be cognitive enti-

ties. Hence concepts are replicators and minds or brains of individuals are vehicles. Memeticists generally use a parasite-host model for the relationship between memes/concepts and the mind or brain of the possessor: Memes are parasites that use the brain (the host) as their vehicle for replication.

The most extended analysis of language change in Dawkinsian memetic terms is by Ritt (2004). Ritt, a historical phonologist, focuses on phonological change. Following Dawkins, linguistic memes are concepts in the mind; specifically, they are some type of replicable brain structure. Ritt argues that phonemes, morphemes, phonotactic patterns, metrical feet, and phonological rules, or more precisely their conceptual representations, are memes. However, linguistic signs (form-meaning pairings) are not replicators because, in Ritt's view, they do not preserve enough structure in replication. Instead, signs are the result of an alliance of replicators.

In the Dawkinsian model, the linguistic behavior that a speaker produces on the basis of her conceptual memes exists for the purpose of replicating the memes, not for communication (Ritt 2004, p. 231); this is the selfish gene/meme theory. The replicators are replicated across speakers by an imitation process (see Blackmore 1999); variation is generated in imperfect imitation. Ritt proposes several selectional pressures for differential replication (i.e., selection), all operating in the mind/brain. He focuses his attention on meme coadaptation as a selectional pressure, using it to account for the interaction between foot structure and vowel changes in the history of English.

Hull adopts Dawkins' concept of replicator but generalizes the role of the organism to an interactor and defines an interactor as any entity that interacts with the environment so as to cause differential replication (that is, selection) of the relevant replicators. Thus, the interactor's interaction with the environment is the locus of selection; it is not a mere vehicle for the replication of the replicator, and Hull does not advocate the selfish gene/meme interpretation that negates the role of the interactor in

Replicator: an entity that is copied and preserves most of its structure in copying

Meme: a cultural replicator

Interactor: an entity that interacts with its environment in such a way as to cause differential replication of the relevant replicators

Lingueme: a
linguistic replicator,
that is, a token of
linguistic structure
produced in an
utterance

evolution. Hull argues that interactors may exist at different levels in the biological hierarchy (gene, cell, organism, even a species), although the organism's interaction with its environment in natural selection is the canonical case. Hull's general analysis of selection is thus centered on the processes by which the interactor's interaction with its environment causes the differential replication of replicators.

Hull (1988, 2001) presents a theory of conceptual change in science in which scientific concepts are replicators and the scientists are interactors. Hull's general analysis of selection does not assume any specific causal relationship from replicator to interactor, so there is no need to invoke a parasite-host model for the concept-scientist relation. However, scientists must be able to cause the differential replication of their ideas/concepts, which they do through publishing, lecturing, and teaching.

The most detailed application of Hull's general analysis of selection to language change is in Croft (2000, 2002, 2006). Croft argues for a model in which the linguistic replicators are behaviors, that is, tokens of linguistic structures in utterances produced by speakers. Croft coins the term lingueme to describe the linguistic replicator. The speakers themselves are interactors. The speaker replicates the replicators in speaking, generating variation in the production and comprehesion of utterances. In Croft's model, linguistic structures evolve via language use, not via language acquisition.

Croft's model, like Hull's, does not specify the mechanisms by which variation is generated. Croft, like all evolutionary biologists and most historical linguists, rejects teleological mechanisms. Croft allows for widely proposed intentional mechanisms, such as expressiveness and avoidance of misunderstanding. Croft also proposes nonintentional mechanisms inspired by theories of sound change, in which speakers or listeners attempt to conform to convention but fail to do so. Speakers are highly variable in the phonetic realization of phonemes (sound linguemes), as noted in much recent phonetic research (e.g., Bybee 2001, Pierrehumbert 2001) and in the verbalization of meaning in grammatical structures (Croft 2008). Listeners are faced with the problem of analyzing the phonemes in an utterance from a complex acoustical signal, and they may reanalyze the mapping between the phonetic signal and the phonological structure, in processes Ohala (2003) calls hypocorrection and hypercorrection. Listeners are also faced with the problem of analyzing the semantic contribution of words, morphemes, and constructions from a complex communicative situation, and they may reanalyze the mapping between form and meaning in those units via different types of form-function reanalysis (Croft 2000, chapters 4–5).

The speaker as interactor is also the locus of selection: The speaker selects a variant to produce. In this respect, Croft's evolutionary model agrees with theories of the propagation of change (selection of variants) developed in sociohistorical linguistics. In the latter theories, investigators propose that various social factors associated with particular sociolinguistic variants in speech communities lead to the propagation (or extinction) of variants, although other factors including the social network structure and the frequency of exposure to variants also play a role. Croft argues that functional pressures operate only in the generation of variation, not in selection; others take the view that functional pressures operate in selection (e.g., Nettle 1999, pp. 30–35).

Some of these models have led to mathematical formalizations and simulations. Nettle (1999) simulates a model in which language change occurs via child language acquisition and argues that the rate of fixation is proportional to the number of speakers in the speech community. Wedel (2006) presents a usage/exemplar-based evolutionary model of sound change, including simulations of inheritance and selection. The work by Baxter et al. (2006) is a formalization of Croft's theory in a statistical physics framework (see also Blythe & McKane 2007).

The model developed in Baxter et al. (2006) shows that some types of selection mechanisms in language change (and other types of cultural evolution) may not exist as such in biological evolution. The classic selection mechanism is a type of replicator selection, that is, differential weighting of replicator variants (their fitness); in language change this is found in the differential social valuation of variants (compare Nettle 1999, pp. 29–30). In neutral evolution (genetic drift, not the same as linguistic drift), random fluctuations lead to change (Nettle 1999, pp. 16–17); these correspond to frequency effects in language change. In addition to these two mechanisms, there is neutral interactor selection, by which differences in the frequency of interaction with other interactors lead to differential replication. Neutral interactor selection corresponds to social network structure effects in language change (Milroy 1987); sexual selection may be an instance of neutral interactor selection in biological evolution. Finally, the model includes weighted interactor selection, in which differential weighting of the interactors with whom one interacts, independent of frequency of interaction, leads to differential replication. Weighted interactor selection is exemplified in the differential social valuation of different speakers; there is no obvious equivalent in biological evolution. Baxter et al. (2008) use their model and simulations based on it to argue that the New Zealand English variety could not have emerged by neutral evolution and neutral interactor selection alone.

Mufwene (2001, 2005) developed an evolutionary model for language change that is similar to Croft's. Mufwene focuses on two aspects of the evolutionary framework not discussed above. First, a language forms a population in the same way that a species does. Mufwene treats a language as a species, specifically a population of linguistic structures that exist in the minds of speakers in communities, because languages are variable, and their spread, extinction, and rates of change are dependent on speaker populations and not on the linguistic system per se. Mufwene follows the parasite-host model for the relationship between a language and its speakers, but his focus is different from the memeticists. The memeticists argue that the linguistic concept (the parasite) uses the speaker (its host) to replicate itself, whereas Mufwene argues that the survival, spread, or extinction of a language is dependent on the survival, spread, or extinction of its host speakers.

The second aspect of evolution that Mufwene exploits is ecology. Languages, and the speakers on which they are dependent, are embedded in an environment, in particular a social environment but also the internal environment of the society and the linguistic varieties found in it. Mufwene uses his framework to analyze the development of creoles and the relationship between creoles and "normal" linguistic transmission. Mufwene argues that creoles emerge from the linguistic varieties available in the earliest stages of colonization, which in the case of European language–based creoles involve nonstandard varieties of the European language(s) and also nonnative European speakers (e.g., Irish nonnative speakers of English, Breton nonnative speakers of French) as well as nonnative speakers of African origin (as in American slave plantations) or indigenous nonnative speakers (as in the Pacific). The emerging creole is a result of natural selection of linguistic structures determined by the ecology of the social and economic situations of the early colonies. Mufwene argues that the emergence of creoles is not different in kind from "normal" language change, but only in degree—the same ecological model fits the development of the Romance languages from Vulgar Latin, for instance.

The emergence of theories of language change based on a generalized theory of evolutionary change is quite recent. Less systematic adaptations of evolutionary concepts in theories of language change continue to be made as well. Evolutionary, usage-based theories of language change are the strongest competitors to the innate-grammar, child-based theories of language change put forward by followers of Chomsky such as Lightfoot (2006).

Comparative method: the
traditional historical linguistic method by which sound correspondences are found among cognates and a protolanguage is reconstructed

Cognate set:
corresponding words in a set of languages that are presumed to have a common ancestor

Sound correspondence: a
systematic correspondence of sounds in the words in a cognate set

PHYLOGENY RECONSTRUCTION AND GENETIC LINGUISTICS

A major potential application of more practical methods from evolutionary biology to historical linguistics is in the area of genetic linguistics, in particular the establishment of language families and their subgroupings. This task parallels what evolutionary biologists call phylogeny reconstruction, the reconstruction of the presumed historical branching of ancestral populations into contemporary populations, of either species or smaller biological groups. Phylogeny reconstruction is accomplished by comparing phenotypic traits of organisms, particularly proteins, or sequences of nucleotides in mitochondrial or nuclear DNA. Breakthroughs in DNA sequencing and the development of mathematical algorithms and computing power to execute those algorithms have led to an explosion of research in phylogeny reconstruction, of which the most famous result is the African Eve hypothesis: that all humans are believed to be descended from an ancestral population in Africa some 100,000–150,000 years ago (Cann et al. 1987, Vigilant et al. 1991).

The connection between phylogeny and language history was made in a paper by Cavalli-Sforza et al. (1988), which attracted a tremendous amount of attention but whose linguistic assumptions were rejected by most linguists. Cavalli-Sforza et al. produce a phylogeny of human populations and compare it with a phylogeny of linguistic populations, that is, the major language families in the world. They note a high degree of congruence of the two phylogenies, suggesting that language spread and diversification have occurred primarily via migration and splitting of speech communities, at least in prehistory. Much of the controversy among linguists is due to the authors' use of language families such as Amerind, Eurasiatic/Nostratic, Altaic, Na-Dene, Austric, and Indo-Pacific, which are not generally accepted among historical lingusts.

One crucial difference between the biological and linguistic data in Cavalli-Sforza et al. is that the biological data have been analyzed quantitatively whereas the linguistic data have not. Since that time an increasing number of researchers have attempted to apply quantitative techniques to the problem of language families and have made other attempts to relate language diversification to prehistoric demography. The remainder of this review focuses on quantitative methods from evolutionary biology applied to comparative historical (genetic) linguistics; owing to topic and length considerations, quantitative methods from other fields are not discussed nor is research on the relationship between prehistoric demography and language families derived by traditional linguistic method.

The Comparative Method and Phylogeny Reconstruction

The comparative method is excellently summarized in the following passage from Ross & Durie (1996, p. 7):

The comparative method (in its strict sense) can be summarized as a set of instructions:

1. Determine on the strength of diagnostic evidence that a set of languages are genetically related, that is, that they constitute a "family."
2. Collect putative cognate sets for the family (both morphological paradigms and lexical items).
3. Work out the sound correspondences from the cognate sets, putting "irregular" cognate sets on one side.
4. Reconstruct the protolanguage of the family as follows:
   a. Reconstruct the protophonology from the sound correspondences worked out in [step] 3, using conventional wisdom regarding the directions of sound changes.
   b. Reconstruct protomorphemes (both morphological paradigms and lexical items) from the cognate sets collected in [step] 2, using the protophonology reconstructed in [step] 4a.
5. Establish innovations (phonological, lexical, semantic, morphological,

morphosyntactic) shared by groups of languages within the family relative to the reconstructed protolanguage.

6. Tabulate the innovations established in [step] 5 to arrive at an internal classification of the family, a "family tree."

7. Construct an etymological dictionary, tracing borrowings, semantic change, and so forth, for the lexicon of the family (or of one language of the family).

Ross & Durie note that the steps in this process are iterated because they are clearly interrelated. For example, what counts as an innovation in sound change in a daughter language or languages depends on what is reconstructed as a protophoneme.

Major similarities exist between the comparative method and phylogeny reconstruction (Greenberg 1992 gives a detailed comparison; see also Lass 1997, chapters 3–4). First, the differentiation of languages and the differentiation of species are assumed to be largely treelike. Nevertheless, both biologists and linguists allow for the possibility of reticulation in phylogenetic trees, certainly for closely related species (hybridization) and languages (dialect mixture). Second, both biologists and historical linguists recognize the important diagnostic value of shared innovations (see steps 5–6 above). These fundamental similarities mean that the tree-building algorithms developed for biological phylogenies are built on the same principles as is historical linguistics and therefore should be applicable to reconstructing linguistic family trees, or language phylogenies.

A major difference between the two domains, however, is that in language, sound change leads the divergence of the phonological forms of words even though they are cognate. Cognate forms are not identical. In genetic comparison, "cognate" sequences of nucleotides are identical. One consequence of this difference is that almost all applications of phylogeny reconstruction algorithms from biology to historical linguistics have used as the input data (character traits) to the phylogeny re-

construction algorithm only lists of established cognates in accepted language families because cognates can be treated as identical. That is, the family tree (the subgrouping) is reconstructed on the basis of the presence versus absence of cognate forms for particular meanings in particular daughter languages. This approach represents a signficant loss of information, but many important issues in historical linguistics can nevertheless be placed in an evolutionary perspective even in this approach.

Some techniques from evolutionary biology are beginning to the applied to the problem of sound correspondence. In particular, techniques from DNA sequencing have been applied to the alignment problem. This is a problem rarely touched on in textbooks on the comparative method: aligning two forms to identify the corresponding sounds. This technique is not straightforward because phonemes may be inserted (epenthesis), deleted, merged, or transposed (metathesis); also, many words contain fossilized affixes that do not correspond with anything in their cognates in the other languages. Computational linguists have addressed the alignment problem for historical comparison, using techniques also found in biology (Covington 1996, 1998; Kessler 1995; Kondrak 2002, 2003; Nerbonne & Heeringa 1997; Oakes 2000). This research is based on minimizing edit distance (Levenshtein distance) between the strings being aligned. Kondrak notes that biologists are beginning to use probabilistic models such as Hidden Markov models and suggests this as a possible new technique to use in historical linguistics (Kondrak 2002, p. 23). Nevertheless, mathematical formalization of the identification of sound correspondences is presently in its infancy.

Mathematical Techniques from Biology

A wide array of techniques from phylogeny reconstruction in biology have been applied to historical linguistics, even given the limitation to cognate judgments that exists only in established language families. This review can give only a broad qualitative description of some of the methods; the mathematics of the methods is described in various references (see also McMahon & McMahon 2003, 2006 for discussion of the methods from a comparative historical linguistics perspective).

Given a set of data such as cognate judgments among a set of genetically related languages, two common ways are used to construct phylogenies. Distance-based methods use an overall pairwise distance measurement between two languages. Historical linguistics has already used a distance-based method to measure the proportion of shared cognates: the lexicostatistical method. (Lexicostatistics has also been used when similar word forms are not known to be cognate; here we discuss only assumed cognacy.) Distance-based methods have the advantage of being computationally very fast. However, this method suffers from a number of defects (Atkinson & Gray 2005, p. 520; Gray & Atkinson 2003, p. 436). The distance measure loses the information about which word forms are cognate. Languages change at different rates (Bergsland & Vogt 1962, Blust 2000, Gray & Atkinson 2003). Individual word meanings also change at different rates (Greenberg 2005, pp. 108–11; Joos 1964; Kruskal et al. 1973; Pagel 2000; Pagel et al. 2007; Pagel & Meade 2006). Finally, borrowing can distort the distance between languages in ways that reflect contact, not common ancestry. However, all these problems can be overcome to some extent with newer phylogenetic techniques, briefly described in this and the following sections.

The loss of information in distance-based methods can be addressed by using character-based methods. In character-based methods, particular cognate forms are used to compute the tree. Character-based methods are most closely associated with cladistics, which distinguishes shared innovations from shared retentions and uses only the former for constructing the tree (subgrouping). Two approaches have been used for determining the best fit of the tree to the data. In maximum parsimony, the algo-rithm minimizes the number of character state changes (in the case of cognate lists, minimizes the number of replacements of word forms). An alternative approach is the compatibility criterion, which minimizes the number of characters that must be assumed to have been innovated more than once. Indo-European trees have been constructed using both maximum parsimony (Rexová et al. 2003) and compatibility (Ringe et al. 2002).

Owing to the complexity of the data, any phylogeny reconstruction algorithm will produce large numbers of trees, measured according to the criteria used (e.g., maximum parsimony). In fact, the space of possible trees is often so large that heuristics must be used to identify the trees to be used in analysis. The traditional approach in both distance-based and character-based methods is to base the result on a set of optimal trees. A consensus tree is produced, typically using a majority rules strategy, which posits the nodes in the consensus tree that are found in at least half the input trees. The robustness of the nodes in the tree relative to the data is commonly tested with a bootstrapping technique (e.g., Holden et al. 2005, p. 60). In bootstrapping, the original data set is sampled with replacement (i.e., one is always sampling from the full original data set) until a new data set of the same size is produced. A pseudoreplicate tree is constructed for the new data set, and the process is repeated many times. The pseudoreplicate trees are compared with the original (consensus) tree, and the robustness of each node in the original tree is the percent of the pseudoreplicate trees that contain the node in question.

More recently, Bayesian methods have been applied to phylogeny reconstruction (Atkinson & Gray 2005, p. 521). In a Bayesian approach, one samples not just the most optimal trees produced, but all possible trees in proportion to their likelihood (Holden et al. 2005, pp. 60–62). Again, a consensus tree is produced from the sample. The proportion of trees with a particular node in the sample is equivalent to the Bayesian posterior probability of that node. A common method used to construct the sample to model the posterior probability distribution of trees is a Markov chain Monte Carlo method (see, for example, Gray & Atkinson 2003, Pagel & Meade 2006). The Bantu languages have been classified using a distance-based method (Bastin et al. 1999), maximum parsimony (Holden 2002, Rexová et al. 2006), and Bayesian methods (Holden et al. 2005, p. 60; Rexová et al. 2006).

Two other facts about phylogeny reconstruction must be noted here. First, trees produced by the algorithms are unrooted: They show groupings but do not indicate which group is the most distant. Rooting is generally established by using an outgroup, a group that is agreed to be most distant from all other members of the data set. Second, the algorithms attempt to construct binary trees. The only way to identify multiple branching is through short binary branches and/or failure to construct statistically robust binary branching in part of the tree.

Differentiating Chance Cognation and Borrowing from Cognates

Step 1 in the comparative method, the identification of a set of languages as forming a language family, poses a basic problem. This selection cannot be done randomly because even with a small number of languages, the number of ways in which they can be classified quickly becomes astronomical (see, e.g., Greenberg 2005, p. 43). Yet most introductions to comparative linguistics assume that the investigator begins with a set of languages that are already related.

Nichols (1996) argues that a single diagnostic trait, or a small set of traits, is sufficient to identify a valid linguistic family, but there are serious statistical problems with this approach (see Kessler 2001, p. 32). It is difficult to find any other technique to identify language families apart from compelling similarities in form and meaning distributed across a set of words among a subset of languages under comparison. This technique is essentially Greenberg's method of multilateral comparison (see the

papers collected in Greenberg 2005). Multilateral comparison has often been misunderstood in the linguistic literature as if Greenberg intended it to replace the comparative method. In fact, he intended it only to be an approach to steps 1 and 2 of the comparative method (Greenberg 2001, p. 127). Step 1 is achieved only jointly with step 2: A set of languages forms a family because of the presence of similar form-meaning pairings that are concluded to be (putative) cognates.

The crucial problem, then, is to differentiate putative cognate forms—those that are phonetically and semantically similar most likely because of common ancestry—from forms in the data that are similar because of contact (borrowing), sound symbolism, or chance. Greenberg's primary contention is that the source of form-meaning similarities in a matrix of word meanings across languages can be fairly accurately determined from the distribution pattern of the form-meaning similarities in the matrix, as well as from phonological patterns in the form-meaning similarities (Greenberg 1957, p. 69; see also Greenberg 2005, chapter 2). Techniques from biology exploiting these distributional patterns can be applied to the problems of chance cognation and borrowing. (Sound symbolism is a fourth source of similarity, but the likelihood of sound symbolism is generally minimized by discounting or excluding meanings that are likely to be sound symbolic—i.e., by exploiting a characteristic distribution pattern across meanings.) This approach differs from the standard assumption among users of the comparative method, namely that only regular sound correspondences can be used to differentiate cognates from borrowing and chance resemblance; therefore, until the establishment of sound correspondences can be formalized, other approaches remain only tentative. Nevertheless, it appears that a considerable amount of information can be extracted from distributional patterns of form-meaning similarities, at least in the relatively shallow language families to which these biological phylogeny reconstruction techniques have been applied.

The likelihood of similarity being due to chance is one that has attracted much attention in historical linguistics, but little can be concluded from the literature on it. Ringe (1992, 1993) and Greenberg & Ruhlen (1992) have proposed methods to evaluate chance cognation, but they are mathematically flawed (Baxter & Manaster Ramer 1996, Greenberg 1993, Kessler 2001, Manaster Ramer & Hitchcock 1996). A more promising approach for evaluating chance cognation is the permutation method, which is not specifically drawn from evolutionary biology (Baxter 1995; Baxter & Manaster Ramer 2000; Justeson & Stephens 1980; Kessler 2001; Oswalt 1970, 1991). The permutation method compares the proportion of form-meaning similarities in the observed data set to random permutations of the forms across the meanings to derive a probability that the observed form-meaning similarities could occur by chance. However, a result indicating that form-meaning similarities in the observed data set are not due to chance gives information only about the data set as a whole. It does not provide information about the validity of particular nodes in the tree. Bootstrapping or Bayesian posterior probabilities, however, can be used to address the chance cognation problem because both give a probability of the validity of each node (genetic grouping) in the tree. Of course, some form-meaning similarities may still be due to chance. The use of character-based methods will provide hypotheses as to which characters (words) are not contributing to the building of the tree and therefore may be chance similarities.

The problem of differentiating borrowing from common ancestry has been addressed in two general ways. The first is to use techniques that assume the data to be treelike and treat anomalous similarities as derived from borrowing. Minett & Wang (2003) examine a distance-based method that compares branch lengths of the tree and lexical distances, but they found that it does not differentiate borrowing from cognates. However, a character-based method using maximum parsimony did allow inference of a likelihood of borrowing for char-

acters (words) among the Chinese languages. Nevertheless, Wang & Minett (2005) formalize Hinnebusch's (1999) proposal that skewing in lexicostatistical percentages may indicate borrowing and suggest that this distance-based approach might be useful.

The second is to use techniques that allow reticulation, that is, they allow branches to rejoin, representing contact relations and creating phylogenetic networks instead of trees. Bryant et al. (2005) use these techniques to represent the conflicting signals of languages that have undergone significant contact. These techniques allow one to ask how treelike the data are, rather than assuming the data are treelike. Bryant et al. show that Indo-European is quite treelike, at least in its basic vocabulary; the same result is reached by Warnow et al. (2006; see also Holden & Gray 2006, discussed below). Ben Hamed (2005) and Ben Hamed & Wang (2006) show that network techniques applied to the complex relationships among dialect differentation, dialect continua, dialect contact, and diglossia in Chinese tend to correlate with known geographical, linguistic, and population history.

One problem with network techniques is that most historical linguists believe that there are few if any instances of true reticulation: One can identify the parent versus the source of contact, and even for so-called mixed languages, the contribution of the two is asymmetric in systematic ways (Croft 2003). Borrowing can be differentiated from common ancestry by the distribution of borrowings and their forms: For instance, some semantic categories are less likely to be borrowed, and borrowing often links the borrowing language to a single source language (e.g., Greenberg 1957, p. 71; 2005, p. 38). McMahon et al. (2005) use different weightings of more versus less stable vocabulary to evaluate the form-meaning resemblances between Quechuan and Aymaran.

Another important route to distinguishing cognates from borrowing is to model the process of word birth, cognate formation, homoplasy (independent convergence, e.g., by chance), borrowing, and word death and compare the results of this model to that of actual language families. Two examples of models including all these processes are Warnow et al. (2006) and Nicholls & Gray (2006; see McMahon & McMahon 2003 for an earlier model that does not allow for homoplasy). Both of these models were used to refine a phylogeny of Indo-European (see below). Bryant (2006) constructs a model comparing radiation (and subsequent isolation) versus "network breaking" (dialect continua followed by gradual divergence) and compares it with linguistic data on Polynesian.

Language Phylogeny and Human Prehistory

The use of techniques from evolutionary biology in historical linguistics is quite new, and current results must be taken as tentative. The review concludes by mentioning some of the more interesting results that have emerged from these techniques. The most intensive work has been done on Indo-European, the most intensively studied language family, and Bantu and Austronesian, the largest present-day language families, which are nevertheless quite shallow.

Ringe et al. (2002) use not only lexical cognates but also morphological and phonological traits from 24 Indo-European languages (the most ancient members of their branches) and a character-based compatability algorithm to derive a phylogeny for Indo-European. Their best tree is rooted with Anatolian as the outgroup, on the (not universally accepted) assumption that Anatolian is the most distant branch. Their phylogeny provides evidence on the following controversial issues in Indo-European phylogeny: that Tocharian is the most distant branch after Anatolian, and that Balto-Slavic, Italo-Celtic, and Greco-Armenian are valid subgroups. The position of Albanian is unclear, and Germanic is problematic; Ringe et al. argue that an eastern Indo-European group later came into contact with western Indo-European. Nakhleh et al. (2005) use a model that includes the possibility of borrowing (see Warnow

et al. 2006) and argue that Germanic was likely in contact with Italic, Balto-Slavic, and possibly Greco-Armenian. Rexová et al. (2003) use maximum parsimony on the 200-word lists for 84 Indo-European languages from Dyen et al. (1992). They conclude that Germanic forms a clade (valid subgroup) with Italic, possibly Celtic, and very possibly Albanian and that there is an eastern satem group consisting of Balto-Slavic and Indo-Iranian. Gray & Atkinson (2003) used Bayesian methods allowing for unequal rates of change (inter alia) to construct a phylogeny and attribute a date and location for proto-Indo-European, specifically Anatolia around 9000 years ago (see also Atkinson & Gray 2006). Their tree treats Tocharian as the most distant branch after Anatolian and provides strong evidence for Balto-Slavic and weaker evidence for Germanic-Italic-Celtic. Atkinson et al. (2005) replicate their result using the data set from Ringe et al. (2002) (see above) and a stochastic-Dollo model of vocabulary evolution, which include the possibility of borrowing (see Nicholls & Gray 2006). Pagel & Meade (2005) use a Bayesian method on a smaller sample of Indo-European languages and use the tree to argue that the ancestral culture likely had monogamy and a dowry system, and shifts away from this system were first to polygyny and then to the absence of a dowry or presence of a bride-price.

Holden et al. (2005) compare a Bayesian phylogeny reconstruction of Bantu with Holden's (2002) maximum parsimony analysis. Both analyses agree that the northwest Bantu groups are most divergent, with the Bayesian analysis suggesting they are paraphyletic (i.e., they do not together form a valid taxon). The east, southeast, and southwest languages form a single clade, within which there is a clear East Bantu group. Holden et al. argue that the migration of the Bantu peoples follows the spread of farming into southern Africa. Rexová et al. (2006) perform maximum parsimony and Bayesian analyses of the same lexical data in combination with phonological and grammatical characters. They also find a single clade for the east, southeast, and southwest groups and conclude that there was a single migration from the equatorial rainforests to the areas south and east. Holden & Gray (2006) use network models to ascertain why the Bantu group is not treelike in certain respects. They conclude that West Bantu languages radiated rapidly but without much contact, whereas East Bantu and east Central Bantu languages appear to have had much contact leading to borrowing. Holden & Mace (2003, 2005) use the maximum parsimony tree to argue that matrilineal descent was lost as cattle were adopted in prehistoric southern Africa.

Gray & Jordan (2000) use a parsimony analysis on 77 Austronesian languages with 5185 lexical items from Blust's unpublished *Austronesian Comparative Dictionary* to argue that the structure of the language family is strongly treelike, with greatest diversity in Taiwan, and that this analysis supports the express train hypothesis of relatively rapid colonization of Oceania by the ancestral Austronesians. However, Greenhill & Gray (2005) show that applying bootstrapping to the original study demonstrates it is not that robust. They use Bayesian methods to construct a tree that fits more closely with the traditional historical linguistic analysis, which still places the origin in Taiwan but does not necessarily entail a rapid expansion across Oceania. A network analysis indicates that the major groups in Austronesian are treelike but that the deeper branchings are less treelike because of the lack of signal in the data set.

Dunn et al. (2005) use a maximum parsimony analysis of typological traits, rather than lexical traits, to construct phylogenies of Oceanic and Papuan languages of Island Melanesia. They compare their analysis to the phylogeny of the Oceanic languages in that area and find a high degree of corroboration. The Papuan languages in the area do not display much lexical resemblance, but Dunn et al. argue that the use of typological traits reveals a phylogeny that is apparently lost owing to lexical replacement. Typological traits are avoided in comparative linguistics because they have few possible values (and are thus highly prone to chance resemblance), they diffuse through contact relatively easily, their values are often not independent (e.g., they are linked by implicational universals), and their values are often externally (functionally) motivated (another source of convergence). Some of these issues are raised in a critique by Donohue & Wichmann (2007); see also the response by Dunn et al. (2007). Although the result from Dunn et al. (2005) is surprising to a historical linguist, it may be that a cluster of typological traits will provide more precision in classification than will individual traits; also some typological traits are quite stable and therefore may be useful indicators of phylogeny. However, Gray (2005) notes some weaknesses in the analysis from Dunn et al., and the use of typological traits in phylogeny reconstruction remains to be investigated further.

As with the employment of qualitative concepts from evolutionary biology in theories of language change, the application of quantitative methods from evolutionary biology to phylogeny reconstruction in comparative linguistics is in its infancy. The application to accepted language families using established cognates provides a new perspective on outstanding problems in those families and allows for a link to human prehistory. However, further progress in adapting methods to linguistic phenomena is required before they can be used confidently to investigate controversial or as yet undiscovered language families.

DISCLOSURE STATEMENT

The author is not aware of any biases that might be perceived as affecting the objectivity of this review.

LITERATURE CITED

Atkinson QD, Gray RD. 2005. Curious parallels and curious connection: phylogenetic thinking in biology and historical linguistics. *Syst. Biol.* 54:513–26

Atkinson QD, Gray RD. 2006. How old is the Indo-European family? Illumination or more moths to the flame? See Forster & Renfrew 2006, pp. 91–109

Atkinson QD, Nicholls GK, Welch D, Gray RD. 2005. From words to dates: water into wine, mathemagic or phylogenetic inference? *Trans. Philol. Soc.* 103:193–219

Bastin Y, Coupez A, Mann M. 1999. Continuity and divergence in the Bantu languages: perspectives from a lexicostatistic study. *Ann. Sci. Hum.* 162:315–17

Baxter GJ, Blythe RA, Croft W, McKane AJ. 2006. Utterance selection model of linguistic change. *Phys. Rev. E* 73.046118

Baxter GJ, Blythe RA, Croft W, McKane AJ. 2008. Modeling language change: an evaluation of Trudgill's theory of the emergence of New Zealand English. *Lang. Var. Change.* In press

Baxter WH. 1995. "A stronger affinity...than could have been produced by accident": a probabilistic comparison of Old Chinese and Tibeto-Burman. In *The Ancestry of the Chinese Language*, J. Chin. Ling. Monogr. Ser. 8, ed. WSY Wang, pp. 1–39. Berkeley: Univ. Calif. Press

Baxter WH, Manaster Ramer A. 1996. Review of Donald A. Ringe, Jr., *On Calculating the Factor of Chance in Language Comparison. Diachronica* 13:371–84

Baxter WH, Manaster Ramer A. 2000. Beyond lumping and splitting: probabilistic issues in historical linguistics. See Renfrew et al. 2000, pp. 167–88

Ben Hamed M. 2005. Neighbour-nets portray the Chinese dialect continuum and the linguistic legacy of China's demic history. *Proc. R. Soc. London B* 272:1015–22

Ben Hamed M, Wang F. 2006. Stuck in the forest: trees, networks and Chinese dialects. *Diachronica* 23:29–60

Bergsland K, Vogt H. 1962. On the validity of glottochronology. *Curr. Anthropol.* 3:115–53

Blackmore S. 1999. *The Meme Machine.* Oxford, UK: Oxford Univ. Press

Blevins J. 2004. *Evolutionary Phonology: The Emergence of Sound Patterns.* Cambridge, MA: Cambridge Univ. Press

Blust R. 2000. Why lexicostatistics doesn't work: the "universal constant" hypothesis and the Austronesian languages. See Renfrew et al. 2000, pp. 311–31

Blythe RA, McKane AJ. 2007. Stochastic models of evolution in genetics, ecology and linguistics. *J. Stat. Mech.* 07-P07018

Boyd R, Richerson PJ. 1985. *Culture and the Evolutionary Process.* Chicago, IL: Univ. Chicago Press

Bryant D. 2006. Radiation and network breaking in Polynesian linguistics. See Forster & Renfrew 2006, pp. 111–18

Bryant D, Filimon F, Gray RD. 2005. Untangling our past: languages, trees, splits and networks. See Mace et al. 2005, pp. 67–83

Bybee JL. 2001. *Phonology and Language Use.* Cambridge, UK: Cambridge Univ. Press

Cann RL, Stoneking M, Wilson AC. 1987. Mitochondrial DNA and human evolution. *Nature* 329:111–12

Cavalli-Sforza LL, Feldman MW. 1981. *Cultural Transmission and Evolution: A Quantitative Approach.* Princeton, NJ: Princeton Univ. Press

Cavalli-Sforza LL, Piazza A, Menozzi P, Mountain J. 1988. Reconstruction of human evolution: bringing together genetic, archaeological, and linguistic data. *Proc. Natl. Acad. Sci. USA* 85:6002–6

Covington MA. 1996. An algorithm to align words for historical comparison. *Comp. Ling.* 22:481–96

Covington MA. 1998. Alignment of multiple languages for historical comparison. *Proc. COLING-ACL'98: Annu. Meet Assoc. Comput. Ling., 36th, Montreal, Canada, and Int. Conf. Comput. Ling., 17th, Montreal, Canada,* pp. 275–80. Morristown: Assoc. Comput. Ling.

Croft W. 2000. *Explaining Language Change: An Evolutionary Approach.* Harlow, Essex, UK: Longman

Croft W. 2002. The Darwinization of linguistics. *Selection* 3:75–91

Croft W. 2003. Mixed languages and acts of identity: an evolutionary approach. In *The Mixed Language Debate*, ed. Y Matras, P Bakker, pp. 41–72. Berlin: Mouton de Gruyter

Croft W. 2006. The relevance of an evolutionary model to historical linguistics. In *Competing Models of Linguistic Change: Evolution and Beyond*, ed. O Nedergård Thomsen, pp. 91–132. Amsterdam: John Benjamins

Croft W. 2008. The origins of grammaticalization in the verbalization of experience. *Linguistics*. In press

Dawkins R. 1982. *The Extended Phenotype*. Oxford, UK: Freeman

Dawkins R. 1989. *The Selfish Gene*. New York: Oxford Univ. Press. 2nd ed.

Donohue M, Wichmann S. 2007. Typology and the linguistic macrohistory of Island Melanesia. *Ocean. Linguist.* 46:348–87

Dunn M, Foley RA, Levinson SC, Reesink G, Terrill A. 2007. Statistical reasoning in the evaluation of typological diversity in Island Melanesia. *Ocean. Linguist.* 46:388–403

Dunn M, Terrill A, Reesink G, Foley RA, Levinson SC. 2005. Structural phylogenetics and the reconstruction of ancient language history. *Science* 309:2072–75

Durham WH. 1991. *Coevolution: Genes, Culture and Human Diversity*. Stanford, CA: Stanford Univ. Press

Durie M, Ross M, eds. 1996. *The Comparative Method Reviewed: Regularity and Irregularity in Language Change*. Oxford, UK: Oxford Univ. Press

Dyen I, Kruskal JB, Black P. 1992. An Indoeuropean classification: a lexicostatistical experiment. *Trans. Am. Philos. Soc.* 82:1–132

Forster P, Renfrew C, eds. 2006. *Phylogenetic Methods and the Prehistory of Languages*. Cambridge, UK: McDonald Inst. Archaeol. Res.

Gray RD. 2005. Pushing the time barrier in the quest for language roots. *Science* 309:2007–8

Gray RD, Atkinson QD. 2003. Language-tree divergence times support the Anatolian theory of Indo-European origin. *Nature* 426:435–39

Gray RD, Jordan FM. 2000. Language trees support the express-train sequence of Austronesian expansion. *Nature* 405:1052–55

Greenberg JH. 1957. Language, diffusion and migration. In *Essays in Linguistics*, pp. 66–74. Chicago, IL: Univ. Chicago Press

Greenberg JH. 1992. Preliminaries to a systematic comparison between biological and linguistic evolution. In *The Evolution of Human Languages*, ed. JA Hawkins, M Gell-Mann, pp. 139–58. Redwood City, CA: Addison Wesley

Greenberg JH. 1993. Observations concerning Ringe's *Calculating the Factor of Chance in Language Comparison*. *Proc. Am. Philos. Soc.* 137:79–90

Greenberg JH. 2001. The methods and purposes of linguistic genetic classification. *Lang. Linguist.* 2:111–36

Greenberg JH. 2005. *Genetic Linguistics: Theory and Method*, ed. W Croft. Oxford, UK: Oxford Univ. Press

Greenberg JH, Ruhlen M. 1992. Linguistic origins of Native Americans. *Sci. Am.* 267(5):94–99

Greenhill SJ, Gray RD. 2005. Testing population dispersal hypotheses: Pacific settlement, phylogenetic trees and Austronesian languages. See Mace et al. 2005, pp. 31–52

Hinnebusch TJ. 1999. Contact and lexicostatics in comparative Bantu studies. In *Bantu Historical Linguistics: Theoretical and Empirical Perspectives*, ed. J-M Hombert, LM Hyman, pp. 173–205. Stanford, CA: Cent. Study Lang. Inf.

Holden CJ. 2002. Bantu language trees reflect the spread of farming across sub-Saharan Africa: a maximum-parsimony analysis. *Proc. R. Soc. London Ser. B* 269:793–99

Holden CJ, Gray RD. 2006. Rapid radiation, borrowing and dialect continua in the Bantu languages. See Forster & Renfrew 2006, pp. 19–31

Holden CJ, Mace R. 2003. Spread of cattle led to the loss of matrilineal descent in Africa: a coevolutionary analysis. *Proc. R. Soc. London Ser. B* 270:2425–33

Holden CJ, Mace R. 2005. "The cow is the enemy of matriliny": using phylogenetic methods to investigate cultural evolution in Africa. See Mace et al. 2005, pp. 217–34

Holden CJ, Meade A, Pagel M. 2005. Comparison of maximum parsimony and Bayesian Bantu language trees. See Mace et al. 2005, pp. 53–65

Hull DL. 1988. *Science as a Process: An Evolutionary Account of the Social and Conceptual Development of Science*. Chicago, IL: Univ. Chicago Press

Hull DL. 2001. *Science and Selection: Essays on Biological Evolution and the Philosophy of Science*. Cambridge, UK: Cambridge Univ. Press

Joos M. 1964. Glottochronology with retention rate homogeneity. *Proc. Int. Congr. Linguist., 9th, Cambridge, Mass.*, ed. HG Lunt, p. 237. The Hague: Mouton

Justeson JS, Stephens LD. 1980. Change cognation: a probabilistic model and decision procedure for historical inference. *Pap. Int. Conf. Hist. Linguist., 4th, Stanford, Calif.*, ed. EC Traugott, R LaBrum, S Shepherd, pp. 37–46. Amsterdam: John Benjamins

Kessler B. 1995. Computational dialectology in Irish Gaelic. *Proc. EACL-95: Conf. Eur. Chapter Assoc. Comput. Linguist., 6th, Dublin, Ireland*, pp. 60–67. San Francisco: Morgan Kaufman

Kessler B. 2001. *The Significance of Word Lists*. Stanford, CA: Cent. Study Lang. Inf.

Kondrak G. 2002. *Algorithms for language reconstruction*. PhD thesis, Univ. Tor. **http://www.cs.ualberta. ca/~kondrak**

Kondrak G. 2003. Phonetic alignment and similarity. *Comput. Hum.* 37:273–91

Kruskal JB, Dyen I, Black P. 1973. Some results from the vocabulary method of reconstructing language trees. In *Lexicostatistics in Genetic Linguistics*, ed. I Dyen, pp. 30–55. The Hague: Mouton

Lass R. 1990. How to do things with junk: exaptation in language change. *J. Linguist.* 26:79–102

Lass R. 1997. *Historical Linguistics and Language Change*. Cambridge, UK: Cambridge Univ. Press

Lightfoot DW. 2006. *How Languages Emerge*. Cambridge, UK: Cambridge Univ. Press

Mace R, Holden CJ, Shennan S, eds. 2005. *The Evolution of Cultural Diversity: A Phylogenetic Approach*. London: UCL Press

Manaster Ramer A, Hitchcock C. 1996. Glass houses: Greenberg, Ringe, and the mathematics of comparative linguistics. *Anthropol. Linguist.* 38:601–19

McMahon AMS, Heggarty P, McMahon R, Slaska N. 2005. Swadesh sublists and the benefits of borrowing: an Andean case study. *Trans. Philol. Soc.* 103:147–70

McMahon AMS, McMahon R. 2003. Finding families: quantitative methods in language classification. *Trans. Philol. Soc.* 101:7–55

McMahon AMS, McMahon R. 2006. *Language Classification by Numbers*. Oxford, UK: Oxford Univ. Press

Milroy L. 1987. *Language and Social Networks*. Oxford: Basil Blackwell. 2nd ed.

Minett JW, Wang WS-Y. 2003. On detecting borrowing: distance-based and character-based approaches. *Diachronica* 20:289–330

Mufwene S. 2001. *The Ecology of Language Evolution*. Cambridge, UK: Cambridge Univ. Press

Mufwene S. 2005. *Créole, Écologie Sociale, Évolution Linguistique*. Paris: L'Harmattan

Nakhleh L, Ringe DJ Jr, Warnow T. 2005. Perfect phylogenetic networks: a new methodology for reconstructing the evolutionary history of natural languages. *Language* 81:382–420

Nerbonne J, Heeringa W. 1997. Measuring dialect distance phonetically. *Proc. SIGPHON-97: Meet. ACL Spec. Interest Group Comput. Phonol., 3rd, Madrid, Spain*. **http://www.cogsci.ed.ac.uk/sigphon**

Nettle D. 1999. *Linguistic Diversity*. Oxford, UK: Oxford Univ. Press

Nicholls GK, Gray RD. 2006. Quantifying uncertainty in a stochastic model of vocabulary evolution. See Forster & Renfrew 2006, pp. 161–71

Nichols J. 1996. The comparative method as heuristic. See Durie & Ross 1996, pp. 39–89

Oakes MP. 2000. Computer estimation of vocabulary in protolanguage from word lists in four daughter languages. *J. Quant. Linguist.* 7:233–43

Ohala JJ. 2003. Phonetics and historical phonology. In *Handbook of Historical Linguistics*, ed. B Joseph, R Janda, pp. 669–86. Oxford, UK: Blackwell

Oswalt RL. 1970. The detection of remote linguistic relationships. *Comp. Stud. Hum. Verbal Behav.* 3:117–29

Oswalt RL. 1991. A method for assessing distant linguistic relationships. In *Sprung from Some Common Source: Investigations into the Prehistory of Languages*, ed. SM Lamb, ED Mitchell, pp. 389–404. Stanford, CA: Stanford Univ. Press

Pagel M. 2000. Maximum-likelihood models for glottochronology and for reconstructing linguistic phylogenies. See Renfrew et al. 2000, pp. 189–207

Pagel M, Atkinson QD, Meade A. 2007. Frequency of word-use predicts rates of lexical evolution throughout Indo-European history. *Nature* 449:717–20

Pagel M, Meade A. 2005. Bayesian estimation of correlated evolution across cultures: a case study of marriage systems and wealth transfer at marriage. See Mace et al. 2005, pp. 235–56

Pagel M, Meade A. 2006. Estimating rates of lexical replacement on phylogenetic trees of languages. See Forster & Renfrew 2006, pp. 173–82

Pierrehumbert JB. 2001. Exemplar dynamics: word frequency, lenition and contrast. In *Frequency and Emergence in Grammar*, ed. JL Bybee, P Hopper, pp. 137–57. Amsterdam: John Benjamins

Renfrew C, McMahon AMS, Trask RL, eds. 2000. *Time Depth in Historical Linguistics*. Cambridge, UK: McDonald Inst. Archaeol. Res.

Rexová K, Bastin Y, Frynta D. 2006. Cladistic analysis of Bantu languages: a new tree based on combined lexical and grammatical data. *Naturwissenschaften* 93:189–94

Rexová K, Frynta D, Zrzavy J. 2003. Cladistic analysis of languages: Indo-European classification based on lexicostatistical data. *Cladistics* 19:120–27

Richerson PJ, Boyd R. 2005. *Not By Genes Alone: How Culture Transformed Human Evolution*. Chicago, IL: Univ. Chicago Press

Ringe DA Jr, Warnow T, Taylor A. 2002. Indo-European and computational cladistics. *Trans. Philol. Soc.* 100:59–129

Ringe DA Jr. 1992. *On Calculating the Factor of Chance in Language Comparison*. Trans. Am. Philos. Soc. Vol. 82, Part 1. Philadelphia: Am. Philos. Soc.

Ringe DA Jr. 1993. A reply to Professor Greenberg. *Proc. Am. Philos. Soc.* 137:91–109

Ritt N. 2004. *Selfish Sounds and Linguistic Evolution: A Darwinian Approach to Language Change*. Cambridge, UK: Cambridge Univ. Press

Ross M, Durie M. 1996. Introduction. See Durie & Ross 1996, pp. 3–38

Vigilant L, Stoneking M, Harpending H, Hawkes R, Wilson AC. 1991. African populations and the evolution of human mitochondrial DNA. *Science* 253:1503–7

Wang WS-Y, Minett JW. 2005. Vertical and horizontal transmission in language evolution. *Trans. Philol. Soc.* 103:121–46

Warnow T, Evans SN, Ringe DA Jr, Nakhleh L. 2006. A stochastic model of language evolution that incorporates homoplasy and borrowing. See Forster & Renfrew 2006, pp. 75–87

Wedel A. 2006. Exemplar models, evolution and language change. *Linguist. Rev.* 23:247–74

Post-Post-Transition Theories: Walking on Multiple Paths

Manduhai Buyandelgeriyn

Department of Anthropology, Massachusetts Institute of Technology, Cambridge, Massachusetts 02139; email: manduhai@mit.edu

Annu. Rev. Anthropol. 2008. 37:235–50

The *Annual Review of Anthropology* is online at anthro.annualreviews.org

This article's doi: 10.1146/annurev.anthro.37.081407.085214

Key Words

ambiguity, postsocialism, neoliberalism, gender, culture

Abstract

This article reviews recent ethnographic works on the former Soviet Union, Eastern and Central Europe, and Mongolia that explore the experiences of people enduring drastic transformations following the collapse of socialism in 1990 and the consequent implementation of a neoliberal "shock therapy." The anthropologists working on postsocialist societies have shown that transition theories are inherently faulty and their implementation often had damaging results. The current condition is not a period of transition or "bridge" between socialism and capitalism. Instead individuals' activities, memory, social networks, and culturally specific values lead to uncertainty as a state of dynamic being. This article argues that uncertainty is a complex conceptual space that offers further opportunities to step away from the evolutionary mode of thinking and to develop theories of multiple ways of being.

INTRODUCTION

The term post-post-transition theories refers to the growing body of anthropological knowledge about the outcomes of the collapse of socialism and the subsequent implementation of neoliberal policies in the 1990s. I use this term in reviewing recent works on the former Soviet Union, Eastern and Central Europe, and Mongolia that reveal the experiences of drastic changes by a variety of actors. The cultures and people in these areas had little in common throughout their separate presocialist histories. Even though the outcomes of socialist and neoliberal policies imposed on them vary, some common experiences allow us to ask similar questions in these areas.

During socialism these countries shared a theory of social evolutionism based on the ideas of Morgan ([1877] 2000), Marx (1973), and Engels (1989) and directed their resources to building socialism and then communism as the highest stage of human civilization. As Hirsch (2005) has shown, the Soviet Union adopted evolutionism at the outset of the twentieth century to disprove German biological determinism—a theory of higher and lower races that placed Russia in a position inferior to the Europeans. Much of the politics of the Soviet Union throughout the twentieth century was directed at expediting their mobility through the unitary path of evolution and arriving at the same final stage as the Europeans. Social evolutionism can be defined as a belief in the power of progress and modernity, a framework for conceptualizing society and history, and a doctrine for legitimizing power and structuring everyday life. The end of socialism was an epistemic, as well as a social and economic, crisis.

Ironically, the end of Marxist-Leninist evolutionism was also the beginning of the transition theories, another version of evolutionism that operates on the assumption that all societies are parts of a global developmental continuum based on a free-enterprise-driven global economy. The practitioners of the transition theory—the neoliberal economists—hold that the road from totalitarianism to capitalism runs through a rupture known as "shock therapy"—a rapid demolition of state enterprises and support systems (Tökés 2000). My engagement with evolutionism in this article is through this specific modern version: the transition theories of neoliberalism. Rooted in evolutionism's previous problematic legacies such as the Enlightenment and Eurocentrism, transition theories mimic a notion of a single modernity as an objective stage of a unilinear history at which all societies arrive at some point through a complete break with the past. Through a reading of select ethnographies of postsocialism, I present the multiplicity of experiences and unprecedented outcomes against the assumption of transition theories' uniformity and certainty. In the process of writing, my engagement with these theories has necessarily also become a moral one. As the ethnographic accounts suggest, the neoliberal policies failed because of the assumption that market rules worked the same everywhere. That assumption was not based on ignorance, however, but on a contemptuous belief that cultural identities, values, and systems are obstacles to progress and that they need to be swept away by the transnational forces of modernization (Tökés 2000). It became clear to me, however, that the cultural differences that the transitologists had dismissed eventually engulfed the transition.

I explore the anthropologists' deconstruction of transition by showing how different aspects of cultures influence market capitalism thus creating unexpected outcomes. My focus is on the unpredictable as the hallmark of the ethnographies of postsocialism from which I derive some theoretical points about post-post-transition theories. In the first part, I focus on anthropologists' tracking of the metamorphoses of market elements as they shift into new sociocultural landscapes. Second, I explore the diversity of gender systems and their unpredictable influence on social changes and also show how a gendered approach affords deeper insights into the trickiest puzzles of postsocialism. I conclude the article by briefly presenting the developments in the studies of culture through specific themes that are directly relevant to evolutionism, such as the notion of "culture," and the transition of memory and history from the realm of the state to a more contested public space. I argue that the interdisciplinary character of postsocialism studies allowed anthropologists to develop insights that contributed to wider anthropological theory and that postsocialist places are increasingly seeing the current situation as a part of a given culture and society with its own dynamics, as opposed to something that is in transition to a version of the contemporary Euro-American world.

Before discussing the ethnographic accounts, it is useful to sort out some of the terminology and frameworks. First, by focusing on the vast area composed of the former Soviet Union, Eastern and Central Europe, and Mongolia, I create a conceptual space to destabilize the problematic division of the area into Asia and Europe. Challenging the boundaries of an established area is also one way to engage with the theory of social evolutionism, as it often has justified colonialism. Marxist theory and the notion of culture as a criterion for placing people on an evolutionary ladder helped to legitimate colonial and semicolonial projects, often under the rubrics of modernizing and civilizing the supposedly less cultured societies. Such projects also contributed to the delineation of geographical regions, which became associated with specific characteristics, assigned by the more "developed" West. Postsocialism does not correspond to a specific study area and is not limited to its institutionalized form as discussed by Hann (1993a), nor is it owned by one—especially with the growing number of studies on postsocialisms on the African continent, as well as in China, South-East Asia, and Latin America among other places—but is claimed as a conceptual space for developing theoretical insights.

The term transition has been debated by a number of anthropologists because it signals evolutionary progress that will arrive at a predetermined destination. In addressing the theories that have developed in response to the notion of transition, I use a double loop in the title post-post-transition. It highlights the complexity of the issue on several levels. Empirically, it shows the multidimensionality of the experiences of the people going through the simultaneous collapse of socialism and the hastily imposed neoliberal changes. The enduring nature of the experiences shows that there is no tangible line between the so-called transition and the so-called expected destination, thus the title begins to deconstuct the transition theories. On the theoretical side, the anthropological critique of interdisciplinary transition theories has led to a rethinking of mainstream anthropological theories as well. This kind of revision is discussed in the section on gender where its placement in a new context demanded reassesment of previous theories. Therefore, the double loop of post-post-transition moves us beyond predetermined ideas of transition to much more nuanced and unexpected newly emerging practices and ideas. The term has an ironic connotation as well: It gestures at the failures of most theories of transition, which incorporate the idea of a "pregiven future," in the form of "textbook capitalism" Burawoy & Verdery (1999). They note that among economists and social scientists who employ different transition theories, the neoliberal economists were convinced that the two grand narratives of modernity, socialism and neoliberal capitalism, must be bridged by "shock therapy," an almost overnight demolition of the socialist state enterprises and support systems. The transition did not lead to the promised world of capitalism. Thus post-post-transition theories are based on the exploration of the experiences of the peoples who accommodate, resist, interpret, and shape their lives in relation to, and despite, the failed transitions brought upon them.

THE METAMORPHOSES OF TRANSITION AND UNPREDICTABILITY

The disintegration of socialism affected all aspects of society, but shock therapy—the rapid dismantling of state enterprises and disorganized privatization—made the changes in the economic sphere much more visible than other aspects of change. Burawoy & Verdery (1999) in their edited volume *Uncertain Transition* were the first to theorize the changes from an anthropological perspective and respond to neoclassical, neoliberal, institutional theories, evolutionary economists, and sociologists. Burawoy & Verdery argue that the post-socialist transition is not a single prescribed road to an objective phase of Western-style capitalism. It is an uncertain process that leads to innovation when new rights and rules enmesh with old values and interests. The authors argue that the aftereffects of shock therapy were often the reincarnations of the very socialist practices that the economists tried to demolish. Many people acted exactly counter to the calculations of the market economists: Privatization was rejected, the market was avoided, and the demolition of the old caused resistance and reinvention of socialist practices in new forms.

Decollectivization in Transylvania (Verdery 1999), for instance, led to the creation of a new association that replaced the demolished collective. Although it was supposed to operate like a capitalist firm to generate revenue for a private ownership, because of the villagers' moral attachments to their assets, private ownership failed in favor of a collective one. Such manifestations of the past in the present (Haney 1999, Zbierski-Salameh 1999) are not nostalgia but a part of a system that works best for some people and they deliberately choose it. But things that seem to be from the past, such as barter relations, have proliferated not as legacies of the past but as outcomes of the monetization of the economy following shock therapy (Woodruff 1999). This is similar to the development of barter owing to the structural failures and the corresponding mistrust and fear discussed by Humphrey elsewhere (2002b). These are only a few examples of the unpredictability of economic life under new conditions. Verdery & Burawoy demonstrated that economy does not operate only through rules, but is influenced also by memories, re-lationships, and historically grounded cultural values.

This kind of theorization against the "therapists" was possible mainly owing to anthropological knowledge about socialism. A few, nonentheless powerful, works (Gellner 1980, Hann 1985, Humphrey 1983, Kligman 1988, Verdery 1983) had shown that socialism was wrought with contradictions, discrepancies, and competing realities behind what seemed to be a rigid totalitarian system. Below I describe what happens when complex, but also morally specific contexts are met with some specific ideas and tools that are supposed to produce definite outcomes.

In the introduction to a collection of her essays, Humphrey (2002a) highlights the fact that concepts such as market, trading, democracy, and global economy come from Euro-American traditions and that they are often taken for granted in those places. When these concepts are transplanted to new contexts, Humphrey finds that they work in bizarrely different ways, often because they receive different (and constantly changing) moral and cultural evaluations. For example, trading goods in the market—a straightforward activity in the Euro-American world—provokes ambivalent reactions in the postsocialist world. Throughout socialism, trade has been considered an immoral activity, a way of making profit without labor. As a result, the contradictions between material interests and socio-moral ones provoke feelings of shame, pride, guilt, collectivity (Heyat 2002, Kaneff 2002, Pine 2002, Watts 2002), and acute discomfort (Konstantinov 1996, Konstantinov et al. 1998, Patico 2005).

In her seminal article "Traders, 'Disorder' and Citizenship Regimes in Provincial Russia," Humphrey (2002b) also traces how the negative attitude toward traders escalated animosity in the city and perpetuated the organization of mafia. Humphrey tracks and weaves together the development of these events. The disintegration of the socialist distributive system opened up spaces for traders to take over the function of providing goods in a Russian provincial town. But the traders were suspicious outsiders who traveled across borders, often several of them in a single trip. They were regarded as parasites in contrast to the workers who produced goods. Trading was often linked with criminal activities associated with mafias and gangs, which alarmed the townspeople who were heavily dependent on the goods provided by the traders. The local government created rules and document requirements to regulate the traders' mobility and carried out crackdowns on shops and businesses. Not only did this visible violence perpetuate the local hostility toward the traders, but it also led to groupings of traders across borders, enhancing their kinship and professional networks. Traders' networks were increasingly transformed to become more like the very mafia and gangs that the locals feared because trading, which in a Euro-American context does not provoke strong emotional and moral reactions, was wrought with negative connotations in the postsocialist world.

Ambiguities surrounded other aspects of the market such as business elites (Humphrey 2002a); ordinary people did not know what to think about them. During the period of inflation and fluctuation, the value, function, and cultural meanings of money became ambiguous (Humphrey 1995; Lemon 1998; Pesmen 1995, 1996, 2000; Ries 2002). In response, goods (Ledeneva 2006), including some as disturbing as home-brewed alcohol, became accepted as currency (Rogers 2005). Even the seemingly positive changes such as privatization of property, especially land, and decollectivization—topics that received much attention (Alexander 2004; Creed 1995; Hann 1993b,c; Kideckel 1995; Lampland 2002; Sneath 2004; Verdery 1994)—provoked dubious reactions. Hann (2006) elaborates on peasants' critical reactions to the outcomes of privatization. Verdery (2003) thoroughly critiques economic theories of privatization, including rational choice, neoliberalism, and neoinstitutionalism. The expectations of privatization were not feasible in practical terms because of the discrepancies in cultural and social understandings of value between socialism and cap-

italism. Property ownership did not automatically lead to development as expected by the transitologists. It was a mistake, Verdery argues, to place the burden of cost-benefit on people who hardly had the resources to bear the costs. Socialism valued relations of reciprocity and obligation. Privatization threatened to undermine these relations through an emphasis on individual advantage and gain. Instead of expected improvement, privatization, at least in the Transylvanian village, brought demodernization and polarization and aggravated the sense of insecurity and economic anxiety.

SURVIVING TRANSITION AND THE MARKET

The same notions of reciprocity, collectivity, and networking, which are juxtaposed to the neoliberal market economy, helped individuals create alternative forms of security during the collapse of the official economy and when the new one cast them aside. Caldwell (2004) explores how, by developing "strategic intimacy" (p. 130) through friendship, holiday celebrations, and interactions in the soup kitchen, Muscovites created a sense of social security. For Muscovites, hunger meant the scarcity of social networks rather than scarcity of food. Help, support, and gift-giving were nonmonetary everyday economic transactions that constitute a part of the economy. Many anthropologists (Bruun & Odgaard 1996; Creed 1998; Hann 2006; Humphrey 2002a; Nazpary 2000; Sneath 1999, 2004) reported different survival strategies. Whereas rural Siberians diversified their herd composition and size (Metzo 2003), Bulgarians engaged in trader-tourism to create social stability, to avoid duties, and to maintain flexible identities (Konstantinov 1996).

With the flow of goods and services, the consumption and production of particular brands shaped, questioned, and structured ethnic, national (Rausing 2002), and class identities, and even spatialized one's belonging to imaginative geographies (Manning & Uplisashvili 2007). Much of a population's consumption then is viewed as a tool for transforming and developing new subjectivities. Yet the scholarship has also shown that people possess cunning strategies to survive without transforming themselves and without changing their previously developed values and ways of life. In Moscow and Poland, Western-style goods, services, and enterprises are appropriated in such a powerful way that the boundary between globalization and localization becomes irrelevant. Not only the French fry (Caldwell 2004), but even industrial enterprises are domesticated. Dunn (2004) explores the process of domesticating a Polish factory by a U.S. enterprise. It is ironic that the U.S. enterprise's attempt to transform Polish workers into post-Fordian flexible capitalist staff often looked more like the opposite: Polish factory workers domesticated Gerber (the U.S. factory) through strategies that they retained from socialism, such as personalizing their work relationships, values, and work space.

As discussed above, transition theories are inherently faulty; postsocialist moral and value systems, when merged with Western ideas, create unpredictable outcomes; and neoliberal principles do not suit the population's moral landscape. By no means has this review thus far addressed the full complexity and range of themes in the literature on postsocialist economy, but the overall direction seems clear. Anthropology's strength comes from talking to people rather than assuming what is best for them, following the life of communities for an extended time through various periods and events. But anthropologists also tend to seek out the marginalized, impoverished, and oppressed, thus exposing the damaging results of the careless policies promoted by neoliberal economists.

Anthropologists critique Western theories of transition, property relations, and policies that economists, sociologists, and political scientists assume are right for a population. They do so by exploring the lives of the people and revealing the metamorphoses of the concepts of the market economy, thus exposing the immateriality behind the assumptions made by other disciplines. Instead of looking for one predeter-

mined path and a single destination, the state of uncertainty and constant change anthropologists uncover offers a chance to explore the multiple paths that ordinary people follow to survive the unexpected changes and manuever through the opaque and shifting landscapes of the new socioeconomic formations.

THE GENDER OF POST-POST-TRANSITION

Although a number of scholars (Bloch 2004; Gal & Kligman 2000a,b; Humphrey 1998; True 2003) have highlighted the fact that men and women have experienced postsocialist transformations in vastly different ways, until recently, gendered analyses have been sparse in the major works on economy, identity, and politics. Fortunately, recent studies have demonstrated that gender has been enmeshed in all aspects of ongoing socioeconomic microprocesses. Because gender is a process and has numerous variations even within one culture, an awareness of gender completely defies the idea of a unified transition. Below, I explore some of this diversity of gender in relation to the dynamics of the past and the present and larger global powers. Then, with two ethnographic examples (Bloch 2004, True 2003) I show how gender provides a necessary lens for comprehending the chaotic and uncertain changes in nuanced ways that might otherwise get overlooked.

A Multiplicity of Gender Systems

Several edited volumes based on the collaboration between Eastern and Euro-American gender and women studies groups have been published since the 1990s. One of the first joint ventures linking women from postsocialist Eastern Europe and Western feminists resulted in an edited volume by Funk & Mueller (1993), *Gender Politics and Post-Communism.* It consists of articles written by Eastern European feminists on a variety of issues including women's oppression under socialism, notions of emancipation, and the problems of combining motherhood duties and work pressures. Each article is methodologically different, reflecting the individual author's scholarly background, personal voice, and political and moral engagements. It is a substantial contribution to the theories of post-post-transition in a number of ways.

These Eastern European scholars challenge the idea of a transition as a unified process that started in the early 1990s. They do so by giving a detailed account of the transformations in gender relations and women's positions throughout all stages of socialism, not just after its collapse. Several diagnostic articles also lay out theories about the failures of socialist feminism. Therefore, by presenting the achievements and the failures of women's struggles for emancipation and equality throughout their recent history, these scholars defy any notion of "transition" as an objective unilinear process with definitive beginnings and endings. Instead, they show that gender politics are uncertain, constantly in flux, incomplete, shifting, and embedded in the historical and political landscape of a particular community or country. Finally, Duhacek's (1993) compelling contribution to the volume explains the failures of women's movements throughout history. Some argue that women's movements constantly failed because they had been attempts at inclusion in linear time only as a part of the history of civilization, but not as autonomous beings in their own rights. The first-generation feminists called for equal rights on the basis that women were rational beings like men. The socialist women demanded equal rights as fighters in a class struggle and as workers of the state. In both cases women demanded equal rights not as human beings in their own right, but because of their potential contributions to movements and causes championed by men. Whether arguing for equality in terms of rationality or class struggle, women did not seek to claim autonomous spaces for themselves, but in a space paved by men and by using the language of the male-dominated discourse. As a collaboration between American and Eastern European feminists, the volume makes a step toward bridging the dichotomy of Us versus Them and loosening the boundaries of the world's hierarchical division into area studies. Fostering an equality of learning and sharing by the two groups, the collection breaks down the offensive borders of "post-Soviet" and "Western" anthropology (a move also suggested by Balzer 1995a, Rethman 1997, and Verdery 1991).

The collection shows a great discrepancy between Eastern European and Western scholars' constructions of gender, values, women's issues, and feminisms. With more emphasis on the sameness between men and women, Western feminism tends to be irrelevant and distant from the concerns and interests of Eastern European women, who emphasize the differences between men and women and do not consider having attributes of femininity and receiving help from men to be a sign of weakness. Even when the Eastern European women try to collaborate and address common issues and problems, differences and barriers in the discourse between the two groups of women inevitably emerge. The two groups discover notable barriers to understanding each other, as well as misconceptions and biases against each other. Even the collection itself shows, therefore, that there is no one gender, and no one single feminism, that would "fit" into one transition.

The dynamic relationship between gender systems and larger structures of power and domination has been explored by Gal & Kligman in their two books (2000a,b), which were produced as collaborative efforts by Eastern European, British, and U.S. scholars. Their goal was to explore how notions of gender are dynamically transformed by nationalist politics, ethnic violence, and the state and to analyze how transition is redefining gender relations and the notions of masculinity and femininity. Because of the fluidity and unpredictability of the way gender affects social processes, the current transformations after socialism do not conform to one predetermined path, but instead take many. The authors show how gender is always influenced by politics such as in abortion law, while politics are also shaped through debates on abortion because the latter are used by electoral candidates as tools for gaining advantage in their campaigns. Reproductive politics affect other spheres of women's life, including work, career, and their relationships with men. Gal and Kligman demonstrate their argument by analyzing the dynamic discrepancies among rhetoric, practices, and women's subjectivities. For example, they trace how, despite socialist state rhetoric's proclamation of women's emancipation, the pronatal policy, on the contrary, had perpetuated the oppression of women. Reproduction has been one of the core analyses in relation to nationalism, especially in Romania. During Ceausescu's regime in Romania, the reproductive capacity of women was utilized for building the body of the nation (Kligman 1998, Verdery 1996). These gender studies are, as in most places, dominated by studies of women. A male crisis has been noted by anthropologists such as Bloch (2004) and True (2003) but has not been pursued in depth.

These explorations of gender systems demonstrate that diversity destabilizes the possibility of an easy transition. Especially once the East and Central European feminists presented their questions, problems, and assumptions, it became clear that the problems of women in one country can be considered emancipation in another, and what some women consider a nuisance may not bother women in other places (or these problems have been interpreted as something else). We cannot yet answer the question, "Transition from what to what?"

Gender Deep

Recent scholarship that examines individuals' subjective experiences through the lens of gender has shed light on the aspects that go beyond the expectations of transition theorists and which otherwise would have remained unexplored. For instance in her ethnography of the residential schools of a far eastern Russian town, Bloch (2004) asks why, despite the brutality of the Soviet system, most people still want to reinstate it. Why is resistance to the state not automatic? I emphasize these questions because other anthropologists have asked

similar questions (e.g., Adams 1999). Bloch's answer stems from her exploration of the gendered politics of residential schooling and labor. She was especially puzzled by particularly strong attachments to Soviet cultural practices among older Evenki women. The Soviets' consistent efforts to emancipate women made them take an active part in building the state. Women were the subjects of transformation more so than men were. Both the residential schools and the specific arrangements of economic production saved women from the tyranny of patriarchy. The state organized reindeer herding and established nomadic camps (brigades). Herding was made into men's work, whereas most women resided in the sedentary center to work in clerical, administrative, service, factory, and cultural jobs. As a result, women were schooled longer and better educated and were considered more cultured, and so they were able to partake in the structures of power. Bloch further explored the range of perspectives regarding the Soviet system among different generations, ranging from nostalgia to accommodation, ambivalence, disapproval, resistance, and maneuvering. Each perspective loosely corresponds to an aspect of the state's power that had more impact on particular individuals' lives. For instance, for the elder Evenkis, the Soviet system was remembered against the backdrop of colonialism by Imperial Russia. The inconsistencies and porosity of state power that impeded work in the community actually allowed intellectuals to partake in activities to strengthen the system, such as designing the school curriculum. Therefore, contrary to the idea that intellectuals were opposed to the state, Bloch's research shows that intellectuals participated in state building. In the recent era of incipient market capitalism, marginalized and impoverished women depended on the school system for resources. But some younger female entrepreneurs who were able to get by without any support resisted the school as a site of creating socialist dependency, and these are the women who felt that school was a place for disciplining and limiting their personal freedom. It is particularly through a gendered approach, then, that Bloch went beyond the dichotomy of power and resistance to locate more subtle and multiple forms through which individuals related to the system.

Aside from the repercussions of socialism, ethnographies have shown that gender is also influenced by globalization, Western-style consumerism, advertising, media, Euro-American and international feminisms, and civil society. True (2003) gave a sustained critique of neoliberalism, Marxism, and institutionalism; these theories all overlook the gendered aspects of transitions and base their analyses on formal political and economic institutions. True was also critical of feminists who have cast women as victims of the market. She offered a gendered but dialectical approach in which women are agents, able to use their resources to accommodate the changes but without necessarily undergoing drastic subjective transformations. She argues that this can occur because in some cases, the Eastern European women are more educated than the feminists from Euro-America. The former have a history of emancipation and participation in labor. They are equipped to work and think about other cultures' impacts on them, and in this way, they are not victims of globalization but can modify and appropriate globalization to suit their interests and needs. A clever example is the Czech transformation of *Cosmopolitan*. The Czech editors of the magazine, a former women's magazine, are much more feminist than their U.S. headquarters. Instead of producing a U.S.-style magazine aimed at fashioning consumers, the Czech version *Cosmopolitan* deviates from the American themes and publishes material that alerts women about issues of sexual harassment, violence, human trafficking, health and the importance of electoral political systems as opposed to promoting consumption. In this way, it is Czech women who have transformed *Cosmopolitan*, not the other way—the intended way—around.

This example illustrates the way the values and principles from socialism were able to appropriate, shape, and modify the allegedly more modern and progressive Western ideas and approaches. By exploring the active modification of the Czech *Cosmopolitan* by Eastern European women, True (2003) emphasizes their empowerment instead of victimization. While one may agree with True (2003) that emphasizing women's suffering as a result of the shock therapy casts them as helpless victims, such portrayal may still be necessary for neoliberal policy-makers to realize the failures of their work.

So far the theoretical concerns of gender studies are neatly related to the state political economy, the chaos and uncertainty of the market, and the reformulation of the notions of femininity and masculinity in the market era. As new rules of the economy, consumption practices, and work demands had been transforming daily lives and structures, women became depicted as new subjects as well. Most notably, women's activities after socialism challenge some taken-for-granted notions about women's empowerment versus marginalization. Consider Russian nightclub entertainers abroad—are they victims of trafficking or entrepreneurs? Bloch (2003) explored the question by conducting an in-depth study of women's backgrounds, education, their relationship with their bosses, and the ways in which they spent their money. Unlike the stereotypical night club dancers who come from uneducated and impoverished backgrounds, these women were mostly university educated. But after socialism, which provided jobs mostly in public service, these women had few opportunities to find satisfying jobs at home. As international night club dancers, they earned enough to support their families back home. Together they felt superior to their bosses who were uneducated and uncouth and who did not speak foreign languages. Instead of feeling oppressed and victimized, these women found travel overseas and audiences exciting and empowering.

Despite such research that offers fresh insights, overall, gender-based analyses have been slow to take off. Scholarship in the 1990s was based mostly on edited volumes that were born from the international conferences that seek to determine future goals, bridging regional, theoretical, and other gaps to foster collaborative research. Some ethnographies (and ethno-graphically informed works) (Bloch 2003, 2004; Dunn 2004; Einhorn 2003; Ghodsee 2005; Rethman 2001; Ries 1997) have been published since the late 1990s. Scholars who are outside of anthropology have adopted ethnographic methods of long-term fieldwork along with interviews.

SITES OF CULTURE

As much as the post-post-transition theories have considered the uncertain transformations in political economy, they have also attended to changes in culture in the broadest sense. The collapse of socialism was an epistemic crisis that challenged the evolutionary scheme of thought. Thus culture is officially no longer an ideolog-ical weapon controlled by the state nor is it a measurement of sophistication and refinement, although such functions remain in practice in these societies overall. What, then, do the an-thropological studies of cultures look like dur-ing a time of uncertainty, rapid transformation, economic anxiety, and instability?

The enormous diversity of themes and issues addressed by anthropologists defies any gener-alizing frameworks. Instead of addressing geo-graphic divisions and corresponding themes, I find that building conversations around themes corresponds to this review's aim to destabilize the taken-for-granted divisions of the world. Therefore, I structure the following brief dis-cussion around the themes of violence, memory, resistance, and identity.

State violence and its memories have been manifested as neurasthenia (Skultans 1998), as ghosts and spirits (Buyandelgeriyn 2007, Jones 1994, Vitebsky 2005), and as fantastic images such as blue elephants (Humphrey 2003). Culturally specific, metaphorical, and re-moved from actual events, these manifestations of memory encompassed a sense of ambiva-lence toward the past, the pain, and the sense of powerlessness against the state that controls memory. They speak to studies of the politics of memory, such as the debates on settling ac-counts (Borneman 1997), the politics of an un-wanted past (Schoeberlein 2004), and the ways the current Mongolian state controls the pub-lic life of memory (Kaplonski 2002). Studies of more recent violence in former Yugoslavia ad-dress different issues. Here, knowledge about death is not metaphorical or distanced, but very specific and tangible: People want to iden-tify the bodies of their dead relatives, see their clothes, and visit the places of death (Hayden 1994, Wagner 2008). As Wagner shows, even the results of DNA testing are contested by the family members of the dead when emotions and memories become part of the knowledge-seeking process. Tishkov's account (2004) on war in Chechnya reveals how the influence of the larger powers has been transformed into the routinization of killing and the erasure of humility among recruits and armed civilians. In her study of the Chernobyl catastrophe, Petryna (2002) provides insight from a medical anthropologist by showing how health or ab-sence of it structures individuals in the matrix of power and citizenry.

Related to violence, the politics of rewriting history, acquiring knowledge, and reconfigur-ing identity have concerned many anthropolo-gists (Bloch 2000, 2001; Bloch & Kendall 2004; Borneman 2004; Boyer 2005; Empson 2007; Grant 1995; Ssorin-Chaikov 2003). Kaplonski's (2004) study of social memory in Mongolia in the midst of shifting and controversial identity formation demonstrated that memory is based on the identities of historical heroes rather than on spaces or places. This was true especially during the time of democratization and when new elites competed for power.

Some intriguing research has emerged on the cultural politics that had flourished in un-official arenas during socialism, outside of the realm of the state. In such areas, the "ethical and aesthetic complexities" took a multitude of "creative, imaginative, and often paradoxi-cal cultural forms" (Yurchak 2006, p. 9). The "evocative transcripts" that could be inter-preted in multiple ways (Humphrey 1994), hidden rituals (Balzer 1992, 1995a; Vitebsky 1995, 2005), ironies, anecdotes, small-scale poems, and the uncanny (Yurchak 2006), politicized, and subversive art (Erjavec & Jay 2003) all constituted counterculture and a cynical critique of negative developments at the outset of the changes in the 1990s that were cast as moral (Ries 2002). The cultural developments among the colonized people of the former Russian Empire differ from those among the people from the European part of Russia. The colonial past of the former is embedded in ambiguous resistance to the Soviet past, which is mediated through rituals, folk medicine, and attitudes toward the state (Balzer 1996, 1999, 2001, 2005; Bloch 2001; Rethman 2001). Sabloff (2001) argued that Mongolia has its own concept of democracy from its distant history. Grant (2005) took up a study of the dominant group. He has shown how Russian colonial settlers reinterpreted their colonial presence in the Caucasus—not as colonizers, but as prisoners—a Russian antidote to colonial sentiments.

The ongoing events of a social, political, and geopolitical nature in various parts of the post-socialist world have directed the studies of culture toward ethnic and nationalist politics, identity formation, state building, religious revival, and conversion. Therefore, the politics of nationalism, ethnicity, and identity (Bulag 1998, Goluboff 2003, Lemon 2000) are about dynamic contestation with other identities and respond to others' prejudices, biases, and stereotypes. The creation of new spaces, borders, and political formations, as well as demolitions of previously existing ones, led to the emergence of the sites of identity politics where culture is used, created, borrowed, or ignored (Abramson 2000, Adams 2005, Berdahl 1999, Bilaniuk 2005, Pelkmans 2006).

Several additional themes taken up by anthropologists include globalization and the penetration of Western-style consumption, which also overlap with gender studies (Berdahl et al. 2000, Urban 2004). Some fruitful scholarship exploring religious politics, conversions, and contestations has begun to emerge (Rasanayagam 2006a,b; Wanner 2007). New and exciting studies include the transformation of the public sphere through film in Poland (Fischer 2003); the politics of emo-

tions in response to the dissatisfaction of the failed promises of "transition" (Hann 2006); the new political- and media-generated spaces of the color-coded "rose revolution" in Georgia (Manning 2007); transformations of the post-socialist city [emergence of homeless, anomie, migrants, and the change of the urban landscape (Alexander et al. 2007)], and informal practices of election campaigns, corruption, shadow economy, double accountancy, and other illegal and semilegal activities in Russia (Ledeneva 2006).

Anthropologists are skilled in deconstructing generalizations, stereotypes, and searches for universal laws. Such skills have been well employed in taking apart transition theories by exploring the specifics of cultural identities. The attack on evolutionary theories and their variants is not new in anthropology. But a number of new aspects are worthy of revisiting in a brief summary. First, in the process of deconstructing "transition," anthropologists have represented political economy as consisting of micropolitics that are uncertain and unpredictable. They have emphasized the fact that individuals' participation, resistance, memory, nostalgia, ways of life, networks, and communities are integral parts of the politico-economic changes. Although this is well understood by anthropologists, it is insufficiently considered by other disciplines.

Second, the vast majority of research shows that the market economy in non-Western contexts operates much more on the basis of the rules of local cultures, kinship, and community rather than the rules in force in Western contexts. Instead of the expected homogenizing of local cultures, the market economy has called into greater prominence the diversity of cultures that were less visible before. Moreover, the new impositions of neoliberalism have created new culturally specific relationships, languages, and practices that have come to be considered traditional.

Third, in this review I emphasize gender as one major component of the post-post-transition theories. This is because gender as a concept and as an analytical tool has offered new insights and findings. A newly established bridge between Western and Eastern European feminists fosters an understanding of each others' differences rather than subsuming them under one theoretical canon. This in turn helps to obliterate the unequal power relations between West and East. The gendered approach once again has demonstrated its relevance by explaining the issues that emerged anew after socialism, such as the situatedness of resistance and women's empowerment in the marginalized and stereotyped space of night clubs.

Fourth, although culture cannot be separated from the political economy and gender, in this review, "culture" is used specifically in relation to the practices that have emerged as consequences of the state's collapse. Because the state is no longer the sole owner of culture, the literature encompasses numerous themes and questions from consumption practices to the transformation of city life and election campaigns. In my attempt to address the issues related directly to the postsocialist state, I emphasize violence and memories, rewriting of history, and unoffical practices during both socialist and neoliberal regimes because the new practices are directly related to and shaped by the repercussions of the socialist state, including the emotional and moral spheres. This brings us back to the question of uncertainty. The past is evoked to serve the uncertain present. Uncertainty helps us revisit our preconceived notions and find an opportunity to understand the diversity of practices from a new angle.

DISCLOSURE STATEMENT

The author is not aware of any biases that might be perceived as affecting the objectivity of this review.

ACKNOWLEDGEMENTS

My very special thanks go to Christopher Kaplonski, Melissa Caldwell, Katrina Moore, Mary Steedly, Nicole Newendorp, and my research assistant Xiyue Wang for consistent and thorough help throughout the long process of conducting research and writing this piece.

LITERATURE CITED

Abramson DM. 2000. Socialism's bastard children. *Polit. Leg. Anthropol. Rev.* 23(1):49–64

Adams LL. 1999. The mascot researcher: identity, power, and knowledge in fieldwork. *J. Contemp. Ethnogr.* 28(4):331–63

Adams LL. 2005. Modernity, postcolonialism, and theatrical form in Uzbekistan. *Slavic Rev.* 64(2):333–54

Alexander C. 2004. Value, relations, and changing bodies: privatization and property rights in Khazakhstan. See Verdery & Humphrey 2004, pp. 251–74

Alexander C, Buchli V, Humphrey C, eds. 2007. *Urban Life in Post-Soviet Russia*. London: Univ. Coll. London Press

Balzer MM. 1992. Turmoil in the Russian mini-empire. *Perspective* 2(3):2–7

Balzer MM, ed. 1995a. *Culture Incarnate: Native Ethnography in Russia*. Armonk, NY: ME Sharpe

Balzer MM. 1995b. Homelands, leadership and self rule: interethnic relations in the Russian Federation North. *Polar Geogr.* 19.4:284–305

Balzer MM. 1996. Changing images of the Shaman: folklore and politics in the Sakha Republic (Yakutia). *Shaman* 4.1–2:1–16

Balzer MM. 1999. *The Tenacity of Ethnicity: A Siberian Saga in Global Perspective*. Princeton, NJ: Princeton Univ. Press

Balzer MM. 2001. Healing Failed Faith? Contemporary Siberian Shamanism. *Anthropol. Humanism* 26.2:134–49

Balzer MM. 2005. Whose Steeple is higher? Religious competition in Siberia. *Relig. State Soc.* 33.1:57–69

Berdahl D. 1999. *Where the World Ended: Reunification and Identity in the German Borderland*. Berkeley: Univ. Calif. Press

Berdahl D, Bunzl M, Lampland M, eds. 2000. *Altering States: Ethnographies of Transition in Eastern Europe and the Former Soviet Union*. Ann Arbor: Univ. Mich. Press

Bilaniuk L. 2005. *Contested Tongues: Language Politics and Cultural Correction in Ukraine*. Ithaca, NY: Cornell Univ. Press

Bloch A. 2000. Authenticating tradition: material culture, youth, and belonging in central Siberia. *Mus. Anthropol.* 23(3):42–57

Bloch A. 2001. Cruise ships and prison camps: reflections from the Russian Far East on museums and the crafting of history. *Pac. Sci.* 55(4):377–88

Bloch A. 2003. Victims of trafficking or entrepreneurial women? Narratives of post-Soviet entertainers in Turkey. *Can. Woman Stud.* 22(3–4):152–58

Bloch A. 2004. *Red Ties and Residential Schools: Indigenous Siberians in a Post-Soviet State*. Philadelphia: Univ. Penn. Press

Bloch A, Kendall L. 2004. *The Museum at the End of the World: Encounters in the Russian Far East*. Philadelphia: Univ. Penn. Press

Borneman J. 1997. *Settling Accounts: Violence, Justice, and Accountability in Postsocialist Europe*. Princeton, NJ: Princeton Univ. Press

Borneman J, ed. 2004. *Death of the Father: An Anthropology of the End in Political Authority*. New York: Berghahn Books

Boyer D. 2005. *Spirit and System: Media, Intellectuals, and the Dialectic in Modern German Culture*. Chicago: Univ. Chicago Press

Bruun O, Odgaard O, eds. 1996. *Mongoliain Transition*. Surrey, UK: Curzon Press

Bulag U. 1998. *Nationalism and Hybridity in Mongolia*. New York: Clarendon

Burawoy M, Verdery K, eds. 1999. *Uncertain Transition: Ethnographies of Change in the Postsocialist World*. Lanham, MD: Rowman & Littlefield

Buyandelgeriyn M. 2007. Dealing with uncertainty: shamans, marginal capitalism, and the remaking of history in postsocialist Mongolia. *Am. Ethnol.* 34(1):127–47

Caldwell ML. 2004. Domesticating the French fry: McDonald's and consumerism in Moscow. *J. Consum. Cult.* 4(1):5–26

Creed G. 1995. An old song in a new voice: decollectivization in Bulgaria. In *East European Communities: The Struggle for Balance in Turbulent Times*, ed. D Kideckel, pp. 25–45. Boulder, CO: Westview

Creed G. 1998. *Domesticating Revolution: From Socialist Reform to Ambivalent Transition in a Bulgarian Village*. University Park: Penn. State Univ. Press

Duhacek D. 1993. Women's time in the former Yugoslavia. See Funk & Mueller 1993, pp. 131–37

Dunn EC. 2004. *Privatizing Poland: Baby Food, Big Business, and the Remaking of Labor*. Ithaca, NY: Cornell Univ. Press

Einhorn B. 2003 [1993]. *Cinderella Goes to Market. Citizenship, Gender, and Women's Movement in East Central Europe*. London: Verso. New ed.

Empson R. 2007. Enlivened memories: recalling absence and loss in Mongolia. In *Ghosts of Memory: Essays on Remembrance and Relatedness*, ed. J Carsten, pp. 58–83. Oxford: Blackwell

Engels F. 1989. *Socialism: Utopian and Scientific*. New York: Pathfinder. 2nd ed.

Erjavec A, Jay M, eds. 2003. *Postmodernism and the Postsocialist Condition: Politicized Art Under Late Socialism*. Berkeley: Univ. Calif. Press

Fischer MMJ. 2003. Post-avant-garde tasks of Polish film: ethnographic *Odklamane*. In *Emergent Forms of Life and the Anthropological Voice*. Durham, NC: Duke Univ. Press

Funk N, Mueller M, eds. 1993. *Gender Politics and Post-Communism: Reflections from Eastern Europe and the Former Soviet Union*. New York: Routledge

Gal S, Kligman G. 2000a. *The Politics of Gender after Socialism: A Comparative Historical Essay*. Princeton, NJ: Princeton Univ. Press

Gal S, Kligman G, eds. 2000b. *Reproducing Gender: Politics, Publics, and Everyday Life after Socialism*. Princeton, NJ: Princeton Univ. Press

Gellner E, ed. 1980. *Soviet and Western Anthropology*. London: Duckworth

Ghodsee K. 2005. *The Red Riviera: Gender, Tourism, and Postsocialism on the Black Sea*. Durham, NC: Duke Univ. Press

Goluboff SL. 2003. *Jewish Russians: Upheavals in a Moscow Synagogue*. Philadelphia: Univ. Penn. Press

Grant B. 1995. *In the Soviet House of Culture: A Century of Perestroika*. Princeton, NJ: Princeton Univ. Press

Grant B. 2005. The good Russian prisoner: naturalizing violence in the Caucasus mountains. *Cult. Anthropol.* 20(1):39–67

Gray PA. 2004. *The Predicament of an Indigenous Movement in Chukotka, Russia's Far North Region*. New York: Cambridge Univ. Press

Haney L. 1999. "But we are still mothers:" gender, the state, and the construction of need in postsocialist Hungary. See Burawoy & Verdery 1999, pp. 151–87

Hann CM. 1985. *A Village Without Solidarity: Polish Peasants in Years of Crisis*. New Haven, CT: Yale Univ. Press

Hann CM, ed. 1993a. *Socialism: Ideals, Ideologies, and Local Practice*. New York: Routledge

Hann CM. 1993b. From production to property: decollectivizationand the family-land relationship in contemporary Hungary. *Man* 28:299–320

Hann CM. 1993c. Property relations in the New Eastern Europe: the case of specialist cooperatives in Hungary. In *The Curtain Rises: Rethinking Culture, Ideology, and the State in Eastern Europe*, ed. HG De Soto, DG Anderson, pp. 99–119. Atlantic Highlands, NJ: Humanities Press

Hann CM. 2006. *"Not the Horse We Wanted!": Postsocialism, Neoliberalism, and Eurasia*. Münster: Lit Verlag

Hayden MR. 1994. Recounting the dead: the rediscovery and redefinition of wartime massacres in late-and post-communist Yugoslavia. See Watson 1994, pp. 167–85

Heyat F. 2002. Women and the culture of entrepreneurship in Soviet and Post-Soviet Azerbaijan. See Mandel & Humphrey 2002, pp. 19–32

Hirsch F. 2005. *Empire of Nations: Ethnographic Knowledge and the Making of the Soviet Union*. Ithaca, NY: Cornell Univ. Press

Humphrey C. 1983. *Karl Marx Collective: Economy, Society and Religion in a Siberian Collective Farm*. Cambridge, UK: Cambridge Univ. Press

Humphrey C. 1994. Remembering and "enemy": the Bogd Khaan in twentieth-century Mongolia. See Watson 1994, pp. 21–41

Humphrey C. 1995. Creating a culture of disillusionment: consumption in Moscow 1993, a chronicle of changing times. In *Worlds Apart*, ed. D Miller, pp. 43–69. London: Routledge

Humphrey C. 1998. *Marx Went Away, but Karl Stayed Behind*. Ann Arbor: Univ. Mich. Press

Humphrey C. 2002a. *The Unmaking of Soviet Life: Everyday Economies after Socialism*. Ithaca, NY: Cornell Univ. Press

Humphrey C. 2002b. Traders, "disorder" and citizenship regimes in Provincial Russia. See Humphrey 2002a, pp. 69–99

Humphrey C. 2003. Stalin and the blue elephant: paranoia and complicity in post-communist metahistories. In *Transparency and Conspiracy: Ethnographies of Suspicion in the New World Order*, ed. HG West, T Sanders, pp. 175–203. Durham, NC: Duke Univ. Press

Jones ES. 1994. Old ghosts and new chains: ethnicity and memory in the Georgian Republic. See Watson 1994, pp. 149–67

Kaneff D. 2002. The shame and pride of market activity: morality, identity and trading in postsocialist rural Bulgaria. See Mandel & Humphrey 2002, pp. 33–52

Kaplonski C. 2002. Thirty thousand bullets: remembering political repression in Mongolia. In *Historical Injustice and Democratic Transition in Eastern Asia and Northern Europe: Ghosts at the Table of Democracy*, ed. K Christie, R Cribb, pp. 155–68. London: RoutledgeCurzon

Kaplonski C. 2004. *Truth, History and Politics in Mongolia: The Memory of Heroes*. London: RoutledgeCurzon

Kideckel D. 1995. *East European Communities: The Struggle for Balance in Turbulent Times*, ed. D Kideckel. Boulder, CO: Westview

Kligman G. 1988. *The Wedding of the Dead: Ritual, Poetics, and Popular Culture in Transylvania*. Berkeley: Univ. Calif. Press

Kligman G. 1998. *The Politics of Duplicity: Controlling Reproduction in Ceausescu's Romania.* Berkeley: Univ. Calif. Press

Konstantinov Y. 1996. Patterns of reinterpretation: trader-tourism in the Balkans (Bulgaria) as a picaresque metaphorical enactment of post-totalitarianism. *Am. Ethnol.* 23(4):762–82

Konstantinov Y, Kressel G, Thuen T. 1998. Outclassed by former outcasts: petty trading in Varna. *Am. Ethnol.* 25(4):729–45

Lampland M. 2002. The advantages of being collectivized: comparative farm managers in the postsocialist economy. In *Postsocialism: Ideals and Practices in Eurasia*, ed. CM Hann, pp. 31–56. London/New York: Routledge

Ledeneva AV. 2006. *How Russia Really Works: The Informal Practices that Shaped Post-Soviet Politics and Business.* Ithaca, NY: Cornell Univ. Press

Lemon A. 1998. "Your eyes are green like dollars": counterfeit cash, national substance, and currency apartheid in 1990s Russia. *Cult. Anthropol.* 13(1):22–55

Lemon A. 2000. *Between Two Fires: Gypsy Performance and Romani Memory from Pushkin to Postsocialism.* Durham, NC: Duke Univ. Press

Mandel R, Humphrey C, eds. 2002. *Markets and Moralities: Ethnographies of Postsocialism.* Oxford: Berg

Manning P. 2007. Rose-colored glasses? Color revolutions and cartoon chaos in postsocialist Georgia. *Cult. Anthropol.* 22(2)171–213

Manning P, Upshlisashvili 2007. "Our beer": ethnographic brands in postsocialist Georgia. *Am. Anthropol.* 109(4):626–41

Marx K. 1973. *Grundrisse.* Harmondsworth: Penguin

Metzo K. 2003. Whither Peasants in Siberia?: agricultural reform, subsistence, and being rural. *Cult. Agric.* 25(1):11–25

Morgan LH. (1877) 2000. *Ancient Society.* New Brunswick, NJ: Transaction

Nazpary J. 2000. Post-soviet chaos: violence and dispossession in Kazakhstan. *Am. Ethnol.* 30(2):328–29

Patico J. 2005. To be happy in a Mercedes: tropes of value and ambivalent visions of marketization. *Am. Ethnol.* 32(3):479–96

Pelkmans M. 2006. *Defending the Border: Identity, Religion, and Modernity in the Republic of Georgia.* Ithaca, NY: Cornell Univ. Press

Pesmen D. 1995. Standing bottles, washing deals, and drinking "for the soul" in a Siberian City. *Anthropol. East Eur. Rev.* 13(2):65–75

Pesmen D. 1996. Do not have a hundred rubles, have instead a hundred friends: money and sentiment in a Perestroika-post-soviet Siberian City. *Ir. J. Anthropol.* 1:3–22

Pesmen D. 2000. "A boggy, soggy, squitchy picture, truly": notes on image making in anthropology and elsewhere. *Anthropol. Humanism* 25(2):111–19

Petryna A. 2002. *Life Exposed: Biological Citizens after Chernobyl.* Princeton, NJ: Princeton Univ. Press

Pine F. 2002. Dealing with money: zlotys, dollars and other currencies in the Polish Highlands. See Mandel & Humphrey 2002, pp. 75–101

Rasanayagam J. 2006a. I'm not a Wahhabi: state power and Muslim orthodoxy in Uzbekistan. In *The Postsocialist Religious Question: Faith and Power in Central Asia and East-Central Europe*, ed. CM Hann, pp. 99–125. Münich: Lit Verlag

Rasanayagam J. 2006b. Post-soviet Islam: an anthropological perspective. *Central Asian Survey* 25(3):219–33

Rausing S. 2002. Re-constructing the 'normal': identity and the consumption of western goods in Estonia. See Mandel & Humphrey 2002, pp. 127–43

Rethman P. 1997. Chto Delat'? Ethnography in the post-Soviet cultural context. *Am. Anthropol.* 99:770–74

Rethman P. 2001. *Tundra Passages: Gender and History in the Russian Far East.* University Park, PA: Penn. State Univ. Press

Ries N. 1997. *Russian Talk: Culture and Conversation Dring Perestroika.* Ithaca, NY: Cornell Univ. Press

Ries N. 2002. "Honest bandits" and "warped people": Russian narratives about money, corruption, and moral decay. In *Ethnography in Unstable Places: Everyday Lives in Contexts of Dramatic Political Change*, ed. C Greenhouse, E Mertz, K Warren, pp. 276–315. Durham, NC: Duke Univ. Press

Rogers D. 2005. Moonshine, money, and the politics of liquidity in rural Russia. *Am. Ethnol.* 32(1):63–81

Schoeberlein J. 2004. Doubtful dead fathers and musical corpses: what to do with the dead Stalin, Lenin, and Tsar Nicholas? In *Death of the Father: An Anthropology of the End in Political Authority*, ed. J Borneman, pp. 201–20. New York/Oxford: Berghahn Books

Skultans V. 1998. *The Testimony of Lives: Narrative and Memory in Post-Soviet Latvia*. London/New York: Routledge

Sneath D. 1999. Mobility, technology, and decollectivization of Pastoralism in Mongolia. In *Landlocked Cosmopolitan: Mongolia in the Twentieth Century*, ed. S Kotkin, BA Elleman, pp. 223–37. Armonk, NY: ME Sharpe

Sneath D. 2004. Property regimes and sociotechnical systems: rights over land in Mongolia's "age of the market." See Verdery & Humphrey 2004, pp. 161–85

Ssorin-Chaikov N. 2003. *The Social Life of the State in Subarctic Siberia*. Stanford, CA: Stanford Univ. Press

Tishkov V. 2004. *Chechnya: Life in a War-Torn Society*. Berkeley: Univ. Calif. Press

Tökés RL. 2000. "Transitology": global dreams and post-Communist realities. *Cent. Eur. Rev.* 2(10): **http://www.ce-review.org/00/10/tokes10.html**

True J. 2003. *Gender, Globalization, and Postsocialism: The Czech Republic after Communism*. New York: Columbia Univ. Press

Urban ME. 2004. *Russia gets the Blues: Music, Culture, and Community in Unsettled Times*. Ithaca, NY: Cornell Univ. Press

Verdery K. 1983. *Transylvanian Villagers*. Berkeley: Univ. Calif. Press

Verdery K. 1991. *National Ideology Under Socialism: Identity and Cultural Politics in Ceausescu's Romania*. Berkeley: Univ. Calif. Press

Verdery K. 1994. The elasticity of land: problems of property restitution in Transylvania. *Slavic Rev.* 53(4):1071–109

Verdery K. 1996. *What was Socialism, and What Comes Next?* Princeton, NJ: Princeton Univ. Press

Verdery K. 2003. *The Vanishing Hectare: Property and Value in Postsocialist Transylvania*. Ithaca, NY: Cornell Univ. Press

Verdery K, Humphrey C, eds. 2004. *Property in Question: Value Transformation in the Global Economy*. Oxford: Berg

Vitebsky P. 1995. From cosmology to environmentalism: shamanism as local knowledge in a global setting. In *Counterworks: Managing the Diversity of Knowledge*, ed. R Fardon, pp. 182–204. London: Routledge

Vitebsky P. 2005. *The Reindeer People: Living with Animals and Spirits in Siberia*. Boston, MA: HoughtonMifflin

Wagner S. 2008. *To Know Where He Lies: DNA Technology and the Search for Srebrenica's Missing*. Berkeley: Univ. Calif. Press

Wanner C. 2007. *Communities of the Converted: Ukrainians and Global Evangelism*. Ithaca, NY: Cornell Univ. Press

Watson RS, ed. 1994. *Memory, History, and Opposition Under State Socialism*. Santa Fe, NM: Sch. Am. Res. Press

Watts J. 2002. Heritage and enterprise culture in Archangel, Northern Russia. See Mandel & Humphrey 2002, pp. 53–75

Woodruff D. 1999. Barter of the bankrupt: the politics of demonetization in Russia's Federal State. See Burawoy & Verdery 1999, pp. 83–124

Yurchak A. 2006. *Everything was Forever, Until it was No More: The Last Soviet Generation*. Princeton, NJ: Princeton Univ. Press

Zbierski-Salameh S. 1999. Polish peasants in the "Valley of Transition": responses to postsocialist reforms. See Burawoy & Verdery 1999, pp. 189–222

The Archaeological Evidence for Social Evolution

Joyce Marcus

Museum of Anthropology, University of Michigan, Ann Arbor, Michigan 48109-1079;
email: joymar@umich.edu

Annu. Rev. Anthropol. 2008. 37:251–66

The *Annual Review of Anthropology* is online at
anthro.annualreviews.org

This article's doi:
10.1146/annurev.anthro.37.081407.085246

Key Words

specific evolution, general evolution, social institutions, ethnogenesis

Abstract

Social evolution can be defined as the appearance of new forms of social or sociopolitical organization. In the case of the prehistoric record,
such changes are perhaps most successfully studied when archaeologists
collaborate with ethnologists or ethnohistorians. Although ethnologists
can provide unequaled detail on agents and institutions, many evolutionary transitions took longer than any ethnologist's lifetime. The archaeological record therefore provides an important proving ground
for evolutionary theory. In this review, I synthesize some of the evidence supporting social evolution from both Old World and New World
archaeology. I also argue that for the study of social evolution to advance,
the field of anthropology must be willing to generalize; to compare and
contrast cultures from different parts of the world; and to search for
common patterns in the ways human societies responded to similar
challenges.

THE ARCHAEOLOGICAL EVIDENCE FOR SOCIAL EVOLUTION

Studies of sociocultural evolution began in the mid-nineteenth century (Morgan 1870, 1877; Spencer 1851, 1857, 1863; Tylor 1870, 1889). These studies were necessarily based on limited and anecdotal ethnographic data from disparate parts of the world. Early evolutionists could not resist proposing terms such as "savagery," "barbarism," and "civilization" for stages of sociocultural development—terms that would not survive the advent of professional anthropology. A second wave of evolutionists (Carneiro 1970; Fried 1967; Sahlins & Service 1960; Service 1960, 1962; Steward 1948, 1949, 1953, 1955) could base their controlled comparisons on richer and more systematically collected ethnographic data. These data began to be compiled in 1949 to form the Human Relations Area Files, a source that continues to yield important results (Bondarenko & Korotayev 2000, Ember 1973, Ember & Ember 1995, Goodenough 1999, Kamp 1998, Peregrine 2001, Peregrine et al. 2004).

In its latest incarnation, evolution is seen as multilinear and can even be divided into topics such as cultural evolution, social evolution, and ethnogenesis. The term cultural evolution is sometimes applied to the divergence of distinct cultures from a common ancestral background, such as occurred when many Polynesian islands were colonized from a "Samoa-Tonga home-land region" (Kirch & Green 2001). The term ethnogenesis is sometimes used when a recognizable ethnic group seems to emerge in the archaeological record, for example, when arguably Eskimo societies began to appear in the Canadian Arctic during the prehistoric Dorset and Thule periods (Maxwell 1984, McGhee 1984).

Social evolution, the focus of this article, can be defined as the appearance of new forms of social or sociopolitical organization, without necessarily implying changes in overall culture or ethnicity. Nearly 50 years ago, Sahlins (1960) identified two modes of social evolu-

tion: specific and general. Specific evolution—by far the most common mode—refers to the small changes that take place over the lifetime of a society, without necessarily transforming it into a larger, more centralized, more hierarchical society. For example, a foraging society with bilateral kinship terms might grow in population to the point at which it became subdivided into multiple clans, reckoning descent unilineally; in every other way, however, it might remain an egalitarian, seminomadic foraging society.

Occasionally, however, what seems initially like a small change can have more profound long-term consequences. For example, should the society described above wind up with multiple clans, one of which emerges as hierarchically above the others—able both to provide leadership to the others and to demand unique privileges—what could result is a foraging society based on rank, like the Calusa of Florida or the Tlingit and Nootka of the Pacific Northwest. Such change, although specific to the group involved, could be considered general not only because it resulted in a more complex society, but also because it can be usefully compared and contrasted with the origins of social hierarchy elsewhere in the world. Despite the fact that general evolutionary change is the less common of the two modes, it remains the one that has most captured archaeologists' imaginations.

When general evolutionists need to ensure that their controlled comparisons and contrasts are being carried out on societies of the same level of complexity or sociopolitical integration, they have tended to create shorthand terms for different social forms or types. No aspect of evolutionary theory is more misunderstood than these social types. They have been attacked as rigid even when they are not, as stages even when they are not, and as unilinear even when they are not.

Sumner & Keller (1927–1928), Wright (1983), Spencer (1990, 1993, 1997), Carneiro (2003), and others have presented cogent arguments showing that some kind of social typology is necessary to facilitate comparisons and contrasts. By way of analogy, imagine the problems that would result if zoologists were forbidden to create categories such as "amphibian," "reptile," and "mammal" and were limited instead to calling every creature "an animal." To carry that analogy further, consider how silly it would be to accuse "reptile" of being a rigid category when we all know it to include creatures as different as snakes, lizards, and turtles, not to mention fossils described as mammal-like reptiles.

THREE REQUIREMENTS OF EVOLUTIONARY THEORY

Wright (1983) proposes three requirements for any social evolutionary theory. First, it must involve "a typology of social forms which *potentially* has some kind of directionality to it" (p. 26, emphasis in original). Second, it must be possible to order these forms of society "in such a way that the probability of staying at the same level of the typology is greater than the probability of regressing." Third, there must be "a positive probability of moving from a given level of the typology to the next higher level."

Wright adds that we must not assume that any society will evolve, regress, or move through a rigid sequence of stages, explaining that "long-term steady states may be more likely than any systematic tendency for movement" (p. 26). This statement is particularly relevant to archaeology because it is long-term steady states that archaeologists tend to recognize as periods or phases in prehistoric sequences. All too often, crucial evolutionary changes appear to have taken place in the much briefer transitions between periods, transitions so rapid as to be nearly unrecognizable at the chronological scale of most archaeology. This is one reason that archaeologists find it so difficult to respond to ethnologists' demands to give more weight to agency in their explanatory schemes. Most chronological periods used by archaeologists are ten times the adult life of an agent. Small wonder that most archaeologists refer to processes, which represent the amalgamated behaviors of multiple agents.

Archaeologists are well aware of such problems and are working on them. To do so, they need to maintain an ongoing dialogue with ethnologists and ethnohistorians, for whom agents are in sharper focus. This collaboration has become increasingly difficult owing to many current anthropologists' antipathy toward generalization, controlled comparison, and the search for universal patterns. Significant exceptions to this trend can be found among social scientists in the former Soviet Union (Artemova 2003, Bondarenko & Korotayev 2003, Grinin et al. 2004, Korotayev 2003, Kradin et al. 2000, Kradin & Lynsha 1995), who not only continue to pursue evolutionary approaches but have even created a new journal, *Social Evolution and History*. Although these scholars welcome constructive criticism of evolutionary archaeology, they also have had no trouble dismissing what they call "the most radically negative attitude to this scheme" (Bondarenko et al. 2004, p. 17). By and large, the archaeologists who spend the most time engaged in active fieldwork seem to have the fewest doubts that social evolution of some kind has taken place, a point to which I return in my conclusions.

THE ROLE OF ARCHAEOLOGY

As suggested above, the study of social evolution should involve collaboration among ethnologists, ethnohistorians, and archaeologists. Each subdiscipline has its role, its strengths, and its weaknesses.

The relationship between ethnology and archaeology is analogous to that between zoology and vertebrate paleontology. Zoologists are able to study both muscle tissue and behavior at a level of detail unavailable to paleontologists. Paleontologists, however, can find the muscle attachments on fossil bones that provide evidence for specific muscles; they can then draw on the zoological literature both on those muscles and on the behavior they reflect. Paleontologists can also elucidate long-term trends and recover the skeletons of transitional species unknown to zoology; such fossils show us the order in which certain structures (and hence behaviors) arose. In an important sense, the fossil record is the proving ground for any theory of change based on comparisons of living species.

The study of social evolution also works best when students of living and fossil societies collaborate. Unfortunately, such collaboration often reveals one of archaeology's weaknesses: It deals with the residues of behavior rather than directly observed behavior. As a result, archaeologists do not really recover types of societies; they recover the residues of social institutions. Fortunately, it is the clusters of social institutions that allow us to reconstruct social forms. What archaeologists must do is patiently accumulate evidence for sets of social institutions (and their associated personnel) until they can make a convincing case for a particular type of society.

A decade ago, Flannery and I argued that for some parts of the world, one could present a kind of "evolution without stages"—a history of change in which emerging social and political institutions, rather than stages, provided the milestones along the way (Marcus & Flannery 1996, p. 236). We further argued that "transition periods—those brief phases of rapid evolution during which the system changed, or the actors deliberately changed it"—might be more crucial to evolutionary analysis than the long, stable periods used for so many social typologies. Here archaeology's long-term perspective is one of its strengths. Archaeologists can observe change over periods many times longer than the lifetime of an ethnologist. The empirical data of archaeology can also provide checks on the accuracy of ethnohistoric documents.

In the remainder of this paper I travel through the archaeological record in chronological order, from the Late Pleistocene until the appearance of the earliest states in the Old and New Worlds, providing a sample of the available archaeological evidence for emerging social institutions. This evidence, much of which has been radiocarbon dated, should make it clear why only the most armchair of archaeologists dispute the existence of social evolution. Fieldworkers—excavating in areas such as the Near East, China, Europe, Mesoamerica, the Andes, or Eastern North America—have seen with their own eyes the evidence for specific and general evolution.

HUNTERS AND GATHERERS

According to one widely held view, our "modern" ancestors left Africa at least 80,000–60,000 years ago, eventually spreading to every major land mass (Mellars 2006). Humans began as hunters and gatherers. By 20,000 years ago, however, at least some of them had adopted a "delayed return" economic strategy that involved various combinations of storage, game management, encouragement of wild plants, and exchange systems that linked human groups into larger symbiotic networks (Woodburn 1988). Eventually, some of these strategies would lead to sedentism, some to agriculture, and some to both.

Archaeologists have frequently used the word "band" to refer to the organization of mobile hunting-gathering groups. An increasing number of ethnologists who work with foragers, however, actually prefer the word "camp." Seldom, they argue, is there a definable "band" that moves from place to place as a group. Fluidity is one of the hallmarks of foragers, and even when a specific camp is occupied repeatedly over several years, it is rarely occupied by the exact same group of people.

A useful evolutionary distinction is the one made by Kelly (2000) into unsegmented vs segmented societies. Kelly points out that hunter-gatherers with no level of organization beyond the local group, relatively impermanent extended families, and little tendency to form segments such as lineages and clans are essentially warless. They may have individual homicides (and capital punishment for them), but group violence is rare. This may explain why there is so little archaeological evidence for group violence in the Old World prior to 15,000 BC and the New World prior to 4000 BC.

The case is different, Kelly notes, among societies divided into equivalent segments, such as patrilineal, matrilineal, or ancestor-based cognatic descent groups, which combine to form progressively more inclusive units. Such segmentary societies display a principle Kelly calls social substitutability: The killing of any member of a segment is considered a group offense and can be avenged by the killing of any member of the offender's segment. Raiding thus began as group versus group social action.

To be sure, archaeologists cannot expect to directly detect changes in social attitudes, such as the principle of social substitutability. What they must try to do is detect the cooccurrence of three social features that are linked in Kelly's model: (*a*) social segments; (*b*) intercommunity raiding; and (*c*) bridewealth, which may join (or replace) bride service when marriage partners are exchanged between social segments. The convergence of these three variables indicates that a society with social substitutability likely exists. Let us now look at some archaeological evidence.

DETECTING EARLY SEGMENTARY SOCIETIES

Perhaps the oldest known archaeological evidence for group violence (and thus for an early segmented society) comes from Jebel Sahaba in the Nile Valley (Wendorf & Schild 2004). Dated by radiocarbon to 15,000 years ago (substantially older if the dates are calibrated), the site consists of 58 burials—men, women, and children—half of whom died violently in a series of ambushes. Some had between 15 and 30 projectile elements embedded in them, a form of homicide Kelly calls "pincushioning." Wendorf & Schild point out that Jebel Sahaba is situated in an area with multiple groups or segments of hunter-gatherers. These foragers evidently competed for localized resources in embayments along the Nile and maintained separate cemeteries, a fact that reinforces our impression of intergroup or intersegment competition.

Although some segmentary societies remained foragers (the aboriginal Australians are a classic example), it was with the growth of population following the origins of agricul-

ture that segmentary societies truly exploded in number. The creation of cemeteries for a corporate segment's dead, already mentioned, can be one archaeological clue. Another clue would be the construction of defensive works, such as ditches or palisades, in response to group-versus-group violence. As mentioned earlier, Kelly also suggests that with the exchange of marriage partners between segments, bridewealth may join or replace bride service. A third clue to social segmentation might therefore be the circulation of goods that could have served as bridewealth.

Archaeologists have found evidence for all three institutions. For example, Tell Maghzaliyah, a Prepottery Neolithic village in northern Iraq, had a stone-and-clay defensive wall (Bader 1993). San José Mogote, an Early Formative agricultural village in southern Mexico, had a palisade of pine posts (Flannery & Marcus 2003, 2005). The latter site also had small cemeteries that may have served different social segments. Any search for possible evidence of bridewealth begins with the brisk trade in marine mollusk shells that characterized so many Late Paleolithic–Early Neolithic societies. The Natufian collectors of wild wheat and barley, who stood on the threshold of agriculture in the Levant, decorated their heads, arms, and ankles with dentalium shells. Mexico's earliest villagers circulated pearl oyster and spiny oyster shells over thousands of square kilometers. The challenge facing archaeologists is to prove that some of this shell was accumulated for bridewealth rather than for mere ornamentation—for example, by demonstrating its association with women of marriageable age.

Service (1962) originally referred to village-based segmentary societies as "tribes." He did not object a few years later, however, when Fried (1966, 1967) abolished the term, in part because it meant different things to different people. This left archaeologists without a term for egalitarian village societies that were organized into lineages, clans, and (sometimes) moieties. Today, many of us follow Townsend (1985, p. 142) and Carneiro (1987, p. 761) in calling these "politically autonomous village societies," meaning that each controlled its own sociopolitical affairs despite its economic links to other villages.

DETECTING THE INSTITUTIONS OF EGALITARIAN VILLAGE SOCIETIES

"Neolithic" societies (*sensu latu*) displayed almost bewildering variation worldwide. That occurred, almost certainly, because there were so many strategies to accomplish the same thing. Societies without strong centralized authority tend to rely heavily on a combination of kinship and achieved status to determine leadership, and there were multiple ways to do this. Village organization often depended on creating opposable segments, then bringing them together via rituals emphasizing common descent, for which there can be countless versions.

In prehistory, such societies might build nuclear family houses (e.g., in Early Formative Mexico), extended family houses (e.g., in the Near East), or multifamily long houses (e.g., in the Bandkeramik culture of Europe). Some village societies also began to build ritual structures, too varied to list under one rubric. At San José Mogote in Mexico there were small lime-plastered buildings that may be men's houses of the "exclusionary" type, that is, too small to accommodate more than an initiated minority of the men (Marcus & Flannery 2004). At Pessejik Depe in Neolithic Turkmenistan (Berdyiev 1968), there were larger "cult buildings" that could have accommodated most of the village's men and were probably less exclusionary.

Some of the most interesting (and precocious) early public buildings are those of Pre-Pottery Neolithic Turkey. The oval, semisubterranean "shrines" at Göbekli Tepe (Schmidt 2006), with their elaborately carved stone pillars, invite comparisons with the most elaborate painted kivas of the U.S. Southwest. One of the stone masonry "cult buildings" at Nevali Çori (Hauptmann 1993), which features sitting benches and accumulations of ancestors' skulls, seems as persuasive an example of a men's house

as textless prehistory can provide. And the sequence of public buildings at Çayönü Tepeşi may well document the step-by-step evolution of the men's house, with its benches and curated ancestors' skulls, into a true Near Eastern temple with its corners aligned to the cardinal points (Özdoğan & Özdoğan 1989, Schirmer 1990).

Which rituals might have characterized such societies? At a minimum, they would include dancing, singing, chanting, and the wearing of costumes, the latter often representing ancestors or supernatural beings. Garfinkel (2003) has documented the evidence (mostly in prehistoric art) for dancing in the Neolithic Near East. Some clay figurines from Formative Mexico show individuals dancing, chanting, or singing (Marcus 1998b). At other New World sites of this era, archaeologists have found flutes, panpipes, ocarinas, whistles, and turtle-shell drums that were apparently played with antler drumsticks. Both Tlatilco in Mexico (García Moll et al. 1991, Piña Chan 1955) and Nahal Hemar in Israel (Bar-Yosef & Alon 1988) have masks of the kind that village societies often use in ritual. Prepottery Neolithic villagers at 'Ain Ghazal in Jordan used lime plaster to model faces on their ancestors' skulls, and they also made large plaster statues of what may be apical or mythological ancestors (Rollefson et al. 1992).

Ethnography tells us that societies featuring multigenerational descent lines sometimes traced those lines back to pairs of contrasting animals or supernaturals, like the Wolf and Raven of the Pacific Northwest. The Mexican equivalents were Earth and Sky, whose angry versions (Earthquake and Lightning) were symbolized on the Formative pottery of 1150–850 BC (Flannery & Marcus 2000, Marcus 1989). In addition to multiple descent lines, some prehistoric Old World villages may have had ethnically contrasting populations. Ma'adi, a very large Late Predynastic village in Egypt's Nile Delta, was occupied by (*a*) people who lived in circular, semisubterranean huts; (*b*) people who lived in rectangular houses built of logs and mud; and (*c*) people who lived in truly subterranean houses, resembling those of Shiqmim in Israel's Negev region (Levy 1987). Corresponding differences in cranial characters have been claimed for the multiple cemeteries at Ma'adi.

DETECTING THE ORIGINS OF HEREDITARY INEQUALITY

A major evolutionary transition—one that has produced a large body of literature over the past two decades—is the replacement (in at least some parts of the world) of egalitarian, politically autonomous village societies where social status is based largely on achievement with societies with hereditary rank, expressed either as a "conical clan" of ranked individuals (Kirchhoff 1955) or as a caste-like hierarchy of chiefly and commoner clans (von Fürer-Haimendorf 1969). Although the differences between achievement-based and rank-based societies can be clearly described by ethnologists, distinguishing their prehistoric counterparts can be so stubborn a problem that some archaeologists have taken to lumping both under the generic term middle range societies (Berezkin 2004, Earle 1997, Price & Feinman 1995, Rousseau 2006).

A few examples should make clear why archaeologists need more refined methods for studying this crucial transition. Archaeologists looking for signs of hereditary rank often focus on what they call "prestige goods," especially sumptuary ornaments of raw materials exotic to the region. Unfortunately, egalitarian societies often accumulate similar exotica for bridewealth or status competition. In response to this problem, some archaeologists concentrate on sumptuary goods buried with infants or children, who, clearly too young to have achieved the right to possess such things, must have inherited their rank.

Many archaeologists believe that they can identify a "chief's house" at their site; yet the fact is that chiefly families, lineages, or clans are often distributed through many houses, sometimes even through different villages. Other archaeologists have tried to associate the man-

power necessary to move huge stone monuments with chiefly authority; yet we know that there were egalitarian societies that could regularly assemble 50–100 men to move multi-ton stones (Hutton 1921). Despite these problems, and others, archaeologists have in fact succeeded in providing us with a number of recent comparative syntheses of rank societies (Drennan & Peterson 2006, Drennan & Uribe 1987, Redmond 1998, Stein & Rothman 1994).

A major focus of recent work on rank societies has been cycling, a long-term process during which chiefly societies arose, collapsed, and rose again. It is now clear, however, that evolutionary oscillations may have been common even at lower and higher levels of social complexity. At a lower level of complexity, for example, Walter and associates (2006) have documented a New Zealand agricultural society that for a time reverted back to hunting and gathering, eventually returning to agriculture. MacNeish (1958) found a similar reversion from agriculture to foraging in the Sierra de Tamaulipas, Mexico. At the level of rank society, archaeologists are, of course, familiar with the oscillations between egalitarian and rank society among the Kachin of Myanmar (Leach 1954). Anderson (1994) has documented analogous cycling between paramount and simple chiefdoms in the Savannah River area of the eastern United States. At a higher level of complexity, cyclic consolidation and dissolution occurred among states in the Maya region (Marcus 1992). More recently, similar cycling has been described for the Andean region and the Near East (Marcus 1998a, Postgate 1992).

RANK SOCIETY: A NEW WORLD CASE

In the Valley of Oaxaca, Mexico, Flannery and I assembled 10 lines of evidence to infer the emergence of rank, arguing that no single line would be sufficient (Marcus & Flannery 1996, p. 110). The evidence for rank society between 900 and 700 BC includes the deliberate cranial deformation of elite children; differential access to jade earspools and magnetite mirrors; differential access to deer meat, pearl oyster, and *Spondylus* shell; a dichotomy between seated/kneeling (elite) burials and prone (lower-status) burials; figurines showing individuals in contrasting positions of authority and obeisance; four-legged stools like those carried by the attendants of chiefs in other New World rank societies; and other clues (Flannery & Marcus 2005).

Carneiro (1991) has made a useful distinction between rank societies where every village remained politically autonomous and societies where the chief's authority extended to smaller villages in the region, creating a territory in which village autonomy was lost. It is only the latter situation that warrants the term chiefdom—a widely misunderstood term because it refers to a territorial unit rather than to a type of society.

To detect this loss of political autonomy by subject villages, archaeologists often turn to settlement patterns, which may show the region's largest village to have been surrounded by smaller satellites. In the Oaxaca case mentioned above, Plog (1976) showed that the satellite villages subject to one large chiefly center tended to share more pottery design elements with the latter than would be predicted by a "gravity" model (one taking both distance and village size into account). For his part, Drennan (1976) showed that the most elite-looking burials at one satellite Oaxaca village were those of women, possibly hypogamous brides from the nearby chiefly center. Finally, large public buildings at that chiefly center contained exotic construction stones from villages up to 5 km distant, suggesting that satellite communities could be called on to supply labor and building material to the local chief.

RANK SOCIETY: AN OLD WORLD CASE

In the Chalcolithic period of the Near East, analogous data for rank can be found among villages of the period 5300–3700 BC. Identifying rank, however, is more difficult in the Near East than in Mesoamerica, in part because

Near Eastern societies were less flamboyant (Flannery 1999a). This lack of flamboyance might reflect a greater reliance on sacred authority than on display. D'Altroy & Earle (1985) suggested that Chalcolithic Near Eastern societies relied more on "staple finance" than on "wealth finance." As a result, Near Eastern rank societies may have made less use of sumptuary goods than did their Mesoamerican counterparts.

That is not to say, of course, that one cannot find cases of Chalcolithic burials with sumptuary goods, including children too young to have achieved their apparent high status. At least three infants at the fortified Samarran village of Tell es-Sawwan on the Tigris were buried with alabaster statuettes bearing inlaid shell eyes and turquoise beads (El-Wailly & Abu al-Soof 1965). At the Halafian site of Yarim Tepe II in northern Iraq, several children 10–13 years of age were given special cremation burials, to which offerings such as alabaster vessels, painted ceramics, necklaces of ground and polished obsidian beads, rock crystal, marine shells, and a stone seal pendant were added (Merpert & Munchaev 1993). And one young woman buried in Chalcolithic levels at Choga Mish in Iran (Delougaz & Kantor 1996, Pl. 69) displayed an artificially deformed skull, not unlike those of some elite women from Formative Mexico. To be sure, no single line of evidence is sufficient to show rank; rather, the more lines, the better the case.

Chalcolithic clues to the loss of village autonomy, leading to the build-up of larger territories administered by chiefly families, can also be found. In the Sinjar-Mosul region of northern Iraq, it is not uncommon to find large (8 ha) Halafian villages surrounded by small (1–3 ha) villages that may be satellite communities (Hijara 1980). The richly painted pottery of the Halafian period, with its scores of motifs, also lends itself to studies of shared designs such as those undertaken by Plog in Mexico. LeBlanc (1971) subjected the painted motifs from seven Halafian sites in Syria, Turkey, and Iraq to a cluster analysis aimed at determining the extent to which villages shared motifs. The strongest coefficients of similarity occurred between the largest Halafian sites—those most likely to have been chiefly centers—regardless of the distance involved. It would appear that, just as in Formative Mexico, important Halafian families exchanged gifts of elegant pottery with their counterparts in neighboring regions (Flannery et al. 2005). As Watson (1983) expresses it, the Halafian sites with the greatest evidence for high pottery craftsmanship were probably "chiefly centers, i.e., places of residence of local strongmen or chiefs."

DETECTING THE ORIGINS OF PRISTINE STATES

Archaeologists in both the New and Old Worlds have been hard at work on ways to detect pristine or first-generation states, those that were the first to arise in their region and did so without having an earlier state as a model. Wright & Johnson (1975) showed that during the Uruk period in southwestern Iran, the rise of the first state was marked by the appearance of a four-tiered site-size hierarchy, the upper three tiers of which had administrative functions. This pattern was discovered through (*a*) full-coverage settlement pattern survey, followed by (*b*) construction of a histogram of site sizes in hectares, and (*c*) the clear emergence of four modes of site sizes—in layman's terms, one city, several towns, a greater number of large villages, and still greater numbers of small villages. Administrative artifacts such as seal impressions in clay (created when jars or bales of commodities were sealed by officials) were found at sites of all sizes, although the seals themselves occurred mainly at the cities and towns where the administrators lived. Johnson (1972) also showed that some Early Dynastic cities in Iraq had regularly spaced "central place lattices" of lower-order sites around them.

Wright & Johnson's approach has proven useful in the New World. Billman (1999) and Wilson (1988) showed that four-tiered site hierarchies appeared in Peru's Moche and Santa Valleys, respectively, during the expansion of the Moche state. Marcus (1973, 1976) found that some Maya secondary centers of AD 700 formed very regular hexagonal central-place lattices around the capital cities to which they were subordinate. Settlement pattern data collected by Kowalewski and his collaborators (1989) can be used to show the presence of analogous central place lattices in the Valley of Oaxaca by the first century AD (Marcus & Flannery 1996, pp. 173–75).

Flannery (1999b) examined five historically documented cases of agents, each of whom created the first state in his region. In all five cases, the first state arose in the context of a group of rival chiefdoms, when one of those chiefdoms managed to gain a competitive advantage and reduce its rivals to subject provinces within a larger polity. Archaeological data suggest that this is what happened in the prehistoric Egyptian and Mexican cases discussed below. In a separate study, Flannery (1998) presented a series of archaeological clues to the presence of an early state, including palaces, royal tombs, and standardized temples for a state religion. These clues work better in some parts of the world (e.g., Mexico) than in others (e.g., the Aegean).

Finally, Spencer (1998) has adapted an equation from the literature on predation to develop a mathematical model showing that primary state formation necessarily involves territorial expansion.

STATE FORMATION: AN OLD WORLD CASE

During the Late Predynastic period (3700–3000 BC), the Nile Valley was occupied by a series of regionally distinct rank societies. Those downstream near the Nile Delta comprised Lower Egypt. Those upstream, at and beyond the great bend of the Nile, comprised Upper Egypt. The societies of Upper Egypt may have included as many as three chiefdoms, with their paramount centers at the sites of Naqada, Hierakonpolis, and This (Kemp 1989, p. 34). At the start of this period, Naqada seems to have been in its ascendancy, its cemeteries rich in sumptuary goods of gold, silver, ivory, and lapis lazuli. Suggestions of hereditary status come from burials like that of Tomb 1863, a young girl accompanied by a Near Eastern cylinder seal (Petrie 1920, p. 40 and Pl. IX), ivory bangles, a slate cosmetic palette, a bone comb, a stone vase, and a pottery dish from the Sudan; she could hardly have achieved the right to such exotic burial offerings in her short life.

In a classic case of chiefly cycling, Hierakonpolis rose to eclipse Naqada between 3400 and 3200 BC. Hierakonpolis's regional population coalesced into fewer but larger settlements (Hoffman et al. 1987); the paramount center constructed a mudbrick defensive wall, an impressive temple complex, and several large tombs, one of which bears a mural showing an unnamed leader smiting an enemy with a mace. By 3200–3100 BC Hierakonpolis had unified all of Upper Egypt, creating a proto-state led by the rulers of what is currently called Dynasty Zero.

Having consolidated their power in Upper Egypt, the rulers of this macrochiefdom or proto-state moved downstream against the Delta, eventually unifying all of Egypt and ushering in Dynasty 1. By 3000 BC a famous carved slate palette from Hierakonpolis depicts a ruler with the hieroglyphic name of Narmer, wearing a double crown that combines the white crown of Upper Egypt and the red crown of the Delta. The unification of Egypt eventually required a new capital at Memphis because Hierakonpolis by then lay too far upstream to administer the whole Egyptian state. There followed a period of territorial expansion in which a vessel made from Egyptian clay and bearing the hieroglyph associated with Narmer reached southern Israel (van den Brink & Levy 2002).

STATE FORMATION: A NEW WORLD CASE

Spencer & Redmond (2004) have recently provided archaeological documentation for the step-by-step formation of the Zapotec state in the Valley of Oaxaca, Mexico. Their work, which complements the earlier research of Blanton (1978) and Kowalewski et al. (1989), brings the Zapotec case in line with examples of pristine state formation elsewhere in the world.

Between 600 and 500 BC, the Valley of Oaxaca (like Predynastic Upper Egypt) was divided into at least three chiefdoms, with their paramount centers at San José Mogote, Yegüih, and San Martín Tilcajete. Rivalry between paramount centers was intense, with San José Mogote enduring the burning of its major temple and carving a stone monument to depict the sacrifice (by heart removal) of a chiefly rival. At roughly 500 BC, at least 2000 people from San José Mogote and its satellite villages moved to a more defensible location, the summit of a 400-m-high mountain called Monte Albán, where they began building 3 km of defensive wall (Blanton 1978, Flannery & Marcus 2003).

Between 500 and 300 BC, nearly a third of the valley's population lived at Monte Albán. They had the support of the entire northern and central valley, the region from which their founders had come. Less than a day's journey to the south, however, lay Tilcajete, an unyielding rival. Tilcajete's response to the founding of Monte Albán was to double its own size (from 25 ha to 52.8 ha); its elite also laid out a civic-ceremonial plaza with an astronomical orientation deliberately chosen to contrast with Monte Albán's (Spencer & Redmond 2004).

At roughly 330 BC, Tilcajete was attacked by Monte Albán and its plaza was burned. Tilcajete refused to capitulate; instead, it drew in supporters and grew to 71.5 ha. Its leaders moved its civic-ceremonial center to a more defensible ridge, defiantly retained the same astronomical orientation, and erected defensive walls. In response, Monte Albán readied itself for a long campaign by concentrating thousands of farmers, artisans, and warriors in 155 satellite villages nearby. Not long after 300 BC, Monte Albán aimed its predatory campaign elsewhere, conquering a less-powerful polity to the north.

Eventually, at roughly 30–20 BC, Monte Albán attacked Tilcajete again, burning its ruler's palatial residence and a nearby temple. Tilcajete did not recover from this attack. It was abandoned, and on a mountaintop nearby, the victorious rulers of Monte Albán built an administrative center subordinate to them (Elson 2007). What resulted from this and other military victories was a unified Zapotec state with a 2150-km^2 heartland, palaces, royal tombs, standardized state temples, and hieroglyphic references to distant places over which Monte Albán claimed hegemony.

The Egyptian and Zapotec examples are but two cases that show how archaeological, ethnohistoric, or historic data can be used to model state formation. Thus far I have seen no convincing case where a single, isolated chiefdom turned into a pristine state. All well-documented cases suggest that pristine states were created out of multiple chiefdoms and that, just as Spencer's mathematical model suggests, territorial expansion was involved. Once a pristine state existed in any region, however, second-generation (or even later) states could and did arise by alternative routes. One possible reason that there is some confusion about the pathways to the state is that a number of authors (e.g., Trigger 2003) have included late, non-pristine states (the Aztec, the Inka, the Akkadians, etc.) in their models. This reliance on later states obscures the process of pristine state formation by throwing the world's first states into the mix of alternative routes followed by second- and third-generation states, rather than keeping the pristine cases separate.

CONCLUSIONS

A great deal remains to be done by those who have sufficient curiosity about social evolution. To begin with, the empirical data of archaeology leave no doubt that such evolution occurred. There were no states 20,000 years ago; indeed, at that period even the evidence for segmentary society is fragmentary. In a world occupied exclusively by hunters and gatherers, signs of institutions such as opposable social segments, bridewealth, and the principle of social substitutability can be very subtle.

The origins of agriculture and animal domestication are considered topics so important that they will continue to be pursued, but the emphasis here is usually on subsistence and eco-nomics. The social changes accompanying early food production were profound, but in recent years they have taken a back seat to the application of new botanical, zoological, and DNA techniques to the study of the plants and animals themselves. In many parts of the world, agriculture created societies larger than any that had ever existed previously. Those societies could no longer be organized the way most foragers are organized. By creating the fiction that large numbers of villagers shared common descent, Neolithic societies focused increased attention on their ancestors, leading to unprecedented ways of treating the dead. They also created rituals both for separating and for recombining social segments; elaborating art, dance, song, and costuming; and necessitating widespread movement of exotic pigments, feathers, shells, and other "nonutilitarian" items. They built structures that were ritual rather than residential and, in many cases, provided potential leaders with ways to raise their prestige through acts of generosity, community service, or status competition.

So varied and remarkable were the feats of Neolithic or Formative societies that they present archaeologists with one of the greatest challenges: devising objective and convincing ways to distinguish achieved versus inherited status. Archaeologists are presented with countless cases of the differential treatment of individuals or families in the prehistoric record. Unfortunately, the reasons for such differential treatment are rarely self-evident. I have the impression that some archaeologists have missed the more subtle signs of hereditary rank, whereas others have underestimated the ability of egalitarian societies to erect public buildings, move multiton stones, produce art, and organize communal labor. This is a line of inquiry in which archaeologists would do well to collaborate with sympathetic ethnologists.

Hierarchical societies appeared relatively late, given the whole sweep of human life on earth. An interesting aspect of the first rank societies, however, is that they seem to have appeared precociously in certain regions, not in terms of absolute radiocarbon dates, but in terms of their timing within the local cultural sequence. Consider, for example, the early village of Caral in Peru's Supe Valley (Shady Solís 2003). At 2200 BC (uncalibrated), a time when agriculture was still at a relatively simple stage, the occupants of Caral were quarrying multiton stones from nearby outcrops and building linear complexes with sunken courts for possible ceremonial processions and associated rites. A great deal of their food seems to have been fish, brought from the Pacific some 23 km away. On the Pacific coast lies an equally impressive early village named Áspero (Moseley & Willey 1973), which harvested the same species of fish carried to Caral. To fish, of course, Áspero needed cotton for nets and gourds for floats, two crops that Caral, 23 km inland, was probably growing with irrigation.

Although it will be years before we know the extent to which Áspero's and Caral's manpower was actually directed by people of hereditary rank, early Supe society looks precocious when compared with its contemporaries in the highlands of Mexico. By 2000 BC, Mexico's indigenous people were cultivating numerous food plants, including maize, beans, squash, chile peppers, and avocados, but they maintained a seminomadic settlement pattern, which makes it difficult to demonstrate the existence of year-round villages or segmentary societies. Andean archaeologists are justifiably proud of Caral and Áspero. They should not forget, however, that by the time both those sites were occupied, Egypt and Mesopotamia had had states for 1000 years.

The origin of the state, like the origin of agriculture, is a topic with such allure for archaeologists that it will be pursued with dedication for decades to come. Proving the existence of a pristine state requires a combination of settlement pattern surveys, broad horizontal excavations, artifact distribution studies, and exposures of the ground plans of buildings associated with state institutions. Just as there are difficulties in distinguishing achieved from hereditary status, so also are there difficulties in separating the achievements of paramount (or "maximal") chiefdoms from those of the first states. One line of evidence will never be enough.

Many of the best-known ancient states, of course, are those for which we have epigraphic, historic, or ethnohistoric data. Unfortunately, almost none of these states evolved from prestate societies. The Aztec and Inka were fourth- or fifth-generation states, building on templates established by earlier states such as Teotihuacan, the Toltec, the Wari, Tiwanaku, and Chimú. Middle Kingdom Egypt, Early Dynastic Sumer, the Akkadians, and the Old Babylonians all had earlier prototypes. We should study their trajectories but not confuse them with first-generation states. The latter seem to have been created by agents who thought that they were just expanding their chiefdom against its rivals, not creating a new social type.

In the analysis and documentation of social evolution, archaeology has the crucial role of providing the fossil record. It badly needs the collaboration of ethnologists and will patiently have to wait until a greater number of them redevelop an interest in comparison, contrast, and generalization. Perhaps the most compelling reason to return to the study of social evolution is because the archaeological record leaves no doubt that it actually happened.

For additional references, I refer the reader to Carneiro (2003), Graber (1995), Johnson & Earle (2000), Pluciennik (2005), Redmond (1994), Rousseau (2006), Sanderson (2001, 2007), Sawyer (2005), Spencer & Redmond (2004), Turner (2003), and Vannelli (2001, 2005).

DISCLOSURE STATEMENT

The author is not aware of any biases that might be perceived as affecting the objectivity of this review.

LITERATURE CITED

Anderson DG. 1994. *The Savannah River Chiefdoms*. Tuscaloosa: Univ. Ala. Press

Artemova O. 2003. Monopolization of knowledge, social inequality, and female status: a cross-cultural study. *Cross-Cult. Res.* 37:62–80

Bader NO. 1993. Tell Maghzaliyah: an early Neolithic site in northern Iraq. See Yoffee & Clark 1993, pp. 7–40

Bar-Yosef O, Alon D. 1988. *Nahal Hemar Cave*. Jerusalem: Dept. Antiq.

Berdyiev OK. 1968. Novii reaskopkii na poselenii Pessedzhik i Chakmakly depe. *Karakumskie Drevnosti* II:10–17

Berezkin YE. 2004. Alternative models of middle range society: "individualistic" Asia vs "collectivistic" America? See Grinin et al. 2004, pp. 61–87

Billman BR. 1999. Reconstructing prehistoric political economies and cycles of political power in the Moche Valley, Peru. In *Settlement Pattern Studies in the Americas: Fifty Years Since Virú*, ed. BR Billman, GM Feinman, pp. 131–59. Washington, DC: Smithson. Inst. Press

Blanton RE. 1978. *Monte Alban*. New York: Academic

Bondarenko DM, Grinin LE, Korotayev AV. 2004. Alternatives of social evolution. In *The Early State*, ed. LE Grinin, RL Carneiro, DM Bondarenko, NN Kradin, AV Korotayev, pp. 3–27. Volgograd, Russia: Uchitel

Bondarenko DM, Korotayev AV. 2000. Family size and community organization: a cross-cultural comparison. *Cross-Cult. Res.* 34:15–89

Bondarenko DM, Korotayev AV. 2003. "Early state" in cross-cultural perspective: a statistical reanalysis of Henri J.M. Claessen's database. *Cross-Cult. Res.* 37:105–32

Carneiro RL. 1970. Scale analysis, evolutionary sequences, and the rating of cultures. In *A Handbook of Methods in Cultural Anthropology*, ed. R Naroll, R Cohen, pp. 834–71. Garden City, NY: Nat. Hist. Press

Carneiro RL. 1987. Cross-currents in the theory of state formation. *Am. Ethnol.* 14:756–70

Carneiro RL. 1991. The nature of the chiefdom as revealed by evidence from the Cauca Valley of Colombia. In *Profiles in Cultural Evolution*, Anthro Pap. No. 85, ed. AT Rambo, K Gillogly, pp. 167–90. Ann Arbor: Univ. Mich. Mus. Anthropol.

Carneiro RL. 2003. *Evolutionism in Cultural Anthropology: A Critical History*. Boulder, CO: Westview

D'Altroy T, Earle T. 1985. Staple finance, wealth finance, and storage in the Inka political economy. *Curr. Anthropol.* 26:187–206

Damas D. 1984. *Handbook of North American Indians*, V. 5: *Arctic*. Washington, DC: Smithsonian Inst.

Delougaz P, Kantor HJ. 1996. *Chogha Mish* Vol. 1: *The First Five Seasons of Excavations, 1961–71*. Oriental Inst. Publ., Vol. 101. Chicago: Orient. Inst., Univ. Chicago

Drennan RD. 1976. *Fábrica San José and Middle Formative Society in the Valley of Oaxaca*. Ann Arbor: Univ. Mich. Mus. Anthropol. Mem. No. 8

Drennan RD, Peterson CE. 2006. Patterned variation in prehistoric chiefdoms. *Proc. Natl. Acad. Sci. USA* 103:3960–67

Drennan RD, Uribe C, eds. 1987. *Chiefdoms in the Americas*. Lanham, MD: Univ. Press Am.

Earle TK. 1997. *How Chiefs Come to Power*. Stanford, CA: Stanford Univ. Press

Elson C. 2007. *Excavations at Cerro Tilcajete*. Ann Arbor: Univ. Mich. Mus. Anthropol. Mem. No. 42

El-Wailly F, Abu al-Soof B. 1965. The excavations at Tell es-Sawwan: first preliminary report. *Sumer* 21:17–32

Ember M. 1973. An archaeological indicator of matrilocal versus patrilocal residence. *Am. Antiq.* 38:177–82

Ember M, Ember CR. 1995. Worldwide cross-cultural studies and their relevance for archaeology. *J. Archaeol. Res.* 3:87–111

Feinman GM, Marcus J, eds. 1998. *Archaic States*. Santa Fe, NM: SAR Press

Flannery KV. 1998. The ground plans of archaic states. See Feinman & Marcus 1998, pp. 15–57

Flannery KV. 1999a. Chiefdoms in the early Near East: why it's so hard to identify them. In *The Iranian World*, ed. A Alizadeh, Y Majidzadeh, S Malek Shahmirzadi, pp. 44–63. Tehran: Iran Univ. Press

Flannery KV. 1999b. Process and agency in early state formation. *Cambridge Archaeol. J.* 9:3–21

Flannery KV, Balkansky AK, Feinman GM, et al. 2005. Implications of new petrographic analysis for the Olmec "mother culture" model. *Proc. Natl. Acad. Sci. USA* 102(32):11219–22

Flannery KV, Marcus J. 2000. Formative Mexican chiefdoms and the myth of the "mother culture." *J. Anthropol. Archaeol.* 19:1–37

Flannery KV, Marcus J. 2003. The origin of war: new ^{14}C dates from ancient Mexico. *Proc. Natl. Acad. Sci. USA* 100:11801–5

Flannery KV, Marcus J. 2005. *Excavations at San José Mogote 1: The Household Archaeology.* Ann Arbor: Univ. Mich. Mus. Anthropol. Mem. No. 40

Fried MH. 1966. On the concepts of "tribe" and "tribal society." *Trans. New York Acad. Sci.* Ser. 2, 28(4):527–40

Fried MH. 1967. *The Evolution of Political Society.* New York: Random House

García Moll R, Juárez Cossio D, Pijoan Aguade C, Salas Cuesta ME, Salas Cuesta M. 1991. *Catálogo de Entierros de San Luis Tlatilco, Mexico.* México: Inst. Nac. Antropol. Hist.

Garfinkel Y. 2003. *Dancing at the Dawn of Agriculture.* Austin: Univ. Tex. Press

Goodenough WH. 1999. Outline of a framework for a theory of cultural evolution. *Cross-Cult. Res.* 33:84–107

Graber RB. 1995. *A Scientific Model of Social and Cultural Evolution.* Kirksville, MO: T. Jefferson Univ. Press

Grinin LE, Carneiro RL, Bondarenko DM, Kradin NN, Korotayev AV, eds. 2004. *The Early State, Its Alternatives and Analogues.* Volgograd, Russia: Uchitel

Hauptmann H. 1993. Ein Kultgebäude in Nevali Çori. In *Between the Rivers and Over the Mountains*, ed. M Frangipane, H Hauptmann, M Liverani, P Matthiae, M Mellink, pp. 37–69. Roma: Dipart. Scienze Storiche Archeol. Antropol. dell'Antichità, Univ. Roma "La Sapienza"

Hijara I. 1980. *The Halaf Period in northern Mesopotamia.* PhD dissertation, Inst. Archaeol., Univ. London

Hoffman MA, Hamroush H, Allen R. 1987. The environment and evolution of an early Egyptian urban center: archaeological and geochemical investigations at Hierakonpolis. *Geoarchaeology* 2(1):1–13

Hutton JH. 1921. *The Sema Nagas.* London: Macmillan

Johnson AW, Earle T. 2000. *The Evolution of Human Societies: From Foraging Group to Agrarian State.* Stanford, CA: Stanford Univ. Press

Johnson GA. 1972. A test of the utility of central place theory in archaeology. In *Man, Settlement and Urbanism*, ed. PJ Ucko, R Tringham, GW Dimbleby, pp. 769–85. London: Duckworth

Kamp KA. 1998. Social hierarchy and burial treatments: a comparative assessment. *Cross-Cult. Res.* 32:79–115

Kelly RC. 2000. *Warless Societies and the Origin of War.* Ann Arbor: Univ. Mich. Press

Kemp BJ. 1989. *Ancient Egypt.* London: Routledge

Kirch PV, Green RC. 2001. *Hawaiki, Ancestral Polynesia.* Cambridge, UK: Cambridge Univ. Press

Kirchhoff P. 1955. The principles of clanship in human society. *Davidson J. Anthropol.* 1:1–10

Korotayev A. 2003. Form of marriage, sexual division of labor, and postmarital residence in cross-cultural perspective: a reconsideration. *J. Anthropol. Res.* 59:69–89

Kowalewski SA, Feinman GM, Finsten L, Blanton RE, Nicholas LM. 1989. *Monte Albán's Hinterland*, Part 2. Ann Arbor: Univ. Mich. Mus. Anthropol. Mem. No. 23

Kradin NN, Korotayev AV, Bondarenko DM, de Munck V, Wason PK, eds. 2000. *Alternatives of Social Evolution.* Vladivostok: FEB RAS

Kradin NN, Lynsha VA, eds. 1995. *Alternative Pathways to the Early State.* Vladivostok: Dal'nauka

Leach ER. 1954. *Political Systems of Highland Burma.* Cambridge, MA: Harvard Univ. Press

LeBlanc SA. 1971. *Computerized, conjunctive archaeology and the Near Eastern Halafian.* PhD diss., Washington Univ., St Louis, MO

Levy TE, ed. 1987. *Shiqmim I.* Oxford, UK: Brit. Arch. Reports

MacNeish RS. 1958. *Preliminary Archaeological Investigations in the Sierra de Tamaulipas, Mexico.* Philadelphia: Am. Phil. Soc.

Marcus J. 1973. Territorial organization of the lowland Classic Maya. *Science* 180:911–16

Marcus J. 1976. *Emblem and State in the Classic Maya Lowlands.* Washington, DC: Dumbarton Oaks

Marcus J. 1989. Zapotec chiefdoms and the nature of Formative religions. In *Regional Perspectives on the Olmec*, ed. RJ Sharer, DC Grove, pp. 148–97. Santa Fe, NM: SAR Press

Marcus J. 1992. Dynamic cycles of Mesoamerican states. *Natl. Geogr. Res. Explor.* 8:392–411

Marcus J. 1998a. The peaks and valleys of ancient states: an extension of the dynamic model. See Feinman & Marcus 1998, pp. 59–94

Marcus J. 1998b. *Women's Ritual in Formative Oaxaca.* Ann Arbor: Univ. Mich. Mus. Anthropol. Mem. No. 33

Marcus J, Flannery KV. 1996. *Zapotec Civilization*. London: Thames and Hudson

Marcus J, Flannery KV. 2004. The coevolution of ritual and society: new ^{14}C dates from ancient Mexico. *Proc. Natl. Acad. Sci. USA* 101:18257–61

Maxwell M. 1984. Pre-Dorset and Dorset prehistory of Canada. See Damas 1984, pp. 359–68

McGhee R. 1984. Thule prehistory of Canada. See Damas 1984, pp. 369–76

Mellars P. 2006. Why did modern human populations disperse from Africa ca 60,000 years ago? A new model. *Proc. Natl. Acad. Sci. USA* 103:9381–86

Merpert NY, Munchaev RM. 1993. Burial practices of the Halaf culture. See Yoffee & Clark 1993, pp. 207–23

Morgan LH. 1870. *Systems of Consanguinity and Affinity of the Human Family*. Washington, DC: Smithson. Inst.

Morgan LH. 1877. *Ancient Society*. London: McMillan

Moseley ME, Willey GR. 1973. Aspero, Peru: a reexamination of the site and its implications. *Am. Antiq.* 38:452–68

Özdoğan M, Özdoğan A. 1989. Çayönü: a conspectus of recent work. *Paléorient* 15(1):65–74

Peregrine PN. 2001. Cross-cultural comparative approaches in archaeology. *Annu. Rev. Anthropol.* 30:1–18

Peregrine PN, Ember C, Ember M. 2004. Universal patterns in cultural evolution: an empirical analysis using Guttman analysis. *Am. Anthropol.* 106:145–49

Petrie WMF. 1920. *Prehistoric Egypt*. London: Bernard Quaritch

Piña Chan R. 1955. *Las Culturas Preclásicas de la Cuenca de México*. México: Fondo Cult. Econ.

Plog S. 1976. Measurement of prehistoric interaction between communities. In *The Early Mesoamerican Village*, ed. KV Flannery, pp. 255–72. New York: Academic

Pluciennik M. 2005. *Social Evolution*. London: Duckworth

Postgate JN. 1992. *Early Mesopotamia*. London: Routledge

Price TD, Feinman GM, eds. 1995. *Foundations of Inequality*. New York: Plenum

Redmond EM. 1994. *Tribal and Chiefly Warfare in South America*. Ann Arbor: Univ. Mich. Mus. Anthropol. Mem. No. 28

Redmond EM, ed. 1998. *Chiefdoms and Chieftaincy in the Americas*. Gainesville: Univ. Press Fla.

Rollefson GO, Simmons AH, Kafafi Z. 1992. Neolithic cultures at 'Ain Ghazal, Jordan. *J. Field Archaeol.* 19:443–70

Rousseau J. 2006. *Rethinking Social Evolution*. Montreal: McGill-Queen's Univ. Press

Sahlins MD. 1960. Evolution: specific and general. See Sahlins & Service 1960, pp. 12–44

Sahlins MD, Service ER, eds. 1960. *Evolution and Culture*. Ann Arbor: Univ. Mich. Press

Sanderson SK. 2001. *The Evolution of Human Sociality*. Lanham, MD: Rowman & Littlefield

Sanderson SK. 2007. *Evolutionism and Its Critics: Deconstructing and Reconstructing an Evolutionary Interpretation of Human Society*. Boulder, CO: Paradigm

Sawyer RK. 2005. *Social Emergence: Societies as Complex Systems*. New York: Cambridge Univ. Press

Schirmer W. 1990. Some aspects of building at the "aceramic Neolithic" settlement of Çayönü Tepeşi. *World Archaeol.* 21(3):363–87

Schmidt K. 2006. *Sie Bauten die Ersten Tempel das Rätselhafte Heiligtum der Steinzeitjäger: Die Archäologische Entdeckung am Göbekli Tepe*. Munich: C.H. Beck

Service ER. 1960. The law of evolutionary potential. See Sahlins & Service 1960, pp. 93–122

Service ER. 1962. *Primitive Social Organization*. New York: Random House

Shady Solís R. 2003. *La Ciudad Sagrada de Caral-Supe*. Lima, Perú: Inst. Nac. Cultura

Spencer CS. 1990. On the tempo and mode of state formation: neoevolutionism reconsidered. *J. Anthropol. Archaeol.* 9:1–30

Spencer CS. 1993. Human agency, biased transmission, and the cultural evolution of chiefly authority. *J. Anthropol. Archaeol.* 12:41–74

Spencer CS. 1997. Evolutionary approaches in archaeology. *J. Archaeol. Res.* 5(3):209–64

Spencer CS. 1998. A mathematical model of primary state formation. *Cult. Dyn.* 10:5–20

Spencer CS, Redmond EM. 2004. Primary state formation in Mesoamerica. *Annu. Rev. Anthropol.* 33:173–99

Spencer H. 1851. *Social Statics*. London: John Chapman

Spencer H. 1857. Progress: its law and cause. *Westminster Rev.* 67:445–85

Spencer H. 1863. *First Principles*. London: Williams and Norgate

Stein G, Rothman M, eds. 1994. *Chiefdoms and Early States in the Near East*. Madison, WI: Prehist. Press

Steward JH. 1948. A functional-developmental classification of American high cultures. In *A Reappraisal of Peruvian Archaeology*, ed. WC Bennett. *Soc. Am. Arch. Mem.* 4:103–4

Steward JH. 1949. Cultural causality and law: a trial formulation of the development of early civilizations. *Am. Anthropol.* 51:1–27

Steward JH. 1953. Evolution and process. In *Anthropology Today*, ed. AL Kroeber, pp. 313–26. Chicago, IL: Univ. Chicago Press

Steward JH. 1955. *Theory of Culture Change*. Urbana: Univ. Ill. Press

Sumner WG, Keller AG. 1927–28. *The Science of Society*, Vol. 4. New Haven, CT: Yale Univ. Press

Townsend JB. 1985. The autonomous village and the development of chiefdoms. In *Development and Decline*, ed. HJM Claessen, P van de Velde, ME Smith, pp. 141–55. South Hadley, MA: Bergin & Harvey

Trigger BG. 2003. *Understanding Early Civilizations*. Cambridge, UK: Cambridge Univ. Press

Turner JH. 2003. *Human Institutions: A Theory of Societal Evolution*. Lanham, MD: Rowman & Littlefield

Tylor EB. 1870. *Researches into the Early History of Mankind*. London: John Murray. 2nd ed.

Tylor EB. 1889. On a method of investigating the development of institutions: applied to laws of marriage and descent. *J. R. Anthropol. Inst.* 18:245–69

Van Den Brink E, Levy TE, eds. 2002. *Egypt and the Levant: Interrelations from the 4th through the early 3rd Millennium BCE*. London: Leicester Univ. Press

Vannelli R. 2001. *Evolutionary Theory and Human Nature*. Boston: Kluwer Acad.

Vannelli R. 2005. *Societies as Complex Systems*. New York: Cambridge Univ. Press

von Fürer-Haimendorf C. 1969. *The Konyak Nagas*. New York: Holt, Rinehart, Winston

Walter R, Smith I, Jacomb C. 2006. Sedentism, subsistence, and socio-political organization in prehistoric New Zealand. *World Archaeol.* 38:274–90

Watson PJ. 1983. The Halafian culture: a review and synthesis. In *The Hilly Flanks and Beyond: Essays on the Prehistory of Southwestern Asia*, ed. TC Young, P Smith, P Mortensen, pp. 231–50. Chicago, IL: Orient. Inst., Univ. Chicago

Wendorf F, Schild R. 2004. Late Paleolithic warfare in Nubia: the evidence and causes. *Adumatu: J. Arab World* 10:7–28

Wilson DJ. 1988. *Prehispanic Settlement Patterns in the Lower Santa Valley, Peru*. Washington, DC: Smithson. Inst.

Woodburn J. 1988. African hunter-gatherer social organization: Is it best understood as a product of encapsulation? In *Hunters and Gatherers*, Vol. 1, ed. T Ingold, D Riches, J Woodburn, pp. 31–64. Oxford: Berg

Wright EO. 1983. Giddens's critique of Marxism. *New Left Rev.* 138:11–35

Wright HT, Johnson GA. 1975. Population, exchange and early state formation in southwestern Iran. *Am. Anthropol.* 77:267–89

Yoffee N, Clark JJ, eds. 1993. *Early Stages in the Evolution of Mesopotamian Civilization*. Tucson: Univ. Ariz. Press

From Resilience to Resistance: Political Ecological Lessons from Antibiotic and Pesticide Resistance

Kathryn M. Orzech and Mark Nichter

Department of Anthropology, University of Arizona, Tucson, Arizona 85721;
email: kmcelvee@email.arizona.edu, mnichter@email.arizona.edu

Annu. Rev. Anthropol. 2008. 37:267–82

First published online as a Review in Advance on June 18, 2008

The *Annual Review of Anthropology* is online at anthro.annualreviews.org

This article's doi:
10.1146/annurev.anthro.37.081407.085205

Key Words

antibiotic misuse, hygiene hypothesis, tragedy of the commons, global health governance

Abstract

This article investigates the interplay of natural and human systems with reference to the growing global problem of antibiotic resistance. Among the diverse causes of antibiotic resistance, we focus broadly on three related causes: pharmaceutical practice and the liberal consumption of antibiotics, the use of antibiotic-containing products in the home, and the use of antibiotics in commercial animal husbandry and agriculture. We draw a parallel between pesticide and antibiotic resistance and examine whether lessons learned from one case may be applicable to the other. Although our main focus is a microecological analysis examining how humans are changing their environments, our conclusion addresses larger implications of this problem for global health. Through the theoretical lens of political ecology, we ask how we may address the "tragedy of the antibiotic commons" through public education and consumer activism as well as global health governance.

INTRODUCTION

The complex adaptive nature of ecosystems means that evolutionary forces are strongest at lower levels of organization; we have learned that the hard way in our continual battles with the evolution of resistance to pesticides and antibiotics, and the unwillingness of microorganisms to take a reasonable approach to making things easy for us. (Levin 2001, p. 17)

Widespread antibiotic resistance is one of the hallmarks of the third epidemiological transition, where populations move from a chronic disease burden back to an increasingly uncontrollable burden of infectious disease (Barrett et al. 1998). Experts have been sounding the alarm about antibiotic resistance for some time (Anderson 2004, Morse 1995), but the many stakeholders involved in the development and spread of antibiotic resistance have been reluctant to take action. A major challenge in addressing antibiotic resistance is that both human and microbial factors contribute to its persistence. This article addresses antibiotic resistance in an evolutionary context by viewing it from both the human and microbe points of view, as well as by taking a broad view of human antibiotic use behavior. The perspective of political ecology is useful here because it combines the examination of ecology with political economy. It looks at the natural world as intertwined with the social, political, and economic world created by humans and explores the unequal power relations that often mediate human-environmental interaction (Bryant 1998, Greenberg & Park 1994). Although humans can anticipate and prepare for the future, biotic systems rely on "the success of past evolutionary experimentation" (Peterson 2000, p. 325), an important distinction to make when exploring the factors contributing to antibiotic resistance and also its potential solutions.

This article draws on Darwin's original definition of evolution as descent with modification (Darwin 1958 [1859]). The modern synthesis of evolution illuminates contemporary ideas of heritability (Mayr 2001), but the focus here is on modifications favored by natural selection that better fit organisms to their environments. This emphasis may differ from other utilizations of evolution because it acknowledges a sometimes pervasive idea that selection should work for the benefit of humans. It is clear from the example of antibiotic resistance, however, that natural selection does not favor one species over another.

Antibiotics have been widespread since the mid-twentieth century, but as soon as an antibiotic is introduced into a hospital or community setting, some resistance typically develops. For example, with penicillin resistance, a few bacteria came into contact with a naturally occurring fungus, and those bacteria that survived passed on this genetic immunity to future generations. Since the 1970s, however, antibiotic resistance has been rising more rapidly than before (Barrett et al. 1998, Harrison & Lederberg 1998, Lewis 1995). According to a Web resource designed to publicize environmental public health research findings, the rate of penicillin resistance increased by more than 300% between 1997 and 2002 (EMS 2002). Although it is beyond the scope of this review, antiviral resistance is also a growing problem, exemplified by the rapidly-evolving human immunodeficiency virus.

The importance of antibiotic resistance as a growing public health problem cannot be overstated (WHO 2001). Mortality, likelihood of hospitalization, and the length of hospital stay are approximately twice as great for individuals with resistant infections, compared with individuals with susceptible strains of bacteria (Holmberg et al. 1987). Disease transmission also increases because people remain infected longer. Antibiotic-resistant infections are more expensive to treat, and sometimes, because of costs or drug scarcity, they may be untreatable (Alliance Prudent Use Antib. 2005). Noting that the presence of resistant bacteria leads to poorer outcomes, however, does not tell the whole story. As resistance rates rise in one area, a switch may be made to a more expensive first-line antibiotic, so even those patients with infections susceptible to the initial antibiotic pay the additional cost to be treated with the

---

Antibiotic resistance: when a bacterial genetic mutation interferes with an antibiotic's ability to effectively control or kill bacteria

Political ecology: theoretical perspective combining ecology with political economy, looking at the natural, social, political, and economic worlds as intertwined

more expensive drug (Howard et al. 2003). The misuse of a common antibiotic resource by a few individuals results in negative consequences for many (Baquero & Campos 2003, Foster & Grundmann 2006), bringing to mind the concept of tragedy of the commons (Hardin 1968).

What Factors Encourage Antibiotic Resistance?

Antibiotic resistance is difficult to control because of the involvement of many different stakeholders. Following Blaikie (1995), **Figure 1** (see color insert) presents a "chain of explanation" for antibiotic resistance. Although many areas of the world have interconnected problems of resistance, this example uses the United States as a specific locus for the problem.

Humans have created an ideal environment for the development of antibiotic resistance. Health care providers often use antibiotics as part of a diagnosis-by-treatment strategy. Antibiotics are also freely available to laypeople over the counter in developing countries, and people often use these drugs to self-medicate (Abellanosa & Nichter 1996, Kamat & Nichter 1998, Nichter & Vuckovic 1994, Saradamma et al. 2000). Individuals may take antibiotics prophylactically, including for a cold or flu or even to reduce the chances of acquiring HIV or anthrax. Natural selection dictates that the selective pressure of antibiotic use will increase the number of resistant bacteria (Lieberman & Wootan 1998), but each of the stakeholders involved sees only a partial picture of the consequences for his/her actions. The situation is complicated by the fact that bacteria may also exist in a benign form in the body. When an individual is treated with a broad-spectrum antibiotic, the bacteria are exposed and resistant strains may be selected (Courvalin 2005). These resistant bacteria can then spread and colonize other people (Lipsitch & Samore 2002).

In addition to ingesting antibiotics, humans may be altering their environments by using antibacterial products in the home. These products, originally developed for use in hospitals, have made their way onto commercial shelves in increasing numbers. From 1990 to 2003, the number of antibacterial products jumped from 23 to more than 700 (Levy 2003). A direct relationship between use of antibacterial products and antibiotic resistance is hard to determine (Aiello & Larson 2003). A major concern remains, however, that relatively harmless bacteria that develop resistance from exposure to household products may transfer their resistance genes to other bacteria that will be more hazardous to human health (Lipsitch & Samore 2002, Tan et al. 2002).

Antibiotic resistance is also promoted through modern animal and plant husbandry. Animals are often raised in very close quarters, and farmers use low levels of antibiotics in animal feed to keep the group of animals healthy. Antibiotics are also often used as growth promoters, and these constant subtherapeutic doses are an ideal environment for the selection of resistance genes. Experts estimate that between 36% and 70% of all antibiotics used in the United States are used on animals (EMS 2002).

Although the numbers presented in **Table 1** are from 1995, they provide a graphic overview of quantities of antibiotics used annually in the United States alone. The 1995 date also indicates the difficulty of finding data across several major sites of antibiotic use in the same time frame.

View from the Microbe

One difficulty in coping with antibiotic resistance is that bacteria acquire and express resistance in diverse ways (**Figure 2**, see color insert). Replication mutations are common in bacteria, as is gene swapping within and between bacterial species (Lemon 2003). Under stress, such as antibiotic exposure, bacteria can increase their mutation rates, which could result in an accelerated rate of selection and produce more resistant organisms (Martinez & Baquero 2000). Cross-resistance, when a bacterial mutation in the presence of one antibiotic proves effective against other antibiotics, may be problematic (Levy 2001).

Tragedy of the commons: conflict over finite resources readily available within the public domain results in tension between self interest and the common good

Selective pressure: the influence of some factor that affects natural selection to promote survival of one organism over another

Broad-spectrum (versus narrow-spectrum) antibiotics: are active against a wider group of bacterial types than are narrow-spectrum antibiotics

Antibacterial products: products containing an antibacterial, a substance that interferes with the growth and reproduction of bacteria

Table 1 Estimated annual antibiotic use in humans and animals in the United States, and resistant pathogens[a]

Target group	Site of use	Uses	Amount	Use estimated as unnecessary	Resistant pathogens
Humans	Hospital	Therapeutic, prophylactic	~190 million annually defined daily doses	25%–45%	Staphylococci, enterococci, gram-negative rods
Humans	Community	Therapeutic, prophylactic	~145 million courses (110 million outpatient, 35 million emergency room)	20%–50%	Pneumococci, gonococci, Group A streptococci, *Escherichia coli*, *Mycobacterium tuberculosis*
Animals	Farm	Therapeutic	~4 million pounds	40%–80%	*Salmonella*, campylobacter
		Prophylactic	~16 million pounds		

[a]This table follows table 3 in Harrison & Lederberg (1998 pp. 40–41), drawn from a September 1995 Congressional Office of Technology Assessment report, *Impacts of Antibiotic-Resistant Bacteria*, OTA-H-629.

Fitness cost:
regarding natural selection, anything that decreases the amount of genetic material an individual can pass on to the next generation

TB: tuberculosis

Recently discovered interspecies communication among bacteria (Federle & Bassler 2003, Waters & Bassler 2005) may also worsen the effects of resistance for humans. The human immune system may be able to mediate some effects of antibiotic resistance but is limited by its own set of biological and social constraints (see sidebar, View from the Immune System).

For a microbe, the evolutionary question is whether the fitness cost is low or high for the genetic changes that mediate resistance. This is still an open question (Levy 1998, Luskin 2001), but research with izonaid-resistant tuberculosis (TB) seems to support the "low cost" side (Cohen et al. 2004).

HUMAN PRESCRIPTION AND CONSUMPTION OF ANTIBIOTICS

General overuse of antibiotics has been documented in both developed and developing countries. Patients may covertly or overtly demand antibiotics from physicians or may purchase antibiotics over the counter or from nonpharmacy sources in many countries (Radyowijati & Haak 2003). Although the ability to purchase antibiotics without a physician prescription may seem to encourage misuse, several authors have addressed the positive side of this practice (Bang et al. 1990, van der Geest 1987).

In competitive health-care markets around the world, doctors look for drugs with a "demonstration effect" so patients feel that they have "really received care" and will return to that practitioner. As a result, doctors may prefer injections and broad-spectrum antibiotics to pills or a narrow-spectrum drug that may not produce as noticeable of an effect (Nichter 2008, Nichter & Vuckovic 1994).

VIEW FROM THE IMMUNE SYSTEM

In early life, stem cells migrate to the thymus, where they mature into T-lymphocytes (T-cells), which mediate cellular immunity against pathogens. When a pathogen enters the body, accessory cells process the antigen and present it to the T-cells that have receptors for that antigen. This action allows the adaptive immune system to identify the pathogen and educate itself to recognize this interloper in the future (Hoffman-Goetz 1986). Immunity also depends on factors such as the life stage of the affected individual and his or her social and economic status. Children are particularly at risk for infections because of immature immune systems, lack of attention to hygiene, and close proximity to other children (Bradley 2003). Breastfeeding increases the infant's maternal antibodies and defense factors (McDade & Worthman 1999). Adequate nutritional resources are required to ensure adequate immune response, but in individuals of lower status, these may be diminished (Bhaskaram 2002). However, affluence and quick physician access may lead to overuse of antibiotics (Lieberman & Wootan 1998). This may result in an immune system that has not been properly "educated" on how to cope with pathogens (for more on this education model of immunity, see Aaby 1995, Cone & Martin 1998).

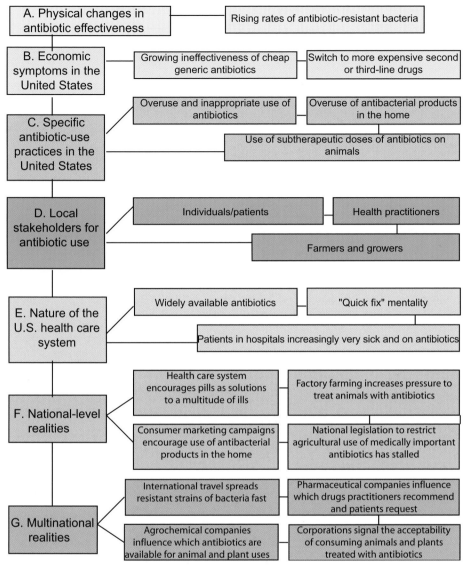

Figure 1

Chain of explanation for antibiotic resistance in the United States.

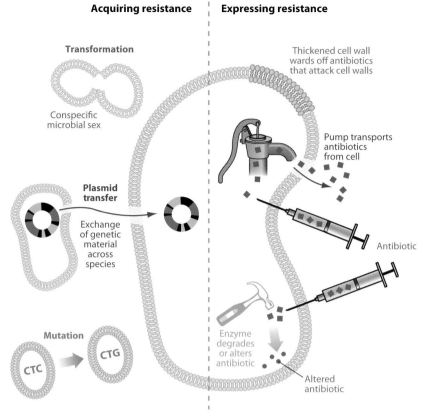

Acquiring resistance

Expressing resistance

Transformation

Conspecific
microbial sex

Thickened cell wall
wards off antibiotics
that attack cell walls

Pump transports
antibiotics
from cell

**Plasmid
transfer**

Exchange
of genetic
material
across
species

Antibiotic

Mutation

CTC → CTG

Enzyme
degrades
or alters
antibiotic

Altered
antibiotic

Figure 2

Ways bacteria acquire and express antibiotic resistance.

Another factor that contributes to overuse of antibiotics is that, especially in countries with an organized insurance scheme, hospital patients are increasingly seriously ill. "At any given time, 25 to 40% of hospital patients are receiving intravenous antibiotics" (Lieberman & Wootan 1998, p. 5). Hospitals use broad-spectrum antibiotics at a high rate rather than waiting the 24 hours necessary to conduct a culture and susceptibility test to determine whether a narrow-spectrum antibiotic might prove more effective (Lieberman & Wootan 1998).

Although many infections are viral in origin and improve without any treatment, practitioners may prescribe inappropriate antibiotics to respond to patient demands (Paredes et al. 1996). Practitioners may be pressed for time and have a desire to help their patients, and writing a prescription for a powerful antibiotic convinces the patient that he or she has "received care" from the practitioner (Nizami et al. 1997). Inadequate provision of practice guidelines and supervision may also play a role in inappropriate prescription of antibiotics (Chalker 2001). Where medication is limited, practitioners may prescribe what the dispensary has on hand rather than the antibiotic most appropriate for the patient's condition.

Failing to complete full courses of antibiotics is a worldwide practice, but especially common in non-Western countries, where it is possible to buy antibiotics over the counter. Individuals may buy an incomplete course of antibiotics because of financial constraints, to test the efficacy of a remedy, or to limit the amount of powerful medicine ingested by a patient (Kamat & Nichter 1998, Simon et al. 1996). By taking an incomplete course, an individual may be left with "extra" antibiotics to use at a later date, causing these drugs to become staples of the home medicine cabinet (Okumura et al. 2002, Stratchounski et al. 2003). Counterfeit drugs are also much more prevalent in developing countries and may contain too little of the active ingredient or different ingredients entirely (Kelesidis et al. 2007, WHO 1999).

The prophylactic use of antibiotics in humans is a worldwide problem that contributes to antibiotic resistance. Patients being prepped for surgery in the United States may receive antibiotics to prevent postsurgical infection, and teenagers with acne may be put on low doses of tetracycline to decrease levels of acne-causing bacteria (Lieberman & Wootan 1998). In other countries, for example, the Philippines and Thailand, individuals may take an antibiotic, often a first-line TB drug, Rifampin, after eating food of questionable hygienic status or as protection against contracting a sexually transmitted disease (STD) after visiting a prostitute (Nichter 2001). With increasing "medicalization" of daily life, prophylactic use of antibiotics and the use of medications to preemptively combat a potential illness will continue to be common practices unless a strong case is made against them.

IMMUNE SYSTEM HARM REDUCTION: ANTIBACTERIAL OVERLOAD AND THE HYGIENE HYPOTHESIS

From 1990 to 2003, the number of available antibacterial products jumped from 23 to more than 700 (Levy 2003). This increase does not reflect just cleaning products infused with an antibacterial agent. Many products are modified to contain triclosan (a common antibacterial agent), including pillows, sheets, towels, and slippers (Levy 2001). Despite a lack of scientific data to support the efficacy of antibiotic-containing products in the home, more than 45% of consumer soaps, for example, contain an antibiotic agent (Tan et al. 2002).

Society's move away from nature, and the microbes such proximity entails, changes a previously held balance. The disadvantage of living in close proximity to animals is zoonotic disease, but the benefit of this nearness may be exposure to antigens early in life that educate our immune systems about what to react to and what to ignore. Epidemiologist David Strachan (1989) codified this idea in the hygiene hypothesis.

The hygiene hypothesis asserts that children exposed to bacterial and viral antigens via

Susceptibility test: a measure of how well an antibiotic affects bacteria. Susceptible bacteria are killed or inhibited by an antibiotic

Hygiene hypothesis: suggests that exposure to antigens via childhood infections educates the immune system and results in a lower prevalence of allergies

infections have a lower prevalence of allergies (atopy). Protective factors against atopy include the presence of siblings and day care attendance early in life (Douwes & Pearce 2002, Strachan 1999). Living on a farm also seems to show a protective effect (Leynaert et al. 2001). More recent studies have affirmed some protective effect of the above-mentioned factors but have not found childhood infections to be a prime protective factor against later atopy (Benn et al. 2004). A 2005 paper introduces an alternative hypothesis that ties increasing rates of childhood asthma (a rise that has paralleled the increase in allergies) to "artificial habitats." This hypothesis suggests that atopy and asthma have not been driven by changes in infection levels from the "environment of evolutionary adaptation," but instead have increased because of a more complicated set of interrelated factors concerning housing and lifestyle (Maziak 2005).

ANTIBIOTIC USE IN ANIMALS AND PLANTS

Each year more than 8 million kilograms (kg) of antibiotics are given to animals and 22,000 kg are applied to fruit trees, representing more than 40%—and perhaps as much as 70%—of the antibiotics manufactured in the United States (Horrigan et al. 2002, Khachatourians 1998). As much as 80%–90% of this total is administered in subtherapeutic doses for growth promotion, improved feed conversion, and disease prevention (EMS 2002, Levy 1998, Lieberman & Wootan 1998; Mellor 2004).

In addition to direct exposure (consumption of animal products harboring resistant bacteria), there are a number of other ways for humans to acquire bacteria from animals. Antibiotic-resistant bacteria may be acquired from crops fertilized by or water contaminated by animal waste (EMS 2002), or bacteria may pass from person to person. A recent study found that ~26% of bacterial isolates taken from swine farm workers harbored resistant bacteria. Those farms that used antibiotic-containing food for their pigs had a higher percentage of resistant isolates, a finding that echoes previous studies of poultry farms (Akwar et al. 2007). Although recent data such as these are alarming, meat producers are often unwilling to change practices for fear that the economic impact will be too great. Evidence suggests, however, that modification of procedures to decrease the use of antibiotics can be performed without a loss in production (Thomke & Elwinger 1997).

Direct links may be made between use of particular antibiotics in animals and a corresponding rise in resistance among bacteria that afflict humans. Fluoroquinolone use in poultry has been tied to fluoroquinolone-resistant *Campylobacter*. The use of the antibiotic avoparcin in food animals and a rise in vancomycin-resistant enterococci (VRE) have also been linked (Keep Antibiot. Work. 2001, Lieberman & Wootan 1998; Wegener 2005). Even more recently, Chinese farmers have been dosing poultry flocks with the antiviral amantadine, potentially selecting for resistant strains of the H5N1 bird flu virus and rendering amantadine useless against human flu cases (Sipress 2005).

The use of antibiotics on crops is also a salient part of antibiotic resistance. Although only a small percentage of antibiotics produced for agriculture are used on plants, the quantity is still large enough for plant pathogens to have developed streptomycin resistance and for non-pathogenic orchard bacteria to have acquired tetracycline resistance (McManus 1999). The main bacterial pathogen for plants is related to other bacteria such as *Escherichia coli*, *Salmonella*, and *Shigella*, all common human pathogens (Lieberman & Wootan 1998). Aspects of this kind of antibiotic application, where antibiotics are applied over physically large areas in ways that may affect both groundwater and fruit supplies, leave the potential danger of this practice open for further investigation (McManus 1999).

THE PESTICIDE RESISTANCE PARALLEL

In 2001, the Food and Agriculture Organization reported more than 700 pest species were resistant to pesticides. A parallel may be drawn between the way that the presence of an antibiotic and the presence of a pesticide both select for resistance in their target species. Bacteria and insects often acquire resistance in the same way, through a single mutation. In the common fruit fly *Drosophila*, one gene change allows the fly to overproduce an enzyme that breaks down dichloro-diphenyl-trichloroethane (DDT) and other poisons. As seems to be the case in at least some instances of antibiotic resistance, removal of the selective agent (the global decline in the use of DDT in this case) does not necessarily cause the insects to revert back to a susceptible state (Major et al. 2003).

Given that pesticide resistance emerged as a problem earlier than did antibiotic resistance, what can we learn from this experience? Two methods to slow the development of resistance in pests are rotating pesticides and using mixtures of chemicals. These methods (and their parallels in antibiotic cycling and combination therapies) ensure that individuals are not repeatedly exposed to the same pesticide and/or antibiotic. Targeting a specific pest or bacterial species through "spot spraying," analogous to using narrow-spectrum antibiotics in humans, also limits exposure for other organisms, reducing cross-resistance. Evaluating the results of treatment can also help farmers or doctors to choose a more effective treatment (Gemplers 2008).

Two places where an antibiotic/pesticide parallel breaks down are in the areas of behavioral modification and creation of "refugia." Whereas insects can modify their behavior (for example, to dwell on the underside of leaves where pesticide concentrations may be lower), bacteria are not capable of this kind of behavior modification. Creating "refugia" where antibiotic-susceptible bacteria could live (parallel to not spraying certain sections of fields to encourage development of pesticide-susceptible insects) (Gemplers 2008) would be unethical because it would mean denying some patients necessary antibiotics. Instead, limiting antibiotic misuse helps to maximize the number of susceptible bacteria.

POTENTIAL SOLUTIONS

To minimize antibiotic resistance, solutions may be drawn from biological, social, and evolutionary realms, with the most effective plans combining elements from all three. See **Table 2** for several possible biological solutions.

Combination therapies are a particularly useful biological solution because with this method each drug attacks bacteria in a different way, minimizing resistance (Kaplan 2003). Antibiotic cycling, on the other hand, may not be as promising a solution because the assumed fitness cost to bacteria for becoming antibiotic resistant seems slight, and true cycling requires a return to the original antibiotic agent or class. When that occurs, resistance to that agent usually resurfaces rapidly (Gerding 2000, Hodges & White 2001).

A variety of social solutions may also help minimize antibiotic resistance (see **Table 3**).

Educating patients on proper antibiotic use is an important first step. Recent research has linked specific antibiotic overuse to specific rises in resistant bacteria within certain countries (Abramson & Givner 1999, Albrich et al. 2004). Each time an antibiotic is ingested, the likelihood increases that the antibiotic will be less effective in the future not only for the person who took the antibiotic, but for others as well (Laxminarayan & Brown 2001). This reality returns us to the tragedy of the commons. By conceptualizing antibiotics as an always-effective global resource, neither patients nor practitioners think about the effects of their antibiotic misuse on the larger population (Simpson et al. 2007).

Encouraging consumers to demand more responsible antibiotic use has proven effective in some cases. McDonalds Corporation now prohibits their direct suppliers from using "medically important antibiotics" as growth

Table 2   Biological solutions[a]

Solution	Methods to achieve solution
Getting the antibiotic right	More bacterial testing of individuals
	Better surveillance of resistant pathogens at the local (Mabey et al. 2004), national (Invasive Bacterial Infection Surveillance (IBIS) Group 1999, Simonsen et al. 2004, Thomas et al. 2003), and global levels (data sharing)
Redefining "a dose" of antibiotics	Calculating appropriate dosage based on the individual
	Social marketing about the meaning of "a dose"
	Blister packs with "a full dose"
Prescribing shorter courses of antibiotics	Confirm effectiveness of shorter (3-day versus 5-day) courses (el Moussaoui et al. 2006); if equally effective these could: 1. increase compliance with treatment, 2. reduce financial burden of taking antibiotics, and 3. diminish selective pressure on bacteria
Combination therapies	"Free combinations" (several different pills are taken together)
	FDCs (more than one drug combined in a single pill)
Antibiotic cycling	Rotating antibiotics to allow bacteria to revert back to a susceptible state (Empey et al. 2002, Schentag 2001)

[a]Abbreviations: FDC, fixed dose combination.

promoters. However, the practice of treating whole flocks or herds for disease when a few animals fall ill is still permitted (UCS 2003). Legislative regulation of antibiotics has generally been less effective, however. In 2005, bills to limit the agricultural use of eight "medically important" antibiotics were introduced in both houses of Congress and referred to committee. In 2007, a modified version of the bill was introduced again, but again stalled in committee. The FDA has recently been spurred to action by a variety of food contamination cases, however, and has curbed the sale of farm-raised fish from China, citing indiscriminate use of antibiotics, particularly fluoroquinolones, by Chinese farmers (Martin 2007).

Finally, two evolutionary solutions may minimize antibiotic resistance (see **Table 4**).

CONCLUSION: WHAT CAN WE LEARN FROM THE RISING TIDE OF RESISTANCE?

The evolution of antibiotic resistance is strongly influenced by the economic behavior of individuals and institutions. The more antibiotics are used (or misused), the greater the selective pressure placed on bacteria to evolve. The problem, therefore, arises from the absence of economic incentives to take into account the negative impact of their use of antibiotics on social welfare. (Laxminarayan & Brown 2001 p. 184)

The age of globalization is the age of universal contagion. (Hardt & Negri 2000, p. 136)

Antibiotic resistance teaches us about the complex interactions among microbes, plants, animals, and humans. One key lesson is that overreliance on quick fixes is often shortsighted, leaving us blindsided by new problems. Antibiotic resistance is a wake-up call for those who have adopted a view of health that pays scant attention to the interaction among species in an ever-changing micro- as well as macroenvironment. Evolutionarily, it is clear that natural selection fits organisms to their environments and does not favor one species over another. Given the multitude of factors contributing to antibiotic resistance, complex systems thinking such as that found in political ecology and ecosocial approaches to epidemiology (Krieger 2001) are needed to account for the impact

Table 3 Social solutions[a]

Solution	Methods to achieve solution
Minimize microbes	Even given the realities of poverty, endeavor to provide clean water and well-ventilated housing (Okeke et al. 1999, Pang & Guindon 2004)
	Encourage better hand-washing practices worldwide (Tierno 2001)
	Implement vaccination programs against common illnesses like pneumonia and measles
Educate patients on proper antibiotic use to avoid misuse	Encourage the use of replacement medications such as vitamins or other needed supplements
	Delay prescription of antibiotics for illnesses that are often viral in origin, perhaps with a safety-net prescription to be filled just in case (Rietveld et al. 2006, Siegel et al. 2003)
	Address patients' "individual" understanding of resistance (Bull 2000) by conducting translational research to express that by not completing a course of antibiotics, patients increase the presence of resistant bacteria, which is a danger to all in the long term
Educate practitioners on appropriate prescribing	Reduce misinformation given to providers about which drugs should be relied upon as first-line drugs
	Focus on practitioner oversight through education and STGs, which have proven effective (2000, Bavestrello & Cabello 2000)
	Make sure practitioners are alert to the possibility of inappropriately curbing antibiotic use (Price et al. 2004)
Minimize influence of pharmaceutical companies	Be aware that most drug information provided to practitioners in developing countries may come from pharmaceutical representatives, who are likely to be biased toward recommending newer and more costly drugs (Lexchin 2000)
	Make efforts to monitor phamaceutical advertising
Consider economic issues	Encourage pharmaceutical companies to invest in new classes of antibiotics (Spellberg et al. 2004) to treat the growing number of multidrug-resistant infections aptly illustrated by the recent flare-up of community-acquired MRSA (Klevens et al. 2007)
Reduce antibiotic use in animals and plants	Encourage consumers to demand an end to the use of antibiotics as growth promoters
	Implement regulations through Congress or the FDA (Keep Antibiot. Work. 2001)

[a]Abbreviations: FDA, Food and Drug Administration; MRSA, multi-drug resistant Staphylococcus aureus; STG: standard treatment guideline.

of political economic policy on medicine use. Attention must be turned to the set of human factors that affect medication use, especially in the private medical sector encouraged by prevailing neoliberal policies across much of the world.

A second key lesson taught to us by antibiotic resistance is just how rapidly the global can be affected by the local in the realm of microecology (Avorn & Solomon 2000, Martin 2006), a lesson we are also learning from emergent diseases such as severe acute respiratory

Table 4 Evolutionary solutions

Solution	Methods to achieve solution
Turn bacteria against themselves	Seek ways to make resistant microbes less fit in their environment (Zhang et al. 2006)
	Follow the example of Daigle and colleagues (1997) who have inhibited bacterial resistance enzymes using a modified protein kinase inhibitor, taking advantage of structural similarities between resistance enzymes and some protein kinases
Encourage an effective immune response in the host	Remember that cells involved in immune response, like the microbes they combat, exist in large, rapidly multiplying populations
	Recognize that the adaptive immune system uses an education model to create antibodies that bind to specific foreign antigens (McDade & Worthman 1999).

syndrome (SARS) and the avian flu. Strains of resistant bacteria that spread rapidly force us to rethink borders and the need for concerted global action in the area of pharmaceutical practice (Fidler 2003). A global sentinel surveillance system is called for to monitor antibiotic sensitivity/specificity as well as drug supply and patterns of use. It is becoming increasingly clear that it is in the best interests of wealthy countries to ensure that less developed countries have access to supplies of essential medicines to treat infectious disease, despite the perception that these diseases are "tropical" and distant from their shores (Nichter 2008).

The same is true for the use of antibiotics in agriculture. The biology of how animals acquire resistant bacteria and how those bacteria may be transferred from plants and animals to humans is becoming increasingly evident. Yet private industry has been notoriously ineffective at regulating its use of antibiotics except when forced to do so. Consumers play their own roles through their purchasing habits and willingness to acquire foods grown under globally irresponsible conditions. Knowledge and perception are beginning to change, however, in countries where quality of food has become a matter of growing public interest and concern.

A final question remains: "Is the often-discussed tragedy of the commons a good metaphor for understanding antibiotic resistance?" Our answer is yes and no. Antibiotics are not a "global public good" because they are privately developed, manufactured, sold, and managed according to the profit motives of pharmaceutical companies. These companies also influence prescribing habits of doctors and government policies. Despite this reservation, however, the tragedy of the commons metaphor brings needed attention to the issue of resistance and encourages patients and practitioners to think beyond their own personal benefit from using (or misusing) antibiotics.

The key to human resilience lies in the unique ability to collect information about microorganisms in an ever-changing environment and the capability to engage in the judicious use

and monitoring of antibiotics. Furthermore, we must involve the public in active strategies that enhance global health in ways that make ecological sense. For meaningful change to take place, transnational attention needs to be turned to global trends of medicine use that indirectly but powerfully affect pharmaceutical effectiveness. Global responsibility for health demands changes in government policy as it pertains to allocation of resources. In addition, global policies need to address pharmaceutical industry marketing practices that encourage antibiotic resistance.

The global elements of a successful strategy against antibiotic resistance include consumer and practitioner education, technical development, legal regulation, and international surveillance of antibiotic use (Khachatourians 1998). We also need to address health care disparities by making essential drugs readily available to the poor at an affordable price. These elements require a coordinated international effort, with some central body providing oversight and accountability so as to minimize conflicts in policy agendas (Fidler 2007).

At least two factors will transform the reality of antibiotic resistance from a biological concern into a biopolitical problem. First, our increasing inability to treat widespread diseases such as TB and malaria with a single drug will make it obvious to various stakeholders that a change in how we view antibiotics is overdue. Second, subpolitics (Beck 1996), which entails political engagement outside and beyond the institutions of the political system of nation-states, encourages conscientious consumption and examination of global commodity chains (Hughes & Reimer 2004). This focus helps individuals realize that by putting pressure on multinational corporations, they can affect how food is grown and raised, to the ultimate benefit of all. Some measure of antibiotic resistance is related to poverty and inappropriate drug use. Far more antibiotic resistance, however, is caused by noncompliance of people and corporations in the agricultural and medical fields and by the pricing of products beyond the reach of those people who would use such products effectively. This kind of biopolitical problem also opens up many issues for anthropologists because the global scope of antibiotic resistance forces us to think on many interconnected levels instead of thinking of individuals, states, or global corporations as isolated causes of this phenomenon.

SUMMARY POINTS

1. A variety of factors, related to both biology and human behavior, impact levels of antibiotic-resistant bacteria in a given area of the world.

2. Although we may think natural selection should operate for the benefit of humans, in reality, selection fits organisms to their environments and makes no distinction between humans and bacteria.

3. Humans worldwide engage in overuse and misuse of antibiotics, for a variety of reasons.

4. Use of antibacterial products in the home may encourage the development of resistant organisms, but more research is needed to determine how detrimental this practice may be to human health.

5. Antibiotic use in animals and plants is an often-overlooked part of the antibiotic resistance equation.

6. Parallels may be drawn between solutions to the longer-standing problem of pesticide resistance and the newer problem of widespread antibiotic resistance.

7. Potential solutions to rising rates of antibiotic resistance may be found at the biological, social, and evolutionary levels.

8. Truly making strides toward solving the antibiotic resistance problem will require a high degree of foresight and international cooperation among the world's governments.

FUTURE ISSUES

1. How do individual patients and community health care workers presently understand antibiotic resistance: as an individual problem related to noncompliance or compatibility, or as a population-based issue? Translational research is needed to improve understanding of public perceptions of antibiotic resistance.

2. How might information about antibiotic resistance rates best be circulated among networks of health practitioners; what might motivate them to alter their prescription practices as members of a community of practice, and why bother?

3. What role might pharmaceutical companies play in national/regional efforts to monitor trends in antibiotic use and emerging antibiotic resistance? What governmental policies and incentives might be introduced to encourage them to share information with health planners and epidemiologists?

4. Research into the political economy of antibiotic use is needed. To begin, researchers might conduct a commodity chain assessment focused on the push-pull dynamics (Fabricant & Hirschhorn 1987) of antibiotic production, marketing, demand, use, and oversight among stakeholders at each node in the chain.

DISCLOSURE STATEMENT

The authors are not aware of any biases that might be perceived as affecting the objectivity of this review.

ACKNOWLEDGMENTS

We offer our thanks to the many colleagues whose scholarship contributed to this review. We apologize in advance to those whose research may have been left out owing to space constraints. Thanks go to Paul Orzech for his initial design work on **Figure 2**.

LITERATURE CITED

2000. Changing prescriber behaviour: Training and treatment guidelines improve prescribing in Uganda. *Essent. Drugs Monit.* 28/29:15, **http://mednet2.who.int/edmonitor/edition/EDM2829en.pdf**

Aaby P. 1995. Assumptions and contradictions in measles and measles immunization research: Is measles good for something? *Soc. Sci. Med.* 41:673–86

Abellanosa I, Nichter M. 1996. Antibiotic prophylaxis among commercial sex workers in Cebu City, Philippines: patterns of use and perceptions of efficacy. *Sex. Transm. Dis.* 23:407–12

Abramson JS, Givner LB. 1999. Bacterial resistance due to antimicrobial drug addiction among physicians. *Arch. Fam. Med.* 8:79–80

Aiello AE, Larson E. 2003. Antibacterial cleaning and hygiene products as an emerging risk factor for antibiotic resistance in the community. *Lancet Infect. Dis.* 3:501–6

Akwar TH, Poppe C, Wilson J, Reid-Smith RJ, Dyck M, et al. 2007. Risk factors for antimicrobial resistance among fecal *Escherichia coli* from residents on forty-three swine farms. *Microb. Drug Resist.* 13:69–76

Albrich WC, Monnet DL, Harbarth S. 2004. Antibiotic selection pressure and resistance in *Streptococcus pneumoniae* and *Streptococcus pyogenes*. *Emerg. Infect. Dis.* 10:514–17

Alliance Prudent Use Antibiot. 2005. Executive summary: global antimicrobial resistance alerts and implications. *Clin. Infect. Dis.* 41(Suppl. 4):S221–23

Anderson W. 2004. Natural histories of infectious disease: ecological vision in twentieth-century biomedical science. *Osiris* 19:39–61

Avorn J, Solomon DH. 2000. Cultural and economic factors that (mis)shape antibiotic use: the nonpharmacologic basis of theraputics. *Ann. Intern. Med.* 133:128–35

Bang AT, Bang RA, Tale O, Sontakke P, Solanki J, et al. 1990. Reduction in pneumonia mortality and total childhood mortality by means of community-based intervention trial in Gadchiroli, India. *Lancet* 336:201–6

Baquero F, Campos J. 2003. The tragedy of the commons in antimicrobial chemotherapy. *Rev. Esp. Quimioter.* 16:11–13

Barrett R, Kuzawa CW, McDade T, Armelagos GJ. 1998. Emerging and re-emerging infectious diseases: the third epidemiologic transition. *Annu. Rev. Anthropol.* 27:247–71

Bavestrello L, Cabello A. 2000. How Chile tackled overuse of antimicrobials. *Essent. Drugs Monit.* 28/29:13–14

Beck U. 1996. World risk society as cosmopolitan society? Ecological questions in a framework of manufactured uncertainties. *Theory Cult. Soc.* 13:1–32

Benn CS, Melbye M, Wohlfahrt J, Bjorksten B, Aaby P. 2004. Cohort study of sibling effect, infectious diseases, and risk of atopic dermatitis during first 18 months of life. *BMJ* 328:1223–27

Bhaskaram P. 2002. Micronutrient malnutrition, infection, and immunity: an overview. *Nutr. Rev.* 60:S40–45

Blaikie P. 1995. Understanding environmental issues. In *People and Environment*, ed. S Morse, M Stocking, pp. 1–30. London: UCL Press

Bradley RH. 2003. Child care and common communicable illnesses in children aged 37 to 54 months. *Arch. Pediatr. Adolesc. Med.* 157:196–200

Bryant RL. 1998. Power, knowledge and political ecology in the third world: a review. *Prog. Phys. Geogr.* 22:79–94

Bull JJ. 2000. Evolutionary biology: technology for the 21st century. **http://www.actionbioscience.org/newfrontiers/bull.html**

Chalker J. 2001. Improving antibiotic prescribing in Hai Phong Province, Viet Nam: the "antibiotic-dose" indicator. *Bull. World Health Organ.* 79:313–20

Cohen T, Becerra MC, Murray MB. 2004. Isoniazid resistance and the future of drug-resistant tuberculosis. *Microb. Drug Resist.* 10:280–85

Cone RA, Martin E. 1998. Chapter 12: Corporeal flows: the immune system, global economies of food and new implications for health. In *The Visible Woman: Imaging Technologies, Gender and Science*, ed. PA Treichler, L Cartwright, C Penley, pp. 321–59. New York: New York Univ. Press

Courvalin P. 2005. Antimicrobial drug resistance: "Prediction is very difficult, especially about the future". *Emerg. Infect. Dis.* 11:1503–6

Daigle DM, McKay GA, Wright GD. 1997. Inhibition of aminoglycoside antibiotic resistance enzymes by protein kinase inhibitors. *J. Biol. Chem.* 272:24755–58

Darwin C. 1958 [1859]. *The Origin of Species by Means of Natural Selection or the Preservation of Favoured Races in the Struggle for Life*. New York: New Am. Libr. World Lit.

Douwes J, Pearce N. 2002. Asthma and the westernization 'package'. *Int. J. Epidemiol.* 31:1098–102

el Moussaoui R, de Borgie CA, Van Den Broek P, Hustinx WN, Bresser P, et al. 2006. Effectiveness of discontinuing antibiotic treatment after three days versus eight days in mild to moderate-severe community acquired pneumonia: randomised, double blind study. *BMJ* 332:1355–58

Empey KM, Rapp RP, Evans ME. 2002. The effect of an antimicrobial formulary change on hospital resistance patterns. *Pharmacotherapy* 22:81–87

EMS. 2002. *Fast facts: antibiotic resistance*. Environmental Media Services. **http://www.ems.org/antibiotics/sub2_antibiotics.html**

Fabricant SJ, Hirschhorn N. 1987. Deranged distribution, perverse prescription, unprotected use: the irrationality of pharmaceuticals in the developing world. *Health Policy Plan.* 2:204–13

Federle MJ, Bassler BL. 2003. Interspecies communication in bacteria. *J. Clin. Invest.* 112:1291–99

Fidler DP. 2003. Chapter 9: Antimicrobial resistance: a challenge for global health governance. In *Health Impacts of Globalization: Toward Global Health Governance*, ed. K Lee, pp. 144–60. New York: Palgrave MacMillan

Fidler DP. 2007. Reflections on the revolution in health and foreign policy. *Bull. World Health Organ.* 85:243–44

Foster KR, Grundmann H. 2006. Do we need to put society first? The potential for tragedy in antimicrobial resistance. *PLoS Med.* 3:e29

Gemplers Inc. 2008. Getting started with IPM (Integrated Pest Management). **http://www.gemplers.com/tech/ipm-intro.htm**

Gerding DN. 2000. Antimicrobial cycling: lessons learned from the aminoglycoside experience. *Infect. Control Hosp. Epidemiol.* 21:S12–17

Greenberg JB, Park TK. 1994. Political ecology. *J. Polit. Ecol.* 1:1–11

Hardin G. 1968. The tragedy of the commons. *Science* 162:1243–48

Hardt M, Negri A. 2000. *Empire*. Cambridge, MA: Harvard Univ. Press

Harrison PF, Lederberg J, eds. 1998. *Antimicrobial Resistance: Issues and Options*. Washington, DC: Natl. Acad. Press. 1–74 pp.

Hodges BM, White RL. 2001. Antimicrobial cycling: the future or a fad? *Ann. Pharmacother.* 35:1224–32

Hoffman-Goetz L. 1986. Malnutrition and immunological function with special reference to cell-mediated immunity. *Yearb. Phys. Anthropol.* 29:139–59

Holmberg SD, Solomon SL, Blake PA. 1987. Health and economic impacts of antimicrobial resistance. *Rev. Infect. Dis.* 9:1065–78

Horrigan L, Lawrence RS, Walker P. 2002. How sustainable agriculture can address the environmental and human health harms of industrial agriculture. *Environ. Health Perspect.* 110:445–56

Howard DH, Scott RD 2nd, Packard R, Jones D. 2003. The global impact of drug resistance. *Clin. Infect. Dis.* 36:S4–10

Hughes A, Reimer S, eds. 2004. *Geographies of Commodity Chains*. London: Routledge

Invasive Bact. Infect. Surveill. (IBIS) Group ICENI. 1999. Prospective multicentre hospital surveillance of *Streptococcus pneumoniae* disease in India. Invasive Bacterial Infection Surveillance (IBIS) Group, International Clinical Epidemiology Network (INCLEN). *Lancet* 353:1216–21

Kamat VR, Nichter M. 1998. Pharmacies, self-medication and pharmaceutical marketing in Bombay, India. *Soc. Sci. Med.* 47:779–94

Kaplan W. 2003. *Effect of fixed dose combination (FDC) drugs on development of clinical antimicrobial resistance: a review paper.* World Health Organization. **http://www.who.int/medicinedocs/en/d/Js6172e/#Js6172e.11.1**

Keep Antibiot. Work. 2001. *Antibiotic resistance—an emerging public health crisis.* Campaign to End Antibiotic Overuse. **http://www.keepantibioticsworking.com/library/uploadedfiles/Antibiotic_Resistance_-_An_Emerging_Public_2.pdf**

Kelesidis T, Kelesidis I, Rafailidis PI, Falagas ME. 2007. Counterfeit or substandard antimicrobial drugs: a review of the scientific evidence. *J. Antimicrob. Chemother.* 60:214–36

Khachatourians GG. 1998. Agricultural use of antibiotics and the evolution and transfer of antibiotic-resistant bacteria. *CMAJ* 159:1129–36

Klevens RM, Morrison MA, Nadle J, Petit S, Gershman K, et al. 2007. Invasive methicillin-resistant *Staphylococcus aureus* infections in the United States. *JAMA* 298:1763–71

Knobler SL, Lemon SM, Najafi M, Burroughs T, eds. 2003. *The Resistance Phenomenon in Microbes and Infectious Disease Vectors: Implications for Human Health and Strategies for Containment: Workshop Summary.* Washington, DC: Natl. Acad. Press

Krieger N. 2001. Theories for social epidemiology in the 21st century: an ecosocial perspective. *Int. J. Epidemiol.* 30:668–77

Laxminarayan R, Brown GM. 2001. Economics of antibiotic resistance: a theory of optimal use. *J. Environ. Econ. Manag.* 42:183–206

Lemon SM. 2003. Summary and assessment. See Knobler et al. 2003, pp. 1–17

Levin SA. 2001. Immune systems and ecosystems. *Conserv. Ecol.* 5:17 **http://www.consecol.org/vol5/iss1/art17**

Levy SB. 1998. Multidrug resistance—a sign of the times. *N. Engl. J. Med.* 338:1376–78

Levy SB. 2001. Antibacterial household products: cause for concern. *Emerg. Infect. Dis.* 7:512–15

Levy SB. 2003. Antibiotic resistance 1992–2002: a decade's journey. See Knobler et al. 2003, pp. 32–43

Lewis R. 1995. The rise of antibiotic-resistant infections. *FDA Consum. Mag.* Sept. **http://www.fda.gov/Fdac/features/795_antibio.html**

Lexchin J. 2000. Promoting resistance? *Essent. Drugs Monit.* 28/29:11

Leynaert B, Neukirch C, Jarvis D, Chinn S, Burney P, Neukirch F. 2001. Does living on a farm during childhood protect against asthma, allergic rhinitis, and atopy in adulthood? *Am. J. Respir. Crit. Care Med.* 164:1829–34

Lieberman PB, Wootan MG. 1998. *Protecting the Crown Jewels of Medicine: A Strategic Plan to Preserve the Effectiveness of Antibiotics.* Washington, DC: Cent. Sci. Public Interest (CPSI)

Lipsitch M, Samore M. 2002. Antimicrobial use and antimicrobial resistance: a population perspective. *Emerg. Infect. Dis.* 8:347–54

Luskin C. 2001. *The implications of antibiotic and antiviral drug resistance for the power of Darwinian evolution.* Intelligent Design and Evolution Awareness (IDEA) Club. **http://www.ideacenter.org/contentmgr/showdetails.php/id/848**

Mabey D, Peeling RW, Ustianowski A, Perkins MD. 2004. Diagnostics for the developing world. *Nat. Rev. Microbiol.* 2:231–40

Major J, Bogwitz M, Perry T. 2003. *Lone gene could force rethink on pest insect control.* Presented at Int. Congr. Genet. Poster, 19th, July 6–11. Referenced in **http://news.bio-medicine.org/biology-news-2/Lone-gene-could-force-re-think-on-pest-insect-control-4295-1/**

Martin A. 2007. FDA curbs sale of 5 seafoods farmed in China. *New York Times* June 29. **http://www.nytimes.com/2007/06/29/business/worldbusiness/29fish.html**

Martin G. 2006. The global health governance of antimicrobial effectiveness. *Glob. Health* 2:7, **http://www.globalizationandhealth.com/content/2/1/7**

Martinez JL, Baquero F. 2000. Mutation frequencies and antibiotic resistance. *Antimicrob. Agents Chemother.* 44:1771–77

Mayr E. 2001. *What Evolution Is.* New York: Basic Books. 318 pp.

Maziak W. 2005. The asthma epidemic and our artificial habitats. *BMC Pulm. Med.* 5:5–11

McDade TW, Worthman CM. 1999. Evolutionary process and the ecology of human immune function. *Am. J. Human Biol.* 11:705–17

McManus PS. 1999. Antibiotic use in plant disease control. *APUA Newsl.* 17:1–3

Mellor S. 2004. *Dairy cattle: alternatives to antibiotics.* Community of International Business Related to Animal Production. **http://www.engormix.com**

Morse SS. 1995. Factors in the emergence of infectious diseases. *Emerg. Infect. Dis.* 1:7–15

Nichter M. 2001. Vulnerability, prophylactic antibiotic use, harm reduction and the misguided appropriation of medical resources: the case of STDs in Southeast Asia. In *Culture and Reproductive Health*, ed. C Obermeyer, pp. 101–27. Oxford, UK: Oxford Univ. Press

Nichter M. 2008. *Global Health: Why Cultural Perceptions, Social Representations and Biopolitics matter.* Tucson: Univ. Ariz. Press

Nichter M, Vuckovic N. 1994. Agenda for an anthropology of pharmaceutical practice. *Soc. Sci. Med.* 39:1509–25

Nizami SQ, Khan IA, Bhutta ZA. 1997. Paediatric prescribing in Karachi. *J. Pak. Med. Assoc.* 47:29–32

Okeke IN, Lamikanra A, Edelman R. 1999. Socioeconomic and behavioral factors leading to acquired bacterial resistance to antibiotics in developing countries. *Emerg. Infect. Dis.* 5:18–27

Okumura J, Wakai S, Umenai T. 2002. Drug utilisation and self-medication in rural communities in Vietnam. *Soc. Sci. Med.* 54:1875–86

Pang T, Guindon GE. 2004. Globalization and risks to health. *EMBO Rep.* 5:S11–16

Paredes P, de la Pena M, Flores-Guerra E, Diaz J, Trostle J. 1996. Factors influencing physicians' prescribing behaviour in the treatment of childhood diarrhoea: knowledge may not be the clue. *Soc. Sci. Med.* 42:1141–53

Peterson G. 2000. Political ecology and ecological resiliance: an integration of human and ecological dynamics. *Ecol. Econ.* 35:323–36

Price DB, Honeybourne D, Little P, Mayon-White RT, Read RC, et al. 2004. Community-acquired pneumonia mortality: a potential link to antibiotic prescribing trends in general practice. *Respir. Med.* 98:17–24

Radyowijati A, Haak H. 2003. Improving antibiotic use in low-income countries: an overview of evidence on determinants. *Soc. Sci. Med.* 57:733–44

Rietveld RP, Bindels PJ, ter Riet G. 2006. Antibiotics for upper respiratory tract infections and conjunctivitis in primary care. *BMJ* 333:311–12

Saradamma RD, Higgenbothan N, Nichter M. 2000. Social factors influencing the acquisition of antibiotics without a prescription in Kerala State, South India. *Soc. Sci. Med.* 50:891–903

Schentag JJ. 2001. Antimicrobial management strategies for Gram-positive bacterial resistance in the intensive care unit. *Crit. Care Med.* 29:N100–7

Siegel RM, Kiely M, Bien JP, Joseph EC, Davis JB, et al. 2003. Treatment of otitis media with observation and a safety-net antibiotic prescription. *Pediatrics* 112:527–31

Simon A, Janabi M, Kalmayem G, Waidubu G, Galia E, et al. 1996. Caretakers' management of childhood acute respiratory infections and the use of antibiotics, Bohol, the Philippines. *Hum. Organ.* 55:76–83

Simonsen GS, Tapsall JW, Allegranzi B, Talbot EA, Lazzari S. 2004. The antimicrobial resistance containment and surveillance approach—a public health tool. *Bull. World Health Organ.* 82:928–34

Simpson SA, Wood F, Butler CC. 2007. General practitioners' perceptions of antimicrobial resistance: a qualitative study. *J. Antimicrob. Chemother.* 59:292–96

Sipress A. 2005. Human drug used on China chickens; antiviral employed to fight bird flu. *Washington Post* June 18:A1

Spellberg B, Powers JH, Brass EP, Miller LG, Edwards JE Jr. 2004. Trends in antimicrobial drug development: implications for the future. *Clin. Infect. Dis.* 38:1279–86

Strachan DP. 1989. Hay fever, hygiene, and household size. *BMJ* 299:1259–60

Strachan DP. 1999. Lifestyle and atopy. *Lancet* 353:1457–58

Stratchounski LS, Andreeva IV, Ratchina SA, Galkin DV, Petrotchenkova NA, et al. 2003. The inventory of antibiotics in Russian home medicine cabinets. *Clin. Infect. Dis.* 37:498–505

Tan L, Nielsen NH, Young DC, Trizna Z. 2002. Use of antimicrobial agents in consumer products. *Arch. Dermatol.* 138:1082–86

Thomas K, Lalitha MK, Steinhoff MC, Ganesan A. 2003. *Temporal trends in antimicrobial resistance patterns of invasive pnuemococci in 7 hospitals in India—a 10 year experience.* Presented at Intersci. Conf. Antimicrob. Agents Chemother.

Thomke S, Elwinger K. 1997. *Report to the Commission on Antimicrobial Feed Additives.* Uppsala: Swedish Univ. Agric.

Tierno P. 2001. *The Secret Life of Germs.* New York: Simon and Schuster

UCS. 2003. *Antibiotic resistance program update.* Union of Concerned Scientists. **http://www.ucsusa.org/food_and_environment/antibiotics_and_food/**

Van Der Geest S. 1987. Self-care and the informal sale of drugs in south Cameroon. *Soc. Sci. Med.* 25:293–305

Waters CM, Bassler BL. 2005. Quorum sensing: cell-to-cell communication in bacteria. *Annu. Rev. Cell Dev. Biol.* 21:319–46

Wegener HC. 2005. *The food chain: antibiotic use in animals.* Wellcome Trust. **http://www.wellcome.ac.uk/stellent/groups/corporatesite/@msh_publishing_group/documents/web_document/wtx026231.pdf**

WHO. 1999. Containing antimicrobial resistance: review of the literature and report of a WHO workshop on the development of a global strategy for the containment of antimicrobial resistance. *WHO/CDS/CSR/DRS/99/2*, World Health Organization, Geneva

WHO. 2001. Executive summary: WHO global strategy for containment of antimicrobial resistance. *WHO/CDS/CSR/DRS/2001/2/EN*, World Health Organization, Geneva

Zhang R, Eggleston K, Rotimi V, Zeckhauser RJ. 2006. Antibiotic resistance as a global threat: evidence from China, Kuwait and the United States. *Global Health* 2:6–19

Violence, Gender, and Subjectivity

Veena Das

Department of Anthropology, Johns Hopkins University, Baltimore, Maryland 21218;
email: veenadas@jhu.edu

Annu. Rev. Anthropol. 2008. 37:283–99

First published online as a Review in Advance on
June 18, 2008

The *Annual Review of Anthropology* is online at
anthro.annualreviews.org

This article's doi:
10.1146/annurev.anthro.36.081406.094430

Key Words

contract, consent, militarization, sexuality, domestic

Abstract

This review examines the interlocking of violence, gender, and subjectivity within the overarching framework of the sexualization of the social contract. Tracking the question of gendered belonging to the nation state, the article discusses the anthropological literature along with feminist and critical theory to shed light on the relation between reproduction and death as a way of giving life to the nation-state. Sexual and reproductive violence are closely linked to the social and cultural imaginaries of order and disorder; and violence, far from being an interruption of the ordinary, is folded into the ordinary.

INTRODUCTION

The ethnographic record shows the concept of violence to be extremely unstable. Instead of policing the definition of violence, this review deems the instability as crucial for understanding how the reality of violence includes its virtuality and its potential to make and unmake social worlds. It also argues that the category of gender is crucial for understanding what connects the national to the domestic, and empires to colonies. The title's third term subjectivity runs through the entire text as we see how the subject comes to be attached to larger collectivities giving expression to an astonishing range of emotions in relation to violence. The centrality of gender in the understanding of violence will show the deep connections between the spectacular and the everyday. The scholarly and popular literature on violence has escalated in recent years as the settled geographies of violence have been questioned. There is an increasing public perception that safe havens no longer exist and that peace-time violence is as debilitating as that of war (Scheper-Hughes 1997, Scheper-Hughes & Bourgois 2003) Sometimes one feels that there is a kind of definitional vertigo in the deployment of the term violence, yet there is merit in the idea that the contests around the question of what can be named as violence are themselves a sign of something important at stake. Therefore, instead of policing the definition of the term violence I hope that by engaging the very instability of this definition, I can show what is at stake in naming something as violence. The title's second term gender has also undergone important conceptual revisions in recent times. The most important of these revisions is that if the category gender was supposed to stand in opposition to sex in the 1960s to show the constructed character of the categories of male and female, today it is the mutual constitution of sex and gender that is considered to be far more productive (Pateman 1990). Certainly in the analysis of violence, I find it much more useful to think of sex and gender as together providing a way to highlight certain aspects of violence that would otherwise remain obscure. Finally, the title's third term subjectivity indicates the importance of the intersubjective character of experience (Biehl et al. 2007a, Das et al. 2000, Kleinman & Fitz-Henry 2007, Rorty 2007) as providing the ground from which I analyze the phenomena of violence. Reading the ethnographic record in light of the anthropological quest to render the specific practices that come to be named as violence, in conjunction with some key texts in feminist and critical theory, serves to unsettle many issues. And although this unsettling might not help us to reach any firm conclusions on the nature of violence, it has, at the very least, the merit of telling us what we do not yet understand.

The main arguments of the paper are as follows. First, I consider the relation between the social contract and the sexual contract as establishing consent to the political order and the domestic order, respectively. I ask what happens when the social contract is sexualized: Consent is forced, even parodied, and the "social savage" is made to appear in times of disorder. What relation does that bear to masculinity and femininity as social constructs and to our understanding of sexuality? The second set of issues follow from the first. If the idea of consent on which political and domestic order are said to be based is in fact a fragile construction, constantly vulnerable to a founding violence that assigns men to the political community and women to the domestic one, then difficulties of naming certain practices of the home as violence are shown to be at the heart of the question of how violence and intimacy (both political and domestic) are interlocked. Third, some key ethnographic texts on the theme of violence show how different affects, emotions, and dispositions present themselves. How is it that we can find references to courage, sacrifice, heroism, cowardice, despair, grief, angst, anger, suffocation, laughter, parody, longing, love, hate, disgust, horror, fear, pain, suffering—in fact, every conceivable kind of emotion or disposition—as part of the experience of violence? Do these emotions and dispositions come to be distributed around categories of gender and of sexuality? How do these affects help us to understand what is a central characteristic of violence, as both actuality and potentiality—that it inheres in everyday life and constitutes a flight from it?

THE POLITICAL AND SOCIAL CONTRACT

Recent literature on the nation-state has unearthed the paradox that while modern states claim legitimacy on the grounds that the rule of law established through their agency has led to enduring social peace, in fact terrible atrocities have been committed on populations that threatened existing perceptions of national unity and security by the agencies of the state (Asad 2003, Naimark 2001). Feminist philosophers, such as Ivekovic (2003) and MacKinnon (1991), argue that it is not so much the ideology of secularism, progress, or biopolitics, but the definition of the state as a masculine state that accounts for the gendered violence of the modern state. Whichever adjectives we attach to the idea of the state under modernity—biopolitical, progressive, secular—the route through which violence becomes part of the subject's attachment to the modern state remains a pressing issue. In this context, the foundational or origin stories that are told about the nation-state within liberal philosophy about giving life to the nation and dying for the nation are important because they seem to normalize violence as part of gendered belonging to the nation-state (Meyer 2000, Yuval-Davis 1997).

One of the places to begin an examination of these foundational stories is to consider the place of nature as inherently violent and the role that this idea plays in the creation of the political. The problem, as I see it, is that once the idea of God as the author of nature and time is displaced and the political body under secularism is seen as subject to death and decay, secular means must be crafted to ensure that the sovereign receives life beyond the lifetime of its individual members (Das 2007b). This entails two obligations. The first obligation is that men should be ready to bear arms for the nation and be ready to die for it (Taylor 2004). The second is that women's reproduction is seen to be rightly belonging to the state (Meyer 2000, Schoenbrun 2003) so that as citizens they are obligated to bear "legitimate" children who will be, in turn, ready to die for the nation (Das 2007b). Thus sex and death, reproduction and war, become part of the same configuration of ideas and institutions through which the nation-state sets up defenses to stave off the uncertainty emanating from dangerous aliens and from the ravages of time. Within this broad picture are, of course, important differences, and historians have shown how ideas about death, preservation, and belonging evolved in specific historical contexts emphasizing regulation in some cases, pedagogy in others (Surkis 2006). Nevertheless, historians and political philosophers demonstrate certain broad agreements about the rights of nation-states to demand different kinds of attachments from their male and female members, which might be usefully delineated here.

Because the state of nature is seen as the point of mythic origin of the state (as in Hobbes), it seems appropriate to begin our own analysis on how Hobbes imagined the emergence of the state as rooted in social contract so that men exchange the perpetual warfare considered normal to the state of nature for the peaceful coexistence within the political community by delegating authority to the state (Hobbes 1981 [1656]). One of the frequently cited passages in Hobbes refers to the mushroom analogy in which we are asked to consider men as sprung out of the earth and suddenly "like mushrooms, come to full maturity, without all kind of engagement to each other." Many feminist scholars have noted the exclusion of the woman from this originary imagination of social order. Thus, Pateman (1980, 1988) notes that the invitation to think of men as springing up like mushrooms is designed to obscure the fact that contractual individualism is grounded in the husband's subjugation of the wife who is consigned to the realm of the domestic without any political rights. Although this line of argumentation is powerful in showing how the profoundly masculine Leviathan is formulated on the explicit exclusion of women, further thinking is required on the conditions under which women come to be included as certain kinds of sexed citizens within the political community.

As many scholars have noted, there is an important shift in Hobbes as compared with Filmer (1991 [1653]) in that consent comes to play an extremely important role in the imagination of Hobbes for the creation of both the political community and the domestic community. Recall that for Filmer, fatherly authority over the family was natural; the father was the head of the family according to the divine law of nature and kingly authority was based on fatherly authority. For Hobbes, in contrast, we have a predication of fatherly authority based on consent rather than something that is natural or originary. But, as Severance (2000) notes, the consent of the family to be ruled by the father is, in effect, to neutralize his power to kill. The sexual contract and the social contract are then two separate realms, but the relation between these two is a vexed one. Certainly, as Severance notes, the idea of the state of nature as that in which every man is in a state of war with every other man should be modified to read as that in which every father as the head of the family is in war against every other father. The members of each individual family "consent" not to the sovereign's but to the father's absolute rule; they are not parties to the "contract" that brings the commonwealth into existence. Unlike the consent to be ruled by the father, which protects the family against him such that political society stops at the door step of the family, the consent to the social contract protects individuals against each other by vesting power in the sovereign but on the condition that they consent to preserve the nation-state by agreeing to be killed in what comes to be regarded as the sacrificial violence offered for the preservation of the nation.

How do these politico-theological ideas translate into the actual practices of war and the way heroic masculinity is imagined in the conduct of warfare?

WAR AND THE HEROIC VIRTUES: THE IMPERATIVES OF THE COLLECTIVE

The theme that violence has been "civilized" in modern warfare owing to the mediation of law and technology is in continuity with the theme of the modern state as the guarantor of peace against diffused violence. The state's monopoly over what Weber called "legitimate" violence does not end violence—it redistributes it (Das & Poole 2004, Weber 1948). The stitching together of the state with the nation makes demands on men to exercise heroic virtues in war to protect the nation. Yet the individual experience of war might be remarkably different from the public celebration of the virtues associated with "civilized" men.

Although philosophers such as Bataille (1957, 1961) think that modern war has lost touch with the passionate visceral experience of hand to hand combat and killing (but see Bourke 1999 for a more historically grounded view), historical and anthropological work reveal that unauthorized massacres, rape, and formation of all kinds of illicit relations on the war front occur in most wars (Karsten 1978, Nordstrom 1997). Thus there is a great disparity between the public celebration of the masculine virtues of heroism and the actual experience of soldiers as they attempt to manage life and death on the war front (Barham 2004). In all major wars since World War I (WWI), processes of censorship have been used to hide from the public and even from the families of soldiers any deviations from the picture of idealized masculinity expected of soldiers (Fussell 1989). An essential element in the contract between the male citizen and the state was the consent to have one's body altered for the state because consent to kill and to die on behalf of the state was assumed (Humphrey 2002). Until recently, the citizens who were asked to bear arms were men, although participation of women as soldiers in both formal armies (Sasson-Levy 2003) and other forms of warfare has increased (De Mel 2003, Trawick 2007). A large number of women have also been involved in war efforts in such capacities as nursing or have been coerced in providing sexual services to soldiers, although scholars have only recently begun attempts to theorize the implications of female participation for a wider understanding of warfare and of militarization of society (Enloe 2000, Moser & Clarke 2001, Peach 1994) that has a serious and long-lasting impact on the lives of men and women (De Mel 2007, Waller & Rycenga 2001).

But even as far as male experience is concerned, much evidence indicates that soldiers did not always consent to the state's demands for injuring or being injured (Humphrey 2002). Fussell (1975) has documented how all injury during WWI was assimilated to heroic sacrifice whatever the circumstances of the injury. Ironically this included soldiers who were shot at the front for desertion but were represented as having incurred war related injuries while fighting the enemy. As early as 1918, W.H.R. Rivers reported that patients suffering from "war neurosis" due to the terrible experiences at the war front found it difficult to converse about their war experiences because they felt defeated by the futility of bringing home the experiences to the hearer (Rivers 1918). I do not discuss here the controversies on the treatment of war-related trauma or posttraumatic stress disorder that emerged after Vietnam veterans began to seek help for such symptoms as recurring nightmares, insomnia, and the inability to relate (Young 1995). I note, however, that it is only through medicalization of their symptoms that soldiers found ways of overcoming the obligation to maintain a stoic and heroic view of their war experiences.

Technological shifts have certainly led to a deployment of high-tech weapons on the part of Western powers, which enables remote warfare with minimal casualties to one's own side. The public tolerance for high casualties has declined considerably in the West as evidenced in not only the antiwar movements in the United States and Europe, but also the disastrous withdrawals from Somalia and the Western refusal to intervene in Rwanda or in Darfur because of the fear of a high rate of casualties. The question of why terms such as courage, heroism, sacrifice, and their opposites continue to circulate in the public arena is a matter of some concern. What functions do these terms perform? In claiming legitimacy for a nation's own wars by demonstrating soldiers' "consent" to pay the ultimate sacrifice on the nation's behalf, such categories, I believe, manage to create boundaries between so-called civilized warfare and savage violence (Ignatieff 1998, Walzer 2004). Such techniques of description and categorization are, of course, not new; they were widely used during colonial wars of pacification (Bley 1971, Colby 1927, Mamdani 2001). What might be new is that techniques of domination have shifted as war becomes more dispersed and all kinds of social groups emerge as mirror reflections of state and empire.

CIVILIZED VERSUS SAVAGE

In relation to the category of "civilized" warfare, I examine two figures that have provoked much reflection in both scholarly and popular literature on what is sometimes characterized as "barbaric"—particularly in Africa—and sometimes as "nihilist" or aimless violence, particularly in relation to the figure of the suicide bomber. At stake in these discussions are the West's assumptions about the legitimacy of its own wars—this much is obvious—but in addition there seem to be unspoken anxieties about what one might call a clash of masculinities.

Harrison's (1993) acute analysis of the tranformation of identity in Sepik warfare provides an example of a different model of sociality and masculinity than that described above for the classic case of war in European theories. Harrison makes a case for, what I would call, the incommensurability (not simply untranslatability) of war practices among the Manambu people of the middle Sepik river and the interpretations of these practices by the colonial Australian authorities. For the Australian authorities, the Manambu were displaying a Hobbesian state of nature when they went into warfare with their closest neighbors with whom they had maintained ties of close sociality. For the Manambu, violence was premised upon preexisting social ties so that warfare was directed toward cutting off social ties. Through the use of body decorations and masks, the warriors converted themselves into dangerous spirits who could kill precisely those with whom they had intimacy that had become unsupportable. In taking on the identities of the spirits, Harrison argues, the men were completely absorbed within the collective—all individual relations were severed. This complex relation between violence and a different kind of sociality was incomprehensible to the Australian colonists who took these kinds of events to be sign of barbarism that had to be eliminated through punitive expeditions. The warrior figure, thus, might draw from different kinds of social and cosmological imaginaries from the ones tied to nation-states described above. For example, rather than emphasizing consent to kill or be killed on behalf of the larger collectivity such as the nation, the warrior might be seen as someone who is waging war not as himself but as an ancestral spirit, as in the Malenesian case. However, as the Australian colonists' response to this form of warfare indicates, such practices came to be measured against the ideas of civilized warfare leading to brutal suppression by colonial authorities. At stake here is the distinction between Western warfare, which was considered rule bound, rational, and masculine, and violence in other places, which was considered anarchic and animal like.

Examples of warfare that deviate from the classical model of war are the so-called low-intensity wars in large parts of Africa, which have some unique features. Mbembe (2000) sees in these wars a crisis of sovereignty and subjectivity, as various kinds of flows of people and weapons, from international organizations, corporations, as well as transborder movements of goods define and remap the region. A defining feature of these wars was the emergence of child soldiers and youth who became ferocious fighters, feared for their brutality. For instance, in Sierra Leone, where war raged for more than a decade, child soldiers were made participants in these wars by all sides of the conflict (Hoffman 2006). The enduring images of this and other wars included limbs amputated by young rebels, hunters adorned with magical protection to make their bodies immune to bullet wounds, blood diamonds, drugs, and abduction of young girls for sexual services (Hoffman 2003).

How are gender relations implicated in this form of militarization of society? For many scholars, the emergence of child soldiers and their brutality in warfare signals a crisis of youth indicating a breakdown of generational connections and traditional patrimonial resources (Boyden & de Berry 2004, Hoffman 2005). However, there was also an aspect of experimentation with different kinds of warrior models in these wars, of which Moran (1995) provides an excellent example. She shows that significant changes occurred in the way youth adopted different models of fighters during the civil war in Liberia. Initially after the 1980 coup, it was the cosmopolitan model of soldierly deportment and ethic that was valued, as soldiers embodied the image of idealized masculinity through which they imagined themselves as participating in a universal worldwide military culture. By 1995, the soldier model was discredited and another model, that of the warrior, was adopted with roots in African traditions in which warfare was ritualized and warrior figures were said to have deep connections with elemental forces of nature, especially the forest. What is intriguing in Moran's analysis of this transition from soldier to warrior is the way in which elements of femininity seem to be parodied as part of the rituals enacted. Thus male warriors in the course of performing war dances wear women's clothing such as bras and negligees, wigs, and other items of Western origin. The description suggests that what, to modern armies, were ludic performances involving personification and parodying of the female body seem to have become part of the imaginary of soldier/warrior figures in Africa

THE SUICIDE BOMBER
AND NIHILISTIC VIOLENCE

The literature on suicide bombing has proliferated since September 11. There seems to be remarkable agreement among scholars that suicide bombing marks a pathology of contemporary Islam and especially of its young men (Benhabib 2001, Bloom 2005, Ètienne 2005, Gambetta 2005, Pedazhur 2005, Strenski 2003; but see Skaine 2006 for a somewhat pedantic survey on female suicide bombers). The typical argument calls such violence nihilist because it assumes that the common motive of the young Islamic militant is to seek a decisive and yet elusive encounter with death. Moreover, suicide bombing is said to evoke horror because the bomber uses his or her own body as a weapon. What is intriguing in such statements is that the internal life of young men who engage in violence of this particular kind is assumed to be transparent. Asad (2007) has persuasively argued that one cannot assume that all men who become suicide bombers, even as jihadists, have the same motives. Surprisingly these theories that talk about the pathology of Islam fail to consider the figure of the female suicide bomber in Sri Lanka, where explanations have ranged from rendering them as engaged in a fight for justice for the cause of Tamil nationalism (Sangarasivam 2003) to considering their participation to be completely coerced by the brutal techniques of Liberation Tigers of Tamil Eelam (LTTE), ranging from abducting youth to forcing families to give at least one child to the militant organization as a form of taxation (Hoglunge 2005).

The distinction between the "just" wars of the West and the nihilist violence of the suicide bombers has enabled some scholars to justify the idea of preemptive war (Benhabib 2001; and for a more nuanced but still problematic view Walzer 2004). Like the defense of colonial occupation in the past as the inevitable burden of the white man, the new wars are also justified on the grounds that they seek to liberate women of these countries from the oppressive practices of Islamic groups such as the Taliban, who have waged war against the "human rights of their own women" (Benhabib 2001). Although the cruelties of the Taliban are not in question, it is intriguing that the theory of just war manages to define many cruelties committed by soldiers (including those on women) as simply "collateral damages," regrettable but not crimes at all. The discursive techniques to make certain kinds of violence by dominant groups (colonizers, occupiers, white races, upper castes) disappear have led to agonizing feminist discussions of the post–September 11 scenario because addressing the violence done to women as part of repressive regimes in some parts of the Islamic world is so often used to make the complicity of Western regimes in supporting those very regimes less visible to the public (Abu-Lughod 2002, Charlesworth & Chinkin 2002, Cooke 2002, Eisenstein 2002).

EMBODYING EMPIRE:
SEXUALIZED VIOLENCE
AND TORTURE

Recent instances of sexualized torture at Abu Ghraib have raised fresh questions about the relation among race, gender, and violence (Greenberg 2006, Strasses 2005). The violence inflicted on Iraqi prisoners by both male and female North American and British soldiers could not be disavowed as only the work of a few "bad apples" as the Army claimed, especially if we take into account not only the actual practices of torture but also the circulation of photographs that recorded these spectacles to friends and family for pleasure (Paur 2004). The theme of humiliating the "enemy" through effeminizing men that has been recorded for many colonial contexts (Krishnaswamy 1998, Sinha 1995) was also witnessed in the Abu Ghraib case. However, the use of women as perpetrators was a new development. The photograph of a young female soldier pointing gleefully at the genitals of a crouching naked Arab man was shocking to many people and especially to feminists who had long argued that war was primarily an affair among men.

Razack (2005) argues that the Abu Ghraib practices of torture, both visual and corporeal, should be understood in terms of the manner in which individuals are interpellated in the structure of empire so that even when they are not themselves dominant within patriarchal and racist hierarchies, they can claim inclusion within the projects of empire by literally embodying it. Some other writers see Abu Ghraib as an instantiation of a contemporary form of torture and do not see any long history embedded in it. They argue for instrumental explanations in that American intelligence agencies' use of sexualized practices, especially through the agency of a woman, was designed to engineer a collapse of the Arab prisoners who, it was assumed, would yield information more quickly if they were sexually humiliated rather than subjected to physical pain. Certain imaginaries of Arab culture as "homophobic" and "misogynist" are at play here. Still others juxtapose the image of torture with that of the beheading carried out by Islamic militants as instantiations of the category of *homo sacer* (as in Agamben 1998) and argue that the images represent a contest over sovereignty (Caton 2006). We are also left with the question of how the senses were trained so that American soldiers, both men and women, could take pleasure in these kinds of sexual humiliation inflicted on the other. After all, the pictures of torture that were circulated were not of grim soldiers performing a distasteful duty but of men and women taking pleasure in the sexual humiliation inflicted on the dominated other.

There is little doubt that the forms of sexualized humiliation witnessed in Abu Ghraib bear similarity to such practices as lynching (Austin 2004), even if direct connections are difficult to establish. The essence of lynching and burning rituals lay in the sense of power and mastery for white men over black subjects (Brown 1975, Harris 1984), while allowing them to obtain intimacy with what was forbidden to desire (Pinar 2001). Cardyn (2002) provides a catalog of practices in lynching such as whipping of distinctive sexualized parts, stripping, simulated forced homoerotic sex, which seem similar to practices at Abu Ghraib. Razack summarizes the theoretical argument by saying that sexualized violence accomplishes the eviction of the tortured from humanity, and it does so as an eviction from masculinity (Mehta 2000 and Mookherjee 2004 for a similar argument for South Asia). White men could then claim their own innocence by masking violence as punishment for black crime (and especially the crime of wanting white women), thus making white violence disappear. Unfortunately, similar analysis of the training of the senses to engage in violent acts such as beheadings or amputation of limbs on the part of young people in militant camps or in guerilla warfare or even a genealogical tracking of such images within other cultural contexts has not been undertaken. Hence some caution has to be exercised in making large theoretical claims. Nevertheless, systematic comparison on the question of sexual humiliation and its link with projects of masculine domination might yield important insights into these troubling phenomena.

THE SOCIAL SAVAGE

The pathology of the sexualization of the social contract becomes most visible in the figure of the abducted woman in times of disorder (Das 2007a, Menon & Bhasin 1998, Mookherjee 2001). Feminist scholars writing on ethnic cleansing and genocide have suggested that the fundamental idea underlying both these forms of collective violence is that of social death (Card 2003). One implication of the notion of social death is that a woman who has been abducted and raped becomes dishonored and either chooses death herself or is rejected by the family (Das 1995). However, as Das (2007a) argues, the collective narratives of honor and shame often conceal from public view the efforts families might make to find ways of offering care to daughters or wives, deviating from the collective scripts of honor and shame. At another level, the concept of social death allows us to recognize that genocidal acts or acts of ethnic cleansing, while often violent, are not always homicidal. Thus forced sterilization of women or men from a targeted group, forcibly separating women from their children for reeducation, as happened to children in indigenous groups in Australia, or even forcibly assimilating them into another group, as has been alleged by Tibet for Chinese policies of forcible assimilation, could all be considered as forms of social death and hence forms of genocide or ethnic cleansing. This would explain why policies of ethnic cleansing or genocide specifically target women and direct both sexual and reproductive violence toward them; women are seen as the cultural and biological repositories of ethnic or religious groups (Fisher 1996). Thus, for instance, sexual or reproductive violence against Bosnian Muslim women was framed by a discourse of revenge and humiliation related to some kind of "Serbization" of the Muslim population. Many feminist scholars have spoken of the "rape regime" in which Bosnian women were forcibly interned in camps and made to carry their pregnancies to term. (Allen 1996, Salzman 2002). Similarly, Pakistani soldiers who raped women during the war for liberation in Bangladesh in 1972 participated in a discourse of the effeminate Islam in Bangladesh, which needed to be invested with more muscular and purer Islam (Mookherjee 2001, Saikia 2004). This situation may be different from the one that prevailed during the partition of India, when there was widespread sexual violence but the discourse of reproductive violence was not in circulation (Das 2007a). Rather, a lot of violence marked the women of the other groups as "spoiled," and violence, actual and fantasized, treated women's bodies as means of humiliating the men of the other community. Mass rape of women, reproductive violence in the form of forcible pregnancies, and abduction for forced marriages are different forms in which the complete annihilation of the other as a collective community is sought in projects of ethnic cleansing and genocide. Return to normalcy draws heavily upon ideas of honor and shame at both familial and national levels.

An important question that arises in this context is whether there are any common assumptions made about male and female sexuality in processes of legal adjudication when judges are confronted with cases of mass rape versus rape (individual or gang rape) as a peace-time crime (Baxi 2007). On the surface, one might think that in times of peace when rape is identified as a "crime," law would function to identify and punish the perpetrator, whereas in the case of mass rapes, which typically take place in times of massive disorder, the problem would be that law itself stands suspended. However, some important structural similarities in assumptions made about male and female sexuality in the functioning of the law show continuity between the peace-time "crime" of rape and the mass rapes, which are taken as the sign of a complete breakdown of law (Baxi 2007).

THE RAPE TRIAL: LAW AND SEXUAL VIOLENCE

Despite differences in the definition of rape in different legal traditions, two ideas seem to be consistently present. The first is that the act of rape consists of some form of penetration of a woman (and, in some cases, a man) and second that this act is forced, without the consent of the woman or man concerned. Whereas some feminist scholars argue that rape is simply an expression of general male violence against women (Brownmiller 1975), others have argued that we need to track more specifically how the legal system functions to authorize male violence against women (Das 2005, Smart 1995). Which kinds of men are punished for the offense of rape, and how does the legal system function to distinguish "good" women from "bad women"? Detailed examination of legal cases and especially what Matoesian (1993) calls "court room talk" reveal that categories of caste, class, and race have a serious impact on the legal decisions on rape. Women are implicitly treated as the property of men so that rape comes to be defined not as an offense against the woman's bodily integrity but as an offense against the property rights of the man who is her guardian. The legal reasoning deployed works with the notion that men are sexual savages, "naturally" positioned to take women, and they have to be controlled through an education of sexual desire. Women, however, are divided into good women and bad women; the former are women who are in the custody of fathers or husbands and have no history of sexual promiscuity. The courts are much more likely to place their trust in women who are thus securely bound within the sanctioned structures of marriage. The bad women, such as prostitutes, by their very profession are seen to be incapable of saying "no" to sex (Baxi 2007, Das 2005). Legal reasoning then works to punish those men who have violated the rights of men, especially those who can be placed in a higher position as compared with the alleged perpetrator (Kannibaran & Kannibaran 2002) and to display publicly the distinction between good women and bad women by pronouncing upon whose "no" to sex can be converted to "consent" because of their sexual history.

Although legal reasoning and court room talk have received the most attention in the analysis of rape, one must remember that most cases do not reach the court room even if rape is reported. Scholars are now beginning to pay attention to forms of sociality that are generated in spaces such as hospital emergency rooms and police stations, where a certain set of assumptions about what is private and what is public and what might stand in a court of law and what might not determines how a case proceeds (Hoyle 1998, Merry 2001, Wood 2005). In terms of ordinary life, the threat of sexual violence has a profound effect on the subjectivity of women who constantly have to consider such factors as reputation and safety in determining how life is to be lived. Yet, statistics on sexual violation reveal that in most cases the perpetrator of sexual violence is someone known or even intimate with a woman rather than a stranger (Gavey 2005, Gelles & Straus 1988, Price 2002). So what is intimate violence? The place to consider in addressing this question is the home.

WHAT IS HOME?

Powerful imageries of the home as a haven, a place of intimacy and nourishment, have informed literary and cultural theory (Bachelard 1964). However, the home is the space of not one but several domesticities. Recent research on violence in the home that has tried to document women's experiences has shown that different people within the home experience it very differently. The home is often the place of masculine dominion in which the man expects the women's labor to secure the peace he craves (Price 2002). The high prevalence of wife beating, child abuse, and female domestic servant abuse in various societies across class has been analyzed by various scholars and tends to show that the home can be a place of terror for many women who are blamed for not being able to maintain the ideal home. Thus male dominion over the home often translates into wife beating: Testimonies of women who have been battered show that they usually cannot anticipate when the blows will come and for what reason. Many women tend to blame themselves for the beatings they received because they have internalized their husbands' accusations of failing to create the ideal home. Others find it impossible to leave the abusive relationship because all their social networks derive from their positions as wives (Abraham 2000, Gelles & Straus 1988, Hoff 1990). Help from state agencies is often hard to obtain because policemen tend to treat violence in the home as a private affair between spouses. As awareness of domestic violence has increased and as it becomes framed as a public health issue, various initiatives from the global and national communities have tried to make this a matter of priority. The conceptual issues of defining what constitutes domestic violence, however, have not all been resolved.

First, the discomfort with the state's intervention into family life is not only a matter of conservative defense of the family. Some feminist scholars have argued that the privacy necessary for intimacy to flourish is deeply compromised by the state's overseeing panoptical surveillance of the home (Kelly 2003).

Because sexual intimacy generates complex emotions, a definition of domestic violence that includes everything from beating to harsh words spoken can lead to a decline in the possibility of intimacy itself. These scholars suggest a community-based pedagogical model of intervention in many cases rather than a punitive model for controlling violence.

Second, the question of consent is as hard to negotiate conceptually in defining domestic violence as in defining soldier's participation in war. On the one side there are scholars who would argue that separating out battered women from other women or violent homes from peaceful homes is fraught with problems because underlying the ideological grid dividing the social contract and the sexual contract is the ever possible presence of male violence in the home (Pateman 1980, Price 2002). The woman's consent to male violence has a taken–for-granted character, which explains why marital rape has been most difficult to legislate in most liberal regimes. On the other side are those who argue that there are specific conditions under which violence is actualized and that strategies such as the battered woman defense are necessary to capture the fact that a woman who lives in constant fear of violence might perceive a reasonable risk to her safety in ways that deviate considerably from the legal norms of a "reasonable person" (Schneider 2000).

Third, recent research has indicated structural connections between wider political and economic processes and the vulnerability of domestic workers as a category subject to abuse within the home (Goldstein 2005, Rafael 2000, Romero 1992). Research will likely show that the categories of mail-order brides, domestic helps, and sexual workers might share certain common conditions deriving from the place of the domestic within transnational economies.

REMAKING THE EVERYDAY

Research on gender and violence is not only about how worlds are unmade by violence but also how they are remade (Das et al. 2001). How does time do its work in allowing people to come to terms with the destruction of their social worlds (Jackson 2002)? How can people inherit a divided past, and what is it to imagine and to work for a possible future? Some studies ask if the obligation of women to convert bad deaths into good deaths (Seremetakis 1991) through mourning and lamentation moves from the spheres of kinship to that of politics so that women are seen as specially obligated to contest the forgetfulness imposed by dominant political actors (especially the state) and to demand justice on behalf of the dead (Butler 2004). The various Truth and Reconciliation Commissions established in various countries such as South Africa, Chile, Peru, and Argentina are premised on the idea that, in addition to the operation of the criminal justice system, which can address culpability of individuals, societies that have undergone state-sponsored massive violence over a long period of time need a public forum in which the atrocities enacted on people can be brought to light outside the strict legal protocols of courts of law (Popkin & Roht-Arriaza 1995, Wilson 2001). Anthropologists working on these commissions have found, however, that despite the freedom to narrate their experiences of violence, women often spoke on behalf of their kin but were unable to give voice to sexual violence done to them personally (Ross 2003).

Although public acknowledgment of harm is important and has received enormous attention in juridical and public policy literature, the work done in the recesses of everyday life, within local communities, kinship networks, and families has received somewhat less attention. Lawrence's (2000) work on possession within a temple complex in Batticaloa, Eastern Sri Lanka, gives a detailed analysis of how a priestess in a temple compound addresses the fear, grief, guilt, and shame of survivors and of those whose loved ones have disappeared in the protracted civil war in Sri Lanka. The coming together of a priestess, the goddess Kali, and the women who seek some direction in relation to their disappeared relatives creates a community of women (though men are not absent from the consultations) who are not necessarily visible to the juridical or public policy communities but whose "work" is nevertheless crucial in that it allows women to move out of their frozen positions and to take other directions in their lives. Other scholars have argued that women might perform private mourning rituals for those killed, often at great risks to themselves, refusing to let a death go unmourned (Das 2007a, Holloway 2003, Walker n.d.).

Whereas the literature on violence and healing emphasizes various aspects of witnessing and memory (Agamben 1999, Bougarel et al. 2007), some innovative work also addresses attempts to keep violence at bay. Argenti-Pillen (2003), for instance, described various linguistic evasion strategies used by women in the home to keep the home insulated from the region's poisonous politics. Some cultural continuities exist in language (use of euphemisms, refusal of naming, indirect speech) through which ritual dangers to the home are addressed and are also extended for keeping political dangers at bay. Although keeping violence at bay is not a matter of forms of discourse alone; the problem of how women and men try to insulate the home from detrimental politics is clearly a very important area of research (Skidmore & Lawrence 2007, Spencer 2000).

Some authors have contested the centrality of trauma discourse and its emphasis on unmastered experience. Thus Das (2007a) considers the manner in which women engage in repair of relationships through ordinary, everyday acts of caring. She thinks of healing through the metaphor of women digesting "poisonous" knowledge so that they learn to reinhabit the world by dwelling again within internal landscapes devastated by violence (see also Mookherjee 2006). Aretxaga (1998) shows how women maintained networks of relationships through everyday acts of borrowing and lending in the divisive politics of Ireland, thus confronting and crossing the political divides in their everyday acts of mutual recognition (see also Walker n.d.).

VIOLENCE AND AFFECT

One can read the ethnographic record to identify a range of affects in the description of violence. Thus although one might expect that fear and horror and sorrow and grief, would be the appropriate emotions in the context of violence (Feldman et al. 1993), one finds that there are also ludic aspects of violence that pose new challenges to how we understand violence. One of the most striking ethnographic account on youth in the LTTE is the recent book by Trawick (2007), who lived in an LTTE village in Eastern Sri Lanka on the border of the forest. Her work shows how categories of war and play become interchangeable in the lives of young LTTE cadres. In her own preface to the project, she says that the LTTE Tigers represented the battles they fought as "child's play," "fully intense, concentrated, and serious, but also elevated above the mundane world, and fun." (Trawick 2007, p. 13). Trawick's explicit theoretical formulation makes a sharp break between representation and experience and is therefore problematic, but the power of this book lies in something akin to reading the novelist Kazuo Ishiguro's novel, *Never Let Me Go*. The novel tells of hopelessness of the lives of clones, bred to be organ "donors", but we come to sense the affects of hopelessness only through the most ordinary of everyday squabbles and childhood politics staged in a typical British public school environment. Could it be that the reality of killing and being killed, which is openly spoken about among the LTTE youth, is both known and yet never fully comprehended? Yet the theoretical move by Trawick that drives a wedge between representation and experience leaves this author at the point at which I understand neither how she would render the longings for escape from the LTTE, recorded in her ethnography, or how the reader should think about moments of grief, in which the young men and women are simply not allowed to indulge. Although I respect Trawick's insistence that the "children" do not wish to be fully accounted for in any theory, there is no place in her text for any perspective from those who fled, for example, from the LTTE. In this respect, the permission given to an anthropologist to work in an area controlled by the LTTE works very much like research visas given by governments who impose strict rules about what can be written about and how it is to be written. These anthropological texts then bear the marks of power in many respects.

Verkaaik (2004), who had worked with the Muttahida Qaumi Movement (MQM) militants in Karachi, also considered the ludic aspects of violence but conveyed the difference between those activists who took the "fun" of militancy as part of their identities and as an escape from the mundane everyday and those who turned back to ordinary lives of careers and marriage and presumably into caring for the next generation. At the opposite end of these affects is Asad's (2007) incisive analysis of horror, which he identifies as the spectacle of the disintegration of the human body and the sense of the dissociation between the soul and the body, seen in the act of killing and being killed in suicide bombing. These three texts provide examples of the pioneering contributions anthropology can make to the understanding of the different affects that constitute and are constituted by violence. As a concluding thought, I propose that it is precisely because the reality of violence includes its virtual (and not only actualized) presence in our lives (Jeganathan 1998, 2000)—its potential to both disrupt the ordinary and become part of the ordinary—that the study of violence continues to challenge and channel our disciplinary desires in profound ways.

DISCLOSURE STATEMENT

The author is not aware of any biases that might be perceived as affecting the objectivity of this review.

ACKNOWLEDGEMENTS

I thank my colleagues and graduate students at the Johns Hopkins University for the stimulating intellectual environment they provide. I am especially grateful to Sylvain Perdigon for his insights into the questions of violence and the ordinary and to Deepak Mehta, whose work on violence continues to open new doors for me.

LITERATURE CITED

Abraham M. 2000. *Speaking the Unspeakable: Marital Violence Among South Asian Immigrants in the United States.* New Brunswick, NJ: Rutgers Univ. Press

Abu-Lughod L. 2002. Do Muslim women really need saving? Anthropological reflections on cultural relativism and its others. *Am. Anthropol.* 104(3):783–90

Agamben G. 1998. *Homo Sacer: Sovereign Power and Bare Life.* Stanford, CA: Stanford Univ. Press

Agamben G. 1999. *Remnants of Aushwitz: The Witness and the Archive.* New York: Zone Books

Allen B. 1996. *Rape Warfare: The Hidden Genocide in Bosnia-Herzegovina and Croatia.* Minneapolis: Univ. Minn. Press

Aretxaga B. 1998. What the border hides: partition and gender politics in Irish nationalism. In *The International Journal of Cultural and Social Practice*, ed. G Ghosh, 42(1):16–33, Spec. issue on Partition, Unification, Nation

Argenti-Pillen A. 2003. *Masking Terror: How Women Contain Violence in Southern Sri Lanka.* Philadelphia: Univ. Penn. Press

Asad T. 2003. *Formations of the Secular: Christianity, Islam, Modernity.* Stanford, CA: Stanford Univ. Press

Asad T. 2007. *On Suicide Bombing.* New York: Columbia Univ. Press

Austin A. 2004. Explanation and responsibility: agency and motive in lynching and genocide. *J. Black Stud.* 34(5):719–33

Bachelard G. 1964. *The Poetics of Space*. New York: Orion

Barham P. 2004. *Forgotten Lunatics of the Great War*. New Haven, CT: Yale Univ. Press

Bataille G. 1957. *L'Erotisme*. Paris: Èd. Minuit

Bataille G. 1961. *The Tears of Eros*. San Francisco: City Light Books

Baxi P. 2007. Adjudicating the riot: communal violence, crowds and public tranquility in India. *Domains: Spec. Issue Riot Discourses* 3:66–101

Benhabib S. 2001. *Unholy politics*. **http://www.ssrc.org/September11**

Biehl J, Good B, Kleinman A. 2007b. Introduction: Rethinking subjectivity. See Biehl et al. 2007b, pp. 1–25

Biehl J, Good B, Kleinman A, eds. 2007b. *Subjectivity: Ethnographic Investigations*. Berkeley: Univ. Calif. Press

Bley H. 1971. *Southwest Africa under German Rule, 1894–1914*, transl. H Ridley. London: Heinemann

Bloom M. 2005. *Dying to Kill: The Lure of Suicide Terror*. New York: Columbia Univ. Press

Bougarel X, Helm E, Duizingo G, eds. 2007. *The New Bosnian Mosaic: Identities, Memories and Moral Claims in a Post-War Society*. Aldershot: Ashgate

Bourke J. 1999. *An Intimate History of Killing: Face to Face Killing in Twentieth Century Warfare*. New York: Basic Books

Boyden J, de Berry J. 2004. *Children and Youth in the Frontline: Ethnography, Armed Conflict and Displacement*. Oxford: Berghahn

Brown RM. 1975. *Strains of Violence: Historical Studies of American Violence*. New York: Oxford Univ. Press

Brownmiller S. 1975. *Against Our Will: Men, Women, and Rape*. New York: Ballentine/Random House

Butler J. 2004. *Precarious Life: The Power of Mourning and Violence*. London: Verso

Card C. 2003. Genocide and social death. *Hypatia* 18(1):63–79

Cardyn L. 2002. Sexualized racisms/gendered violence: outraging the body politic in the Reconstruction South. *Mich. Law Rev.* 100(4):675–867

Caton S. 2006. Coatzee, Agamben, and the pain of Abu Ghraib. *Am. Anthropol.* 108(1):114–23

Charlesworth H, Chinkin C. 2002. Sex, gender and September 11. *Am. J. Int. Law* 96(3):783–90

Colby CE. 1927. How to fight savage tribes. *Am. J. Int. Law* 21(2):279–88

Cooke M. 2002. Saving brown women. *Signs* 28(1):468–73

Das V. 1995. National honour and practical kinship. In *Critical Events: An Anthropological Perspective on Contemporary India*, Chapter 3. Delhi: Oxford Univ. Press

Das V. 2005. Sexual violence, discursive formations and the state. In *States of Violence*, ed. F Coronil, J Skurski, pp. 323–425. Michigan: Univ. Mich. Press

Das V. 2007a. *Life and Words: Violence and the Descent into the Ordinary*. Berkeley: Univ. Calif. Press

Das V. 2007b. The figure of the abducted woman: the citizen as sexed. In *Political Theologies: Public Religions in a Post-Secular World*, ed. H de Vries, LE Sullivan, pp. 209–27. Delhi: Soc. Sci. Orient Longman

Das V, Kleinman A, Lock M, Ramphele M, Reynolds P, eds. 2001. *Remaking a World: Violence, Social Suffering and Recovery*. Berkeley: Univ. Calif. Press

Das V, Kleinman A, Ramphele M, Reynolds P, eds. 2000. *Violence and Subjectivity*. Berkeley: Univ. Calif. Press

Das V, Poole D, eds. 2004. *Anthropology in the Margins of the State*. Santa Fe, NM: Sch. Am. Res.

De Mel N. 2003. Agent or victim? The Sri Lankan woman militant in the interregnum. In *Feminists Under Fire: Exchanges Across War Zones*, ed. W Giles, M de Alwis, E Klein, N Silva, pp. 55–70. Ontario: Between the Lines

De Mel N. 2007. *Militarizing Sri Lanka: Popular Culture, Memory, and Narrative in the Armed Conflict*. Colombo: Int. Cent. Ethn. Stud.

Eisenstein Z. 2002. Feminism in the aftermath of September 11. *Soc. Text.* 20(3):72–99

Enloe C. 2000. *The International Politics of Militarizing Women's Lives*. Berkeley: Univ. Calif. Press

Ètienne B. 2005. *Les Combattants Suicidaire*s. Paris: Ed. Aub

Feldman LC, Prisa A, Senkovic R, eds. 1993. *Fear, Death and Resistance: An Ethnography of War, Croatia 1991–1992*. Zagreb: Inst. Ethnol. Folk. Res.

Filmer SR. 1991 [1653]. *Patriarcha and Other Writings*, ed. JP Sommerville. Cambridge, UK: Cambridge Univ. Press

Fisher SK. 1996. Occupation of the womb: forced impregnation as genocide. *Duke Law J.* 46(1):91–133

Fussell P. 1975. *The Great War and Modern Memory*. London: Oxford Univ. Press

Fussell P. 1989. *Wartime: Understanding and Behaviour in the Second World War*. New York: Oxford Univ. Press

Gambetta D, ed. 2005. *Making Sense of Suicide Missions*. New York: Oxford Univ. Press

Gavey N. 2005. *Just Sex? The Cultural Scaffolding of Rape*. New York: Routledge

Gelles R, Straus MA. 1988. *Intimate Violence*. New York: Simon and Schuster

Goldstein D. 2005. *Laughter Out of Place: Race, Class, Violence and Sexuality in a Rio Shantytown*. Berkeley: Univ. Calif. Press

Greenberg KJ, ed. 2006. *The Torture Debate in America*. Cambridge, UK: Cambridge Univ. Press

Harris T. 1984. *Exorcising Blackness: Historical and Literary Lynching and Burning Rituals*. Bloomington: Ind. Univ. Press

Harrison S. 1993. *The Mask of War: Violence, Ritual and the Self in Melanesia*. Manchester, UK: Manchester Univ. Press

Hobbes T. 1981 [1656]. *Leviathan*. London: Penguin

Hoff LA. 1990. *Battered Women as Survivors*. New York: Routledge

Hoffman D. 2003. Like beasts in a bush: synonyms of childhood and youth in Sierra Leone. *Postcolonial Stud.* 6(3):295–308

Hoffman D. 2005. Military patrimonialism and child soldiers clientialism in the Liberian and Sierra Leonian Civil Wars. *Afr. Stud. Rev.* 46(2):61–87

Hoffman D. 2006. Disagreement: dissent politics and the war in Sierra Leone. *Afr. Today* 52(2):3–22

Hoglunge K. 2005. Violence and the peace process in Sri Lanka. *Civil Wars* 7(9):156–70

Hoyle C. 1998. *Negotiating Domestic Violence: Police, Criminal Justice, Violence*. Oxford: Oxford Univ. Press

Holloway KFC. 2003. *Passed On: African-American Mourning Stories*. Durham, NC: Duke Univ. Press

Humphrey M. 2002. *The Politics of Atrocity and Reconciliation: From Terror to Trauma*. London: Routledge

Ignatieff M. 1998. *The Warrior's Honour: Ethnic War and the Modern Conscience*. New York: Metropolitan/Holt

Ivekovic R. 2003. *Le Sexe de la Nation*. Paris: Léo Scheer

Jackson M. 2002. *The Politics of Story Telling: Violence, Transgression and Intersubjectivity*. Copenhagen: Tiscaulanum Mus.

Jeganathan P. 1998. "Violence" as an analytical problem: Sri Lankanist anthropology in the wake of a riot. *Nethra: J. Int. Cent. Ethn. Stud.* 4(2):2–42

Jeganathan P. 2000. A space for violence: anthropology, politics and the location of a Sinhala practice of masculinity. In *Community, Gender and Violence: Subaltern Studies XI*, ed. P Chatterjee, P Jeganathan, pp. 37–65. Delhi: Permanent Black

Kannibaran K, Kannibaran V. 2002. *De-Eroticizing Assault: Essays on Modernity, Hinduism and Power*. Delhi: Popular Prakashan

Karsten P. 1978. *Law, Soldiers and Combat*. Westport: Greenwood

Kelly KA. 2003. *Domestic Violence and the Politics of Privacy*. Ithaca: Cornell Univ. Press

Kleinman A, Fitz-Henry E. 2007. The experiential basis of subjectivity. See Biehl et al. 2007b, pp. 52–66

Krishnaswamy R. 1998. *Effeminism: The Economy of Colonial Desire*. Ann Arbor: Univ. Mich. Press

Lawrence P. 2000. Violence, suffering, Amman: the work of oracles in Sri Lanka's Eastern war zone. See Das et al. 2000, pp. 171–205

MacKinnon C. 1991. *Toward a Feminist Theory of the State*. Cambridge, MA: Harvard Univ. Press

Mamdani M. 2001. A brief history of genocide. *Transition* 10(3):26–47

Matoesian GM. 1993. *Reproducing Rape: Domination Through Talk in the Courtroom*. Chicago: Univ. Chicago Press

Mbembe A. 2000. At the edge of the world: boundaries, territoriality and sovereignty in Africa. *Public Cult.* 12(1):259–84

Mehta D. 2000. Circumcision, body, masculinity: the ritual wound and collective violence. See Das et al. 2000, pp. 79–102

Menon U, Bhasin K. 1998. *Borders and Boundaries: Women in India's Partition*. New Brunswick, NJ: Rutgers Univ. Press

Merry SE. 2001. Spatial governmentality and the new urban social order: controlling gender violence through law. *Am. Anthropol* 103(1):16–29

Meyer T, ed. 2000. *Ironies of Nationalism: Sexing the Nation*. London: Routledge

Mookherjee N. 2001. *A lot of history: sexual violence, public memory, and the Bangladesh Liberation War of 1971.* PhD diss. Sch. Orient. Afr. Stud., Univ. London

Mookherjee N. 2004. 'My *man* (honour) is lost but I still have my *iman* (principle)': sexual violence and articulation of masculinity. In *South Asian Masculinities*, ed. R Chopra, C Osella, F Osilla, pp. 130–59. Delhi: Kali for Woman

Mookherjee N. 2006. "Remembering to forget': public secrecy and memory of sexual violence in the Bangladesh war of 1971. *J. R. Anthropol. Inst.* 12(2):433–50

Moran M. 1995. Warriors or soldiers? Masculinity and ritual transvestism in the Liberian civil war. In *Situated Lives: Gender and Culture in Everyday Life*, ed. L Lamphere, H Ragoné, P Zavella, pp. 440–68. New York: Routledge

Moser CON, Clarke FC, eds. 2001. *Victims. Perpetrators or Actors? Gender, Armed Conflict and Political Violence.* London: Zed Books

Naimark NW. 2001. *Fires of Hatred: Ethnic Cleansing in Twentieth-Century Europe.* Cambridge, MA: Harvard Univ. Press

Nordstrom C. 1997. *A Different Kind of War Story.* Philadelphia: Univ. Penn. Press

Pateman C. 1980. Women and consent. *Polit. Theory* 149–68

Pateman C. 1988. *The Sexual Contract.* Cambridge, UK: Polity Press

Pateman C. 1990. Review of *Feminism Unmodified: Discourses on Life and Law. Ethics* 1000(2):398–407

Paur JK. 2004. Abu Ghraib: arguing against exceptionalism. *Feminist Stud.* 30(2):522–34

Peach LJ. 1994. An alternative to pacifism? Feminism and Just War Theory. *Hypatia* 9:152–72

Pedazhur A. 2005. *Suicide Terrorism.* Cambridge, UK: Polity Press

Rafael VL. 2000. *White Love and Other Events in Filipino History.* Durham, NC: Duke Univ. Press

Pinar WF. 2001. *The Gender of Racial Politics and Violence in America: Lynching, Prison Rape and the Crisis of Masculinity.* New York: Counterpoints

Popkin M, Roht-Arriaza N. 1995. Truth or justice: investigative commissions in Latin America. *Law Soc. Inq.* 20(1):79–116

Price JM. 2002. The apotheosis of home and maintenance of spaces of violence. *Hypatia* 17(4):39–70

Razack SH. 2005. How is white supremacy embodied? Sexualized racial violence at Abu Ghraib. *Can. J. Women Law* 17(2):341–63

Rivers WHR. 1918. The repression of war experiences. *Lancet.* **http://www.panix.com**

Romero M. 1992. *Maid in the USA.* New York: Routledge

Rorty A. 2007. The vanishing subject: the many faces of subjectivity. See Biehl et al. 2007b, pp. 25–34

Ross F. 2003. *Bearing Witness: Women and the Truth and Reconciliation Commission.* London: Pluto

Saikia Y. 2004. Beyond the archive of silence: narratives of violence of the 1971 liberation war of Bangladesh. *Hist. Workshop J.* 58:275–87

Salzman TA. 2002. Rape camps as a means of ethnic cleansing: religious, cultural and ethical responses to rape victims in former Yugoslavia. *Hum. Rights Q.* 20(2):345–75

Sangarasivam Y. 2003. Militarizing the female body: women's participation in the Tamil nationalist struggle. In *Violence and the Body: Race, Gender and the State*, ed. AJ Aldama, pp. 39–59. Bloomington: Indiana Univ. Press

Sasson-Levy O. 2003. Feminism and military practice: Israeli women soldiers in "masculine" roles. *Sociol. Inq.* 73(3):440–65

Schoenbrun DL. 2003. *Politics of the Womb: Women, Reproduction and the State in Kenya.* Berkeley: Univ. Calif. Press

Scheper-Hughes N. 1997. Peace-time crimes. *Soc. Identities* 3(3):471–98

Scheper-Hughes N, Bourgois P, eds. 2003. *Violence in War and Peace.* London: Blackwell

Schneider EM. 2000. *Battered Women and Feminist Lawmaking.* New Haven, CT: Yale Univ. Press

Seremetakis NC. 1991. *The Last Word: Women, Death and Divination in Inner Mani.* Chicago: Univ. Chicago Press

Severance ML. 2000. Sex and the social contract. *Engl. Lit. Hist.* 67(2):453–513

Sinha M. 1995. *Colonial Masculinity: The 'Manly Englishman' and the 'Effeminate Bengali' in the Late Nineteenth Century.* Manchester, UK: Manchester Univ. Press

Skaine R. 2006. *Female Suicide Bombers*. Jefferson, NC: MacFarland

Skidmore M, Lawrence P. 2007. *Women and the Contested State: Religion, Violence and Agency in South and Southeast Asia*. Notre Dame: Univ. Notre Dame Press

Smart C. 1995. *Law, Crime and Sexuality: Essays in Feminism*. London: Sage

Spencer J. 2000. On not becoming a "terrorist": problems of memory, agency and community in the Sri Lankan conflict. See Das et al. 2000, pp. 120–41

Strasses S, ed. 2005. *The Abu Ghraib Investigations*. New York: Public Aff.

Strenski I. 2003. Sacrifice, gift and the logic of Muslim human bombers. *Terror. Polit. Violence* 15(3):1–34

Surkis J. 2006. *Sexing the Citizen: Morality and Masculinity in France*. Ithaca: Cornell Univ. Press

Taylor C. 2004. *Modern Social Imaginaries*. Durham, NC: Duke Univ. Press

Trawick M. 2007. *Enemy Lines: Warfare, Childhood and Play in Batticaloa*. Berkeley: Univ. Calif. Press

Verkaaik O. 2004. *Migrants and Militants. Fun and Urban Violence in Pakistan*. Princeton, NJ: Princeton Univ. Press

Walker B. n.d. *Trust and "every-other-day-violence": daily realities on Sri Lanka's East Coast*. Unpublished, Univ. Edinburgh. 30 pp.

Waller MR, Rycenga J, eds. 2001. *Frontline Feminism: Women, War and Resistance*. New York: Routledge

Walzer M. 2004. *Arguing About War*. New Haven, CT: Yale Univ. Press

Weber M. 1948. *From Max Weber: Essays in Sociology*. New York: Routledge

Wilson R. 2001. *The Politics of Truth and Reconciliation in South Africa: Legitimizing the Post-Apartheid State*. Cambridge, UK: Cambridge Univ. Press

Wood K. 2005. Contextualizing group rape in post-apartheid South Africa. *Cult. Health Sex.* 7(4):303–17

Young A. 1995. *The Harmony of Illusions: Inventing Post Traumatic Stress Disorder*. Princeton, NJ: Princeton Univ. Press

Yuval-Davis N. 1997. *Gender and Nation*. London: Sage

Demographic Transitions and Modernity

Jennifer Johnson-Hanks

Departments of Demography and Sociology, University of California, Berkeley,
California 94720-2120; email: johnsonhanks@demog.berkeley.edu

Annu. Rev. Anthropol. 2008. 37:301–15

First published online as a Review in Advance on
June 18, 2008

The *Annual Review of Anthropology* is online at
anthro.annualreviews.org

This article's doi:
10.1146/annurev.anthro.37.081407.085138

0084-6570/08/1021-0301$20.00

Key Words

birthrate, population, governmentality, rationality

Abstract

Much contemporary anthropology is concerned with the origin, character, and consequences of late modernity. Surprisingly absent in this literature is the importance of population size, structure, and process. In particular, the demographic transition—or historical change from a high to a low equilibrium of birth and death rates—is an important component of modernity that deserves greater anthropological engagement. This review outlines demographic transition and transition theory, then discusses two ways in which transition intersects with literatures on modernity: through individual rationality and governmentality. Confronting both the material of population and the theories about it has the potential to significantly reconfigure anthropologies of the present.

INTRODUCTION

Cultural and social anthropologists have paid scant attention to population size, structure, and dynamics, particularly in recent years.[1] New work on risk, aggregation, statistics, and population as a discursive formation has made this absence more problematic. Through a discussion of demographic transition, I argue that a real understanding of population dynamics not only enriches and alters our understanding of modernity, but also offers a compelling argument against methodological individualism in social science. Thus, an anthropology of the present will benefit from a deeper engagement with the material of population and with demographic theory.

The term demographic transition has two primary meanings. It refers first to the historically specific change from high to low rates of fertility and mortality that many human populations have undergone since 1750, and second to a set of theories regarding the causes and mechanisms behind that change (e.g., Caldwell 1976, Coale 1973, Davis 1963, Jones et al. 1997, Kirk 1996, Notestein 1945). I distinguish between the empirical change and the theories about its causes by using the term demographic transition to indicate the first definition and the term theories of demographic transition (TDT) to indicate the second one.[2] Nearly all these theories treat demographic transition as a consequence of modernity under some guise, although they differ in attributing particular causal force to changing modes of production; rising aspirations of consumption; increasing secularization and individualism; or changing conceptions of sex, gender, and family. Central to most TDT is the concept of individual choice, often formulated with the assumptions of rational choice theory. Some TDT also treat the declining vital rates as causes of further social, political, or economic change (e.g., Binion 2000, Van Krieken 1997, Zhao 1996; c.f. Reisman 2002).

Theories of demographic transition have generally presupposed that the move from high to low vital rates is both a one-time event in the history of a given population and an inevitable one. These assumptions are partly the product of the theory's proximal origin in early post-WWII demography in the United States, when scholars with backgrounds in engineering and agricultural science turned their attention to population change. They sought, and therefore found, the same principle of unilineal progress that their contemporaries had identified in technology, governmental form, and human development: As societies developed and modernized, their populations would invariably undergo transition. Over the past 60 years, however, it has become abundantly clear that there is no coherent, comparable metric of societies' modernity. Whether, how, and how well proxy measures of modernity or development predict vital rates remain open, and hotly contested, empirical questions. There is wide agreement among population scholars that transition is associated with modernization or modernity, but little agreement about how or why.

DEMOGRAPHIC TRANSITIONS IN HISTORY

The decline of demographic rates over the past 250 years represents one of the most dramatic changes in known human experience (Flinn 1981, Gillis et al. 1992, Heuveline 1999, Lee 2003). In the early eighteenth century, cohort life expectancy was approximately 30 years in most European countries, meaning that half of all people died by that age, mostly in infancy. The cohort total fertility rate (TFR), which can be loosely understood as the average number of births per woman, was greater than 8.5. Starting in France, and then across the continent, mortality and fertility fell precipitously over the next

---

Demographic transition: a historically specific change from high to low rates of fertility and mortality that many human populations have undergone since 1750

Theories of demographic transition (TDT): set of related theories regarding the causes and mechanisms of the historical decline of fertility and mortality, usually focused on modernization as a primary driver

Modernization: a general term used in theories of transition to refer collectively and loosely to rising urbanization, industrialization, individualism, and secularism

Total fertility rate (TFR): the number of children that a woman would bear if she survived through the ages of childbearing and gave birth at the age-specific rates of the time period

---

[1] A generation ago this was far less true. See Cowgill 1975, Hall 1972, Hammel et al. 1979, Handwerker 1983, Howell 1979, and review in Howell 1986.

[2] Szreter (1993) argues that there are four distinct meanings of the term demographic transition. In this review, I conflate what he calls a theory, a historical model, and a proscriptive model, considering all three TDT.

200 years. By 1960, European life expectancy approached 70 years and the TFR for the continent lay between 2 and 3. European-descended populations in North America and Australia underwent parallel changes. Populations across Latin America and Asia have undergone equivalent, but far more rapid, changes in the twentieth century. Wherever it occurs, this empirical reduction in rates of fertility and mortality is called demographic transition.

A demographic transition is a special kind of change in vital rates—a movement from one demographic equilibrium to another. Before transition, fertility and mortality rates are high but approximately balanced so that populations neither grow nor shrink. During transition, populations grow considerably. After transition, the vital rates are again in equilibrium, with population growth rates near zero. Thus, two different rates of demographic metabolism (Ryder 1964) both produce negligible rates of population growth. Because equilibria are central to the concept of demographic transition, most TDT incorporate homeostatic mechanisms, that is, processes that function to synchronize birth and death rates (Lee 1987, Reher 1999, Teitelbaum & Winter 1988). These homeostatic mechanisms may take a variety of forms from Malthusian checks (Coleman & Schofield 1986, Malthus 1960) to what Davis (1963) called multiphasic response.

Demographic transitions imply dramatic changes in many domains, including the economy, disease environment, and household organization. For example, the changes in overall levels of mortality are associated with changes in its character: Infant and child deaths, and deaths due to infectious causes, decline most as death becomes concentrated in a narrow band of older ages. Thus, an epidemiologic transition is integrally related to the demographic one (Omran 1977). Lower infant mortality means that children are more likely to survive to adulthood, but this effect can be overwhelmed by a decline in birthrates. Falling fertility rates almost always result in a decline in the number of siblings for any given child and therefore a decline in the numbers of aunts, uncles,

and cousins a generation later.[3] Such declines also yield a decrease in the variation of sibling set size. As a whole, falling rates of birth and death mean far less uncertainty about when and how death will come and about the number of children one will parent. Slower demographic metabolism at the population level means greater predictability for the individual: a longer and clearer horizon for the life plans central to Giddens's theory of the modern self (1991).

THEORIES OF DEMOGRAPHIC TRANSITION

The first theories of transition assumed that mortality rates would fall before fertility rates (**Figure 1**). This figure shows an idealization of the demographic transition after Notestein (1945) and Thompson (1929), rather than the trajectory of any specific population. Note in particular that the x-axis is labeled modernization, but could just as well be labeled development, or even time. As Ferguson (2006, p. 178) has argued, the concept of modernity conflates time and status, and this arguement applies to TDT as much as to modernization theories in political science or sociology. Modernization is an essential causal force in nearly all theories of TDT (see Goldscheider 1971); however, most theories give surprisingly short shrift to what modernization means. Some scholars lump together "growing individualism and rising levels of popular aspirations," urbanization, and the fact that "the family lost many of its functions to the factory, the school, and commercial enterprises" (Notestein 1945, p. 40; see also Coale 1973, pp. 64–65). Others, mostly for practical reasons in a quantitative analysis, take gross national product (GNP), proportion urbanized, women's literacy, secularization, or another single variable as a proxy for whatever it is about modernity that matters. Not only do

Demographic metabolism: turnover within a population through births and deaths. Occurs quickly in pretransition populations and slowly in posttransition ones

Homeostatic mechanism: any process or force that functions to synchronize birth and death rates in a population over time

GNP: gross national product

---

[3]In theory population-level fertility could decline without this consequence if an increasing number of women remained childless. Empirically, however, most of fertility decline results from a reduction in higher-order births.

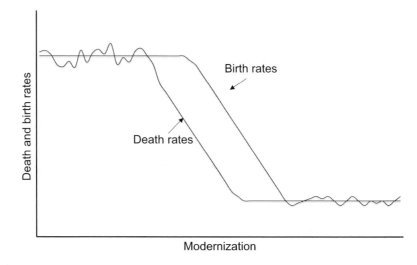

Figure 1

Stylized representation of demographic transition theory adapted from Notestein (1945) and Thompson (1929).

ethnographers stand to benefit from an engagement with population studies, but transition theorists could also learn from anthropological work on modernity.

Even the theories that agree that mortality should fall before fertility offer conflicting causal explanations. Notestein (1945, p. 41) argued that people would naturally deploy the advantages of modernity to reduce death rates, but that fertility rates would be stalled by cultural factors that would only slowly give way. Davis (1963), in contrast, posited that modernization would lead to lower infant death rates, in turn creating a social crisis, particularly around inheritance (see also Macunovich 2000). People would respond to this crisis in varied ways (multiphasic response), including emigration, infanticide, and fertility limitation. In Notestein's depiction, therefore, modernity exerts a direct effect on both mortality and fertility, whereas for Davis fertility decline is an only indirect consequence of modernity, mediated by mortality.

The basic outline of TDT as developed by Notestein and Davis corresponds well with microeconomic theories of demographic behavior, in which fertility decline results from the changing costs and benefits of children as

a result of economic development, education, and women's employment (Becker 1991, Easterlin 1975,[4] Easterlin & Crimmins 1985, Leibenstein 1975, Pritchett 1994). The kind of modernity that matters in these microeconomic theories is a material one, grounded in the division of labor and the increased productivity that it affords. In the cross section, microeconomic theories of fertility are supported by evidence: There is a generally negative association between economic development and fertility at the aggregate level (see **Figure 2**). In this figure, each country is represented by a line that connects the values of GNP and fertility at three points in time. The overall shape of the data—sloping downward from left to right—shows the generally negative association between the variables. A similarly negative but weak relationship holds for education and fertility in the aggregate. At the individual level, too,

---

[4]Easterlin's model differs from the others by focusing not only on the demand for children, but also on their supply and the cost of fertility regulation. It thus makes explicit a characteristic inherent to all these models, namely the extension of the economic concept of demand to something for which there is no market (births, or in Becker's case child services), and which arises as a consequence of action taken for another purpose entirely (see Potts 1997).

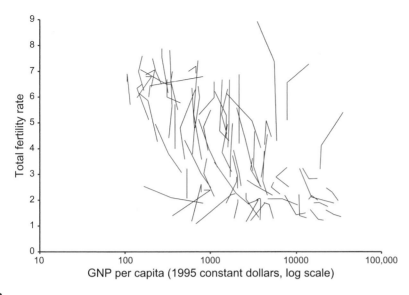

Figure 2

Fertility in 120 countries as a function of GNP per capita in 1980, 1990, and 2000. (Data from the World Bank International Database.)

income and education are associated with fertility outcomes in nearly every context (Bledsoe et al. 1999, Martin 1995; see discussion in Johnson-Hanks 2006, pp. 4–8). However, TDT that rely on economic modernization have also faced considerable contrary evidence.

Some of this evidence is visible in **Figure 2**: There is substantial variation in fertility rates for different countries with the same GNP per capita. Countries with a gross domestic profit (GDP) per capita of ~$4000 have TFRs ranging from 1.3 to 8.9. Even when the outliers are excluded, the range in fertility at a given level of GNP is more than six children, or more than two-thirds of the range of the complete data. Although there is a negative association between the variables, the predictive power of GDP for fertility is weak. The economic trajectories of specific countries, too, suggest that economic modernization does not adequately explain fertility decline. Patterns of economic growth between 1980 and 2000 do not predict changes in fertility. The paths in some countries do slope downward from left to right, consistent with an economic modernization explanation, but others slope upward, are essentially vertical or horizontal, or make v-shapes with varying orienta-

tions. All these suggest that something other than economic modernization influences fertility decline.

Between the late 1960s and the early 1980s, Coale and his students at Princeton conducted a detailed analysis of demographic transition in Europe (Coale et al. 1979, 1986; Knodel 1974; Lesthaeghe 1977; Livi Bacci 1971, 1977; Teitelbaum 1984; van de Walle 1974). The results of the European Fertility Project dramatically transformed thinking about transition in two ways: It showed that mortality decline did not always precede fertility decline and that speakers of the same language generally experienced fertility transition at the same time, regardless of economic development (but see Brown & Guinnane 2007, Guinnane et al. 1994 for methodological critiques). These findings led to what has been called the diffusionist model, which treats fertility decline as a consequence of the spread of new ideas, largely independent of changes in mortality and economic development (for overviews of the microeconomic-diffusionist debate, see Bulatao & Casterline 2001, Hirschman 1994, Mason 1997, Pollak & Watkins 1993). Watkins exemplifies the diffusionist perspective, writing "in the end it is individuals who act in the privacy of their bedroom; I propose, however, that even when the couple is literally alone in the bedroom, the echoes of conversations with kin and neighbors influence their actions" (Watkins 1990, p. 242). As a result of the Princeton project, culture, identity, and social interaction all became legitimate objects of analysis in demography. Indeed, many saw them as the key drivers of, or potential obstacles to, fertility decline. For the diffusionists, fertility decline is the product of modern ideas and identities, which circulate through social networks, enhanced by mass media and interventions such as family planning clinics (e.g., Bongaarts & Watkins 1996, Cleland & Wilson 1987, Kincaid 2000, Montgomery & Casterline 1996, Watkins 2000).

The post-Princeton body of work provides a potentially fruitful point of contact for ethnographers and linguistic anthropologists. Watkins places the circulation of discourse at the beginning of a causal chain leading from discourse to ideas to individual vital decisions in the bedroom. Both the promise and the potential pitfalls of this view will be evident to anthropologists familiar with the history of diffusion theories in North American anthropology (see Stocking 1982).

Several authors have proposed models of fertility decline that use ideas associated with both the microeconomic and the diffusionist schools. Two are of particular importance. Caldwell's theory of the direction of wealth flows posits that in pretransition societies children are a net economic benefit to their parents, whereas in posttransition societies they are a net cost (1976, 2005). This model is not a strictly microeconomic one, however, because Caldwell argues that the structural change is caused by new values and norms about childhood, consumption, and discipline, particularly as a result of mass primary education (see especially Caldwell 1980).[5] Coale (1973) advo-

cates a model in which fertility fell when child numbers entered into the "calculus of conscious choice," fertility limitation was desirable (as a result of largely economic incentives), and the means of fertility control were available. Building on Coale's three preconditions, Lesthaeghe and his coauthors have argued in a series of papers that couples must be ready, willing, and able to reduce fertility, and that any of these three can serve as a bottleneck and delay decline (see Lesthaeghe & Moors 1994, Lesthaeghe & Neels 2002).

TRANSITION AND RATIONALITY

The emergence of a new, calculating rationality is often considered one of the hallmarks of modernity (e.g., Weber 1958; see Lash 1999, p. 1). This view is echoed in both microeconomic and diffusionist theories of transition. Microeconomic perspectives on fertility transition assert that the material conditions under which people make reproductive decisions change with modernization, but that the process of decision making is rational before and after transition. That is, pretransition populations have high fertility because individuals in those populations choose to have large families (Pritchett 1994, p. 4). Diffusionists, by contrast, assert that modernity transforms the grounds or process of decision making itself, such as by moving reproduction from the realm of custom to a legitimate object of rational choice (see LeVine et al. 1991, Lesthaeghe 1980).

A key example of the centrality of rationality to theories of transition is Coale's (1973) idea that reproduction, in the form of completed family size, must enter the calculus of conscious choice before fertility will fall. Coale posits that prior to transition, couples did not make conscious choices about child numbers, or even consider doing so (see also van de Walle 1992). Fertility decline in his model relies on a specific form of calculating rationality focused on the number of children conceived in marriage, as opposed to—for example—the timing and spacing of births, marriage postponement, or child attributes. Indeed, nearly all the

---

[5] Empirical analyses have not generally supported Caldwell's claim. See Lee & Kramer (2002), Stecklov (1997).

existing literature treats fertility decline as equivalent to the emergence of parity-specific fertility control, that is, the limitation of marital fertility once a specific target number of children has been attained (see Carter 1995, p. 84 for a critique).

Insofar as fertility decline is subsumed into parity-specific control and parental rationality, the debate about the causes of fertility decline becomes a debate about the causes of changing reproductive intentions. In a classic paper, Henry (1961, p. 91) writes that fertility "control is said to exist when the behavior of the couple is bound to the number of children already born and is modified when this number reaches the maximum which the couple does not want to exceed." Similarly, Knodel (1983, table 1) identifies "deliberate stopping with the intent to limit family size" as the sine qua non of controlled fertility; that is, fertility falls because couples think about their fertility and choose to limit the number of children they bear: reproduction is the product of reasoned action. Most scholars of fertility transition would thus agree with a recent review that asserts, "fertility decline is a largely rational process" driven by "the desire for smaller families" (Bulatao 2001, p. 11), regardless of whether that desire arises from material conditions or diffusion processes.

Thus, in the standard view described above, people intend to have three children in the same way that they intend to buy breakfast cereal, hire an assistant, or open a window. The conceptual problem with this view is that fertility does not resemble opening a window in any of the relevant ways. People do not necessarily have explicit plans of action in reference to reproduction. The plans that do exist may change before they are accomplished. They may also be vague, underspecified, or relatively unimportant compared with other simultaneous plans. Actions with reproductive consequences also have other, even more important, motivations. People must collaborate with others in the relevant actions. Even when people have clear intentions, biology often thwarts their achievement. At some basic level, reproduction remains partially outside the calculus of conscious choice, even in posttransition societies. The conceptual problems are echoed by empirical fact: At the individual level, reproductive intentions predict outcomes quite poorly.

A growing number of studies, building on Ryder's and Westoff's pioneering work in the 1970s, examine the relationship between stated fertility intentions and subsequent reproductive outcomes at the individual level (Bankole & Westoff 1998; Campbell & Campbell 1997; De Silva 1992; Jones et al. 1980; Miller & Pasta 1995; Morgan 1981, 1982; Nair & Chow 1980; Quesnel-Vallee & Morgan 2004; Schoen et al. 1999, 2000; Symeonidou 2000; Tan & Tey 1994; Vlassoff 1990; Westoff & Ryder 1977; Williams et al. 1999). The results of these studies are mixed, partly because of varying research methods and partly because of the different socioeconomic contexts in which the studies were conducted. But this literature gives reason to doubt that fertility outcomes are the product of reasoned action oriented to completed family size, even in posttransition populations. For example, Westoff & Ryder (1977) found that in their sample of married, college-educated, fecund, white, American women—arguably the subpopulation most able to achieve their intentions—more than 20% had reproductive experiences within a five-year period that contradicted their stated intentions. Even higher levels of discordance are found in posttransition Taiwan (Nair & Chow 1980).

If posttransition fertility outcomes are not primarily the product of intentional, reasoned action oriented toward child numbers, how should we explain them? A growing body of work argues that reproductive action is oriented by ethics and aspirations in high- and low-fertility populations alike, and that rationality matters only as a culturally meaningful portrayal of reproductive action, and not as an empirical description of it. Bledsoe (2002, Bledsoe et al. 1998) argues that Gambian women orient their reproduction not toward total child numbers, but toward physically and socially appropriate birth timing. Johnson-Hanks (2002) has made a similar argument about the reproductive practices of urban, educated

Cameroonians, emphasizing the importance of women's honor. Fisher (2006) uses life history interviews to make the case that working-class English couples in the first half of the twentieth century reduced their fertility without formulating intended family sizes; fertility fell, she argues, without child numbers entering the calculus of conscious choice. Together, these recent works suggest that fertility transition results from changing conceptions of value, time, and ethics, rather than from the transformation of reproduction from the domain of values to the domain of rational calculation. A study of posttransition fertility thus offers a new perspective on rationality and modernity.

TRANSITION, MODERNITY, AND GOVERNMENTALITY

Although most TDT treat modernization or modernity as its key cause, these theories offer surprisingly thin discussions of modernity. Equally surprising is how completely the leading theorists of modernity in anthropology ignore demographic change: Changes in vital rates or in population size and structure are almost completely absent from anthropological writings on the modern, the postmodern, the postcolonial, and the contemporary (see Fischer 1999 for a review; partial exceptions include Schneider & Schneider 1996, Setel 1999, Szreter et al. 2004). This is surprising for three reasons. First, demographic changes are empirically some of the most dramatic transformations in the human condition recorded in the past three centuries: that the average person should have one sibling instead of seven, should expect to live into adulthood without experiencing the death of a parent or sibling, should have few enough kin to be able to know each of them, and should be able to plan a life trajectory neither centered on raising children nor colored with the constant risk of death. The emergence of cyberspace, futures options, and new reproductive technologies pales in comparison. Second, demographic changes are closely intertwined with the social, political, and technological changes that do draw considerable research

attention. Imagine, for example, a "'regime of the self' as a prudent yet enterprising individual, actively shaping his or her life course through acts of choice," (Rose & Novas cited in Collier & Ong 2003, p. 423) in a population where life expectancy is below 30: not impossible, but dramatically less likely. Third, there are vibrant literatures at the margins of population processes, both on the discourses of population and biopower/biopolitics (e.g., Agamben 1998; Foucault 1990, 1997, 2004; Greenhalgh 2003; Greenhalgh & Winckler 2005; Hacking 1990; Horn 1994; Krause 2005; Paxson 2004; Rose 1996, 2007) and on birth and death as individual experiences, meaningful symbols, and elements in a political economy (e.g., Clarke 1998, Franklin & Lock 2003, Ginsburg & Rapp 1995, Inhorn 1994, Kaufman & Morgan 2005, Lock 2002, Loizos & Heady 1999, Sargent 1989, Scheper-Hughes 1992, van Hollen 2003). These literatures would be greatly enhanced by direct engagement with the study of population size, structure, and rates of change, that is, with the materiality of population, and not only the discourses about it.

As a primary example, the idea of population plays a central role in Foucault's conceptualization of modern governmentality. In a variety of works, he makes the argument that "one of the great innovations in the techniques of power in the 18th century was the emergence of 'population' as an economic and political problem. . . . Governments perceived that they were not dealing simply with subjects, or even with a 'people,' but with a 'population'" (Foucault 1990, p. 25; see also Foucault 1990, p. 139; 1997, pp. 242–44). Indeed, for Foucault, population "is the pivot on which turned the transition from rule based on sovereign authority to a 'governmentalized' rule . . . [which is] triangulated around practices of sovereignty-discipline-government and [has] as its essential object the population" (Curtis 2002, p. 506). Building on Foucault, Hacking (1986) treats demographic categorization as a prototypical case of the rise of statistical forms under modern rule, whereby official classifications, such as from the census, enter people's own understandings of themselves and others, altering the character of social relations. In the past decade, numerous scholars have investigated migration, family planning policies, and public health systems through a Foucauldian lens (e.g., Greene 1999, Inda 2005, Petersen & Bunton 1997).

Governing China's Population by Greenhalgh & Winckler (2005), perhaps the most demographically astute of these recent works, argue that the project of population is central to power and politics in post-Mao China, particularly through the one-child policy and its precursors. Indeed, the decline of fertility in China was linked to an explicit program of modernization, making China at once a paradigmatic and exceptional case. Greenhalgh & Winckler gloss Foucault's triangle as "governance over and through government in the conventional sense . . . , governance through 'intermediate' disciplinary institutions, usually run by professionals on the basis of particular expertise . . . , [and] self-governance by individuals of themselves" (Greenhalgh & Winckler 2005, p. 23). This last category is of critical importance with regard to demographic transition. Whereas institutions within and beyond the state clearly influence fertility and mortality rates, births and deaths are, in the end, individual-level events, and their comprehensive analysis must extend to that level. Demographic transition turns on the questions of when and how specific reproductive actors change their behavior.

For Foucault, sovereignty-discipline-government exists as a palimpsest in which self-regulation emerges out of the disciplining of conduct through nonstate institutions, which in turn builds on sovereign power. Each new modality coexists with the earlier ones rather than displacing them (see Moore 2005, especially chapters 2 and 3). The self-monitoring of individual conduct thus emerges out of the ongoing expert administration of populations aimed at optimizing individual and collective life and health. In this view, the emergence of fertility limitation should follow—both temporally and conceptually—the disciplining of reproduction by demographers, public

health experts, and other participants in an institutionalized politics of life. For China, as analyzed by Greenhalgh & Winckler (2005), this explanation may hold, although much of what they describe resembles pure sovereign power more than governmentality as conventionally understood. However, most of the fertility decline in the North Atlantic occurred long before any such formation existed, starting by the 1750s in France and by 1850 in most of the rest of Europe and North America. At the time, governments were strongly pronatalist in discourse, policies were neutral or pronatalist, and the disciplining of reproduction, for example by demographers, had not yet begun. That is, fertility fell through the transformation of individual conduct without the mirroring, monitoring, or reinforcement of the state.

Parish registers, through a technique known as family reconstitution, serve as the primary data source for the period before European state collection of birth records [for details on the method and use of family reconstitution, see Henry & Fleury (1956), Wrigley & Schofield (1989)]. Churches recorded baptisms, marriages, and funerals out of concern for souls rather than as part of the power to make live and let die; we therefore have information about population changes before, and at least partially independent of, the knowledge/power oriented to their control (see Wilke 2004). Based on these sources, it is clear that fertility began falling in specific communities in France by 1750 (Hadeishi 2003) and decline was well established throughout the country by 1790 (Flinn 1981, p. 86; Weir 1994), that is, by the time of the first demographic analyses of the birthrate[6] and more than a century before the liberalization of laws against abortion. What is more, reproductive conduct

---

[6]Among these earliest publications in France is Laplace (1786). A couple of earlier studies of fertility were published in England (Arbuthnot 1710) and Germany (Süssmilch 1742), arguing that the sex ratio at birth showed evidence of God's providence. Studies of mortality began much earlier, also in England, and were well developed by 1800. For discussions, see Daston (1988), Dupâquier & Dupâquier (1985), and Hacking (1975).

in many European countries was already self-monitored and managed well before the onset of the demographic transition, albeit in relation to the timing rather than the numbers of births (Bengtsson & Dribe 2006, van de Walle & Muhsam 1995; see Friedlander et al. 1999, pp. 508–11 for a review). Similarly, in what would become the United States, fertility decline began around the time of the revolution, before knowledge of the birthrate, before disciplinary institutions that were oriented to its management, and even before the establishment of a state that could authorize such management (Binion 2000, Main 2006). Demographic transition should be a paradigmatic example of biopower, but at least in France and the United States, new kinds of individual self-regulation, visible in birthrates, preceded the relevant forms of knowledge/power by decades. A study of population rates thus alters how we think about discourses of population.

CONCLUSION

Much of contemporary anthropology seeks to understand the contemporary condition as a product of neoliberalism, modernity, and its aftermath. Although, looking comparatively, no single aspect of modernity seems either necessary or sufficient for demographic transition to occur, the change from high to low rates of fertility and mortality was everywhere intertwined with the emergence of the modern. Transition is not only a consequence of modern institutions and forms of personhood, but also one of their sources. The life plans that play such an important role in Giddens's (1991) theory of the modern self, for example, require a posttransition demographic regime.

Generalizing beyond demographic transition, population size, structure, and dynamics constitute the conditions of possibility for much of social life. Discourses about rates, statistics, and populations matter (see, e.g., Krause 2001, Urla 1993), but actual rates and ratios matter, too. For example, contemporary concerns about European identity and immigration are fueled by the fact that birthrates are below replacement; within a generation, all countries in Europe would likely experience population decline were it not for immigration. The very high sex ratio at birth in China means that many men will be unable to find native-born wives. Rising life expectancy and falling birthrates combine with legal and economic factors to create the social security shortfall. And fertility postponement up against the limits of fecundability generates markets in IVF, donor gametes, and surrogacy. In sum, populations have systematic properties that emerge only at the aggregate level, making them natural objects for anthropological investigation. When so many of the social sciences are gravitating to methodological individualism or reducing the social to an epiphenomenon of brain structure, population dynamics offer an unassailable example of why that path can never be sufficient.

DISCLOSURE STATEMENT

The author is not aware of any biases that might be perceived as affecting the objectivity of this review.

LITERATURE CITED

Agamben G. 1998. *Homo Sacer: Sovereign Power and Naked Life*. Stanford, CA: Stanford Univ. Press. 228 pp.
Arbuthnot J. 1710. An argument for divine providence, taken from the regularity observ'd in the birth of both sexes. *Philos. Trans. R. Soc. London* 27:186–90
Bankole A, Westoff C. 1998. The consistency and validity of reproductive attitudes: evidence from Morocco. *J. Biosoc. Sci.* 30:439–55
Becker G. 1991. *A Treatise on the Family*. Cambridge, MA: Harvard Univ. Press. Enlarge. ed.
Bengtsson T, Dribe M. 2006. Deliberate control in a natural fertility population: southern Sweden 1766–1864. *Demography* 43(4):727–46

Binion R. 2000. Marianne in the home. Political revolution and demographic transition in France and the United States. *Population* 55(1):81–104

Bledsoe C. 2002. *Contingent Lives: Fertility, Time and Aging in West Africa*. Chicago: Univ. Chicago Press. 353 pp.

Bledsoe C, Banja F, Hill A. 1998. Reproductive mishaps and western contraception: an African challenge to fertility theory. *Popul. Dev. Rev.* 24:15–57

Bledsoe C, Casterline J, Johnson-Kuhn J, Haaga J, eds. 1999. *Critical Perspectives on Schooling and Fertility in the Developing World*. Washington, DC: Natl. Acad. Press. pp. 1–23

Bongaarts J, Watkins SC. 1996. Social interactions and contemporary fertility transitions. *Popul. Dev. Rev.* 22:639–83

Brown JC, Guinnane TW. 2007. Regions and time in the European fertility transition: problems in the Princeton project's statistical methodology. *Econ. Hist. Rev.* 60(3):574–95

Bulatao R. 2001. Introduction. See Bulatao & Casterline 2001, pp. 1–16

Bulatao R, Casterline J, eds. 2001. *Global Fertility Transition*. New York: Popul. Counc. 338 pp.

Caldwell J. 1976. Toward a restatement of demographic transition theory. *Popul. Dev. Rev.* 2:321–66

Caldwell J. 1980. Mass education as a determinant of the timing of fertility decline. *Popul. Dev. Rev.* 6:225–55

Caldwell JC. 2005. On net intergenerational wealth flows: an update. *Popul. Dev. Rev.* 31(4):721–40

Campbell EK, Campbell PG. 1997. Family size and sex preferences and eventual fertility in Botswana. *J. Biosoc. Sci.* 29:191–204

Carter A. 1995. Agency and fertility: for an ethnography of practice. In *Situating Fertility: Anthropological and Demographic Inquiry*, ed. S Greenhalgh. pp. 55–85. Cambridge, UK: Cambridge Univ. Press

Clarke A. 1998. *Disciplining Reproduction: Modernity, American Life Sciences and "The Problems of Sex."* Berkeley: Univ. Calif. Press. 438 pp.

Cleland J, Wilson C. 1987. Demand theories of fertility transition: an iconoclastic view. *Popul. Stud.* 41:5–30

Coale A. 1973. The demographic transition reconsidered. *Prec. Int. Popul. Conf.* pp. 53–72. Liege, Belgium: IUSSP

Coale A, Anderson B, Harm E. 1979. *Human Fertility in Russia Since the 19th Century*. Princeton, NJ: Princeton Univ. Press. 536 pp.

Coale A, Watkins SC, eds. 1986 . *The Decline of Fertility in Europe: The Revised Proceedings of a Conference on the Princeton European Fertility Project*. Princeton, NJ: Princeton Univ. Press. 484 pp.

Coleman D, Schofield R. 1986. *The State of Population Theory: Forward from Malthus*. Oxford: Blackwell. 299 pp.

Collier S, Ong A. 2003. Oikos/Anthropos: rationality, technology, infrastructure; a workshop report. *Curr. Anthropol.* 44(3):421–26

Cowgill G. 1975. On causes and consequences of ancient and modern population changes. *Am. Anthropol.* 77:505–25

Curtis B. 2002. Foucault on governmentality and population: the impossible discovery. *Can. J. Sociol.* 27(4):505–33

Daston L. 1988. *Classical Probability in the Enlightenment*. Princeton, NJ: Princeton Univ. Press. 386 pp.

Davis K. 1963. The theory of change and response in modern demographic history. *Popul. Index* 29:345–66

De Silva W. 1992. Achievement of reproductive intentions in Sri Lanka, 1982–1985: a longitudinal study. *Soc. Biol.* 39:123–38

Dupâquier J, Dupâquier M. 1985. *Histoire de la Démographie*. Paris: Libr. Acad. Perrin. 386 pp.

Easterlin RA. 1975. An economic framework for fertility analysis. *Stud. Fam. Plan.* 6:54–63

Easterlin RA, Crimmins EM. 1985. *The Fertility Revolution*. Chicago: Univ. Chicago Press. 191 pp.

Ferguson J. 2006. *Global Shadows: Africa in the Neoliberal World Order*. Durham, NC/London: Duke Univ. Press. 227 pp.

Fischer MMJ. 1999. Emergent forms of life: anthropology of late or postmodernities. *Annu. Rev. Anthropol.* 28:455–78

Fisher K. 2006. *Birth Control, Sex, and Marriage in Britain 1918–1960*. Oxford: Oxford Univ. Press. 243 pp.

Flinn MW. 1981. *The European Demographic System*. Baltimore, MD: Johns Hopkins Univ. Press. 175 pp.

Foucault M. 1990. *The History of Sexuality*. Vol. 1. New York: Vintage. 159 pp.

Foucault M. 1997. *Society Must Be Defended: Lectures at the Collège de France 1975–1976*. New York: Picador. 289 pp.

Foucault M. 2004. *Security, Territory, Population: Lectures at the College de France 1977–1978*. New York: Palgrave. 358 pp.

Franklin S, Lock MM, eds. 2003. *Remaking Life and Death: Toward an Anthropology of the Biosciences*. Santa Fe, NM: Sch. Am. Res. Press. 396 pp.

Friedlander D, Okun B, Segal S. 1999. The demographic transition then and now: processes, perspectives, and analyses. *J. Fam. Hist.* 24(4):493–533

Giddens A. 1991. *Modernity and Self-Identity. Self and Society in the Late Modern Age*. Cambridge, UK: Polity. 178 pp.

Gillis J, Tilly L, Levine D, eds. 1992. *The European Experience of Declining Fertility, 1850–1970*. Cambridge, MA/Oxford: Blackwell. 370 pp.

Ginsburg F, Rapp R. 1995. *Conceiving the New World Order: The Global Politics of Reproduction*. Berkeley: Univ. Calif. Press. 439 pp.

Goldscheider C. 1971. *Population, Modernization, and Social Structure*. Boston: Little, Brown. 325 pp.

Greene RW. 1999. *Malthusian Worlds: US Leadership and the Governing of the Population Crisis*. Boulder: Westview. 273 pp.

Greenhalgh S. 2003. Planned births, unplanned persons: "population" in the making of Chinese modernity. *Am. Ethnol.* 30:196–215

Greenhalgh S, Winckler E. 2005. *Governing China's Population: From Leninist To Neoliberal Biopolitics*. Stanford, CA: Stanford Univ. Press. 341 pp.

Guinnane T, Okun B, Trussell J. 1994. What do we know about the timing of fertility transitions in Europe? *Demography* 31:1–20

Hacking I. 1975. *The Emergence of Probability: A Philosophical Study of Early Ideas about Probability, Induction and Statistical Inference*. Cambridge, UK: Cambridge Univ. Press. 185 pp.

Hacking I. 1986. Making Up People. In *Reconstructing Individualism: Autonomy, Individuality, and the Self in Western Thought*, ed. by Weller, Sosna, and Wellbery, Stanford Univ. Press

Hacking I. 1990. *The Taming of Chance*. Cambridge, UK: Cambridge Univ. Press. 256 pp.

Hadeishi H. 2003. Economic well-being and fertility in France, 1744–1792. *J. Econ. Hist.* 63:489–505

Hall R. 1972. Demographic transition: stage 4. *Curr. Anthropol.* 13(2):349–383

Hammel E, McDaniel C, Wachter K. 1979. Demographic consequences of incest tabus. *Science* 205:972–77

Handwerker WP. 1983. The first demographic transition: an analysis of subsistence choices and reproductive consequences. *Am. Anthropol.* 85(1):5–27

Henry L. 1961. Some data on natural fertility. *Eugen. Q.* 8:81–91

Henry L, Fleury M. 1956. *Des Registres Paroissiaux à l'histoire de la Population. Manuel de Dépouillement et d'exploitation de l'état civil Ancien*. Paris: INED

Heuveline P. 1999. The global and regional impact of mortality and fertility transitions, 1950–2000. *Popul. Dev. Rev.* 25:681–702

Hirschman C. 1994. Why fertility changes. *Annu. Rev. Sociol.* 20:203–33

Horn DG. 1994. *Social Bodies: Science, Reproduction, and Italian Modernity*. Princeton, NJ: Princeton Univ. Press. 208 pp.

Howell N. 1979. *Demography of the Dobe !Kung*. New York, NY: Academic. 442

Howell N. 1986. Demographic anthropology. *Annu. Rev. Anthropol.* 15:219–46

Inda J, ed. 2005. *Anthropologies of Modernity: Foucault, Governmentality, and Life Politics*. Malden, MA: Blackwell Publ. 266 pp.

Inhorn M. 1994. *Quest for Conception: Gender, Infertility, and Egyptian Medical Traditions*. Philadelphia: Univ. Penn. Press. 394 pp.

Johnson-Hanks J. 2002. The modernity of traditional contraception. *Popul. Dev. Rev.* 28:229–49

Johnson-Hanks J. 2006. *Uncertain Honor: Modern Motherhood in an African Crisis*. Chicago: Univ. Chicago Press. 324 pp.

Jones E, Paul L, Westoff C. 1980. Contraceptive efficacy: the significance of method and motivation. *Stud. Fam. Plan.* 11:39–50

Jones G, Caldwell J, Douglas R, D'Souza R, eds. 1997. *The Continuing Demographic Transition*. Oxford: Oxford Univ. Press

Kaufman S, Morgan L. 2005. The anthropology of the beginnings and endings of life. *Annu. Rev. Anthropol.* 34:317–41

Kincaid DL. 2000. Social networks, ideation, and contraceptive behavior in Bangladesh: a longitudinal analysis. *Soc. Sci. Med.* 50:215–31

Kirk D. 1996. Demographic transition theory. *Popul. Stud.* 50(3):361–87

Knodel J. 1983. Natural fertility: age patterns, levels and trends. In *Determinants of Fertility in Developing Countries*, ed. RA Bulatao, RD Lee. 1-642. New York: Academic

Knodel J. 1974. *The Decline of Fertility in Germany, 1871–1939*. Princeton, NJ: Princeton Univ. Press. 262 pp.

Krause E. 2001. "Empty cradles" and the quiet revolution: demographic discourse and cultural struggles of gender, race, and class in Italy. *Cult. Anthropol.* 16(4):576–611

Krause E. 2005. *A Crisis of Births: Population Politics and Family-Making in Italy*. Belmont, CA: Thomson/ Wadsworth. 198 pp.

Laplace PS. 1786. Sur les naissances, les marriages et les morts à Paris, depuis 1771 jusqu'en 1784. *Mémoires de l'Académie royale des Sciences, Année 1783*, pp. 693–702

Lash S. 1999. *Another Modernity, A Different Rationality*. Oxford: Blackwell. 415 pp.

Lee R. 1987. Population dynamics of humans and other animals. *Demography* 24:443–65

Lee R. 2003. The demographic transition: three centuries of fundamental change. *J. Econ. Perspect.* 17:167–90

Lee R, Kramer K. 2002. Children's economic roles in the Maya family life cycle: Cain, Caldwell and Chayanov revisited. *Popul. Dev. Rev.* 28:475–99

Leibenstein H. 1975. Economic theory of fertility decline. *Q. J. Econ.* 89(1):1–31

Lesthaeghe RJ. 1977. *The Decline of Belgian Fertility, 1800–1970*. Princeton, NJ: Princeton Univ. Press. 232 pp.

Lesthaeghe R. 1980. On the social control of human reproduction. *Popul. Dev. Rev.* 6:527–48

Lesthaeghe RJ, Moors G. 1994. Explaining the diversity of family and domestic types: economic theory of cultural influence. *Population* 49(6):1503–25

Lesthaeghe R, Neels K. 2002. From the first to the second demographic transition: an interpretation of the spatial continuity of demographic innovation in France, Belguim and Switzerland. *Eur. J. Popul.* 18(4):325–60

LeVine RA, Levine SE, Richman A, Uribe FMT, Correa CS, Miller PM. 1991. Women's schooling and child care in the demographic transition: a Mexican case study. *Popul. Dev. Rev.* 17:186–91

Livi Bacci M. 1971. *A Century of Portuguese Fertility*. Princeton, NJ: Princeton Univ. Press. 131 pp.

Livi Bacci M. 1977. *A History of Italian Fertility During the Last Two Centuries*. Princeton, NJ: Princeton Univ. Press. 311 pp.

Lock M. 2002. *Twice Dead: Organ Transplants and the Reinvention of Death*. Berkeley: Univ. Calif. Press. 389 pp.

Loizos P, Heady P, eds. 1999. *Conceiving Persons: Ethnographies of Procreation, Fertility, and Growth*. London/ New Brunswick, NJ: Athlone. 242 pp.

Macunovich DJ. 2000. Relative cohort size: source of a unifying theory of global fertility transition? *Popul. Dev. Rev.* 26(2):235–61

Main GL. 2006. Rocking the cradle: downsizing the New England family. *J. Interdiscip. Hist.* 37(1):35–58

Malthus T. 1960. A summary view of the principle of population. In *On Population: Three Essays*, pp. 13–59. New York: Mentor

Martin TC. 1995. Women's education and fertility: results from 26 demographic and health surveys. *Stud. Fam. Plan.* 26:187–202

Mason K. 1997. Explaining fertility transitions. *Demography* 34:443–55

Miller WB, Pasta DJ. 1995. Behavioral intentions: Which ones predict fertility behavior in married couples? *J. Appl. Psychol.* 25:530–55

Montgomery MR, Casterline JB. 1996. Social learning, social influence and new models of fertility. *Popul. Dev. Rev.* 22:151–75

Moore D. 2005. *Suffering for Territory: Race, Place and Power in Zimbabwe*. Durham, NC: Duke Univ. Press. 399 pp.

Morgan SP. 1981. Intention and uncertainty at later stages of childbearing: the United States 1965 and 1970. *Demography* 18:267–85

Morgan SP. 1982. Parity-specific fertility intentions and uncertainty: the United States, 1970–1976. *Demography* 19:315–34

Nair NK, Chow LP. 1980. Fertility intentions and behavior: some findings from Taiwan. *Stud. Fam. Plan.* 11:255–63

Notestein F. 1945. Population—the long view. In *Food for the World*, ed. TW Schultz, pp. 36–57. Chicago: Univ. Chicago Press

Omran A. 1977. The epidemiologic transition: a theory of the epidemiology of population change. *Milbank Mem. Fund Q.* 49:509–37

Paxson H. 2004. *Making Modern Mothers: Ethics and Family Planning in Urban Greece.* Berkeley: Univ. Calif. Press. 291 pp.

Petersen A, Bunton R, eds. 1997. *Foucault, Health and Medicine.* London/New York: Routledge. 294 pp.

Pollak R, Watkins SC. 1993. Cultural and economic approaches to fertility: proper marriage or *mésalliance*? *Popul. Dev. Rev.* 19:467–96

Potts M. 1997. Sex and the birth rate: human biology, demographic change, and access to fertility-regulation methods. *Popul. Dev. Rev.* 23:1–39

Pritchett L. 1994. Desired fertility and the impact of population policies. *Popul. Dev. Rev.* 20:1–55

Quesnel-Vallee A, Morgan SP. 2004. Missing the target? Correspondence of fertility intentions and behavior in the US. *Popul. Res. Pol. Rev.* 22:497–525

Reher D. 1999. Back to the basics: mortality and fertility interactions during the demographic transition. *Contin. Chang.* 14:9–31

Reisman D. 2002. David Reisman on phases of population growth and social character. *Popul. Dev. Rev.* 28(2):313–28

Rose N. 1996. *Inventing Our Selves.* Cambridge, UK: Cambridge Univ. Press. 232 pp.

Rose N. 2007. *The Politics of Life Itself: Biomedicine, Power, and Subjectivity in the Twenty-First Century.* Princeton, NJ: Princeton Univ. Press. 372 pp.

Ryder NB. 1964. Notes on the concept of a population. *Am. J. Sociol.* 69:447–62

Sargent CF. 1989. *Maternity, Medicine and Power: Reproductive Decision in Urban Benin.* Berkeley: Univ. Calif. Press. 231 pp.

Scheper-Hughes N. 1992. *Death Without Weeping: Everyday Violence in Brazil.* Berkeley: Univ. Calif. Press. 556 pp.

Schneider J, Schneider PT. 1996. *Festival of the Poor: Fertility Decline and the Ideology of Class in Sicily, 1860–1980.* Tucson: Univ. Ariz. Press. 283 pp.

Schoen R, Astone NM, Kim YJ, Nathanson CA, Fields JM. 1999. Do fertility intentions affect fertility behavior? *J. Marriage Fam.* 61:790–99

Schoen R, Astone NM, Nathanson CA, Kim YJ, Murray N. 2000. The impact of fertility intentions on behavior: the case of sterilization. *Soc. Biol.* 47:61–76

Setel P. 1999. *A Plague of Paradoxes: AIDS, Culture and Demography in Northern Tanzania.* Chicago: Univ. Chicago Press. 249 pp.

Stecklov G. 1997. Intergenerational resource flows in Cote d'Ivoire: empirical analysis of aggregate flows. *Popul. Dev. Rev.* 23:525–53

Stocking G. 1982. *Race, Culture, and Evolution: Essays in the History of Anthropology.* Chicago: Univ. Chicago Press. 412 pp.

Süssmilch JP. 1742. *Die göttliche Ordnung in den Veränderungen des menschlichen Geschlechts.* Berlin: D.A. Gohls.

Symeonidou H. 2000. Expected and actual family size in Greece: 1983–1997. *Eur. J. Popul.* 16:335–52

Szreter S. 1993. The idea of demographic transition and the study of fertility change: a critical intellectual history. *Popul. Dev. Rev.* 19:659–701

Szreter S, Sholkamy H, Dharmalingam A, eds. 2004. *Categories and Contexts: Anthropological and Historical Studies in Critical Demography.* Oxford: Oxford Univ. Press. 395 pp.

Tan PC, Tey NP. 1994. Do fertility intentions predict subsequent behavior? Evidence from peninsular Malaysia. *Stud. Fam. Plan.* 25:222–31

Teitelbaum M. 1984. *The British Fertility Decline: Demographic Transition in the Crucible of the Industrial Revolution.* Princeton, NJ: Princeton Univ. Press. 269 pp.

Teitelbaum M, Winter J, eds. 1988. *Population and Resources in Western Intellectual Traditions.* Cambridge, UK: Cambridge Univ. Press. 310 pp.

Thompson W. 1929. Population. *Am. J. Sociol.* 34(6):959–75

Urla J. 1993. Cultural politics in an age of statistics: numbers, nations, and the making of Basque identity. *Am. Ethnol.* 20(4):818–43

van de Walle E. 1974. *The Female Population of France in the Nineteenth Century.* Princeton, NJ: Princeton Univ. Press. 483 pp.

van de Walle E. 1992. Fertility transition, conscious choice, and numeracy. *Demography* 29:487–502

van de Walle E, Muhsam HV. 1995. Fatal secrets and the French fertility transition. *Popul. Dev. Rev.* 21:261–79

Van Hollen C. 2003. *Birth on the Threshold: Childbirth and Modernity in South India.* Berkeley: Univ. Calif. Press. 310 pp.

Van Krieken R. 1997. Sociology and the reproductive self: demographic transitions and modernity. *Sociology* 31:445–72

Vlassoff C. 1990. Fertility intentions and subsequent behavior: a longitudinal study in rural India. *Stud. Fam. Plan.* 21:216–25

Watkins SC. 1990. From local to national communities: the transformation of demographic regimes in Western Europe, 1870–1960. *Popul. Dev. Rev.* 16:241–72

Watkins SC. 2000. Local and foreign models of reproduction in Nyanza Province, Kenya. *Popul. Dev. Rev.* 26:725–59

Weber M. 1958. *The Protestant Ethic and the Spirit of Capitalism.* New York: Charles Scribner's Sons. 289 pp.

Weir DR. 1994. New estimates of nuptiality and marital fertility in France, 1740–1911. *Popul. Stud.* 48(2):307–31

Westoff C, Ryder N. 1977. The predictive validity of reproductive intentions. *Demography* 14:431–53

Wilke J. 2004. From parish register to the historical table. *Hist. Fam.* 9(1):63–79

Williams L, Abma J, Piccinino LJ. 1999. The correspondence between intentions to avoid childbearing and subsequent fertility: a prospective analysis. *Fam. Plan. Perspect.* 31:220–27

Wrigley EA, Schofield RS. 1989. *The Population History of England 1541–1871: A Reconstruction.* Cambridge, UK: Cambridge Univ. Press. 2nd ed. 779 pp.

Zhao ZW. 1996. The demographic transition in Victorian England and changes in English kinship networks. *Contin. Chang.* 11(Pt. 2):243–72

Sexuality Studies in Archaeology

Barbara L. Voss

Department of Anthropology, Stanford University, Stanford, California 94305-2034;
email: bvoss@stanford.edu

Annu. Rev. Anthropol. 2008. 37:317–36

First published online as a Review in Advance on
June 18, 2008

The *Annual Review of Anthropology* is online at
anthro.annualreviews.org

This article's doi:
10.1146/annurev.anthro.37.081407.085238

Key Words

reproduction, sexual identity, prostitution, institutions, queer theory,
gender

Abstract

Does sexuality have a past? A growing body of archaeological research
on sexuality demonstrates that the sexual politics of the past were as
richly varied and complex as those of the present. Furthermore, investigations of past sexualities have much to say about conventional
archaeological topics such as state formation, subsistence and settlement systems, and the emergence and elaboration of symbolic systems,
and they have made methodological and theoretical contributions to
the archaeology of social identities and visual representations. To date,
most research has clustered into five groupings: reproduction management, sexual representations, sexual identities, prostitution, and the sexual politics of institutions. The most intriguing new development is the
growing application of queer theory as an archaeological methodology for investigating nonsexual as well as sexual matters. In particular,
queer theory provides a methodological bridge between archaeological
research on sexuality and research on other aspects of social identity.

INTRODUCTION

Less than 15 years ago, a review of sexuality studies in archaeology would have merited little more than a substantial footnote. With the exception of a few pioneering studies, discussion of sexuality was generally subsumed under "fertility" and associated "cults" of phallic or goddess worship. More commonly, archaeological interpretations relied on latent sexual narratives that portrayed people in the past as monogamous heterosexual couples whose sex lives were oriented entirely toward reproduction. This view was supported by a legacy of sex negativity in archaeology, which has suppressed evidence of sexual diversity in the past. In many parts of the world, sexually explicit artifacts, especially those portraying same-sex sexual acts, have been destroyed because of their illicit content. Others have been sequestered in private collections or in restricted-access museum assemblages (such as the famous Cabinet of Obscene Objects in the Naples Archaeological Museum) and censored from archaeological publications (Clarke 1998, p. 148; Davis 2001; Taylor 2006, pp. 73–74).

It is not yet clear whether this situation has significantly changed. Most archaeological texts still read as if they were written to be approved by a morals committee for the promotion of family values. When sex is mentioned, it is still largely discussed in terms of reproduction. These archaeological narratives reify the mistaken notion that the complex sexual politics of the present are a uniquely modern phenomenon, divorced from the rich cultural traditions of the past. Fortunately, the trope of universal, reproductive heterosexuality is no longer the only perspective available. In the past two decades, a broad corpus of archaeological scholarship has emerged that takes sexuality seriously. This work is not only transforming our archaeological interpretations of past societies but also challenging conventional understandings of sexuality itself.

ARCHAEOLOGY REDISCOVERS SEXUALITY

The current wave of scholarship represents both a continuation of and a break from archaeology's long entanglement with sexuality studies. The formulation of modern concepts of sexuality has deep roots in the archaeological past. For example, the term pornography (literally, whore-writing) was coined in 1850 by German archaeologist C. O. Müller to classify a diverse set of objects and images found at Pompeii; this archaeological term rapidly migrated into nineteenth-century law through edicts such as the British Obscene Publications Act of 1857 (Clarke 2003, pp. 11–12). J. J. Winckelmann's eighteenth-century studies of ancient art and John Symonds's *A Problem in Greek Ethics* (1901) were instrumental points of reference for sexologists who formulated current medico-psychological theories of sexual orientation (Davis 1996, Verstraete & Provencal 2006). Other nineteenth-century Europeans turned to Egyptology for countercultural models of sexual potency, bisexuality, gender ambiguity, and homoeroticism (Meskell 1998a). Sigmund Freud, whose psychological theories located human subject formation in the struggle to resolve conflicting sexual drives, was an avid antiquities collector and made extensive use of archaeological terminology and metaphors (Ucko 2001). North America's most prominent twentieth-century sexologist, Alfred Kinsey, also collected erotic artifacts and collaborated in Larco Hoyle's (1965) analysis of prehistoric Peruvian ceramics. Today, both advocates and opponents of homosexual and transgendered human rights cite historic precedents as justification for their positions. As a result of these entanglements, there is no clear boundary between "our" (modern) sexualities and "their" (ancient) sexualities because current understandings of our sexual selves have been formed in no small part through engagement with the archaeological record.

What distinguishes the recent florescence of sexuality research in archaeology is a sincere effort to attend to the cultural and historical specificity of sexuality rather than to interpret archaeological finds as evidence of universal principles of human sexual behavior. In this vein, some have cogently argued that "sexuality" is perhaps the wrong starting point for this enterprise (e.g., Halperin et al. 1990; Joyce 2004; Meskell 1999, p. 88, 2002; Voss 2005). Ethnographic studies have long demonstrated that what is considered "sexual" varies radically across and within cultural groups (Boellstorff 2007). Foucault's (1978) now-familiar argument locates the formation of a cultural field of sexuality in the eighteenth- and nineteenth-century shift from religious to medico-juridical regulation of sexual practices. Thus alongside considerations of cultural difference, most archaeological contexts are also chronologically "before sexuality" in that the cultural poetics of desire in many past societies were not categorized into a unitary field labeled "sexuality" (Halperin et al. 1990, pp. 4–6). For example, Meskell (1999) demonstrates that scholars of ancient Egypt might better approach the subject through a study of the "libidinal economy" of bodily fluids and boundaries, including but not limited to those considered sexual in our own culture. Archaeological research increasingly defamiliarizes modern sexuality and reveals the particularity of present-day assumptions about human sexuality.

The archaeological turn toward questions of sexual difference began in classical archaeology. In 1970, Brendel (1970) contrasted erotic representations from classical Greece and Rome with those from pre-Columbian Peru and medieval India. Next, Dover's landmark *Greek Homosexuality* (1978) analyzed painted ceramics and classical texts to argue that male-male sexual relationships in ancient Greece were not equivalent to twentieth-century homosexuality; instead, Greek male-male sexuality was an expression of broader sexual hierarchies between insertive adult male citizens and their subordinate receptive partners (youths, slaves, foreigners, and women). Praise and criticism of Dover's conclusions launched a veritable explosion of classical scholarship on sexual-

ity (e.g., Clarke 1998, Halperin et al. 1990, Kampen 1996, Richlin 1992, Winkler 1989). Although most research in classical archaeology has focused on male sexuality, two texts—*Naked Truths* (Koloski-Ostrow & Lyons 1997) and *Among Women* (Rabinowitz & Auanger 2002)—have brought greater attention to female sexuality in the classical world. Today, the study of classical sexualities has become sufficiently incorporated into the mainstream to warrant an undergraduate textbook on the subject (Skinner 2005).

Despite anthropology's long tradition of frank engagement with questions of sexuality, anthropological archaeologists have been much slower to investigate sexuality. Studies of sexuality in anthropological archaeology initially developed through applications of feminist theory to archaeological research (Voss 2000b). Early research in this tradition framed sexuality as a product of gender relations. The first text to break from this mold was Taylor's *The Prehistory of Sex* (1996). Three edited collections soon followed: *Archaeologies of Sexuality* (Schmidt & Voss 2000); *Indecent Exposure* (Bevan 2001a); and "Queer Archaeologies," a special issue of the journal *World Archaeology* (Dowson 2000). Additionally, several recent monographs provide in-depth studies of sexuality in a variety of archaeological contexts (e.g., Bourget 2006, Gilchrist 1994, Joyce 2000b, Meskell 1999, Meskell & Joyce 2003, Strassburg 2000, Voss 2008a). In 2004, the University of Calgary hosted the first conference dedicated to the subject, "Que(e)rying Archaeology," the proceedings of which are currently in press. Over time, queer theory has become increasingly prominent in archaeological studies of sexual matters. As a result, gender, sexuality, the body, and personhood have become increasingly intertwined in archaeological interpretations (Joyce 2005).

REPRODUCTION MANAGEMENT

Archaeological studies of reproduction foreground the complicated relationship between biology and culture in sexuality research.

Biological reproduction, necessary to the survival of the species, is commonly understood to be one of the most universal and "natural" aspects of human sexuality. Yet for most primates, including hominids, reproduction constitutes a relatively small aspect of sexual activities and relationships. "As extreme K-strategists, with heavy parental investment in very few offspring... the amount of reproductive sex required for a person to pass on their genes effectively is minimal" (Taylor 2006, p. 97). Because primate and hominid sexual activities include a wide suite of nonreproductive behaviors, sexuality is more appropriately viewed as a learned source for the exploration of pleasure, power, and sociality alongside its reproductive aspects (Abramson & Pinkerton 1995, Vasey 1998).

The mistaken assumption that all sexual acts are, or should be, oriented toward reproduction has been exemplified by the archaeological tendency to interpret representations of the unclothed body and of sexual acts as evidence of fertility rites. Recent critiques of this widespread practice (e.g., Bailey 2005, Clark 2003, Hays-Gilpin 2004, Meskell 2007) are careful not to discount human concerns with reproduction. Rather, the concept of "reproduction management" is more inclusive, including both the prevention and the promotion of conception as well as measures taken to interrupt or support the development of the embryo or fetus and to care for the birthing mother and infant before, during, and after delivery. Reproduction management thus provides a means by which the reproductive consequences of some sexual activities can be either enhanced or suppressed within a broader cultural context.

There is good archaeological evidence that from ~5000 BP onward, communities in many parts of the world produced various material devices for enhancing or repressing sexual reproduction, including plant-based medicines and suppositories, caustic and blocking vaginal pessaries, and tools used in abortions (Taylor 1996, pp. 85–96). This corresponds with what some archaeologists have argued is an increase in sexual images and artifacts during the onset of agriculture and herding, as people became more directly involved in the reproductive cycles of plants and animals (Bolger 1996, Ellis 2001, Kauffman Doig 2001, Kokkinidou & Nikolaidou 1997, Taylor 2006). More speculatively, some researchers have argued that cultural management of reproduction began during early hominid bipedalism, about four million years ago, because corresponding morphological changes to the pelvis required social involvement in birthing to ensure the survival of the mother and child (Adovasio et al. 2007); plant-based fertility medicines, abortion, barrier contraception, and infanticide are argued to have been a consistent feature of human reproductive management since 40,000 BP (Bentley 1996, Taylor 1996).

In historical archaeology, discoveries of preserved condoms, pessaries, diaphragms, and prophylactic medicines have garnered new information about the standardization and commercialization of reproduction management technologies from the seventeenth century to the present (e.g., Gaimster et al. 1996, Karskens 1999, Meyer et al. 2005). Wilkie's (2000, 2003) research on nineteenth-century African American sexual magic and midwifery makes a distinctive contribution by investigating the ways that women made decisions "to mother or not to mother" (Wilkie 2003, p. 147) in a climate of racial oppression. Wilkie found that spiritual and medicinal practices were seamlessly integrated in an "ethnomedical tool kit" (Wilkie 2000, p. 138) that women and men employed to prevent and promote childbearing and to mediate tensions between the sexes. "The contents of a single jar of Vaseline could have been bought for use as a hair pomade, used to help cure a bout of impotence, and then used to treat a diaper rash... All of these magical-medical cures indicated from the midwifery site incorporated symbols that were strongly connected with regulating sexual activity or treating the consequences of such activity" (Wilkie 2000, pp. 133, 139). Wilkie's study illustrates that the conceptual shift from fertility to reproduction management has not decoupled sexuality from its reproductive aspects, but rather created new possibilities to investigate the complex and culturally contingent relationships between sex and reproduction.

REPRESENTATIONS

Representations of the body in general, and of sexual organs and sexual activity in particular, constitute the most prominent source of evidence through which archaeologists have studied past sexualities. However, identifying what is "sexual" is itself a challenge. On one hand, archaeologists have tended to downplay the sexual content of the archaeological record. Paradoxically, at other times it seems that archaeologists see sex everywhere, interpreting every carved baton or incised line as phallic and every triangle, curved groove, or oval as vulvaform. Fortunately, a consensus is slowly emerging around a set of best practices in analysis of bodily representations and sexual imagery (Bahn 1986, Bailey 2005, Clarke 1998, Frontisi-Ducroux & Lissarrague 1990, Hays-Gilpin 2004, Joyce 2005, Kampen 1996, Meskell 2007, Yates 1993). The first principle is that what is viewed as sexual in our society may not be so in other cultures, and vice versa. Display of the clothed or unclothed body, or of particular body parts, may or may not be sexualized. Not all sexual representations are erotic, that is, designed to stimulate a sexual response in the viewer; sexual images may also be apotropaic, political, comical, or religious. It follows that attention to context is critical: Clarke (1998, p. 11) enjoins archaeologists studying sexual images and objects to establish who made it (artist), who sponsored it (patronage), when it was created (temporal context), who looked at it (intended and unintended audience), where people looked at it (physical context), under what circumstances (social and functional context), and what else it looks like (iconographic models).

The second widely shared principle is to avoid the fallacy of representation: the trap of assuming that sexual representations are snapshots of real bodies and lived sexual practices rather than creative interpretations and ideological presentations. "The job of representation, if we can call it that, is to reconfigure the world; in the process it may help to challenge or to reproduce social arrangements" (Kampen 1997, p. 267). Furthermore, the "polysemantic nature of symbols" (Hays-Gilpin 2004, p. 19) means that sexual images are inherently ambiguous. Thus viewing is an active process in which the viewer participates in constructing the sexual narrative of representations. Some of the most interesting archaeological research on sexual representations considers how desire influences the relationship between representations and social practice, for example, how the seductive allure of a representation might foster conditions in which the viewer, "oblivious to the membrane of the medium, engages in a quasi-corporeal relationship with the image" (Winter 1996, p. 21; see also Bailey 2005, Joyce 2000a, Kampen 1997).

In prehistoric archaeology, both figurines and rock art have functioned as "Rorschach" tests with regard to sexuality. The ambiguity of many anthropomorphic painted and pecked images and carved or molded figures creates interpretive dilemmas about even the most basic aspects of sexuality: "With surprising frequency, one encounters figures with something fancy between the legs that can't readily be assigned to one of two categories, neither penis nor vagina" (Hays-Gilpin 2004, pp. 15–16). When two or more figures are entwined, sexual relationships become even more difficult to decipher.

Anthropomorphic prehistoric figurines, such as the so-called goddess figurines of prehistoric Europe and the Middle East, exemplify the tangled relationship between reproduction and sexuality. Longstanding interpretations of these objects as fertility charms used in worship of the Mother Goddess have been widely challenged (Bailey 2005, pp. 12–24; Conkey & Tringham 1995; Meskell 1998b; Talalay 1994), with alternative interpretations emphasizing themes of embodiment, sexual pleasure, and sexual control. In an analysis of figurines from the Balkan Neolithic, Bailey (2005, p. 180) argues that whether these objects were perceived in terms of reproduction or pleasure, female figurines with exaggerated genitalia and breasts "made Neolithic people think about their bodies and about the bodies of others in especially sexual ways." Similarly Meskell (2007, p. 147) is studying figurines found in Çatalhöyük, Turkey, to investigate "whether the Neolithic was a sexual revolution, a period of 'self' exploration at a level not experienced before." In North America, recent studies of prehistoric rock art have turned away from facile accounts of "fertility magic" to explore how the act of creating rock art is involved in creating and renegotiating gender and sexual identities (Hays-Gilpin 2004, Sundstrom 2004).

Peruvian "sex pots," recovered from Moche and other Andean early states, provide another example of the changing approach to sexual representations. These functional ceramic vessels depict "lively little figures engaged in a startling variety of acts involving the hands, nipples, genitals, anus, mouth, and tongue" (Weismantel 2004, p. 495). Most Moche pots depict masturbation, fellatio, and anal sex. The scarcity of representations of heterosexual intercourse puzzled researchers, who initially interpreted the pots as portrayals of birth control techniques, admonitions against taboo sexual practices, or representations of funerary sex rituals [see Kauffman-Doig (2001, pp. 18–22) and Bourget (2006, pp. 66–73) for syntheses of earlier research]. More recent studies have drawn attention to the sex pots' archaeological context as funerary offerings in high-ranking tombs. Weismantel (2004, p. 502) argues that the vessels "alter the definition of the reproductive act" by depicting intergenerational transfers of reproductive fluids outside of penile-vaginal intercourse. For example, ceramics depicting belly-to-back anal sex often include a tiny third figure breastfeeding on the woman's chest; through this position, one reproductive fluid (semen) is transformed into breast milk and transferred through the woman to the infant. Vessels shaped like masturbating skeletons facilitated the transfer of reproductive bodily fluids from ancestors to the living. These and other sexual images may have worked to consolidate powerful elite lineages by emphasizing continuity of substance from one generation to the next. Gero (2004) provides an alternative reading of the Moche vessels by comparing them with contemporary "copulation pots" found in Andean Recuay mortuary contexts. The Recuay pots depict heterosexual pairs copulating belly to belly, often in public buildings with an attending audience. This difference between the Moche and Recuay ceramics suggests that sexual politics were very different in the two adjacent polities: The Recuay emphasized complementary male-female sexuality, and the Moche celebrated the solitary male orgasm as a powerful political act. Finally, Bourget's (2006) analysis of the Moche sex pots draws attention to the performative dimensions of sexual and nonsexual acts depicted on the ceramic vessels. Bourget concludes that the sex pots represent elite funerary rituals involving sexual congress with sacrificial victims. These victims become physically connected to ruling elite through sexual and violent acts and serve as transitional individuals who facilitate ancestral involvement in human, plant, and animal fertility.

What is particularly striking about Weismantel, Gero, and Bourget's divergent interpretations of the Moche sex pots is that all three turn to the ways that sexuality participates in political projects, such as state formation and the consolidation of power among ruling lineages. Similarly, several archaeologists have concluded that flourishing representations of the body in prehistoric Mesoamerica, especially of the sexualized male body and of the disembodied phallus, were implicated in state ideologies that linked virility and self-sacrifice to political power and imposed idealized ideologies of masculinity on young men (Ardren & Hixson 2006; Joyce 2000a,b; Perry & Joyce 2001).

As in the prehistoric examples given above, new attention to context, ambiguity, and desire is challenging conventional interpretations of sexual representations from ancient Greece and Rome. For example, scholars long assumed that black- and red-figured Greek ceramics, dating to ~570–470 BCE, were made for use in the male homosocial environment of the Greek symposium. However, most extant vases with sexual content were actually recovered from Etruscan tombs in central and southern Italy, raising questions about whether the vessels can be used to study Athenian sexuality (Skinner 2005, pp. 80–81). Common themes in erotic Greek pottery scenes are abduction, the sexual practices of satyrs, heterosexual sex between citizens and courtesans, and homoerotic and homosexual scenes between adult citizens and youths. New scholarship on these painted vessels is notable for its attention to the contextual analysis of posture, gesture, and gaze, both among the figures depicted on the pots and the postures and gazes of the vessels' users (e.g., Elsner 1996, Frontisi-Ducroux 1996). Rabinowitz's (2002) attention to gaze and gesture has been particularly instrumental in identifying overlooked depictions of female homosocial and homoerotic imagery.

Research on sexuality in ancient Rome has focused heavily on the frescos, mosaics, and artifacts uncovered in Pompeii and Herculaneum, two Roman cities destroyed by volcanic eruption in AD 79. Continuing the theme of gaze and gesture, Clarke's *Looking at Lovemaking* (1998, pp. 1–4) presents a core thesis shared by many scholars that Roman sexuality was "a sexual culture that operated under rules completely different from our own . . . where sexual pleasure and its representation stood for positive social and cultural values." Clarke convincingly argues that many Roman sexual representations, although widespread, were not erotic: For example, recurring macrophallic imagery in mosaics, jewelry, and everyday household objects used the comedy of the grotesque to guard against the evil eye. Other sexual representations, such as small paintings of lovemaking, were likely acquired to signal the wealth and sophistication of the owner. Clark is inclined to view Roman sexuality as liberated and free of guilt, a stance that focuses on the sexual pleasures of citizen men. A contrasting view of Roman sexual imagery is provided by Richlin (1992), whose attention to noncitizens (women, slaves, foreigners, and prostitutes) reveals stark power differentials. Roman representations often portrayed sexuality as an act that involved the degradation of the weaker by the stronger and conflated the violent and the sexual. The contrast between Clarke and Richlin's interpretations of similar imagery exemplifies a pervasive question in classical archaeology, namely, the degree to which the ancient Greeks and Romans were like "us" in sexual matters. Overall, those studying male sexuality tend to argue for radical difference, whereas studies of female sexuality trace historical continuities in patterns of sexual violence and objectification of the female body (Brown 1997, Richlin 1992, Salomon 1997).

IDENTITIES

The relationship between past and present sexualities is especially fraught in the question of identities. On one hand, there has been a persistent interest in "finding" homosexuals and transsexuals in the past to counter political charges that same-sex sexuality and gender bending are uniquely modern phenomena. However, present-day sexual taxonomies, e.g., the categorizing of all those who have sex with members of the same gender as "homosexual," can be traced to the formation of the medico-juridical field of sexology in the late nineteenth century. Some have argued that before the nineteenth century, there were no sexual identities, only sexual acts. Others distinguish the concept of sexual orientation as a universalizing theory of innate physical/psychological drives from sexual identities and subjectivities that form in particular cultural and historical contexts (Boellstorff 2007, Halperin 2002, Rabinowitz 2002, Voss 2005). A second core issue is the relationship between gender and sexuality. The current emphasis on sexuality as a determinant of social identity appears to be a relatively modern and Western phenomenon, with many present and past cultures emphasizing gendered difference more than sexual partner choice. Queer theory, which foregrounds the interdependence of gendered and sexual identities, facilitates an integrated approach to this question (Boellstorff 2007, Halperin 2002, Joyce 2000c, Voss 2006a).

Archaeological research on past sexual identities has focused on the classical Greek/Roman *kinaidos/cinaedus* and the Native American two-spirit. In classical Athens, the kinaidos was an Athenian citizen who had prostituted himself; in the Roman Empire, cinaedii were men who liked to be penetrated by other men, whether or not for pay. The Greek/Roman kinaidos/cinaedus presents a particular paradox to modern theories of sexual identity: In societies where nearly all men participated in same-sex sexual activities, how did some men come to be categorized and stigmatized by their sexual involvement with other men? Furthermore, did kinaidos/cinaedus constitute a shared identity, or did the terms refer to only to the stigmatized sexual act itself? Archaeological research on kinaidos/cinaedus identities relies heavily on painted ceramics and preserved classical texts. The most prominent interpretation is the penetrative hypothesis, which argues that ancient Greeks and Romans viewed sex as a zero-sum game in which shame accrued to the penetrated (Dover 1978, Halperin 1990). Citizen adult men who allowed or even enjoyed penetration were stigmatized because they had failed to hold up the distinction between honorable citizens and those who were routinely penetrated because of their social status (youths, women, slaves, foreigners, prostitutes). However, representations depicting kinaidoi/cinaedii penetrating women and other men have been interpreted as indications that the kinaidos/cinaedus was defined not through sexual acts but through gender liminality, as persons who straddled the boundary between masculinity and femininity (Gleason 1990, Skinner 2005, Winkler 1990). A third argument particular to ancient Greece argues that the regulation of sexuality was not oriented toward partner choice, active/passive roles, or gender conformity but toward the management of appetites, whether for money, food, drink, or sex; a citizen who prostituted himself displayed an inability to restrain his own desires (Davidson 1997). Regardless, substantial evidence indicates that kinaidoi/cinaedii participated in distinct subcultures if not a shared identity (Clarke 2006,

Richlin 2006). Additionally, new studies of sculpture and architecture emphasize other pervasive aspects of Greek and Roman male homoeroticism, such as idealization of the male body and reciprocal male-male sexuality (Clarke 2006, Davidson 2001, Eger 2007).

In North America, studies of Native American two-spirits (also *berdache* and third- and fourth-gender) figure prominently in archaeological studies of sexual identity. The term two-spirit encompasses a wide range of tribally specific identities associated with transgendered dress and occupations, same-sex sexual practices, hermaphrodism, and specialized spiritual roles (Jacobs et al. 1997). Archaeologists first studied two-spirit identities through mortuary analyses that identified individuals whose cultural gender (as identified by grave goods and musculoskeletal stress markers) differed from their physical sex (Hollimon 1997, Perry 2004, Whelan 1991), an approach that emphasizes transsexuality as the determining characteristic of two-spirit identity. Research has recently broadened to incorporate architecture, rock art, occupation, craft, and ritual. For example, the Chumash 'Aqi were members of an undertaking guild that included transsexual biological men, men who have sex with men, men without children, celibates, and postmenopausal women. Becoming a Chumash 'Aqi required abstention from procreative sex acts rather than a specific sexual or gender identity. The antiquity of the 'Aqi undertaker guild is suggested by the long history of well-defined cemeteries and systematic treatment of the dead in the Chumash region since ~7500 BP (Hollimon 2000, 2001). Perry's (2004, Perry & Joyce 2001) research on Pueblo prehistory links the development of large plaza settlements ~1100 CE to the cultural codification of the two-spirit *Lhamana* identity. The large central plazas of new Pueblo settlements were used for both repetitive everyday activities and ceremonial ritual acts, including the public ritual performance of the transgendered Katsina, Kolhamana. Prine (2000) has similarly examined architecture to investigate two-spirit Hidatsa *miati*, who were identified as male at birth but later adopted aspects of women's gender roles, assumed particular spiritual responsibilities, and created households through relationships with men. Hidatsa *miati* played a key role in earth lodge-building ceremonies, mediating the tension between feminine earth and masculine sky. Also in the Northern Plains, Sundstrom (2004) has studied Lakota and Dakota rock art to reconstruct the practices involved in Double Woman dream rituals, in which some male dreamers are instructed to live as women. Finally, gender ambiguity among images of gods, rulers, and warriors is well-documented in prehistoric Mesoamerica (Looper 2002, McCafferty & McCafferty 1994, Stockett 2005). What is striking about these recent studies is the degree to which many two-spirit identities appear to be formed predominantly in reference to spiritual roles and occupational specialties. These identities reference, but are not entirely defined through, sexuality. Nor do they appear to be transgressive or abject because although two-spirits cross and link gender dualism, these roles are sanctioned by dual-gendered deities and institutionalized roles that can be filled only by two-spirits.

In Europe, several mortuary studies have investigated gender and sexual diversity within prehistoric cemetery populations [e.g., Halsall 2001, Lucy 1997, Rega 1997; see Arnold (2002) and Schmidt (2002, 2005) for discussions of methodology]. Schmidt (2000, 2002) and Strassburg (2000) have emphasized the relationship between shamanism and gender and sexual variability in prehistoric northern Europe, where shamans harnessed both male and female sexual potentials. Paradoxically, although shamanistic identities may have crossed gender and sexual norms, such ritual practitioners likely contributed to the stability of sexual norms (Strassburg 2000, p. 110), perhaps similar to the way that celibate Catholic priests enact marriage rites today. Other researchers in Europe and India have reanalyzed rock art, figurines, and other imagery to identify representations of same-sex couplings and transgendered and ambiguously gendered persons (Clark 2003, Danielsson 2002, Vasey

1998, Yates 1993). More than anything, the wide range of gendered and sexual expressions of identity found in the archaeological record demonstrates the limitations of modern sexual identity theories. If gender and sexual variability in the past did not fit neatly within the modern categories of homosexual and transsexual, then cross-sex sexualities were also likely configured quite differently from what we consider heterosexuality.

PROSTITUTION

Archaeological studies of prostitution concentrate on brothels in only two contexts: first-century Pompeii, and nineteenth-century North America. In Pompeii, McGinn (2002) investigated the extent to which Pompeii (and by extension, other Roman cities) practiced moral zoning. He found that brothels were located throughout the city, in both elite and impoverished residential and commercial neighborhoods. However, one cluster of buildings, including the largest brothel in the town (the Lupenar at VII), was a hub of commercial sexual activity, with a large hotel, a sizeable tavern, and a bathhouse adjacent to the brothel. Clarke's study of the famous wall paintings in the Lupenar at VII argues that these visual representations of sexual activity contributed to an environment of fantasy in an atmosphere of "rough-and-ready sexual commerce" (Clarke 1998, p. 206).

The study of prostitution in North America has been driven largely by the discovery of nineteenth-century brothel sites during modern urban redevelopment projects. The rise of commercial sex generally, and brothel prostitution specifically, has long been noted as a characteristic of the post-1800 North American industrial city. Red-light districts in rapidly growing cities provided a precedent for modern urban planning and zoning ordinances. As in Pompeii, excavations of North American brothels are contributing new perspectives on the sexual politics of urbanism (Hardesty 1994; Seifert 1991, 2005). Initial research focused on identifying the material characteristics that distinguished brothel sites: elevated frequencies of artifacts associated with women's fancy dress, grooming, and hygiene; large numbers of men's buttons, presumably lost during the rapid removal of clothing; and, frequently, expensive household goods and imported foods. However, although brothel assemblages are generally different from neighboring kin-based households, no single brothel pattern has been identified because "brothels of different periods and statuses are different from each other" (Seifert & Balicki 2005, p. 65). Distinct regional differences exist: For example, brothel and saloon deposits in western North America overlap considerably, as both were places where male sociality was fostered by drinking, gambling, and sexual entertainment, whereas eastern brothels are more distinct (Dixon 2005, Spude 2005). Crib prostitution, in which small rooms were rented by the shift to prostitutes who lived elsewhere, was also more common in western cities (Meyer et al. 2005).

One core research topic has been the economic status of brothel prostitutes relative to their nonbrothel neighbors. A widely used methodology developed by Seifert (1991) uses pattern analysis to compare artifacts and food remains recovered at brothel sites with those recovered from nonbrothel households and boarding houses (Meyer et al. 2005, Seifert 1994, Seifert & Balicki 2005, Spude 2005, Yamin 2005). These studies have consistently found that brothels display higher levels of conspicuous consumption and more abundant, diverse, and high-quality food remains than their neighbors. This finding was initially interpreted as evidence that prostitutes enjoyed a higher standard of living than did nonprostitute working-class women, but recent studies have questioned this conclusion. In St. Paul, Minnesota, archaeologists excavated trash deposits from the front entryway of a brothel site, where patrons would have gathered, and general refuse deposits from the rear yard. They found a sharp bifurcation in artifact distribution, with expensive dishes and exotic meats clearly consumed by patrons, whereas the brothel residents consumed inexpensive foods

served on plain dishes [Ketz et al. 2005; see also Meyer et al. (2005) and Yamin (2005) for similar cases in Los Angeles and New York]. These findings challenge the assumption that brothel residents enjoyed the trappings of middle- and upper-class life: "When the women were not working they lived no better than their sisters in the tenements ... The duality reveals exploitation as well as economic well-being and pain as well as pleasure" (Yamin 2005, p. 4).

The occupational hazards of prostitution are also attested to by the high frequency of health-related personal items found in brothel deposits, such as douching paraphernalia, female urinals, pessaries, improvised barrier contraception devices, bulk quantities of prophylactic fluids, and an abundance of opium- and alcohol-rich patent and prescription medicines, all suggesting "the relative seriousness of ailments suffered by the women" (Ketz et al. 2005, p. 80). Nursing shields, baby bottles, marbles, dolls, and other toys document the presence of children in brothel life. Whereas most research on brothels has focused somewhat narrowly on the economic aspects of the commercial sex trade, two studies (Costello 2000, Dawdy & Weyhing 2008) have used self-reflexive and narrative methodologies to explore the complicated webs of desire involved in the archaeological study of prostitution. Additionally, brothel research has focused rather narrowly on female prostitutes and madams, ignoring male patrons and men and boys who worked in the sex trade as prostitutes, pimps, procurers, entertainers, and servants. Despite these limitations, the rich body of archaeological evidence gathered on nineteenth-century North American brothels demonstrates that the "world's oldest profession" was also historically and culturally contingent, participating in the industrialization, urbanization, and commercialization of life in North American cities.

INSTITUTIONS

Institutions of religion, conversion, and reform have been the focus of archaeological investigations of institutional sexuality. This work has been deeply influenced by Foucault's (1978) histories of the formation and regulation of sexual subjectivities in institutional contexts. Like Foucault, archaeologists have emphasized the importance of architecture in fostering patterns of movement and constraint. Gilchrist's (1994, 2000) research on British medieval nunneries is a case in point: She demonstrates that the celibate sexuality of medieval religious women was conditioned through the materiality of physical enclosure and visual imagery, both of which elevated the senses and fostered ecstatic states of consciousness involving contemplation of union with Christ. Celibacy, although shared between male and female religious, was not a uniform practice: Nuns were more tightly cloistered and had poorer sanitation and less contact with nonreligious, indicating a greater abnegation of the body among female religious.

Institutions of religious and governmental reform often built on the monastic model of sexual control. Eighteenth-century religious missions in Spanish-colonial California used architecture to monitor and regulate Native Californian sexuality, for example, by sequestering unmarried women and girls in locked wards (Voss 2000a). The nineteenth-century Magdalen Society home for "fallen women" in Philadelphia used the spatial grammar of the middle-class home to effect sexual reform: A succession of entryways, passages, and enclosed stairs "physically and symbolically marked the Magdalen's progressive ritual passage from a fallen state to one of moral rectitude" (De Cunzo 2001, p. 26). Casella's (2000a, 2000b) research on the Ross Female Factory in convict-era Australia reveals that similar architectural patterns were used to reform female convicts. The Ross Female Factory is significant because it is the only archaeological study to date that has investigated the materiality of female same-sex sexual relationships and desire. Excavation of the prison revealed evidence of a rich black market economy. Spatial analysis of contraband items and buttons used as currency showed that the apex of the underground prison economy was the solitary cells, which had been built particularly to reform women involved in same-

sex relationships. "Within the Van Diemen's Land penal colony, female sexual activity transformed into a mode of exchange, as it was inextricably intertwined with dynamics of access, allocation, and distribution of resources" (Casella 2000b, p. 215). Casella's findings highlight the paradoxical nature of sexual relationships in institutional contexts: sometimes predatory, sometimes strategic, sometimes economic, and sometimes affectionate.

A very different kind of sexual reform was institutionalized in the Narkomfin Communal House in Moscow, constructed by Bolshevik elite in 1929. Intending to ease the residents' transition toward fully socialized life, the building's designers drew on archaeological studies of Paleolithic dwellings to envision new architectural forms that would disarticulate heterosexual relations from the relations of production. Buchli's (2000a,b) diachronic study of the occupation of the Narkomfin Communal House shows that as the Communist party's vision of the relationship between architecture and household changed, so too did expectations for heterosexual relationships. Rather than transforming heterosexualities, the building itself became transformed as its inhabitants adapted the structure to meet new expectations. Buchli's study hints at the contribution archaeology can make to better understanding the sexual politics of a wider range of institutions, from military fortifications (Voss 2008a) to college fraternities (Wilkie 2001).

OTHER TOPICS

Archaeologists studying European colonization of the Americas have a long history of investigating interracial sexual relationships, especially heterosexual marriage, as a central mechanism of cultural exchange between colonizing and indigenous populations (e.g., Deagan 1983). More recent work has broadened the question of colonial encounters to include same-sex relationships (Byrne 2007) and concubinage, slavery, and sexual violence (Lightfoot 2005; Rothschild 2003; Voss 2000a, 2008a,b). Archaeological studies of sexual violence have also addressed representations of abduction in classical Greece (Cohen 1996), slave plantations in the Americas (Delle 2000), and mortuary analysis in Europe (Scott 2001). Other notable topics include puberty (Bevan 2001b, Hays-Gilpin 2004, Joyce 2000c, Sundstrom 2004) and polygamy (Chase 1991). Finally, at least two ethnoarchaeological studies (Buchli & Lucas 2001b, Hohmann 1975) of late twentieth- and early twenty-first-century urban contexts have demonstrated that explicit material references to sexual activity and desire comprise a significant part of the presently forming archaeological record.

QUEER ARCHAEOLOGIES

Queer archaeology is not always about sexuality, and sexuality research in archaeology is not always queer, yet the queer focus on retheorizing sexual politics and sexual identities draws the two together. Queer theory emerged from work by activists and scholars to address the particular sexual and gender politics of the late twentieth and early twenty-first centuries. As a body of scholarship, queer theory is perhaps best described as a poststructuralist intervention into feminist theories of gender and sexuality, most famously associated with Butler (1990). One core project in queer theory has been a critique of the conventional divisions among physical sex, cultural gender, and sexuality, instead exploring the ways that sex, gender, and sexuality are mutually constituted.

A widely shared tenet in queer theory is that gendered and sexual categories are inherently unstable and that normative genders and sexualities are constituted by what they exclude (for example, that heterosexuality is constituted by the abjectification of homosexuality and transsexuality). Sexes, genders, and sexualities are thus negotiated through an ongoing dance of identification and misidentification. These iterations are often conceptualized as "performances" that mimic, reproduce, or trouble gendered and sexual norms (Morris 1995). Archaeologists have turned to performance theory as a methodology for the diachronic study of iden-

tify formation: "Since gender performance is by definition a repetition or citation of a precedent [. . .], the kinds of material regularities that archaeologists document in the media of performance can be profitably viewed as mechanisms for the regulation of gender" (Perry & Joyce 2001, pp. 65–66). Joyce's (2000b,c) analyses of life cycle rituals and representations of the body in prehistoric Mesoamerica have powerfully demonstrated that archaeological materials and settings were the media and stages for gendered and sexual performances. Alberti (2001) has argued that similarities among Bronze Age figurines in Knossos can be explained as a result of performative citation of prior practices, rather than sexual universals. Voss (2008a) has used performance theory to show how Spanish-colonial labor regimes fostered repetitive social interactions that heightened gendered differences among colonial and indigenous men.

Other archaeologists have turned to queer heritage as a way to commemorate the ways that people with marginalized gender and sexual identities were able to inhabit landscapes dominated by normative heterosexuality. Rubin (2000) draws on settlement pattern analysis and central place theory to reconstruct the landscapes occupied by gay male leathermen in twentieth-century San Francisco. Byrne (2005) documents places in the Asia-Pacific region where "the gay community has a long history of using them and a quite strong sense of ownership of them" (Byrne 2005, p. 3), such as gay beaches, drag clubs, cruising areas in public parks, and rural retreats. Archaeologists excavating the peace camps surrounding Greenham Common Airbase have argued that these sites are queer not only because they were occupied by feminists, lesbians, and pacifists, but also because the transient and illicit occupation of the site by protesters poses unconventional challenges to heritage management (Schofield & Anderton 2000). Matthews (1999) suggests that the Roman city walls of Chester, England, may have great antiquity as a site of gay male cruising, perhaps back to medieval or even Roman periods, whereas Eger (2007) uses an ethnographic analogy from present-day gay male bathhouses to argue for a queering of ancient Roman bathhouses as places where male intimacy and reciprocity could occur.

Many texts and films written by nonarchaeologists also posit far-reaching connections between present-day queer communities and sexual variability in deep antiquity (e.g., Feinberg 1996, Schmidt 2002). This aspect of queer heritage is troublesome for archaeologists and historians who hold that sexual and gender identities are culturally constructed. For example, same-sex sexuality appears to have meant very different things in classical Rome and prehistoric Scandinavia than in the present day. Yet the impulse to turn to the past for citational precedents of queerness is understandable: "If you are a minority group, heritage visibility is often an issue of struggle.... So if we fail to record the heritage of homosexuality then it is that much easier for governments and empowered majorities to pretend or assert that homosexuality has not existed in the past and this makes it that much easier to deny its legitimacy in the present" (Byrne 2005, p. 6). The challenge, as Halperin (2002, p. 16) has written, is "to recruit the queerness of past historical periods not in order to justify one or another partisan model of gay life in the present but rather to acknowledge, promote, and support a heterogeneity of queer identities, past *and* present."

A third emphasis in queer archaeology is challenging heteronormativity in archaeological practice and interpretation. Several scholars have soundly critiqued the ways that dominant archaeological interpretations presume the universality of heterosexuality, marriage, and the nuclear family, falsely imposing heteronormative gender and sexual structures on past cultures (Cobb 2005, Flatman 2003, Reeder 2000, Schmidt 2002). For example, Dowson's (2007) analysis of museum dioramas shows that such displays typically serve more to promote an idea of the family unit as unchanging and constant than to present information about social relations in the past. Solli's (1999) reanalysis of white stone artifacts associated with Viking-era shamanism demonstrates that although con- ventional archaeological interpretations have categorized such stones as either phallic or vulvaform, the artifacts actually intermix symbols of male and female power. Here, queer theory enables archaeologists to embrace gender ambiguity and sexual fluidity.

More broadly, many have turned to queer theory's focus on abjection and "the constitutive outside, premised on exclusion and otherness, [that] forms the corona of difference through which identities are enunciated" (Meskell 2002, p. 280). This shift away from sexuality, specifically, to abjection, generally, is an important move in queer archaeology because it recognizes that sexual and gendered differences were not necessarily stigmatized in all past societies. Thus queer studies of past cultures "would be focused on ways in which the normative and deviant have been defined, not specifically in sexual behavior but in all social structures" (Ardren 2008, p. 19). For example, in prehistoric Mesoamerica, "mixed performances, inter-species hybrids, and the dwarf—beings presented as incompletely human—occupy the edges of embodied abjection.... [T]he anxiety of the Mesoamerican tradition is engaged not with sexuality, but with humanity" (Perry & Joyce 2001, p. 73). Strassburg's (2000) analysis of burial grounds in prehistoric northwest Europe concludes that the undead—people who died a nonnormative death—were viewed as a queer force that disrupted the sexualities of the living. Communities protected themselves by disciplining the corpses posthumously through dressing and feeding the corpses in ritualized ways and postmortem "killings" through blows to the head and placement of weighty stones in graves.

Most broadly, queer theory has been cited to challenge normative archaeological research practices, whether or not such practices are directly related to sexuality. Recent polemics have charged that certain subfields (rock art research, maritime archaeology) are queer because of their marginalization and that certain research practices, such as excavation or artifact dating, enforce normative values in archaeology (Croucher 2005, Dowson 2001, Ransley

2005). Strassburg's *Shamanic Shadows* (2000) convincingly demonstrates that conventional archaeological practice tends to emphasize norms in the archaeological record and, in doing so, suppresses unique materials and evidence of social variation in the past. Resistance to normalization, Strassburg notes, is a powerful force for cultural change by constantly opening up alternative desires and social practices in any sociocultural world. Strassburg's empirically rich and methodologically innovative study of postglacial hunter-gatherer archaeology in northwest Europe offers one of the most successful examples of how queer critiques of the discipline may transform archaeological practices.

IMPLICATIONS AND FUTURE DIRECTIONS

The innovative body of work that has emerged in the past 20 years has demonstrated that the archaeology of sexuality is about far more than interpersonal relationships or individual identities. Sexuality research is contributing new perspectives on topics as diverse as state formation, urban planning, economic systems, and settlement practices and is fostering broad methodological innovations in archaeological investigations of place, representations, and material culture. The scholarship reviewed above has demonstrated that human sexuality was as richly varied in the past as it is in the present day, so much so that current theories of human sexuality may be inadequate to characterize past social relationships and sexual identities. Indeed, archaeology's most important contribution to sexuality studies may lie precisely in its ability to demonstrate that "sexuality" as it is commonly understood today may have been configured quite differently in the past.

The biggest challenge facing sexuality studies in archaeology is the lack of attention given to opposite-sex sexual relationships, the forms of which are known to have changed significantly in recent centuries and which likely varied considerably throughout prehistory as well. Scholarship on sexualities that are marginalized in our own society—homosexuality, transsexuality, prostitution, etc.—needs to be balanced with thoughtful research on heterosexuality. The most intriguing, and promising, innovation in the past decade is the growing use of queer theory as an archaeological methodology for investigating nonsexual as well as sexual matters in the past. Queer theory was developed to better understand the ways that normative social structures are promulgated and reproduced, and it may be that queer theory will provide the conceptual tools archaeologists need to investigate heterosexual institutions and other sexual norms in past cultures.

DISCLOSURE STATEMENT

The author is not aware of any biases that might be perceived as affecting the objectivity of this review.

ACKNOWLEDGMENTS

My first thanks are offered to all the researchers whose scholarly and political work pioneered the study of sexuality in archaeology. Owing to journal limitations, I was not able to cite directly all the fine work that has been done on this topic, and at times, could mention only highlights of richly textured and complex projects. Although it is not possible to thank by name all those whose perspectives on the topic have informed my own, I wish to acknowledge particularly Traci Ardren, Tom Boellstorff, Bryan Burns, Shannon Dawdy, Sandy Hollimon, Kate McCaffrey, and Lynn Meskell, who generously provided advance copies of their publications; Maura Finkelstein for bibliographic research; and Deb Cohler and Kathleen Hull for their unflagging encouragement.

LITERATURE CITED

Abramson PR, Pinkerton SD, eds. 1995. *Sexual Nature, Sexual Culture*. Chicago: Univ. Chicago Press

Adovasio JM, Soffer O, Page J. 2007. *The Invisible Sex: Uncovering the True Roles of Women in Prehistory*. Washington, DC: Smithson. Books

Alberti B. 2001. Faience goddesses and ivory bull-leapers: the aesthetics of sexual difference at Late Bronze Age Knossos. *World Archaeol.* 33:189–205

Ardren T. 2008. Studies of gender in the prehispanic Americas. *J. Archaeol. Res.* 16:1–35

Ardren T, Hixson DR. 2006. The unusual sculptures of Telantunich, Yucatán: phalli and the concept of masculinity among the ancient Maya. *Camb. Archaeol. J.* 16:7–25

Arnold B. 2002. "Sein und Werden": gender as process in mortuary ritual. In *Pursuit of Gender: Worldwide Archaeological Approaches*, ed. SM Nelson, M Rosen-Ayalon, pp. 239–56. Walnut Creek, CA: AltaMira

Bahn PG. 1986. No sex, please, we're Aurignacians. *Rock Art Res.* 3:99–120

Bailey DW. 2005. *Prehistoric Figurines: Representation and Corporeality in the Neolithic*. London: Routledge

Bentley GR. 1996. How did prehistoric women bear "man the hunter"? Reconstructing fertility from the archaeological record. In *Gender and Archaeology*, ed. RP Wright, pp. 23–51. Philadelphia: Univ. Penn. Press

Bevan L, ed. 2001a. *Indecent Exposure: Sexuality, Society, and the Archaeological Record*. Glasgow: Cruithne

Bevan L. 2001b. Sex and death: sexual differentiation in mortuary ritual and grave goods as sexual symbols. See Bevan 2001a, pp. 122–29

Boellstorff T. 2007. Queer studies in the house of anthropology. *Annu. Rev. Anthropol.* 36:17–35

Bolger D. 1996. Figurines, fertility, and the emergency of complex society in prehistoric Cyprus. *Curr. Anthropol.* 37:365–73

Bourget S. 2006. *Sex, Death, and Sacrifice in Moche Religion and Visual Culture*. Austin: Univ. Tex. Press

Brendel OJ. 1970. The scope and temperment of erotic art in the Greco-Roman world. In *Studies in Erotic Art*, ed. T Bowie, CV Christenson, pp. 3–69. New York: Basic Books

Brown S. 1997. "Ways of seeing" women in antiquity: an introduction to feminism in classical archaeology and ancient art history. See Koloski-Ostrow & Lyons 1997, pp. 12–42

Buchli V. 2000a. *An Archaeology of Socialism*. Oxford: Berg

Buchli V. 2000b. Constructing utopian sexualities: the archaeology and architecture of the early Soviet state. See Schmidt & Voss 2000, pp. 236–49

Buchli V, Lucas G, eds. 2001a. *Archaeologies of the Contemporary Past*. London: Routledge

Buchli V, Lucas G. 2001b. The archaeology of alienation: a late twentieth-century British council house. See Buchli & Lucas 2001a, pp. 158–67

Butler J. 1990. *Gender Trouble: Feminism and the Subversion of Identity*. New York: Routledge

Byrne D. 2005. Excavating desire: queer heritage in the Asia-Pacific region. *Perm. Arch. Sex. Gend. Rights in Asia: 1st Int. Conf. Asian Queer Stud.* Bangkok: Res. Sch. Pac. & Asian Stud., Aust. Natl. Univ., **http://bangkok2005.anu.edu.au/**

Byrne D. 2007. Excavating desire: dissonant heritage at Campuan, Bali. Presented at Aust. Archaeol. Conf., Sydney

Casella EC. 2000a. Bulldaggers and gentle ladies: archaeological approaches to female homosexuality in convict-era Australia. See Schmidt & Voss 2000, pp. 143–59

Casella EC. 2000b. "Doing trade": a sexual economy of nineteenth-century Australian female convict prisons. *World Archaeol.* 32:209–21

Casella EC, Fowler C, eds. 2005. *The Archaeology of Plural and Changing Identities: Beyond Identification*. New York: Kluwer/Plenum

Chase SM. 1991. Polygyny, architecture and meaning. *Archaeol. Gend: Proc. Annu. Conf. Archaeol. Assoc. Univ. Calgary, 22nd*, ed. D Walde, ND Willows, pp. 150–58

Clark SR. 2003. Representing the Indus body: sex, gender, sexuality, and the anthropomorphic terracotta figurines from Harappa. *Asian Perspect.* 42:304–28

Clarke JR. 1998. *Looking at Lovemaking: Constructions of Sexuality in Roman Art, 100 B.C.–A.D. 250*. Berkeley: Univ. Calif. Press

Clarke JR. 2003. *Roman Sex, 100 B.C. to A.D. 250*. New York: Abrams

Clarke JR. 2006. Representations of the *Cinaedus* in Roman art: evidence of 'gay' subculture? See Verstraete & Provencal 2006, pp. 271–98

Cobb H. 2005. Straight down the line? A queer consideration of hunter-gatherer studies in north-west Europe. *World Archaeol.* 37:630–36

Cohen A. 1996. Portrayals of abduction in Greek art: rape or metaphor. See Kampen 1996, pp. 117–35

Conkey MW, Tringham RE. 1995. Archaeology and the goddess: exploring the contours of feminist archaeology. In *Feminisms in the Academy*, ed. DC Stanton, AJ Stewart, pp. 199–247. Ann Arbor: Univ. Mich. Press

Costello JG. 2000. Red light voices: an archaeological drama of late nineteenth-century prostitution. See Schmidt & Voss 2000, pp. 160–75

Croucher K. 2005. Queerying Near Eastern archaeology. *World Archaeol.* 37:610–20

Danielsson I-MB. 2002. (Un)masking gender—gold foil (dis)embodiedments in Late Iron Age Scandinavia. In *Thinking through the Body: Archaeologies of Corporeality*, ed. Y Hamilakis, M Pluciennik, S Tarlow, pp. 179–99. New York: Kluwer/Plenum

Davidson J. 1997. *Courtesans and Fishcakes: The Consuming Passions of Classical Athens*. New York: St. Martins

Davidson J. 2001. Dover, Foucault and Greek homosexuality: penetration and the truth of sex. *Past Present* 170:3–51

Davis W. 1996. Winckelmann's "homosexual" teleologies. See Kampen 1996, pp. 262–76

Davis W. 2001. Homoerotic art collection from 1750 to 1920. *Art Hist.* 24:247–77

Dawdy SL, Weyhing R. 2008. Beneath the rising sun: "Frenchness" and the archaeology of desire. *Int. J. Hist. Archaeol.* 12:In press

Deagan K. 1983. The mestizo minority: archaeological patterns of intermarriage. In *Spanish St. Augustine: The Archaeology of a Colonial Creole Community*, ed. K Deagan, pp. 99–124. New York: Academic

De Cunzo LA. 2001. On reforming the "fallen" and beyond: transforming continuity at the Magdalen Society of Philadelphia, 1845–1916. *Int. J. Hist. Archaeol.* 5:19–43

Delle JA. 2000. Gender, power, and space: negotiating social relations under slavery on coffee plantations in Jamaica, 1790–1834. In *Lines that Divide: Historical Archaeologies of Race, Class, and Gender*, ed. JA Delle, SA Mrozowski, R Paynter, pp. 168–201. Knoxville: Univ. Tenn. Press

Dixon KJ. 2005. *Boomtown Saloons: Archaeology and History in Virginia City*. Reno: Univ. Nev. Press

Dover KJ. 1978. *Greek Homosexuality*. Cambridge, MA: Harvard Univ. Press

Dowson TA, ed. 2000. Special issue, *Queer Archaeologies*. *World Archaeol.* 32(2)

Dowson TA. 2001. Queer theory and feminist theory: towards a sociology of sexual politics in rock art research. In *Theoretical Perspectives in Rock Art Research*, ed. K Helskog, pp. 312–29. Oslo: Novus

Dowson TA. 2007. Archaeologists, feminists, and queers: sexual politics in the construction of the past. In *Feminist Anthropology: Past, Present, and Future*, ed. PL Geller, MK Stockett, pp. 89–102. Philadelphia: Univ. Penn. Press

Eger AA. 2007. Age and male sexuality: 'queer space' in the Roman bath-house. *J. Rom. Archaeol., Suppl. Ser.* 65:131–51

Ellis P. 2001. Sexual metaphors in the Neolithic. See Bevan 2001a, pp. 56–63

Elsner J. 1996. Naturalism and the erotics of the gaze: imitations of Narcissus. See Kampen 1996, pp. 247–61

Feinberg L. 1996. *Transgender Warriors: Making History from Joan of Arc to RuPaul*. Boston: Beacon

Flatman J. 2003. Cultural biographies, cognitive landscapes, and dirty old bits of boat: 'theory' in maritime archaeology. *Int. J. Naut. Archaeol.* 32:143–57

Foucault M. 1978. *The History of Sexuality*. Volume I: *An Introduction*. New York: Random House

Frontisi-Ducroux F. 1996. Eros, desire, and the gaze. See Kampen 1996, pp. 81–100

Frontisi-Ducroux F, Lissarrague F. 1990. From ambiguity to ambivalence: a dionysiac excursion through the "anakreontic" vases. See Halperin et al. 1990, pp. 211–56

Gaimster D, Boland P, Linnane S, Cartwright C. 1996. The archaeology of private life: the Dudley Castle condoms. *Post-Mediev. Archaeol.* 30:129–42

Gero JM. 2004. Sex pots of ancient Peru: post-gender reflections. In *Combining the Past and the Present: Archaeological Perspectives on Society*, ed. T Oestigaard, N Anfinset, T Saetersdal, pp. 3–22. Oxford: BAR Int. Ser. 1210.

Gilchrist R. 1994. *Gender and Material Culture: The Archaeology of Religious Women*. London: Routledge

Gilchrist R. 2000. Unsexing the body: the interior sexuality of medieval religious women. See Schmidt & Voss 2000, pp. 89–103

Gleason MW. 1990. The semiotics of gender: physiognomy and self-fashioning in the second century C.E. See Halperin et al. 1990, pp. 389–415

Halperin DM. 1990. *One Hundred Years of Homosexuality and Other Essays on Greek Love*. New York: Routledge

Halperin DM. 2002. *How to Do the History of Homosexuality*. Chicago, IL: Univ. Chicago Press

Halperin DM, Winkler JJ, Zeitlin FI, eds. 1990. *Before Sexuality: The Construction of Erotic Experience in the Ancient Greek World*. Princeton, NJ: Princeton Univ. Press

Halsall G. 2001. Material culture, sex, gender and transgression in sixth-century Gaul: some reflections in the light of recent archaeological debate. See Bevan 2001a, pp. 130–46

Hardesty DL. 1994. Class, gender strategies, and material culture in the mining west. See Scott 1994, pp. 129–45

Hays-Gilpin KA. 2004. *Ambiguous Images: Gender and Rock Art*. Walnut Creek, CA: AltaMira

Hohmann JW. 1975. Determining if patterned behavior occurs at the ends of roads by observation of trash deposits. Manuscr. on file. Ariz. State Mus., Univ. Ariz., Tucson

Hollimon SE. 1997. The third gender in native California: two-spirit undertakers among the Chumash and their neighbors. In *Women in Prehistory: North American and Mesoamerica*, ed. C Claassen, RA Joyce, pp. 173–88. Philadelphia: Univ. Penn. Press

Hollimon SE. 2000. Archaeology of the ʻAqi: gender and sexuality in prehistoric Chumash society. See Schmidt & Voss 2000, pp. 179–96

Hollimon SE. 2001. Death, gender, and the Chumash peoples: mourning ceremonialism as an integrative mechanism. *Archaeol. Pap. Am. Anthropol. Assoc.* 10:41–55

Jacobs SE, Thomas W, Lang S, eds. 1997. *Two-Spirit People: Native American Gender Identity, Sexuality, and Spirituality*. Urbana: Univ. Ill. Press

Joyce RA. 2000a. A precolumbian gaze: male sexuality among the ancient Maya. See Schmidt & Voss 2000, pp. 263–83

Joyce RA. 2000b. *Gender and Power in Prehispanic Mesoamerica*. Austin: Univ. Tex. Press

Joyce RA. 2000c. Girling the girl and boying the boy: the production of adulthood in ancient Mesoamerica. *World Archaeol.* 31:473–83

Joyce RA. 2004. Embodied subjectivity: gender, femininity, masculinity, sexuality. In *A Companion to Social Archaeology*, ed. L Meskell, RW Preucel, pp. 82–95. Oxford: Blackwell

Joyce RA. 2005. Archaeology of the body. *Annu. Rev. Anthropol.* 34:139–58

Kampen NB, ed. 1996. *Sexuality in Ancient Art: Near East, Egypt, Greece, and Italy*. Cambridge, UK: Cambridge Univ. Press

Kampen NB. 1997. Epilogue: gender and desire. See Koloski-Ostrow & Lyons 1997, pp. 267–77

Karskens G. 1999. *Inside the Rocks: The Archaeology of a Neighborhood*. Alexandria, Aust.: Hale

Kauffman Doig F. 2001. *Sexo y Magia Sexual en el Antiguo Perú/Sex and Sexual Magic in Ancient Peru*. Lima: Merkatus

Ketz KA, Abel EJ, Schmidt AJ. 2005. Public image and private reality: an analysis of differentiation in a nineteenth-century St. Paul bordello. *Hist. Archaeol.* 39:74–88

Kokkinidou D, Nikolaidou M. 1997. Body imagery in the Aegean Neolithic: ideological implications of anthropomorphic figurines. See Moore & Scott 1997, pp. 88–112

Koloski-Ostrow AO, Lyons CL, eds. 1997. *Naked Truths: Women, Sexuality, and Gender in Classical Art and Archaeology*. London: Routledge

Larco Hoyle R. 1965. *Checán: Essay on Erotic Elements in Peruvian Art*. Geneva: Nagel

Lightfoot KG. 2005. *Indians, Missionaries, and Merchants: The Legacy of Colonial Encounters on the California Frontiers*. Berkeley: Univ. Calif. Press

Looper MG. 2002. Women-men (and men-women): Classic Maya rulers and the third gender. In *Ancient Maya Women*, ed. T Ardren, pp. 171–202. Walnut Creek, CA: AltaMira

Lucy SJ. 1997. Housewives, warriors and slaves? Sex and gender in Anglo-Saxon burials. See Moore & Scott 1997, pp. 150–68

Matthews K. 1999. The material culture of the homosexual male: a case for archaeological exploration. In *Gender and Material Culture in Archaeological Perspective*, ed. M Donald, L Hurcombe, pp. 3–19. London: Macmillan

McCafferty SD, McCafferty GG. 1994. The conquered women of Cacaxtla: gender identity or gender ideology? *Anc. Mesoam.* 5:159–72

McGinn TA. 2002. Pompeian brothels and social history. *J. Rom. Archaeol. Suppl.* 47:7–46

Meskell L. 1998a. Consuming bodies: cultural fantasies of ancient Egypt. *Body Soc.* 4:63–76

Meskell L. 1998b. Oh, my goddess! Archaeology, sexuality, and ecofeminism. *Archaeol. Dialogues* 5:126–42

Meskell L. 1999. *Archaeologies of Social Life: Age, Sex, Class et cetera in Ancient Egypt.* Oxford: Blackwell

Meskell L. 2002. The intersections of identity and politics in archaeology. *Annu. Rev. Anthropol.* 31:279–301

Meskell L. 2007. Refiguring the corpus at Çatalhöyük. In *Material Beginnings: A Global Prehistory of Figurative Representation*, ed. C Renfrew, I Morley, pp. 143–56. Cambridge, UK: McDonald Inst. Monogr.

Meskell L, Joyce RA. 2003. *Embodied Lives: Figuring Ancient Maya and Egyptian Experience.* London: Routledge

Meyer MD, Gibson ES, Costello JG. 2005. City of angels, city of sin: archaeology in the Los Angeles red-light district ca. 1900. *Hist. Archaeol.* 39:107–25

Moore J, Scott E, eds. 1997. *Invisible People and Processes: Writing Gender and Childhood into European Archaeology.* London: Leic. Univ. Press

Morris RC. 1995. All made up: performance theory and the new anthropology of sex and gender. *Annu. Rev. Anthropol.* 24:567–92

Perry EM. 2004. *Bioarchaeology of labor and gender in the prehispanic American Southwest.* PhD thesis. Univ. Ariz, Tucson. 442 pp.

Perry EM, Joyce RA. 2001. Providing a past for "Bodies That Matter": Judith Butler's impact on the archaeology of gender. *Int. J. Sex. Gend. Stud.* 6:63–76

Prine E. 2000. Searching for third genders: towards a prehistory of domestic spaces in middle Missouri villages. See Schmidt & Voss 2000, pp. 197–219

Rabinowitz NS. 2002. Excavating women's homoeroticism in ancient Greece: the evidence from Attic vase painting. See Rabinowitz & Auanger 2002, pp. 106–66

Rabinowitz NS, Auanger L, eds. 2002. *Among Women: From the Homosocial to the Homoerotic in the Ancient World.* Austin: Univ. Tex. Press

Ransley J. 2005. Boats are for boys: queering maritime archaeology. *World Archaeol.* 37:621–29

Reeder G. 2000. Same-sex desire, conjugal constructs, and the tomb of Niankhkhnum and Khnumhotep. *World Archaeol.* 32:193–208

Rega E. 1997. Age, gender and biological reality in the Early Bronze Age cemetery at Mokrin. See Moore & Scott 1997, pp. 229–47

Richlin A, ed. 1992. *Pornography and Representation in Greece and Rome.* Oxford, UK: Oxford Univ. Press

Richlin A. 2006. Sexuality in the Roman Empire. In *A Companion to the Roman Empire*, ed. DS Potter, pp. 327–53. Oxford: Blackwell

Rothschild NA. 2003. *Colonial Encounters in a Native American Landscape: The Spanish and Dutch in North America.* Washington, DC: Smithson. Books

Rubin G. 2000. Sites, settlements, and urban sex: archaeology and the study of gay leathermen in San Francisco, 1955–1995. See Schmidt & Voss 2000, pp. 62–88

Salomon N. 1997. Making a world of difference: gender, asymmetry, and the Greek nude. See Koloski-Ostrow & Lyons 1997, pp. 197–219

Schmidt RA. 2000. Shamans and northern cosmology: the direct historical approach to mesolithic sexuality. See Schmidt & Voss 2000, pp. 220–35

Schmidt RA. 2002. The iceman cometh: queering the archaeological past. In *Out in Theory: The Emergence of Lesbian and Gay Anthropology*, ed. E Lewin, WL Leap, pp. 155–85. Chicago: Univ. Ill. Press

Schmidt RA. 2005. The contribution of gender to personal identity in the southern Scandinavian Mesolithic. See Casella & Fowler 2005, pp. 79–108

Schmidt RA, Voss BL, eds. 2000. *Archaeologies of Sexuality.* London: Routledge

Schofield J, Anderton M. 2000. The queer archaeology of Green Gate: interpreting contested space at Greenham Common Airbase. *World Archaeol.* 32:236–51

Scott E. 2001. The use and misuse of rape in prehistory. See Bevan 2001a, pp. 1–18

Scott EM, ed. 1994. *Those of Little Note: Gender, Race, and Class in Historical Archaeology*. Tucson: Univ. Ariz. Press

Seifert DJ. 1991. Within site of the White House: the archaeology of working women. *Hist. Archaeol.* 25:82–107

Seifert DJ. 1994. Mrs. Starr's profession. See Scott 1994, pp. 149–73

Seifert DJ, ed. 2005. Thematic issue, *Sin City*. *Hist. Archaeol.* 39(1)

Seifert DJ, Balicki J. 2005. Mary Ann Hall's House. *Hist. Archaeol.* 39:59–73

Skinner M. 2005. *Sexuality in Greek and Roman Culture*. Oxford: Blackwell

Solli B. 1999. Odin the *queer*? On *ergi* and shamanism in Norse mythology. In *Glyfer Och Arkeologiska Rum: En Vanbok*, ed. J Nordblach, pp. 341–49. Goteborg: Goteborg Univ.

Spude CH. 2005. Brothels and saloons: an archaeology of gender in the American west. *Hist. Archaeol.* 39:89–106

Stockett MK. 2005. On the importance of difference: re-envisioning sex and gender in ancient Mesoamerica. *World Archaeol.* 37:566–78

Strassburg J. 2000. *Shamanic Shadows: One Hundred Generations of Undead Subversion in Southern Scandinavia, 7,000–4,000 BC*. Stockholm: Stockh. Univ. Stud. Archaeol.

Sundstrom L. 2004. *Storied Stone: Indian Rock Art in the Black Hills Country*. Norman: Univ. Okla. Press

Symonds JA. 1901. *A Problem in Greek Ethics, Being an Inquiry into the Phenomenon of Sexual Inversion Addressed Especially to Medical Psychologists and Jurists*. London: Areopagitiga Soc.

Talalay LE. 1994. A feminist boomerang: the great goddess of Greek prehistory. *Gend. Hist.* 6:165–83

Taylor T. 1996. *The Prehistory of Sex: Four Million Years of Human Sexual Culture*. New York: Bantam

Taylor TF. 2006. The origins of human sexual culture: sex, gender and social control. *J. Psychol. Hum. Sex.* 18:69–105

Ucko P. 2001. Unprovenanced material culture and Freud's collection of antiquities. *J. Mater. Cult.* 6:269–322

Vasey PL. 1998. Intimate sexual relations in prehistory: lessons from the Japanese macaques. *World Archaeol.* 29:407–25

Verstraete BC, Provencal V, eds. 2006. *Same-Sex Desire and Love in Greco-Roman Antiquity and in the Classical Tradition of the West*. New York: Hayworth

Voss BL. 2000a. Colonial sex: archaeology, structured space, and sexuality in Alta California's Spanish-colonial missions. See Schmidt & Voss 2000, pp. 35–61

Voss BL. 2000b. Feminisms, queer theories, and the archaeological study of past sexualities. *World Archaeol.* 32:180–92

Voss BL. 2005. Sexual subjects: identity and taxonomy in archaeological research. See Casella & Fowler 2005, pp. 55–78

Voss BL. 2006a. Engendered archaeology: men, women, and others. In *Historical Archaeology*, ed. M Hall, S Silliman, pp. 107–27. London: Blackwell

Voss BL. 2006b. Sexuality in archaeology. In *The Handbook of Gender in Archaeology*, ed. SM Nelson, pp. 365–400. Lanham, MD: AltaMira

Voss BL. 2008a. *The Archaeology of Ethnogenesis: Race and Sexuality in Colonial San Francisco*. Berkeley: Univ. Calif. Press

Voss BL. 2008b. Domesticating imperialism: sexual politics and the archaeology of empire. *Am. Anthropol.* 110:191–203

Weismantel M. 2004. Moche sex pots: reproduction and temporality in ancient South America. *Am. Anthropol.* 106:495–505

Whelan MK. 1991. Gender and historical archaeology: eastern Dakota patterns in the 19th century. *Hist. Archaeol.* 25:17–32

Wilkie LA. 2000. Magical passions: sexuality and African-American archaeology. See Schmidt & Voss 2000, pp. 129–42

Wilkie LA. 2001. Black sharecroppers and white frat boys: living communities and the appropriation of their archaeological pasts. See Buchli & Lucas 2001a, pp. 108–18

Wilkie LA. 2003. *The Archaeology of Mothering: An African-American Midwife's Tale*. New York: Routledge

Winkler JJ. 1989. *The Constraints of Desire: The Anthropology of Sex and Gender in Ancient Greece*. New York: Routledge

Winkler JJ. 1990. Laying down the law: the oversight of men's sexual behavior in classical Athens. See Halperin et al. 1990, pp. 171–209

Winter IJ. 1996. Sex, rhetoric, and the public monument: the alluring body of Naram-Sin of Agade. See Kampen 1996, pp. 11–26

Yamin R. 2005. Wealthy, free, and female: prostitution in nineteenth-century New York. *Hist. Archaeol.* 39:4–18

Yates T. 1993. Frameworks for an archaeology of the body. In *Interpretive Archaeology*, ed. C Tilley, pp. 31–72. London: Berg

Reproduction and Preservation of Linguistic Knowledge: Linguistics' Response to Language Endangerment

Nikolaus P. Himmelmann

Institut für Allgemeine Sprachwissenschaft, Westfälische Wilhelms-Universität Münster, D-48143 Münster, Germany; email: nikolaus.himmelmann@uni-muenster.de

Annu. Rev. Anthropol. 2008. 37:337–50

First published online as a Review in Advance on June 24, 2008

The *Annual Review of Anthropology* is online at anthro.annualreviews.org

This article's doi: 10.1146/annurev.anthro.37.081407.085226

Key Words

fieldwork ethics, language documentation, linguistic structuralism

Abstract

In responding to the globally accelerating rate at which linguistic varieties are disappearing, structural linguistics is confronted with a number of challenges for which it is ill-equipped because of limitations in its basic conceptualization of linguistic knowledge. In addition to providing a brief history of the recent promotion of language endangerment to a major concern of the discipline as a whole, this article discusses three such challenges: (*a*) new demands on linguistic fieldwork practices, (*b*) rhetorical tensions arising from the need to address a multiplicity of audiences; (*c*) the limits of the traditional descriptive trilogy and its replacement by the concept of language documentation. On a theoretical level, these challenges are all linked to the problem that the structuralist conception of linguistic structures lacks adequate grounding in the social realities of the speech community, a problem that has accompanied linguistic structuralism since its inception.

INTRODUCTION

Reproduction is not a term or concept that has much currency in linguistics because most branches of modern linguistics investigate linguistic behavior and knowledge almost exclusively in abstract structural or cognitive terms. Consequently, the replication of linguistic knowledge in a given community is generally discussed in terms of acquisition, transmission, or inheritance. That is, children acquire the language(s) of their parents; a variety is intergenerationally transmitted; and structural features, differences in register, and conversational routines are inherited from older generations. Linguistic knowledge is thus likened to some kind of object that is passed down through generations and is not seen as something that is socially constructed and reproduced.

For most research areas of concern to core linguistics, e.g., grammatical theory or typology, it is not clear to what extent the disregard for social aspects of language structure and use compromises research goals and outcomes. However, this disregard is indeed harmful to a number of topic areas. One of these areas is large-scale language endangerment, which has become a topic of major concern for mainstream structural linguistics since the early 1990s. After briefly recounting in the next section the (re)discovery of this topic, this article reviews the following three major challenges that emerged when linguists started to address the fact that linguistic varieties are currently disappearing at a vastly accelerated rate.

First, work on endangered languages generally involves fieldwork. Anthropology and other social sciences have been critically reviewing the ethics of their fieldwork practices since the middle of the twentieth century, but structural linguistics largely ignored ethical issues until fieldwork on endangered languages finally forced the issue, as further discussed in Language Maintenance and Fieldwork Ethics, below.

Second, attempts to articulate the challenge of language endangerment—both for the field of linguistics itself and the general public—involve a number of themes and concepts, which are double-edged when considered from the point of view of noncore linguistic audiences, in particular communities where an endangered variety is still in use. This is further discussed in Rhetorical Challenges.

Third, confronting the challenge of language endangerment raises the issue of whether the traditional model for describing languages, which focuses on structures and neglects actual practices, is adequate for a long-term documentation of endangered languages. This issue is discussed in Multifunctional Long-Term Documentation.

For all three topics, the challenges faced by structural linguistics apparently arise from the need to speak to, and address concerns of, noncore linguistic audiences. But it would be wrong to consider these challenges merely communicative challenges relating to the strategic representation and promotion of the field within academia and the wider public. Instead, they reflect the essentially a-social conceptualization of linguistic knowledge within mainstream structural linguistics, which has delegated to the subfield of sociolinguistics (broadly conceived, including anthropological linguistics) the investigation of all social aspects of language structure and use. In putting language endangerment on the mainstream agenda, structural linguistics has added another issue to the growing list of items that second guess the wisdom of excluding from its core agenda almost all regard for the ways in which linguistic knowledge is socially constructed and reproduced, as briefly discussed in the final section.

To appreciate the dynamics of the professional discourse on language endangerment detailed in the following sections, it is useful to note that the primary agents in highlighting language endangerment as a key issue in the field in the 1990s were not sociolinguists specializing in the topics of language shift and language maintenance but rather were typologically oriented core linguists interested in crosslinguistic comparisons, some of these also involved in fieldwork on minority languages (historical detail is provided in the following section). Because I belong to the latter camp, this review reflects the views of a typologically oriented structuralist linguist with only superficial knowledge of the work being done under the label of sociolinguistics.

THE (RE)DISCOVERY OF LANGUAGE ENDANGERMENT AS A TOPIC OF CONCERN FOR LINGUISTS

Many of the thousands of linguistic varieties still in use all over the world will disappear in the next decades. This fact is usually communicated in terms of "languages" with statements such as "at the rate things are going—the coming century will see either the death or the doom of 90% of mankind's languages" (Krauss 1992, p. 7), but this is also true for innumerable dialects and special registers. That linguistic varieties become obsolete is a natural process in the sense that it has happened at all times and in all places. As such it has been a perhaps not central but well-established topic in linguistic research under the headings of language death or language obsolescence (Dorian 1981, 1989; Dressler 1972, 1988; Dressler & Wodak 1977; Gal 1979; Sasse 1992). Scholars widely agree that the speed and pervasiveness of language obsolescence have dramatically increased in the twentieth century. The realization of this fact poses a number of challenges for linguistics and has made language endangerment a topic of major concern for the discipline at large. To understand and contextualize better the way these challenges have been addressed within linguistics, it is useful to recount briefly the history of how language endangerment became a central issue in linguistics in the 1990s.

The trigger for a series of events that led to the establishment of language endangerment as a major topic of concern in mainstream linguistics was a short presentation by Johannes Bechert to the section on universals and typology at the fourteenth International Congress of Linguists in East Berlin in 1987. This presentation on universals research and ethnocentrism, later published as Bechert

(1990), starts with a quote from Mühlhäusler's (1985) review of Schmidt (1985), which likens the prospect that 200 of Australia's 250 Aboriginal languages still spoken at the time European colonization began will have disappeared by the end of the twentieth century to "the large-scale destruction of natural gene pools such as that in the tropical rain forests" and predicts that languages "and the philosophies and world views encoded in them, are increasingly becoming a vanishing resource" (Mühlhäusler 1985, p. 1005). If that is indeed the case, Bechert asks, why is it that linguists in general are not concerned about this imminent loss of a major part of their empirical basis, and he cites the example of biologists who at the time had already been very successful in making the large-scale extinction of biological species a well-established topic of concern to the public.

An immediate reaction to this presentation was a motion drafted by Christian Lehmann, which was presented to the business meeting of the Comité International Permanent des Linguistes (CIPL) at the same conference. This motion, signed by more than 200 of the linguists present, urged the committee to take action with the goal of bringing the issue of language endangerment to the attention of professional linguists and the general public. It did this primarily in two ways. First, it made language endangerment one of the two central themes of its fifteenth International Congress of Linguists in Quebec in 1992, and it continues to hold panels on endangered languages at every congress. Second, it commissioned a volume taking stock of the extent of language endangerment in all parts of the world. This volume, published as Robins & Uhlenbeck (1991), was put together in collaboration with Stephen Wurm, at the time president of the Conseil International de la Philosophie et des Sciences Humaines (CIPSH), a suborganization of UNESCO, which also published a part of the collection in its journal *Diogènes* (1991). Thus endangered languages became part of the UNESCO agenda, resulting inter alia in the inauguration of an Endangered Languages Program in 1993 (http://portal.unesco.org/culture/en/ev.php-URL_ID=8270&URL_DO=DO_TOPIC&URL_SECTION=201.html).

In the wake of these events, many professional organizations of linguists took measures to promote the issue of language endangerment. Most importantly perhaps, the 1991 annual meeting of the Linguistic Society of America (LSA) included a symposium on Endangered Languages organized by Kenneth Hale, major contributions to which were published a year later in the field's leading journal *Language* (Hale et al. 1992). Another major event was the creation of a committee on endangered languages by the DGfS, the German linguistic society, which in 1993 organized the first summer school dedicated to the topic and engineered the first major funding initiative in the field, the Dokumentation bedrohter Sprachen (DoBeS) program of the Volkswagen Foundation inaugurated in 1999. In the same year, the project Endangered Languages of the Pacific Rim (http://www.elpr.bun.kyoto-u.ac.jp/index_e.html) started in Japan. By the year 2000, language endangerment was firmly established as an active field of research in linguistics as evidenced by the usual indicators such as regular and manifold conferences, a steady stream of articles and books, new societies and funds dedicated to the documentation and maintenance of endangered languages, and a special mailing list.[1]

In terms of its uptake within the profession, the 1987 motion was thus considerably more successful than a very similar one dating from 1962, when more than 50 Scandinavian linguists urged their national UNESCO committees to demand that the General Assembly of UNESCO take measures to protect the rapidly increasing number of languages in danger of disappearing. The call was drafted by Swedish linguist Pierre Naert and published under the title of "Pour la défense des langues des minorités" in the journal *Europa Ethnica* (1962).

Kloss (1969, pp. 287–304) provides an extended critique of the parallelization with nature conservation, which guides this call in the same way as it does the more recent campaigning for the preservation of endangered languages (see also England 2002, p. 142). When pointing to the relatively greater success biologists have had in focusing public and political attention on the issue of species extinction, which appears in most linguistic writing on language endangerment, ignored is the fact that the more widespread concern for species extinction may have been engineered in part by business interests (agro-chemical industry, genetic engineering). To date, no similar business interests have supported linguists' concerns regarding accelerating language shift.

Naert's call led to the establishment of a society [the Association internationale pour la défense des langues et cultures menacées (AIDLCM)] but seems to have had little impact within the profession. Specifically, both the motion itself as well as the AIDLCM have been completely ignored in the recent flurry of language endangerment–related activities. It thus seems most likely that the rediscovery of the topic of language endangerment in the late 1980s would not have been so successful if the topic had not been in the air at the time, as it were. Of importance in this regard were ongoing discussions among fieldworking linguists who were forced to reflect on the relevance and implications of their work for the communities speaking endangered varieties, as further discussed in the next section.

LANGUAGE MAINTENANCE AND FIELDWORK ETHICS

The issue of language endangerment has had probably its most profound impact on structural linguistics with regard to fieldwork practices. Unlike anthropology and other social sciences, where ethical issues pertaining to the

---

[1] Tasaku Tsunoda maintains an online resource, Bibliography on Language Endangerment and Language Revitalization (http://www.tooyoo.l.u-tokyo.ac.jp/BibLE/). The Online Resources For Endangered Languages (OREL) provide "links to web resources on revitalising or documenting endangered languages, including links on language endangerment and revitalisation, technology and techniques, ethical issues, and funding sources" (OREL 2008).

relation between researchers and the people studied have been a concern for decades,[2] linguistics, for most of the twentieth century, conceived of linguistic fieldwork as something that was of no particular concern to the people being studied. Most important, it was widely held by fieldworking linguists that linguistic fieldwork was neutral in that regard. Fieldwork, that is, could cause no harm, but it also would not provide any particular benefit to anyone outside academia.[3] Specifically, the outcomes of linguistic fieldwork were seen to be of no particular interest to the speakers (unless they also happened to be linguists), and hence no obligations existed with regard to sharing these results with them. Inasmuch as obligations were felt to be involved at all, they pertained to remunerations for the time invested by speakers in talking to the linguist.

This view of fieldwork, I believe, is closely linked to the essentially a-social conceptualization of language in structural linguistics. In descriptive, grammar-oriented fieldwork, one does not have to deal with speech communities; instead, it is largely sufficient to tap the linguistic knowledge of one or two speakers. In actual practice, and unlike anthropologists, linguists rarely spent extended periods of time in a community. Inasmuch as fieldwork actually involved getting close to the speech community— Bloomfield's fieldwork on Tagalog happened in his office at the University of Illinois—it often consisted in taking the main informants out of the noisy environment of their homes and villages and working with them in a guest house, trailer, or hotel nearby.

This basic approach was challenged by work with communities speaking an endangered variety, especially where community and researcher(s) were part of the same larger political and socioeconomic setting as in the case of indigenous communities in Australia and northern America. Individual speakers and representative bodies of the communities began to ask what the purpose of linguistic research actually was and how it could help them in their struggle to maintain their cultural and linguistic identity. Perhaps the most intensive and coherent debate about the answers to these questions took place in Australia, where linguistic fieldwork has been a main concern of linguistic research since the 1960s. Organizations of Aborigines such as the Aboriginal Languages Association started to articulate community expectations regarding language-related research projects, and a large number of PhD students working on grammatical descriptions as topics of their theses were directly confronted with these issues and expectations in the late 1970s and early 1980s.

It is thus not by chance that the most profound and radical discussion of ethical issues in linguistic fieldwork is Wilkins' (1992, 2000) report and reflection on his work in Arrernte communities in central Australia, starting in 1982. In 1983, Wilkins and fellow graduate students at the Australian National University drafted the "Statement of Professional Ethics for Linguists Doing Research in Aboriginal Communities" in response to a statement of linguistic rights of Aboriginal and Islander communities prepared by the Aboriginal Languages Association (Wilkins 1992, p. 174). The Australian Linguistic Society adopted a statement of ethics in 1989 (**http://www.als.asn.au/Policies**), and the Applied Linguistics Association of Australia followed with their "Statement of Good Practice" in 1997 (**http://www.latrobe.edu.au/alaa/goodprac.htm**). To date, these two bodies appear to be the only professional organizations of linguists that have their own codes of ethics.[4]

In the 1990s, the rising concern about language endangerment prominently included the

---

[2] On its Web site (**http://www.aaanet.org/stmts/ethstmnt.htm**), for example, the American Anthropological Society documents statements on ethics dating from 1948 onward.

[3] One possible exception are situations in which use of an officially forbidden variety is actively prosecuted and punished by government agencies (e.g., use of Kurmanci and other minority languages in Turkey), and hence fieldwork on this variety may be dangerous for both the participating speaker(s) and the researcher(s).

[4] Musgrave & Thieberger (2006, p. 2) also provide copies of the 1984 and 1989 statements in an appendix.

call for linguists to engage in fieldwork on endangered varieties. A broader segment of the profession was consequently forced to engage with the problem of what constitutes responsible linguistic fieldwork. This process was helped by the fact that a related discussion, centering on the notions of advocacy and empowerment, emerged among sociolinguists working with minority groups in Europe and North America. The most comprehensive statement of the relevant issues and positions may be found in Cameron et al. (1992), which discusses language-related fieldwork issues in sociolinguistics, anthropology, and sociology.[5] Works specifically concerning fieldwork in endangered language communities include, Wilkins (1992, 2000), England (1992), Craig (1992), McLaughlin & Sall (2001), Florey (2001), Grinevald (2003), Hill (2006, pp. 119–27), Mosel (2006), and Musgrave & Thieberger (2006).

Control and obligation are the core issues in this debate: Who participates in choosing research topic and methods? Who determines the overall and the daily work flow and time schedule? Who controls the dissemination of results? Which obligations do researchers have vis-à-vis their collaborators and the speech community? Do these obligations extend beyond matters directly related to the research objective? Beyond language-related matters? These issues are complex and do not allow for straightforward and universally applicable answers. But the following tenets and observations may be widely shared.

■ Individual speakers and the community at large should be involved in the design of the research project and the work flow as much and as early as possible. That is, fieldwork projects should be designed essentially as cooperative enterprises between equal parties. Although almost certainly rendering the fieldwork

process more time consuming and potentially significantly more complicated, a collaborative design also tends to make it much more profitable and productive, as already noted by Wilkins (1992, pp. 183–86; see also McLaughlin & Sall 2001, Mosel 2006).

■ Speakers and communities should have a say with regard to the dissemination of research results, in particular where and whenever they could be affected by it. This aspect has recently attained increased importance and attention in the context of the establishment of multimedia archives for materials on endangered languages. Determining restrictions on access to such materials and answering questions about ownership and the protection of intellectual property rights have turned out to be core problems inhibiting dissemination. All major archives have codes of conduct and ethical guidelines.[6]

■ Work in communities where an endangered variety is in use includes the obligation to contribute to the maintenance of this variety inasmuch as this is wanted by the community. This may involve obligations not directly related to the research goal at hand (e.g., producing an alphabet primer in a project concerned with discourse structures; see Hinton & Hale 2001 and Grenoble & Whaley 2006 for more examples and extensive discussion). Fieldwork in countries with many endangered varieties may also have to respond to a demand to participate in training local researchers and in setting up and maintaining local documentation and language maintenance

---

[5] Issue 13.2 of the journal *Language & Communication* contains a succinct summary of the argument (Cameron et al. 1993) with peer review.

[6] Most digital archives for materials on endangered languages are joined in the Digital Endangered Languages and Musics Archives Network (DELAMAN, http://www.delaman.org/). Relevant examples for statements on ethics, intellectual property rights, etc., can be found on many of the sites of individual archives listed there.

structures (England 1992, 2007; Florey & Himmelmann 2008).

- The major problem for responsible field-work is the fact that more often than not it is difficult if not impossible to identify the relevant parties with whom researchers could enter into mutually binding agreements. Specifically, who has the right and the authority to represent the community in these matters? What happens when there are multiple and conflicting claims in this regard?

- Another frequent problem pertains to ensuring informed consent by speakers and communities who, because they lack familiarity with western academia and media and the global impact and accessibility of the Internet, cannot seriously gauge the possible impact of a given research goal or dissemination option (e.g., allowing a recording to be freely available in an archive accessible via the Internet).

RHETORICAL CHALLENGES

One major challenge in the attempt to raise awareness about language endangerment pertains to the fact that multiple and very heterogeneous audiences need to be addressed, including linguistic scholars and students, the major academic funding bodies, the general public, speakers of endangered varieties and their communities, government agencies, and international policy-making agencies such as UNESCO. These audiences have widely diverging and, in part, contradictory expectations and interests. Consequently, campaigns addressed to one audience run into the danger of alienating another (Hill 2002, Errington 2003).

The major tensions arising here pertain to themes and rhetorical figures deemed to be effective with respect to funding bodies, government and policy-making agencies, and the wider (western) public, but which may be counterproductive when overheard by local groups and speakers. As England (2002, p. 141) notes, the term endangered language itself is felt by some speakers to contribute to the marginalization of those languages. Furthermore, as discussed by Hill (2002, pp. 121–23), the rhetoric of endangered language advocacy often involves reference to the idea that the disappearance of a language constitutes a loss for all of humankind. Although this notion is true when seen from a general humanistic (and, in particular, a linguist's) point of view, such an assertion may be perceived by speakers and communities as dispossessing them of their heritage language, which in many communities is seen as the locally created and maintained core pillar of their identity.

A related theme, called "hypervalorization" by Hill (2002, p. 123), pertains to the idea that every language is a unique and "priceless treasure" bearing witness to the beauty of the human mind. Although this is again true when seen from the point of view of a linguistic connoisseur, speakers and local communities may perceive this as transforming their linguistic practices into commodities in a "rarefied linguistic marketplace . . . inaccessible to ordinary speakers" (Hill 2002, p. 125). Furthermore, as Dorian (2002) notes, the features of a given variety that, from a speaker's point of view, are most distinctive and effective in a given linguistic ecology may not be particularly rare in cross-linguistic perspective and hence may not be of special interest to the professional linguist.

Perhaps the clearest example of the contradictions arising in the global conversation about language endangerment is the following paradox emerging in the context of competition for funding. In this context, increased endangeredness becomes something positive because, more often than not, funding is channeled toward what are judged to be the most endangered varieties. This is a defensible position when seen purely from a data-gathering point of view: Try to obtain as much data as possible for this variety as long as there are still speakers around. This practice is obviously counterproductive and demoralizing when seen from the points of view of speakers and communities struggling to maintain their heritage language.

The preceding points may be largely addressed by paying more attention to rhetorical packaging and adjusting the themes accordingly (see Hill 2002, p. 129, for some suggestions). In this regard it will be useful for linguists "to think about lessons that cultural anthropologists have already learned about multiplying meanings and interpretations of research and writing outside an academic ingroup" (Errington 2003, p. 723). There is still considerable resistance to confronting such lessons, as shown, for example, by Chafe's (2003) rejoinder to Hill's challenges. Chafe's counterarguments are largely convincing from a purely professional point of view, but they completely neglect the possibility of a differing point of view taken by a nonacademic speaker of a minority variety.

Apart from the rhetorical problems arising from the multiplicity of audiences, there is a somewhat deeper and more principled issue at stake here that again relates to the inability of structural linguistics to address adequately the social nature of linguistic knowledge. The fundamental issue is that the endangerment discourse of professional linguists is geared at individual languages conceived of as objects that are transmitted within well-defined communities. However, what actually is at stake are complex linguistic ecologies with fuzzy external boundaries and intricate and overlapping internal groupings. This point has been made most emphatically in the work of Mühlhäusler (1992, 1996), and it is of utmost importance for all serious attempts to reverse language shift (Fishman 1991; 2001; 2002, p. 147), but it also underlies the theme of "enumeration" discussed by Hill (2002, p. 127) and her commentators and the attempts to "factorize" assessments of language vitality.

One good example of the latter is a UNESCO (2003) document entitled "Language Vitality and Endangerment," put together by an ad hoc expert group on endangered languages and finalized in March 2003. In a section called "Assessing Language Endangerment and Urgency for Documentation," the document lists the following nine major evaluative factors of language vitality, all but one accompanied by an assessment grid in the form of a grading scale:

> Factor 1. Intergenerational language transmission (scale)
> Factor 2. Absolute number of speakers (real numbers)
> Factor 3. Proportion of speakers within the total population (scale)
> Factor 4. Trends in existing language domains (scale)
> Factor 5. Response to new domains and media (scale)
> Factor 6. Materials for language education and literacy (scale)
> Factor 7. Governmental and institutional language attitudes and policies, including official status and use (scale)
> Factor 8. Community members' attitudes toward their own language (scale)
> Factor 9. Amount and quality of documentation (scale)

Apart from obvious and superficial inconsistencies such as the fact that amount and quality of documentation (factor 9) is irrelevant for assessing language vitality, the major shortcoming of these kinds of lists is that they misleadingly presume to systematize and factorize realities that, in fact, are too complex for such a factorization. In the list above, for example, transmission (factor 1) and use of a variety in different domains (factor 4) appear to be unrelated matters. But the two actually systematically belong together because use of a variety in interactions with children is but one of the existing language domains.

The list also mixes causes and symptoms for decreasing vitality. Strictly speaking, reductions in the number and quality of usage domains (here somewhat arbitrarily distributed across factors 1, 4, and 5) are symptoms, and hence the major diagnostics, for decreasing vitality. The other factors (except 9) may be argued to contribute to the causes for such reductions and hence endangerment, but they are at best contributing factors of widely diverging relevance. Speaker number and proportions (factors 2 and 3), for example, have no necessary relation to language endangerment because, in fact, there are several examples of smallish minority groups that have maintained their traditional varieties (e.g., the Arizona Tewa; see Kroskrity 1993). The most important causes for language shift, i.e., socioeconomic factors, are conspicuously absent from the above list, probably because they are difficult to factorize.

As explicitly argued in Himmelmann (2008) and perhaps best illustrated in the detailed case study by Kulick (1992), typologizing endangerment scenarios, instead of attempting to factorize language vitality, would be a more appropriate approach. In a scenario approach, language endangerment is seen as the result of a specific and complex constellation of varied factors, some of which may be conducive to language shift and others to language maintenance. The scenario approach thus explicitly focuses on the fact that endangered varieties generally belong to complex linguistic ecologies and cannot be adequately addressed in terms of grading scales targeting a single, easily isolated variety in a well-defined community.

MULTIFUNCTIONAL LONG-TERM DOCUMENTATION

When confronted with the global extent of current language endangerment, the first and most widespread reaction among linguists was to emphasize the need for descriptive work on varieties for whom speakers are still available. The primary model for this urgently needed descriptive work was the structuralist model of language description, which in its classic form consists of a trilogy: a grammar, a dictionary, and a text collection. These three parts are not equal in several ways, including the time needed to compile them (here dictionaries far outrank grammars and text collections) and the status they have as academic achievements (only grammars have recently been accorded again some prestige within the core linguistic community, after an almost total disregard for descriptive work in linguistics during the second half of the twentieth century). Because of these inequalities, descrip-

tive efforts came to focus almost exclusively on grammars during the twentieth century (see Himmelmann 1996 for a brief history of relevant developments).

Hence, the call for salvage work on endangered languages appearing frequently around 1990 was, in the first instance, a call for writing descriptive grammars, the empirical pillar of all crosslinguistic research. But very soon it became clear that an exclusive focus on grammatical description was not tenable for both practical and theoretical reasons. One reason is because, once again, there are tensions between the interests and goals of speech communities and professionals. Although grammars are highly valued among linguists, they have little practical value for speakers and speech communities, especially when written in an international language unknown to them. Hence, the potential value that descriptive grammars may have for language preservation in many communities is purely symbolic in that having a grammar may be of use for raising the status of a given variety.

In literate communities, however, dictionaries and text collections may have practical uses in addition to purely symbolic ones. Among other things, text collections and—provided they include ample exemplification of lexeme uses in context—dictionaries record ways in which a given variety is actually used and thus may become a resource in attempts to stabilize or even reverse an ongoing language shift. But, as Hinton & Weigel (2002) show, with regard to dictionary production, tensions are certain to arise between community expectations and academic standards and goals (see also other contributions in Frawley et al. 2002).

Thus in general all three parts of the structuralist descriptive trilogy are of limited direct practical use for local speakers and communities. Inasmuch as the future of an endangered variety has become a topic of concern within the speech community itself, fieldwork in such a community is now usually confronted with demands to engage in activities directly supporting the vitality of the variety, as discussed above.

Another reason why the structuralist descriptive trilogy is probably not the "best record"[7] for an endangered variety pertains to systematic holes that tend to occur in such descriptions. As argued by Grace (1981, 1987) and Pawley (1985, 1993), structuralist descriptions do not capture the specific way of expressing oneself idiomatically in a given variety. That is, even if a truly comprehensive descriptive grammar and dictionary existed for a given variety, one would still not know how actual utterances are formed because the descriptive resources are typically overgenerative—they allow for a number of alternative ways of expressing complex ideas, only one of which happens to be the standard or normal way of rendering a particular idea. For example, the following expressions are all grammatically well-formed and can also be understood by native speakers of English: half past twelve, half before one, twelve and two quarters, eleven plus two hours minus half an hour. But only the first one is the normal, idiomatic way of telling the time.

To capture the standard way of saying things in a given variety, one would have to be able to include a systematic description of speech formulae in the description of a given variety. Although formulaic speech has recently made it from a marginal oddity to a more central concern of mainstream linguistics, involving quite a few different approaches and subdisciplines as documented, for example, in Wray (2002) and Pawley (2007), there is still no standard methodology or theoretical model for incorporating it into structuralist language descriptions.

The lack of an adequate way to address formulaic language is but one of a number of deficiencies of the structuralist model of language description, possibly the most significant one. It generally holds that structuralist descriptions can only be as good as current grammatical theory. Only those categories and structures that can be recognized and represented with the available theoretical apparatus are described. But there is no guarantee that the apparatus allows for a complete identification of all structural units and regularities. In fact, older descriptions generally lack adequate treatments of some topics of major current interest (e.g., pre-Chomskyan descriptive grammars are usually quite terse with regard to syntactic structures). This is, of course, no problem as long as the variety being described continues to be used and new data can be collected when needed. But when the task is to provide the last ever possible description, the problems of completeness and comprehensiveness take center stage.

Many of these problems can be addressed by redefining and enlarging the role of the text collection in the descriptive trilogy, which had never been clarified and theorized before language endangerment became a major concern in the discipline. One way of doing this is to stick with the trilogy but make text collection a more systematic and comprehensive enterprise, as proposed by Lehmann (2001, 2002, 2003). A more radical proposal, developed and discussed by Himmelmann (1996, 1998, 2006) and from a more anthropological linguistics point of view in Woodbury (1998, 2003), is to separate text collection from the other two components and turn it into a scientific enterprise of its own.

This enterprise, now widely called language documentation as opposed to language description, is no longer based on the structuralist notion of a language system that must be captured in as economical a set of abstract units and rules as possible. Language documentations, instead, focus on observable linguistic behavior and knowledge. The goal is a lasting, multifunctional record of the linguistic practices attested at a given time in a given speech community and the knowledge speakers have about these practices. Multifunctional means that such a data compilation is of use not only for linguists, but also for researchers from other disciplines (anthropology, oral history, etc.), educators and policy makers, and the speech community itself. But this, of course, also means that the documentation contains annotated but otherwise raw data, which must be further processed

_____

[7]David Wilkins organized a workshop with this title at the Max Planck Institute in Nijmegen in 1995.

by each user group before they can serve their specific purposes. Thus language documentations are not purely or even primarily linguistic projects, but interdisciplinary projects, which ideally reach beyond academia and actively involve, and become involved in, the speech community.

That language documentation is not a purely linguistic enterprise does not mean that descriptive techniques and concepts do not have a role to play in it. On the contrary, the transcription and further annotation of recordings, which constitute the major workload in a documentation project, essentially depend on these techniques and concepts. But the role of description is an ancillary one in documentation, i.e., to make a compilation of records of linguistic practices accessible to, and useful for, a broad range of users. It is no longer the main goal as it used to be in the descriptive trilogy.

CONCLUSION

When Saussure was trying to delimit the proper object of study for linguistics, he determined that this object, *langue*, "n'existe parfaitement que dans la masse" (Saussure 1972 [1916], p. 30). *Langue* is a socially constructed and attested phenomenon that is realized in individual acts and psychologically manifest only in individual brains (*parole*). Consequently, in distinguishing *langue* from *parole*, one needs to separate, inter alia, "ce qui est social de ce qui est individuel" (Saussure 1972 [1916]). How exactly this separation is to be done and what exactly it means to say that language—as studied in linguistics—is a *fait social* remain unclear in Saussure's exposition and have never been satisfactorily resolved in mainstream structural linguistics. In fact, starting with Bloomfield's operationalization of the structuralist program, structural linguistics has replaced "social" first with "psychological" and then with "cognitive" in the conceptualization of the supraindividual nature of its object of study, attempting to relate its abstract units, rules, and generalizations to the cognitive endowment of human beings. Concomitantly, as already noted in the

introduction, the investigation of all social aspects of language structure and use was delegated to the subfield of sociolinguistics (broadly conceived).

Although the exclusion of the social has arguably not done fatal damage to its core project, structural linguistics periodically encounters problems resulting from its neglect of social aspects of linguistic knowledge. This review has identified a number of such problems relating to its dealings with language endangerment. But similar problems arise in other areas as well. Thus, for example, the fact that linguistic items and structures tend to diffuse areally also raises doubts about the idea that languages are essential wholes that are handed down across generations (Enfield's 2005 review in this series). Another example is the fact that recent grammatical theory struggles to provide a place for frequency effects of various kinds in its overall model of grammatical knowledge, where it does not have a natural place under the standard assumption that grammar as an abstract system is essentially homogeneous across a speech community (e.g., Bybee 2006; Gahl & Garnsey 2004, 2006; Pierrehumbert 2001; and, for a critical stance, see Newmeyer 2006).

Such periodically emerging problems have occasionally led to calls for abandoning the structural approach in linguistics altogether. But this does not seem to be the most promising venue to take. Instead, the challenge at hand is to maintain structuralist core ideas and concepts that have stood the test of time (e.g., the phoneme, distributional analysis, the distinction between substance and form) and to develop them further so that they explicitly allow for a socially negotiated construction and reproduction of linguistic structures, as perhaps most brilliantly exemplified in the work of Silverstein (e.g., Silverstein 1976a,b; 1986). Useful theoretical grounding for this enterprise is provided by Millikan's philosophy of language (Millikan 2005, especially chapter 2, "In Defense of Public Language"), which puts social functions at the center of the theory and makes reproducibility a core characteristic of linguistic conventions.

DISCLOSURE STATEMENT

N.H. serves as president of Gesellschaft für Bedrohte Sprachen (German Society for Endangered Languages). He is also a recipient of multiple grants from the Documentation of Endangered Languages program of the Volkswagen Foundation.

ACKNOWLEDGMENTS

I am grateful to Nick Evans and Christian Lehmann for checking historical detail and to Fred Bertz for critically reading the manuscript.

LITERATURE CITED

1962. Pour la défense des langues des minorités. *Eur. Ethnica* 19.4:182–85

Austin P, ed. 2003. *Language Documentation and Description*, Vol. 1. London: SOAS

Bechert J. 1990. Universalienforschung und Ethnozentrismus. *Proc. Int. Congr. Linguists 1987, Berlin/GDR, 14th*, 3 vols., ed. W Bahner, J Schildt, D Viehweger, pp. 2350–52. Berlin: Akademie Verlag

Bybee JL. 2006. From usage to grammar: the mind's response to repetition. *Language* 82:711–33

Bybee JL, Hopper P, eds. 2001. *Frequency and the Emergence of Linguistic Structure*. Amsterdam: Benjamins

Cameron D, Frazer E, Harvey P, Rampton B, Richardson K. 1992. *Researching Language. Issues of Power and Method*. London: Routledge

Cameron D, Frazer E, Harvey P, Rampton B, Richardson K. 1993. Ethics, advocacy and empowerment: issues of method in researching language. *Lang. Commun.* 13(2):81–94

Chafe W. 2003. On the rhetorics of linguists. *J. Linguist. Anthropol.* 12:234–38

Craig C. 1992. Fieldwork on endangered languages: a forward look at ethical issues. *Proc. Int. Congr. Linguists, XVth*, ed. A Cochetiere, JC Boulanger, C Ouellon, pp. 33–42. Quebec: Press. Univ. Laval

Dorian NC. 1981. *Language Death: The Life Cycle of a Scottish Gaelic Dialect*. Philadelphia: Univ. Penn. Press

Dorian NC, ed. 1989. *Investigating Obsolescence*. Cambridge, UK: Cambridge Univ. Press

Dorian NC. 2002. Commentary: broadening the rhetorical and descriptive horizons in endangered-language linguistics. *J. Linguist. Anthropol.* 12:134–40

Dressler W. 1972. On the phonology of language death. *Chicago Linguist. Soc.* 8:448–57

Dressler W. 1988. Language death. In *Linguistics: The Cambridge Survey*, ed. F Newmeyer, pp. 184–92. Cambridge, UK: Cambridge Univ. Press

Dressler W, Wodak R, eds. 1977. Thematic issue, *Language Death. Int. J. Sociol. Lang.* Vol. 12

Enfield NJ. 2005. Areal linguistics and mainland southeast Asia. *Annu. Rev. Anthropol.* 34:181–206

England NC. 1992. Doing Mayan linguistics in Guatemala. *Language* 68:29–35

England NC. 2002. Commentary: Further rhetorical concerns. *J. Linguist. Anthropol.* 12:141–43

England NC. 2007. The influence of Maya-speaking linguists on the state of Mayan linguistics. In *Endangered Languages [Linguistische Berichte Sonderheft* 14], ed. P Austin, A Simpson, pp. 93–111. Hamburg: Buske

Errington J. 2003. Getting language rights: the rhetorics of language endangerment and loss. *Am. Anthropol.* 105:723–32

Fishman J. 1991. *Reversing Language Shift*. Clevedon: Multiling. Matters

Fishman J, ed. 2001. *Can Threatened Languages Be Saved?* Clevedon: Multiling. Matters

Fishman J. 2002. What a difference 40 years make! *J. Linguist. Anthropol.* 12:144–49

Florey M. 2001. Community aspirations towards language renewal among Moluccan migrants in the Netherlands. In *Language Maintenance for Endangered Languages: An Active Approach*, ed. D Bradley, M Bradley, pp. 257–271. London: Curzon

Florey M, ed. 2008. *Endangered Languages of Austronesia*. Oxford, UK: Oxford Univ. Press. In press

Florey M, Himmelmann NP. 2008. New directions in field linguistics: training strategies for language documentation in Indonesia. See Florey 2008. In press

Frawley W, Hill KG, Munro P, eds. 2002. *Making Dictionaries: Preserving Indigenous languages of the Americas*. Berkeley: Univ. Calif. Press

Gahl S, Garnsey SM. 2004. Knowledge of grammar, knowledge of usage: syntactic probabilities affect pronunciation variation. *Language* 80:748–75

Gahl S, Garnsey SM. 2006. Knowledge of grammar includes knowledge of syntactic probabilities. *Language* 82:405–10

Gal S. 1979. *Language Shift: Social Determinants of Linguistic Change in Bilingual Austria*. New York: Academic

Gippert J, Himmelmann NP, Mosel U, eds. 2006. *Essentials of Language Documentation*. Berlin: Mouton de Gruyter

Grace GW. 1981. *An Essay on Language*. Columbia, SC: Hornbeam

Grace GW. 1987. *The Linguistic Construction of Reality*. New York: Croom Helm

Grenoble LA, Whaley LJ. 2006. *Saving Languages*. Cambridge, UK: Cambridge Univ. Press

Grinevald C. 2003. Speakers and documentation of endangered languages. See Austin 2003, pp. 52–72

Hale K, Krauss M, Watahomigie L, Yamamoto A, Craig C, et al. 1992. Endangered languages. *Language* 68:1–42

Hill JH. 2002. "Expert rhetorics" in advocacy for endangered languages: Who is listening and what do they hear? *J. Linguist. Anthropol.* 12:119–33

Hill JH. 2006. The ethnography of language and language documentation. See Gippert et al. 2006, pp. 113–28

Himmelmann NP. 1996. Zum Aufbau von Sprachbeschreibungen. *Linguist. Berichte* 164:315–33

Himmelmann NP. 1998. Documentary and descriptive linguistics. *Linguistics* 36:161–95

Himmelmann NP. 2006. Language documentation: What is it and what is it good for? See Gippert et al. 2006, pp. 1–30

Himmelmann NP. 2008. Language endangerment scenarios: a case study from northern Central Sulawesi. See Florey 2008. In press

Hinton L, Hale K. 2001. *The Green Book of Language Revitalization in Practice*. San Diego: Academic

Hinton L, Weigel W. 2002. A dictionary for whom? Tensions between academic and nonacademic functions of bilingual dictionaries. In Frawley et al. 2002, pp. 155–70

Kloss H. 1969. *Grundfragen der Ethnopolitik im 20. Jahrhundert. Die Sprachgemeinschaften zwischen Recht und Gewalt*. Wien: Braumüller

Krauss M. 1992. The world's languages in crisis. *Language* 68:4–10

Kroskrity PV. 1993. *Language History and Identity: Ethnolinguistic Studies of the Arizona Tewa*. Tucson: Univ. Ariz. Press

Kulick D. 1992. *Language Shift and Cultural Reproduction: Socialization Self and Syn Syncretism in a Papua New Guinean Village*. Cambridge, UK: Cambridge Univ. Press

Lehmann C. 2001. Language documentation: a program. In *Aspects of Typology and Universals*, ed. W Bisang, pp. 83–97. Berlin: Akademie Verlag

Lehmann C. 2002. Structure of a comprehensive presentation of a language: with particular reference to the interface between text, grammar and lexicon. In *Basic Materials in Minority Languages 2002*, ed. T Tsunoda, pp. 5–33. Osaka: Osaka Gakuin Univ.

Lehmann C. 2003. Documentation of grammar. In *Lectures on Endangered Languages 4. From Kyoto Conference 2001*, ed. O Sakiyama, F Endo, H Watanabe, F Sasama, pp. 61–74. Osaka: Osaka Gakuin Univ.

McLaughlin F, Sall TS. 2001. The give and take of fieldwork: noun classes and other concerns. In Newman & Ratliff 2001, pp. 189–210

Millikan RG. 2005. *Language: A Biological Model*. Oxford: Oxford Univ. Press

Mosel U. 2006. Sketch grammar. In Gippert et al. 2006, pp. 301–9

Mühlhäusler P. 1985. Review of *Young People's Dyirbal* by A. Schmidt. *Linguistics* 23:1005–8

Mühlhäusler P. 1992. Preserving languages or language ecologies? A top-down approach to language survival. *Ocean. Linguist.* 31:163–80

Mühlhäusler P. 1996. *Linguistic Ecology. Language Change and Linguistic Imperialism in the Pacific Region*. London: Routledge

Musgrave S, Thieberger N. 2006. Ethical challenges in documentary linguistics. In *Selected Papers from the 2005 Conference of the Australian Linguistic Society*, ed. K Allan. **http://www.als.asn.au**

Newman P, Ratliff M, eds. 2001. *Linguistic Fieldwork*. Cambridge, UK: Cambridge Univ. Press

Newmeyer FJ. 2006. On Gahl and Garnsey on grammar and usage. *Language* 82:405–10

OREL. 2008. *Online resources for endangered languages*. **http://www.hrelp.org/languages/resources/orel/**

Pawley AK. 1985. On speech formulas and linguistic competence. *Lenguas Modernas* 12:84–104

Pawley AK. 1993. A language which defies description by ordinary means. In *The Role of Theory in Language Description*, ed. WA Foley, pp. 87–129. Berlin: de Gruyter

Pawley AK. 2007. Developments in the study of formulaic language since 1970: a personal view. In *Phraseology and Culture in English*, ed. P. Skandera, pp. 3–34. Berlin: Mouton de Gruyter

Pierrehumbert JB. 2001. Exemplar dynamics: word frequency lenition and contrast. In Bybee & Hopper 2001, pp. 137–57

Robins RH, Uhlenbeck EM, eds. 1991. *Endangered Languages*. Oxford/New York: Berg

Sasse HJ. 1992. Theory of language death. In *Language Death: Factual and Theoretical Explorations with Reference to East Africa*, ed. M. Brenzinger, pp. 7–30. Berlin: de Gruyter

Saussure F de. 1978 [1916]. *Cours de Linguistique Générale*, ed. T de Mauro. Paris: Payot

Schmidt A. 1985. *Young People's Dyirbal: An Example of Language Death from Australia*. Cambridge, UK: Cambridge Univ. Press

Silverstein M. 1976a. Hierarchy of features and ergativity. In *Grammatical Categories in Australian Languages*, ed. RMW Dixon, pp. 112–71. Canberra: AIAS

Silverstein M. 1976b. Shifters, linguistic categories, and cultural description. In *Meaning in Anthropology*, ed. KH Basso, HA Selby, pp. 11–55. Albuquerque: Univ. N. M. Press

Silverstein M. 1986. Classifiers, verb classifiers, and verbal categories. *Proc. Berkeley Linguist. Soc., 12th*, 12:497–514

UNESCO. 2003. *Language vitality and endangerment*. **http://www.unesco.org/culture/ich/doc/src/00120-EN.pdf**

Wilkins DP. 1992. Linguistic research under aboriginal control: a personal account of fieldwork in central Australia. *Aust. J. Linguist.* 12:171–200

Wilkins DP. 2000. Even with the best of intentions: some pitfalls in the fight for linguistic and cultural survival. In *As Linguas Amazoncas Hoje*, ed. F Queixalos, O Renault-Lescure Odile. São Paolo/Paris: Instituo Ambiental/IRD

Woodbury AC. 1998. Documenting rhetorical, aesthetic, and expressive loss in language shift. In *Endangered Languages*, ed. LA Grenoble, LJ Whaley, pp. 234–58. Cambridge: Cambridge Univ. Press

Woodbury AC. 2003. Defining documentary linguistics. See Austin 2003, pp. 35–51

Wray A. 2002. *Formulaic Language and the Lexicon*. Cambridge, UK: Cambridge Univ. Press

The Anthropology of Crime and Criminalization

Jane Schneider[1] and Peter Schneider[2]

[1]PhD Program in Anthropology, Graduate Center, City University of New York, New York, NY 10024; email: Schneider.jane@gc.cuny.edu

[2]Department of Anthropology and Sociology, Fordham University, Bronx, New York 10458; email: Schneider@fordham.edu

Annu. Rev. Anthropol. 2008. 37:351–73

First published online as a Review in Advance on June 24, 2008

The *Annual Review of Anthropology* is online at anthro.annualreviews.org

This article's doi: 10.1146/annurev.anthro.36.081406.094316

0084-6570/08/1021-0351$20.00

Key Words

crime talk, banditry, street gangs, trafficking, racketeering, mafias

Abstract

The ambiguity of the concept of crime is evident in the two strands of anthropological research covered in this review. One strand, the anthropology of criminalization, explores how state authorities, media, and citizen discourse define particular groups and practices as criminal, with prejudicial consequences. Examples are drawn from research on peasant rebellion, colonialism, youth, and racially or ethnically marked urban poor. The other strand traces ethnographic work on more or less organized illegal and predatory activity: banditry, rustling, trafficking, street gangs, and mafias. Although a criminalizing perspective tends to conflate these diverse forms of "organized" crime, in particular erasing the boundary between street gangs and drug trafficking, the forms have discrete histories and motivations. Their particularities, as well as their historical interactions, illuminate everyday responses to crime and suggest ways to put in perspective the "crime talk" of today, which borders on apocalyptic.

INTRODUCTION

Amidst the powerful transformations of industrial capitalism and imperialism in nineteenth-century Europe, the word "crime," already burdened by an uneasy mix of moral and legal implications, became the focus of the new science of criminology. Criminological discourse linked criminal activity—defined as a violation of public law and/or harm to public welfare—mainly to the "dangerous classes," whose uprooting, dispossession, congregation in cities, and potential for rebellion threatened the forming bourgeois, and colonial, social order (Beirne 1993). The resulting close association between criminality and marginalized elements of society was reinforced by the pioneering urban ethnographies of the Chicago School of sociology in the 1930s, creating a conceptual challenge that is difficult to overcome. Tending to criminalize powerless groups, above all their "deviant" male youth, such a construction inflates the significance of property crimes committed by have-nots while bracketing off other relevant phenomena for separate consideration, the following in particular: entrepreneurially creative, more-or-less professionalized white collar and organized crime (Braithwaite 1985, Reynolds 1995); crimes of state and capitalist enterprise whose harm can be horrific (Mattei & Nader 2008, Nordstrom 2007); illegal activities inexorably flowing from coercive or prohibitionist legal orders, possibly paving the way for normative change (Durkheim 1933, Naylor 2002); and the sneaky thrills of transgression that, although subject to cultural and spatial constraints, do not bear the stamp of any group and may have little to do with material acquisition (Hayward 2004).

Anthropologist editors of recent collections on crime have confronted these effects of power through a comparative and historical perspective. For Heyman & Smart (1999), "state-illegality relations," understood as interactive and changeable over time, underscore how states, "claiming to act in the name of collective opinion" (Greenhouse 2003, p. 276), selectively ignore or sponsor some illegal activities while vigorously prosecuting others that many consider licit or morally just. For Parnell (2003), crime and law, both social constructs, are created as people differentially experience wrenching historical processes. Produced along somewhat separate lines, the two interconnect in complex ways. For Comaroff & Comaroff (2006), the post–Cold War expansion of democratic governance and privatization of economic resources have generated a "dialectic" of law and disorder in which "crime and politics ... endlessly redefine each other" (p. 11). Although pertaining to first world countries, and quite markedly to the second world of the former Soviet Bloc, the interplay manifests itself most intensely in the third world's postcolonies, whose histories include having experienced the law as a cover for colonial predation.

Here, we pursue two lines of anthropological inquiry, both also informed by a sense of comparative history. One is the study of criminalization: the processes by which states, media, and fearful citizens define particular groups and practices as "criminal," evoking a threatening criminal imaginary. The other is ethnographic attention to forms of illegal predation—banditry, rustling, theft, racketeering, and trafficking—whose specific trajectories are entangled with the destabilizing effects of state-legitimated political economies. Taken together, these themes enable us to provide a concluding reflection on global crime, experienced as increasingly virulent and dangerous in many parts of our contemporary world and an issue that urgently awaits anthropology's contribution. (For want of space, we only touch on adjacent anthropological literatures on law, violence, racism, human rights, borders, prisons, policing, corruption, informal economies, youth, poverty and prostitution.)

PARADIGMS OF CRIMINOLOGY

The founding text of Western criminology, Beccaria's 1764 *Essay on Crimes and Punishments*, had, as its central purpose, disaggregating crime as "harm to society" from sin as "offense to God" and establishing a system of punishment that eschewed crowd-pleasing bodily pain and torture (Beirne 1993, pp. 22–26). Influenced by the Enlightenment idea of a social contract between sovereign and populace, the latter conceptualized as an aggregate of self-seeking individuals moved by material and sensual passions, Beccaria proposed that violators of the contract were equally responsible and deserved equal punishment proportionate to their crimes. Along with this prescription for punitive reform, he hinted at a "pre-sociological" theory of crime, interpreting theft as an outgrowth of the "misery and desperation" of the propertyless and warning about the "murky and mysterious rapture" of "turbulent mobs" (pp. 45–46).

Over the course of the nineteenth century, as European states began to collect statistics on their subjects, it became apparent that persons prosecuted for crimes came disproportionately from certain classes and regions. With his 1876 publication of *L'Uomo Delinquente* (*Criminal Man*), Italian army psychiatrist and self-styled anthropologist Cesare Lombroso, a leading advocate of positivist methods, introduced an hypothesis that would be debated in international congresses of criminal anthropology throughout the 1880s. For Lombroso and his followers the specific challenge was to explain the higher rate of crime in southern compared with northern Italy. They were aware of the miserable condition of the South's landless laborers and were prepared to explore every imaginable cause of their law-breaking, from climate to religion. Under the influence of the late Victorian social Darwinist hegemony, however, and alarmed by the growing immigrant communities in Italy's industrializing northern cities, they settled on a genetic factor. Like all of the "savage races," who "regard homicide as a mere incident, and as glorious in case it is the outcome of revenge," southern Italian men were said to harbor a congenital "Latin" weakness for fury, vengeance, carnal love, and drunkenness, making them, in effect, "born criminals" (quoted in Baker 1998, p. 58; see also Gibson 1998; Jones 1986, pp. 82–105; Rafter & Gibson 2004; Taylor et al. 1973).

Positivist criminology is not necessarily racist; criticized by contemporaries in France and Italy, Lombroso himself demoted the significance of biology in subsequent research (Beirne 1993, p. 154). Twentieth-century practitioners endlessly tested relations between deprivation and delinquent behavior. In the 1970s, however, Foucault's influential *Discipline and Punish* (1977) folded into a single trajectory even the "softest" variants, including a Marxist criminological tradition. Beccaria had begot Bentham, whose utopian prison design, the Panopticon, was a metaphor for the modern disciplinary society, in which ideas of prisoner rehabilitation coexisted with ideas of draconian punishment. Criminals could be monstrous or juridical subjects, possibly even exonerated by underlying circumstances. Either way, the crime rate did not diminish. Himself a prison reformer, Foucault detailed how the surveillance, categorizing, and labeling practices of the French penal authorities produced crime and made recidivism inevitable.

The civil rights and anticolonial movements of the 1960s and 1970s, so important to Foucault's thinking, underwrote a new, "critical criminology." Birmingham School researchers, for example, explored how "moral entrepreneurs," using the press and media, engineered public responses to youth delinquency that were vastly disproportionate to any "actual" danger, creating a politically resonant "moral panic" (Cohen 1972, Goode & Ben-Yehuda 1994, Hall et al. 1978; see also Scheingold 1991). The dynamics of fear, the effects of labeling, and the perspectives of incriminated persons entered research design (e.g., Chancer 2005). Notwithstanding this paradigm shift, however, the "modern" criminal justice systems of Western capitalist societies maintained an overall coherence in which abnormal psychology, theories of anomie and relative deprivation, "subculture theory," and the theory of labeling jockeyed for position within a broader set of arguments about whether to locate responsibility for crime with defective persons and families or with morbid social conditions (see Garland 2001). Either way, the crime problem involved the lower classes.

Displacing critical criminology is what Garland calls a "crime complex," emerging since the 1970s from the risks and insecurities of neoliberal capitalism and welfare state decline. In both the United States and England, which he compares, the rehabilitative ideal has given way to "expressive justice," evident in a populist language of condemnation and punishment. Criminologists place new emphasis on the symbolism of penal sanctions, while philosophers create rationales for retribution—the more so as an angry public, righteously demanding strong punishments, routinely evokes the figure of the victim and the victim's kin (Garland 2001, pp. 9–13). Simon, in *Governing through Crime* (2007), examines the implications of these changes for the United States, where the frayed safety net has left individuals ever more responsible for their own stability amid dramatic economic and demographic change. Criminals are those who refuse to "responsibilize" themselves, threatening national and local security. The effects have been devastating for poor, minority, and immigrant communities, but it is Simon's argument that all classes and groups are affected by the fear of crime—as targets of criminal justice, as "eager consumers" of public and private mechanisms for lowering risk, and as subjects of a government allowed to become more authoritarian. Wacquant (1999, 2002) draws similar conclusions for France.

CRIMINOLOGY AND ANTHROPOLOGY

Lombroso's scientific study of the "body, mind and habits" of the "born" criminal rested on the premise, familiar to early evolutionist anthropology, that crime among the "civilized races" was an "atavistic" throwback to "savage custom" (see Stocking 1987, p. 223). His *Criminal Woman* was translated into English in 1895; in 1911 Gina Lombroso, his daughter, made *Criminal Man* accessible through a compilation of its main ideas. Together these texts bestowed scientific authority on U.S. "criminal anthropologists" who, like Frederick Starr in 1897 and E.A. Hooten in 1927, explained the dispropor-

tionate incarceration of Blacks compared with native-born and foreign-born Whites in terms of Blacks' "natural" predisposition to criminal activity (Baker 1998, pp. 58–59; Jones 1986, pp. 108–25). This tawdry genealogy aside, until the 1950s, anthropological research was oriented toward small-scale societies in which deviance had a moral rather than legal status, and violators of norms were shamed, ridiculed, held up for retribution, or punished as witches or sorcerers. Such a framework seemed, at the time, to be an archaic inheritance from the past, destined to be superseded by modern criminal jurisprudence (e.g., Malinowski 1926; but see Comaroff & Comaroff 2004).

Much of what early ethnographers documented under the rubric of witchcraft and sorcery resonates with the crimes most feared today: assault, theft, burglary, and the perverse dissemination of addictive substances and pleasures. This is because predatory takings and seductions are not isomorphic with modern relations of property and markets but assume myriad forms, including the occult removal of bodily fluids and stores of food that underpin health and well-being, skills and harvests, trusting relationships and viable offspring—in short, good fortune itself (Favret-Saada 1980). Victims feel violated in their person, home, circle of dependents, and sense of security, regardless of the content of the loss or its cause. Underscoring this resonance is the parallel between criminologists' debates over criminal responsibility and Evans-Pritchard's (1937) classic effort to distinguish witchcraft from sorcery: Witches derive their power from an inherent condition they cannot control, whereas sorcerers' acts are deliberate.

More to the point is Geschiere's argument in *The Modernity of Witchcraft* (1997), that indigenous concepts of occult takings and seductions, far from residues of premodern "tradition," have developed with the dynamics of capital accumulation and political competition under postcolonial conditions. We see, below, that property crime may be justified in the name of equity, as a brake on sudden accumulations of wealth that appear to come from nowhere and taunt those whose fortunes are in decline. Conversely, it may be justified as clever enterpreneurship. Interpretations of the covert, magical depletion of another's vitality and vital relationships similarly reference moral criticisms of both (accumulative) greed and (leveling) envy and are a suitably ambiguous clue to rapidly transforming social hierarchies (e.g., Kelly 1994, Knauft 1985). With the expansion of neoliberal capitalism, the world has seen a coincident spike in both crime rates and accusations of witchcraft and sorcery, including a "spectacular rise" of "witch burnings" and "zombie conjurings" (Comaroff & Comaroff 1999, 2000).

ANTHROPOLOGY AND CRIMINALIZATION

In the 1960s and 1970s, as sociologists explored the dynamics of labeling and moral panic, anthropologists became engaged with peasant studies, a field influenced by Marxist social history. A key text at the time was Eric Hobsbawm's *Primitive Rebels* (1959), in which he introduced "social bandits": persons defined by the state as criminals who, however, spring from, represent, and are protected by peasant communities beset by crises of livelihood and oppression. Blurring the line between crime and rebellion, bandits were sheltered by villagers who identified with their defiance. In a controversial move, Hobsbawm described them as "prepolitical," driven by inchoate rage.

The social bandit concept, although developed primarily in relation to nineteenth-century agrarian struggles in the Mediterranean and Latin America, was soon applied to anticolonial resistance movements in Africa and Asia. Contributors to a volume edited by Crummey on African rebellion (1986) recount the careers of "heroic criminals" whose exploits were entangled with social protest but who were pejoratively labeled "bandits" by the authorities. In his chapter on early-twentieth-century Namibia, Gordon (1986), for example, reconstructs how the word "Bushman" arose as a criminalizing, blame-the-victim designation

for people who, having lost land to, and been compelled to work for, German settler farmers, absconded with these farmers' cattle and goats into "the bush."

Also widely read was E. P. Thompson's *Whigs and Hunters*, which blamed the intensification of poaching in eighteenth-century England on stiffened game law enforcement that favored landlords' claims to deer and ambition to enclose their estates. Crime, Thompson insisted, is problematic "when we simply take over the definitions of those who own property, control the state, and pass the laws which 'name' what shall be crimes" (1975, pp. 193–94). Linebaugh, Thompson's student, subsequently analyzed the records of persons taken to the hangman at Tyburn in London between 1750 and 1776. New overkill legislation had defined as theft punishable by death the customary artisanal and outworker practice of gleaning leftover materials from the shop floor (1991).

Like Hobsbawm, Thompson and his students inspired new ways of approaching crime in Europe's colonies and former colonies. One example is Colin Sumner (1982), a comparative criminologist of "underdevelopment" who considered *Whigs and Hunters* to be "possibly the best historical study of crime and justice in a metropolitan country." Sumner praised Thompson above all for demonstrating the "dwarfed" significance of poaching when compared with Britain's legally sanctioned slaving and military imperialism of the same epoch (p. 9). Africa's newly independent nations, he feared, were making criminality synonymous with poor youth gangs, conveniently overlooking what Ugandan criminologist Mashanga summarized as the "mass murders, massacres, genocide and general brutality and terrorism against civilians by those in power" (quoted on p. 2).

Guha, a pioneer of subaltern studies, criticized Hobsbawm for rendering banditry as "prepolitical." His 1983 book on peasant insurgency in Bengal does, however, respect both his and Thompson's insights into criminalization processes, presenting crime and rebellion as two contrasting "codes" for defining the same phenomenon. To peasants the dacoit Lodhas of western Bengal were mythic champions of justice who kidnapped or stole from greedy moneylenders, officials, and landlords; conversely, persons with property and power described the dacoits as terrifying threats to public order. In a similar vein, Martin (2003) traces how the elites and press of Morelos used Lombrosian criminal anthropology to construct Emiliano Zapata as an animalistic criminal rather than a leader of the Mexican revolution.

Thompson's (1967) "Time, Work Discipline, and Industrial Capitalism" informs Merry's (1998) overview of European colonizers' attempts to criminalize the everyday practices of their colonial subjects, applying the unfamiliar legal framework of "harm to society" as distinct from harm to specific others punishable through compensation. Ordinances typically interdicted gambling, drinking, and dancing; festivals; sexuality; and a "vagrant" lack of industrial discipline. In addition to synthesizing a range of case studies (e.g., Chanock 1985, Cole & Chaikin 1990, Cooper 1987, Gordon & Meggitt 1985, Roberts & Mann 1991, Snyder & Hay 1987), Merry uses Hawaiian court records to document a shift from the criminalization of "vice" to the severe interdiction of "work violations" as British and U.S. planters set up the sugar economy (Merry 1998, pp. 33–34). Several anthropologists of colonialism note a comparable stance toward the "dangerous classes" in the metropolitan societies from which the colonists hailed. Everywhere, it seemed, authorities were rattled by "outlaws" who hovered at the edges of protest; who disappeared into unfamiliar territory, including taverns and gambling halls; who, cloaked in disguises, evaded recognition; or who, as "vagrants," slipped across political jurisdictions, embarrassing the quest for orderly rule and labor productivity (e.g., Arnold 1985, Freitag 1985, Rafael 1999, Stoler 1985, Tolen 1991).

Like studies of peasants and colonial "others," anthropological research on contemporary youth flags the construction of criminality. Studies of hang-around or hooligan youth, and youth incivility in Europe, for example,

highlight the role of media in stigmatizing "naughty areas" where young people congregate and make note of older people's anger with the police for their seeming lack of urgency when called upon to intervene (Bailleau 1998, pp. 99–100; Girling et al. 1998, pp. 316–17; Martineau 2006; Pearson 1983). Recent essays on African youth (e.g., Cole 2004, Mains 2007, Walsh 2003, Weiss 2002) illustrate how such attitudes preclude understanding of "late modern" youth entrapment: the condition of having no work (or respected work), being unable to marry according to community expectations, and wallowing in unstructured time while surrounded by images of glittering consumer emporia. These conditions, not criminal intent, explain why so many young people hold polite society ransom to a "riotous return of the repressed" (Comaroff & Comaroff 2000, pp. 306–9).

Criminalizing processes are a familiar theme in literature on the United States, whose "war on drugs" has exposed pervasive racism. Rather than attempting to understand the crack "epidemic" of the 1980s in the context of economic restructuring and associated collapse of government services, the public and the authorities preferred to blame Black crack users and incarcerate them at rates 100 times higher than the more affluent (mostly White) users of powder cocaine—an approach that contributed not only to the tripling of the U.S. prison population since the 1970s, but also to the staggering, recent statistic that 1 in every 9 African American men between the ages of 20 and 34 is behind bars (see Bourgois 1995, 1997; Feldman 1994; Mauer 1999; Mullings 2003; Reinarman & Levine 1997; Tonry 1995). Today, images of methamphetamine fuel criminalizing sentiments against Mexican immigrants (Garriott 2008, Pine 2007), compounding what Inda (2006) discovered: that media and policy initiatives constructing Mexicans as illegal have elevated their risk of death in border crossings.

Caldeira's (2000) ethnography of crime and insecurity in São Paulo, Brazil, around 1990 highlights criminalization processes that shade into vigilantism. Coincident with the liberalization of the Brazilian economy, shift to democratic rule, and spread of drug use and trafficking, the city charted an increase in muggings, robberies, car-jackings, and kidnappings, but "crime talk" functioned mainly to stereotype poor *favela* dwellers, recent immigrants from the Northeast, youth, and women of dark complexion. Fear propelled a reshaping of the urban landscape, evident in aggressive slum clearance, the multiplication of "restricted enclaves" (see also Low 2001), and the view that human rights should bow before extra-legal violence on the part of the police or private security guards. Taussig, a witness to the 2001 paramilitary *limpieza* or cleansing of "criminals" from the lawless Cuaca Valley of Colombia, documents a similar contempt for the penal code and populist support for free-lance murder and brutality (2003, pp. 22–47).

As a criminalization process, vigilantism is ambiguous. For Linger (2003), the extrajudicial executions of democratic Brazil reenact the "wild power" of the now defunct military dictatorship, effective for instilling terror even when actual assaults are only sporadic. Scheper-Hughes (2006, p. 157), researching the phenomenon in a market town of Brazil's Northeast, cites the "complicity of the middle classes" in unleashing death squads to "sweep the streets of . . . social garbage." But the lower classes were collusive, too, illustrating what Caldeira calls "one of the most perverse ironies"—that supporters of police who kill "come from the same social group as the victims of the police: the poor residents of the neighborhoods in the peripheries" (2006, p. 109). According to Goldstein (2005), who studied "flexible self-help justice" in Cochabamba, the angry residents who episodically gather to lynch suspected criminals, tying them up for beatings or stonings, generally belong to the poorest barrios, are of indigenous origin, and have suffered mightily from Bolivia's neoliberal restructuring.

BANDITS AND RUSTLERS

Analyses of criminalization are at times constructionist—crime is a "danger on the borders . . . how we explain it and whom we blame are highly symptomatic of who we are and how we organize our relations with others" (Girling et al. 1998, p. 305)—at times exonerative: Criminal acts occur, but they are rooted in poverty and marginalization and thus overlap with legitimate resistance. Neither of these logics precludes the possibility that criminalization may respond to "actual" predations by more or less organized groups whose affiliates include rogue entrepreneurs, variously "crazy," cunning, swashbuckling, picaresque, violent. This approach to crime as an entrepreneurial force complicates the moral and political clarity of a straightforward criminalization paradigm and can be traced, in anthropology, to Blok's "The Peasant and the Brigand; Social Banditry Reconsidered" (1972).

Based on the archival and ethnographic research underlying his *The Mafia of a Sicilian Village* (1974), Blok challenged Hobsbawm's romanticism for obscuring how "social" bandits also prey on peasants, become landlords' retainers, and depend on landlords and corrupt officials for protection, all the while proferring a Robin Hood myth as ideology. [Hobsbawm, in response (1972, p. 504), claimed never to have generalized about all bandits, and to have always insisted that ambiguity was "the crucial fact of the bandit's social situation."] Following Blok, Vanderwood characterized Mexican bandits as "self interested individuals . . . who found themselves excluded from the possibilities and opportunities, not to mention the benefits, of society at large, and who promoted disorder as a lever to enter a system reserved for a few." In his account, bandits morphed into policemen and vice versa, both being "highly motivated opportunists . . . colorful, deadly, and interchangeable" (Vanderwood 1992, p. xvi; see also Gilbert 1990 and, for late 1800s Java, Nordholt & van Till 1999). Having interviewed road bandits along the multiple national borders of the Chad Basin, Roitman (2006) also eschews romantic imagery. The characters in question engaged in economic activities—smuggling, counterfeiting, cattle rustling, theft—that, although illegal, had redistributive effects and were widely considered "licit." Yet they did not think of themselves as Robin Hoods, agents of social justice or rebel proponents of an oppositional moral universe. Financed by local businessmen and protected by government agents, including impersonator-agents in counterfeit uniforms, they merely participated "in recognized modes of governing the economy," simultaneously feared and revered (p. 259).

Herzfeld's *The Poetics of Manhood* (1985), about a "nexus" of animal raiders in the highlands of Crete around 1980, belongs to this discussion. Throughout Crete's Turkish occupation (1669–1913), highlanders had descended to the plains to rustle the invaders' livestock; in addition, they stole from patron-landowners on whom they depended for grazing rights. But rivalry among rustlers further led to reciprocal raiding within the cluster of villages that constituted the nexus. Through narrating these close-to-home incidents, shepherds established a reputation for ferociously protecting their own property, at the same time recruiting allies and deflecting future raids. Significantly, during Herzfeld's fieldwork, some thieves acquired trucks for transporting stolen livestock to cities. The government in Athens had earlier tolerated Crete's "brigands," wary of otherwise delivering them to the Communist Party. Now, as it attempted to suppress this commerce, a handful of politicians subverted the effort, no doubt because they benefited from the proceeds (1985, pp. 33, 266–68).

Sant Cassia (1993), finding the Hobsbawm-Blok debate too narrow, raises a question about the kinds of rural structure that encourage a "psychology and sociology of terror" (p. 773). In nineteenth-century Cyprus, the site of his case study, the pastoral sector produced bandits when cultivators, backed by Ottoman power, put pressure on grazing land. Neither "primitive rebels," nor individual opportunists—nor, as Blok would have it, the henchmen of rural potentates—the outlaws in question moved between these tendencies, at the same time engaging in "an aggressive form of . . . adventurist capital accumulation" (p. 793). Regions whose histories embraced large estates, impoverished smallholder peasants, and pastoralist intermediaries were, Sant Cassia proposed, historically ripe for this dynamic, a suggestion supported by Poole's (1988, 1994) analysis of southern Peru's high provinces where, still today, "folkloric traditions, songs, legends, and spectacles . . . celebrate the livestock, horses, arms and masculine bravado"—in short, the performative violence—that constituted nineteenth-century local power (1994, pp. 18–19).

Sidel (1999) reiterates the myths surrounding a famed Filipino bandit of the 1950s and 1960s whose powers were believed to derive from magical amulets and Masonic charms. That this colorful personage respected local taboos against stealing peasants' draft animals, raping their women, and poisoning fish ponds was also in his favor. Ironically, however, he relied on the police and politicians for franchises and protection, as do today's car thieves, cattle rustlers, illegal loggers, lottery operators, bank robbers, kidnappers, and distributors of arms and drugs. Sidel characterizes the bandits (and gangsters) of the Philippines as close to mafiosi, defined, following Blok (1974), as "entrepreneurs who use private, formally unlicensed violence as a means of social control and economic accumulation" (Sidel 1999, pp. 71–72).

This reference to "mafia" points to the potential for everyday forms of rural banditry to scale up into organized crime formations of some historical consequence, even if the institutional scope and capacity of the Sicilian Mafia, considered below, is unusual. In a pioneering study of policing in newly independent Uganda, Tanner laid out the "complicated organization of the cattle raid," which required spies, persons to hide and feed the rustlers, others to perform religious rituals, and rear guards to protect the getaway. Raids conducted by 100+ men were not uncommon (1970, p. 54; see also Roitman 2006, p. 252). Such leaps of scale seem often to have involved increased competition for grazing land; expanding urban markets for wool, hides, or meat; and state-making processes that relied, locally, on the fire power or muscle of clientelistic factions. Fleisher's (2000) study of Kuria cattle raiders in northern Tanzania near Kenya adds the additional elements of available arms and porous national borders. Banditry, it seems, is consistently energized when states decommission their armies after wars.

Taken together, the writings on banditry support Gallant's (1999) argument regarding the interplay of "brigandage, piracy, capitalism and state formation." Brigands and pirates flourish in challenging geographies (rugged mountains and deserts, the high seas, remote borders, and now the Internet). Such difficult-to-police spaces are promising environments for outlaws, just as great river systems and fertile plains are congenial to state-makers. In addition to geography, large-scale processes of accumulation and enclosure undertaken by states, corporations, or other bodies that enjoy the cover of state-enforced law generate organized thievery. To the extent that whole populations are destabilized by these (often colonial) megatakings—Mattei & Nader (2008) refer to them as "plunder"—emergent bandits find ready audiences for the claim that theft is licit if not entirely just. One does not need the social bandit concept to appreciate the social as well as physical resources that shore up the infrastructures— the webs of protected routes and locales, tolerant neighbors, and corruptible officials—so important to "stealing back." According to Gallant (1999), this does not mean that pirates, bandits, and military adventurers are "fighting a rearguard action against the encroachment of the modern world"; like the pirates who became the privateers of empire, they belong to that world and are useful to it (p. 25). Taking the same long view, Tilly places "banditry, piracy, gangland rivalry, policing, and war-making . . . on the same continuum," defining states as "quintessential protection rackets with the advantage of legitimacy" (1985, p 169).

TRAFFICKERS AND GANGSTERS

Although borders render a state real, laws that specify what and who may cross are bound to be broken, as are laws that govern internal circulation. This is partly because such interdictions invite transgression. Depending on the relations in play, border guards (or their mimics) either bend to bribery and intimidation or intimidate and extort for a piece of the smugglers' action (see McMurray 2003; Roitman 2006, p. 254; Taussig 2003, p. 197). When particular interdictions enjoy a substantial moral consensus, possibly garnered through social and religious movements, or the activism of moral entrepreneurs, smuggling becomes more difficult and costly, although not impossible. What Scheper-Hughes (2000) aptly calls the "rotten trades"—widely condemned traffics in "orphans," sex workers, slaves, body parts, blood diamonds, endangered species, nuclear materials, antiquities, toxic waste—alas persist because of the gravitational pull of specific pockets of demand and the fast money to be made from supplying them.

Prohibitionist legislation is also at times the residue of struggles in which the interests and values of some are imposed on others, leading to restraints that lack consensus and cannot be enforced. Such conflicts of interest and values are obvious in the case of laws curtailing labor migration, a reality that makes people-smuggling inexorable (e.g., Kwong 1997). Similarly, thriving urban markets for affordable meat and music render the suppression of animal rustling and CD piracy quite challenging. Puritanical controls placed on potentially addictive substances and services—alcohol, tobacco, drugs, gambling, prostitution, and pornography—are particularly ineffectual, given the different ways these so-called vices intersect with everyday life. Governments swing between relaxed and extremely prohibitive stances, at times repressing them (as happened in Europe's colonies), but at other times permitting, and taxing, them. (Taxed vices may then become candidates for smuggling, e.g., cigarettes.)

In its most draconian moments (dating to the early twentieth-century), the United States has demonized both alcohol and drugs by associating them with feared or rejected groups, defunding public health approaches to addiction, and promoting prohibitionism internationally (Booth 1996, 2004; Courtwright 1995; Gootenberg 1999; Kerr 1985; Musto 1999; Musto & Korsmeyer 2002; Nadelmann 2008). Such over-reaching, captured by the expression "war on drugs," inevitably fosters an infrastructure for capital accumulation on the part of trafficking enterprises. It did so during the Prohibition era of the 1920s and is doing so again—in both instances facilitated by the deregulation of financial markets and the lavish availability of improved, and unsecured, firearms following World War I and the Cold War, respectively.

Such conjunctures are the foundation for some astonishingly hypocritical, covert alliances between traffickers and political actors. McCoy (2003) links anticommunist operatives of the Central Intelligence Agency (CIA), and its forerunner, the Office of Strategic Services (OSS), to Kuomintang opium traffickers in Southwest China and Burma, to successor traffickers of the Golden Triangle at the time of the Vietnam War, to Afghan warlords following the Soviet invasion, and cocaine smugglers in Central and South America. Rebel insurgents such as the Fuerzas Armadas Revolucionarias de Colombia (FARC) in Colombia, the Irish Republican Army (IRA) in Northern Ireland, and the Taliban in Afghanistan have raised money through trafficking, as have the counterinsurgents who would suppress them. Historians of opium in China and Southeast Asia document how the political manipulation of smuggling networks, dating to the time of the Opium Wars, tainted the British, Dutch, and Japanese, as well as the American, empires with scandal (e.g., Booth 1996; McCoy 2003; Meyer & Parssinen 1998, pp. 192–95; Rush 1990; Trocki 1990).

Reference to the war on drugs conjures the image of the kingpin, mythic figures like Kuhn Sa of Burma and Pablo Escobar of Colombia who own costly transportation assets (light aircraft, landing strips, speed boats, and fast cars) and who have the military capacity, in the form of heavily armed lieutenants and foot soldiers, to protect these assets from confiscation by authorities or hijacking by competitors (see McCoy 1999, Roldan 1999). According to Paoli, however, most couriers and smugglers of illegal drugs are small-scale and transient, leveraged mainly by personalized, kin-based networks, geographically extended through immigration. The enterprises they create, and the entrepreneurs who invest in them, rise and fall in a competitive maelstrom that is no less variegated and unstable than the whole of business history. Rarely does a coherent enterprise control the arc from source to destination (Paoli 2002, pp. 69–71; see also Chu 2000; Naylor 2002; Nordstrom 2007, pp. 139–46). The effects, however, are huge. Border regions, both between and within nation-states, and the rural producers of trafficked goods and services deserve attention (e.g., Morales 1989), as do "mafia syndicates" (see below). Here we consider cities.

Some cities, especially but not exclusively port or border cities, are culturally shaped by the presence of a thriving underworld. Eighteenth-century New Orleans, evolving in the interstices of an ambitious French Empire whose mercantilist edicts were unenforceable, is diagnostic. Dawdy (2008), introducing the concept "rogue colonialism," traces how the city's full-fledged smuggling economy created an atmosphere in which the swagger of lawbreakers was considered romantically anarchic—the dark and thrilling side of personal charisma—while an innuendo of criminal conspiracy enveloped the seats of power. Ethnographic descriptions of late-twentieth-century Hong Kong (Chu 2000), Vladivostok (Holzlehner 2007), Naples (Pardo 1996; Pine 2005), Palermo (Schneider & Schneider 2003), Marseilles (McCoy 2003), Mexico City (Lomnitz 2003), São Paulo (Caldeira 2000), Kingston (Gray 2003, Robotham 2003), and several Colombian cities (Roldan 2003, Taussig 2003) convey similar mysteries and poisons. So do accounts of Chicago in the 1920s and 1930s (Reynolds 1995).

With regard to illegal narcotics, a more general urban effect flows from the by-now-familiar interface between trafficking enterprises and street gangs—phenomena that are often conflated but have discrete roots and motivations. In a recent overview, Vigil (2003) attributes "urban violence and street gangs" to the multiple marginalizations of poor modern youth—second-generation migrants in first-world cities and, more broadly, victims of neoliberal restructuring. Constrained to live in the ugliest and least serviced of neighborhoods, they lack work and opportunity; their families are in crisis; and they are not reached by schools and other institutions of the wider society. Perhaps 10% of impoverished youth join sodalities of the street; an even smaller percent become the energized "crazy" heroes of these formations. But, from Port Moresby to Paris, gangs of "rascals" and "baddies" are a notable urban presence (see Cole 2004; Comaroff & Comaroff 2000, pp. 306–9; Dinnen 2001; Gigengack 1999, 2000; Gray 2003; Harriott 2003; Hunt et al. 2005; Pitts 2002; Vigil 2007; Weiss 2002).

At the core of many street gangs is a complex interplay of hustling for a livelihood and hanging out. Banter and gossip, their entertainment value raised by drinking beer, smoking dope, sniffing glue, throwing dice—also by consuming the images, music, and dance of transnational celebrity gangstas—create solidarity. So, too, do rites of initiation, enforced rules of loyalty and silence, insider nicknames, and embodied signs of belonging such as gestures, handshakes, tattoos or special clothing. Although girls may participate (Vigil 2003, p. 227), and there are known girl gangs (e.g., Venkatesh 1998), such groupings have usually been both male and masculinist, their members obliged—not unlike the sheep thieves of Crete—to prove themselves capable of defending their turf, attracting allies, and warding off disrespect. Leadership structures are at best incipient and related to age; membership coalesces and dissolves through time. That a sodality exists does, however, mitigate tensions surrounding competition for girlfriends, incursions from other gangs, and the everyday uncertainty of pulling off small-scale heists without being caught.

Transnational drug trafficking enterprises thrive on setting up retail operations in the territories of street gangs. Gang members constitute a pool of malleable labor and entrepreneurial talent (especially accessible if they are coethnics) in neighborhoods that are potential marketplaces. In addition, the erratic policing of gangs renders "their" corners and storefronts commercially suited for drive-by sales that service the narcotics habits of society's other classes. Jensen (2000), a critic of the South African Prevention of Organized Crime Act for eliding the difference between street gangs and traffickers, examines how the two interact in a Greater Capetown neighborhood.

His case begins with the 1990s scaling up of local Cape Flats gangs. Prisons—"universities of crime"—were integral to the process, fostering disciplined drug gangs and bestowing on inmates a network of criminal contacts, useful upon graduation. [In *Monster: The Autobiography of an L.A. Gang Member*, Shakur (1994) describes spending prison time poring over *The Godfather* for behavioral models (pp. 207–8)]. Unlike street gang members whose reputations were enhanced by confronting the police, affiliates of drug gangs had the wherewithal to bribe authorities. Regulating the street gangs' unruly quarrels, they ostentatiously donated money to local schools and causes. Venkatesh's (2000) study of a Chicago housing project similarly references "the ideology of the benevolent and socially inclined drug dealer who supports his community" (Jensen 2000, p. 108).

But malign processes are also evident. Cape Flats drug dealers exploited youthful gang members, remunerating them poorly for the risks they took in peddling narcotics to outsiders and breaking their limbs over transactions gone awry. Oriented toward their home territory, the youths lacked the translocal networks of the (somewhat older) dealers, not to mention their firepower. Some of them became addicted and in this condition were less able to defend themselves, their gang-mates, or their turf (Jensen 2000; see also Anderson 2002, Venkatesh 2000). Bourgois's (1997) ethnography of the 1980s circulation of crack cocaine in East Harlem attributes a rising incidence of homicides to unregulated market competition and distrust among and between dealers and youthful retailers, the latter hungry for the intoxicating allure of danger and opportunity to acquire symbols of opulence that are the rewards of trafficking (pp. 66–67).

Traffickers introduce new resources to the local arena: guns, most noticeably, but also gifts and money. They may, as noted above, self-consciously burnish an image of themselves as Robin Hood. Communities, broken by the ramifying effects of "conjugated" (multiple and overlapping) oppressions (Bourgois 1997), and aware that they are categorically criminalized by the wider society, may lionize these figures in popular culture. But the economic pressures of trafficking at the same time prompt street gang members to become more mercenary and uncaring. We find them burglarizing a relative's apartment when earlier they might have thieved only from outsiders; challenging neighbors' efforts to organize community policing; taking sexual advantage of women addicts desperate for money; and wielding more lethal weapons on their own streets (Anderson 2002; Gigengack 1999, 2000; Jensen 2000; Leeds 1996; Venkatesh 2000; see also Strathern 1992).

MAFIAS

Compared with trafficking enterprises and street gangs, crime syndicates are institutionalized and have deep histories. Yakuza is traceable to itinerant bands of gamblers and peddlers in early-eighteenth-century Japan (Kaplan & Dubro 2003); the Chinese Triads to secret societies that emerged from conditions of rural displacement and landlessness in southern Fujian province in the late eighteenth-century then spread to Guangdong, Taiwan, and abroad through Fujianese migrations (Chu 2000, Murray & Qin 1994). As it became a unified state after 1860, Italy, whose central and northern regions were the historic cradle of capitalism, produced not one but three crime syndicates south of Rome: the Neapolitan Camorra, the Calabrian 'Ndrangheta, and the Sicilian Mafia (Allum 2006, Paoli 2003). Beginning in the 1880s, fugitives from Italian

prosecutors and traffickers in contraband found shelter in the trans-Atlantic pathways of Sicilian immigration. Alcohol prohibition, in effect in the United States by constitutional amendment from 1919 to 1933, gave particular leverage to Sicilian mafiosi, who, competing successfully with Jewish, Irish, and other southern Italian bootleggers, were able to consolidate the Sicilian-American Mafia. Ironically, the famed Chicago School of urban sociology, although it produced numerous monographs on crime and delinquency in the 1920s and 1930s, turned a blind eye to organized crime, as if Al Capone were not a neighbor (Reynolds 1995). But Hollywood and the U.S. media paid close attention, which may be why the word mafia has become a generic for the syndicate form worldwide.

Mafia formation occurs when a group of people, by common accord, engages in a continuing, reproducible, conspiracy to monopolize illegal enterprises and use illegal means to control legal enterprises. Operating without the benefit of state-enforced contracts, those involved generate a durable subculture for creating trust and enforcing rules. Similar to street gangs, the cultural practices in question revolve around localized fraternal sodalities, replete with initiations, a founding myth, and esoteric marks of belonging. The resulting brotherhoods or metaphorical families—as Paoli (2003) shows, the salience of biological kinship varies with the mafia in question—are, however, considerably more structured than street gangs, having two or more leadership ranks, life-long membership, and intergenerational continuity. Leaders coordinate predations on the surrounding economy, distribute the take, regulate the use of violence, and support members and their (biological) families in the event of prosecution and imprisonment. From our experience in Sicily (Schneider & Schneider 2003), seconded by Holzlehner's (2007) description of the mafia in Vladivostok and Chu's of the Triads in Hong Kong (2000), we imagine that leaders also galvanize rounds of extravagant hospitality and transgressive horsing around.

Mafias are not readily accessible to ethnographers. In the 1960s, we, along with Blok, did personally know a few mafiosi in the Sicilian towns we studied. As Tilly wrote in the introduction to Blok's book, however, at the time we believed that "the Mafia supergang is a simplifying fiction, invented by publicists and by Fascist officials charged with eliminating Southern Italian lawlessness.... The sum of [the] actions [of mafiosi] makes up the phenomenon called *mafia*" (Tilly 1974, p. xiv). We were even skeptical that initiation rites existed; to acknowledge them gave too much credence to popular criminalizing models. Subsequent research by historians and journalists, and the recent depositions of justice collaborators, point, rather, to a well-formed fraternity with boundaries, structure, and goals and to a consistently practiced rite of entry, possibly learned from Freemasons in nineteenth-century prisons. In it, novices hold the burning image of a saint while their sponsor pricks their finger and, mixing the blood and ashes, exacts an oath of loyalty and secrecy until death (see Paoli 2003, Schneider & Schneider 2003).

Considering how so coherent an institution could develop, two ingredients—both also central to the histories of other mafias—seem decisive. First are ongoing, reliable flows of (urban as well as rural) revenue. Extortion—the exaction of tribute in exchange for peace—is the bread and butter of mafia syndicates, reflecting their historical connections with bandits or gangsters who threaten unprotected properties and businesses. Other typical enterprises include loan sharking; running, or servicing illegal businesses (prostitution and gambling are especially familiar); poaching the resources of legal businesses; regulating entry to crowded labor markets and other forms of labor racketeering; and brokering contracts for public works and construction.

The second ingredient is a precondition for the first: the collusive participation of the legitimate institutions of society, creating what Italians call "that wicked deal." Political connections, extending into the criminal justice sector, are especially necessary to avert arrests, abort

police investigations and trials, and procure licenses to conduct business and carry arms. Although mafia leaders deploy money bribes, they are more likely to ingratiate themselves with political, economic, and religious elites by mediating local elections, inviting officials to their banquets, and policing small-scale troublemakers in the name of peace. During the Cold War, the governments of Japan, Taiwan, France, Italy, and the United States sporadically prosecuted organized crime. Paradoxically, however, pieces of these governments also engaged mafia syndicates in the repression of "communism" and labor militancy, tolerating their criminal activities, including drug trafficking, and giving them a new lease on life (see Blok 1974; Block 1980, 1994; Chubb 1996; Kaplan & Dubro 2003; Maruko 2003; Murray & Qin 1994; Paoli 2003; Schneider & Schneider 2003).

Like secret societies generally, mafia brotherhoods are replicable over wide, transnational geographies without much coordination. Attempts at centralization are, if anything, a predictable source of internecine jealousy and conflict. Clearly, a far-flung network of chapters fostering mutual recognition is an asset for members who involve themselves in trafficking. Even the best capitalized kingpins, although avid cultivators of multisited connections, lack the advantage of instant fraternal support that mafia membership confers (Paoli 2002). Mafiosi, however, may have historically lagged behind well-capitalized businessmen-traffickers when it came to counterfeiting documents and laundering profits (see Chu 2000, pp. 107–21; Paoli 2002).

This distinction between organized crime formations anchored, on the one hand, in local racketeering and, on the other hand, in the globalized commerce of illegal goods and services resonates with Block's categories, applied to the American Mafia, of "power syndicate" and "enterprise syndicate" (1980, 1994), but the contrast should not be overdrawn. Already in the late 1800s, the Sicilian Mafia lived off extortion but simultaneously encouraged individual members to market stolen livestock in the regional capital and to transport morphine and heroin to the United States. Members of Japanese Yakuza, equally territorial in its historical formation, were also, historically, conduits for trafficked sex workers in much of Asia (Kaplan & Dubro 2003). Both commerce in opium and local racketeering are old and intertwined enterprises in the organized crime traditions of Taiwan, Hong Kong, Fujian Province, and overseas Chinese communities (Chu 2000, Murray & Qin 1994).

In the 1990s, Russia and the former Soviet Republics became sites of attention for "mafiologists." Not only did former Cold Warriors from East and West converge to produce a "mafiya" discourse—what Verdery calls a "conceptual mafia" (1996, p. 219; see also Wedel 2003)—but the abrupt privatization (or "grabitization," pp. 228–29) of state-owned resources in the absence of a supportive institutional matrix created a niche for protection racketeering. Sociologist Diego Gambetta, having developed a market model to account for the Sicilian Mafia—he called it a "private protection industry"—applied the same reasoning to Russia: When the state legislates private property without guaranteeing its integrity, mafiosi will surface to meet the demand for security (1993; see also Chu 2000, Chubb 1996, Varese 2001).

Ries (2002) offers a more complex ethnographic picture for Yaroslavl, northeast of Moscow, where, in the mid-1990s, everyone had a tale of lying, cheating, and swindling going on around them. Many (especially elderly) citizens were barely scraping by, but a minority flaunted sudden wealth. Pyramid schemes, in which a handful of early entrants raked in windfalls at the expense of thousands who lost their life savings, dramatized the unfairness. In such a context, people welcomed the *banditi* who offered a *krysha* or "roof." Businessmen (especially if they engaged in illegal transactions) depended on such "roofs" to collect debts, recover stolen goods, and enforce contractual arrangements; to ordinary citizens, the *banditi* (whose funerals they attended in droves) were providers of social and moral or-

der, the means by which avarice and corruption might be reined in. And yet, Ries suspected, the "demand" for protection was in part created by the protectors: Cut me in or it will be worse for you. Murders, bombings, and assassinations, reported in newspapers with no more fanfare than car accidents, impinged on everyday experience. Strikingly, those who offered "roofs" had a muscular pedigree. Just as in Volkov's (2002) analysis of "violent entrepreneurs in the making of Russian capitalism," a "bandit" Reis befriended belonged to the "sportsmeny," members of boxing clubs whose devotion to pumping iron was already a contribution to criminal enterprise during Soviet times.

Humphrey (1999) rejects interpretations that reduce the phenomenon of protection racketeering to a recent emergency of public order, pointing to another strand of Russian mafia history: the prerevolutionary bandits who, under Bolshevik repression in Siberian prisons, created a full-fledged fraternity, defined by allegiance to a "thieves' law" (see also Rawlingson 1997). Like the competing sportsmeny, the fractious descendants of this tradition display a predatory cultural energy not easily captured by a market model. Holzlehner (2007) encountered both strands in Vladivostok, initially through the larger–than-life etchings of murdered "godfathers" on the tombstones in the local cemetery, and subsequently through discovering how much of the local economy, culture, and politics they controlled.

LIVING WITH IT (OR AGAINST IT)

The varied forms of organized crime, coupled with processes of criminalization, raise the question how people cope when caught between these phenomena. That scaled-up syndicates and trafficking enterprises are entangled with states and legitimate business further ups the ante, adding the element of sponsored criminality. Ethnographic studies have captured an array of adjustments, shaped not only by the local interplay of banditry, gangsterism, protection racketeering, and trafficking, but also by local cultural practices and specific historical conjunctures.

In Merry's (1981) study of a "crime-ridden" Philadelphia neighborhood in the late 1970s, African American residents, although statistically more vulnerable to robberies and assaults than other groups, displayed the least fear, managing apprehension through "befriending even those they distrust and making sure not to treat them with suspicion and hostility, at least overtly" (p. 140). Reflecting their shared anger over the injustices that create desperate thieves, they even baked cookies for drug addicts whom they dared not invite into their homes. Reciprocally, youthful hustlers were disinclined to steal from people who acknowledged their existence as human beings, showed them respect, and did not "bother" them. As Siegel notes, referring to rural Indonesians of the same period, people know the local thieves, and how to guard against them, just as they know how to guard against ghosts (Siegel 1999, p. 221).

But, theft and assault became more threatening in Indonesia, as in many places, in the 1980s and 1990s. A Javanese lawyer interviewed by Pemberton (1999) referenced the transition this way: In the past, pickpockets and robbers lived by the principle "don't shit in your own room"; today they violently trespass their own rooms with the collaboration of the police. Tellingly, in the early 1980s, the word for thief, *maling*, which encompassed magical talents as well as professional skills, was supplemented by a new, Western-inspired word, *kriminalitas* (Pemberton 1999, pp. 207–8; Siegel 1999, p. 217). Barker (1999) studied the concomitant marginalization of a traditional community policing system in Bandung, the capital of Western Java, and its displacement, not by the state's surveillance apparatus so much as by resort to extralegal protectors. Exacting tribute on local businesses, these figures also engaged in reciprocities with ordinary people who, although deeply ambivalent toward them, wanted a "good relationship"; it was as if they owned the territory and everyone else paid rent (Barker 1999, p. 121).

Intimidated by both lawless youth and the police, and criminalized by outsiders, residents of the *favelas* studied by Caldeira (2000; see also Scheper-Hughes 2006) similarly turned to *justiceiros*—thuggish allies of gangs and drug dealers, redefined as heroes. Such "devil's bargains," in which the strongest medicine is harvested from the sickest source, are grist for the mill of protection rackets, as suggested by the *banditi* of Yaroslavl. In their desire to harness hidden powers and deflect revenge, the people who negotiate them also evoke the ethnography of witchcraft and sorcery.

Pardo's (1996) study of the *popolino* of Naples describes a set of guideposts for "managing existence," given that the Camorra is an entrenched institution in the Neapolitan region, thoroughly entwined with business and politics. People should exercise caution in relation to the vast illegal, and sometimes violent, "informal economy." In negotiating the gray areas of tax evasion, off-the-books lotteries, unwanted services, and informal usury, they should not proceed lightly, or in defiance of their wider moral framework of favors and reciprocities. Most important, they should mind their own business (Pardo 1996). These prescriptions, also applicable in Sicily, are captured by the famed code of *omertà*, whose meaning goes beyond "silence before the law," or refusal to snitch. At its core, *omertà* valorizes keeping to one's own affairs and ignoring, or pretending to ignore, the *embrogli*—the complicities and disputes—of others, in part out of fear of coming to know too much (Blok 1974; Pine 2005, 2008). This psychologically demanding practice of not knowing is particularly hard on women who, as the arbiters of family reputation, depend on evaluative gossip, especially with other women. Turning a blind eye, feigning ignorance, offers an escape from the twisted threads of responsibility, but it can be an awkward impediment to candid conversation (Schneider 2006, Siebert 1996).

From the late 1970s through the early 1990s, as Sicilian mafiosi became heavily involved in heroin refining and international drug trafficking, and in the midst of a bloody internecine war among mafia factions for control of that traffic, a broad-based antimafia social movement coalesced, whose main thrust was to insulate honest police and prosecutors from the wicked deal of corrupt criminal justice. Palermo and Naples, centers of this mobilization, witnessed the "turning" of many mafiosi into justice collaborators, rupturing *omertà*. A series of "maxi" trials, although controversial, convicted a number of powerful bosses without seriously violating the due process guarantees of Italy's democratic constitution or resorting to populist, criminalizing vigilantism (Jacquemet 1996, Jameison 2000, Paoli 2003, Schneider & Schneider 2003, Siebert 2003, Stille 1995). Incipient antimafia processes are evident in other cities similarly whipsawed by trafficking and violence, for example Kingston, as described by Johnson & Soeters (2008).

OUR TIMES: APOCALYPTIC CRIME TALK

To many observers, the nation-state system, losing its integrity in the face of neoliberal pressures and awash in errant AK-47s since the collapse of the Soviet Union, will soon be inundated by crime; Rapley (2006) calls this "remedievalization." Garland, citing increased rates of property crime, violent crime, and drug offences since the 1980s, characterizes late modern societies as "crime prone" (2001, pp. 90–93). Several recent books suggest a powerful new synergism of supply and demand for illegal commodities, including enslaved or commodified human beings: for example, journalist Glenny's investigation of trafficked women from Eastern Europe since the fall of Communism reported in *McMafia: Crime without Frontiers* (2008); and sociologist Hayward's (2004) analysis of postmodern consumer culture in which the desire for instant gratification, status, and recognition is often expressed through daring illegal adventurism and trophies shown off to peers.

Meanwhile, policy analysts worry about extreme disorder in "weak," postcolonial democracies such as Papua New Guinea (Dinnen 2001, Pitts 2002) and Jamaica (Harriott 2003),

where politicians deploy criminal gangs to get out (or suppress) the vote. Or they sound alarms regarding the Mara Salvatrucha gang, argued to be scaling up in El Salvador as a consequence of the deportation of members from Los Angeles prisons (Arana 2005). The Strategic Studies Institute of the U.S. Army War College warns that this, and similar "posses," constitute a "new urban insurgency" (Manwaring 2005). Scarier still, since 9/11, the criminal imaginary has exploded with images of traffickers interacting with terrorists (see Garriott 2008).

Nordstrom (2007), having pursued ethnographic research at multiple, specific junctures of outlaw networks, finds it is impossible to answer the question, "who are the criminals of the twenty-first-century?" The trillions of dollars that grease the "extrastate" economy "flow through millions of hands, thousands of institutions, and hundreds of borders," leaving us dangerously in the dark about "a series of power grids that shape the fundamental econo-political dynamics of the world today" (pp. xvi–xvii). And yet crime talk—now taking on an apocalyptic tone—is itself dangerous. Under its cover, governments engage in criminal violence, or authorize criminal proxies to "eradicate crime," using such terrifying methods as killing street children, abducting gang members, leaving the murdered bodies of presumed criminals at large for others to see, and dehumanizing victims of police brutality through media representations (Feldman 1994; Caldeira 2000; Chancer 2005; Inda 2006; Linger 2003; Scheper–Hughes 2006; Siegel 1998, 1999; Taussig 2003; Van der Kroef 1985). An anthropological approach, historically informed and comparative, challenges the paradigm of "governing through crime" in a few specific ways.

First, although mafia syndicates historically developed out of—and trafficking enterprises exploit—lower-level formations such as bands and gangs, these forms are not the same. To conflate them is to obscure the consistent reasons for banditry and gangsterism in the first place: political/demographic economies that wrench people from their accustomed places in the world, marginalize them in multiple ways, and leave them without a path to a decent existence. As Robotham (2003) argues for Jamaica, governments must again intervene in their societies, supported where possible by supranational institutions, to redress the vast disequilibria that have enriched a few while robbing millions over the past few decades. Second, however, it is problematic to leave our thinking in "primitive rebel" mode; the business history of violent entrepreneurship points equally to the need for states to recruit, train, and professionalize a criminal justice apparatus that is both capable of independent investigations and respectful of human rights.

Third, harmful predation is not new in the world; it has a vibrant past. Nor has it ever been separable from either local communities with all their apprehensions, desires, and jealousies, or the persons and clienteles of politicians, judges, bankers, religious authorities, secret service operatives, and others "above suspicion." In some times and places—the Prohibition era in the United States, the Cold War on several continents—entanglements with power have sabotaged criminal justice, decisively contributing to the virulence of organized crime. Transparency regarding sponsored criminality would seem an essential precondition for reducing the threats of the present. This is equally true of the kinds of crime to which anthropologists may have little access, but can follow through the courageous reporting of investigative journalists: white collar crime, the crimes of pharmaceutical and mining corporations, the crimes of states.

But fourth, and perhaps most telling, we should recognize something historically new in the war on drugs. This global set of arrangements, promoted by the United States, is not the first attempt to create a worldwide regime of interdictions based on moral as well as political concerns. Others, however—the nineteenth-century conventions against slavery and piracy—mobilized a much wider consensus (although both have undergone troubling reversals since the 1980s). Or, they flatly failed as did the attempt to prohibit alcohol in North America and around the world in the 1920s. That the United States has been able to organize a global prohibitionist regime against addictive narcotics, including marijuana, and in the face of multiple pressures to the contrary, in itself cries out for historical and comparative analysis (see Nadelmann 2008). Similar to the war on terror, the war on drugs is extraordinarily productive of what it is supposed to defeat, namely, criminal enterprise.

DISCLOSURE STATEMENT

The authors are not aware of any biases that might be perceived as affecting the objectivity of this review.

ACKNOWLEDGMENTS

An earlier draft of this article was read and discussed by members of a faculty seminar in the Anthropology PhD Program at CUNY. Convergent criticisms helped sharpen our thinking about the place of urban poverty in the Western history of ideas about crime. In addition, we benefited from the close reading and bibliographic suggestions of Will Garriott, Mary Gibson, Rob Gordon, Shirley Lindenbaum, and Jason Pine.

LITERATURE CITED

Allum F. 2006. *Camorristi, Politicians, and Businessmen: The Transformation of Organized Crime in Post-War Naples*. Leeds, UK: North. Univ. Press

Allum F, Siebert R, eds. 2003. *Organized Crime and the Challenge to Democracy*. London/New York: Routledge

Anderson E. 2002. *Code of the Street: Decency, Violence, and the Moral Life of the Inner City*. New York: Norton

Arana A. 2005. How the street gangs took Central America. *Foreign Aff.* 84(3):98–111

Arnold D. 1985. Crime and crime control in Madras, 1885–1947. See Yang 1985, pp. 62–68

Bailleau F. 1998. A crisis of youth or of juridical response? See Ruggiero et al. 1998, pp. 95–104

Baker LD. 1998. *From Savage to Negro: Anthropology and the Construction of Race, 1896–1954*. Berkeley/Los Angeles: Univ. Calif. Press

Barker J. 1999. Surveillance and territoriality in Bandung. See Rafael 1999, pp. 95–127

Beirne P. 1993. *Inventing Criminology: Essays on the Rise of "Homo Criminalis."* Albany: State Univ. N. Y. Press

Block AA. 1980. *East Side–West Side: Organizing Crime in New York, 1930–1950*. Cardiff, UK: Univ. Coll. Cardiff Press

Block AA. 1994. *Space, Time and Organized Crime*. New Brunswick, NJ: Transaction. 2 ed.

Blok A. 1972. The peasant and the brigand: social banditry reconsidered. *Comp. Stud. Soc. Hist.* 14:495–504

Blok A. 1974. *The Mafia of a Sicilian Village, 1860–1960: A Study of Violent Peasant Entrepreneurs*. New York: Harper and Row

Booth M. 1996. *Opium: A History*. London: Simon and Schuster

Booth M. 2004. *Cannabis: A History*. New York: St. Martin's Press

Bourgois P. 1995. *In Search of Respect: Selling Crack in El Barrio*. Cambridge, UK: Cambridge Univ. Press

Bourgois P. 1997. In search of Horatio Alger: culture and ideology in the crack economy. See Reinarman & Levine 1997, pp. 57–75

Braithwaite J. 1985. White collar. *Annu. Rev. Sociol.* 11:1–25

Caldeira TPR. 2000. *City of Walls: Crime, Segregation, and Citizenship in São Paulo*. Berkeley/Los Angeles: Univ. Calif. Press

Caldeira TPR. 2006. "I came to sabotage your reasoning!": violence and resignifications of justice in Brazil. See Comaroff & Comaroff 2006, pp. 102–50

Chancer L. 2005. *High-Profile Crimes: When Legal Cases Become Social Causes*. Chicago: Univ. Chicago Press

Chanock M. 1985. *Law, Custom, and Social Order: The Colonial Experience in Malawi and Zambia*. Cambridge, UK: Cambridge Univ. Press

Chu YK. 2000. *The Triads as Business*. London/New York: Routledge

Chubb J. 1996. The Mafia, the market and the state in Italy and Russia. *J. Mod. Hist.* 1:273–91

Cohen S. 1972. *Folk Devils and Moral Panics: The Creation of Mods and Rockers*. New York: St. Martin's Press

Cole J. 2004. Fresh contact in Tamatave, Madagascar: sex, money, and intergenerational transformation. *Am. Ethnol.* 31(4):573–88

Cole D, Chaikin I. 1990. *An Iron Hand Upon the People: The Law Against the Potlatch on the Northwest Coast*. Seattle: Univ. Wash. Press

Comaroff J, Comaroff JL. 1999. Occult economies and the violence of abstraction: notes from the South African postcolony. *Am. Ethnol.* 26:279–303

Comaroff J, Comaroff JL. 2000. Millenial capitalism: first thoughts on a second coming. *Publ. Cult.* 12(2):291–343

Comaroff JL, Comaroff J. 2004. Criminal justice, cultural justice: the limits of liberalism and the pragmatics of difference in the new South Africa. *Am. Ethnol.* 31:188–205

Comaroff J, Comaroff JL, eds. 2006. *Law and Disorder in the Postcolony*. Chicago/London: Univ. Chicago Press

Comaroff JL, Comaroff J. 2006. Law and disorder in the postcolony: an introduction. See Comaroff & Comaroff 2006, pp. 1–57

Cooper F. 1987. *On the African Waterfront: Urban Disorder and the Transformation of Work in Colonial Mombasa*. New Haven: Yale Univ. Press

Courtwright DT. 1995. The rise and fall and rise of cocaine in the United States. In *Consuming Habits: Drugs in History and Anthropology*, ed. J Goodman, PE Lovejoy, A Sherratt, pp. 206–29. London: Routledge

Crummey D. 1986. *Banditry, Rebellion and Social Protest in Africa*. London/Portsmouth, NH: J. Currey/Heinemann

Dawdy SL. 2008. *The Devil's Empire: Engineers, Rogues, and Creoles in French Colonial New Orleans, 1718–1769*. Chicago: Univ. Chicago Press

Dinnen S. 2001. *Law and Order in a Weak State: Crime and Politics in Papua New Guinea*. Honolulu: Univ. Hawaii Press

Durkheim E. 1933 [1893]. *The Division of Labor in Society*, transl. G Simpson. New York/London: Free Press/Macmillan

Evans-Pritchard EE. 1937. *Witchcraft, Oracles and Magic Among the Azande*. Oxford: Clarendon

Favret-Saada J. 1980. *Deadly Words: Witchcraft in the Bocage*. Cambridge, UK: Cambridge Univ. Press

Feldman A. 1994. On cultural anesthesia: from Desert Storm to Rodney King. *Am. Ethnol.* 21:404–18

Fleisher ML. 2000. Kuria cattle raiding: capitalist transformation, commoditization, and crime formation among an East African agro-pastoral people. *Comp. Stud. Soc. Hist.* 42:745–69

Foucault M. 1977. *Discipline and Punish: The Birth of the Prison*, transl. A Sheridan. New York: Pantheon

Freitag SB. 1985. Collective crime and authority in North India codification. See Yang 1985, pp. 140–63

Gallant TW. 1999. Brigandage, piracy, capitalism, and state formation: transnational crime from a historical world-systems perspective. See Heyman 1999, pp. 25–63

Gambetta D. 1993. *The Sicilian Mafia: The Business of Protection*. Cambridge, MA: Harvard Univ. Press

Garland D. 2001. *The Culture of Control: Crime and Social Order in Contemporary Society*. Chicago, IL: Univ. Chicago Press

Garriott W. 2008. *Terrorists, drug dealers and other criminals: the discourse of criminality and the paradox of hypersecurity*. Work. Pap., Dep. Anthropol., Princeton Univ.

Geschiere P. 1997. *The Modernity of Witchcraft: Politics, and the Occult in Postcolonial Africa*. Charlottesville: Univ. Va. Press

Gibson M. 1998. Race and southern "deviancy" in the writings of Italian criminologists, 1880–1920. In *Italy's "Southern Question": Orientalism in One Country*, ed. J Schneider, pp. 99–117. Oxford: Berg

Gigengack R. 1999. The Buca boys from metro Juàrez: leadership, gender and age in Mexico City's youthful street culture. *Etnofoor* 12(2):101–24

Gigengack R. 2000. La banda de Gari: the street community as a bundle of contradictions and paradoxes. *Focaal* 36:117–42

Gilbert JM. 1990. On the trail of Latin American bandits: a reexamination of peasant resistance. *Latin Am. Res. Rev.* 15:7–55

Girling E, Loader I, Sparks R. 1998. Crime and the sense of one's place: globalization, restructuring and insecurity in an English town. See Ruggiero et al. 1998, pp. 304–23

Glenny M. 2008. *McMafia: Crime without Frontiers*. London: Bodley Head

Goldstein DM. 2005. Flexible justice: neoliberal violence and "self-help" security in Bolivia. *Crit. Anthropol.* 25(4):389–411

Goode E, Ben-Yehuda N. 1994. *Moral Panics: The Social Construction of Deviance*. Malden, MA: Blackwell

Gootenberg P, ed. 1999. *Cocaine: Global Histories*. London/New York: Routledge

Gordon RJ. 1986. Bushman banditry in twentieth-century Namibia. See Crummey 1986, pp. 173–93

Gordon RJ, Meggitt MJ. 1985. *Law and Order in the New Guinea Highlands: Encounters with Enga*. Hanover, VT: Univ. Press N. Engl.

Gray O. 2003. Badness-honour. See Harriott 2003, pp. 13–47

Greenhouse CJ. 2003. Solidarity and objectivity. Re-reading Durkheim. See Parnell & Kane 2003, pp. 269–93

Guha R. 1983. *Elementary Aspects of Peasant Insurgency in Colonial India*. Delhi: Oxford Univ. Press

Hall S, Critcher C, Jefferson T, Clarke J, Roberts B. 1978. *Policing the Crisis: Mugging, the State and Law and Order*. New York: Holmes and Meier

Harriott A. 2003. The Jamaican crime problem: new developments and new challenges for public policy. See Harriott 2003, pp. 1–13

Harriott A, ed. 2003. *Understanding Crime in Jamaica: New Challenges for Public Policy*. Kingston: Univ. West Indies Press

Hayward KJ. 2004. *City Limits: Crime, Consumer Culture and the Urban Experience*. London: Glasshouse

Herzfeld M. 1985. *The Poetics of Manhood: Contest and Identity in a Cretan Mountain Village*. Princeton, NJ: Princeton Univ. Press

Heyman JMcC, ed. 1999. *States and Illegal Practices*. Oxford: Berg

Heyman JMcC, Smart A. 1999. States and illegal practices: an overview. See Heyman 1999, pp. 1–25

Hobsbawm E. 1959. *Primitive Rebels: Studies of Archaic Forms of Social Movement in the 19th and 20th Centuries.* Manchester, UK: Manchester Univ. Press

Hobsbawm E. 1972. Social bandits: reply (to Blok). *Comp. Stud. Soc. Hist.* 14(4):503–5

Holzlehner T. 2007. "The harder the rain, the tighter the roof": evolution of organized crime networks in the Russian Far East. *Sibirica* 6(2):51–86

Humphrey C. 1999. Russian protection rackets and the appropriation of law and order. See Heyman 1999, pp. 199–233

Hunt GP, MacKenzie K, Joe-Laidler K. 2005. Alcohol and masculinity. In *Drinking Cultures: Alcohol and Identity*, ed. TM Wilson, pp. 225–50. Oxford: Berg

Inda JX. 2006. *Targeting Immigrants: Government, Technology, and Ethics.* Oxford: Blackwell

Jacquemet M. 1996. *Credibility in Court: Communicative Practices in the Camorra Trials.* Cambridge, UK: Univ. Cambridge Press

Jameison A. 2000. *The Antimafia: Italy's Fight Against Organized Crime.* London: Macmillan

Jensen S. 2000. Of drug dealers and street gangs: power, mobility, and violence on the Cape Flats. *Focaal* 36:105–16

Johnson HN, Soeters JL. 2008. Jamaican dons, Italian godfathers and the chances of a "reversible destiny". *Polit. Stud.* 56(1):166–91

Jones DA. 1986. *History of Criminology: A Philosophical Perspective.* New York/Westport, CT: Greenwood

Kaplan DE, Dubro A. 2003. *Yakuza: Japan's Criminal Underworld.* Berkeley/Los Angeles: Univ. Calif. Press

Kelly RC. 1994. *Constructing Inequality: The Fabrication of a Hierarchy of Virtue Among the Etoro.* Ann Arbor: Univ. Mich. Press

Kerr KA. 1985. *Organized for Prohibition: A New History of the Anti-Saloon League.* New Haven, CT: Yale Univ. Press

Knauft BM. 1985. *Good Company and Violence: Sorcery and Social Action in Lowland New Guinea Society.* Berkeley/Los Angeles: Univ. Calif. Press

Kwong P. 1997. *Forbidden Workers: Illegal Chinese Immigrants and American Labor.* New York: Norton

Leeds E. 1996. Cocaine and parallel polities in the Brazilian urban periphery. *Latin Am. Res. Rev.* 31:47–83

Linebaugh P. 1991. *The London Hanged: Crime and Civil Society in the Eighteenth-Century.* London: Penguin

Linger DT. 2003. Wild power in postmilitary Brazil. See Parnell & Kane 2003, pp. 99–125

Lomnitz C. 2003. The depreciation of life during Mexico City's transition into "the crisis." See Schneider & Susser 2003, pp. 47–71

Low S. 2001. The edge and the center: gated communities and the discourse of urban fear. *Am. Anthropol.* 103(1):45–58

Mains D. 2007. Neoliberal times: progress, boredom, and shame among young men in urban Ethiopia. *Am. Ethnol.* 34(4):659–74

Malinowski B. 1926. *Crime and Custom in Savage Society.* London: Kegan Paul/Trench/Trubner

Manwaring MG. 2005. *Street Gangs: The New Urban Insurgency.* Carlisle PA: Strat. Stud. Inst., U.S. Army War Coll. **http://www.carlisle.army.mil/ssi**

Martin J. 2003. Criminal instabilities: narrative interruptions and the politics of criminality. In *Crime's Power: Anthropology and the Ethnography of Crime*, ed. PC Parnell, SC Kane, pp. 173–95. New York: Palgrave Macmillan

Martineau E. 2006. *Too much tolererance: hang-around youth, public space, and the problem of freedom in the Netherlands.* PhD diss. Grad. Cent., City Univ. N. Y.

Maruko E. 2003. Mediated democracy: *Yakuza* and Japanese political leadership. See Allum & Siebert 2003, pp. 202–19

Mattei U, Nader L. 2008. *Plunder: When the Rule of Law is Illegal.* Malden, MA/Oxford: Blackwell

Mauer M. 1999. *Race to Incarcerate.* New York: New Press

McCoy AW. 1999. Requiem for a drug lord: state and commodity in the career of Khun Sa. See Heyman 1999, pp. 129–69

McCoy AW. 2003 (1972). *The Politics of Heroin: CIA Complicity in the Global Drug Trade (Afghanistan, Southeast Asia, Central America, Colombia).* Chicago: Lawrence Hill

McMurray DA. 2003. Recognition of state authority as a cost of involvement in Moroccan border crime. See Parnell & Kane 2003, pp. 125–45

Merry SE. 1981. *Urban Danger: Life in a Neighborhood of Strangers*. Philadelphia: Temple Univ. Press

Merry SE. 1998. The criminalization of everyday life. In *Everyday Practices and Trouble Cases*, ed. A Sarat, M Constable, D Engel, V Hans, S Lawrence, pp. 14–40. Evanston, IL: Northwest. Univ. Press

Meyer K, Parssinen T. 1998. *Webs of Smoke: Smugglers, Warlords, Spies, and the History of the International Drug Trade*. Lanham, MD: Rowman and Littlefield

Morales E. 1989. *Cocaine: White Gold Rush in Peru*. Tucson/London: Univ. Ariz. Press

Mullings L. 2003. The prison-industrial complex in the contemporary United States. See Schneider & Susser 2003, pp. 173–203

Murray DH, Qin B. 1994. *Origins of the Tiandihui: The Chinese Triads in Legend and History*. Stanford, CA: Stanford Univ. Press

Musto D. 1999 [1973]. *The American Disease: Origins of Narcotic Control*. New York/Oxford: Oxford Univ. Press

Musto D, Korsmeyer P. 2002. *The Quest for Drug Control: Politics and Federal Policy in a Period of Increasing Substance Abuse, 1963–1981*. New Haven: Yale Univ. Press

Nadelmann EA. 2008. Global prohibition regimes: the evolution of norms in international society. In *Transnational Crime*, ed. N Passas, pp. 1–25. **http://www.criminology.fsu.edu/transcrime/ articles/GlobalProhibitionRegimes.htm**

Nader L. 2003. Crime as a category. See Parnell & Kane 2003, pp. 55–77

Naylor TR. 2002. *Wages of Crime: Black Markets, Illegal Finance, and the Underworld Economy*. Ithaca: Cornell Univ. Press

Nordholt HS, van Till M. 1999. Colonial criminals in Java, 1870–1910. See Rafael 1999, pp. 47–70

Nordstrom C. 2007. *Global Outlaws: Crime, Money, and Power in the Contemporary World*. Berkeley/Los Angeles: Univ. Calif. Press

Paoli L. 2002. The paradoxes of organized crime. *Crime Law Soc. Change* 37:51–97

Paoli L. 2003. *Mafia Brotherhoods: Organized Crime, Italian Style*. Oxford, UK: Oxford Univ. Press

Pardo I. 1996. *Managing Existence in Naples*. Cambridge, UK: Cambridge Univ. Press

Parnell PC. 2003. Introduction. See Parnell & Kane 2003, pp. 1–33

Parnell PC, Kane SC, eds. 2003. *Crime's Power: Anthropologists and the Ethnography of Crime*. New York: Palgrave Macmillan

Pearson G. 1983. *Hooligan: A History of Respectable Fears*. Basingstoke: Macmillan

Pemberton J. 1999. Open secrets: excerpts from conversations with a Javanese lawyer, and a comment. See Rafael 1999, pp. 193–209

Pine JA. 2005. *Omertà: the melodramatic aesthetic and its moral/political economy in Naples*. PhD diss. Univ. Tex. Austin

Pine JA. 2007. Economy of speed: the new narco-capitalism. *Public Cult.* 19(2):357–66

Pine JA. 2008. Contact, complicity, conspiracy: affective communities and economies of affect in Naples. *Law, Culture Humanit.* 4:201–23

Pitts M. 2002. *Crime, Corruption and Capacity in Papua New Guinea*. Canberra: Aust. Natl. Univ., Asia Pac. Press

Poole D. 1988. Landscapes of power in a cattle-rustling culture of southern Andean Peru. *Dialect. Anthropol.* 12:367–98

Poole D. 1994. Introduction: anthropological perspectives on violence and culture–a view from the Peruvian high provinces. In *Unruly Order: Violence, Power, and Cultural Identity in the High Provinces of Southern Peru*, ed. D Poole, pp. 1–31. Boulder, CO/San Francisco/Oxford, UK: Westview

Rafael VL, ed. 1999. *Figures of Criminality in Indonesia, the Philippines, and Colonial Vietnam*. Ithaca, NY: Cornell Univ. Press

Rafael VL. 1999. Introduction: criminality and its others. See Rafael 1999, pp. 9–23

Rafter NH, Gibson M. 2004 [1893]. Translators' introduction. In *Criminal Woman, The Prostitute and the Normal Woman*, ed. C Lombroso, G Ferrero, pp. 3–35. Transl. NH Rafter, M Gibson. Durham/London: Duke Univ. Press

Rapley J. 2006. The new middle ages. *Foreign Aff.* 85(3):95–105

Rawlingson P. 1997. Russian organized crime: a brief history. In *Russian Organized Crime: A New Threat?* ed. P Williams, pp. 28–51. London: Frank Cass

Reinarman CR, Levine HG, ed. 1997. *Crack in America: Demon Drugs and Social Justice*. Berkeley/Los Angeles: Univ. Calif. Press

Reynolds M. 1995. *From Gangs to Gangsters: How American Sociology Organized Crime, 1918–1994*. Albany, NY: Harrow and Heston

Ries N. 2002. "Honest" bandits and "warped people": Russian narratives about money, corruption, and moral decay. In *Ethnography in Unstable Places: Everyday Lives in the Context of Dramatic Political Change*, ed. CJ Greenhouse, E Mertz, KB Warren, pp. 276–315. Durham, NC: Duke Univ. Press

Roberts R, Mann K. 1991. *Law in Colonial Africa*. Portsmouth, NH: Heinemann

Robotham D. 2003. Crime and public policy in Jamaica. See Harriott 2003, pp. 197–239

Roitman J. 2006. The ethics of illegality in the Chad Basin. See Comaroff & Comaroff 2006, pp. 247–73

Roldan M. 1999. Colombia: cocaine and the "miracle" of modernity in Medellin. See Gootenberg 1999, pp. 165–82

Roldan M. 2003. Wounded Medellin: narcotics traffic against a backdrop of industrial decline. See Schneider & Susser 2003, pp. 129–49

Ruggiero V, South N, Taylor I, eds. 1998. *The New European Criminology: Crime and Social Order in Europe*. London/New York: Routledge

Rush JR. 1990. *Opium to Java: Revenue Farming and Chinese Enterprise in Colonial Indonesia, 1860–1910*. Ithaca/London: Cornell Univ. Press

Sant Cassia P. 1993. Banditry, myth and terror in Cyprus and other Mediterranean societies. *Comp. Stud. Soc. Hist.* 35:773–95

Scheingold SA. 1991. *The Politics of Street Crime: Criminal Process and Cultural Obsession*. Philadelphia: Temple Univ. Press

Scheper-Hughes N. 2000. The global traffic in human organs. *Curr. Anthropol.* 41:191–224

Scheper-Hughes N. 2006. Death squads and democracy in Northeast Brazil. See Comaroff & Comaroff 2006, pp. 150–88

Schneider J. 2006. Women in the mob. *Glob. Crime* 7(1):127–33

Schneider J, Schneider P. 2003. *Reversible Destiny: Mafia, Antimafia, and the Struggle for Palermo*. Berkeley/Los Angeles: Univ. Calif. Press

Schneider J, Susser I, eds. 2003. *Wounded Cities: Destruction and Reconstruction in a Globalized World*. Oxford: Berg

Shakur S (aka Monster Kody Scott). 1994. *Monster: The Autobiography of an L.A. Gang Member*. New York: Penguin

Sidel J. 1999. The usual suspects: Nardong Putik, Don Pepe Oyson, and Robin Hood. See Rafael 1999, pp. 70–95

Siebert R. 1996. *Secrets of Life and Death: Women and the Mafia*, transl. L Heron. London/New York: Verso

Siebert R. 2003. Mafia and anti-Mafia: the implications for everyday life. See Allum & Siebert 2003, pp. 39–55

Siegel JT. 1998. *A New Criminal Type in Jakarta: Counter-Revolution Today*. Durham/London: Duke Univ. Press

Siegel JT. 1999. A new criminal type in Jakarta: the nationalization of death. See Rafael 1999, pp. 210–31

Simon J. 2007. *Governing Through Crime: How the War on Crime Transformed American Democracy and Created a Culture of Fear*. Oxford/New York: Oxford Univ. Press

Snyder F, Hay D. 1987. *Law, Labour, and Crime: An Historical Perspective*. London/New York: Tavistock

Stille A. 1995. *Excellent Cadavers: The Mafia and the Death of the First Italian Republic*. New York: Vintage

Stocking GW. 1987. *Victorian Anthropology*. New York: Free Press

Stoler A. 1985. Perceptions of protest: defining the dangerous in colonial Sumatra. *Am. Ethnol.* 12:642–58

Strathern A. 1992. Let the bow go down. In *Expanding States and Indigenous Warfare*, ed. RB Ferguson, NL Whitehead, pp. 230–50. Santa Fe, NM: Sch. Am. Res. Press

Sumner C. 1982. Crime, justice and underdevelopment: beyond modernization theory. In *Crime, Justice and Underdevelopment*, ed. C Sumner, pp. 1–40. London: Heinemann

Tanner RES. 1970. *Three Studies of East African Criminology: Crime in East Africa*. Uppsala: Scand. Inst. Afr. Stud.

Taussig MT. 2003. *Law in a Lawless Land: Diary of a Limpieza in Colombia*. New York: New Press

Taylor I, Walton P, Young J. 1973. *The New Criminology: For a Social Theory of Deviance*. New York: Harper Torchbooks

Thompson EP. 1967. Time, work-discipline, and industrial capitalism. *Past Present* 38:56–97

Thompson EP. 1975. *Whigs and Hunters: The Origin of the Black Act*. London: Penguin

Tilly C. 1974. Foreword. In *The Mafia of a Sicilian Village*, A Blok, pp. xiii–xxiv. Oxford: Basil Blackwell

Tilly C. 1985. The state as organized crime. In *Bringing the State Back In*, ed. P Evans, D Rueschemeyer, T Skocpol, pp. 169–91. Cambridge, UK: Cambridge Univ. Press

Tolen RJ. 1991. Colonizing and transforming the criminal tribesman: the Salvation Army in British India. *Am. Ethnol.* 18:106–26

Tonry M. 1995. *Malign Neglect: Race, Crime, and Punishment in America*. New York: Oxford Univ. Press

Trocki CA. 1990. *Opium and Empire: Chinese Society in Colonial Singapore, 1800–1910*. Ithaca/London: Cornell Univ. Press

Van Der Kroef JM. 1985. "Petrus:" patterns of prophylactic murder in Indonesia. *Asian Survey* 25:745–59

Vanderwood PJ. 1992. *Disorder and Progress: Bandits, Police and Mexican Development*. Wilmington, DE: Sch. Resour. Books

Varese F. 2001. *The Russian Mafia: Private Protection in a New Market Economy*. Oxford: Oxford Univ. Press

Venkatesh SA. 1998. Gender and outlaw capitalism: a historical account of the black sisters united "Girl Gang." *Signs* 23:683–709

Venkatesh SA. 2000. *American Project: The Rise and Fall of a Modern Ghetto*. Cambridge, MA: Harvard Univ. Press

Verdery KV. 1996. *What Was Socialism and What Comes Next?* Princeton, NJ: Princeton Univ. Press

Vigil JD. 2003. Urban violence and street gangs. *Annu. Rev. Anthropol.* 32:225–42

Vigil JD. 2007. *The Projects: Gang and Non-Gang Families in East Los Angeles*. Austin: Univ. Tex. Press

Volkov V. 2002. *Violent Entrepreneurs: The Use of Force in the Making of Russian Capitalism*. Ithaca, NY: Cornell Univ. Press

Wacquant L. 1999. How penal common sense comes to Europeans: notes on the transatlantic diffusion of neoliberal doxa. *Eur. Soc.* 1(3):319–52

Wacquant L. 2002. *Prisons of poverty*. Minneapolis: Univ. Minn. Press

Walsh A. 2003. "Hot money" and daring consumption in a northern Malagasy sapphire-mining town. *Am. Ethnol.* 30(2):290–305

Wedel JR. 2003. Mafia without malfeasance, clans without crime: the criminality conundrum. See Parnell & Kane 2003, pp. 221–45

Weiss B. 2002. Thug realism: inhabiting fantasy in urban Tanzania. *Cult. Anthropol.* 17(1):93–124

Yang AA, ed. 1985. *Crime and Criminality in British India*. Tucson: Univ. Ariz. Press

Alternative Kinship, Marriage, and Reproduction

Nancy E. Levine

Department of Anthropology, University of California, Los Angeles, California 90095-1553;
email: nelevine@anthro.ucla.edu

Annu. Rev. Anthropol. 2008. 37:375–89

First published online as a Review in Advance on
June 24, 2008

The *Annual Review of Anthropology* is online at
anthro.annualreviews.org

This article's doi:
10.1146/annurev.anthro.37.081407.085120

Key Words

family, new reproductive technologies, gay, lesbian

Abstract

This review examines the implications of new kinship practices for anthropological theory, with a special focus on recent research in gay and lesbian kinship and assisted reproduction. The article begins with an account of the theoretical contexts in which kinship studies have been conducted and a brief survey of some of the older literature on alternative systems of marriage and family formation in preindustrial and modern societies. The emphasis then turns to current discussions of how gay men and lesbian women are creating meaningful networks of kin and families and the ways in which these practices both follow and challenge traditional expectations for family life. The final section surveys the ways in which the new reproductive technologies have been utilized in Euro-American societies and how cultural ideas and values concerning kin relationships have shaped the transfer of these technologies to and their utilization in other societies.

INTRODUCTION:
THEORETICAL CONTEXTS

Anthropology, in its modernist heyday, combined research on exotic, preindustrial societies with a search for what was traditional, normative, and internally concordant. These emphases were especially prominent in studies of kinship systems. The classic kinship studies displayed impeccable detail; they were closely argued and highly abstract and demanded technical knowledge of abstruse theory. Their concerns were systems and structures, integration and stability, and groups and the relationships between groups, conceptualized in terms of paradigms of descent and alliance. Beginning in the 1950s, kinship theory began to be subjected to a series of critiques (Bloch 1973; Goody 1973; Kuper 1982; Leach 1961, 1968; Lewis 1965; Needham 1971; Worsley 1956), of which the most devastating and most productive for future research were published by Schneider (1965, 1972, 1980, 1984).

In his papers and in two influential books, Schneider moved the study of kinship from a focus on function, social structure, rules, and types of societies to a study of culture and meaning, essentially, what kin relationships mean to people (Carsten 2004). His influence, which was felt most strongly in the United States, motivated new ethnographic research and analyses of Euro-American and other societies. Schneider's key arguments were simply stated. For the Americans he surveyed, kinship was based on ideas about "shared bio-genetic substance" and "enduring diffuse solidarity." These elements provided the basis for three categories of kin—relatives by blood, in law, and in nature—which derived from the master symbol of sexual intercourse and linked parents to their children and husbands to their wives. Not surprisingly, as subsequent research has shown, these broad generalizations do not fit Americans of all classes, ethnicities, and sexual identities equally well (Peletz 1995, p. 347; Schneider 1980, p. 122; Smith 1987; Weston 1991; Yanagisako 1978). Schneider (1972) went on to argue that ideas about kinship were part of

two more general categories of American culture: the "order of nature" and the "order of law."

Schneider also contended that Americans' references to biology in their discussions of family and relatives had no necessary relationship to biology as a natural process (1972, p. 45), but rather were cultural constructs and essentially symbolic (1980, p. 116), arguments that were consistent with the emerging theory of culture at the time. Accordingly, he criticized assumptions that kinship is based, in a literal sense, on the facts of biology and human reproduction and that it should be treated as a distinctive domain of social relationships, assumptions that were prevalent among the era's leading kinship theorists (for example, Fortes 1969, pp. 220–29; Fortes 1972, 1978; Gellner 1963; Scheffler 1973, p. 749). Questions about the universality of biological and genealogical reckoning had been raised at the very outset of cross-cultural kinship analyses (Malinowski 1913, 1929; Westermarck 1922) and were still being debated at mid-century, most notably the ideas about procreation held in Australia and the Trobriand Islands (Delaney 1986; Leach 1966; Montague 1971; Spiro 1968; Weiner 1976, pp. 121–23). Schneider contended that the view that "blood was thicker than water" naively reflected Euro-American thinking on kinship and was inapplicable to societies other than our own. He went on to suggest that kinship was a figment of the anthropological imagination and an artifact of a bad theory and that comparative studies of kinship had to be based on "some other, firm ground, or abandoned" (Schneider 1980, p. 119; 1984, p. 177). It is testament to the power of Schneider's arguments, the weight of his accusation of ethnocentrism, and his influence in the field that this critique led to what has been described as a 20-year decline in kinship studies (Peletz 1995; Stone 2001, 2006) and also undermined the classic project of cross-cultural comparison (Carsten 2004, p. 22).

Kinship has seen a resurgence in recent years, spurred partly by interest in allied fields, such as studies of gender, sexuality, demography, social history, and evolutionary theory, and by new research. The classic kinship studies that have fallen into desuetude were based on intensive participant observation conducted in nonwestern preindustrial societies, sometimes described as kin-based societies, where kin statuses were seen as all-encompassing and fixed irrevocably by birth. By contrast, more recent studies have focused on globalizing or developed societies and have stressed the fluid and contingent nature of kin relationships and how they are instituted and nurtured over time through various actions. In place of system and structure, the new analyses stress practice and process (Carsten 1995; Howell 2003; Stone 2006, p. 21; Weismantel 1995). The research considered here has thus been sparked by both paradigmatic and topical shifts: changes in marriage, reproduction, and families in highly developed societies; responses to the new reproductive technologies; and efforts by gays and lesbians to create meaningful networks of kin and independent families.

Thirteen years ago, when Peletz wrote "Kinship Studies in Late Twentieth-Century Anthropology" for the *Annual Review of Anthropology* (1995), he described developments in studying gay and lesbian kinship and assisted reproduction as part of a larger disciplinary shift, which turned the attention of anthropologists to their own societies. He depicted the scholarship at the time as challenging existing preconceptions about the flexibility of concepts of family and kin and destabilizing concepts of relatedness and concluded that these postmodern developments had "profoundly subversive potential" (pp. 362, 365). The more recent literature, however, suggests that the models constructed by gay and lesbian families, parents, and partners and the parents of children born of new technologies draw equally on conventional ideas and radical ones, and often draw on ideas about kinship that reference biogenetic connections.

ALTERNATIVE KINSHIP, MARRIAGE, AND REPRODUCTION: PRECEDENTS

In her studies of the American family (1996, 1998), Stacey described a revolution in domestic life that was generated by diverse social and economic changes in American society. These changes undid the prototypical modern family, which involved self-contained nuclear household units and complementary male and female roles and which was succeeded by an assortment of alternative family forms. These alternatives, characterized by Stacey as "postmodern," have now become part of the mainstream; they include families headed by never-married or divorced mothers, unmarried couples raising children, families with more gender-egalitarian roles, and gay and lesbian families.

Although the notion of alternative marriages and families may be attracting more attention, and though they may be more common nowadays, alternative kinship practices are found across time and place. The rarity of ethnographic, cross-cultural literature featuring kinship alternatives may be due to earlier preoccupations with the normative and conventional, with social systems and structure, and with male perspectives. It took Gough's feminist reanalysis of Evans-Pritchard's materials on the Nuer, for example, to draw attention to types of marriage that provided other options to women in that society—including woman-woman marriage, ghost marriage, and women leaving husbands for lovers; this reanalysis also called into question Evans-Pritchard's elegant model of a social structure based on patrilineal descent (Evans-Pritchard 1940, 1951, pp. 107–18; Gough 1971; Hutchinson 1996, pp. 61, 175; Scheffler 2001, p. 92).

Many alternative practices in preindustrial societies are motivated by "strategies of heirship," in Goody's phrasing, meant to ensure heirs for persons who predecease their spouses or who prove infertile or to offer to the childless the promise of old-age security (Goody 1976). Yet other practices attempt to secure preferable conjugal relationships or enhanced women's status. Woman-woman marriage, which was widespread in Africa, seems to have produced both results. It provided heirs to wealthy childless women and gave them certain advantages that normally accrue to men. It also provided an attractive option for the women who became their wives, who may not have been able to marry otherwise or who preferred the greater sexual and social freedom offered by this kind of marriage (Greene 1998, Oboler 1980). Other instances of alternative kin and marital relationships illustrate how individuals can manipulate the range of options available to them to secure personally desirable marital and familial arrangements. Such examples are offered by the forms of marriage resistance found in the Canton Delta of China a century ago (Stockard 1989) and by marriage avoidance currently in practice among Tibetan pastoralists and farmers (Clarke 1992, Levine 1994). Examples of highly unorthodox conjugal relationships can be found among the *hijras* of India and the American Indian *berdache*, who adopt female identities, clothing, and occupations and occasionally take men as sexual partners, who may be described as their husbands (Nanda 1999; Reddy 2005; Weston 1993, pp. 351–52).

European societies have a long history of alternative marriage arrangements. One example is agreed-upon celibate marriage, sometimes for the duration of the marriage and sometimes after the birth of children, reportedly exercised for ascetic, spiritual purposes. These practices seem to have suspended the gender inequities of traditional marriages (Boswell, 1994, Elliott 1993). Another example is same-sex unions, which were solemnized by the clergy and publicly celebrated. The ceremonies involved some of the same activities found in heterosexual weddings. It is not clear whether these unions were always or sometimes sexual in nature, but they clearly entailed an intended lifelong commitment between two "friends."

Not unlike our own times, the mid-nineteenth century in the United States pro-duced a variety of kinship alternatives. These were times of rapid social change involving the transition from a preindustrial to a modern economy. As in the present, economic changes were accompanied by the development of new religions, reconfigured gender relations, and new forms of marriage and family life. The most widely documented cases include the Shakers, who were celibate, the Oneida community, which practiced "complex marriage," a community-based form of group marriage, and Mormons, who practiced polygyny (Foster 1981, 1991). The Mormon Church abandoned polygyny in response to legal sanctions in 1890; nonetheless, communities of rural, culturally isolated, fundamentalist Mormons remain polygynous to this day. People living on the Arizona-Utah border numbered ~10,000 in the mid-1990s (Altman & Ginat 1996) and are linked to groups in other western states and Canada. All face periodic intense media scrutiny and legal action.

The most far-reaching transformation ever instituted in family organization occurred in the kibbutz movement. This was a collectivist social and economic experiment that was intended to create a new kind of person and a new kind of society, which were to be economically and socially egalitarian and in which the family was a unit of neither production nor child rearing. Instead, the socialization of children was the responsibility of nurses and the peer group rather than of their parents. The more extreme social experiments were short-lived, however. As kibbutzim expanded and became more stable, the family grew stronger and reverted to more traditional Euro-American practices (Spiro 1965, Talmon 1972). No other experiments in communal living have instituted such radical means of handling child socialization. In the groups that have been studied, children sometimes lived with nonfamily members or were schooled apart from their parents, but none of these groups developed programs of collective child rearing (Berger 1981, Daner 1976, Weisner 2001).

RECONFIGURING FAMILIES AMONG GAY MEN AND LESBIAN WOMEN

The new kinship practices forged by gay men and lesbian women have attracted growing scholarly attention in recent decades. As in many emerging areas of inquiry, this research seems to be motivated more by documentary than by theoretical goals (Weston 1993). This research has also been hampered by logistical problems, such as gaining access to representative samples, given the fact that gay and lesbian individuals may be difficult to identify, reluctant to talk to people they do not know, or reticent about politically and socially charged issues. For these reasons, the subjects of recent research come mostly from the same sorts of class and ethnic backgrounds as the academics who have written about them, and they live mostly in cosmopolitan urban settings that have large self-identified gay and lesbian populations.

One of the most influential contributions to the new literature is Weston's *Families We Choose* (1991), a book in which the point of departure is Schneider's model of American kinship. Weston noted that the relationships that lesbian women and gay men recognize fit uneasily into Schneider's typology of relatives related by blood and marriage, by natural substance and code for conduct, and by the core symbol of heterosexual intercourse (Schneider 1980). She stated that gay Americans have contested assumptions that families must be defined on the basis of genetics and procreative sexuality and have created an alternative kinship paradigm and a distinctive family type, that is, chosen families, which are based on friendship, love, and individual choice and a variety of sexual, social, and economic relationships (Weston 1991). From one perspective, chosen families provide surrogate kin ties in that they entail enduring diffuse solidarity (Schneider 1980, p. 50). Thus they are modeled after the conventional meanings that surround kinship in American culture (Lewin 1993, p. 183). From another perspective, they provide a countervailing model to straight kinship and a critique of the privilege accorded to a biogenetically grounded mode of determining which relationships count as kin.

Weston (1991) described chosen families, not surprisingly, as fluid networks of individuals who are easily replaced as personal choice and circumstances dictate (pp. 108–13). She noted that not all the individuals to whom she spoke considered their lovers and friends as kin. Arguably those that did were utilizing what Scheffler (1976) has described as "metaphoric extensions." Weston also noted that although the lesbian "baby boom" has provided another way of challenging the centrality of heterosexual intercourse and the two-person, opposite gender model of parenthood, having babies involves a reincorporation of ideas about biological ties and procreation.

Carrington (1999) examined everyday life in households of lesbian, bisexual, and gay families, defined as people who engage in a consistent and reciprocal pattern of loving and caring activities. He noted, however, that many individuals lack the time, money, and personal networks to create alternative families based on choice and that many African American, Asian American, and Latina/o lesbians and gay men in his sample maintained strong connections to their birth relatives, perhaps because they were less mobile and lived nearby. Carrington argued that the sorts of jobs held by the people to whom he spoke can stymie ideals of equality. Many scholars suggest that same-sex couples are egalitarian because of the lack of fixed roadmaps for the division of domestic labor—this roadmap must be negotiated anew for each couple—and because partnerships between persons of the same gender are presumed to transcend conventional, heterosexual power inequities (Hayden 1995; Murray 2000; Short 2007, p. 61; Stacey & Biblarz 2001). However, one partner having a better paid or more demanding job may create inequitable situations. Carrington found these conditions to be so ideologically fraught that people nearly universally asserted splitting domestic work 50/50, even where he found evidence of differentiation and inequality in their domestic lives (1999, p. 217).

ALTERNATIVE MODELS OF PARENTING: STUDIES OF LESBIAN MOTHERS

In the past, when adoption was not a realistic option and the new reproductive technologies were less advanced and less widely available, most lesbian women and gay men became parents in heterosexual relationships. Lewin (1993) began her research at a time when lesbian women were losing custody of their children in contentious divorce cases; thus her goal was to show that these women were as devoted and competent as heterosexual mothers and that their identities as mothers superseded an identity based on sexual orientation. She found lesbian mothers maintaining ties with birth kin and with the fathers of their children to better their children's circumstances and to provide biological moorings. In more recent years, many lesbian women have used donor insemination to have children. They often do so in ways that maximize biogenetic ties within their families or that approximate such ties. A woman may use the same donor so all her children will be related, choose her partner's brother to be the donor to give both women a genetic link to the child, choose a donor whose physical characteristics resemble those of the partner who is to be the comother of the child, or have her partner actively participate in the process of donor insemination (Hayden 1995, p. 54; Sullivan 2004). Gay men have more limited choices of adoption or the costly and complex process of surrogacy. As Benkov (1994, pp. 160–62) has noted, the families so created both challenge and mimic conservative cultural models of gender and parent-child relationships. Yet, as Hicks (2005, 2006) has argued, these seemingly contradictory views on the family may simply involve divergent responses to different situations. Lesbian women and gay men are, for example, more likely to voice conventional family values when applying to foster or adopt children and to voice more radical views when concerned with new identities and communities of support.

Sullivan (2004), who studied dual-mother lesbian families, found that the women sought equal involvement in their children's lives, and other studies have confirmed success in achieving this goal (Short 2007, Stacey & Biblarz 2001). Dual-mother families also try to tie in the nonbirth mother by second-parent adoptions, which were accorded legal recognition in 11 states when Sullivan's book was written and now are available in 25 states. Many of these women also choose to expand their children's kin networks with members of the sperm donor's family or with other lesbian coparent families who have used the same donor. These ideas demonstrate the resilience of biogenetic thinking about kinship—ideas that stand out even more noticeably in the context of reconfigured family forms and the emphasis on choice in gay kinship (Sullivan 2004, p. 209).

SAME-SEX MARRIAGE

No discussion of alternative marriage is complete without a critique of Lévi-Strauss's foundational work *The Elementary Structures of Kinship* (1969) and its presumption of male dominance in heterosexual marital exchange, its misrecognition of women's marital strategies, and the distortion it imposes on matrilineal societies, a notable example being the Moso, who have noncontractual, nonexclusive conjugal relationships (Barnes 2006, Blackwood 2005, Butler 2002, Cai 2001, Godelier 2004, Shih 2000). Gay marriage poses challenges not only to certain anthropological theories but also to legal statutes and so-called traditional values, which have led to efforts to prevent it in the United States, including the drafting of a federal law, the Defense of Marriage Act, in 1996. The American Anthropological Association's response to this debate is the "Statement on Marriage and the Family," which declares that viable social orders do not depend on marriage as an exclusively heterosexual institution (Exec. Board Am. Anthropol. Assoc. 2004).

Same-sex civil unions and marriages offer numerous possibilities for future research, including studies of everyday practices in these marriages and partnerships, their characteristic patterns of interpersonal relationships, and their durability compared with heterosexual unions among people of comparable socioeconomic circumstances and demographic characteristics. These questions remain to be answered, but it is already clear that many gay men and lesbian women are seeking formal recognition of their relationships as marriages, and not only for pragmatic reasons, such as access to employer-paid health care, rights to inheritance, or designations as next of kin in case of an emergency. Hull (2006) argued that same-sex couples do so because marriage is a powerful relationship model in American culture and because of the power of law in American society to validate relationships—and thus to offer recognition and social legitimacy to homosexual relationships. Hull's data are drawn from public documents and interviews with individuals who participated in public commitment ceremonies. What she concluded is that these couples draw heavily from widely shared cultural meanings and often use traditional symbols of marriage to mark their relationships. She found class, gender, and previous marital history to be correlated with the decision to hold a public commitment ritual (2006, p. 109). Among the couples surveyed, some displayed dichotomous and others undifferentiated roles in their relationships (pp. 40–41). These diverse gay relationship models have been described as involving a complex layering of gender signifiers and as having been influenced by shifting fashions in gay identities over the past half century (Carrington 1999, p. 12; Weston 1991, p. 146, 1993, p. 354).

THE IMPACT OF THE NEW REPRODUCTIVE TECHNOLOGIES

The first child produced by in-vitro fertilization (IVF) was born in the United Kingdom in 1978; this and other advances in the field of human reproduction have prompted the convening of appointed committees and legislative debates about their social, ethical, and legal implications (Franklin 1993, Riviére 1985, Shore 1992). The introduction of such innovations provides a natural social experiment for discerning what constitutes relatedness for their users, for unpacking the meanings of key kinship concepts and kin terms, and for testing the adequacy of anthropological theories about kinship cross-culturally (Godelier 2004, pp. 569–75; Strathern 1992).

To generalize broadly, there are two strains of writing on the kinship implications of the new reproductive technologies (NRTs). Some scholars argue that they have changed our understandings of relatedness, whereas others show how their utilization is strongly shaped by traditional kinship ideas. Edwards (2000) and Strathern (1995), for example, have taken the former view and have pointed out how the NRTs, despite being used by a small number of individuals, have altered ideas about procreation in the population at large. Strathern (1995) suggested that the sorts of changes that have occurred confirm Schneider's earlier prediction that new scientific findings would lead Americans to revise their understandings of biogenetic relationships (Schneider 1980, p. 23), a change that Franklin (1995) attributed partly to the role of medical professionals in managing these technologies and access to them.

As cultures change, so do regulatory systems. Dolgin (2000) found that the NRTs have had an impact on family law. In place of the view of families as holistic social units that supersede the identities of individual members, we now find a stress on autonomous individuality and discussions of the domestic arena in terms once reserved for life in the marketplace: choice and intention. Intention has been privileged in various recent disputes over children born of complex reproductive technologies involving gamete donation and surrogacy, with custody granted to those individuals who first put into motion the efforts that created the child (Dolgin 2000; Ragoné 1994; Strathern 1995, 2005).

Some scholars have argued that these technologies are conceptualized in terms of traditional notions of kinship. Modell, for example, noted how women undergoing IVF emphasize their "normal" and "natural" pregnancies, childbirth, and conventional parenthood and how individuals using their own sperm and eggs stress the importance of bilateral blood ties (Modell 1989). Other accounts of how people come to terms with the NRTs have shown that users rationalize the procedures they have initiated by naturalizing them. Women who use egg donation highlight maternity achieved through gestation and downplay the role of genetics, whereas those who use a surrogate for gestation highlight the importance of their genetic contribution (Cussins 1998; Ragoné 2003, p. 217; Teman 2003, pp. 79–80). Individuals using donor insemination conversely stress social, over biological, parenthood (Becker 2002).

In many cultural contexts, egg and even embryo donation raise fewer problems than does sperm donation because of ideas about the experience of birth and maternal bonding during pregnancy (see Riviére 1985 on the United Kingdom). This is the case in certain patrilineal societies, such as Vietnam, where gestation confers relatedness regardless of genetic ties (Pashigian 2008). In China, egg donation is more accepted than sperm donation because of patriarchal values and concerns about patrilineage continuity (Handwerker 2002). Quite the opposite situation prevails in Israel, where Jewish identity is established through the mother. Egg donation there raises genealogical conundrums, whereas sperm donation is unproblematic (Kahn 2000).

Cultural constructions of gender also affect ideas about egg and sperm donation. In Britain and the United States, sperm donation is seen as sexualized—perhaps because the donation crosses gender lines—whereas egg donation is seen as asexual and altruistic (Haimes 1993). For this reason, people planning egg donation may consider a family member an acceptable choice, which is not the case for sperm donation (Becker 2000). Familial relationships notwithstanding, people seek as sperm and egg donors individuals who are physically similar to the so-cial parent-to-be, following the cultural expectation that children should resemble their parents. Where family members are unavailable as egg donors, friends sometimes are viewed as suitable substitutes because they may have similar ethnicities or similar backgrounds and life experiences and, in one reported instance, because donating an egg was seen to be similar to helping out with the care of an infant (Cussins 1998).

The literature on the NRTs also includes discussions of how women personally experience these procedures, which are arduous and stressful, which often, inexplicably, fail, and to which women respond by trying to exert as much control over the process as possible (Cussins 1996, Franklin 1997, Greil 2002, Modell 1989). The women who donate, by contrast, have been described both as detached from and ambivalent about these procedures, seeing themselves as offering a means for another person to have a child rather than as utilizing their own unique reproductive capacities (Konrad 1998; Ragoné 2003, pp. 222–23; Teman 2003).

RESPONSES TO SURROGACY

Surrogacy was utilized as far back as Biblical times, when childless Rachel sent her maidservant to her husband. The child born was accounted to Rachel, and similar practices are found in a number of contemporary southern African societies (Fortes 1969, p. 256). Surrogacy, nonetheless, lacks legal recognition in most countries and in many states of the United States and is viewed as a particularly problematic form of assisted reproduction. Perhaps this is because surrogacy, more unambiguously than any other NRT, introduces contractual arrangements into private affairs, fragments motherhood (into genetic, gestational, and social components), and implies an adulterous relationship. It has also raised concerns about women being exploited, reproduction being commodified, and children being trafficked (Blyth & Potter 2003, Cook et al. 2003, Fox 1993, Lacayo 1987, Lane 2003,

Markens 2007, Pashigian 2008, Rothman 1988, Teman 2003).

Ragoné (1994) studied surrogate motherhood programs in the United States and found all parties in the endeavor—program employees, surrogates, and couples—to highlight those aspects of surrogacy that are consistent with conventional reproduction and American kinship ideology. In genetic, or "traditional," surrogacy, for example, Ragoné found a stress on social motherhood, which was seen as comprising intentionality, choice, and nurturance and as more important than biological motherhood (pp. 109–10). Nonetheless, some of the mothers reported the lack of a physical tie to their child as creating a sense of exclusion, which echoes the importance of bilateral ties in American kinship (Modell 1989, p. 134).

THE ECONOMIC DIMENSIONS OF MEDICALIZED REPRODUCTION

Since public debate on the NRTs began, concerns have been raised about the ways in which these technologies introduce the issue of commerce into what formerly was the private family domain. Thus the NRTs are seen as breaching the divide between acts undertaken for love and those undertaken for money and between the public domain of self-interested commerce and the private domain of generalized reciprocity (Franklin 1993, 1995, p. 336; Markens 2007, pp. 174–76; Riviére 1985). Another difference between conventional reproduction and gamete donation and surrogacy is that third parties are involved in the creation of a child.

Yet one should keep in mind that economic calculations have always been a consideration in childbearing. In premodern conditions, children were valued for their economic contributions to their parents (Arnold et al. 1975, Fawcett 1983, Nag et al. 1978). Microeconomic analyses of fertility describe children in highly developed societies, by contrast, as the ultimate consumption good (Becker 1960, Cochrane 1975). Individuals who utilize NRTs appear to have goals for their families that are no more consumer-oriented than any other individuals who wish to reproduce. Nor does the way in which children are conceived alter expectations about the emotional relationships that will develop between parents and children. As Kahn (2000) argues for Israel, an infertile couple's or single woman's decision to use the NRTs does not evolve out of a consumerist impulse, but out of the desire to have children and to meet social and religious expectations to be fruitful and multiply. The service providers, however, operate out of commercial motives and act as gatekeepers by controlling access to these procedures and deciding which sorts of individuals are best suited to serve as gamete donors to which sorts of clients (Kahn 2000, pp. 38–39; Schmidt & Moore 1998).

GLOBALIZATION: TECHNOLOGY TRANSFERS MADE MEANINGFUL

Studies of NRTs around the world provide fascinating illustrations of the power of culture to channel how such technologies are interpreted and selectively utilized, and these findings are of special interest here, given their implications for core kinship concepts and intimate family life. Kahn's (2000) study of the NRTs in Israel is especially strong in this regard. She showed how local attitudes, a proactive medical community, supportive government policies, and rabbinic pronouncements have contributed to a growing trend of single Israeli Jewish women conceiving via anonymous sperm donation. Children born to unmarried women in this society are not considered illegitimate according to Jewish law and suffer none of the stigma associated with Euro-American notions of bastardy. Another rabbinic interpretation of Jewish law designates non-Jewish sperm donors as the best choice for women whose husbands are infertile. Because there is no recognition of non-Jewish paternity in traditional religious law, no trace of relatedness is left and the husband can establish paternity through his intentions. Kahn argued that the ways in which the NRTs are used in Israel are certainly innovative and may affect ideas about marriage and the nuclear family, but they do not destabilize foundational assumptions about kinship.

Inhorn (2003) described the very different, and far less permissive, accommodations made for the NRTs in Egypt. Egyptians seeking assisted reproduction face multiple constraints, including economic barriers to access, shortages of supplies, and problems of technological competence, in addition to local theories of procreation and religious prohibitions, which have contributed to various legislative restrictions. Third-party donation is disallowed because of ideas about adultery, inadvertent incest among offspring, and a strong emphasis on genealogical connection. Adoption is disapproved for the same reasons. Instead, Egyptians attempt the delicate procedure of intracytoplasmic sperm injection (which involves injecting sperm into the egg) for male infertility. The case of Egypt clearly illustrates how the NRTs are used in conformity with existing cultural and religious values and need not alter ideas about kinship and moral conduct.

Another example of how cultural models of kinship affect the utilization of the NRTs can be found in Sri Lanka. Infertile couples regularly ask to use the sperm of a close relative, usually the husband's brother, to achieve pregnancy. An infertile man requesting to use his brother's sperm is antithetical to Euro-American thinking (Haimes 1993) but is socially accepted in Sri Lanka in light of attitudes persisting from traditions of polyandrous marriage (Simpson 2004). In China, where an array of NRTs is available, positive attitudes toward technology and modernity have contributed to the view that technologically assisted conceptions can create superior offspring (Handwerker 2002).

A final illustration of how reproductive technologies are used in conformity with existing cultural values concerns the handling of embryos. In the United States and in coastal Ecuador, embryos are considered by some to be human life and to be autonomous entities that may be stored or donated to other individuals. By contrast, in highland Ecuador, practitioners and patients prefer that embryos stay within the family and not be given over to an unknown fate, leading them to avoid cryopreservation (Roberts 2007). Muslim Egyptians prefer to destroy extra embryos rather than to donate them to other couples, which risks mixing genealogical relations and incest (Inhorn 2003, pp. 86, 112).

PRACTICES OF DISCLOSURE

Parents availing themselves of high-tech reproduction commonly conceal this fact, both from members of their extended families and from the children born through these procedures. Concealment even has been reported for less controversial technologies, such as IVF, which uses the parents' own genetic contributions, because it is considered unorthodox and could stigmatize the child (Modell 1989). Such concerns may have decreased by now, given the widespread use of IVF. Donor insemination, nonetheless, remains problematic because it runs up against expectations of biogenetic connections between parents and their children and because of the shame attached to male infertility, which calls into question a man's virility and masculinity. For these reasons, disclosure has been a pressing concern for heterosexual parents planning to use donor insemination. Those intending to hide this fact justified their decision out of fear that such a revelation would distress their child and that the child would love his/her father less. Those intending to reveal this information spoke of the value of open communication or their concern about their child later inadvertently learning how he or she was conceived (Becker 2002). Needless to say, lesbian and single mothers, who invariably reported planning to disclose to their children how they had been conceived, do not share these concerns (Golombok 2006). There have been longstanding debates about the advisability of disclosure and policies concerning the release of donor identities (Haimes 1992), and even today, after the move toward more openness in adoption, debates continue about whether these facts should be revealed to children. Although the policies and recommendations of regulatory agencies vary dramatically around the world, the overall trend is moving toward open disclosure, and some evidence indicates that telling children how they were conceived makes a positive contribution to family relationships (Lycett et al. 2004, MacDougall et al. 2007, Snowden et al. 1983).

The same trends are affecting policies of donor anonymity (Frith 2001). In Great Britain, donor offspring had, for many years, the right to access genetic information about their donors when they reached age 18, but they could not access the donor's identity. This policy changed in 2005, and children born after that date now have the right to access an egg or sperm donor's identity upon reaching age 18, although donors do not have the reciprocal right to find a child. There was concern that the new policy would result in reluctance to donate, but in fact the numbers of men registering to be donors increased (BBC News 2005, 2007). Clearly, these trends reflect the notion that personal genetic information is intrinsically valuable in enhancing knowledge about oneself as an individual (Strathern 1995). They also reflect beliefs about biogenetic connection automatically confering relatedness and the importance of acting on this information. Some Internet sites aid individuals seeking their donors, offspring, or any half-siblings who may exist, and they facilitate "reunions" with kin, as have been sought by children given up for adoption (Modell 1994). As they come of age, individuals conceived through donor procedures are beginning to speak out on these issues (for example, Clark 2006). Efforts of this kind show the persisting cultural emphasis on biogenetic connection in Euro-American and other societies, as providing a basis for common identity, as conferring irrevocable kinship, and as offering relationships that anthropologists have described as entailing enduring solidarity (Schneider 1980) and prescriptive altruism (Fortes 1972).

DISCLOSURE STATEMENT

The author is not aware of any biases that might be perceived as affecting the objectivity of this review.

LITERATURE CITED

Altman I, Ginat J. 1996. *Polygamous Families in Contemporary Society*. Cambridge, UK: Cambridge Univ. Press, 512 pp.

Arnold F, Bulatao RA, Buripakdi C, Chung B, Fawcett J, et al. 1975. *The Value of Children. A Cross National Study: Introduction and Comparative Analysis*. Honolulu: E-W Pop. Inst. 251 pp.

Banton M, ed. 1965. *The Relevance of Models for Social Anthropology*. London: Tavistock

Barnes RH. 2006. Maurice Godelier and the metamorphosis of kinship, a review essay. *Comp. Stud. Soc. Hist.* 48(2):326–58

BBC News. 2005. *Sperm donor anonymity ends*. **http//news.bbc.co.uk/2/hi/health/4397249.stm**

BBC News. 2007. *UK sperm donor numbers increase*. **http://news.bbc.co.uk/2/hi/health/6618977.stm**

Becker G. 2000. *The Elusive Embryo: How Women and Men Approach New Reproductive Technologies*. Berkeley: Univ. Calif. Press. 320 pp.

Becker G. 2002. Deciding whether to tell children about donor insemination: an unresolved question in the United States. See Inhorn & van Balen 2002, pp. 119–33

Becker GS. 1960. An economic analysis of fertility. In *Demographic and Economic Change in Developed Countries*, ed. Natl. Bur. Econ. Res., pp. 209–13. Princeton, NJ: Princeton Univ. Press

Benkov L. 1994. *Reinventing the Family: The Emerging Story of Lesbian and Gay Parents*. New York: Crown. 289 pp.

Berger BM. 1981. *The Survival of a Counterculture: Ideological Work and Everyday Life among Rural Communards*. Berkeley: Univ. Calif. Press. 264 pp.

Blackwood E. 2005. Wedding bell blues: marriage, missing men, and matrifocal follies. *Am. Ethnol.* 32(1):1–19

Bloch M. 1973. The long term and the short term: the economic and political significance of the morality of kinship. See Goody 1973, pp. 75–87

Blyth E, Potter C. 2003. Paying for it? Surrogacy, market forces and assisted conception. See Cook & Sclater 2003, pp. 227–42

Boswell J. 1994. *Same-Sex Unions in Premodern Europe*. New York: Villard. 412 pp.

Butler J. 2002. Is kinship always already heterosexual? *Differ.: J. Fem. Cult. Stud.* 15(1):14–44

Cai H. 2001. *A Society Without Fathers or Husbands: The Na of China*. New York: Zone. 505 pp.

Carrington C. 1999. *No Place Like Home*. Chicago, IL: Univ. Chicago Press. 273 pp.

Carsten J. 1995. The substance of kinship and the heat of the hearth: feeding, personhood, and relatedness among Malays in Pulau Langkawi. *Am. Ethnol.* 22(2):223–41

Carsten J. 2004. *After Kinship*. Cambridge, UK: Cambridge Univ. Press. 216 pp.

Clark K. 2006. *My father was an anonymous sperm donor*. **http://www.washingtonpost.com/wp-dyn/content/article/2006/12/15/AR2006121501820.html**

Clarke GE. 1992. Aspects of the social organisation of Tibetan pastoral communities. In *Tibetan Studies*, Vol. 2, ed. S Ihara, Z Yamaguchi, pp. 393–411. Narita, Japan: Naritasan Shinshoji

Cochrane SH. 1975. Children as by-products, investment goods and consumer goods: a review of some microeconomic models of fertility. *Popul. Stud.* 29(3):373–90

Cook R, Sclater SD, eds. 2003. *Surrogate Motherhood: International Perspectives*. Oxford: Hart

Cook R, Sclater SD, Kaganas F. 2003. Introduction. See Cook & Sclater 2003, pp. 1–19

Cussins C. 1996. Ontological choreography: agency through objectification in infertility clinics. *Soc. Stud. Sci.* 26(3):575–610

Cussins C. 1998. Quit sniveling, cryo-baby: We'll work out which one's your mother. See Davis-Floyd & Dumit 1998, pp. 40–66

Daner JD. 1976. *The American Children of Kṛṣṇa: A Study of the Hare Kṛṣṇa Movement*. New York: Holt, Rinehart & Winston. 118 pp.

David-Floyd R, Dumit J, eds. 1998. *Cyborg Babies: From Techno-Sex to Techno-Tots*. New York: Routledge

Delaney C. 1986. The meaning of paternity and the virgin birth debate. *Man* 21(3):494–513

Dolgin JL. 2000. Choice, tradition, and the new genetics: the fragmentation of the ideology of family. *Conn. L. Rev.* 32:523–66

Edwards J. 2000. *Born and Bred: Idioms of Kinship and New Technologies in England*. Oxford, UK: Oxford Univ. Press. 264 pp.

Elliott D. 1993. *Spiritual Marriage: Sexual Abstinence in Medieval Wedlock*. Princeton, NJ: Princeton Univ. Press. 375 pp.

Evans-Pritchard EE. 1940. *The Nuer: A Description of the Modes of Livelihood and Political Institutions of a Nilotic People*. Oxford, UK: Clarendon. 271 pp.

Evans-Pritchard EE. 1951. *Kinship and Marriage among the Nuer*. Oxford, UK: Clarendon. 183 pp.

Exec. Board Am. Anthropol. Assoc. 2004. *Statement on marriage and the family*. **http://www.aaanet.org/press/ma_stmt_marriage.htm**

Fawcett JT. 1983. Perceptions of the value of children: satisfaction and costs. In *Determinants of Fertility in Developing Countries*, ed. RA Bulatao, RD Lee, pp. 429–57. New York: Academic

Fortes M. 1969. *Kinship and the Social Order: The Legacy of Lewis Henry Morgan*. Chicago, IL: Aldine. 347 pp.

Fortes M. 1972. Kinship and the social order: précis and reply. *Curr. Anthropol.* 13(2):285–96

Fortes M. 1978. An anthropologist's apprenticeship. *Annu. Rev. Anthropol.* 7:1–30

Foster L. 1981. *Religion and Sexuality: Three American Communal Experiments of the Nineteenth Century*. New York: Oxford Univ. Press. 363 pp.

Foster L. 1991. *Women, Family and Utopia: Communal Experiments of the Shakers, The Oneida Community, and The Mormons*. Syracuse, NY: Syracuse Univ. Press. 353 pp.

Fox R. 1993. *Reproduction and Succession: Studies in Anthropology, Law and Society*. New Brunswick: Transaction. 269 pp.

Franklin S. 1993. Making representations: the parliamentary debate on the human fertilisation and embryology act. In *Technologies of Procreation*, ed. J Edwards, S Franklin, E Hirsch, F Price, M Strathern, pp. 96–131. Manchester: Manchester Univ. Press

Franklin S. 1995. Postmodern procreation: a cultural account of assisted reproduction. See Ginsburg & Rapp 1995, pp. 323–45

Franklin S. 1997. *Embodied Progress: A Cultural Account of Assisted Conception*. London: Routledge

Frith L. 2001. Gamete donation and anonymity: the ethical and legal debate. *Hum. Reprod.* 16(5):818–24

Gellner E. 1963. Nature and society in social anthropology. *Philos. Sci.* 27:187–204

Ginsburg FD, Rapp R, eds. 1995. *Conceiving the New World Order: The Global Politics of Reproduction*. Berkeley: Univ. Calif. Press

Godelier M. 2004. *Métamorphoses de la Parenté*. Paris: Fayard. 678 pp.

Golombok S. 2006. New family forms. In *Families Count: Effects on Child and Adolescent Development*, ed. A Clarke-Stewart, J Dunn, pp. 273–98. Cambridge, UK: Cambridge Univ. Press

Goody JR, ed. 1973. *The Character of Kinship*. London, UK: Cambridge Univ. Press. 251 pp.

Goody JR. 1976. *Production and Reproduction: A Comparative Study of the Domestic Domain*. Cambridge, UK: Cambridge Univ. Press. 157 pp.

Gough EK. 1971. Nuer kinship: a re-examination. In *The Translation of Culture*, ed. TO Beidelman, pp. 79–121. London: Tavistock

Greene B. 1998. The institution of woman-marriage in Africa: a cross-cultural analysis. *Ethnology* 37(4):395–412

Greil AL. 2002. Infertile bodies: medicalization, metaphor, and agency. See Inhorn & van Balen 2002, pp. 101–18

Haimes E. 1992. Gamete donation and the social management of genetic origins. In *Changing Human Reproduction: Social Science Perspectives*, ed. M Stacey, pp. 119–47. London: Sage

Haimes E. 1993. Issues of gender in gamete donation. *Soc. Sci. Med.* 36(1):85–93

Handwerker L. 2002. The politics of making modern babies in China: reproductive technologies and the "new" eugenics. See Inhorn & van Balen 2002, pp. 298–314

Hayden CP. 1995. Gender, genetics, and generation: reformulating biology in lesbian kinship. *Cult. Anthropol.* 10(1):41–63

Hicks S. 2005. Queer genealogies: tales of conformity and rebellion amongst lesbian and gay foster carers and adopters. *Qual. Soc. Work* 4(3):293–308

Hicks S. 2006. Genealogy's desire: practices of kinship among lesbian and gay foster-carers and adopters. *Brit. J. Soc. Work* 36:761–76

Howell S. 2003. Kinning: the creation of life trajectories in transnational adoptive families. *J. R. Anthropol. Inst.* 9(3):465–84

Hull KE. 2006. *Same-Sex Marriage: The Cultural Politics of Love and Law*. Cambridge, UK: Cambridge Univ. Press. 277 pp.

Hutchinson SE. 1996. *Nuer Dilemmas. Coping with Money, War, and the State*. Berkeley: Univ. Calif. Press. 408 pp.

Inhorn MC. 2003. *Local Babies, Global Science: Gender, Religion, and In Vitro Fertilization in Egypt*. New York: Routledge. 310 pp.

Inhorn MC, van Balen F, eds. 2002. *Infertility Around the Globe: New Thinking on Childlessness, Gender, and Reproductive Technologies*. Berkeley: Univ. Calif. Press. 347 pp.

Kahn SM. 2000. *Reproducing Jews: A Cultural Account of Assisted Conception in Israel*. Durham, NC: Duke Univ. Press. 227 pp.

Konrad M. 1998. Ova donation and symbols of substance: some variations on the theme of sex, gender and the partible person. *J. R. Anthropol. Inst.* 4(4):643–67

Kuper A. 1982. Lineage theory: a critical retrospect. *Annu. Rev. Anthropol.* 11:71–95

Lacayo R. 1987. Whose child is this? Baby M. and the agonizing dilemma of surrogate motherhood. *Time* Jan. 19:56–58

Lane M. 2003. Ethical issues in surrogacy arrangements. See Cook & Sclater 2003, pp. 121–39

Leach ER. 1961. *Rethinking Anthropology*. London: Athlone. 143 pp.

Leach ER. 1966. Virgin birth. *Proc. R. Anthropol. Inst.* 1966:39–49

Leach ER. 1968. *Pul Eliya: A Village in Ceylon: A Study of Land Tenure and Kinship*. Cambridge, UK: Cambridge Univ. Press. 343 pp.

Levine NE. 1994. The demise of marriage in Tibet. In *Tibetan Studies*, ed. P Kvaerne, pp. 468–80. Oslo: Inst. Comp. Res. Hum. Cult.

Lévi-Strauss C. 1969 [1949]. *The Elementary Structures of Kinship*. Boston: Beacon. 541 pp.

Lewin E. 1993. *Lesbian Mothers: Accounts of Gender in American Culture*. Ithaca, NY: Cornell Univ. Press. 232 pp.

Lewis IM. 1965. Problems in the comparative study of unilineal descent. See Banton 1965, pp. 86–112

Lycett E, Daniels K, Curson R, Golombok S. 2004. Offspring created as a result of donor insemination: a study of family relationships, child adjustment, and disclosure. *Fertil. Steril.* 82(1):172–79

MacDougall K, Becker G, Scheib JE, Nachtigall RD. 2007. Strategies for disclosure: how parents approach telling their children that they were conceived with donor gametes. *Fertil. Steril.* 87(3):524–33

Malinowski B. 1913. *The Family among the Australian Aborigines: A Sociological Study*. London: Univ. London Press. 322 pp.

Malinowski B. 1929. *The Sexual Life of Savages in North-Western Melanesia*. New York: Eugenics. 603 pp.

Markens S. 2007. *Surrogate Motherhood and the Politics of Reproduction*. Berkeley: Univ. Calif. Press. 272 pp.

Modell J. 1989. Last chance babies: interpretations of parenthood in an in vitro fertilization program. *Med. Anthropol. Q.* 3(2):124–38

Modell J. 1994. *Kinship with Strangers: Adoption and Interpretations of Kinship in American Culture*. Berkeley: Univ. Calif. Press. 280 pp.

Montague S. 1971. Trobriand kinship and the virgin birth controversy. *Man* 6(3):353–68

Murray SO. 2000. *Homosexualities*. Chicago, IL: Univ. Chicago Press. 507 pp.

Nag M, White BNF, Peet RC. 1978. An anthropological approach to the study of the economic value of children in Java and Nepal. *Curr. Anthropol.* 19(2):293–306

Nanda S. 1999. *Neither Man nor Woman: The Hijras of India*. Belmont, CA: Wadsworth. 186 pp.

Needham R. 1971. Remarks on the analysis of kinship and marriage. In *Rethinking Kinship and Marriage*, ed. R Needham, pp. 1–34. London: Tavistock

Oboler RS. 1980. Is the female husband a man? Woman/woman marriage among the Nandi of Kenya. *Ethnology* 19(1):69–88

Pashigian M. 2008. Inappropriate relations: the ban on surrogacy with in vitro fertilization and the limits of state renovation in contemporary Vietnam. In *Assisting Reproduction, Testing Genes: Global Encounters with New Biotechnologies*, ed. D Birenbaum-Carmeli, MC Inhorn. New York: Berghahn. In press

Peletz MG. 1995. Kinship studies in late twentieth-century anthropology. *Annu. Rev. Anthropol.* 24:343–72

Ragoné H. 1994. *Surrogate Motherhood: Conception in the Heart*. Boulder, CO: Westview. 215 pp.

Ragoné H. 2003. The gift of life: surrogate motherhood, gamete donation and constructions of altruism. See Cook & Sclater 2003, pp. 209–26

Reddy G. 2005. *With Respect to Sex: Negotiating Hijra Identity in South India*. Chicago, IL: Univ. Chicago Press. 310 pp.

Riviére P. 1985. Unscrambling parenthood: the Warnock report. *Anthropol. Today* 1(4):2–7

Roberts EFS. 2007. Extra embryos: the ethics of cryopreservation in Ecuador and elsewhere. *Am. Ethnol.* 34(1):181–99

Rothman BK. 1988. Reproductive technology and the commodification of life. *Women Health* 13(1/2):95–100

Scheffler HW. 1973. Kinship, descent and alliance. In *Handbook of Social and Cultural Anthropology*, ed. JJ Honigmann, pp. 747–93. Chicago, IL: Rand McNally

Scheffler HW. 1976. The "meaning" of kinship in American culture: another view. In *Meaning in Anthropology*, ed. KH Basso, HA Selby, pp. 57–91. Albuquerque: Univ. N. M. Press

Scheffler HW. 2001. *Filiation and Affiliation*. Boulder, CO: Westview. 202 pp.

Schmidt M, Moore LJ. 1998. Constructing a "good catch," picking a winner: the development of technosemen and the deconstruction of the monolithic male. See Davis-Floyd & Dumit 1998, pp. 21–39

Schneider DM. 1965. Some muddles in the models: or, how the system really works. See Banton 1965, pp. 25–85

Schneider DM. 1972. What is kinship all about? In *Kinship Studies in the Morgan Centennial Year*, ed. P Reining, pp. 32–63. Washington, DC: Anthropol. Soc. Wash.

Schneider DM. 1980 [1968]. *American Kinship: A Cultural Account*. Chicago, IL: Univ. Chicago Press. 137 pp. 2nd ed.

Schneider DM. 1984. *A Critique of the Study of Kinship*. Ann Arbor: Univ. Mich. Press. 208 pp.

Shih C. 2000. *Tisese* and its anthropological significance: issues around the visiting sexual system among the Moso. *L'Homme* 154/5:697–712

Shore C. 1992. Virgin birth and sterile debates. *Curr. Anthropol.* 33(3):295–314

Short L. 2007. Lesbian mothers living well in the context of heterosexism and discrimination: resources, strategies and legislative change. *Fem. Psychol.* 17(1):57–74

Simpson B. 2004. Acting ethically, responding culturally: framing the new reproductive and genetic technologies in Sri Lanka. *Asia Pac. J. Anthropol.* 5(3):227–43

Smith RT. 1987. Kinship and class in Chicago. In *Cities of the United States*, ed. L Mullings, pp. 292–313. New York: Columbia Univ. Press

Snowden R, Mitchell GD, Snowden EM. 1983. *Artificial Reproduction: A Social Investigation*. London: Allen and Unwin. 188 pp.

Spiro ME. 1965 [1958]. *Children of the Kibbutz: A Study in Child Training and Personality*. New York: Schocken. 500 pp.

Spiro ME. 1968. Virgin birth, parthenogenesis and physiological paternity: an essay in cultural interpretation. *Man* 3(2):242–61

Stacey J. 1996. *In the Name of the Family: Rethinking Family Values in the Postmodern Age*. Boston: Beacon. 194 pp.

Stacey J. 1998 [1990]. *Brave New Families: Stories of Domestic Upheaval in Late Twentieth-Century America*. Berkeley: Univ. Calif. Press. 328 pp. 2nd ed.

Stacey J, Biblarz TJ. 2001. (How) does the sexual orientation of parents matter? *Am. Sociol. Rev.* 66(2):159–83

Stockard JE. 1989. *Daughters of the Canton Delta: Marriage Patterns and Economic Strategies in South China, 1860–1930*. Stanford, CA: Stanford Univ. Press. 221 pp.

Stone L. 2001. Introduction: theoretical implications of new directions in anthropological kinship. In *New Directions in Anthropological Kinship*, ed. L Stone, pp. 1–20. Lanham, MD: Rowman & Littlefield

Stone L. 2006. *Kinship and Gender: An Introduction*. Boulder, CO: Westview. 322 pp. 3rd ed.

Strathern M. 1992. *Reproducing the Future*. New York: Routledge. 200 pp.

Strathern M. 1995. Displacing knowledge: technology and the consequences for kinship. See Ginsburg & Rapp 1995, pp. 346–63

Strathern M. 2005. *Kinship, Law and the Unexpected: Relatives Are Always a Surprise*. Cambridge, UK: Cambridge Univ. Press. 229 pp.

Sullivan M. 2004. *The Family of Woman: Lesbian Mothers, Their Children, and the Undoing of Gender*. Berkeley: Univ. Calif. Press. 312 pp.

Talmon Y. 1972. *Family and Community in the Kibbutz*. Cambridge, MA: Harvard Univ. Press. 266 pp.

Teman E. 2003. The medicalization of "nature" in the "artificial body": surrogate motherhood in Israel. *Med. Anthropol. Q.* 17(1):78–98

Weiner AB. 1976. *Women of Value, Men of Renown: New Perspectives in Trobriand Exchange*. Austin: Univ. Tex. Press. 299 pp.

Weismantel M. 1995. Making kin: kinship theory and Zumbagua adoptions. *Am. Ethnol.* 22(4):685–704

Weisner TS. 2001. The American dependency conflict: continuities and discontinuities in behavior and values of countercultural parents and their children. *Ethos* 29(3):271–95

Westermarck E. 1922. *The History of Human Marriage*, Vol. 1. New York: Allerton. 571 pp. 5th ed.

Weston K. 1991. *Families We Choose: Lesbians, Gays, Kinship*. New York: Columbia Univ. Press. 261 pp.

Weston K. 1993. Lesbian/gay studies in the house of anthropology. *Annu. Rev. Anthropol.* 22:339–67

Worsley PM. 1956. The kinship system of the Tallensi: a revaluation. *J. R. Anthropol. Inst.* 86(1):37–75

Yanagisako SJ. 1978. Variance in American kinship: implications for cultural analysis. *Am. Ethnol.* 5(1):15–29

Cumulative Indexes

Contributing Authors, Volumes 29–37

Good I, 30:209–26
Goodenough WH, 32:1–12
Gravlee CC, 34:231–52
Gremillion H, 34:13–32
Grine FE, 35:209–28
Güldemann T, 37:93–109
Gupta D, 34:409–27
Gusterson H, 36:155–75
Guyer JI, 33:499–523

H

Haeri N, 29:61–87
Hames R, 36:177–90
Hammer MF, 31:303–21
Hancock AM, 37:197–217
Hanks WF, 34:67–83
Hann C, 37:145–58
Hansen KT, 33:369–92
Hansen TB, 35:295–315
Harrell S, 30:139–61
Hay J, 36:89–103
Hayashida FM, 34:43–65
Hayes MG, 29:217–42
Hill K, 34:639–65
Himmelmann NP, 37:337–50
Hodder I, 36:105–20
Hogle LF, 34:695–716
Holloway RL, 37:1–19
Holtzman JD, 35:361–78
Houston SD, 33:223–50
Hurtado AM, 34:639–65
Hutchinson JF, 30:85–108

I

Igoe J, 35:251–77
Inhorn MC, 37:177–96

J

Jablonski NG, 33:585–623
Jackson JE, 34:549–73
James P, 34:639–65
Johnson-Hanks J, 37:301–15
Johnstone B, 29:405–24
Joyce RA, 34:139–58

K

Kane S, 30:457–79
Kaufman SR, 34:317–41

Keyes CF, 31:233–55
King SR, 30:505–26
Koo KS, 33:297–317
Korbin JE, 32:431–46
Kulick D, 29:243–85
Kyratzis A, 33:625–49

L

Lamb Z, 34:619–38
Lambourne CA, 34:639–65
Lansing JS, 32:183–204
LaRoche CJ, 34:575–98
Lemon A, 31:497–524
Leonard WR, 34:121–38; 451–71
Leone MP, 34:575–98
Levine NE, 37:375–89
Lindenbaum S, 30:363–85;
    33:475–98
Lofink H, 35:337–60
Lomnitz C, 34:105–20
Lovejoy CO, 32:85–109

M

Maffi L, 34:599–617
Mahon M, 29:467–92
Marcus J, 37:251–66
Maskovsky J, 32:315–38
Mason T, 30:457–79
Mathur S, 29:89–106
Maurer B, 35:15–36
Mazzarella W, 33:345–67
McCollum MA, 32:85–109
McDade TW, 34:495–521
McHenry HM, 29:125–46
Mencher JP, 29:107–24
Merlan F, 34:473–94
Merry SE, 35:99–116
Mertz E, 36:337–53
Meskell L, 31:279–301
Meyer B, 33:447–74
Michael L, 31:121–45
Mills MB, 32:41–62
Mintz SW, 31:99–119
Monaghan L, 31:69–97
Montgomery H, 36:391–405
Moore SF, 34:1–11
Moran K, 30:505–26
Moreland J, 35:135–51
Morgan LM, 34:317–41
Morgen S, 32:315–38

Morris RC, 36:355–89
Mufwene SS, 33:201–22
Mühlhäusler P, 35:457–79
Mullings L, 34:667–93

N

Nazarea VD, 35:317–35
Nelson DL, 36:191–209
Nguyen V-K, 32:447–74
Nichter M, 37:267–82

O

Okongwu AF, 29:107–24
O'Rourke DH, 29:217–42
Ortiz S, 31:395–417
Orzech KM, 37:267–82
Oths KS, 34:231–52

P

Paley J, 31:469–96
Palmié S, 35:433–56
Panter-Brick C, 31:147–71
Parker R, 30:163–79
Peace A, 35:457–79
Peregrine PN, 30:1–18
Perry SE, 35:171–90
Peschard K, 32:447–74
Peterson LC, 31:449–67
Phillips L, 35:37–57
Poe MR, 36:301–36
Pollard AM, 36:245–59
Poole D, 34:159–79
Povinelli EA, 30:319–34

R

Redmond EM, 33:173–99
Reischer E, 33:297–317
Renfrew C, 34:343–61
Reno PL, 32:85–109
Reyes-García V, 34:121–38
Rhodes LA, 30:65–83
Richards M, 32:135–62
Robbins J, 33:117–43
Rogers SC, 30:481–504
Rosenman BA, 32:85–109
Ross CF, 29:147–94
Rubertone PE, 29:425–46
Ruff C, 31:211–32

S

Safari L, 36:391–405
Sapolsky RM, 33:393–418
Scheinsohn V, 32:339–61
Schell LM, 32:111–34
Scheyd GJ, 34:523–48
Schildkrout E, 33:319–44
Schneider J, 37:351–73
Schneider P, 37:351–73
Schoenemann PT, 35:379–406
Schoepf BG, 30:335–61
Schurr TG, 33:551–83
Senghas RJ, 31:69–97
Sharp LA, 29:287–328
Shepherd N, 31:189–209
Shennan S, 37:75–91
Sheridan TE, 36:121–38
Sherzer J, 31:121–45
Shukla S, 30:551–72
Sidnell J, 36:229–44
Siikala J, 35:153–70
Silk JB, 31:21–44
Silverman EK, 33:419–45
Silverstein M, 35:481–96
Silverstein PA, 34:363–84
Slice DE, 36:261–81
Smart A, 32:263–85
Smart J, 32:263–85
Smedley A, 30:xvii–xxxii
Smith EA, 29:493–524
Smith ME, 33:73–102
Snodgrass JJ, 34:451–71
Sorensen MV, 34:451–71
Spencer CS, 33:173–99

Spencer J, 29:1–24
Spindler GD, 29:xv–xxxviii
Stahl AB, 33:145–72
Stanish C, 30:41–64
Stark MT, 35:407–32
Stepputat F, 35:295–315
Stocks A, 34:85–104
Stokes M, 33:47–72
Stoneking M, 37:93–109
Strathern M, 33:1–19
Strier KB, 37:21–36
Strong PT, 34:253–68
Stronza A, 30:261–83
Swisher CC, 33:271–96

T

Tainter JA, 35:59–74
Taylor JS, 34:741–56
Teaford MF, 35:209–28
Threlkeld B, 34:619–38
Trevathan WR, 36:139–54
Trinkaus E, 34:207–30

U

Ulijaszek SJ, 35:337–60
Ungar PS, 35:209–28

V

Vadez V, 34:121–38
Vail G, 35:497–519

van der Veer P, 31:173–87
Van Esterik P, 31:257–78
Van Wolputte S, 33:251–69
Varki A, 36:191–209
Vigil JD, 32:225–42
Vitzthum VJ, 37:53–73
Voss BL, 37:317–36

W

Walker PL, 30:573–96
Walsh M, 34:293–315
Warren KB, 34:549–73
Watkins J, 34:429–49
Wells JCK, 31:323–38
West P, 35:251–77
Wichmann S, 35:279–94
Wilson ML, 32:363–92
Wilson SM, 31:449–67
Wishnie M, 29:493–524
Wolfe TC, 29:195–216
Wortham S, 37:37–51
Wrangham RW, 32:363–92

Y

Yelvington KA, 30:227–60
Yon DA, 32:411–29

Z

Zegura SL, 31:303–21
Ziegler TE, 31:45–67

Chapter Titles, Volumes 29–37

ANNUAL REVIEWS

Intelligent Synthesis of the Scientific Literature

Annual Reviews – Your Starting Point for Research Online
http://arjournals.annualreviews.org

- Over 1150 Annual Reviews volumes—more than 26,000 critical, authoritative review articles in 35 disciplines spanning the Biomedical, Physical, and Social sciences—available online, including all Annual Reviews back volumes, dating to 1932

- Current individual subscriptions include seamless online access to full-text articles, PDFs, Reviews in Advance (as much as 6 months ahead of print publication), bibliographies, and other supplementary material in the current volume and the prior 4 years' volumes

- All articles are fully supplemented, searchable, and downloadable—see http://anthro.annualreviews.org

- Access links to the reviewed references (when available online)

- Site features include customized alerting services, citation tracking, and saved searches

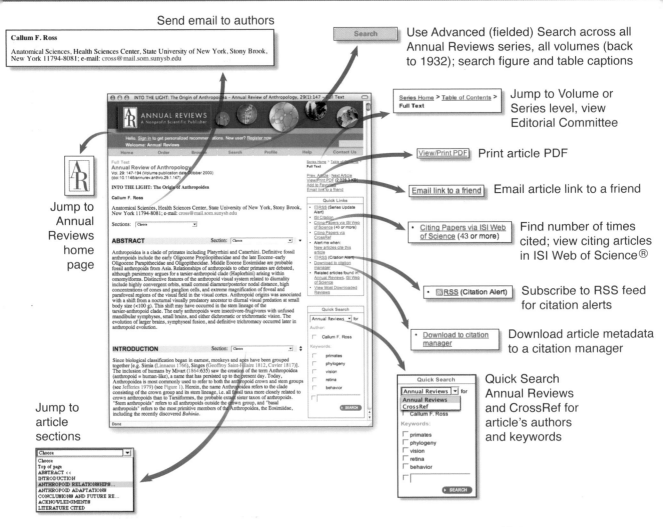

Send email to authors

Use Advanced (fielded) Search across all Annual Reviews series, all volumes (back to 1932); search figure and table captions

Callum F. Ross
Anatomical Sciences, Health Sciences Center, State University of New York, Stony Brook, New York 11794-8081; e-mail: cross@mail.som.sunysb.edu

Jump to Volume or Series level, view Editorial Committee

Jump to Annual Reviews home page

Print article PDF

Email article link to a friend

Find number of times cited; view citing articles in ISI Web of Science®

Subscribe to RSS feed for citation alerts

Download article metadata to a citation manager

Quick Search Annual Reviews and CrossRef for article's authors and keywords

Jump to article sections